RAND McNALLY

the WORLD

Afghanistan to Zimbabwe

RAND McNALLY

the WORLD

Afghanistan to Zimbabwe

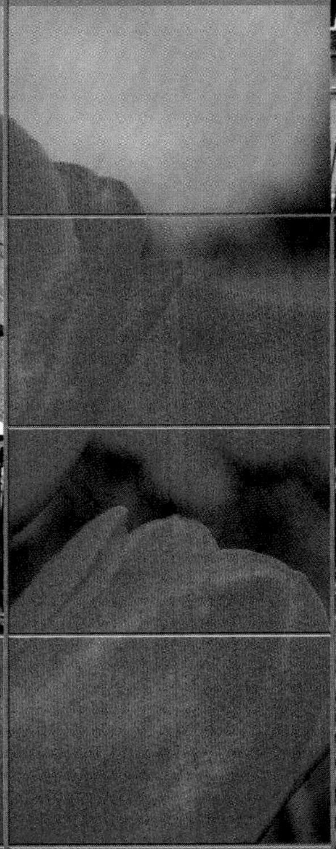

**Vice President,
Rand McNally
Map & Atlas Publishing**
Jayne L. Fenton

Editors
Jon M. Leverenz
Brett R. Gover

Art Direction
John C. Nelson

Design
Donna M. McGrath
Melanie Alden-Roberts

Production
Jennifer A. Herrick

Jacket Design
Vincent R. DePinto

Cartographic Direction
V. Patrick Healy

Cartographic Staff
Robert K. Argersinger
Audrey S. Curry
W. Kay Fisher
Wanda L. McDonald
Patty A. Porter
James A. Purvis
Barbara M. Smith
L. Charlene Smith
Stephen F. Steiner
David C. Zapenski

Research
Susan K. Hudson
Winifred V. Farbman

**Locator Maps and
Other Graphics**
Thomas F. Vitacco
Robert L. Merrill
Barbara L. Strassheim
Dara L. Thompson

**Writer, Country
Introductions
and Captions**
Ryan Ver Berkmoes

Production Coordination
James E. Hernandez

Marketing Manager
David M. Collins

Photo Research
Feldman & Associates, Inc.

Illustration
Mike Yurkovic
(pages 2-5)

⊕ RAND McNALLY

The World, Afghanistan to Zimbabwe
Copyright © 1996 by Rand McNally
1998 Revised Edition

www.randmcnally.com

Published and printed in the U.S.A.

Library of Congress Catalog Number: 95-074681

ISBN: 0-528-83773-7

Photo Credits
[l=left; r=right; c=center; t=top; b=bottom]

Aurora:
© R. Caputo, 33 (t)

Black Star:
© C. Morris, 26 (both); © C. Sillitoe, 33 (c); © M. Coyne, 33 (b), 188 (b); © S. Rutherford, 98 (b both), 99 (b l); © R. Falco, 128 (b); © B&C Alexander, 155 (b l); © F. Charton, 198 (b)

© Cameramann International, Ltd.:
178 (c l & b)

© Liz Chilsen:
136 (t & b)

DDB Stock Photo:
© V. DeWitt, 80 (t)

© Victor Englebert:
32 (t & c), 35 (b), 39 (t)

© Ric Ergenbright: 188 (t)

FPG International:
© A. Montes de Oca, 41 (2 photos); © G.Marche, 52

© Peter French Photography: A-18 (b), 6 (l)

H. Armstrong Roberts:
28 (t), 85 (c), 102 (b), 117 (c), 150; © K. Scholz, A-18 (r) 7, 8 (b), 83 (t), 98 (t), 196 (b); © R. Kord, A-23 (b), 54 (b), 176 (b), 195 (b r); © G. Hunter, 2 (t), 20 (b), 36 (t l), 37 (t), 51 (t), 184 (b), 200 (b); © M. Thonig, 4 (t), 74 (t), 75 (b l), 122 (b r), 133 (t), 205 (t); © D. Bell, 9 (b); © Zefa-U.K., 10 (t), 54 (2 photos), 191 (t r), 111 (t), 175 (b); © J. Messerschmidt, 10 (c), 20 (t r); © Sunak/Zefa, 11 (t); © Smith/Zefa, 14 (l); © A. Tovy, 14 (Sydney), 22 (t l), 42 (t); © R. Waldkirch, 16 (t); © M. Koene, 25 (b, 57 (c)); © Blumebild, 34 (b); © E. R. Degginger, 46 (b), 195 (t); © M. Spector, 44 (b l); © Damm/Zefa 51 (c); © Photo Media, 53 (b); © Geopress, 57 (t), 86 (t), 100 (t & b l), 129 (t), 140 (b); © Honkanen/Zefa, 61; © Kotoh/Zafa, 63; © K. Reno, 64 (t); © Braennhage/Zefa, 65 (b r); © M. Schneider, 70 (t), 166, 176 (t); © M. Berman, 92 (t); © R. Opfer, 94 (2 photos); © W. Bertsch, 97 (c),194 (b r); © R. Krubner, 127 (b); © R. Watts, 142 (b); © M. T. O'Keefe, 144; © Sekal/Zefa, 148; © W. Metzen, 151 (b); © E. Pozsonyi, 153 (b); © Camerique, 164 (b), 172 (c); © B. Pogue, 165 (2 photos); © H. Sutton, 170 (t l); © Kreuger/Zefa, 184 (t); © E. Cooper, 193 (t); © F. Gordon, 196 (c r); © P. Royer, 205 (b)

© Dave G. Houser:
49 (both), 126 (b)

© Randall Hyman:
156 (Lena River & Neva River); 189 (2 photos)

© Wolfgang Kaehler:
89 (t), 101 (c), 117 (t), 125 (t), 129 (b), 162 (b), 194 (l), 201 (t)

Lauré Communications:
© M. Lauré, 6 (t); © J. Lauré, 207 (t)

© Carol Lee:
80 (b), 81 (t), 82 (t)

© Patrick Morrow:
69 (t)

© Vincent J. Musi/National Geographic Image Collection, 126 (t)

Odyssey Chicago:
© R. Gordon, 88 (b), 89 (c); © R. Frerck, 95 (t), 169 (b), 170 (b l), 196 (t l); © T. Wagner, 98 (c l); © K.O. Mooney, 195 (Chicago skyline)

© Chip & Rosa Maria de la Cueva Peterson:
A-24 (t), 145 (3 photos), 197 (2 photos)

Photo 20-20:
© D. Downie, A-19 (t), 105 (b), 116, 185 (t); © Esbin-Anderson, 70 (Walled City); © T. Streshinsky, 95 (b); © R. S. Gerometta, 96 (t)

Photri:
12 (c t & b), 17 (t), 19 (r), 106 (b), 138 (t), 149 (t r), 155 (l), 179 (t)

© Kevin Schafer/Martha Hill, 126 (t l):

© Kevin Schafer, 130 (t)

© Eugene G. Schulz: 17 (b)

SuperStock International, Inc.:
© N. & M. Jansen, 3 (2 photos), © F. Wood, 136 (t l)

Terraphotographics/BPS:
© Robert E. Ford, 32 (b)

Tony Stone Images:
122 (b l); © N. Faridani, 2 (b), 90 (t); © S. Grandadam, A-24 (b l), 4 (b), 93; © R. Planck, 8 (t); © O. Benn, 9 (t r); © D. Spiro, (t l); © J. Warden, 10 (b); © P & K Smith, 11 (b); © P. Tweedie, 14 (b), 128 (t r); © P. Chesley, 15 (b r); © C. Ehlers, 16 (b), 140 (t), 175 (t & c), 174; © B. Krist, (t l); © G. Allison, (t r), 74 (c), 135, 133 (t c), 195 (b c); © R. Elliot, 22 (b), 100 (b l); © J. Janqoux, 25 (t), 206 (3 photos); © C. Harvey, 27 (t & b l); © M. Surowiak, 27 (b r); © T. Cazabon, 29 (b r), 44 (t r); © R. Evans, 31 (2 photos), 177 (t); © Traveler's Resource, 34 (t), 131; © J. Kobalenko, 36 (t r); © D. Nausbaum, 37 (b), 78 (t r); © D. E. Cox, 43 (t r); © M. Uemura, 44 (b r); © R. Frerck, 46 (2 photos), 146 (t), 151 (t), 171 (r); © Churchill & Klehr, 50 (t); © D. Madison, 51 (b); © J. Pickerell, 64 (b); © F. Ivaldi, 65 (t); ;© A. Neal, 65 (b l); © M. Busselle, 66 (t), 171 (l); © B. De Hogues, 66 (b);© B. Seed, 72 (2 photos); © M. Segal, 73, 75 (t), 168(t & b r); © C. Lee, 81 (b); © B. Pogue, 84 (t); © C. Slattery, 85 (b); © G. Brettnacher, 88 (c); © D. Smetzer, 90 (b); © O. Benn, 97 (t) © P. Kenward, 102 (c l); © R.E. Daemmrich, 104 (b); © A. Smith, 108 (b); © D. Bayes, 111 (c); © E. Simpson, 121 (t), 146 (b); © D. Hiser, 122 (t); © D. & P. Valenti, 127 (t); © C. Melloan, 132, 181 (r); © A. Wolfe, 142 (t), 156 (t c & c c); © K. Wood, 143; © J. S. Hibbert, 153 (t); © J. Balog, 156 (b); © J. Lewis, 161 (t), 177 (b); © C. Arnesen, 164 (t); © M. Mehlig, 170 (t r); © M. Rogers 172 (t); © P. Timmermans, 172 (b); © J. Johnson, 180; © D. Austen, 181 (l); © H. Sitton, 185 (b); © W. Clay, 196 (c l); © H. R. Johnston, 193 (b); © C. Clifton, 194 (t r); © S. Cohen, 194 (c b); © P. Grebliunas, 195 (b l); © D. Maisel, 196 (t r); © Z. Kaluzhny, 200 (t); © K. Heacox, 208 (t l); © K. Schafer, 208 (c)

Travel Stock:
© Buddy Mays, 101 (b)

Trip:
© D. Saunders, 19 (l), 97 (b); © V. Shuba, 21 (t); © M. Barlow, 21 (b), 166 (b); © W. Jacobs, 35 (t, c r, c l), 84 (b), 115, 137 (t), 149 (l); © M. Jelliffe, 39 (b), 117 (b); © R. Powers, 82 (b); © T. Lester, 88 (t), 107 (b); © Trip, 101 (t); © C. C., 106 (t); © V. Kolpakov, 108 (t), 198 (t); © H. Rogers, 109 (2 photos), 178 (t); © R. Musallam, 111 (b); © C. Slater, 125 (b); © M. Pepperell, 130 (b); © N & J Wiseman, 141 (2 photos); © I. Deineko, 154 (t); © V. Sidoropolev, 155 (t l), 156 (t l); © Heath, 156 (t l); © A. Dalton, 162 (t); © S Harris, 168 (b l); © C. Rennie, 186 (t); © I. Burgandivov, 186 (b); © P. Rauter, 192 (b); © R. Squires, 201 (b)

Tropix:
© J. Lee, 179 (b)

Valan:
© C. Osborne, 105 (t)

Viesti Associates, Inc.:
© M. Downey, 86 (b); © Tettoni, Cassio & Associates Pte Ltd, 87 (t); © J. Viesti, 147, 191 (t l & b r); © M. Cooper, 173 (3 photos); © E. Wessman, 190 (b)

Westlight:
© D. & J. Heaton, 71 (l); © J. Zuckerman, 71 (r)

© Nik Wheeler:
91 (3 photos)

CONTENTS

Contents continued

WORLD SUPERLATIVES AND INFORMATION TABLES

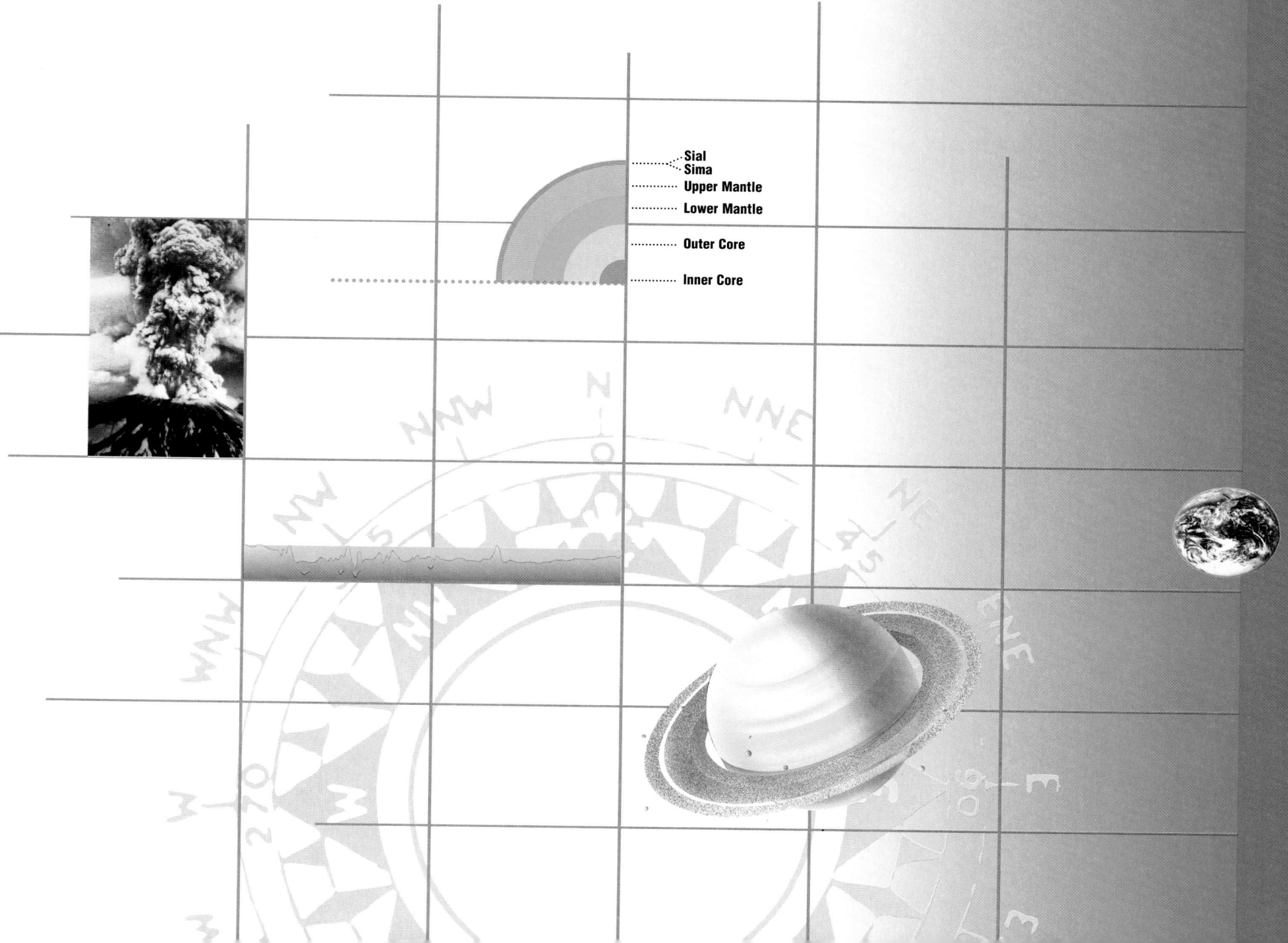

Sial
Sima
Upper Mantle
Lower Mantle
Outer Core
Inner Core

THE UNIVERSE AND SOLAR SYSTEM

The Milky Way Galaxy

Our star, the Sun, is one of 200 billion stars banded together in the enormous gravitational spiral nebula called the Milky Way Galaxy, which is but one of millions of known galaxies in the universe.

The Milky Way is huge; it would take light — which travels at 186,000 miles per second — 100,000 years to go from one end of the galaxy to the other. In addition to the billions of stars, Earth shares the Milky Way with eight other known planets.

Statistical Data for the Milky Way Galaxy

Diameter: 100,000 light-years

Mass: About 200 billion suns

Distance between spiral arms: 6,500 light years

Thickness of galactic disk: 1,300 light-years

Satellite galaxies: 2 (visible only in the southern sky)

Sun

The Sun's diameter — more than 865,000 miles — is 109 times greater than that of the Earth. Even so, the Sun is actually a fairly small star. Somewhere in the vastness of the universe astronomers have located a star that is 3,500 times larger than the Sun.

Diameter: 865,000 miles (1,392,000 km)
Mass: 333,000 times that of the Earth
Surface temperature: 10,300° F (5,700° C)
Central temperature: 27 million° F (15 million° C)
Composition: 70% hydrogen, 27% helium
Spin (at equator): 26 days, 21 hours

Mercury

Distance from the Sun: 35,985,000 miles (57,909,000 km), or 39% that of the Earth
Diameter: 3,031 miles (4,878 km), or 38% that of the Earth
Average surface temperature: 340° F (171° C)
Atmosphere: Extremely thin, contains helium and hydrogen
Length of day: 58 days, 15 hours, 30 minutes
Length of year: 87.97 days
Satellites: None

Venus

Distance from the Sun: 67,241,000 miles (108,209,000 km), or 72% that of the Earth
Diameter: 7,521 miles (12,104 km), or 95% that of the Earth
Surface temperature: 867° F (464° C)
Surface pressure: 90 times that of the Earth, equivalent to the pressure at a water depth of 3,000 feet (900 meters)
Atmosphere: 96% carbon dioxide
Length of day: 243 days, 14 minutes. The planet spins opposite to the rotation of the Earth.
Length of year: 224.7 days
Satellites: None

Earth

Distance from the Sun: 92,960,000 miles (149,598,000 km)
Diameter: 7,926 miles (12,756 km)
Average surface temperature: 58° F (14° C)
Surface pressure: 1 atmosphere
Atmosphere: 78% nitrogen, 21% oxygen
Length of day: 23 hours, 56 minutes and 4 seconds
Length of year: 365.25 days
Satellites: 1

The Moon

The Moon is the Earth's only natural satellite. About 2,160 miles (3,746 km) across, the Moon is an airless, waterless world just one-fourth the size of the Earth. It circles the planet once every 27 days at an average distance of about 238,000 miles (384,000 km).

Mars

Distance from the Sun: 141,642,000 miles (227,940,000 km), about 1.5 times that of the Earth
Diameter: 4,222 miles (6,794 km), or 53% that of the Earth
Average surface temperature: –13° F (–25° C)
Surface pressure: 0.7% (1/150 th) that of the Earth
Atmosphere: 95% carbon dioxide, 2.7% nitrogen
Length of day: 24 hours, 37 minutes
Length of year: 1 year, 321.73 days
Satellites: 2

Jupiter

By any measure, Jupiter is the solar system's giant. To equal Jupiter's bulk would take 318 Earths. Over 1,300 Earth-sized balls could fit within this enormous planet.

Distance from the Sun: 483,631,000 miles (778,292,000 km), or 5.2 times that of the Earth
Diameter: 88,700 miles (142,800 km), or 11.3 times that of the Earth
Temperature at cloud tops: –234° F (–148° C)

Spatial Relationships of the Sun and the Planets

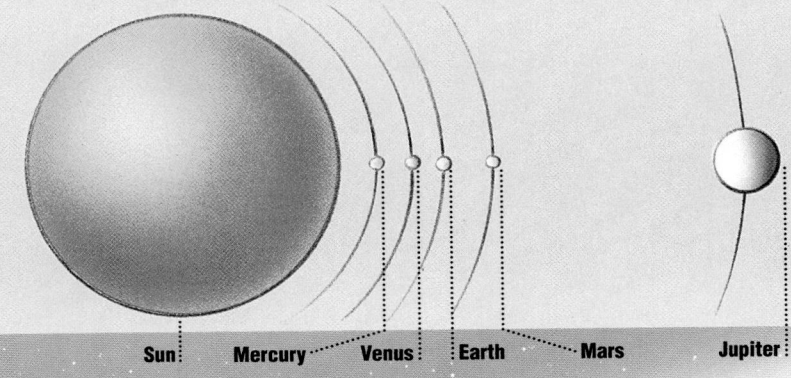

Sun · Mercury · Venus · Earth · Mars · Jupiter · Saturn

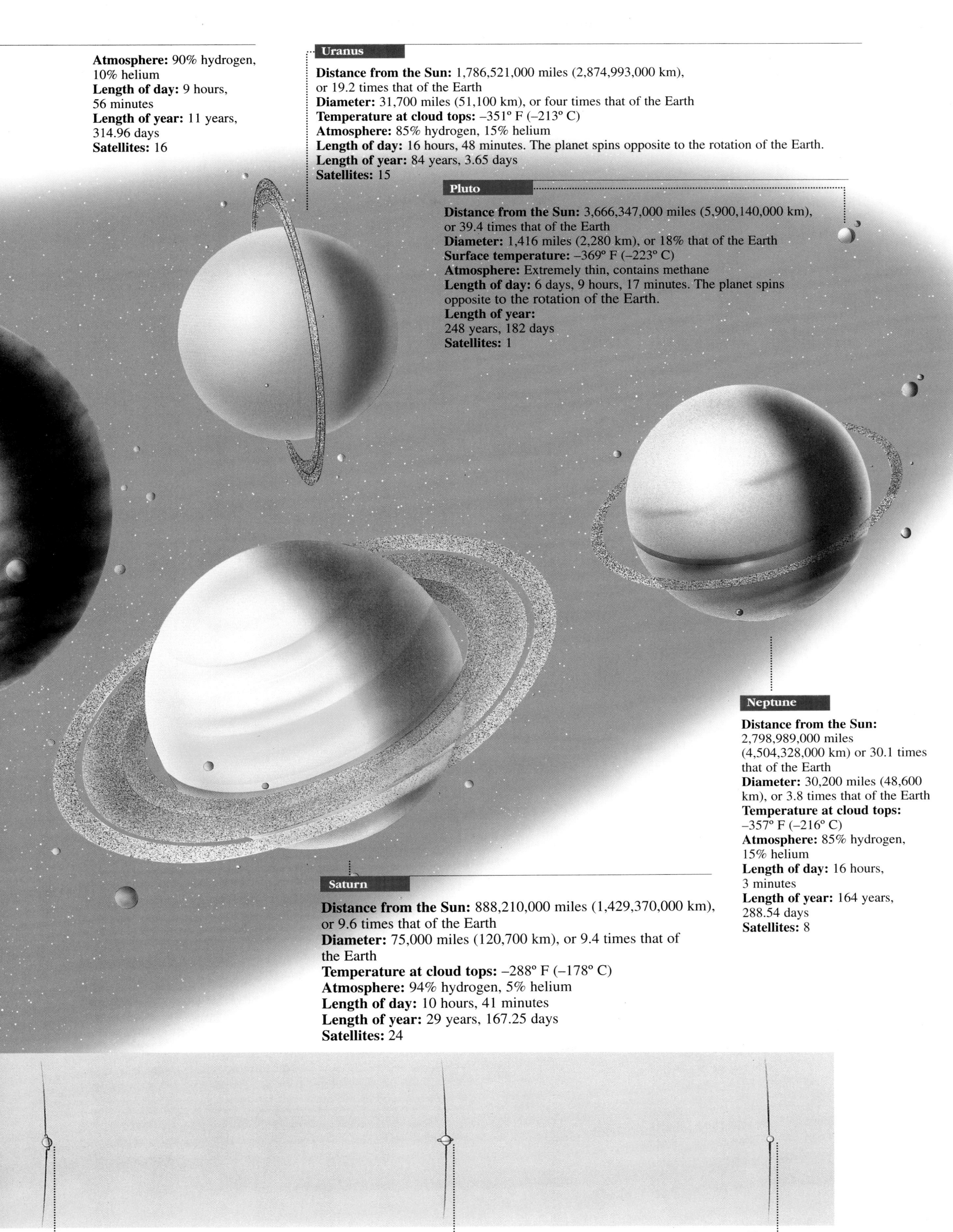

Atmosphere: 90% hydrogen, 10% helium
Length of day: 9 hours, 56 minutes
Length of year: 11 years, 314.96 days
Satellites: 16

Uranus

Distance from the Sun: 1,786,521,000 miles (2,874,993,000 km), or 19.2 times that of the Earth
Diameter: 31,700 miles (51,100 km), or four times that of the Earth
Temperature at cloud tops: –351° F (–213° C)
Atmosphere: 85% hydrogen, 15% helium
Length of day: 16 hours, 48 minutes. The planet spins opposite to the rotation of the Earth.
Length of year: 84 years, 3.65 days
Satellites: 15

Pluto

Distance from the Sun: 3,666,347,000 miles (5,900,140,000 km), or 39.4 times that of the Earth
Diameter: 1,416 miles (2,280 km), or 18% that of the Earth
Surface temperature: –369° F (–223° C)
Atmosphere: Extremely thin, contains methane
Length of day: 6 days, 9 hours, 17 minutes. The planet spins opposite to the rotation of the Earth.
Length of year: 248 years, 182 days
Satellites: 1

Neptune

Distance from the Sun: 2,798,989,000 miles (4,504,328,000 km) or 30.1 times that of the Earth
Diameter: 30,200 miles (48,600 km), or 3.8 times that of the Earth
Temperature at cloud tops: –357° F (–216° C)
Atmosphere: 85% hydrogen, 15% helium
Length of day: 16 hours, 3 minutes
Length of year: 164 years, 288.54 days
Satellites: 8

Saturn

Distance from the Sun: 888,210,000 miles (1,429,370,000 km), or 9.6 times that of the Earth
Diameter: 75,000 miles (120,700 km), or 9.4 times that of the Earth
Temperature at cloud tops: –288° F (–178° C)
Atmosphere: 94% hydrogen, 5% helium
Length of day: 10 hours, 41 minutes
Length of year: 29 years, 167.25 days
Satellites: 24

Uranus   **Neptune**   **Pluto**

THE EARTH

History of the Earth

Estimated age of the Earth:
At least 4.6 billion (4,600,000,000) years.

Formation of the Earth:
It is generally thought that the Earth was formed from a cloud of gas and dust (A) revolving around the early Sun. Gravitational forces pulled the cloud's particles together into an ever denser mass (B), with heavier particles sinking to the center. Heat from radioactive elements caused the materials of the embryonic Earth to melt and gradually settle into core and mantle layers. As the surface cooled, a crust formed. Volcanic activity released vast amounts of steam, carbon dioxide and other gases from the Earth's interior. The steam condensed into water to form the oceans, and the gases, prevented by gravity from escaping, formed the beginnings of the atmosphere (C).

The calm appearance of our planet today (D) belies the intense heat of its interior and the violent tectonic forces which are constantly reshaping its surface.

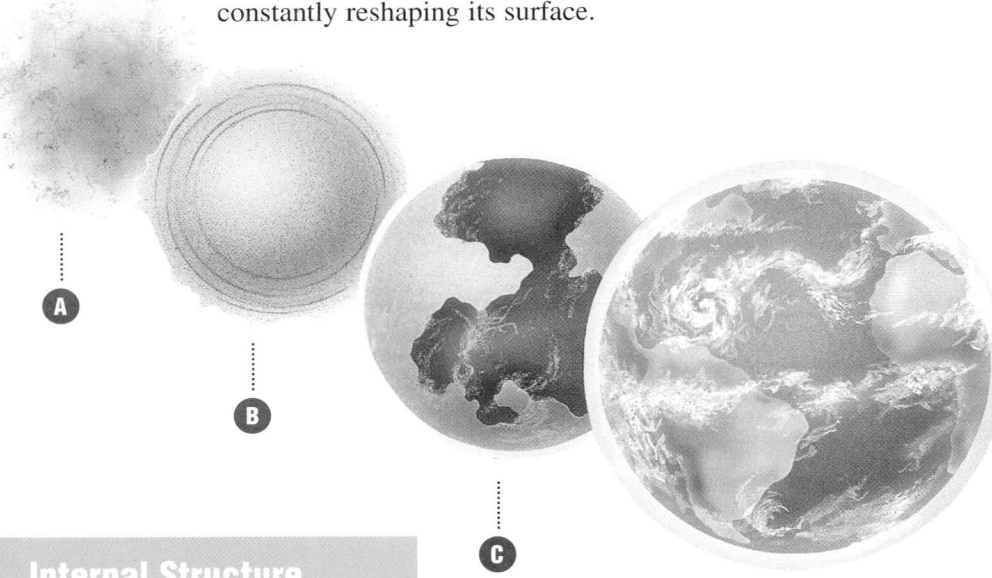

Periods in Earth's history

Earth's history is divided into different **eras**, which are subdivided into **periods**.

The most recent periods are themselves subdivided into **epochs**. The main divisions and subdivisions are shown below.

	Began	Ended	
	(million years ago)		
Precambrian Era			
Archean Period	3,800	2,500	Start of life
Proterozoic Period	2,500	590	Life in the seas
Paleozoic Era			
Cambrian Period	590	500	Sea life
Ordovician Period	505	438	First fishes
Silurian Period	438	408	First land plants
Devonian Period	408	360	Amphibians
Carboniferous Period	360	286	First reptiles
Permian Period	286	248	Spread of reptiles
Mesozoic Era			
Triassic Period	248	213	Reptiles and early mammals
Jurassic Period	213	144	Dinosaurs
Cretaceous Period	144	65	Dinosaurs, dying out at the end
Cenozoic Era			
Tertiary Period			
Paleocene	65	55	Large mammals
Eocene	55	38	Primates begin
Oligocene	38	25	Development of primates
Miocene	25	5	Modern-type animals
Pliocene	5	2	*Australopithecus* ape, ancestor to the human race
Quaternary Period			
Pleistocene	2	0.01	Ice ages; true humans
Holocene	0.01	Present	Modern humans

Source: *Atlas of the Universe* by Patrick Moore, Reed International Books Limited, 1994.

Internal Structure of the Earth

In its simplest form, the Earth is composed of a crust, a mantle with an upper and lower layer, and a core, which has an inner region.

Temperatures in the Earth increase with depth, as is observed in a deep mine shaft or bore-hole, but the prediction of temperatures within the Earth is made difficult by the fact that different rocks conduct heat at different rates: rock salt, for example, has 10 times the heat conductivity of coal. Also, estimates have to take into account the abundance of heat-generating atoms in a rock. Radioactive atoms are concentrated toward the Earth's surface, so the planet has, in effect, a thermal blanket to keep it warm. The temperature at the center of the Earth is believed to be approximately 5,400° F (3,000° C).

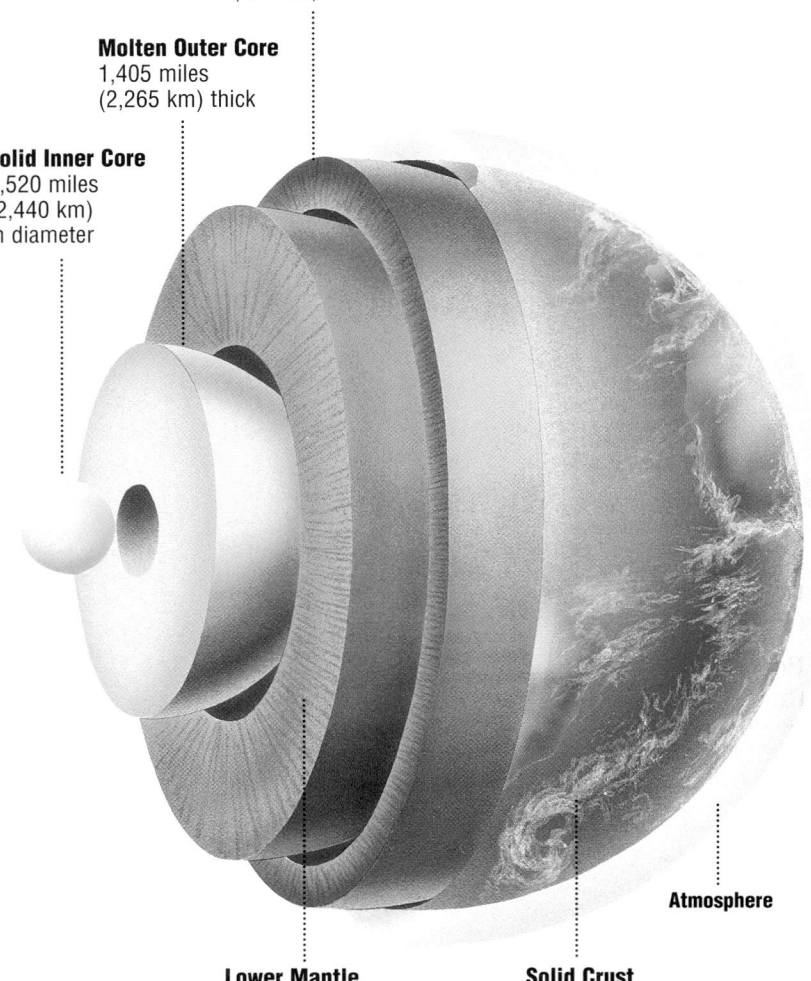

Upper Mantle
415 miles
(667 km) thick

Molten Outer Core
1,405 miles
(2,265 km) thick

Solid Inner Core
1,520 miles
(2,440 km)
in diameter

Atmosphere

Lower Mantle
1,365 miles
(2,200 km) thick

Solid Crust
0–19 miles
(0–33 km) thick

Chemical composition of the Earth:

The chemical composition of the Earth varies from crust to core. The upper crust of continents, called sial, is mainly granite, rich in aluminum and silicon. Oceanic crust, or sima, is largely basalt, made of magnesium and silicon. The mantle is composed of rocks that are rich in magnesium and iron silicates, whereas the core, it is believed, is made of iron and nickel oxides.

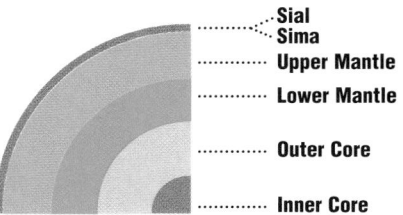

- Sial
- Sima
- Upper Mantle
- Lower Mantle
- Outer Core
- Inner Core

A. Silicon
B. Aluminum
C. Iron
D. Calcium
E. Magnesium
F. Nickel
G. Other

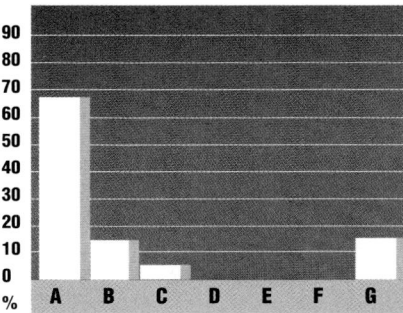

Sial (upper crust of continents)

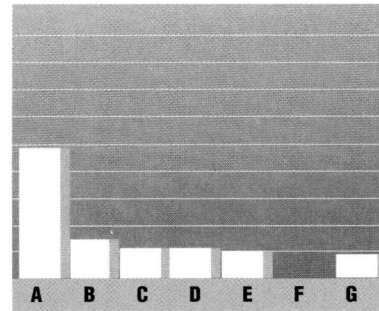

Sima (oceanic crust)

Mantle

Core

Measurements of the Earth

Equatorial circumference of the Earth: 24,901.45 miles (40,066.43 km)

Polar circumference of the Earth: 24,855.33 miles (39,992.22 km)

Equatorial diameter of the Earth: 7,926.38 miles (12,753.54 km)

Polar diameter of the Earth: 7,899.80 miles (12,710.77 km)

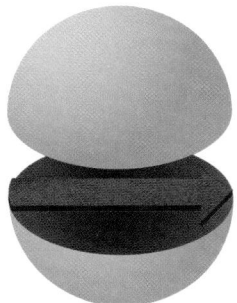

Equatorial radius of the Earth: 3,963.19 miles (6,376.77 km)

Polar radius of the Earth: 3,949.90 miles (6,355.38 km)

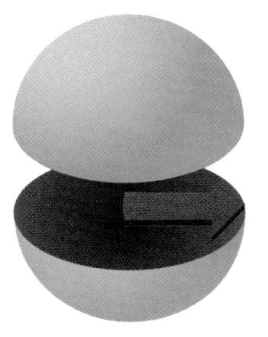

Estimated weight of the Earth:

6,600,000,000,000,000,000,000 tons, or 6,600 billion billion tons (5,940 billion billion metric tons)

Total surface area of the Earth: 197,000,000 square miles (510,230,000 sq km)

Total land area of the Earth (including inland water and Antarctica): 57,900,000 square miles (150,100,000 sq km)

Total ocean area of the Earth: 139,200,000 square miles (360,528,000 sq km), or 70% of the Earth's surface area

Total area of the Earth's surface covered with water (oceans and all inland water): 147,750,000 square miles (382,672,500 sq km), or 75% of the Earth's surface area

Types of water: 97% of the Earth's water is salt water; 3% is fresh water

Life on Earth

Number of plant species on Earth: About 350,000

Number of animal species on Earth: More than one million

Estimated total human population of the Earth: 5,628,000,000

Movements of the Earth

Mean distance of the Earth from the Sun: About 93 million miles (149.6 million km)

Period in which the Earth makes one complete orbit around the Sun: 365 days, 5 hours, 48 minutes, and 46 seconds

Speed of the Earth as it orbits the Sun: 66,700 miles (107,320 km) per hour

Period in which the Earth makes one complete rotation on its axis: 23 hours, 56 minutes and 4 seconds

Equatorial speed at which the Earth rotates on its axis: More than 1,000 miles (1,600 km) per hour

The Shape of the Earth

Comparing the Earth's equatorial and polar dimensions reveals that our planet is actually not a perfect sphere but rather an oblate spheroid, flattened at the poles and bulging at the equator. This is the result of a combination of gravitational and centrifugal forces.

An even more precise term for the Earth's shape is "geoid" — the actual shape of sea level, which is lumpy, with variations away from spheroid of up to 260 feet (80 m). This lumpiness reflects major variations in density in the Earth's outer layers.

The Seasons
(Northern Hemisphere)

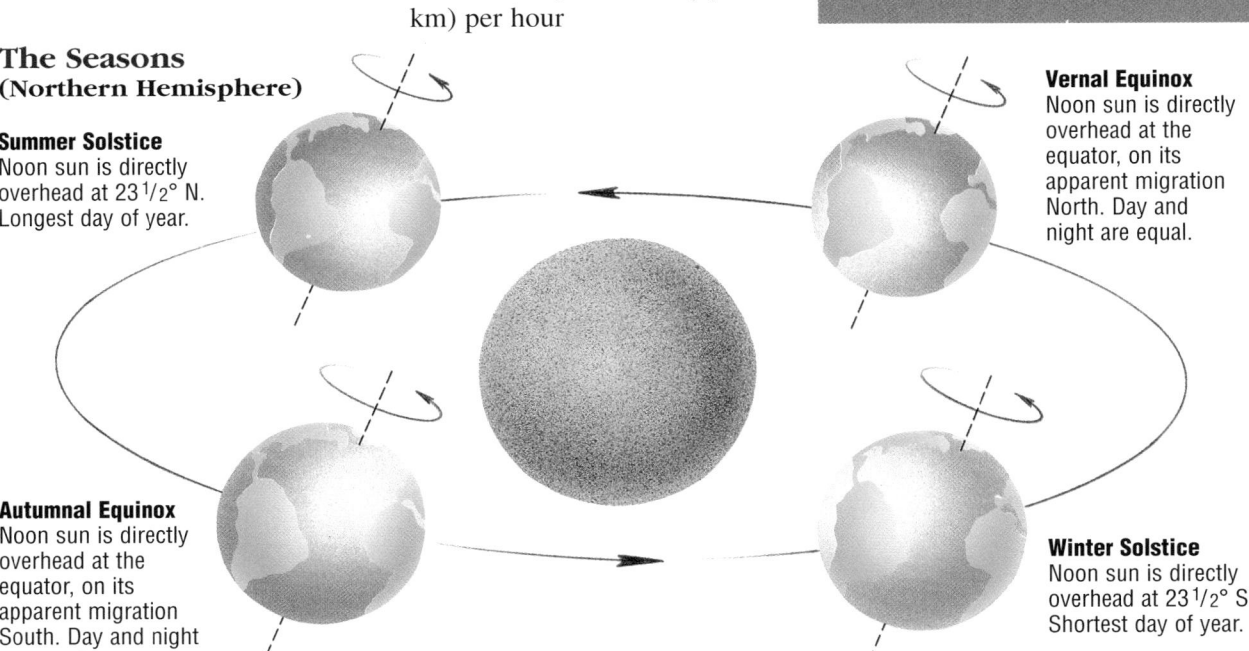

Summer Solstice
Noon sun is directly overhead at 23 1/2° N. Longest day of year.

Vernal Equinox
Noon sun is directly overhead at the equator, on its apparent migration North. Day and night are equal.

Autumnal Equinox
Noon sun is directly overhead at the equator, on its apparent migration South. Day and night are equal.

Winter Solstice
Noon sun is directly overhead at 23 1/2° S. Shortest day of year.

CONTINENTS AND ISLANDS

The word "continents" designates the largest continuous masses of land in the world.

For reasons that are mainly historical, seven continents are generally recognized: Africa, Antarctica, Asia, Australia, Europe, North America, and South America. Since Asia and Europe actually share the same land mass, they are sometimes identified as a single continent, Eurasia.

The lands of the central and south Pacific, including Australia, New Zealand, Micronesia, Melanesia, and Polynesia, are sometimes grouped together as Oceania.

The Continents

Africa

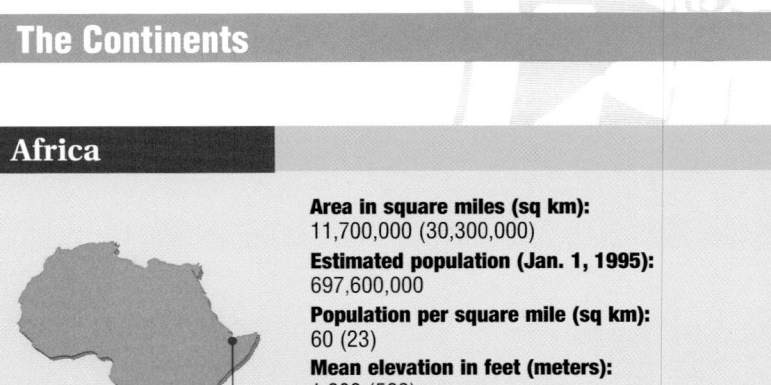

Area in square miles (sq km):
11,700,000 (30,300,000)

Estimated population (Jan. 1, 1995):
697,600,000

Population per square mile (sq km):
60 (23)

Mean elevation in feet (meters):
1,900 (580)

Highest elevation in feet (meters):
Kilimanjaro, Tanzania, 19,340 (5,895)

Lowest elevation in feet (meters):
Lac Assal, Djibouti, 515 (157) below sea level

Antarctica

Area in square miles (sq km):
5,400,000 (14,000,000)

Estimated population (Jan. 1, 1995):
Uninhabited

Population per square mile (sq km):
0 (0)

Mean elevation in feet (meters):
6,000 (1,830)

Highest elevation in feet (meters):
Vinson Massif, 16,066 (4,897)

Lowest elevation in feet (meters):
Deep Lake, 184 (56) below sea level

Asia

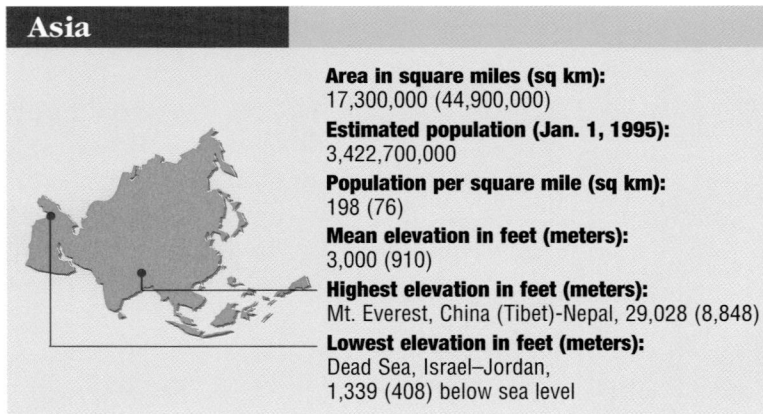

Area in square miles (sq km):
17,300,000 (44,900,000)

Estimated population (Jan. 1, 1995):
3,422,700,000

Population per square mile (sq km):
198 (76)

Mean elevation in feet (meters):
3,000 (910)

Highest elevation in feet (meters):
Mt. Everest, China (Tibet)-Nepal, 29,028 (8,848)

Lowest elevation in feet (meters):
Dead Sea, Israel–Jordan,
1,339 (408) below sea level

Australia

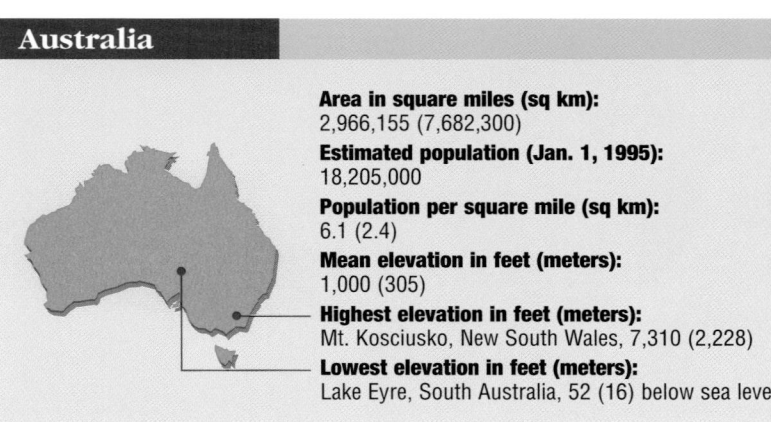

Area in square miles (sq km):
2,966,155 (7,682,300)

Estimated population (Jan. 1, 1995):
18,205,000

Population per square mile (sq km):
6.1 (2.4)

Mean elevation in feet (meters):
1,000 (305)

Highest elevation in feet (meters):
Mt. Kosciusko, New South Wales, 7,310 (2,228)

Lowest elevation in feet (meters):
Lake Eyre, South Australia, 52 (16) below sea level

Europe

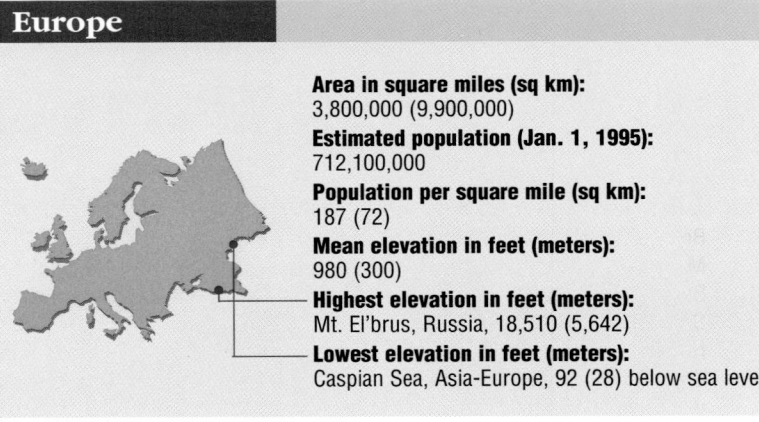

Area in square miles (sq km):
3,800,000 (9,900,000)

Estimated population (Jan. 1, 1995):
712,100,000

Population per square mile (sq km):
187 (72)

Mean elevation in feet (meters):
980 (300)

Highest elevation in feet (meters):
Mt. El'brus, Russia, 18,510 (5,642)

Lowest elevation in feet (meters):
Caspian Sea, Asia-Europe, 92 (28) below sea level

North America

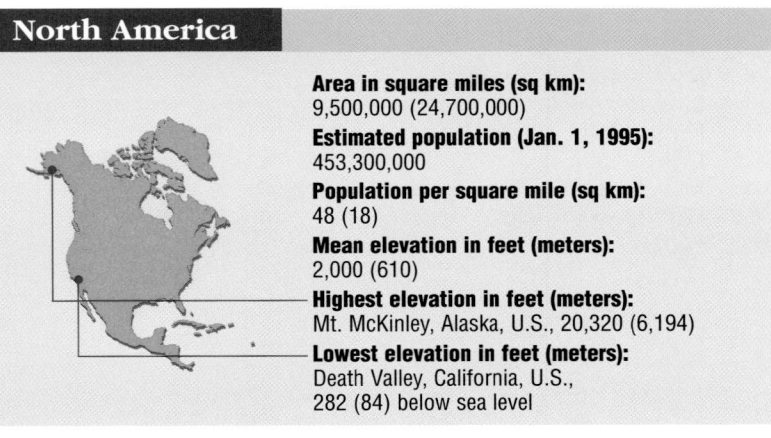

Area in square miles (sq km):
9,500,000 (24,700,000)

Estimated population (Jan. 1, 1995):
453,300,000

Population per square mile (sq km):
48 (18)

Mean elevation in feet (meters):
2,000 (610)

Highest elevation in feet (meters):
Mt. McKinley, Alaska, U.S., 20,320 (6,194)

Lowest elevation in feet (meters):
Death Valley, California, U.S.,
282 (84) below sea level

Oceania (incl. Australia)

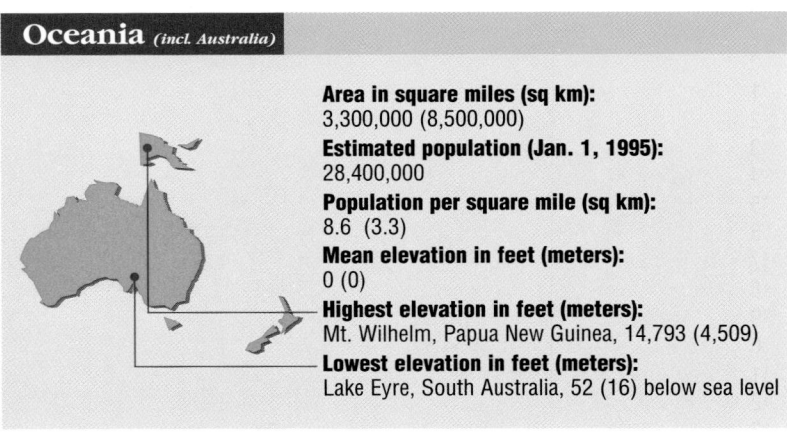

Area in square miles (sq km):
3,300,000 (8,500,000)

Estimated population (Jan. 1, 1995):
28,400,000

Population per square mile (sq km):
8.6 (3.3)

Mean elevation in feet (meters):
0 (0)

Highest elevation in feet (meters):
Mt. Wilhelm, Papua New Guinea, 14,793 (4,509)

Lowest elevation in feet (meters):
Lake Eyre, South Australia, 52 (16) below sea level

South America

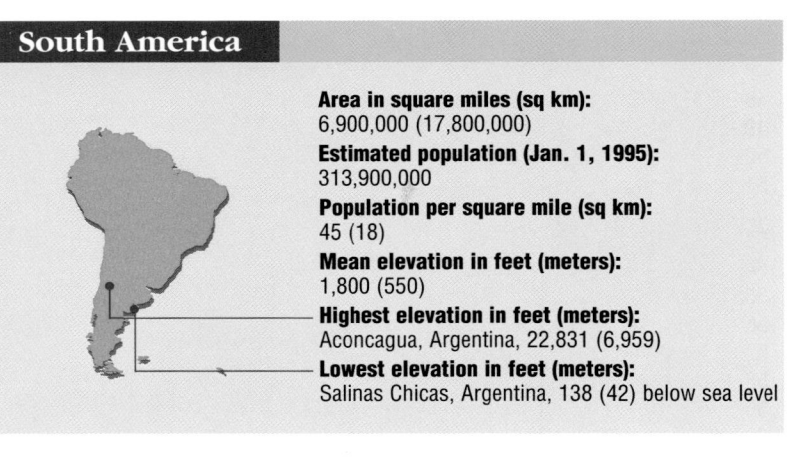

Area in square miles (sq km):
6,900,000 (17,800,000)

Estimated population (Jan. 1, 1995):
313,900,000

Population per square mile (sq km):
45 (18)

Mean elevation in feet (meters):
1,800 (550)

Highest elevation in feet (meters):
Aconcagua, Argentina, 22,831 (6,959)

Lowest elevation in feet (meters):
Salinas Chicas, Argentina, 138 (42) below sea level

World

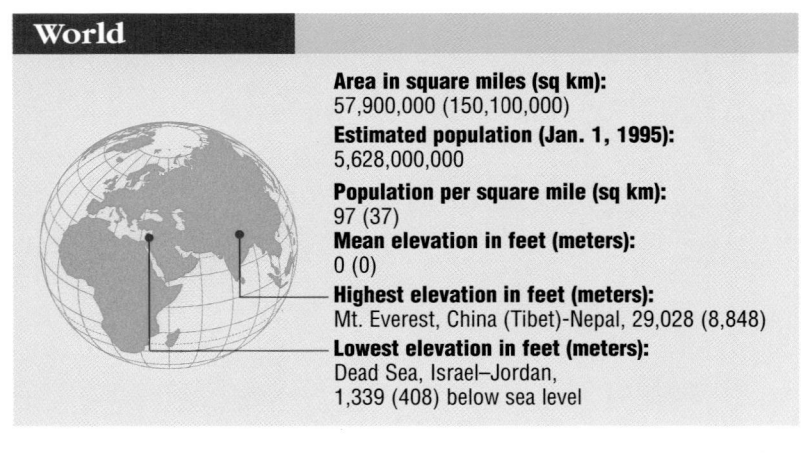

Area in square miles (sq km):
57,900,000 (150,100,000)

Estimated population (Jan. 1, 1995):
5,628,000,000

Population per square mile (sq km):
97 (37)

Mean elevation in feet (meters):
0 (0)

Highest elevation in feet (meters):
Mt. Everest, China (Tibet)-Nepal, 29,028 (8,848)

Lowest elevation in feet (meters):
Dead Sea, Israel–Jordan,
1,339 (408) below sea level

Largest Islands

Rank	Name	Area square miles	Area square km
1	Greenland, North America	840,000	2,175,600
2	New Guinea, Asia-Oceania	309,000	800,000
3	Borneo (Kalimantan), Asia	287,300	744,100
4	Madagascar, Africa	226,500	587,000
5	Baffin Island, Canada	195,928	507,451
6	Sumatra (Sumatera), Indonesia	182,860	473,606
7	Honshū, Japan	89,176	230,966
8	Great Britain, United Kingdom	88,795	229,978
9	Victoria Island, Canada	83,897	217,291
10	Ellesmere Island, Canada	75,767	196,236
11	Celebes (Sulawesi), Indonesia	73,057	189,216
12	South Island, New Zealand	57,708	149,463
13	Java (Jawa), Indonesia	51,038	132,187
14	North Island, New Zealand	44,332	114,821
15	Cuba, North America	42,800	110,800
16	Newfoundland, Canada	42,031	108,860
17	Luzon, Philippines	40,420	104,688
18	Iceland, Europe	39,800	103,000
19	Mindanao, Philippines	36,537	94,630
20	Ireland, Europe	32,600	84,400
21	Hokkaidō, Japan	32,245	83,515
22	Sakhalin, Russia	29,500	76,400
23	Hispaniola, North America	29,400	76,200
24	Banks Island, Canada	27,038	70,028
25	Tasmania, Australia	26,200	67,800
26	Sri Lanka, Asia	24,900	64,600
27	Devon Island, Canada	21,331	55,247
28	Berkner Island, Antarctica	20,005	51,829
29	Alexander Island, Antarctica	19,165	49,652
30	Tierra del Fuego, South America	18,600	48,200
31	Novaya Zemlya, north island, Russia	18,436	47,764
32	Kyūshū, Japan	17,129	44,363
33	Melville Island, Canada	16,274	42,149
34	Southampton Island, Canada	15,913	41,214
35	Axel Heiberg, Canada	15,498	40,151
36	Spitsbergen, Norway	15,260	39,523
37	New Britain, Papua New Guinea	14,093	36,500
38	Taiwan, Asia	13,900	36,000
39	Hainan Dao, China	13,100	34,000
40	Prince of Wales Island, Canada	12,872	33,339
41	Novaya Zemlya, south island, Russia	12,633	32,730
42	Vancouver Island, Canada	12,079	31,285
43	Sicily, Italy	9,926	25,709
44	Somerset Island, Canada	9,570	24,786
45	Sardinia, Italy	9,301	24,090
46	Bathurst Island, Canada	7,600	19,684
47	Shikoku, Japan	7,258	18,799
48	Ceram (Seram), Indonesia	7,191	18,625
49	North East Land, Norway	6,350	16,446
50	New Caledonia, Oceania	6,252	16,192
51	Prince Patrick Island, Canada	5,986	15,509
52	Timor, Indonesia	5,743	14,874
53	Sumbawa, Indonesia	5,549	14,377
54	Ostrov Oktyabr'skoy Revolyutsii, Russia	5,511	14,279
55	Flores, Indonesia	5,502	14,250
56	Samar, Philippines	5,100	13,080
57	King William Island, Canada	4,961	12,853
58	Negros, Philippines	4,907	12,710
59	Thurston Island, Antarctica	4,854	12,576
60	Palawan, Philippines	4,550	11,785

Islands, Islands, Everywhere

Four islands — Hokkaidō, Honshū, Kyūshū, and Shikoku —
constitute 98% of Japan's total land area, but the country is actually
comprised of more than 3,000 islands. Similarly, two islands —
Great Britain and Ireland — make up 93% of the total land area of
the British Isles, but the island group also includes more than 5,000
smaller islands.

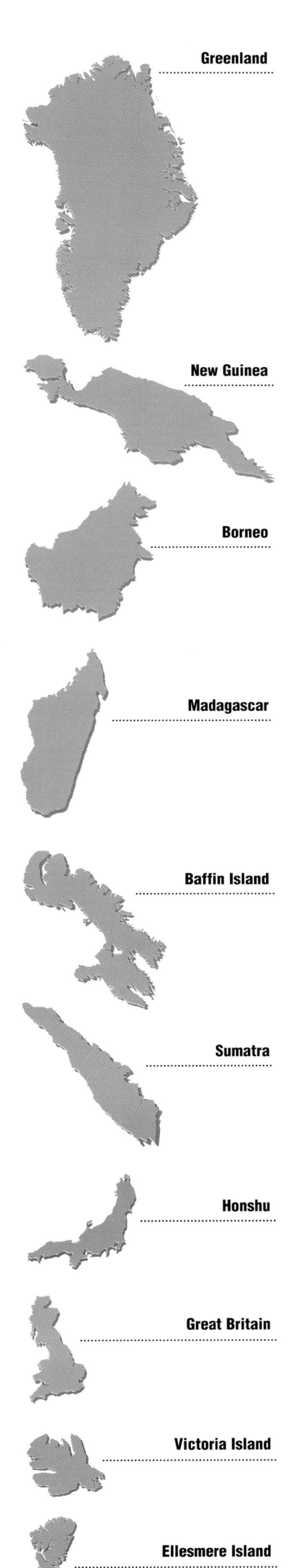

Greenland

New Guinea

Borneo

Madagascar

Baffin Island

Sumatra

Honshu

Great Britain

Victoria Island

Ellesmere Island

Major World Island Groups

Aleutian Islands (Pacific Ocean)

Alexander Archipelago
(Pacific Ocean)

Azores (Atlantic Ocean)

Bahamas (Atlantic Ocean)

Balearic Islands
(Mediterranean Sea)

British Isles (Atlantic Ocean)

Bismarck Archipelago
(Pacific Ocean)

Canary Islands (Atlantic Ocean)

Cape Verde Islands
(Atlantic Ocean)

Dodecanese (Mediterranean Sea)

Faeroe Islands (Atlantic Ocean)

Falkland Islands (Atlantic Ocean)

Fiji Islands (Pacific Ocean)

Galapagos Islands (Pacific Ocean)

Greater Sunda Islands (Indian/Pacific
Oceans)

Hawaiian Islands (Pacific Ocean)

Ionian Islands
(Mediterranean Sea)

Japan (Pacific Ocean)

Cyclades (Mediterranean Sea)

Kuril Islands (Pacific Ocean)

Lesser Sunda Islands
(Indian Ocean)

Moluccas (Pacific Ocean)

New Hebrides (Atlantic Ocean)

New Siberian Islands
(Arctic Ocean)

Novaya Zemlya (Arctic Ocean)

Philippine Islands (Pacific Ocean)

Ryukyu Islands (Pacific Ocean)

Severnaya Zemlya (Arctic Ocean)

Solomon Islands (Pacific Ocean)

Spitsbergen (Arctic Ocean)

Contrasting Population Densities

Some islands are among
the most densely populated
places on Earth, while
others are among the least
densely populated. This
fact is dramatically
illustrated by
the following
comparison of
five islands:

Manhattan, N.Y., U.S., (pop. 1,488,000)	67,636/ sq mile (26,105/ sq km)
Singapore Island, Singapore (pop. 2,921,000)	11,874/ sq mile (4,593/ sq km)
Long Island, N.Y., U.S. (pop. 6,863,000)	4,984/ sq mile (1,925/ sq km)

Population per square mile (sq km)

Baffin Island, Canada (pop. 8,800) 0.04/ sq mile (0.02/ sq km)	Greenland (pop. 57,000) 0.07/ sq mile (0.03/ sq km)

MOUNTAINS, VOLCANOES, AND EARTHQUAKES

The Tallest Mountain in the World

With its peak reaching 29,028 feet (8,848 m) above sea level, Mt. Everest ranks as the *highest* mountain in the world, but not the *tallest*. That title goes to Mauna Kea, one of the five volcanic mountains that make up the island of Hawaii. From its base on the floor of the Pacific Ocean, Mauna Kea rises 33,476 feet (10,210 m)—more than six miles—although only the top 13,796 feet (4,205 m) are above sea level.

Seafloor Atop Mt. Everest

When Sir Edmund Percival Hillary and Tenzing Norgay reached the summit of Mt. Everest in 1953, they probably did not realize they were standing on the seafloor.

The Himalayan mountain system was formed through the process of plate tectonics. Ocean once separated India and Asia, but 180 million years ago the Indo-Australian crustal plate, on which India sits, began a northward migration and eventually collided with the Eurasian plate. The seafloor between the two landmasses crumpled and was slowly thrust upward. Rock layers that once lay at the bottom of the ocean now crown the peaks of the highest mountains in the world.

Principal Mountain Systems and Ranges of the World

Alaska Range (North America)
Alps (Europe)
Altai (Asia)
Andes (South America)
Apennines (Europe)
Atlas Mountains (Africa)
Appalachian Mountains (North America)
Brooks Range (North America)
Carpathian Mountains (Europe)
Cascade Range (North America)
Caucasus (Europe/Asia)
Coast Mountains (North America)
Coast Ranges (North America)
Great Dividing Range (Australia)
Greater Khingan Range (Asia)
Himalayas (Asia)
Hindu Kush (Asia)
Karakoram Range (Asia)
Kunlun Shan (Asia)
Madre Occidental, Sierra (North America)
Madre Oriental, Sierra (North America)
Nevada, Sierra (North America)
Pamir (Asia)
Pyrenees (Europe)
Rocky Mountains (North America)
Sayan Mountains (Asia)
Southern Alps (New Zealand)
Tien Shan (Asia)
Ural Mountains (Europe)
Zagros Mountains (Asia)

Principal Mountains of the World
Δ = Highest mountain in range, region, country, or state named

Location	Height Feet	Meters
Africa		
Kilimanjaro, Δ Tanzania (Δ Africa)	19,340	5,895
Kirinyaga (Mount Kenya), Δ Kenya	17,058	5,199
Margherita Peak, Δ Uganda-Δ D.R.C.	16,763	5,109
Ras Dashen Mtn., Δ Ethiopia	15,158	4,620
Meru, Mount, Tanzania	14,978	4,565
Karisimbi, Volcan, Δ Rwanda-D.R.C.	14,787	4,507
Elgon, Mount, Kenya-Uganda	14,178	4,321
Toubkal, Mt., Δ Morocco (Δ Atlas Mts.)	13,665	4,165
Cameroon Mountain, Δ Cameroon	13,451	4,100
Antarctica		
Vinson Massif, Δ Antarctica	16,066	4,897
Kirkpatrick, Mount	14,856	4,528
Markham, Mount	14,049	4,282
Jackson, Mount	13,747	4,190
Sidley, Mount	13,717	4,181
Wade, Mount	13,399	4,084
Asia		
Everest, Mount, Δ China-Δ Nepal (Δ Tibet; Δ Himalayas; Δ Asia; Δ World)	29,028	8,848
K2 (Qogir Feng), China-Δ Pakistan (Δ Kashmir; Δ Karakoram Range)	28,250	8,611
Kanchenjunga, Δ India-Nepal	28,208	8,598
Makalu, China-Nepal	27,825	8,481
Dhaulagiri, Nepal	26,810	8,172
Nanga Parbat, Pakistan	26,660	8,126
Annapurna, Nepal	26,504	8,078
Gasherbrum, China-Pakistan	26,470	8,068
Xixabangma Feng, China	26,286	8,012
Nanda Devi, India	25,645	7,817
Kamet, China-India	25,447	7,756
Namjagbarwa Feng, China	25,446	7,756
Muztag, China (Δ Kunlun Shan)	25,338	7,723
Tirich Mir, Pakistan (Δ Hindu Kush)	25,230	7,690
Gongga Mt., China	24,790	7,556
Kula Kangri, Δ Bhutan	24,784	7,554
Communism Peak, Δ Tajikistan (Δ Pamir)	24,590	7,495
Nowshak, Δ Afghanistan-Pakistan	24,557	7,485
Pobedy, Pik, China-Russia	24,406	7,439
Chomo Lhari, Bhutan-China	23,997	7,314
Muztag, China	23,891	7,282
Lenin Peak, Δ Kyrgyzstan-Tajikistan	23,406	7,134
Api, Nepal	23,399	7,132
Kangrinboqê Feng, China	22,028	6,714
Hkakabo Mt., Δ Myanmar	19,296	5,881
Mt. Daimavend, Δ Iran	18,386	5,604
Agri Dagi (Mount Ararat), Δ Turkey	16,854	5,137
Fuladi, Kuh-e, Afghanistan	16,847	5,135
Jaya Peak, Δ Indonesia (Δ New Guinea)	16,503	5,030
Klyuchevskaya Sopka Volcano, Russia (Δ Kamchatka Peninsula)	15,584	4,750
Trikora Peak, Indonesia	15,584	4,750
Mt. Belukha, Kazakhstan-Russia	14,783	4,506
Turgen, Mount, Mongolia	14,311	4,362
Kinabalu, Mt., Δ Malaysia (Δ Borneo)	13,455	4,101
Yü Mtn., Δ Taiwan	13,114	3,997
Erciyes, Mount, Turkey	12,851	3,917
Kerinci, Mount, Indonesia (Δ Sumatra)	12,467	3,800
Fuji, Mt., Δ Japan (Δ Honshu)	12,388	3,776
Rinjani, Mount, Indonesia (Δ Lombok)	12,224	3,726
Semeru, Mount, Indonesia (Δ Java)	12,060	3,676
Nabi Shuayb, Mt., Δ Yemen (Δ Arabian Peninsula)	12,008	3,660
Australia / Oceania		
Wilhelm, Mt., Δ Papua New Guinea	14,793	4,509
Giluwe, Mt., Papua New Guinea	14,330	4,368
Bangeta, Mt., Papua New Guinea	13,520	4,121
Victoria, Mt., Papua New Guinea (Δ Owen Stanley Range)	13,238	4,035
Cook, Mt., Δ New Zealand (Δ South Island)	12,316	3,754
Europe		
Elbrus, Mount, Δ Russia (Δ Caucasus; Δ Europe)	18,510	5,642
Dykhtau, Mt., Russia	17,073	5,204
Blanc, Mont (Monte Bianco) Δ France-Δ Italy (Δ Alps)	15,771	4,807

Location	Height Feet	Meters
Dufourspitze, Italy-Δ Switzerland	15,203	4,634
Weisshorn, Switzerland	14,783	4,506
Matterhorn, Italy-Switzerland	14,692	4,478
Finsteraarhorn, Switzerland	14,022	4,274
Jungfrau, Switzerland	13,642	4,158
Écrins, Barre des, France	13,458	4,102
Viso, Monte, Italy (Δ Cottian Alps)	12,602	3,841
Grossglockner, Δ Austria	12,457	3,797
Teide Peak, Δ Spain (Δ Canary Is.)	12,188	3,715
North America		
McKinley, Mt., Δ Alaska (Δ United States; Δ North America)	20,320	6,194
Logan, Mt., Δ Canada (Δ Yukon; Δ St. Elias Mts.)	19,551	5,959
Orizaba, Pico de, Δ Mexico	18,406	5,610
St. Elias, Mt., Alaska-Canada	18,008	5,489
Popocatépetl, Mexico	17,930	5,465
Foraker, Mt., Alaska	17,400	5,304
Iztaccíhuatl, Mexico	17,159	5,230
Lucania, Mt., Canada	17,147	5,226
Fairweather, Mt., Alaska-Canada (Δ British Columbia)	15,300	4,663
Whitney, Mt., Δ California	14,494	4,418
Elbert, Mt., Δ Colorado (Δ Rocky Mts.)	14,433	4,399
Massive, Mt., Colorado	14,421	4,396
Harvard, Mt., Colorado	14,420	4,395
Rainier, Mt., Δ Washington (Δ Cascade Range)	14,410	4,392
Williamson, Mt., California	14,370	4,380
La Plata Pk., Colorado	14,361	4,377
Blanca Pk., Colorado (Δ Sangre de Cristo Mts.)	14,345	4,372
Uncompahgre Pk., Colorado (Δ San Juan Mts.)	14,309	4,361
Grays Pk., Colorado (Δ Front Range)	14,270	4,349
Evans, Mt., Colorado	14,264	4,348
Longs Pk., Colorado	14,255	4,345
Wrangell, Mt., Alaska	14,163	4,317
Shasta, Mt., California	14,162	4,317
Pikes Pk., Colorado	14,110	4,301
Colima, Nevado de, Mexico	13,991	4,240
Tajumulco, Volcán, Δ Guatemala (Δ Central America)	13,845	4,220
Gannett Pk., Δ Wyoming	13,804	4,207
Mauna Kea, Δ Hawaii	13,796	4,205
Grand Teton, Wyoming	13,770	4,197
Mauna Loa, Hawaii	13,679	4,169
Kings Pk., Δ Utah	13,528	4,123
Cloud Pk., Wyoming (Δ Bighorn Mts.)	13,167	4,013
Waddington, Mt., Canada (Δ Coast Mts.)	13,163	4,012
Wheeler Pk., Δ New Mexico	13,161	4,011
Boundary Pk., Δ Nevada	13,140	4,005
Robson, Mt., Canada (Δ Canadian Rockies)	12,972	3,954
Granite Pk., Δ Montana	12,799	3,901
Borah Pk., Δ Idaho	12,662	3,859
Humphreys Pk., Δ Arizona	12,633	3,851
Chirripó, Volcán, Δ Costa Rica	12,530	3,819
Columbia, Mt., Canada (Δ Alberta)	12,294	3,747
Adams, Mt., Washington	12,276	3,742
Gunnbjørn, Mtn., Δ Greenland	12,139	3,700
South America		
Aconcagua, Δ Argentina (Δ Andes; Δ South America)	22,831	6,959
Ojos del Salado, Mt., Argentina-Δ Chile	22,615	6,893
Bonete, Cerro, Argentina	22,546	6,872
Huascarán, Δ Peru	22,133	6,746
Llullaillaco, Volcán, Argentina-Chile	22,110	6,739
Yerupaja, Nevado, Peru	21,765	6,634
Tupungato, Cerro, Argentina-Chile	21,555	6,570
Sajama, Volcano, Bolivia	21,463	6,542
Illampu, Nevado, Bolivia	21,066	6,421
Illimani, Nevado, Bolivia	20,741	6,322
Chimborazo, Δ Ecuador	20,702	6,310
Antofalla, Volcano, Argentina	20,013	6,100
Cotopaxi, Ecuador	19,347	5,897
Misti, Volcano, Peru	19,101	5,822
Huila, Mt., Colombia (Δ Cordillera Central)	18,865	5,750
Bolívar Peak, Δ Venezuela	16,427	5,007

Notable Volcanic Eruptions

Eruption of Mt. St. Helens in 1980

Year	Volcano Name, Location	Comments
ca. 4895 B.C.	Crater Lake, Oregon, U.S.	Collapse forms caldera that now contains Crater Lake.
ca. 4350 B.C.	Kikai, Ryukyu Islands, Japan	Japan's largest known eruption.
ca. 1628 B.C.	Santorini (Thira), Greece	Eruption devastates late Minoan civilization.
79 A.D.	Vesuvius, Italy	Roman towns of Pompeii and Herculaneum are buried.
ca. 180	Taupo, New Zealand	Area measuring 6,200 square miles (16,000 sq km) is devastated.
ca. 260	Ilopango, El Salvador	Thousands killed, with major impact on Mayan civilization.
915	Towada, Honshu, Japan	Japan's largest historic eruption.
ca. 1000	Baitoushan, China/Korea	Largest known eruption on Asian mainland.
1259	Unknown	Evidence from polar ice cores suggests that a huge eruption, possibly the largest of the millennium, occurred in this year.
1586	Kelut, Java	Explosions in crater lake; mudflows kill 10,000.
1631	Vesuvius, Italy	Eruption kills 4,000.
ca. 1660	Long Island, Papua New Guinea	"The time of darkness" in tribal legends on Papua New Guinea.
1672	Merapi, Java	Pyroclastic flows and mudflows kill 3,000.
1711	Awu, Sangihe Islands, Indonesia	Pyroclastic flows kill 3,000.
1760	Makian, Halmahera, Indonesia	Eruption kills 2,000; island evacuated for seven years.
1772	Papandayan, Java	Debris avalanche causes 2,957 fatalities.
1783	Lakagigar, Iceland	Largest historic lava flows; 9,350 deaths.
1790	Kilauea, Hawaii	Hawaii's last large explosive eruption.
1792	Unzen, Kyushu, Japan	Tsunami and debris avalanche kill 14,500.
1815	Tambora, Indonesia	History's most explosive eruption; 92,000 deaths.
1822	Galunggung, Java	Pyroclastic flows and mudflows kill 4,011.
1856	Awu, Sangihe Islands, Indonesia	Pyroclastic flows kill 2,806.
1883	Krakatoa, Indonesia	Caldera collapse; 36,417 people killed, most by tsunami.
1888	Ritter Island, Papua New Guinea	3,000 killed, most by tsunami created by debris avalanche.
1902	Mont Pelee, West Indies	Town of St. Pierre destroyed; 28,000 people killed.
1902	Santa Maria, Guatemala	5,000 killed as 10 villages are buried by volcanic debris.
1912	Novarupta (Katmai), Alaska	Largest 20th-century eruption.
1914	Lassen, California, U.S.	California's last historic eruption.
1919	Kelut, Java	Mudflows devastate 104 villages and kill 5,110 people.
1930	Merapi, Java	1,369 people are killed as 42 villages are totally or partially destroyed.
1943	Paricutín, Mexico	Fissure in cornfield erupts, building cinder cone 1,500 feet (460 m) high within two years. One of the few volcano births ever witnessed.
1951	Lamington, Papua New Guinea	Pyroclastic flows kill 2,942.
1963	Surtsey, Iceland	Submarine eruption builds new island.
1977	Nyiragongo, Dem. Rep. of the Congo	One of the shortest major eruptions and fastest lava flows ever recorded.
1980	St. Helens, Washington, U.S.	Lateral blast; 230-square-mile (600 sq km) area devastated.
1982	El Chichón, Mexico	Pyroclastic surges kill 1,877.
1985	Ruiz, Colombia	Mudflows kill 23,080.
1991	Pinatubo, Luzon, Philippines	Major eruption in densely populated area prompts evacuation of 250,000 people; fatalities number fewer than 800. Enormous amount of gas released into stratosphere lowers global temperatures for more than a year.
1993	Juan de Fuca Ridge, off the coast of Oregon, U.S.	Deep submarine rift eruptions account for three-fourths of all lava produced; this is one of the very few such eruptions that have been well-documented.

Sources: Smithsonian Institution Global Volcanism Program; Volcanoes of the World, Second Edition, by Tom Simkin and Lee Siebert, Geoscience Press and Smithsonian Institution, 1994.

Significant Earthquakes through History

Year	Estimated Magnitude	Number of Deaths	Place
365		50,000	Knossos, Crete
844		50,000	Damascus, Syria; Antioch, Turkey
856		150,000	Damghan, Kashan, Qumis, Iran
893		150,000	Caucasus region
894		180,000	western India
1042		50,000	Palmyra, Baalbek, Syria
1138		230,000	Aleppo, Gansana, Syria
1139	6.8	300,000	Gandzha, Kiapas, Azerbaijan
1201		50,000	upper Egypt to Syria
1290	6.7	100,000	eastern China
1556		820,000	Shaanxi Province, China
1662		300,000	China
1667	6.9	80,000	Caucasus region, northern Iran
1668		50,000	Shandong Province, China
1693		93,000	Sicily, Italy
1727		77,000	Tabriz, Iran
1731		100,000	Beijing, China
1739		50,000	China
1755		62,000	Morocco, Portugal, Spain
1780	6.7	100,000	Tabriz, Iran
1868	7.7	70,000	Ecuador, Colombia
1908	7.5	83,000	Calabria, Messina, Italy
1920	8.5	200,000	Gansu and Shaanxi provinces, China

Year	Estimated Magnitude	Number of Deaths	Place
1923	8.2	142,807	Tokyo, Yokohama, Japan
1927	8.3	200,000	Gansu and Qinghai provinces, China
1932	7.6	70,000	Gansu Province, China
1970	7.8	66,794	northern Peru
1976	7.8	242,000	Tangshan, China
1990	7.7	50,000	northwestern Iran

Some Significant U.S. Earthquakes

Year	Estimated Magnitude	Number of Deaths	Place
1811–12	8.6, 8.4, 8.7	<10	New Madrid, Missouri (series)
1886	7.0	60	Charleston, South Carolina
1906	8.3	3,000	San Francisco, California
1933	6.3	115	Long Beach, California
1946	7.4	5 ‡	Alaska
1964	8.4	125	Anchorage, Alaska
1971	6.8	65	San Fernando, California
1989	7.1	62	San Francisco Bay Area, California
1994	6.8	58	Northridge, California

‡ A tsunami generated by this earthquake struck Hilo, Hawaii, killing 159 people.
Sources: Lowell S. Whiteside, National Geophysical Data Center; Catalog of Significant Earthquakes 2150 B.C.—1991 A.D. by Paula K. Dunbar, Patricia A. Lockridge, and Lowell S. Whiteside, National Geophysical Data Center, National Oceanic and Atmospheric Administration.

OCEANS AND LAKES

Oceans, Seas, Gulfs, and Bays

	Area sq. miles	Area sq. km.	Volume of water cubic miles	Volume of water cubic km.	Mean depth feet	Mean depth meters	Greatest known depth feet	Greatest known depth meters	
Pacific Ocean	63,800,000	165,200,000	169,650,000	707,100,000	12,987	3,957	35,810	10,922	Mariana Trench
Atlantic Ocean	31,800,000	82,400,000	79,199,000	330,100,000	11,821	3,602	28,232	8,610	Puerto Rico Trench
Indian Ocean	28,900,000	74,900,000	68,282,000	284,600,000	12,261	3,736	23,812	7,258	Weber Basin
Arctic Ocean	5,400,000	14,000,000	4,007,000	16,700,000	3,712	1,131	17,897	5,453	Lat. 77° 45'N, long. 175°W
Coral Sea	1,850,000	4,791,000	2,752,000	11,470,000	7,857	2,394	30,079	9,165	
Arabian Sea	1,492,000	3,864,000	2,416,000	10,070,000	8,973	2,734	19,029	5,803	
South China Sea	1,331,000	3,447,000	943,000	3,929,000	3,741	1,140	18,241	5,563	
Caribbean Sea	1,063,000	2,753,000	1,646,000	6,860,000	8,175	2,491	25,197	7,685	Off Cayman Islands
Mediterranean Sea	967,000	2,505,000	901,000	3,754,000	4,916	1,498	16,470	5,023	Off Cape Matapan, Greece
Bering Sea	876,000	2,269,000	911,000	3,796,000	5,382	1,640	25,194	7,684	Off Buldir Island
Bengal, Bay of	839,000	2,173,000	1,357,000	5,616,000	8,484	2,585	17,251	5,261	
Okhotsk, Sea of	619,000	1,603,000	316,000	1,317,000	2,694	821	1,029	3,374	Lat. 146° 10'E, long. 46° 50'N
Norwegian Sea	597,000	1,546,000	578,000	2,408,000	5,717	1,742	13,189	4,022	
Mexico, Gulf of	596,000	1,544,000	560,000	2,332,000	8,205	2,500	14,370	4,382	Sigsbee Deep
Hudson Bay	475,000	1,230,000	22,000	92,000	328	100	850	259	Near entrance
Greenland Sea	465,000	1,204,000	417,000	1,740,000	4,739	1,444	15,899	4,849	
Japan, Sea of	413,000	1,070,000	391,000	1,630,000	5,037	1,535	12,041	3,669	
Arafura Sea	400,000	1,037,000	49,000	204,000	646	197	12,077	3,680	
East Siberian Sea	357,000	926,000	14,000	61,000	216	66	508	155	
Kara Sea	349,000	903,000	24,000	101,000	371	113	2,034	620	
East China Sea	290,000	752,000	63,000	263,000	1,145	349	7,778	2,370	
Banda Sea	268,000	695,000	511,000	2,129,000	10,056	3,064	24,418	7,440	
Baffin Bay	263,000	681,000	142,000	593,000	2,825	861	7,010	2,136	
Laptev Sea	262,000	678,000	87,000	363,000	1,772	540	9,780	2,980	
Timor Sea	237,000	615,000	60,000	250,000	1,332	406	10,863	3,310	
Andaman Sea	232,000	602,000	158,000	660,000	3,597	1,096	13,777	4,198	
Chukchi Sea	228,000	590,000	11,000	45,000	252	77	525	160	
North Sea	214,000	554,000	12,000	52,000	315	96	2,655	809	
Java Sea	185,000	480,000	5,000	22,000	147	45	292	89	
Beaufort Sea	184,000	476,000	115,000	478,000	3,295	1,004	12,245	3,731	
Red Sea	174,000	450,000	60,000	251,000	1,831	558	8,648	2,635	
Baltic Sea	173,000	448,000	5,000	20,000	157	48	1,506	459	
Celebes Sea	168,000	435,000	380,000	1,586,000	11,962	3,645	19,173	5,842	
Black Sea	166,000	431,000	133,000	555,000	3,839	1,170	7,256	2,211	
Yellow Sea	161,000	417,000	4,000	17,000	131	40	344	105	
Sulu Sea	134,000	348,000	133,000	553,000	5,221	1,591	18,300	5,576	
Molucca Sea	112,000	291,000	133,000	554,000	6,242	1,902	16,311	4,970	
Ceram Sea	72,000	187,000	54,000	227,000	3,968	1,209	17,456	5,319	
Flores Sea	47,000	121,000	53,000	222,000	6,003	1,829	16,813	5,123	
Bali Sea	46,000	119,000	12,000	49,000	1,349	411	4,253	1,296	
Savu Sea	41,000	105,000	43,000	178,000	5,582	1,701	11,060	3,370	
White Sea	35,000	91,000	1,000	4,400	161	49	1,083	330	
Azov, Sea of	15,000	40,000	100	400	29	9	46	14	
Marmara, Sea of	4,000	11,000	1,000	4,000	1,171	357	4,138	1,261	

Source: Atlas of World Water Balance, *USSR National Committee for the International Water Decade and UNESCO, 1977.*

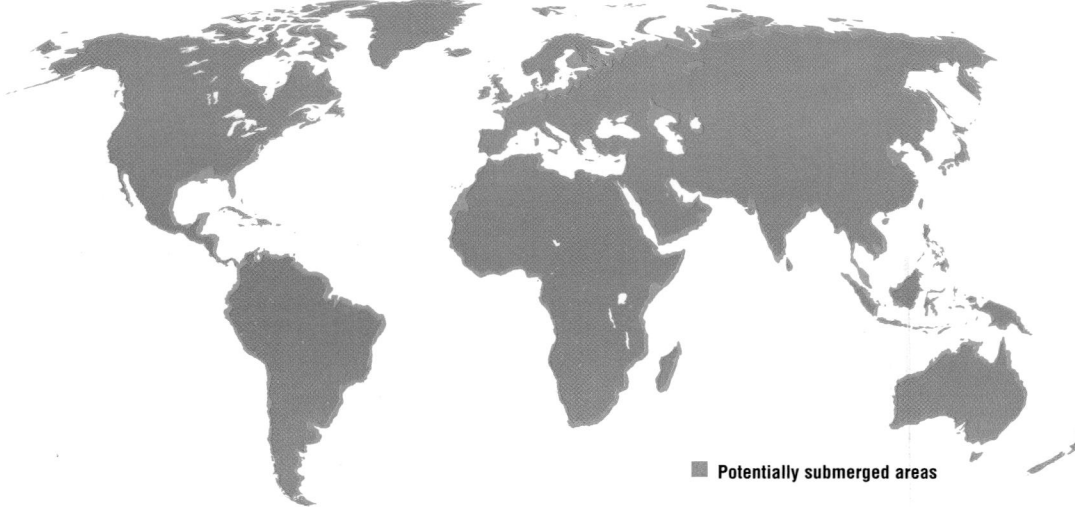

Potentially submerged areas

Fluctuating Sea Level

Changes in the Earth's climate have a dramatic effect on the sea level. Only 20,000 years ago, at the height of the most recent ice age, a vast amount of the Earth's water was locked up in ice sheets and glaciers, and the sea level was 330 feet (100 meters) lower than it is today. As the climate warmed slowly, the ice began to melt and the oceans began to rise.

Today there is still a tremendous amount of ice on the Earth. More than nine-tenths of it resides in the enormous ice cap which covers Antarctica. Measuring about 5.4 million square miles (14 million sq km) in surface area, the ice cap is on average one mile (1.6 km) thick but in some places is nearly three miles (4.8 km) thick. If it were to melt, the oceans would rise another 200 feet (60 m), and more than half of the world's population would have to relocate.

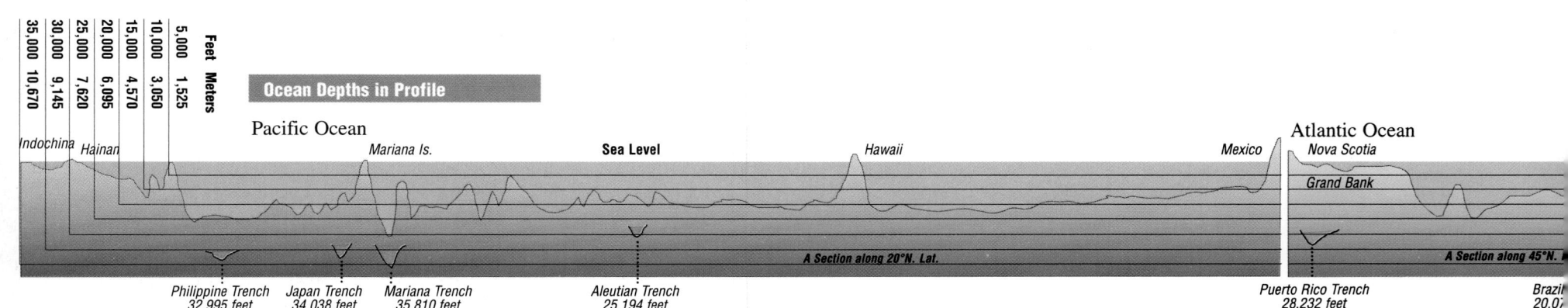

Ocean Depths in Profile

Pacific Ocean · Indochina · Hainan · Mariana Is. · Sea Level · Hawaii · Mexico · Atlantic Ocean · Nova Scotia · Grand Bank

A Section along 20°N. Lat.

A Section along 45°N.

Philippine Trench 32,995 feet (10,063 m)
Japan Trench 34,038 feet (10,375 m)
Mariana Trench 35,810 feet (10,922 m)
Aleutian Trench 25,194 feet (8,100 m)
Puerto Rico Trench 28,232 feet (8,611 m)
Brazil 20,0 (6,1

	Lake	Greatest depth feet	meters
1	Baikal, Lake, Russia	5,315	1,621
2	Tanganyika, Lake, Africa	4,800	1,464
3	Caspian Sea, Asia-Europe	3,363	1,025
4	Nyasa, Lake (Lake Malawi), Malawi-Mozambique-Tanzania	2,317	706
5	Issyk-Kul, Lake, Kyrgyzstan	2,303	702
6	Great Slave Lake, NWT, Canada	2,015	614
7	Matana, Lake, Indonesia	1,936	590
8	Crater Lake, Oregon, U.S.	1,932	589
9	Toba, Lake, Indonesia	1,736	529
10	Sarez, Lake, Tajikistan	1,657	505
11	Tahoe, Lake, California-Nevada, U.S.	1,645	502
12	Kivu, Lake, Rwanda-D.R.C.	1,628	496
13	Chelan, Lake, Washington, U.S.	1,605	489
14	Quesnel Lake, BC, Canada	1,560	476
15	Adams Lake, BC, Canada	1,500	457

Lakes with the Greatest Volume of Water

	Lake	Volume of water cubic mi	cubic km
1	Caspian Sea, Asia-Europe	18,900	78,200
2	Baikal, Lake, Russia	5,500	23,000
3	Tanganyika, Lake, Africa	4,500	18,900
4	Superior, Lake, Canada-U.S.	2,900	12,200
5	Nyasa, Lake (Lake Malawi), Malawi-Mozambique-Tanzania	1,900	7,725
6	Michigan, Lake, U.S.	1,200	4,910
7	Huron, Lake, Canada-U.S.	860	3,580
8	Victoria, Lake, Kenya-Tanzania-Uganda	650	2,700
9	Issyk-Kul, Lake, Kyrgyzstan	415	1,730
10	Ontario, Lake, Canada-U.S.	410	1,710
11	Great Slave Lake, Canada	260	1,070
12	Aral Sea, Kazakhstan-Uzbekistan	250	1,020
13	Great Bear Lake, Canada	240	1,010
14	Ladoga, Lake, Russia	220	908
15	Titicaca, Lake, Bolivia-Peru	170	710

Sources for volume and depth information: Atlas of World Water Balance, USSR National Committee for the International Water Decade and UNESCO, 1977; Principal Rivers and Lakes of the World, National Oceanic and Atmospheric Administration, 1982.

Principal Lakes

	Lake	Area sq mi	sq km
1	Caspian Sea, Asia-Europe	143,240	370,990
2	Superior, Lake, Canada-U.S.	31,700	82,100
3	Victoria, Lake, Kenya-Tanzania-Uganda	26,820	69,463
4	Aral Sea, Kazakhstan-Uzbekistan	24,700	64,100
5	Huron, Lake, Canada-U.S.	23,000	60,000
6	Michigan, Lake, U.S.	22,300	57,800
7	Tanganyika, Lake, Africa	12,350	31,986
8	Baikal, Lake, Russia	12,200	31,500
9	Great Bear Lake, Canada	12,095	31,326
10	Nyasa, Lake (Lake Malawi), Malawi-Mozambique-Tanzania	11,150	28,878
11	Great Slave Lake, Canada	11,030	28,568
12	Erie, Lake, Canada-U.S.	9,910	25,667
13	Winnipeg, Lake, Canada	9,416	24,387
14	Ontario, Lake, Canada-U.S.	7,540	19,529
15	Balkhash, Lake, Kazakhstan	7,100	18,300
16	Ladoga, Lake, Russia	6,833	17,700
17	Chad, Lake (Lac Tchad), Cameroon-Chad-Nigeria	6,300	16,300
18	Onega, Lake, Russia	3,753	9,720
19	Eyre, Lake, Australia	3,700	9,500
20	Titicaca, Lake, Bolivia-Peru	3,200	8,300
21	Nicaragua, Lake, Nicaragua	3,150	8,158
22	Mai-Ndombe, Lake, D.R.C.	3,100	8,000
23	Athabasca, Lake, Canada	3,064	7,935
24	Reindeer Lake, Canada	2,568	6,650
25	Tonle Sap, Cambodia	2,500	6,500
26	Rudolf, Lake, Ethiopia-Kenya	2,473	6,405
27	Issyk-Kul, Ozero, Kyrgyzstan	2,425	6,280
28	Torrens, Lake, Australia	2,300	5,900
29	Albert, Lake, Uganda-D.R.C.	2,160	5,594
30	Vänern, Sweden	2,156	5,584
31	Nettilling Lake, Canada	2,140	5,542
32	Winnipegosis, Lake, Canada	2,075	5,374
33	Bangweulu, Lake, Zambia	1,930	4,999
34	Nipigon, Lake, Canada	1,872	4,848
35	Urmia, Lake, Iran	1,815	4,701
36	Manitoba, Lake, Canada	1,785	4,624
37	Woods, Lake of the, Canada-U.S.	1,727	4,472
38	Kyoga, Lake, Uganda	1,710	4,429
39	Great Salt Lake, U.S.	1,680	4,351

Lake Baikal

Russia's Great Lake

On a map of the world, Lake Baikal is easy to overlook — a thin blue crescent adrift in the vastness of Siberia. But its inconspicuousness is deceptive, for Baikal is one of the greatest bodies of fresh water on Earth.

Although lakes generally have a life span of less than one million years, Baikal has existed for perhaps as long as 25 million years, which makes it the world's oldest body of fresh water. It formed in a rift that tectonic forces had begun to tear open in the Earth's crust. As the rift grew, so did Baikal. Today the lake is 395 miles (636 km) long and an average of 30 miles (48 km) wide. Only seven lakes in the world have a greater surface area.

Baikal is the world's deepest lake. Its maximum depth is 5,315 feet (1,621 m) — slightly over a mile, and roughly equal to the greatest depth of the Grand Canyon. The lake bottom lies 4,250 feet (1,295 m) below sea level and two-and-a-third miles (3.75 km) below the peaks of the surounding mountains. The crustal rift which Baikal occupies is the planet's deepest land depression, extending to a depth of more than five-and-a-half miles (9 km). The lake sits atop at least four miles (6.4 km) of sediment, the accumulation of 25 million years.

More than 300 rivers empty into Baikal, but only one, the Angara, flows out of it. Despite having only 38% of the surface area of North America's Lake Superior, Baikal contains more water than all five of the Great Lakes combined. Its volume of 5,500 cubic miles (23,000 cubic km) is greater than that of any other freshwater lake in the world and represents approximately one-fifth of all of the Earth's unfrozen fresh water.

Caspian Sea ·············

Lake Superior ·············

Lake Victoria ·············

Aral Sea ·············

Lake Huron ·············

Lake Michigan ·············

Lake Tanganyika ·············

Lake Baikal ·············

Great Bear Lake ·············

Lake Nyasa (Malawi) ·············

France | Mediterranean Sea | Indian Ocean | Arctic Ocean | Pacific Ocean | South Pole

Gibraltar Malta Israel | Sea Level | Sumba | North Pole | 65°N 65°S

A Section along 10°N. Lat.

RIVERS

World's Longest Rivers

Rank	River	Length Miles	Length Kilometers	Rank	River	Length Miles	Length Kilometers
1	Nile, Africa	4,145	6,671	36	Murray, Australia	1,566	2,520
2	Amazon-Ucayali, South America	4,000	6,400	37	Ganges, Asia	1,560	2,511
3	Yangtze (Chang), Asia	3,900	6,300	38	Pilcomayo, South America	1,550	2,494
4	Mississippi-Missouri, North America	3,740	6,019	39	Euphrates, Asia	1,510	2,430
5	Huang (Yellow), Asia	3,395	5,464	40	Ural, Asia	1,509	2,428
6	Ob-Irtysh, Asia	3,362	5,410	41	Arkansas, North America	1,459	2,348
7	Río de la Plata-Paraná, South America	3,030	4,876	42	Colorado, North America (U.S.-Mexico)	1,450	2,334
8	Congo (Zaïre), Africa	2,900	4,700	43	Aldan, Asia	1,412	2,273
9	Paraná, South America	2,800	4,500	44	Syr Darya, Asia	1,370	2,205
10	Amur-Argun, Asia	2,761	4,444	45	Dnieper, Europe	1,350	2,200
11	Lena, Asia	2,700	4,400	46	Araguaia, South America	1,350	2,200
12	Mackenzie, North America	2,635	4,241	47	Cassai (Kasai), Africa	1,338	2,153
13	Mekong, Asia	2,600	4,200	48	Tarim, Asia	1,328	2,137
14	Niger, Africa	2,600	4,200	49	Kolyma, Asia	1,323	2,129
15	Yenisey, Asia	2,543	4,092	50	Orange, Africa	1,300	2,100
16	Missouri-Red Rock, North America	2,533	4,076	51	Negro, South America	1,300	2,100
17	Mississippi, North America	2,348	3,779	52	Ayeyarwady (Irrawaddy), Asia	1,300	2,100
18	Murray-Darling, Australia	2,330	3,750	53	Red, North America	1,270	2,044
19	Missouri, North America	2,315	3,726	54	Juruá, South America	1,250	2,012
20	Volga, Europe	2,194	3,531	55	Columbia, North America	1,240	2,000
21	Madeira, South America	2,013	3,240	56	Xingu, South America	1,230	1,979
22	São Francisco, South America	1,988	3,199	57	Ucayali, South America	1,220	1,963
23	Grande, Rio (Río Bravo), North America	1,885	3,034	58	Saskatchewan-Bow, North America	1,205	1,939
24	Purús, South America	1,860	2,993	59	Peace, North America	1,195	1,923
25	Indus, Asia	1,800	2,900	60	Tigris, Asia	1,180	1,899
26	Danube, Europe	1,776	2,858	61	Don, Europe	1,162	1,870
27	Brahmaputra, Asia	1,770	2,849	62	Songhua, Asia	1,140	1,835
28	Yukon, North America	1,770	2,849	63	Pechora, Europe	1,124	1,809
29	Salween (Nu), Asia	1,750	2,816	64	Kama, Europe	1,122	1,805
30	Zambezi, Africa	1,700	2,700	65	Limpopo, Africa	1,120	1,800
31	Vilyuy, Asia	1,647	2,650	66	Angara, Asia	1,105	1,779
32	Tocantins, South America	1,640	2,639	67	Snake, North America	1,038	1,670
33	Orinoco, South America	1,615	2,600	68	Uruguay, South America	1,025	1,650
34	Paraguay, South America	1,610	2,591	69	Churchill, North America	1,000	1,600
35	Amu Darya, Asia	1,578	2,540	70	Marañón, South America	995	1,592

The World's Greatest River

Although the Nile is slightly longer, the Amazon surpasses all other rivers in volume, size of drainage basin, and in nearly every other important category. If any river is to be called the greatest in the world, surely it is the Amazon.

It has been estimated that one-fifth of all of the flowing water on Earth is carried by the Amazon. From its 150-mile (240-km)-wide mouth, the river discharges 6,180,000 cubic feet (174,900 cubic m) of water per second — four-and-a-half times as much as the Congo, ten times as much as the Mississippi, and fifty-six times as much as the Nile. The Amazon's tremendous outflow turns the waters of the Atlantic from salty to brackish for more than 100 miles (160 km) offshore.

Covering more than one-third of the entire continent of South America, the Amazon's vast drainage basin measures 2,669,000 square miles (6,915,000 sq km), nearly twice as large as that of the second-ranked Congo. The Amazon begins its 4,000-mile (6,400-km) journey to the Atlantic from high up in the Andes, only 100 miles (160 km) from the Pacific. Along its course it receives the waters of more than 1,000 tributaries, which rise principally from the Andes, the Guiana Highlands, and the Brazilian Highlands. Seven of the tributaries are more than 1,000 miles (1,600 km) long, and one, the Madeira, is more than 2,000 miles (3,200 km) long.

The depth of the Amazon throughout most of its Brazilian segment exceeds 150 feet (45 m). Depths of more than 300 feet (90 m) have been recorded at points near the mouth. The largest ocean-going vessels can sail as far inland as Manaus, 1,000 miles (1,600 km) from the mouth. Freighters and small passenger vessels can navigate to Iquitos, 2,300 miles (3,700 km) from the mouth, even during times of low water.

Drainage basin of the Amazon River

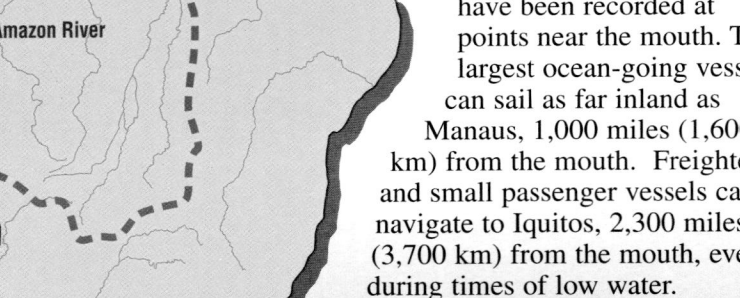

Rivers with the Greatest Volume of Water

Rank	River Name	Flow of water per second at mouth cubic feet	Flow of water per second at mouth cubic meters
1	Amazon, South America	6,180,000	174,900
2	Congo, Africa	1,377,000	39,000
3	Negro, South America (tributary of Amazon)	1,236,000	35,000
4	Orinoco, South America (trib. of Amazon)	890,000	25,200
5	Río de la Plata-Paraná, South America	809,000	22,900
6	Yangtze (Chang), Asia;	770,000	21,800
	Madeira, South America (trib. of Amazon)	770,000	21,800
7	Missouri, North America (trib. of Mississippi)	763,000	21,600
8	Mississippi, North America*	640,300	18,100
9	Yenisey, Asia	636,000	18,000
10	Brahmaputra, Asia	575,000	16,300
11	Lena, Asia	569,000	16,100
12	Zambesi, Africa	565,000	16,000
13	Mekong, Asia	500,000	14,100
14	Saint Lawrence, North America	460,000	13,000
15	Ayeyarwady (Irrawaddy), Asia	447,000	12,600
16	Ob-Irtysh, Asia; Ganges, Asia	441,000	12,500
17	Amur, Asia	390,000	11,000
18	Para-Tocantins, South America (joins Amazon at mouth)	360,000	10,200
19	Salween, Asia	353,000	10,000
20	Cassai (Kasai), Africa (trib. of Congo)	351,000	9,900
21	Mackenzie, North America	343,000	9,700
22	Volga, Europe	271,000	7,700
23	Ohio, North America (trib. of Mississippi)	257,000	7,300
24	Yukon, North America	240,000	6,800
25	Indus, Asia	235,000	6,600
26	Danube, Europe	227,000	6,400
27	Niger, Africa	215,000	6,100
28	Atchafalaya, North America	181,000	5,100
29	Paraguay, South America	155,000	4,400
30	Ob-Katun, Asia	147,000	4,200
31	São Francisco, South America	120,000	3,400
32	Tunguska, Asia	118,000	3,350
33	Huang (Yellow), Asia	116,000	3,300
34	Nile, Africa	110,000	3,100

*Approximately one-third of the Mississippi's water is diverted above Baton Rouge, Louisiana, and reaches the Gulf of Mexico via the Atchafalaya River.

Principal Rivers of the Continents

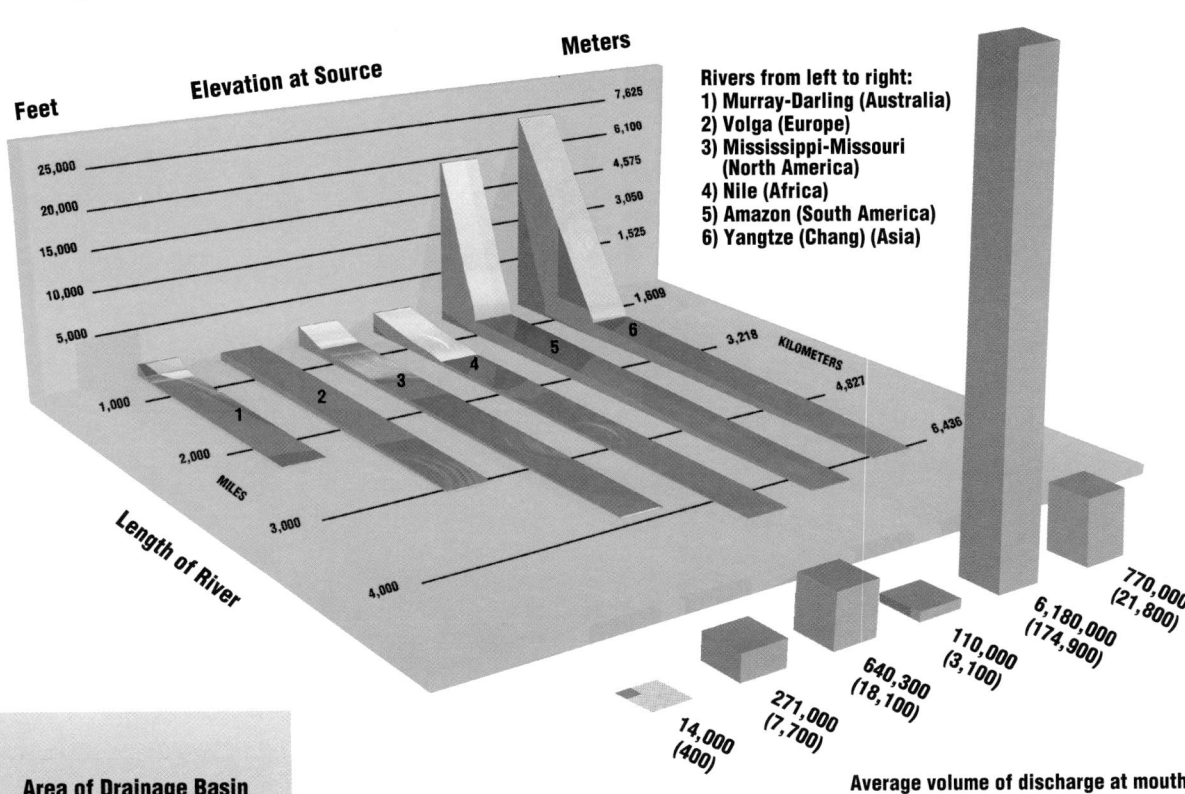

Rivers from left to right:
1) Murray-Darling (Australia)
2) Volga (Europe)
3) Mississippi-Missouri (North America)
4) Nile (Africa)
5) Amazon (South America)
6) Yangtze (Chang) (Asia)

Average volume of discharge at mouth, in cubic feet (cubic meters) per second

Rivers with the Largest Drainage Basins

Rank	River	Area of Drainage Basin Square Miles	Area of Drainage Basin Square Kilometers
1	Amazon, South America	2,669,000	6,915,000
2	Congo (Zaire), Africa	1,474,500	3,820,000
3	Mississippi-Missouri, North America	1,243,000	3,220,000
4	Río de la Plata-Paraná, South America	1,197,000	3,100,000
5	Ob-Irtysh, Asia	1,154,000	2,990,000
6	Nile, Africa	1,108,000	2,870,000
7	Yenisey-Angara, Asia	1,011,000	2,618,500
8	Lena, Asia	961,000	2,490,000
9	Niger, Africa	807,000	2,090,000
10	Amur-Ergun, Asia	792,000	2,051,300
11	Yangtze (Chang), Asia	705,000	1,826,000
12	Volga, Europe	525,000	1,360,000
13	Zambesi, Africa	513,500	1,330,000
14	St. Lawrence, North America	503,000	1,302,800
15	Huang (Yellow), China	486,000	1,258,700

Sources for volume and drainage basin information: Atlas of World Water Balance, USSR National Committee for the International Hydrological Decade and UNESCO, 1977; Principal Rivers and Lakes of the World, National Oceanic and Atmospheric Administration, 1982.

CLIMATE AND WEATHER

Temperature Extremes by Continent

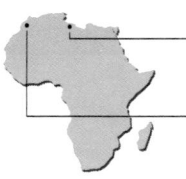

Africa
Highest recorded temperature
Al 'Azīzīyah, Libya, September 13, 1922:
136° F (58° C),
Lowest recorded temperature
Ifrane, Morocco, February 11, 1935:
-11° F (-24° C)

Antarctica
Highest recorded temperature
Vanda Station, January 5, 1974:
59° F (15° C)
Lowest recorded temperature
Vostok, July 21, 1983:
-129° F (-89° C)

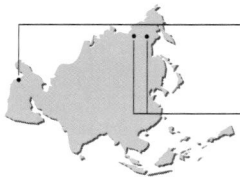

Asia
Highest recorded temperature
Tirat Zevi, Israel, June 21, 1942:
129° F (54° C)
Lowest recorded temperature
Oymyakon and Verkhoyansk,
Russia, February 5 and 7, 1892,
and February 6, 1933: -90° F (-68° C)

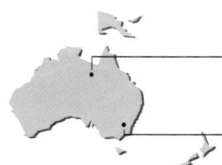

Australia / Oceania
Highest recorded temperature
Cloncurry, Queensland, January 16, 1889:
128° F (53° C)
Lowest recorded temperature
Charlottes Pass, New South Wales,
June 14, 1945, and July 22, 1947: -8° F (-22° C)

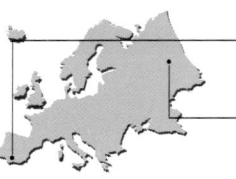

Europe
Highest recorded temperature
Seville, Spain, August 4, 1881:
122° F (50° C)
Lowest recorded temperature
Ust' Ščugor, Russia, (date not known):
-67° F (-55° C)

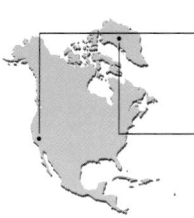

North America
Highest recorded temperature
Death Valley, California, United States,
July 10, 1913: 134° F (57° C)
Lowest recorded temperature
Northice, Greenland, January 9, 1954:
-87° F (-66° C)

South America
Highest recorded temperature
Rivadavia, Argentina, December 11, 1905:
120° F (49° C)
Lowest recorded temperature
Sarmiento, Argentina, June 1, 1907:
-27° F (-33° C)

World
Highest recorded temperature
Al 'Azīzīyah, Libya, September 13, 1922:
136° F (58° C)
Lowest recorded temperature
Vostok, Antarctica, July 21, 1983:
-129° F (-89° C)

World Temperature Extremes

Highest mean annual temperature Dalol, Ethiopia, 94° F (34° C)
Lowest mean annual temperature Plateau Station, Antarctica: -70° F (-57° C)

Greatest difference between highest and lowest recorded temperatures
Verkhoyansk, Russia. The highest temperature ever recorded there is 93.5° F (34.2° C); the lowest is -89.7° F (−67.6° C)
— a difference of 183° F (102° C).

Highest temperature ever recorded at the South Pole 7.5° F (-14° C) on December 27, 1978

Most consecutive days with temperatures of 100° F (38° C) or above Marble Bar, Australia, 162 days: October 30, 1923 to April 7, 1924

Greatest rise in temperature within a 12-hour period
Granville, North Dakota, on February 21, 1918. The temperature rose 83° F (46° C) from -33° F (-36° C)
in early morning to +50° F (10° C) in late afternoon

Greatest drop in temperature within a 12-hour period
Fairfield, Montana, on December 24, 1924. The temperature dropped 84° F (46° C), from 63° F (17° C)
at noon to -21° F (-29° C) by midnight

Temperature Ranges for 14 Major Cities around the World

| | Mean Temperature | | | Mean Temperature | |
City	Coldest Winter Month	Hottest Summer Month	City	Coldest Winter Month	Hottest Summer Month
Bombay, India	Jan: 74.3° F (23.5° C)	May: 85.5° F (29.7° C)	Moscow, Russia	Feb: 14.5° F (-9.7° C)	Jul: 65.8° F (18.8° C)
Buenos Aires, Argentina	Aug: 51.3° F (10.7° C)	Jan: 75.0° F (23.9° C)	New York City, U.S.	Jan: 32.9° F (0.5° C)	Jul: 77.0° F (25.0° C)
Calcutta, India	Jan: 67.5° F (19.7° C)	May: 88.5° F (31.4° C)	Osaka, Japan	Jan: 40.6° F (4.8° C)	Aug: 82.2° F (27.9° C)
London, England	Feb: 39.4° F (4.1° C)	Jul: 63.9° F (17.7° C)	Rio de Janeiro, Brazil	Jul: 70.2 ° F (21.2° C)	Jan: 79.9° F (26.6° C)
Los Angeles, U.S.	Jan: 56.3° F (13.5° C)	Jul: 74.1° F (23.4° C)	São Paulo, Brazil	Jul: 58.8° F (14.9° C)	Jan: 71.1° F (21.7° C)
Manila, Philippines	Jan: 77.7° F (25.4° C)	May: 84.9° F (29.4° C)	Seoul, South Korea	Jan: 23.2° F (-4.9° C)	Aug: 77.7° F (25.4° C)
Mexico City, Mexico	Jan: 54.1° F (12.3° C)	May: 64.9° F (18.3° C)	Tokyo, Japan	Jan: 39.6° F (4.2° C)	Aug: 79.3° F (26.3° C)

Precipitation

Greatest local average annual rainfall
Mt. Waialeale, Kauai, Hawaii,
460 inches (1,168 cm)

Lowest local average annual rainfall
Arica, Chile, .03 inches (.08 cm)

Greatest rainfall in 12 months
Cherrapunji, India, August 1860 to August 1861:
1,042 inches (2,647 cm)

Greatest rainfall in one month
Cherrapunji, India, July 1861: 366 inches (930 cm)

Greatest rainfall in 24 hours
Cilaos, Reunion, March 15 and 16, 1952:
74 inches (188 cm)

Greatest rainfall in 12 hours
Belouve, Reunion, February 28 and 29, 1964:
53 inches (135 cm)

Most thunderstorms annually
Kampala, Uganda, averages 242 days per
year with thunderstorms

Between 1916 and 1920, Bogor, Indonesia,
averaged 322 days per year with thunderstorms

Longest dry period
Arica, Chile, October, 1903
to January, 1918 — over 14 years

Largest hailstone ever recorded
Coffeyville, Kansas, U.S., September 3, 1970:
circumference 17.5 inches (44.5 cm)
diameter 5.6 inches (14 cm),
weight 1.67 pounds (758 grams)

Heaviest hailstone ever recorded
Kazakhstan, 1959: 4.18 pounds (1.9 kilograms)

North America's greatest snowfall in one season
Rainier Paradise Ranger Station, Washington,
U.S., 1971–1972: 1,122 inches (2,850 cm)

North America's greatest snowfall in one storm
Mt. Shasta Ski Bowl, California, U.S.,
February 13 to 19, 1959: 189 inches (480 cm)

North America's greatest snowfall in 24 hours
Silver Lake, Colorado, U.S., April 14 and 15, 1921:
76 inches (192.5 cm)

N. America's greatest depth of snowfall on the ground
Tamarack, California, U.S., March 11, 1911:
451 inches (1,145.5 cm)

Foggiest place on the U.S. West Coast
Cape Disappointment, Washington,
averages 2,552 hours of fog per year

Foggiest place on the U.S. East Coast
Mistake Island, Maine, averages
1,580 hours of fog per year

Wind

Highest 24-hour mean surface wind speed
Mt. Washington, New Hampshire, U.S.,
April 11 and 12, 1934: 128 mph (206 kph)

Highest 5-minute mean surface wind speed
Mt. Washington, New Hampshire, U.S.,
April 12, 1934: 188 mph (303 kph)

Highest surface wind peak gust:
Mt. Washington, New Hampshire, U.S.,
April 12, 1934: 231 mph (372 kph)

Windiest U.S. Cities

Chicago is sometimes called "The Windy City."
It earned this nickname because of long-winded politicians,
not because it has the strongest gales.

The windiest cities in the U.S. are as follows:

| | Average wind speed | |
Cities	mph	kph
Great Falls, Montana	13.1	21.0
Oklahoma City, Oklahoma	13.0	20.9
Boston, Massachusetts	12.9	20.7
Cheyenne, Wyoming	12.8	20.6
Wichita, Kansas	12.7	20.4

Chicago ranks 16th, with a 10.4 mph (16.7 kph) average.

Deadliest Hurricanes in the U.S. since 1900

Rank	Place	Year	Number of Deaths
1	Texas (Galveston)	1900	>6,000
2	Louisiana	1893	2,000
3	Florida (Lake Okeechobee)	1928	1,836
4	South Carolina, Georgia	1893	>1,000
5	Florida (Keys)	1919	>600
6	New England	1938	600
7	Florida (Keys)	1935	408
8	Southwest Louisiana, north Texas— "Hurricane Audrey"	1957	390
	Northeast U.S.	1944	390
9	Louisiana (Grand Isle)	1909	350
10	Louisana (New Orleans)	1915	275

Tornadoes in the U.S., 1950—1993

Rank	State	Total Number of Tornadoes	Yearly Average	Total Number of Deaths
1	Texas	5,303	120	471
2	Oklahoma	2,259	51	217
3	Kansas	2,068	47	199
4	Florida	1,932	44	81
5	Nebraska	1,618	37	51
	U.S. Total	33,120	753	4,045

Deadliest Floods in the U.S. since 1900

Rank	Place	Year	Number of Deaths
1	Ohio River and tributaries	1913	467
2	Mississippi Valley	1927	313
3	Black Hills, South Dakota	1972	237
4	Texas rivers	1921	215
5	Northeastern U.S., following Hurricane Dianne	1955	187
6	Texas rivers	1913	177
7	James River basin, Virginia	1969	153
8	Big Thompson Canyon, Colorado	1976	139
9	Ohio and Lower Mississippi river basins	1937	137
10	Buffalo Creek, West Virginia	1972	125

POPULATION

During the first two million years of our species' existence, human population grew at a very slow rate, and probably never exceeded 10 million. With the development of agriculture circa 8000 B.C., the growth rate began to rise sharply: by the year A.D. 1, the world population stood at approximately 250 million.

By 1650 the population had doubled to 550 million, and within only 200 years it doubled again, reaching almost 1.2 billion by 1850. Each subsequent doubling has taken only about half as long as the previous one: 100 years to reach 2.5 billion, and 40 years to reach 5.2 billion.

Experts have estimated that today's world population of 5.6 billion represents 5.5% of all of the people who have ever lived on Earth.*

* Population Today, *Population Reference Bureau, February 1995*

World Population

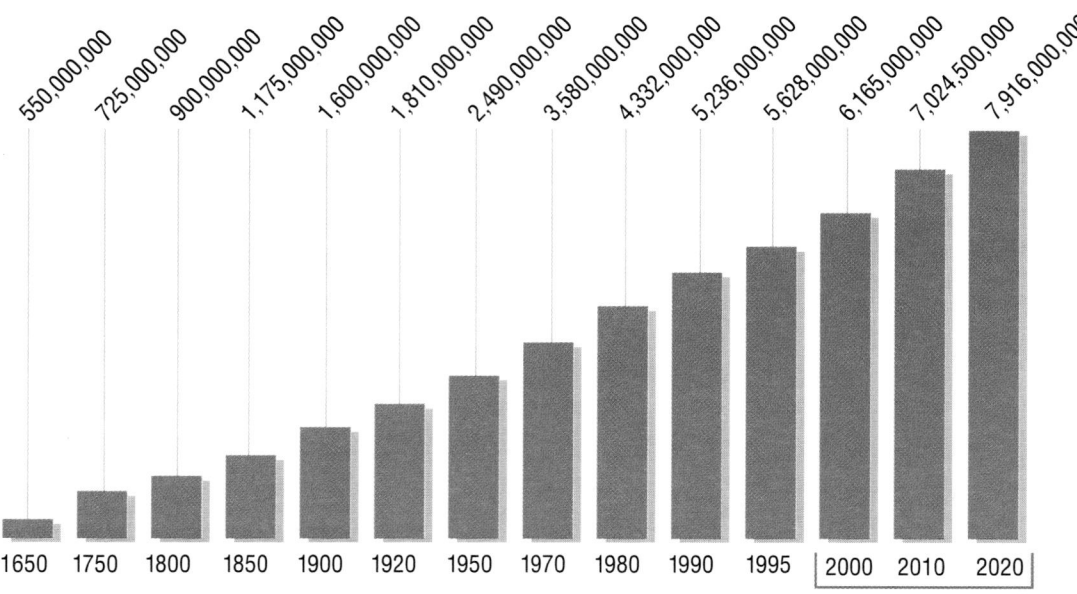

| 550,000,000 | 725,000,000 | 900,000,000 | 1,175,000,000 | 1,600,000,000 | 1,810,000,000 | 2,490,000,000 | 3,580,000,000 | 4,332,000,000 | 5,236,000,000 | 5,628,000,000 | 6,165,000,000 | 7,024,500,000 | 7,916,000,000 |

| 1650 | 1750 | 1800 | 1850 | 1900 | 1920 | 1950 | 1970 | 1980 | 1990 | 1995 | 2000 | 2010 | 2020 |

Projected Population

The World's Estimated Population (as of January 1, 1995): 5,628,000,000
Population Density: 97 people per square mile (37 people per square kilometer)

Historical Populations of the Continents and the World

Year	Africa	Asia	Australia	Europe	North America	Oceania, incl. Australia	South America	World
1650	*100,000,000*	335,000,000	*<1,000,000*	*100,000,000*	*5,000,000*	*2,000,000*	*8,000,000*	*550,000,000*
1750	*95,000,000*	476,000,000	*<1,000,000*	*140,000,000*	*5,000,000*	*2,000,000*	*7,000,000*	*725,000,000*
1800	*90,000,000*	593,000,000	*<1,000,000*	*190,000,000*	*13,000,000*	*2,000,000*	*12,000,000*	*900,000,000*
1850	*95,000,000*	754,000,000	*<1,000,000*	265,000,000	*39,000,000*	*2,000,000*	*20,000,000*	*1,175,000,000*
1900	*118,000,000*	932,000,000	4,000,000	400,000,000	106,000,000	6,000,000	38,000,000	*1,600,000,000*
1920	*140,000,000*	1,000,000,000	6,000,000	453,000,000	147,000,000	9,000,000	61,000,000	*1,810,000,000*
1950	199,000,000	1,418,000,000	8,000,000	530,000,000	219,000,000	13,000,000	111,000,000	*2,490,000,000*
1970	346,900,000	2,086,200,000	12,460,000	623,700,000	316,600,000	19,200,000	187,400,000	3,580,000,000
1980	463,800,000	2,581,000,000	14,510,000	660,000,000	365,000,000	22,700,000	239,000,000	4,332,000,000
1990	648,300,000	3,156,100,000	16,950,000	688,000,000	423,600,000	26,300,000	293,700,000	5,236,000,000

Figures for years prior to 1970 are rounded to the nearest million. Figures in italics represent rough estimates.

The 50 Most Populous Countries

Rank	Country	Population	Rank	Country	Population	Rank	Country	Population
1	China	1,196,980,000	18	United Kingdom	58,430,000	35	Algeria	27,965,000
2	India	909,150,000	19	Egypt	58,100,000	36	Morocco	26,890,000
3	United States	262,530,000	20	France	58,010,000	37	Sudan	25,840,000
4	Indonesia	193,680,000	21	Italy	57,330,000	38	Korea, North	23,265,000
5	Brazil	159,690,000	22	Ethiopia	55,070,000	39	Peru	23,095,000
6	Russia	150,500,000	23	Ukraine	52,140,000	40	Uzbekistan	22,860,000
7	Pakistan	129,630,000	24	Myanmar	44,675,000	41	Romania	22,745,000
8	Japan	125,360,000	25	Korea, South	44,655,000	42	Venezuela	21,395,000
9	Bangladesh	119,370,000	26	South Africa	44,500,000	43	Nepal	21,295,000
10	Nigeria	97,300,000	27	Dem. Rep. of the Congo	43,365,000	44	Taiwan	21,150,000
11	Mexico	93,860,000	28	Spain	39,260,000	45	Iraq	20,250,000
12	Germany	81,710,000	29	Poland	38,730,000	46	Afghanistan	19,715,000
13	Vietnam	73,760,000	30	Colombia	34,870,000	47	Malaysia	19,505,000
14	Philippines	67,910,000	31	Argentina	34,083,000	48	Uganda	18,270,000
15	Iran	63,810,000	32	Kenya	28,380,000	49	Sri Lanka	18,240,000
16	Turkey	62,030,000	33	Tanzania	28,350,000	50	Australia	18,205,000
17	Thailand	59,870,000	34	Canada	28,285,000			

Most Densely Populated Countries

Rank	Country (Population)	Population per Square Mile	Population per Square Kilometer
1	Monaco (31,000)	44,286	16,316
2	Singapore (2,921,000)	11,874	4,593
3	Vatican City (1,000)	5,000	2,500
4	Malta (368,000)	3,016	1,165
5	Maldives (251,000)	2,183	842
6	Bangladesh (119,370,000)	2,147	829
7	Guernsey (64,000)	2,133	821
8	Bahrain (563,000)	2,109	815
9	Jersey (86,000)	1,911	741
10	Barbados (261,000)	1,572	607
11	Taiwan (21,150,000)	1,522	587
12	Mauritius (1,121,000)	1,423	550
13	Nauru (10,000)	1,235	476
14	Korea, South (44,655,000)	1,168	451
15	Puerto Rico (3,625,000)	1,031	398

Least Densely Populated Countries

Rank	Country (Population)	Population per Square Mile	Population per Square Kilometer
1	Greenland (57,000)	0.07	0.03
2	Mongolia (2,462,000)	4.1	1.6
3	Namibia (1,623,000)	5.1	2.0
4	Mauritania (2,228,000)	5.6	2.2
5	Australia (18,205,000)	6.1	2.4
6	Botswana (1,438,000)	6.4	2.5
7	Iceland (265,000), Suriname (426,000)	6.7	2.6
8	Canada (28,285,000)	7.3	2.8
9	Libya (5,148,000)	7.6	2.9
10	Guyana (726,000)	8.7	3.4
11	Gabon (1,035,000)	10.1	3.9
12	Chad (6,396,000)	12.9	5.0
13	Central African Republic (3,177,000)	13.0	5.1
14	Bolivia (6,790,000)	16.0	6.2
15	Kazakhstan (17,025,000)	16.3	6.3

Most Highly Urbanized Countries

Country	Urban pop. as a % of total pop.
Vatican City	100%
Singapore	100%
Monaco	100%
Belgium	96%
Kuwait	96%
San Marino	92%
Israel (excl. Occupied Areas)	92%
Venezuela	91%
Iceland	91%
Qatar	90%
Uruguay	89%
Netherlands	89%
United Kingdom	89%
Malta	87%
Argentina	86%

Least Urbanized Countries

Country	Urban pop. as a % of total pop.
Bhutan	5%
Burundi	5%
Rwanda	6%
Nepal	11%
Oman	11%
Uganda	11%
Ethiopia	12%
Cambodia (Kampuchea)	12%
Malawi	12%
Burkina Faso	15%
Eritrea	15%
Grenada	15%
Solomon Islands	15%
Bangladesh	16%
Northern Mariana Islands	16%

World's Largest Metropolitan Areas

Rank	Name	Population
1	Tokyo-Yokohama, Japan	30,300,000
2	New York City, U.S.	18,087,000
3	São Paulo, Brazil	16,925,000
4	Osaka-Kobe-Kyoto, Japan	16,900,000
5	Seoul, South Korea	15,850,000
6	Los Angeles, U.S.	14,531,000
7	Mexico City, Mexico	14,100,000
8	Moscow, Russia	13,150,000
9	Bombay, India	12,596,000
10	London, England	11,100,000
11	Rio de Janeiro, Brazil	11,050,000
12	Calcutta, India	11,022,000
13	Buenos Aires, Argentina	11,000,000
14	Paris, France	10,275,000
15	Jakarta, Indonesia	10,200,000

Fastest-Growing and Slowest-Growing Countries

A country's rate of natural increase is determined by subtracting the number of deaths from the number of births for a given period. Immigration and emigration are not included in this formulation.

The highest rate of natural increase among major countries today is Syria's 3.74%. At this rate, Syria's 1995 population of 14,100,000 will double in 19 years and triple in 30 years.

In Hungary and Ukraine deaths currently outnumber births, and the two countries share the same negative rate of natural increase, -0.026%, the lowest in the world.

When all of the countries of the world are compared, pronounced regional patterns become apparent. Of the 35 fastest-growing countries, 30 are found in either Africa or the Middle East. Of the 45 slowest-growing countries, 42 are found in Europe.

The following table lists the most populous cities of the world by continent and in descending order of population. It includes all cities with central city populations of 500,000 or greater. Cities with populations of less than 500,000 but with metropolitan area populations of 1,000,000 or greater have also been included in the table.

The city populations listed are the latest available census figures or official estimates. For a few cities, only unofficial estimates are available. The year in which the census was taken or to which the estimate refers is provided in parentheses preceding the city population. When comparing populations it is important to keep in mind that some figures are more current than others.

Figures in parentheses represent metropolitan area populations — the combined populations of the cities and their suburbs.

The sequence of information in each listing is as follows: city name, country name (metropolitan area population) (date of census or estimate) city population.

Cairo, Egypt

Africa

Cairo (Al Qāhirah),
Egypt (9,300,000) ('86) 6,068,695
Kinshasa, Dem. Rep. of the Congo ('86) . 3,000,000
Alexandria (Al Iskandarīyah),
Egypt (3,350,000) ('86) 2,926,859
Casablanca (Dar-el-Beida),
Morocco (2,475,000) ('82) 2,139,204
Abidjan, Cote d'Ivoire ('88) 1,929,079
Addis Ababa, Ethiopia (1,990,000) ('90) . 1,912,500
Giza (Al Jīzah), Egypt ('86) 1,883,189
Algiers (El Djazaïr),
Algeria (2,547,983)('87) 1,507,241
Nairobi, Kenya ('90) 1,505,000

Dakar, Senegal ('88) 1,490,450
Luanda, Angola ('89) 1,459,900
Antananarivo, Madagascar ('88) 1,250,000
Lagos, Nigeria (3,800,000) ('87) 1,213,000

Lagos, Nigeria

Rural Nigerians move to Lagos at a rate of 200,000 a year. The government cannot cope with this influx, and thus the city is one of the world's most overcrowded and problem-ridden, with recurrent food shortages, severe pollution, and a chronic shortage of housing.

Ibadan, Nigeria ('87) 1,144,000
Dar es Salaam, Tanzania ('85) 1,096,000
Maputo, Mozambique ('89) 1,069,727
Lusaka, Zambia ('90) 982,362
Accra, Ghana (1,390,000) ('87) 949,113
Cape Town,
South Africa (1,900,000) ('91) 854,616
Conakry, Guinea ('86) 800,000
Kampala, Uganda ('91) 773,463
Durban, South Africa (1,740,000) ('91) . . . 715,669
Shubrā al Khaymah, Egypt ('86) 714,594
Johannesburg,
South Africa (4,000,000) ('91) 712,507
Douala, Cameroon ('87) 712,251
Brazzaville, Congo ('89) 693,712
Harare, Zimbabwe (955,000) ('83) 681,000
Bamako, Mali ('87) 658,275
Oran, Algeria ('87) 628,558
Mogadishu (Muqdisho), Somalia ('84) 600,000

Luanda, Angola: waterfront at night

Bangui, Central African Republic ('89) 596,800
Tunis, Tunisia (1,225,000) ('84) 596,654
Soweto, South Africa ('91) 596,632
Tripoli (Ṭarābulus),
Libya (960,000) ('88) 591,062
Ogbomosho, Nigeria ('87) 582,900
Lubumbashi, Dem. Rep. of the Congo ('84) 564,830
Yaoundé, Cameroon ('87) 560,785
Kano, Nigeria ('87) 538,300

The Most Populous City in the World, through History

With more than 30 million people, Japan's Tokyo-Yokohama agglomeration ranks as the most populous metropolitan area in the world today. New York City held this title from the mid-1920's through the mid-1960's. But what city was the most populous in the world five hundred years ago? Five *thousand* years ago?

The following time line represents one expert's attempt to name the cities that have reigned as the most populous in the world since 3200 B.C. The time line begins with Memphis, the capital of ancient Egypt, which was possibly the first city in the world to attain a population of 20,000.

Listed after each city name is the name of the political entity to which the city belonged during the time that it was the most populous city in the world. The name of the modern political entity in which the city, its ruins, or its site is located, where this entity differs from the historic political entity, is listed in parentheses.

For the purpose of this time line, the word "city" is used in the general sense to denote a city, metropolitan area, or urban agglomeration.

It is important to note that reliable census figures are not available for most of the 5,200 years covered by this time line. Therefore the time line is somewhat subjective and conjectural.

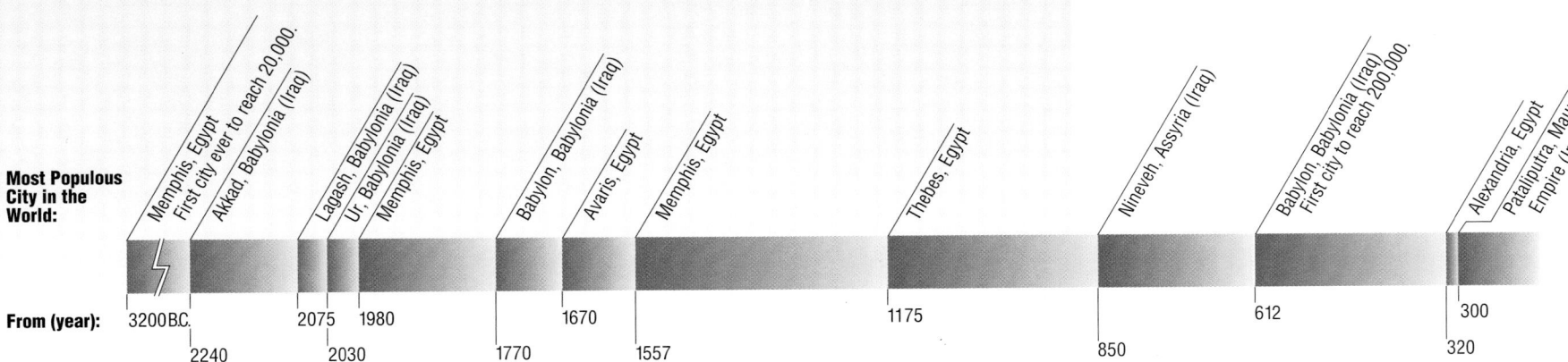

Most Populous City in the World:

Memphis, Egypt. First city ever to reach 20,000. | Akkad, Babylonia (Iraq) | Lagash, Babylonia (Iraq) | Ur, Babylonia (Iraq) | Memphis, Egypt | Babylon, Babylonia (Iraq) | Avaris, Egypt | Memphis, Egypt | Thebes, Egypt | Nineveh, Assyria (Iraq) | Babylon, Babylonia (Iraq). First city to reach 200,000. | Alexandria, Egypt | Pataliputra, Mauryan Empire (India)

From (year): 3200 B.C. | 2240 | 2075 | 2030 | 1980 | 1770 | 1670 | 1557 | 1175 | 850 | 612 | 320 | 300

Istanbul, Turkey: view of city, with Galeta Bridge in foreground

Mombasa, Kenya ('90) 537,000
Cotonou, Benin ('92) 533,212
Omdurman (Umm Durmān),
   Sudan ('83) 526,192
Pretoria, South Africa (1,100,000) ('91) . . 525,583
Rabat, Morocco (980,000) ('82) . . . 518,616
Lomé, Togo ('87) 500,000
N'Djamena, Chad ('88) 500,000
Khartoum (Al Khartūm),
   Sudan (1,450,000) ('83) 473,597

Asia

Bombay, India

Originally built on seven islands, Bombay now occupies a great expanse along the Arabian Sea. The islands have long since been surrounded by landfill as India's largest city looks for more land. Every night over 100,000 people sleep on small plots of rented sidewalk.

Seoul (Söul),
   South Korea (15,850,000) ('90) 10,627,790
Bombay (Mumbai),
   India (12,596,243) ('91) 9,925,891
Jakarta, Indonesia (10,200,000) ('90) . . . 8,227,746
Tokyo, Japan (30,300,000) ('90) 8,163,573
Shanghai, China (9,300,000) ('88) 7,220,000
Delhi, India (8,419,084) ('91) 7,206,704
Beijing (Peking),
   China (7,320,000) ('88) 6,710,000
Istanbul, Turkey (7,550,000) ('90) 6,620,241
Tehran, Iran (7,550,000) ('86) 6,042,584

Bangkok (Krung Thep),
   Thailand (7,060,000) ('91) 5,620,591
Tianjin (Tientsin), China ('88) 4,950,000
Karachi, Pakistan (5,300,000) ('81) 4,901,627
Calcutta, India (11,021,918) ('91) 4,399,819
Shenyang (Mukden), China ('88) 3,910,000
Madras (Chennai),
   India (5,421,985) ('91) 3,841,396
Baghdad, Iraq ('87) 3,841,268
Pusan, South Korea (3,800,000) ('90) . . . 3,797,566
Dhaka (Dacca),
   Bangladesh (6,537,308) ('91) 3,637,892
Wuhan, China ('88) 3,570,000
Yokohama, Japan ('90) 3,220,331
Guangzhou (Canton), China ('88) 3,100,000
Hyderabad, India (4,344,437) ('91) 3,043,896
Ahmadabad, India (3,312,216) ('91) 2,876,710
Ho Chi Minh City (Saigon),
   Vietnam (3,300,000) ('89) 2,796,229
Harbin, China ('88) 2,710,000
Lahore, Pakistan (3,025,000) ('81) 2,707,215
Taipei, Taiwan (6,130,000) ('92) 2,706,453
Singapore, Singapore (3,025,000) ('90) . . 2,690,100
Bangalore, India (4,130,288) ('91) 2,660,088
Osaka, Japan (16,900,000) ('90) 2,623,801

Seoul, South Korea: Tongdaemun Market

Guangzhou, China

Guangzhou is one of China's fastest-growing cities. Its status since 1979 as an economically independent zone has fueled its boom. Each day, hundreds of people arrive from China's countryside in hopes of sharing in the new wealth. The city, which dates back to the 3rd century B.C., had a population of close to 1,000,000 in 1900.

Ankara, Turkey (2,650,000) ('90) 2,559,471
Yangon (Rangoon),
   Myanmar (2,650,000) ('83) 2,513,023
Chongqing (Chungking), China ('88) 2,502,000
Surabaya, Indonesia ('90) 2,473,272
Nanjing (Nanking), China ('88) 2,390,000
Pyongyang, North Korea ('81) 2,355,000
Dalian (Dairen), China ('88) 2,280,000
Taegu, South Korea ('90) 2,228,834
Xi'an (Sian), China ('88) 2,210,000
Nagoya, Japan (4,800,000) ('90) 2,154,793

Xi'an, China: Huaching Hot Springs

Tashkent,
   Uzbekistan (2,325,000) ('91) 2,113,300
Bandung, Indonesia (2,220,000) ('90) . . . 2,058,122
Chengdu (Chengtu), China ('88) 1,884,000
Kanpur, India (2,029,889) ('91) 1,874,409
Changchun, China ('88) 1,822,000
Inchŏn, South Korea ('90) 1,818,293
Izmir, Turkey (1,900,000) ('90) 1,757,414
Medan, Indonesia ('90) 1,730,052
Taiyuan, China ('88) 1,700,000
Sapporo, Japan (1,900,000) ('90) 1,671,742
Quezon City, Philippines ('90) 1,666,766
Nagpur, India (1,664,006) ('91) 1,624,752
Lucknow, India (1,669,204) ('91) 1,619,115
Manila, Philippines (9,650,000) ('90) . . . 1,598,918
Aleppo, Syria (1,640,000) ('94) 1,591,400
Poona (Pune), India (2,493,987) ('91) . . 1,566,651

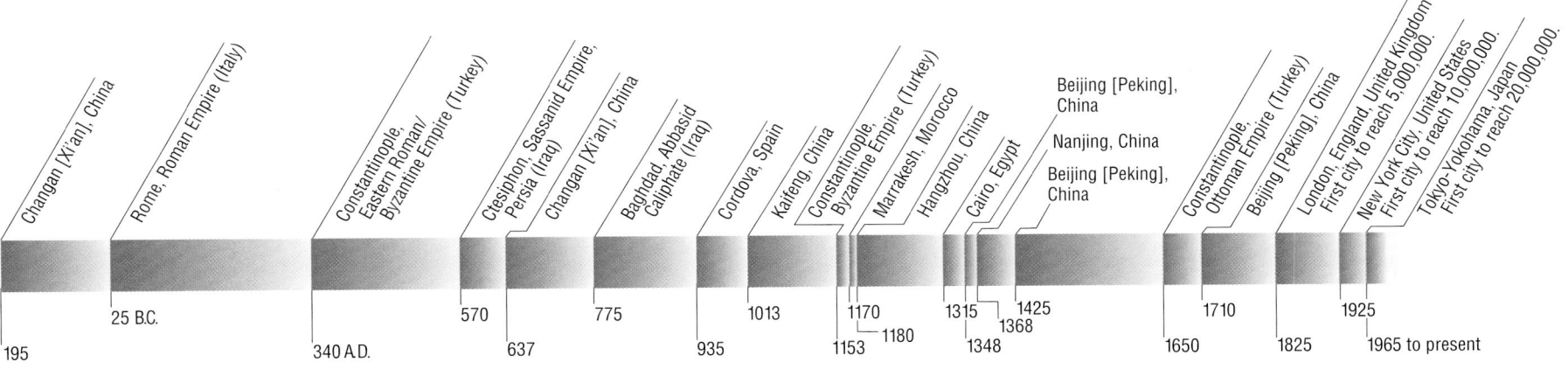

Source: Four Thousand Years of Urban Growth by Tertius Chandler, Edwin Mellen Press, 1987.

Chittagong, Bangladesh (2,342,662) ('91) 1,566,070
Damascus (Dimashq),
Syria (2,230,000) ('94) 1,549,932

Damascus, Syria

Damascus, capital of Syria, is believed to be the oldest continually occupied city in the world. It originated as a desert oasis commercial center as early as 2000 B.C. The city is mentioned in the biblical book of Genesis and in 4,000-year-old Egyptian records.

Jinan (Tsinan), China ('88) 1,546,000
Xinjiulong (New Kowloon),
China ('86) 1,526,910
Surat, India (1,518,950) ('91) 1,498,817
Kobe, Japan ('90) 1,477,410
Mashhad, Iran ('86) 1,463,508
Kyoto, Japan ('90) 1,461,103
Jaipur, India (1,518,235) ('91) 1,458,483
Novosibirsk, Russia (1,600,000) ('91) . . 1,446,300
Kabul, Afghanistan ('88) 1,424,400
Kaohsiung, Taiwan (1,845,000) ('92) . . . 1,401,239
Anshan, China ('88) 1,330,000
Kunming, China ('88) 1,310,000
Jiddah, Saudi Arabia ('80) 1,300,000
Qingdao (Tsingtao), China ('88) 1,300,000
Lanzhou (Lanchow), China ('88) 1,297,000
Hangzhou (Hangchow), China ('88) 1,290,000
Fushun (Funan), China ('88) 1,290,000
Tbilisi, Georgia (1,460,000) ('91) 1,279,000

Jiulong, China: skyline at night

Hangzhou, China: tea cultivation

Xianggang (Hong Kong),
China (4,770,000) ('91) 1,250,993
Riyadh (ar-Riyad), Saudi Arabia ('80) . . . 1,250,000
Semarang, Indonesia ('90) 1,249,230
Fukuoka, Japan (1,750,000) ('90) 1,237,062

Tbilisi, Georgia: one of the city's ubiquitous street sweepers

Changsha, China ('88) 1,230,000
Shijiazhuang, China ('88) 1,220,000
Jilin (Kirin), China ('88) 1,200,000
Yerevan, Armenia (1,315,000) ('89) 1,199,000
Qiqihar (Tsitsihar), China ('88) 1,180,000
Kawasaki, Japan ('90) 1,173,603
Omsk, Russia (1,190,000) ('91) 1,166,800
Almaty, Kazakhstan (1,190,000) ('91) . . . 1,156,200
Zhengzhou (Chengchow), China ('88) . . . 1,150,000
Chelyabinsk, Russia (1,325,000) ('91) . . 1,148,300
Kwangju, South Korea ('90) 1,144,695
Palembang, Indonesia ('90) 1,144,047
Baotou (Paotow), China ('88) 1,130,000
Faisalabad (Lyallpur), Pakistan ('81) . . . 1,104,209
Indore, India (1,109,056) ('91) 1,091,674
Nanchang, China ('88) 1,090,000
Hiroshima, Japan (1,575,000) ('90) 1,085,705
Baku (Bakı),
Azerbaijan (2,020,000) ('91) 1,080,500
Tangshan, China ('88) 1,080,000
Bhopal, India ('91) 1,062,771
Taejon, South Korea ('90) 1,062,084
Ürümqi, China ('88) 1,060,000
Ludhiana, India ('91) 1,042,740
Vadodara, India (1,126,824) ('91) 1,031,346
Guiyang (Kweiyang), China ('88) 1,030,000
Kitakyushu, Japan (1,525,000) ('90) 1,026,455
Kalyan, India ('91) 1,014,557
Isfahan, Iran (1,175,000) ('86) 986,753
Tabriz, Iran ('86) 971,482
Howrah, India ('91) 950,435
Ujungpandang (Makasar), Indonesia ('90) 944,372
Madurai, India (1,085,914) ('91) 940,989
Amman, Jordan (1,625,000) ('89) 936,300
Varanasi (Benares), India (1,030,863) ('91) 929,270
Krasnoyarsk, Russia ('91) 924,400

Kuala Lumpur

One of the world's fastest growing cities is also one of its youngest. Kuala Lumpur, or KL as it is commonly called, was founded in 1860 by a band of prospectors looking for tin. Its name means "Muddy Estuary," after its location at the confluence of the Kelang and Gombak Rivers.

Kuala Lumpur, Malaysia (1,475,000) ('80) . 919,610
Sendai, Japan (1,175,000) ('90) 918,398
Patna, India (1,099,647) ('91) 917,243
Adana, Turkey ('90) 916,150
Fuzhou, China ('88) 910,000
Hanoi, Vietnam (1,275,000) ('89) 905,939
Agra, India (948,063) ('91) 891,790
Wuxi (Wuhsi), China ('88) 880,000
Handan, China ('88) 870,000
Xuzhou (Süchow), China ('88) 860,000
Benxi (Penhsi), China ('88) 860,000
Shiraz, Iran ('86) 848,289

Agra, India: Taj Mahal

Zibo (Zhangdian), China ('88) 840,000
Yichun, China ('88) 840,000
Bursa, Turkey ('90) 834,576
Chiba, Japan ('90) 829,455
Coimbatore, India (1,100,746) ('91) 816,321
Datong, China ('88) 810,000
Sakai, Japan ('90) 807,765

Bursa, Turkey: Yeşil Türbe, 15th-century mosque containing the tomb of Sultan Mehmed I

Thana, India ('91) 803,369
Allahabad, India (844,546) ('91) 792,858
T'ai-chung, Taiwan ('92) 785,182
Jiulong (Kowloon), China ('86) 774,781
Caloocan, Philippines ('90) 761,011
Luoyang (Loyang), China ('88) 760,000
Meerut, India (849,799) ('91) 753,778
Vishakhapatnam, India (1,057,118) ('91) . 752,037
Jabalpur, India (888,916) ('91) 741,927
Suzhou (Soochow), China ('88) 740,000
Hefei, China ('88) 740,000
Nanning, China ('88) 720,000
Jinzhou (Chinchou), China ('88) 710,000
Amritsar, India ('91) 708,835
Hyderabad, Pakistan (800,000) ('81) 702,539
Vijayawada, India (845,756) ('91) 701,827
Fuxin, China ('88) 700,000

Tel Aviv, Israel

Jixi, China ('88) 700,000
Huainan, China ('88) 700,000
Multan, Pakistan (732,070) ('81) 696,316
Malang, Indonesia ('90) 695,089
T'ai-nan, Taiwan ('92) 692,116
Gwalior, India (717,780) ('91) 690,765
Ulsan, South Korea ('90) 682,978
Liuzhou, China ('88) 680,000
Hohhot, China ('88) 670,000
Bucheon, South Korea ('90) 667,777
Jodhpur, India ('91) 666,279
Nashik, India (725,341) ('91) 656,925
Mudanjiang, China ('88) 650,000
Hubli-Dharwar, India ('91) 648,298
Vladivostok, Russia ('91) 648,000
Suwon, South Korea ('90) 644,968
Homs, Syria ('94) 644,204
Irkutsk, Russia ('91) 640,500
Daqing, China ('88) 640,000
Bishkek, Kyrgyzstan ('91) 631,300
Phnom Penh, Cambodia ('90) 620,000
Xining (Sining), China ('88) 620,000
Faridabad, India ('91) 617,717
Basra (Al Basrah), Iraq ('85) 616,700
Khabarovsk, Russia ('91) 613,300
Colombo, Sri Lanka (2,050,000) ('89) 612,000
Cebu, Philippines (825,000) ('90) 610,417
Karaganda, Kazakhstan ('91) 608,600
Barnaul, Russia (673,000) ('91) 606,800
Solapur, India (620,846) ('91) 604,215
Gaziantep, Turkey ('90) 603,434
Novokuznetsk, Russia ('91) 601,900
Khulna, Bangladesh (966,096) ('91) 601,051
Gujranwala, Pakistan (658,753) ('81) 600,993

Ranchi, India (614,795) ('91) 599,306
Srinagar, India (606,002) ('81) 594,775
Okayama, Japan ('90) 593,730
Hegang, China ('86) 588,300
Bareilly, India (617,350) ('91) 587,211
Gauhati, India ('91) 584,342
Dushanbe, Tajikistan ('91) 582,400
Ahvaz, Iran ('86) 579,826
Dandong, China ('86) 579,800
Kumamoto, Japan ('90) 579,306
Ulan Bator, Mongolia ('91) 575,000

Ulan Bator, Mongolia

Situated high on a windswept plateau in Mongolia, Ulan Bator is one of the coldest of the world's large cities. Its average annual temperature is under 25 degrees Fahrenheit. However, the city enjoys an average of 240 clear, sunny days each year, and rarely sees rain or snow.

Aurangabad, India (592,709) ('91) 573,272
Mosul, Iraq ('85) 570,926
Ningbo, China ('88) 570,000
Cochin, India (1,140,605) ('91) 564,589
Bakhtaran (Kermānshāh), Iran ('86) 560,514
Shantou (Swatow), China ('88) 560,000
Rajkot, India (654,490) ('91) 559,407
Mecca (Makkah), Saudi Arabia ('80) 550,000
Qom, Iran ('86) 543,139
Songnam, South Korea ('90) 540,764
Taipeihsien, Taiwan ('91) 538,954
Kota, India ('91) 537,371
Kagoshima, Japan ('90) 536,752
Hamamatsu, Japan ('90) 534,620
Funabashi, Japan ('90) 533,270
Mandalay, Myanmar ('83) 532,949
Sagamihara, Japan ('90) 531,542
Jerusalem (Yerushalayim) (Al-Quds),
    Israel (560,000) ('91) 524,500
Trivandrum, India (826,225) ('91) 524,006
Changzhou (Changchow), China ('86) 522,700
Davao, Philippines ('90) 521,525
Kemerovo, Russia ('91) 520,700
Higashiosaka, Japan ('90) 518,319
Chonju, South Korea ('90) 517,104
Pimpri-Chinchwad, India ('91) 517,083
Quanwan (Tsuen Wan), China ('86) 514,241
Konya, Turkey ('90) 513,346
Jallandar, India ('91) 509,510
Beirut (Bayrūt), Lebanon (1,675,000) ('82) 509,000
Peshawar, Pakistan (566,248) ('81) 506,896
Tomsk, Russia ('91) 505,600
Gorakhpur, India ('91) 505,566

Srinagar, India: vegetable merchant on Dal Lake

Chandigarh, India (575,829) ('91) 504,094
Surakarta, Indonesia (590,000) ('90) 503,827
Zhangjiakou (Kalgan), China ('88) 500,000
Rawalpindi, Pakistan (1,040,000) ('81) . . . 457,091
Tel Aviv-Yafo, Israel (1,735,000) ('91) 339,400
Kuwait (Al-Kuwayt),
    Kuwait (1,375,000) ('85) 44,335

Australia and Oceania

Brisbane, Australia (1,334,017) ('91) 751,115
Perth, Australia (1,143,249) ('91) 80,517
Melbourne, Australia (3,022,439) ('91) 60,476
Adelaide, Australia (1,023,597) ('91) 14,843
Sydney, Australia (3,538,749) ('91) 13,501

Sydney, Australia

The city commonly known as Sydney is actually a collection of towns stretching for 40 miles along the coast of the Tasman Sea. Sydney proper is a small area at the core of the city on an inlet of the ocean. Its population of 13,501 accounts for less than 0.4% of the total metropolitan area population of 3.5 million.

Sydney, Australia: Opera House and downtown skyline

Europe

Moscow (Moskva),
    Russia (13,150,000) ('91) 8,801,500
London, England, U.K. (11,100,000) ('81) 6,574,009
Saint Petersburg (Leningrad),
    Russia (5,525,000) ('91) 4,466,800
Berlin, Germany (4,150,000) ('91) 3,433,695

London, England: Tower Bridge

Madrid, Spain (4,650,000) ('88) 3,102,846
Rome (Roma), Italy (3,175,000) ('91) . . 2,693,383
Kiev (Kyyiv), Ukraine (3,250,000) ('91) . . 2,635,000
Paris, France (10,275,000) ('90) 2,152,423
Bucharest (Bucureşti),
  Romania (2,300,000) ('92) 2,064,474
Budapest, Hungary (2,515,000) ('90) . . . 2,016,774
Barcelona, Spain (4,040,000) ('88) 1,714,355

Rome, Italy: Spanish Steps

Hamburg, Germany (2,385,000) ('91) . . . 1,652,363
Warsaw (Warszawa),
  Poland (2,312,000) ('93) 1,644,500
Minsk, Belarus (1,694,000) ('91) 1,633,600
Kharkiv (Kharkov),
  Ukraine (2,050,000) ('91) 1,622,800
Vienna (Wien), Austria (1,900,000) ('91) . 1,539,848
Nizhny Novgorod (Gorky),
  Russia (2,025,000) ('91) 1,445,000

Barcelona, Spain: Las Ramblas

Yekaterinburg, Russia (1,620,000) ('91) . 1,375,400
Milan (Milano), Italy (3,750,000) ('91) . . 1,371,008
Samara (Kuybyshev),
  Russia (1,505,000) ('91) 1,257,300
Munich (München),
  Germany (1,900,000) ('91) 1,229,026
Prague (Praha),
  Czech Republic (1,328,000) ('91) 1,212,010
Dnipropetrovs'k,
  Ukraine (1,600,000) ('91) 1,189,300
Sofia (Sofiya), Bulgaria (1,205,000) ('89) 1,136,875
Belgrade (Beograd),
  Yugoslavia (1,554,826) ('91) 1,136,786
Donets'k, Ukraine (2,125,000) ('91) 1,121,300
Perm', Russia (1,180,000) ('91) 1,110,400
Kazan', Russia (1,165,000) ('91) 1,107,300
Odesa, Ukraine (1,185,000) ('91) 1,100,700
Ufa, Russia (1,118,000) ('91) 1,097,000
Rostov-na-Donu,
  Russia (1,165,000) ('91) 1,027,600

Naples (Napoli), Italy (2,875,000) ('91) . 1,024,601
Birmingham,
  England, U.K. (2,675,000) ('81) 1,013,995
Volgograd (Stalingrad),
  Russia (1,360,000) ('91) 1,007,300
Turin (Torino), Italy (1,550,000) ('91) . . . 961,916
Cologne, Germany (1,810,000) ('91) 953,551
Lódź, Poland (950,000) ('93) 938,400
Saratov, Russia (1,155,000) ('91) 911,100
Riga, Latvia (1,005,000) ('91) 910,200
Voronezh, Russia ('91) 900,000
Zaporizhzhya, Ukraine ('91) 896,600
Lisbon (Lisboa), Portugal (2,250,000) ('81) 807,167
L'viv (L'vov), Ukraine ('91) 802,200
Marseille, France (1,225,000) ('90) 800,550
Athens (Athínai), Greece (3,096,775) ('91) . 748,110
Kraków, Poland (823,000) ('93) 744,000
València, Spain (1,270,000) ('88) 743,933
Kryvyy Rih, Ukraine ('91) 724,000
Amsterdam, Netherlands (1,875,000) ('92) . 713,407

Amsterdam, Netherlands: canal scene

Zagreb, Croatia ('87) 697,925
Palermo, Italy ('91) 697,162
Glasgow, Scotland, U.K. (1,800,000) ('90) . 689,210
Kishinev (Chişinău), Moldova ('91) 676,700
Genoa (Genova), Italy (805,000) ('91) 675,639
Stockholm, Sweden (1,491,726) ('91) 674,452
Seville, Spain (945,000) ('88) 663,132
Tolyatti, Russia ('91) 654,700
Ulyanovsk, Russia ('91) 648,300
Izhevsk, Russia ('91) 646,800
Frankfurt (Frankfurt am Main),
  Germany (1,935,000) ('91) 644,865
Wrocław (Breslau), Poland ('93) 640,700
Yaroslavl, Russia ('91) 638,100
Krasnodar, Russia ('91) 631,200

Essen, Germany (5,050,000) ('91) 626,973
Dortmund, Germany ('91) 599,055
Vilnius, Lithuania ('92) 596,900
Rotterdam, Netherlands (1,120,000) ('92) . 589,707
Poznań, Poland (666,000) ('93) 582,900
Zaragoza, Spain ('88) 582,239
Stuttgart, Germany (2,005,000) ('91) 579,988
Düsseldorf, Germany (1,225,000) ('91) . . . 575,794
Málaga, Spain ('88) 574,456
Orenburg, Russia ('91) 556,500
Bremen, Germany (790,000) ('91) 551,219
Penza, Russia ('91) 551,100
Tula, Russia (640,000) ('91) 543,600
Liverpool, England, U.K. (1,525,000) ('81) . 538,809
Duisburg, Germany ('91) 535,447
Ryazan, Russia ('91) 527,200
Mariupol' (Zhdanov), Ukraine ('91) 521,800
Hannover, Germany (1,000,000) ('91) 513,010
Astrakhan, Russia ('91) 511,900
Mykolayiv, Ukraine ('91) 511,600
Leipzig, Germany (720,000) ('91) 511,079
Naberezhnyye Chelny,
  Russia ('91) 510,100
Luhans'k, Ukraine (650,000) ('91) 503,900
Gomel', Belarus ('91) 503,300
Dublin, Ireland (1,140,000) ('86) 502,749
Helsinki (Helsingfors),
  Finland (1,045,000) ('93) 501,514
Nürnberg, Germany (1,065,000) ('91) 493,692

Dublin, Ireland: street scene

Antwerp, Belgium (1,140,000) ('91) 467,518
Copenhagen (København),
  Denmark (1,670,000) ('92) 464,566
Leeds, England, U.K. (1,540,000) ('81) . . . 445,242
Manchester, England, U.K. (2,775,000) ('81) 437,612
Lyon, France (1,335,000) ('90) 415,487
Katowice, Poland (2,770,000) ('93) 359,900

Frankfurt, Germany: Romerberg Square, Old Town

New York, NY, U.S.: skyline at sunset, looking downtown

San Francisco, U.S.
In 1900, San Francisco was the eighth-largest city in the United States. It has been slipping down the list since then; presently it ranks 14th. Surrounded on three sides by the waters of its bay and the Pacific Ocean, and hemmed in by other cities to its south, San Francisco has no room left to grow.

Tlalnepantla, Mexico ('90)	702,270
Tijuana, Mexico ('90)	698,752
Managua, Nicaraqua ('85)	682,000
Zapopan, Mexico ('90)	668,323
Toronto, On., Canada (3,893,046) ('91)	635,395
Jacksonville, Fl., U.S. (906,727) ('90)	635,230
Columbus, Oh., U.S. (1,377,419) ('90)	632,910
Milwaukee, Wi., U.S. (1,607,183) ('90)	628,088
Winnipeg, Mb., Canada (652,354) ('91)	616,790
Edmonton, Ab., Canada (839,924) ('91)	616,741
Memphis, Tn., U.S. (981,747) ('90)	610,337

Porto, Portugal (1,225,000) ('81)	327,368
Mannheim, Germany (1,525,000) ('91)	310,411
Newcastle upon Tyne, England, U.K. (1,300,000) ('81)	199,064
Lille, France (1,050,000) ('90)	172,142
Brussels (Bruxelles), Belgium (2,385,000) ('91)	136,42

Helsinki, Finland: floating market

North America

Mexico City, Mexico
Mexico City is built over the ruins of Tenochtitlán, the Aztec capital. At the time of the Spanish Conquest in 1519, Tenochtitlán had a population of perhaps 150,000, which was not only greater than any other city in the Americas but also greater than any European city at the time. Today, Mexico City and its environs rank as the world's seventh most-populous metropolitan area, with a total population of over 14 million. The population has doubled since 1970 and may well do so again by 2025.

Mexico City (Ciudad de México), Mexico (14,100,000) ('90)	8,235,744
New York, N.Y., U.S. (18,087,251) ('90)	7,322,564
Los Angeles, Ca., U.S. (14,531,529) ('90)	3,485,398
Chicago, Il., U.S. (8,065,633) ('90)	2,783,726
Santo Domingo, Dominican Republic ('90)	2,411,900
Havana (La Habana), Cuba (2,210,000) ('91)	2,119,059
Guadalajara, Mexico (2,325,000) ('90)	1,650,042
Houston, Tx., U.S. (3,711,043) ('90)	1,630,553
Philadelphia, Pa., U.S. (5,899,345) ('90)	1,585,577
Nezahualcóyotl, Mexico ('90)	1,255,456
Ecatepec, Mexico ('90)	1,218,135
San Diego, Ca., U.S. (2,949,000) ('90)	1,110,549
Monterrey, Mexico (2,015,000) ('90)	1,068,996
Guatemala, Guatemala (1,400,000) ('89)	1,057,210
Detroit, Mi., U.S. (4,665,236) ('90)	1,027,974
Montreal, P.Q., Canada (3,127,242) ('91)	1,017,666
Puebla, Mexico (1,200,000) ('90)	1,007,170
Dallas, Tx., U.S. (3,885,415) ('90)	1,006,877
Phoenix, Az., U.S. (2,122,101) ('90)	983,403
San Antonio, Tx., U.S. (1,302,099) ('90)	935,933
Naucalpan de Juárez, Mexico ('90)	845,960
Port-au-Prince, Haiti (880,000) ('87)	797,000
Ciudad Juárez, Mexico ('90)	789,522
San Jose, Ca., U.S. (1,497,577) ('90)	782,248
León, Mexico ('90)	758,279
Baltimore, Md., U.S. (2,382,172) ('90)	736,014
Indianapolis, In., U.S. (1,249,822) ('90)	731,327
San Francisco, Ca., U.S. (6,253,311) ('90)	723,959
Calgary, Ab., Canada (754,033) ('91)	710,677

Washington, D.C., U.S.: the Capitol

Washington, D.C., U.S. (3,923,574) ('90)	606,900
Kingston, Jamaica (890,000) ('91)	587,798
Tegucigalpa, Honduras ('88)	576,661
Boston, Ma., U.S. (4,171,643) ('90)	574,283
North York, On., Canada ('91)	562,564
Guadalupe, Mexico ('90)	535,332
Scarborough, On., Canada ('91)	524,598
Mérida, Mexico ('90)	523,422
Seattle, Wa., U.S. (2,559,164) ('90)	516,259
Chihuahua, Mexico ('90)	516,153
Acapulco, Mexico ('90)	515,374
El Paso, Tx., U.S. (1,211,300) ('90)	515,342
Cleveland, Oh., U.S. (2,759,823) ('90)	505,616
New Orleans, La., U.S. (1,238,816) ('90)	496,938

Montreal, Canada

Vancouver, B.C., Canada (1,602,502) ('91) . 471,844
Denver, Co., U.S. (1,848,319) ('90) 467,610
Fort Worth, Tx., U.S. (1,332,053) ('90) 447,619
Portland, Or., U.S. (1,477,895) ('90) 437,319
Kansas City, Mo., U.S. (1,566,280) ('90) . . 435,146
San Juan, Puerto Rico (1,877,000) ('90) . 426,832
Saint Louis, Mo., U.S. (2,444,099) ('90) . . 396,685
Charlotte, N.C., U.S. (1,162,093) ('90) 395,934
Atlanta, Ga., U.S. (2,833,511) ('90) 394,017
Oakland, Ca., U.S. (2,082,914) ('90) 372,242
Pittsburgh, Pa., U.S. (2,242,798) ('90) 369,879
Sacramento, Ca., U.S. (1,481,102) ('90) . . 369,365
Minneapolis, Mn., U.S. (2,464,124) ('90) . 368,383
Cincinnati, Oh., U.S. (1,744,124) ('90) 364,040
Miami, Fl., U.S. (3,192,582) ('90) 358,548
Buffalo, N.Y., U.S. (1,189,288) ('90) 328,123
Tampa, Fl., U.S. (2,067,959) ('90) 280,015
San José, Costa Rica (1,355,000) ('88) . . . 278,600
Newark, N.J., U.S. (1,824,321) ('90) 275,221
Anaheim, Ca., U.S. (2,410,556) ('90) . . . 266,406
Norfolk, Va., U.S. (1,396,107) ('90) 261,229
Rochester, N.Y., U.S. (1,002,410) ('90) . . . 231,636
Riverside, Ca., U.S. (2,588,793) ('90) 226,505
Orlando, Fl., U.S. (1,072,748) ('90) 164,693
Providence, R.I., U.S. (1,141,510) ('90) . . . 160,728
Salt Lake City, Ut., U.S. (1,072,227) ('90) . 159,936
Fort Lauderdale, Fl., U.S. (1,255,488) ('90) 149,377
Hartford, Ct., U.S. (1,085,837) ('90) 139,739

South America

São Paulo, Brazil (16,925,000) ('91) 9,393,753
Rio de Janeiro, Brazil (11,050,000) ('91) . 5,473,909

Rio de Janeiro, Brazil: Ipanema Beach

Bogotá (Santa Fe de Bogotá),
　Colombia (4,260,000) ('85) 3,982,941
Buenos Aires,
　Argentina (11,000,000) ('91) 2,960,976
Salvador, Brazil (2,340,000) ('91) 2,070,296
Caracas, Venezuela (4,000,000) ('90) . . 1,824,654
Belo Horizonte, Brazil (3,340,000) ('91) . 1,529,566
Brasília, Brazil ('91) 1,513,470
Guayaquil, Ecuador ('90) 1,508,444
Medellín, Colombia (2,095,000) ('85) . . . 1,468,089
Cali, Colombia (1,400,000) ('85) 1,350,565

Belo Horizonte, Brazil

São Paulo, Brazil

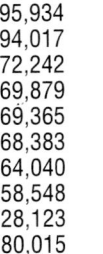

*Founded in 1554, São Paulo
remained a small town for three
centuries. Since the late 1800s,
however, its population has
increased by about 200 times.
Today, the São Paulo metropolitan
area is the third most populous in
the world, and the fastest-growing.
Its position as Latin America's
most important industrial center
has made it an irresistible lure for
rural dwellers seeking jobs.
Construction and services have
not been able to keep up with the
mushrooming population, and a
large number—perhaps half—of
São Paulo's inhabitants live in
squalid slums.*

Montevideo, Uruguay: Independence Park, Palacio Salvo,
and downtown skyline

Recife, Brazil (2,880,000) ('91) 1,296,995
Montevideo, Uruguay (1,550,000) ('85) . 1,251,647
Maracaibo, Venezuela ('90) 1,249,670
Porto Alegre, Brazil (2,850,000) ('91) . . . 1,247,352
Córdoba, Argentina (1,260,000) ('91) . . . 1,148,305
San Justo, Argentina ('91) 1,111,811

Belém, Brazil: fishermen unloading catch

Quito, Ecuador (1,300,000) ('90) 1,100,847
Manaus, Brazil ('91) 1,005,634
Goiânia, Brazil (1,130,000) ('91) 912,136
Valencia, Venezuela ('90) 903,621
Barranquilla, Colombia (1,140,000) ('85) . 899,781
Rosario, Argentina (1,190,000) ('91) 894,645
Curitiba, Brazil (1,815,000) ('91) 841,882
Belém, Brazil (1,355,000) ('91) 765,476
Campinas, Brazil (1,290,000) ('91) 759,032
Fortaleza, Brazil (2,040,000) ('91) 743,335

La Paz, Bolivia

*La Paz, Bolivia, is the world's high-
est capital. Some parts of the city
lie at elevations above 13,000 feet.
It generally takes several days for
visitors from lower altitudes to
acclimate to the thin atmosphere.*

La Paz, Bolivia (1,120,000) ('92) 713,378
Santa Cruz de la Sierra, Bolivia ('92) 697,278
General Sarmiento (San Miguel),
　Argentina ('91) 646,891
Morón, Argentina ('91) 641,541
Barquisimeto, Venezuela ('90) 625,450
Lomas de Zamora, Argentina ('91) 572,769
Osasco, Brazil ('91) 566,949
Nova Iguaçu, Brazil ('91) 562,062
Teresina, Brazil (665,000) ('91) 556,073
Maceió, Brazil ('91) 554,727
São Bernardo do Campo, Brazil ('91) 550,030
Guarulhos, Brazil ('91) 546,417
Cartagena, Colombia ('85) 531,426
La Plata, Argentina ('91) 520,449
Mar del Plata, Argentina ('91) 519,707
Santo André, Brazil ('91) 518,272
Campo Grande, Brazil ('91) 516,403
Quilmes, Argentina ('91) 509,445

Lima, Perú: Plaza San Martin

Asunción, Paraguay (700,000) ('92) 502,426
Santos, Brazil (1,165,000) ('91) 415,554
Lima, Perú (4,608,010) ('81) 371,122
Santiago, Chile (4,100,000) ('82) 232,667

THE WORLD, CONTINENTS, AND OCEANS

Land Features

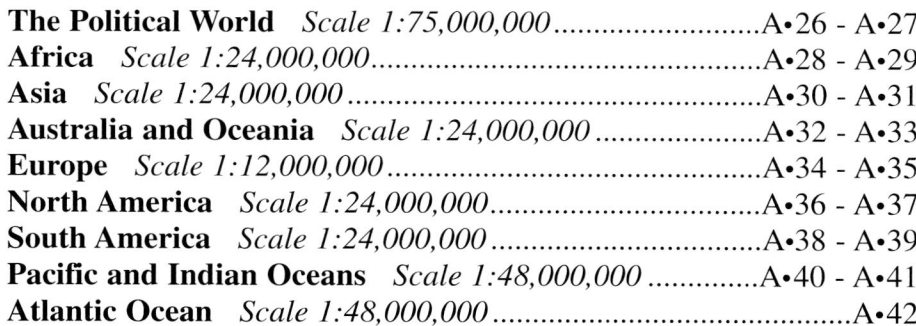

Matterhorn △ 4478	Elevation Above Sea Level
76 ▽	Elevation Below Sea Level
Mount Cook ▲ 3754	Highest Elevation in Country
133 ▼	Lowest Elevation in Country
	Elevations and Depths are given in meters.
	Highest elevation and lowest elevation of a continent are underlined.
A N D E S	Mountain Range
BAFFIN ISLAND	Island
POLUOSTROV KAMAČATKA	Peninsula, Cape, Point, etc.

Water Features

	Shoreline
	Undefined or Fluctuating Shoreline
Amur	River, Stream
	Intermittent Stream
764 ▽	Depth of Water
8428 ▼	Greatest Depth (Atlantic, Pacific, and Indian Oceans)
L. Victoria	Lake, Reservoir
	Intermittent Lake, Reservoir
Tuz Golu	Salt Lake

Inhabited Localities

· 0—100,000	The symbol size represents the approximate number of inhabitants within the locality.
⊙ 100,000—1,500,000	
■ >1,500,000	
Kiruna	The size of the type indicates the relative economic and political importance of the locality.
Bordeaux	
Frankfurt	
BARCELONA	
LONDON	Capitals of political entities are underlined.

International Political Boundaries

As symbolized on Political Maps:	As symbolized on Portrait Maps	
		Demarcated, Undemarcated, and Administrative
		Disputed De Jure
		Indefinite or Undefined
		Demarcation Line
FAEROE ISLANDS (Den.)	Administering country is shown in parentheses.	
MOSKVA MOSCOW	Unless a feature is international in scope, the name form used on the map is the country's local official form for the feature. For certain unfamiliar names the English form is also printed with the local form.	

This section of the atlas opens with a map of the world that shows the countries as they are linked together to make up the total world community. The map is primarily political – that is, political boundaries are given greater emphasis than other features. Gray relief shading provides a general representation of the Earth's terrain.

Following the world map are six continent maps. Five of these maps are drawn at the consistent scale of 1:24,000,000, approximately the same scale as a globe 20 inches in diameter. The size of the continent maps on these printed pages is roughly equivalent to the size at which the actual continents would appear if viewed from 4,000 miles out in space. Use of a consistent scale enables the reader to easily compare the sizes, shapes, and relationships of the world's physical and political features.

Since Europe covers a smaller area than the other continents, it is drawn at a scale of 1:12,000,000. This smaller scale allows the continent to be mapped in greater detail.

The last two maps in the section are Portrait Maps, one depicting the Pacific and Indian Oceans and adjacent lands, the other depicting the Atlantic Ocean and adjacent lands. The colors and shading on these maps portray the surface of the Earth, its broad terrain and vegetative environments, as if viewed from space during the growing season. Underwater features and varying water depths are represented by shading and different color tones.

The legend on this page provides keys to the symbols, type, color tones, and shading that appear on the maps in this section.

Vegetative Environments depicted on the Portrait Maps

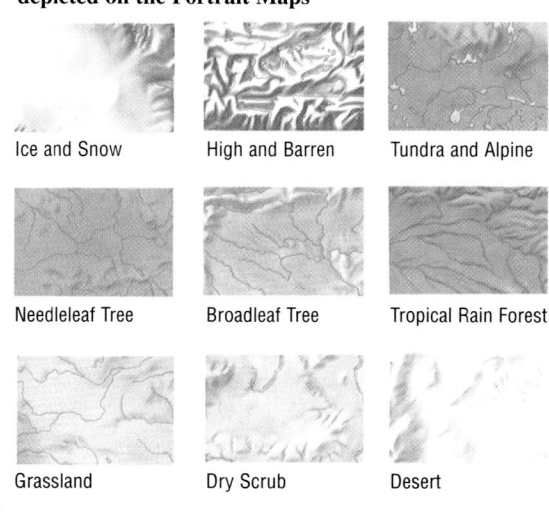

Ice and Snow   High and Barren   Tundra and Alpine

Needleleaf Tree   Broadleaf Tree   Tropical Rain Forest

Grassland   Dry Scrub   Desert

Water and Submarine Features depicted on the Portrait Maps

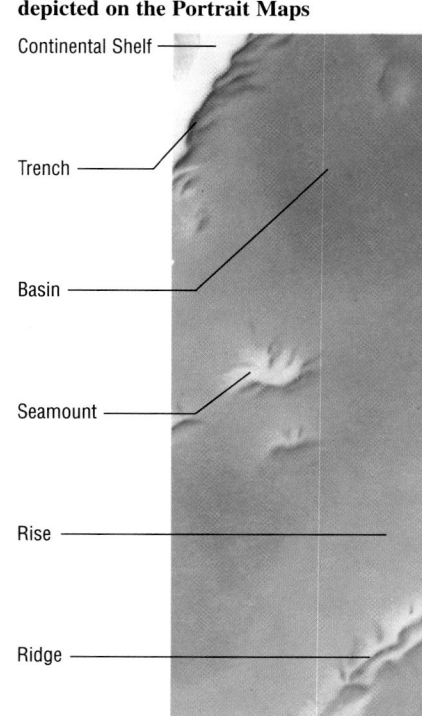

Continental Shelf

Trench

Basin

Seamount

Rise

Ridge

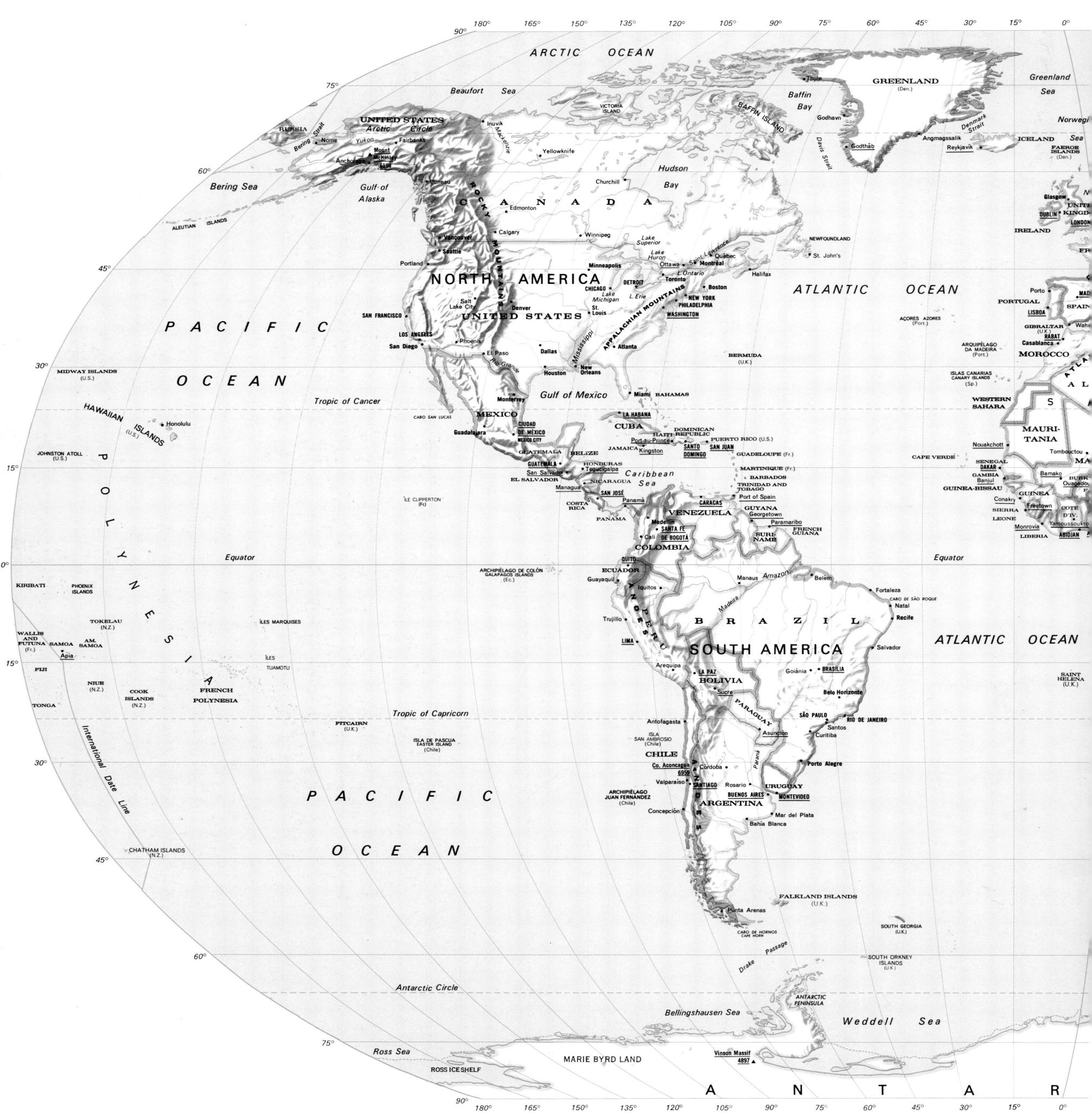

One centimeter represents 750 kilometers.
One inch represents approximately 1200 miles.
Robinson Projection
Scale 1:75,000,000

One centimeter represents approximately 240 kilometers.
One inch represents approximately 380 miles.
Lambert Azimuthal Equal-Area Projection

Scale 1:24,000,000

Mi.
800
600
400
200
0
Km.
800
600
400
200
0

Kilometers
Statute Miles

Copyright by Rand McNally & Co.
Map prepared by Rand McNally & Co.
A-519394-264

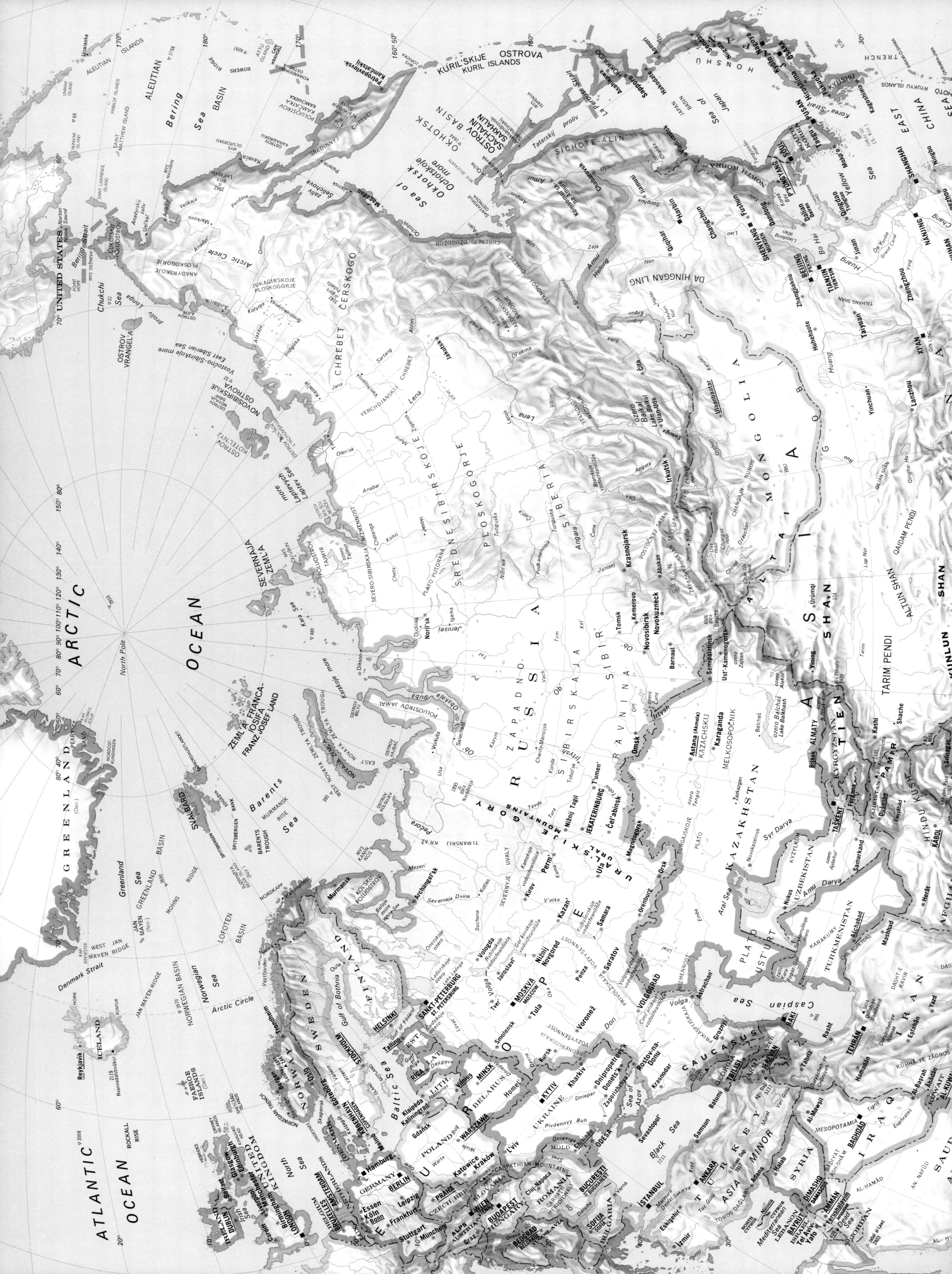

Guadalupe Seamount
▽ 6890
▽ 1316
▽ 1477

KURE ATOLL
MIDWAY ISLANDS (U.S.)
PEARL AND HERMES ATOLL
LISIANSKI ISLAND
LAYSAN ISLAND
Paul Seamount
GARDNER PINNACLES
NECKER ISLAND
NIHOA
FRENCH FRIGATE SHOALS

HAWAIIAN ISLANDS (U.S.)
MOLOKAI FRACTURE ZONE
Tropic of Cancer

HAWAIIAN RIDGE
NECKER RIDGE

KAUAI
NIIHAU
Honolulu
OAHU
MOLOKAI
LANAI
MAUI
Hilo
Mauna Kea 4205
HAWAII
KA LAE
Loihi Seamount 969

UNITED STATES
Swordfish Seamount
▽ Pensacola Seamount 1057
Karin Seamount
JOHNSTON ATOLL (U.S.)
Horizon Tablemount
Hess Tablemount ▽ 859
Cape Johnson Tablemount
SCHJETMAN REEF

WAKE ISLAND (U.S.)

PACIFIC   MOUNTAINS

TAONGI

MARSHALL ISLANDS

BIKAR
BIKINI
UTIRIK
ENEWETAK
RONGELAP
AILUK
WOTHO
KWAJALEIN
WOTJE
MALOELAP
UJAE
LAE
RALIK
LIB
NAMU
ARNO
AILINGLAPALAP
JALUIT
MILI
NAMORIK
KILI
EBON
PINGELAP
KOSRAE

MARSHALL   ISLANDS

RATAK CHAIN
MAJURO

6519
CENTRAL

PACIFIC

BASIN

PACIFIC

CHRISTMAS RIDGE
KINGMAN REEF (U.S.)
PALMYRA ATOLL (U.S.)
TERAINA
TABUAERAN

POLY

P   A   C   I   F   I   C

▽ 4809

MELANESIAN
▽ 4462

NAURU
BASIN

BUTARITARI
TARAWA
ABEMAMA
KURIA
KIRIBATI

BANABA
NONOUTI
BERU
NIKUNAU
TABITEUEA
ONOTOA
TAMANA
ARORAE

NAMU

▽ 1737

SOLOMON ISLANDS

ISLANDS
MALAITA
GUADALCANAL

TUVALU

NANUMEA
NUTAO
NANUMANGA
NUI
VAITUPU
NUKUFETAU
FUNAFUTI
NUKULAELAE

NIULAKITA

HOWLAND ISLAND (U.S.)
BAKER ISLAND (U.S.)
WINSLOW REEF
▽ 11

KIRIBATI
PHOENIX
BIRNIE
ISLANDS
ORONA
NIKUMARORO
KANTON ENDERBURY
RAWAKI
MANRA

KIRITIMATI

JARVIS ISLAND (U.S.)

▽ 5349

Equator

MALDEN

STARBUCK

▽ 6469
▽ 5029

VOSTOK
CAROLINE
Merlin Seamount

▽ 5029

LINE

OCEAN

ISLANDS

SAN CRISTOBAL
▽ 6879
SANTA CRUZ BASIN
8322
9175
NENDO
UTUPUA
VANIKOLO
SANTA CRUZ ISLANDS

ÎLES TORRES
▽ 1188
ÎLES BANKS
VANUA LAVA
SANTA MARIA

VANUATU
MAEWO
PENTECÔTE
AMBRYM
MALAKULA
EPI
NEW
Port Vila
ESPÍRITU SANTO
EFATÉ
HEBRIDES
ERROMANGO
TANNA
ANATOM

NEW CALEDONIA (Fr.) NOUVELLE-CALÉDONIE
Nouméa
ÎLES LOYAUTÉ
OUVÉA
LIFOU
MARÉ

NORTH FIJI BASIN

ROTUMA

WALLIS AND FUTUNA (Fr.)
ÎLES WALLIS
ÎLE FUTUNA
ÎLE ALOFI

Combe Bank
Home Seamount

SWAINS ISLAND
AMERICAN SAMOA ISLANDS
NASSAU ISLAND
NORTHERN
MANIHIKI

SAMOA
SAVAII
Apia
UPOLU
Pago Pago
TUTUILA
ROSE ISLAND
TAFAHI

PENRHYN

COOK   ISLANDS
SUWARROW

FIJI ISLANDS
VANUA LEVU
NEW HEBRIDES
TAVEUNI
VITI LEVU
Suva
Koro Sea
KANDAVU ISLAND

FIJI

LAU GROUP

TOKU ISLAND
VAVAU
VAVAU GROUP
TONGA ISLANDS
NIUE (N.Z.)

SAMOA BASIN
▽ 7314
COOK ISLANDS (N.Z.)
PALMERSTON

MOTU ONE
MANUAE
MAUPIHAA
BORA-BORA
TAHAA
MATANA
SOCIETY RIDGE
MAKATEA

ÎLES DU DÉSAPPOINTEMENT
ÎLES DU ROI GEORGES
ÎLE TIKEI

NEW CALEDONIA
ÎLE HUNTER
HUNTER TRENCH
▽ 3580
TONGATAPU GROUP
TONGATAPU
Nuku'alofa
EUA
ONO-ILAU
ATA
10800
TONGA TRENCH
TONGA RIDGE
TONGA
LAU RIDGE
LAU BASIN

VAVAU
▽ 4846

AITUTAKI
MANUAE
MITIARO
TAKUTEA
ATIU
MAUKE
SOUTHERN COOK ISLANDS
RAROTONGA
MANGAIA

MAUPITI
MOOREA
TETIAROA
MEHETIA
TAHITI
Papeete
RAIATEA
ARCHIPEL DE LA SOCIÉTÉ
SOCIETY ISLANDS

KAUKURA
FAKARAVA
RARAKA
ANAA
MAKEMO
TUAMOTU RIDGE
HIKUERU
MARUTEA
HARAIKI
RAVAHERE
AMANU
HAO
NENGONENGO
MANUHANGI
ANUANU
TUAMOTU ARCHIPELAGO
AHUNU
VANAVANA

TUAMOTU

FRENCH POLYNESIA

▽ 5303
SOUTH FIJI BASIN

ÎLES MARIA
MANGAIA
RURUTU

ÎLES AUSTRALES

FRENCH POLYNESIA

NORFOLK RIDGE

NEW CALEDONIA BASIN

NORFOLK ISLAND (Austl.)

LORD HOWE ISLAND (Austl.)
LORD HOWE RISE

THREE KINGS IS.
NORTH CAPE
TAUROA POINT
▽ 1518
GREAT BARRIER ISLAND
RAOUL ISLAND
KERMADEC ISLANDS
CURTIS ISLAND
10047

KERMADEC RIDGE
KERMADEC TRENCH

LOUISVILLE RIDGE
Currituck Seamount
Seafox Seamount
Louisville Seamount
Burton Seamount

SOUTHWEST

FABERT Seamount
Osbourn Seamount

RIMATARA
TUBUAI
RAIVAVAE
RAPA
ÎLES MAROTIRI
TEMATANGI
Tropic of Capricorn

AUSTRAL SEAMOUNTS

▽ 1088

PACIFIC

BASIN

Auckland
NEW
New Plymouth
CAPE EGMONT
CAPE FAREWELL
▽ 497
ZEALAND
NORTH ISLAND
Bay of Plenty
EAST CAPE
Mount Ruapehu 2797
Napier
Hawke Bay
Wellington
CAPE PALLISER
Cook Strait
▽ 8009

Mount Cook 3754
Christchurch
SOUTH ISLAND
Canterbury Bight
WEST CAPE
Dunedin
Invercargill
SOUTH WEST CAPE
STEWART ISLAND
SNARES ISLANDS

CHATHAM RISE
CHATHAM ISLAND
CHATHAM ISLANDS (N.Z.)
BOUNTY TROUGH

▽ 4755

Tasman Sea
▽ 457
man BASIN

CAMPBELL PLATEAU
ANTIPODES ISLANDS (N.Z.)
BOUNTY ISLANDS (N.Z.)

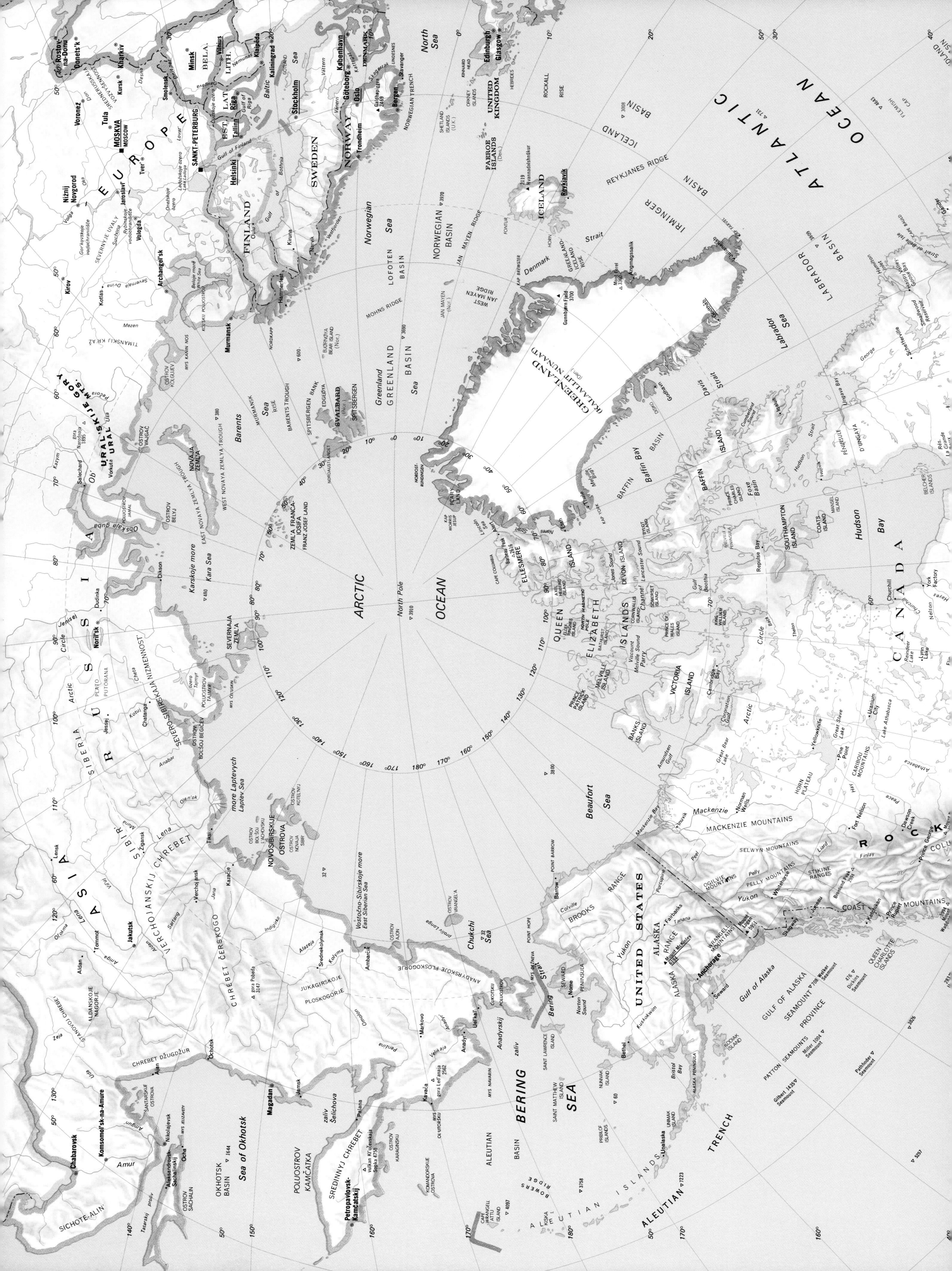

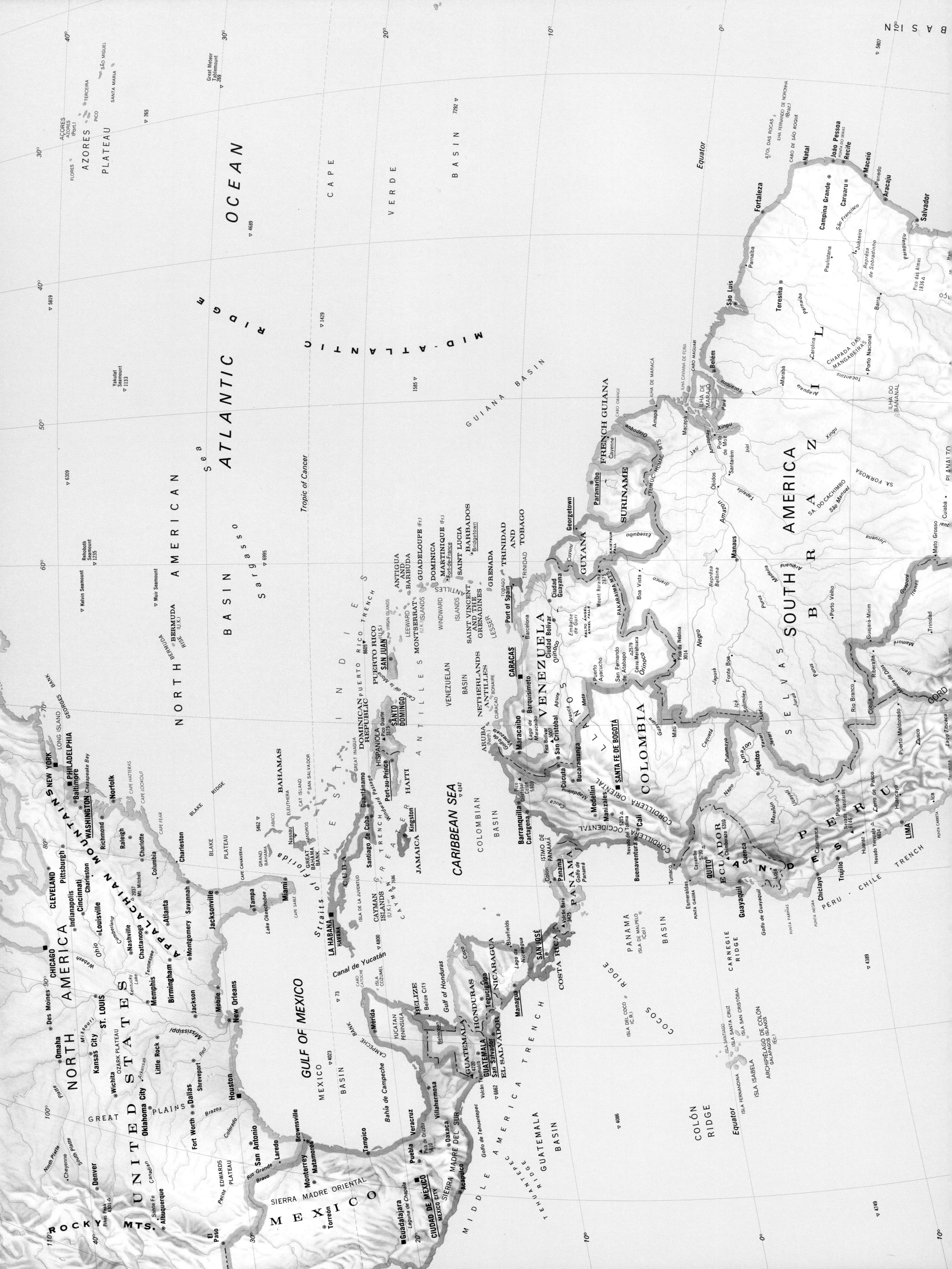

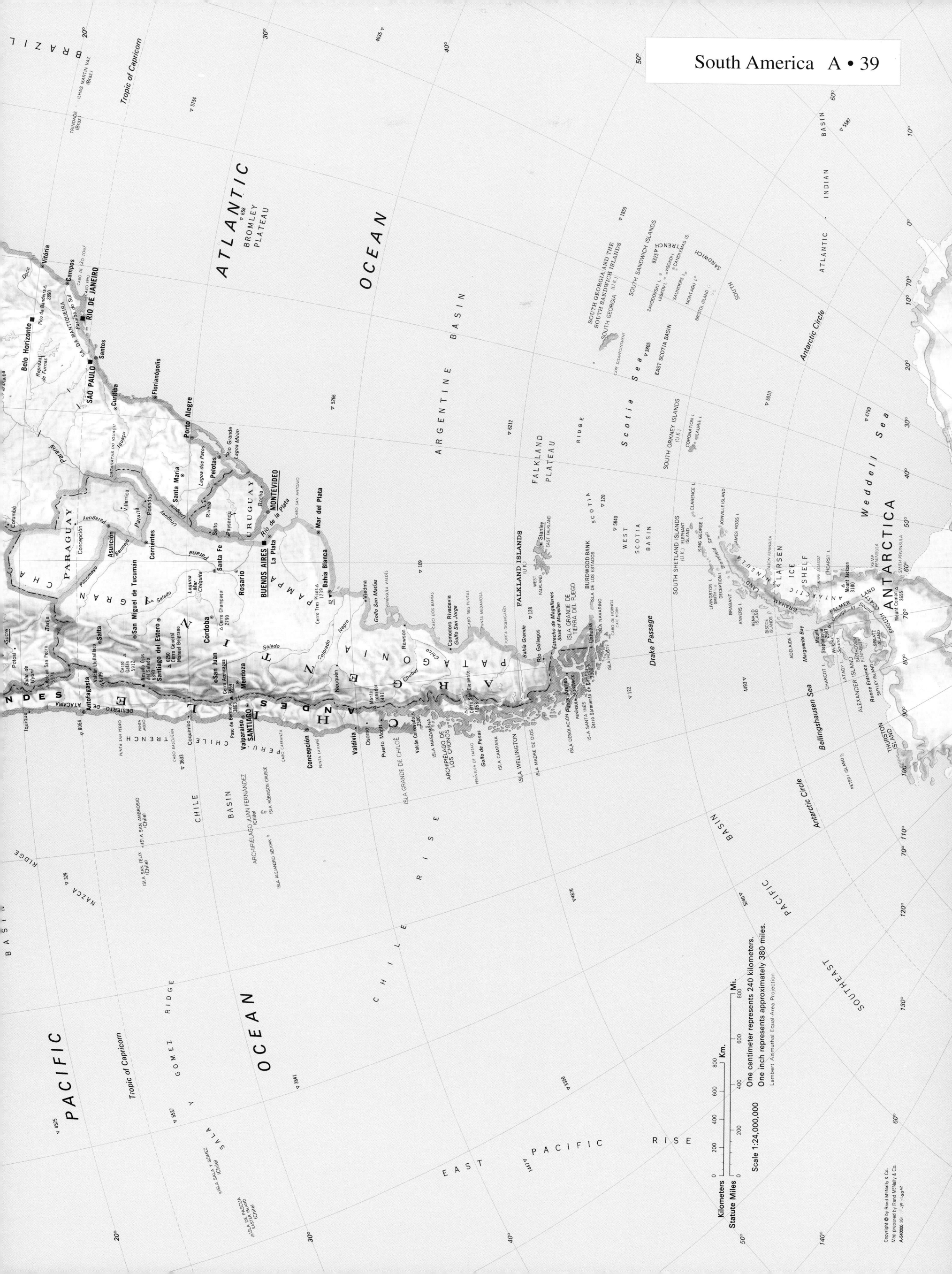

ARCTIC OCEAN

Ostrov Vrangelja

Proliv Longa

Chukchi Sea

POINT BARROW   Beaufort   Sea   Mackenzie Bay   BANKS ISLAND   PRINCE OF WALES ISLAND   VICTORIA ISLAND   Amundsen Gulf   SOMERSET ISLAND   BAFFIN ISLAND   Gulf of Boothia

Anadyr'   Anadyrskij zaliv   Point Hope   Nome   BROOKS RANGE   Inuvik   Cambridge Bay   KING WILLIAM ISLAND   Arctic Circle

SAINT LAWRENCE ISLAND   Fairbanks   OGILVIE MOUNTAINS   MACKENZIE MOUNTAINS   Yellowknife   Back   Thelon

BERING SEA   NUNIVAK ISLAND   Mount McKinley 6191   Anchorage   Mount Logan 5959   SELWYN MOUNTAINS   Great Bear Lake   Great Slave Lake   SOUTHAMPTON ISLAND   COATS ISLAND   MANSEL ISLAND   Hudson   Strait

Kavača   PRIBILOF ISLANDS   KODIAK ISLAND   ALASKA PENINSULA   Juneau   COAST MOUNTAINS   Lake Athabasca   Churchill   BELCHER ISLANDS   Hudson   Bay   UNGAVA BAY   PÉNINSULE D'UNGAVA

GREENLAND   Godthåb   Reykjavik   ICELAND   Julianehåb   KAP FARVEL

ALEUTIAN BASIN   ALEUTIAN ISLANDS   ALEUTIAN TRENCH   Bristol Bay   Gulf of Alaska   QUEEN CHARLOTTE ISLANDS   Prince Rupert   ROCKY MOUNTAINS   Peace   Lake Winnipeg   Nelson   Churchill   MONTS OTISH   Labrador

BEAUFORT SEA

KOMANDORSKIJE OSTROVA   Gilbert Seamount 1435   VANCOUVER ISLAND   Vancouver   Edmonton   Calgary   Winnipeg   Lake of the Woods   Thunder Bay   Lake Nipigon   Happy Valley-Goose Bay   CAPE BAULD   NEWFOUNDLAND   Gander   FLEMISH CAP

Seattle   Mount Rainier 4392   Portland   COLUMBIA   Spokane   Missouri   Duluth   Lake Superior   Sault Ste. Marie   LE D'ANTICOSTI   NEWFOUNDLAND   St. John's   GRAND BANKS OF NEWFOUNDLAND   NEWFOUNDLAND BASIN

NORTH AMERICA   Minneapolis   CHICAGO   DETROIT   Buffalo   Lake Michigan   Lake Huron   Toronto   Ottawa   Montréal   Québec   Gulf of Saint Lawrence   PRINCE EDWARD ISLAND   CAPE BRETON ISLAND   Halifax   CAPE SABLE   ATLANTIC   OCEAN

Cobb Seamount   5257   3826   SIERRA NEVADA   GREAT BASIN   Great Salt Lake   Salt Lake City   Denver   UNITED STATES   St. Louis   Ohio   Lake Erie   Cleveland   BOSTON   NEW YORK   PHILADELPHIA   WASHINGTON   Baltimore   CAPE COD

PACIFIC OCEAN

949   7022   5257   MENDOCINO FRACTURE ZONE   SAN FRANCISCO   Pikes Peak 4301   GREAT PLAINS   APPALACHIAN MOUNTAINS   Norfolk   ATLANTIC   OCEAN

292   5120   Mount Whitney 4418   LOS ANGELES   San Diego   Phoenix   El Paso   Gila   Dallas   Memphis   Atlanta   Charleston   NORTH AMERICAN BASIN   BERMUDA (U.K.)   6309

MIDWAY ISLANDS (U.S.)   LISIANSKI ISLAND   HAWAIIAN RIDGE   HAWAIIAN ISLANDS (U.S.)   Tropic of Cancer   ISLA GUADALUPE (Mex.)   3008   BAJA CALIFORNIA SEAMOUNT PROVINCE   Jacksonville   New Orleans   Houston   Gulf of   Mexico   Tampa   Miami   CAPE CANAVERAL   CAPE SABLE   Straits of Florida   LA HABANA   Nassau   BAHAMAS   BERMUDA RISE   6995   Sargasso Sea   WEST INDIES

WAKE ISLAND (U.S.)   KAUAI   OAHU   Honolulu   MAUI   Hawaii   859   Hess Tablemount   Johnston Atoll   1057   Pensacola Seamount   4809   ISLAS REVILLAGIGEDO (Mex.)   MEXICO   BAJA CALIFORNIA   Golfo de California   SIERRA MADRE OCCIDENTAL   Monterrey   MEXICO BASIN   4023   Tampico   Bahía de Campeche   Veracruz   YUCATAN PENINSULA   CUBA   GREATER ANTILLES   HISPANIOLA   DOM. REP.   PUERTO RICO   SAN JUAN   PUERTO RICO TRENCH   8605

TAONGI   MOUNTAINS   SCHJETMAN REEF   CHRISTMAS RIDGE   CLARION FRACTURE ZONE   GUADALAJARA   CIUDAD DE MEXICO   SIERRA MADRE DEL SUR   Pico de Orizaba 5610   GUATEMALA   BELIZE   HAITI   Port-au-Prince   JAMAICA   Kingston   SANTO DOMINGO   4347

BIKAR   CENTRAL PACIFIC BASIN   KINGMAN REEF (U.S.)   PALMYRA ATOLL (U.S.)   TERAINA   TABUAERAN   5720   CLIPPERTON FRACTURE ZONE   LE CLIPPERTON (Fr.)   4086   Caribbean   Sea   VENEZUELAN BASIN   Maracaibo   CARACAS

MARSHALL ISLANDS   EBON   BUTARITARI   TARAWA   KIRIBATI   HOWLAND ISLAND (U.S.)   BAKER ISLAND (U.S.)   KANTON   JARVIS ISLAND (U.S.)   MALDEN   5349   Equator   4809   ISLA DEL COCO (C.R.)   ISLA DEL MALPELO (Col.)   ARCHIPIÉLAGO DE COLÓN GALAPAGOS ISLANDS (Ec.)   Cali   COLOMBIA   QUITO   Negro

4462   BANABA   PHOENIX ISLANDS   TUVALU   6469   TOKELAU (N.Z.)   PENRHYN   VOSTOK   5029   HIVA OA   ÎLES MARQUISES MARQUESAS ISLANDS   5485   EAST PACIFIC RISE   5851   CARNEGIE RIDGE   ECUADOR   Guayaquil   Chimborazo 6310   Iquitos   Marañón   SOUTH   BRAZIL   AMERICA

SANTA CRUZ ISLANDS   ÎLES TORRES   NORTH FIJI BASIN   VANUA LEVU   MANIHIKI   SUWARROW   NASSAU ISLAND   NORTHERN COOK ISLANDS   UPOLU   SAMOA   SAMOA ISLANDS   SAVAI'I   AMERICAN SAMOA   7314   MANUA IS.   ÎLES MARQUISES   FRENCH POLYNESIA   ÎLES DU DÉSAPPOINTEMENT   ARCHIPEL DE LA SOCIÉTÉ   PERU   PERU BASIN   4525   PERU-CHILE TRENCH   Trujillo   6746   Nevado Huascarán   LIMA   329   8064

VANUATU   VITI LEVU   Suva   FIJI   WALLIS AND FUTUNA (Fr.)   COOK ISLANDS (N.Z.)   PALMERSTON   SOUTHERN COOK ISLANDS   Tahiti   ÎLES TUAMOTU   MURUROA   ÎLES GAMBIER   ÎLES AUSTRALES   Tropic of Capricorn   PITCAIRN ISLAND   HENDERSON ISLAND   PITCAIRN   RAPA   ÎLES MAROTIRI   Arequipa   Nevado Sajama 6542   LA PAZ   Lago Titicaca   BOLIVIA   Sucre   PARAGUAY   GRAN CHACO   Asunción

NEW HEBRIDES   HUNTER RIDGE   TONGA RIDGE   TONGA TRENCH   NIUE (N.Z.)   RAROTONGA   FABERT SEAMOUNT   10800   5303   SOUTH FIJI BASIN   KERMADEC TRENCH   1088   3841   ARCH. JUAN FERNÁNDEZ (Chile)   ISLA SALA Y GÓMEZ (Chile)   ISLA DE PASCUA EASTER ISLAND (Chile)   5537   ISLA SAN FÉLIX (Chile)   ISLA SAN AMBROSIO (Chile)   6893   Nevado Ojos del Salado   Córdoba   6959   Cerro Aconcagua   Rosario   URUGUAY   Paraná   PAMPA

NORFOLK RIDGE   NORFOLK ISLAND (Austl.)   KERMADEC ISLANDS (N.Z.)   NORTH CAPE   1518   Auckland   Bay of Plenty   EAST CAPE   NORTH ISLAND   Wellington   Mount Ruapehu 2797   PACIFIC   RISE   Valparaíso   SANTIAGO   BUENOS AIRES   MONTEVIDEO   Mar del Plata   ARGENTINA

NEW ZEALAND   CHATHAM RISE   CHATHAM ISLANDS (N.Z.)   4755   PACIFIC   OCEAN   Concepción   Bahía Blanca   Río Negro   Golfo San Matías   ARGENTINE BASIN   5266

3754   Mount Cook   SOUTH ISLAND   Christchurch   BOUNTY TROUGH   3977   1447   Monte Tronador 3491   ISLA GRANDE DE CHILOÉ   ARCHIPIÉLAGO DE LOS CHONOS   PATAGONIA   Golfo San Jorge   CABO TRES PUNTAS   109

STEWART ISLAND   BOUNTY ISLANDS (N.Z.)   ANTIPODES ISLANDS (N.Z.)   3350   4876   4058   Cerro San Clemente   Estrecho de Magallanes Strait of Magellan   FALKLAND ISLANDS (U.K.)   FALKLAND ISLANDS PLATEAU   6212

CAMPBELL PLATEAU   SOUTHWEST PACIFIC BASIN   5249   4706   Punta Arenas   TIERRA DEL FUEGO   ISLA HOSTE   CABO DE HORNOS CAPE HORN   NORTH SCOTIA RIDGE   SOUTH GEORGIA (U.K.)   8325

CAPE ADARE   International Date Line   PACIFIC-ANTARCTIC RIDGE   Drake Passage   5240   SOUTHEAST PACIFIC BASIN   WEST SCOTIA BASIN   Scotia Sea   SOUTH ORKNEY ISLANDS (U.K.)   SOUTH SANDWICH TRENCH   EAST SCOTIA BASIN

Kilometers   0   400   800   1200   1600   Km.
Statute Miles   0   400   800   1200   1600   Mi.
Scale 1:48,000,000
at 35° latitude
One centimeter represents 480 kilometers.
One inch represents approximately 760 miles.
Modified Cylindrical Projection

Copyright © by Rand McNally & Co.
Map prepared by Rand McNally & Co.
A-914700-784   41

Ross Sea   Antarctic Circle   Amundsen Sea   Bellingshausen Sea   THURSTON ISLAND   Ronne Entrance   ENGLISH COAST   Weddell   Sea   CAPE NORVEGIA   PRINCESS MARTHA COAST

EIGHTS COAST   Mount Jackson 4190   PALMER LAND   GRAHAM LAND   ANTARCTIC PENINSULA   LARSEN ICE SHELF   ALEXANDER ISLAND   MARGUERITE BAY   ATLANTIC-INDIAN BASIN   SOUTH SHETLAND ISLANDS (U.K.)   5636

GAZETTEER OF THE COUNTRIES OF THE WORLD

Global Locator Maps
Above each County Name is a small map of the globe, with the subject country highlighted in pink. Some very small countries that are difficult to see at this scale are encircled by a pink ring.

Country Names
For each country, the name shown is the short form of the English translation of the official name.

Flags
In many countries two or more versions of the national flag exist. The flag versions shown in this atlas are the ones that each country has chosen to fly at the United Nations.

A**fter decades of peace,** the republic of Bosnia and Herzegovina has been shattered by violent ethnic strife...

Introductory paragraphs
Where space permits, short introductory paragraphs are included. In some cases these paragraphs provide concise overviews of the countries; in others they point out unusual features of the country, important historical events, or current trends.

Japan at a glance

"At a glance" fact blocks
These statistical lists give quick overviews of each country's **People, Politics, Economy,** and **Land.** *Ethnic groups, Religions, Trade partners, Exports,* and *Imports* are listed in order of decreasing size and/or importance. *Languages* are similarly organized, with official language(s) listed first. *Political Parties* are cited alphabetically, as are *Memberships.* In this last category, acronyms for the following organizations appear:

Arab League (AL)
Association of South East Asian Nations (ASEAN)
Commonwealth of Independent States (CIS)
Commonwealth of Nations (CW)
European Union (EU)
North Atlantic Treaty Organization (NATO)
Organization for Economic Cooperation and Development (OECD)
Organization of African Unity (OAU)
Organization of American States (OAS)
Organization of Petroleum Exporting Countries (OPEC)
United Nations (UN)

For certain countries, reliable facts are not available, and therefore information has not been included in some of the "at a glance" categories.

Articles
The descriptive articles for each country in the atlas are segmented in a consistent fashion to allow quick access to the information.

People

This section describes the country's populace, often touching upon ethnicity, religion, language, and social problems, as well as other important factors.

Economy and the Land

General overviews of the country's economy, terrain and climate are presented in this section.

History and Politics

The significant events that have shaped the country, and important current events and trends, are related here.

Getting the most from the Gazetteer pages

In this atlas, each of the world's countries and other major political entities is described in a unit of anywhere from one-third of a page to four pages, depending upon its size and relative importance. For each country, the atlas provides a global locator map, a representation of the national flag, an "at a glance" fact block, a regional locator map and/or a reference map, and an article discussing the people, economy, land, history, and politics. For many of the countries, additional information and graphics are also included.

This page offers a list and brief description of all of the items that appear on the pages of the Gazetteer section.

Regional Locator Maps
These maps show the location of subject countries in relation to neighboring countries and major bodies of water. As with the Global Locator Maps, subject countries are highlighted in pink.

Reference Maps
Each Reference Map presents a wealth of information, including: country boundaries; principal cities and towns; railroads; terrain elevations and depths; and major geographic features such as rivers, lakes, mountain ranges, deserts, and plains. Accompanying each reference map is a **Caption** highlighting interesting information about the country's geography or geology.

A comprehensive 15-page **Index** at the back of the atlas provides the page number and geographic coordinates for places and features named on the Reference Maps.

Size Comparison Maps
These unique maps show how each subject country compares in size to the U.S. A pink silhouette map of the subject country is overlaid onto a green silhouette map of the U.S.

Population and GDP Comparison Bar Graphs
These graphs compare the subject country's population and Gross Domestic Product to those of the U.S.

Ethnic Groups Pie Charts
The ethnic makeup of the subject country's populace can be seen at a glance on these colorful charts.

Urban/Rural Bar Graphs
These graphs show how each country's population breaks down with regard to urban dwellers and rural dwellers.

Map Legend
The following symbols are found on the reference maps in the Gazetteer. In addition to this master legend, most maps have an individual legend.

	Major Urban Area
Clayton •	City type size indicates
Evansville •	the relative importance
Oakland •	of the places.
Seattle •	
Pittsburgh •	
New York •	
Washington	Capital (underlined)
	International Boundary
	Secondary Boundary (states, provinces, etc.)
	Autonomous Region Boundary
	Occupied Territory
	Lake
	River
	Canal or Waterway
	Dike
	Glacier
	Ice Cap
	Ice Shelf
+ Mt. Wade 4083m	Spot Elevation or Depth
	Railroad*
••••••••••••	Major Oil Pipeline
▲	Major Oil Field

* For island maps on pages 5, 9, 13, 40, 48, 55, 67, 77, 93, 103, 119, 123, 134, 139, 143, 158, 159, 164, 199, and 202, the red lines indicate roads.

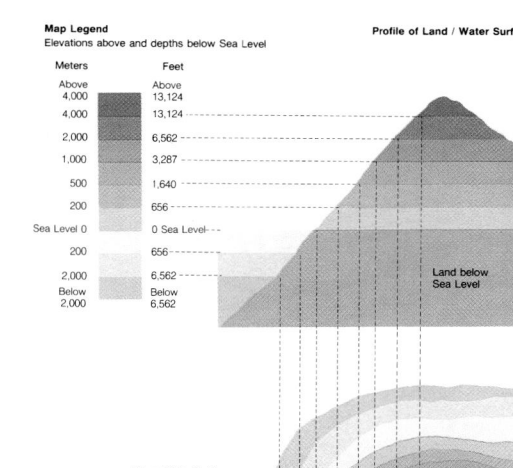

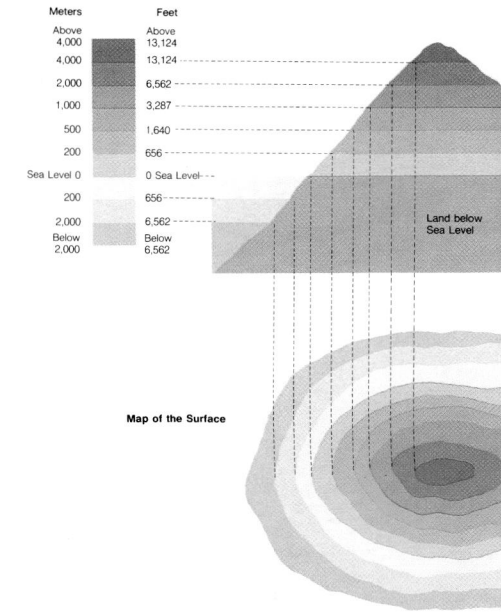

Map Legend
Elevations above and depths below Sea Level

Profile of Land / Water Surface

Meters	Feet
Above 4,000	Above 13,124
4,000	13,124
2,000	6,562
1,000	3,287
500	1,640
200	656
Sea Level 0	0 Sea Level
200	656
2,000	6,562
Below 2,000	Below 6,562

Land below Sea Level

Map of the Surface

Elevations and Depths
Elevations and depths can be determined by referring to the color bar on each map. The different colors represent areas of different elevations. The darker the color, the higher the elevation and the lower the depth. Thus the colors provide a symbolized depiction of the Earth's terrain as well as ocean and sea depths.

To the left is a color bar legend and a diagram showing its relationship to the Earth's terrain and depths and to the reference maps in the Gazetteer.

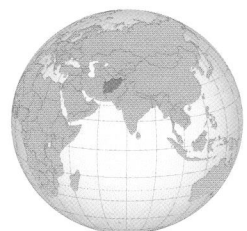

AFGHANISTAN

A 175-foot Buddha carved in the cliffs above the town of Bamian is dwarfed by the rugged terrain of central Afghanistan.

A primitive and undeveloped land, Afghanistan is peopled by a loose confederation of rival clans and tribes. Since the Soviet Union withdrew in 1989 after a 10-year occupation, the tenuous unity among the *mujahidin*—Islamic guerrillas—who fought the Soviets has broken down into internecine warfare. The hostilities have done little to help the economy, which consists mostly of subsistence agriculture.

People

Afghanistan shares borders with China, Iran, Pakistan, Tajikistan, Turkmenistan, and Uzbekistan. This crossroads position has created a population that is ethnically and linguistically diverse. Religion, however, plays a strong unifying role. Most Afghans are Muslim, and Islamic laws and customs determine lifestyles and beliefs, both religious and secular. The population is mainly rural, consisting primarily of farmers and a small nomadic group.

Economy and the Land

The main force behind Afghanistan's underdevelopment is agriculture and the recent civil war. Subsistence farming and animal husbandry account for much of the agricultural activity. Irrigation systems have aided crop production. A terrain of mountains and valleys, including the Hindu Kush, separates the desert region of the southwest from the more fertile north, an area of higher population density and the site of natural gas deposits. Increased development has made natural gas an important export. Winters are generally cold, and summers are hot and dry.

History and Politics

Once part of the Persian Empire, the area of present-day Afghanistan saw invasions by Persians, Macedonians, Greeks, Turks, Arabs, Mongols, and other peoples. An Arab invasion in A.D. 652 introduced Islam. In 1747 Afghan tribes led by Ahmad Shah Durrani united the area and established today's Afghanistan. Power remained with the Durrani tribe for more than two centuries. In the nineteenth and early twentieth centuries Britain controlled Afghanistan's foreign affairs. A Durrani tribe member and former prime minister led a military coup in 1973 and set up a republic, ending the country's monarchical tradition. The new government's failure to improve economic and social conditions led to a 1978 revolution that established a Marxist government and brought Soviet aid. Intraparty differences and citizenry dissent led to a Soviet invasion in 1979. Fighting erupted between government forces and the *mujahidin* guerrillas. In 1988 the Soviets agreed to remove their military forces and in 1991 the United States and Russia stopped all military assistance to the warring factions. Fighting, however, continues.

POPULATION COMPARISON
Afghanistan=8% of U.S.

United States

GDP COMPARISON
Afghanistan=0.05% of U.S.

United States

ETHNIC GROUPS

Other
Uzbek
Pathan
Hazara
Tajik

POPULATION DISTRIBUTION
Urban — Rural

Bande Amir, a lake in the Hesar Mountains

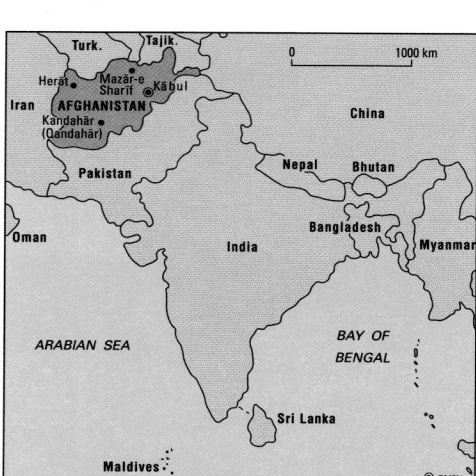

About 80 percent of Afghanistan is mountainous, and much of the country has an elevation higher than 4,000 feet. Harsh terrain and a land-locked location have fostered the nation's isolation.

AFGHANISTAN

— Railroad
⊥⊥ Canal or Waterway
Glacier
+ Spot Elevation

National capitals are underlined
City type size indicates relative importance

Meters Above	Feet Above
4000	13124
2000	6562
1000	3281
500	1640
200	656
0	0

Scale 1:9,750,000

0 50 100 150 200 250 km
0 50 100 150 mi

Afghanistan at a glance

Official name	Islamic State of Afghanistan

People

Population	19,715,000
Density	78/mi² (30/km²)
Urban	18%
Capital	Kabul, 1,424,400
Ethnic groups	Pathan 38%, Tajik 25%, Hazara 19%, Uzbek 6%
Languages	Dari, Pashto, Uzbek, Turkmen
Religions	Sunni Muslim 84%; Shiite Muslim 15%; Hindu, Sikh, and other 1%
Life expectancy	44 female, 43 male
Literacy	29%

Politics

Government	Islamic republic
Parties	Islamic, Islamic Revolutionary Movement, Islamic Society, Islamic Union, National Liberation Front, others
Suffrage	None
Memberships	UN
Subdivisions	30 provinces

Economy

GDP	$3,000,000,000
Per capita	$205
Monetary unit	Afghani
Trade partners	Exports: Former Soviet republics, Pakistan, India Imports: Former Soviet republics, Japan
Exports	Natural gas, fruits and nuts, carpets, wool, cotton, hides, pelts
Imports	Food, petroleum

Land

Description	Southern Asia, landlocked
Area	251,826 mi² (652,225 km²)
Highest point	Nowshāk, 24,557 ft (7,485 m)
Lowest point	Along Amu Darya River, 850 ft (259 m)

Greek ruins of
Apollonia, Fier

ALBANIA

For four decades after World War II, Albania was a closed society, cut off from the rest of the world. Since the death of longtime communist ruler Enver Hoxha in 1985, successive governments have liberalized the society and opened the country to foreign visitors. Unhappy living in Europe's poorest country, Albanians have taken to the polls and the streets to protest their economic conditions.

A farmer walks with his donkey near Tiranë. Although this road is paved, most in Albania are not.

Albania at a glance

Official name	Republic of Albania

People

Population	3,394,000
Density	306/mi² (118/km²)
Urban	36%
Capital	Tiranë, 238,100
Ethnic groups	Albanian (Illyrian) 90%, Greek 8%
Languages	Albanian, Greek
Religions	Muslim 70%, Greek Orthodox 20%, Roman Catholic 10%
Life expectancy	77 female, 71 male
Literacy	72%

Politics

Government	Republic
Parties	Democratic, Omonia, Republican, Socialist
Suffrage	Universal, over 18
Memberships	UN
Subdivisions	26 districts

Economy

GDP	$3,300,000,000
Per capita	$998
Monetary unit	Lek
Trade partners	Italy, Macedonia, Germany
Exports	Asphalt, metals and metallic ores, electricity, crude oil, vegetables.
Imports	Machinery, consumer goods, grains

Land

Description	Southeastern Europe
Area	11,100 mi² (28,748 km²)
Highest point	Korabit Peak, 9,035 ft (2,754 m)
Lowest point	Sea level

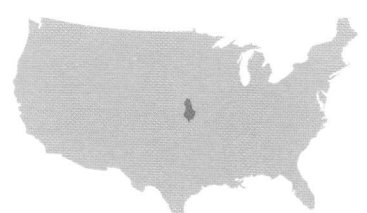

POPULATION COMPARISON
Albania=1% of U.S.

United States

GDP COMPARISON
Albania=0.05% of U.S.

United States

ETHNIC GROUPS

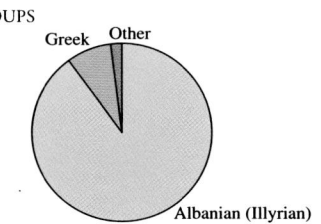

Greek Other

Albanian (Illyrian)

POPULATION DISTRIBUTION

Urban   Rural

People

A homogeneous native population characterizes Albania, where Greeks are the main minority. Five centuries of Turkish rule shaped much of the culture and led many Albanians to adopt Islam. Since 1944 an increased emphasis on education has more than tripled the literacy rate. From 1967 until 1990 religious institutions were banned.

Economy and the Land

The poorest country in Europe, Albania has tried to shift its economy from agriculture to industry. Farms employ about 50 percent of the work force, a significant decrease from more than 80 percent before 1944. Agriculture has expanded since economic reforms resulted in the privatization of 90 percent of the farm land. Mineral resources make mining the chief industrial activity. The terrain consists of forested hills and mountains, and the climate is mild.

History and Politics

Early invaders and rulers included Greeks, Romans, Goths, and others. In 1468 the Ottoman Turks conquered the area, and it remained part of their empire until the First Balkan War in 1912. Albania was invaded by Italy and occupied by Germany during World War II. A communist government was established after the war. The failure of Soviet communism increased instability within Albania and in 1991 the communist government resigned. Elections in 1992 provided Albania with its first democratic president. Living conditions are poor but land has been privatized and the economy has begun to grow. Relations with Greece have been deteriorating.

ALBANIA		Meters	Feet
		4000	13124
		2000	6562
――― Railroad	National capitals are underlined	1000	3281
·―· Oil Pipeline		500	1640
▲ Major Oil Field	Scale 1:2,474,000	200	656
+ Spot Elevation or Depth		0	0
		200	656
		2000	6562

Work has begun to reestablish the road and rail links to Albania's neighbors that were severed during the Communist era. The mild climate and many miles of unspoiled coastline may eventually be a major draw for tourists.

Life-giving wells are few and far between in the sparsely populated Sahara Desert. Where there is water, plants and animals flourish.

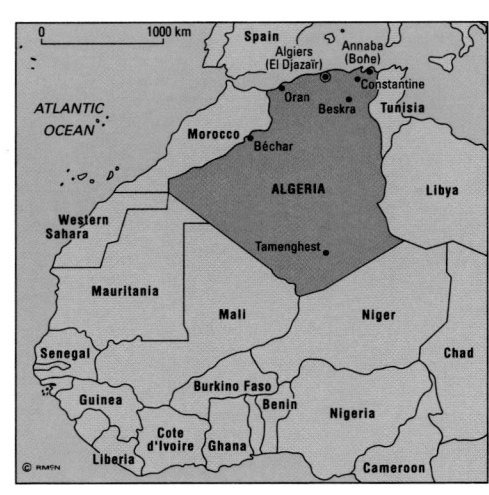

ALGERIA

Man praying in front of small mosque

Algeria has been shattered by civil war since the government cancelled 1992 elections to prevent Islamic fundamentalists from taking power. Foreigners, government officials and Algerians with higher education have all been targets of attacks by the fundamentalists. In response, security forces have launched harsh crack-downs.

People

Indigenous Berbers and invading Arabs shaped modern Algeria's culture, and today most of the population is Muslim and of Arab-Berber descent. European cultural influences, evidence of over a century of French control, exist in urban areas. Since independence in 1962, free medical care has been instituted and the educational system has been greatly improved.

Economy and the Land

A member of the Organization of Petroleum Exporting Countries (OPEC), Algeria produces oil and natural gas. Agriculture is divided between state and privately-owned farms. The government continues to emphasize gas production and exportation, while it maintains a socialistic economy and promotes development of private business. Algeria's terrain is varied. The Tell, Arabic for hill, is a narrow Mediterranean coastal region that contains the country's most fertile land and highest population. South of this lie high plateaus and the Atlas Mountains, which give way to the Sahara Desert. The climate is temperate along the coast and dry and cool in the plateau region.

History and Politics

In the eighth and eleventh centuries, invading Arabs brought their language and religion to the native Berbers. The Berbers and Arabs together became known as Moors, and conflicts between Moors, Turks, and Spaniards erupted periodically over several centuries. France began conquering Algeria in 1830, and by 1902 the entire country was under French control. The revolution against French rule began in 1954, but it was not until 1962 that the country was declared independent. Since a bloodless coup in 1965, the political situation has been relatively stable. A 1989 referendum approved a new constitution allowing multiparty elections. The first free national elections since independence were held in 1991. The fundamentalist Islamic Salvation Front (ISF) won in a landslide victory, prompting a military takeover. In 1992 the government banned ISF and jailed its leaders, but Muslim militants continue their opposition.

Algeria at a glance

Official name   Democratic and Popular Republic of Algeria

People

Population	27,965,000
Density	30/mi² (12/km²)
Urban	52%
Capital	Algiers, 1,507,241
Ethnic groups	Arab-Berber 99%
Languages	Arabic, Berber dialects, French
Religions	Sunni Muslim 99%, Christian and Jewish 1%
Life expectancy	67 female, 65 male
Literacy	57%

Politics

Government	Provisional military government
Parties	Islamic Salvation Front, National Liberation Front, Socialist Forces Front, others
Suffrage	Universal, over 18
Memberships	AL, OAU, OPEC, UN
Subdivisions	48 departments

Economy

GDP	$89,000,000,000
Per capita	$3,305
Monetary unit	Dinar
Trade partners	Exports: France, U.S., Italy Imports: France, Germany, U.S.
Exports	Petroleum, natural gas
Imports	Machinery, manufactures

Land

Description	Northern Africa
Area	919,595 mi² (2,381,741 km²)
Highest point	Tahat, 9,541 ft (2,908 m)
Lowest point	Chott Melrhir, -131 ft (-40 m)

POPULATION COMPARISON
Algeria=11% of U.S.

United States

GDP COMPARISON
Algeria=1% of U.S.

United States

ETHNIC GROUPS

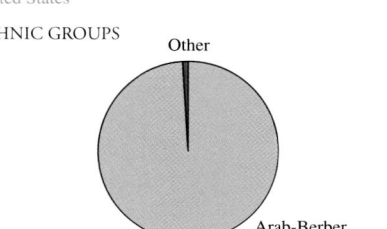

Other

Arab-Berber

POPULATION DISTRIBUTION
Urban   Rural

ALGERIA

	Meters	Feet
Railroad	4000	13124
Oil Pipeline	2000	6562
Major Oil Field	1000	3281
Spot Elevation or Depth	500	1640
	200	656
	0	Sea Level

National capitals are underlined

Scale 1:12,985,000

	0	0
	200	656
	Below 2000	Below 6562

0   100   200   300 km
0   50   100   150   200 mi

The coastal capital of Algiers is filled with the architectural legacy of over 100 years of French rule. Elsewhere, Algeria is mostly undeveloped, from the high plateau in the north to the Sahara Desert in the south.

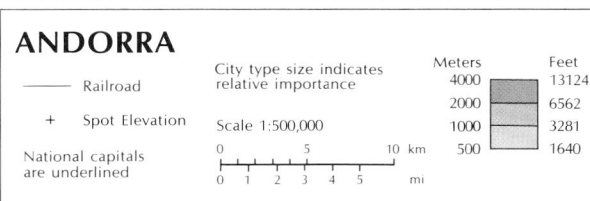

Five of the islands—Tutuila, Aunuu, Tau, Ofu and Olosega—are volcanic in origin and have rich soils and rainfalls that approach 300 inches a year. The other two islands, Rose and Swains, are low-lying coral reefs.

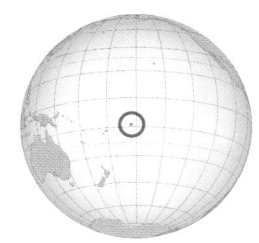

AMERICAN SAMOA

American Samoa at a glance

Official name	Territory of American Samoa

People

Population	56,000
Density	727/mi² (281/km²)
Urban	47%
Capital	Pago Pago, Tutuila I., 3,518
Ethnic groups	Samoan 89%, Caucasian 2%, Tongan 4%
Languages	Samoan, English
Religions	Congregationalist 50%, other Protestant 30%, Roman Catholic 20%
Life expectancy	75 female, 71 male
Literacy	97%

Politics

Government	Unincorporated territory (U.S.)
Parties	None
Suffrage	Universal, over 18
Memberships	None
Subdivisions	3 districts

Economy

GDP	$128,000,000
Per capita	$3,048
Monetary unit	U.S. dollar
Trade partners	U.S., Japan, New Zealand
Exports	Canned tuna
Imports	Machinery, food, petroleum products

Land

Description	South Pacific islands
Area	77 mi² (199 km²)
Highest point	Lata Mountain, 3,160 ft (963 m)
Lowest point	Sea level

People

Ethnically and linguistically, the people of American Samoa are the same as those of Samoa: mainly Samoan-speaking Polynesians, with a minority of Samoan-European descent. The majority of American Samoans are bilingual, speaking English in addition to Samoan. Most live in rural villages on Tutuila, the main island and location of the capital of Pago Pago, but more American Samoans live on the United States mainland and in Hawaii than live on the islands themselves.

Economy and the Land

American Samoa's industry is based on fishing, and activities include tuna canning and producing fish products. Most farming is on the subsistence level. In the 1960s an economic expansion program, funded by the United States, improved transportation systems, medical and educational facilities, and the tourist and fish industries. Many benefits were short-lived, however. The seven islands are part of the South Pacific island chain that includes Samoa. Tutuila, Aunuu, and the Manua group—Tau, Ofu, and Olosega—are volcanic in origin, and Rose and Swains islands are coral atolls. The terrain is mostly mountainous, and the climate is tropical.

History and Politics

More than two thousand years ago the first inhabitants of the Samoan Islands probably migrated from eastern Melanesia. The first Europeans arrived at the islands in the early 1700s. Foreign competition for influence resulted in the division of the islands between the United States and Germany in 1900, with the United States receiving the eastern islands of Tutuila, Aunuu, and the Manua group. Swains Island was annexed in 1925. In 1976 American Samoans voted to elect their own governor, who had previously been appointed by the Secretary of the Interior.

Andorra at a glance

Official name	Principality of Andorra

People

Population	59,000
Density	337/mi² (130/km²)
Urban	63%
Capital	Andorra, 20,437
Ethnic groups	Spanish 61%, Andorran 30%, French 6%
Languages	Catalan, Spanish (Castilian), French
Religions	Roman Catholic
Life expectancy	81 female, 75 male

Politics

Government	Parliamentary co-principality (Spanish and French protection)
Parties	Liberal Union, National Coalition, National Democratic Group
Suffrage	Universal, over 18
Memberships	UN
Subdivisions	7 parishes

Economy

GDP	$760,000,000
Per capita	$14,074
Monetary unit	French franc, Spanish peseta
Trade partners	France, Spain
Exports	Electricity, tobacco products, furniture
Imports	Manufactures, food

Land

Description	Southwestern Europe, landlocked
Area	175 mi² (453 km²)
Highest point	Coma Pedrosa Peak, 9,665 ft (2,946 m)
Lowest point	Along Valira River, 2,756 ft (840 m)

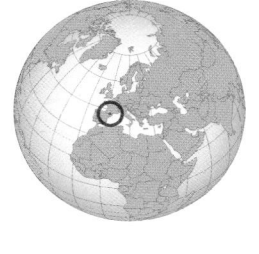

ANDORRA

ANDORRA

—— Railroad	
+ Spot Elevation	
National capitals are underlined	

City type size indicates relative importance

Scale 1:500,000

Meters	Feet
4000	13124
2000	6562
1000	3281
500	1640

Located high in the Pyrenees, Andorra is cool in the summer and cold in the winter. Until transportation routes were improved in this century, it was isolated and ignored.

People

Much of Andorran life and culture has been shaped by its mountainous terrain and governing countries, France and Spain. Population is concentrated in the valleys, and despite a tourism boom in past decades, the peaks and valleys of the Pyrenees have isolated the small country from many twentieth-century changes. Catalan is the official language, and cultural and historic ties exist with the Catalonian region of northern Spain. The majority of the population is Spanish; Andorran citizens are a minority.

Economy and the Land

The terrain has established Andorra's economy as well as its lifestyle. Improved transportation routes together with other factors have resulted in a thriving tourist industry—a dramatic shift from traditional sheepherding and tobacco growing. In addition, duty-free status has made the country a European shopping mecca. Tobacco is still the main agricultural product, though only about four percent of the land is arable. Climate varies with altitude; winters are cold and summers are cool and pleasant.

History and Politics

Tradition indicates that Charlemagne freed the area from the Moors in A.D. 806. A French count and the Spanish bishop of Seo de Urgel signed an agreement in the 1200s to act as co-princes of the country, establishing the political status and boundaries that exist today. The co-principality is governed by the president of France and the bishop of Seo de Urgel. In 1994 Andorra adopted a new constitution, ending a system of government in effect since the 13th century.

Angola

Angola has not known peace for a generation. After winning a 14-year war for independence from Portugal in 1975, the country plunged into a civil war which continued despite numerous attempts at peace. Large numbers of civilians have died both from the fighting and from starvation caused by the ruined economy.

Offshore oil rig, Cabinda

ANGOLA

A church dominates a rural town near the coast. The Catholicism practiced by 38 percent of Angolans is a legacy of Portuguese colonists.

People
Angola is made up mostly of various Bantu peoples—mainly Ovimbundu, Mbundu, Kongo, and others. Despite influences from a half-century of Portuguese rule, Angolan traditions remain strong, especially in rural areas. Each group has its own language, and although Portuguese is the official language, it is spoken by a minority. Many Angolans, retaining traditional indigenous beliefs, worship ancestral spirits.

Economy and the Land
A 1975 civil war, the resultant departure of skilled European labor, and continuing guerrilla activity have taken their toll on Angola's economy. The country has been working toward recovery, however, encouraging development of private industries and foreign trade. Although not a member of the Organization of Petroleum Exporting Countries (OPEC), Angola is a large oil producer. Cabinda, an enclave separated from the rest of the country by the Democratic Republic of the Congo, is the main site of oil production. Diamond mining remains an important activity, as does agriculture. Much of the land is forested, however, and is therefore not suited for commercial farming. The flat coastal area gives way to inland plateaus and uplands. The climate varies from tropical to subtropical.

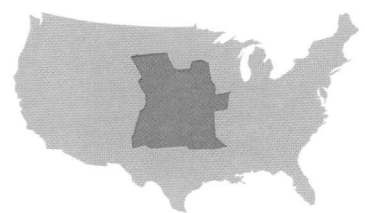

History and Politics
Bantu groups settled in the area prior to the first century A.D. In 1483 a Portuguese explorer became the first European to arrive in Angola, and slave trade soon became a major activity. Portuguese control expanded and continued almost uninterrupted for several centuries. In the 1960s ignored demands for popular rule led to two wars for independence. Three nationalist groups emerged, each with its own ideology and supporters. In 1974 a coup in Portugal resulted in independence for all Portuguese territories in Africa, and Angola became independent in 1975. A civil war ensued, with the three groups fighting for power. By 1976, with the assistance of Cuban military personnel, the Popular Movement for the Liberation of Angola (PMLA) had established control. Angola, Cuba, and South Africa signed an accord in 1988 providing for Cuban troop withdrawals by July 1991. The country's first democratic elections were held in 1992 but were disputed. Fragile peace treaties and intermittent civil war have plagued the country since.

POPULATION COMPARISON
Angola=4% of U.S.

United States

GDP COMPARISON
Angola=0.09% of U.S.

United States

ETHNIC GROUPS

Other
European
Mulatto
Kongo
Ovimbundu
Mbundu

POPULATION DISTRIBUTION
Urban   Rural

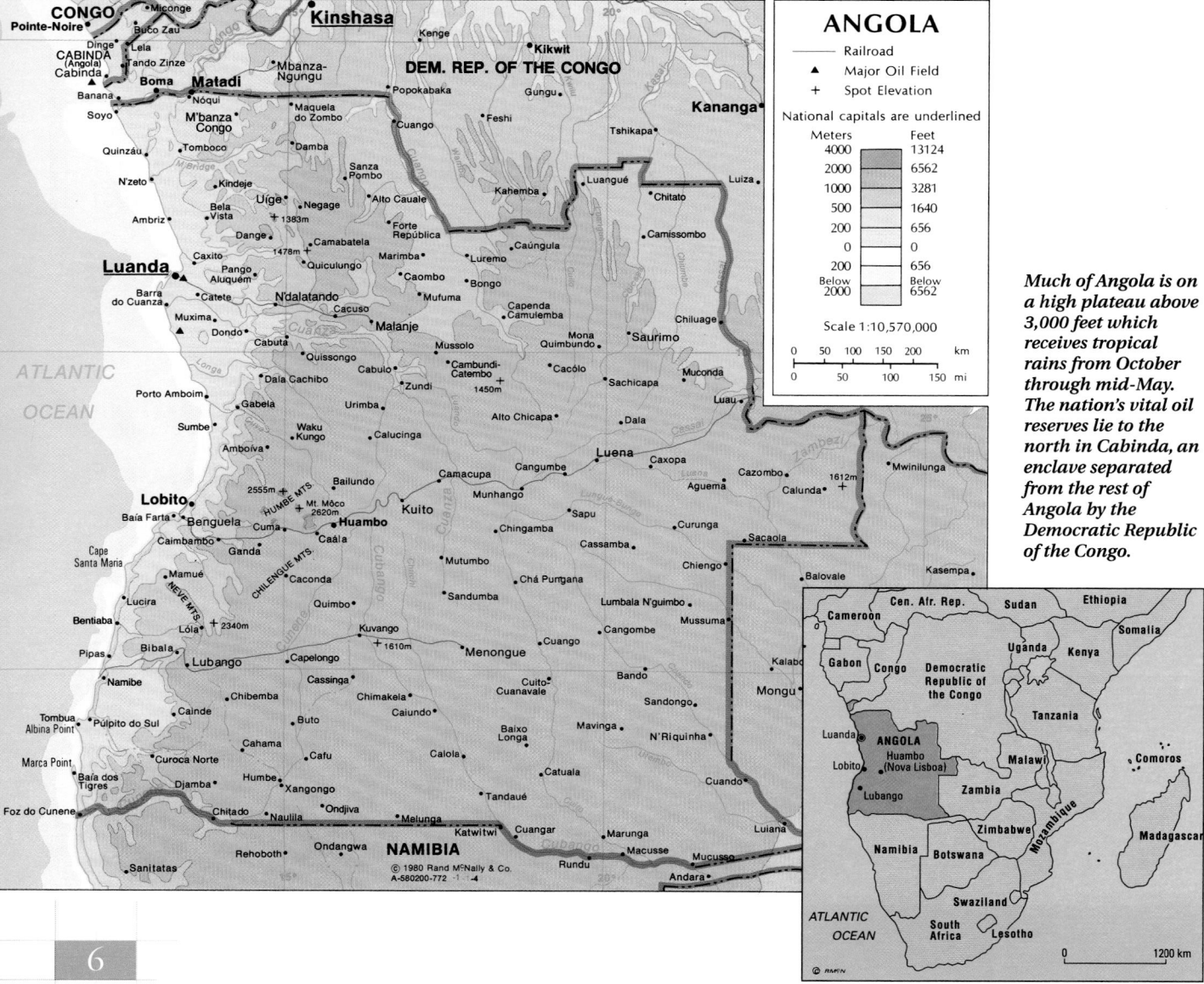

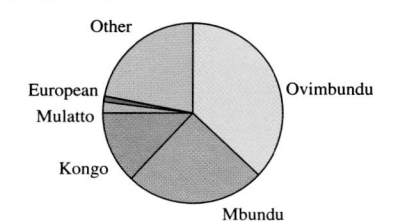

Much of Angola is on a high plateau above 3,000 feet which receives tropical rains from October through mid-May. The nation's vital oil reserves lie to the north in Cabinda, an enclave separated from the rest of Angola by the Democratic Republic of the Congo.

Angola at a glance
Official name   Republic of Angola

People

Population	10,690,000
Density	22/mi² (8.6/km²)
Urban	28%
Capital	Luanda, 1,459,900
Ethnic groups	Ovimbundu 37%, Mbundu 25%, Kongo 13%, mulatto 2%, European 1%
Languages	Portuguese, indigenous
Religions	Animist 47%, Roman Catholic 38%, Protestant 15%
Life expectancy	48 female, 45 male
Literacy	42%

Politics

Government	Republic
Parties	National Union for the Total Independence of Angola, Popular Movement for Liberation, others
Suffrage	Universal, over 18
Memberships	OAU, UN
Subdivisions	18 provinces

Economy

GDP	$5,700,000,000
Per capita	$531
Monetary unit	Kwanza
Trade partners	Exports: U.S., Bahamas Imports: U.S., France, Brazil, Portugal
Exports	Petroleum, diamonds, coffee, sisal, fish, lumber, cotton
Imports	Machinery and electrical equipment, food, transportation equipment

Land

Description	Southern Africa
Area	481,354 mi² (1,246,700 km²)
Highest point	Mt. Môco, 8,596 ft (2,620 m)
Lowest point	Sea level

Anguilla at a glance

Official name   Anguilla

People

Population	7,100
Density	203/mi² (78/km²)
Capital	The Valley, 1,042
Ethnic groups	Black
Languages	English
Religions	Anglican 40%, Methodist 33%, Seventh Day Adventist 7%, Baptist 5%
Life expectancy	77 female, 71 male
Literacy	95%

Politics

Government	Dependent territory (U.K. protection)
Parties	Democratic, National Alliance, United
Suffrage	Universal, over 18

Economy

GDP	$47,000,000
Per capita	$6,714
Monetary unit	East Caribbean dollar
Trade partners	U.K. and other European countries, Canada, U.S., Puerto Rico
Exports	Lobsters, salt

Land

Description	Caribbean island
Area	35 mi² (91 km²)
Highest point	Crocus Hill, 225 ft (69 m)
Lowest point	Sea level

People

Most of the inhabitants of Anguilla are descendants of black Africans, who were brought to the region to work as plantation slaves during the early colonial period. A dependency of the United Kingdom, Anguilla has a majority language of English, and the main religion is Anglican. The Valley, a village area, serves as capital, and most Anguillans live in rural communities scattered over the island. Many people are poor, and fewer than one-tenth of the population has a telephone.

Economy and the Land

Many Anguillans work as subsistence farmers, although only 5 percent of the land is cultivable: soils are poor and rainfall low and unpredictable. Some people raise livestock such as cattle and goats, which they trade with inhabitants of nearby islands. Other activities include fishing, lobstering, producing sea salt, and boat building. Jobs have been scarce, however, and this has led to a high rate of emigration. Tourism is an economic contributor and offers potential for expansion. Amenities include a warm climate, tempered by trade winds, and more than thirty white-coral beaches, but hotel facilities and air transportation need to be expanded. Other sectors with potential for economic expansion include light industry and offshore banking, with the island's lack of income tax as incentive. Anguilla is a low-lying coral island, with a mostly flat, scrub-covered terrain. Uninhabited Dogs Island lies off the east coast, Scrub Island off the Northeast, and tiny Anguillita off the southwestern tip. Anguilla has a topical climate subject to occasional hurricanes.

History and Politics

Artifacts of an Indian culture dating back to around 100 B.C. and petroglyphs in the Fountain, a cave currently under excavation, are reminders of Anguilla's ancient history. The island's early inhabitants were probably the Arawak Indians, who were most likely conquered by the more aggressive Caribs. In 1493 Christopher Columbus arrived on the island, naming it Anguila, Spanish for "eel," because of its long, narrow shape. Anguilla became a British colony in 1650, and in 1796 the French landed at Rendezvous Bay in an unsuccessful attempt to take the island from Britain. In 1882 Britain united Anguilla with St. Kitts and Nevis, and subsequent years saw St. Kitts, Nevis, and Anguilla administered as a single colony. Many Anguillans rebelled against this status, and dissatisfaction led to unilateral secession from the state in 1967 and British military intervention in 1969. The Anguilla Act of 1980 formally established Anguilla as a separate dependency of Britain, although the de facto separation had been in effect for some time. A new constitution became effective in 1982, and Anguilla continues to be governed by an appointee of the Crown.

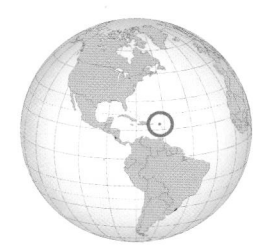

ANGUILLA

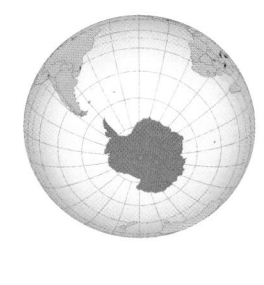

A low-lying coral island, Anguilla boasts miles of white beaches and crystal clear waters. Because of the arid climate, little is grown. The fishing, however, is excellent.

ANTARCTICA

Penguins watch a few of the hardy tourists who journey to the frozen continent each year during the short and comparatively mild summer.

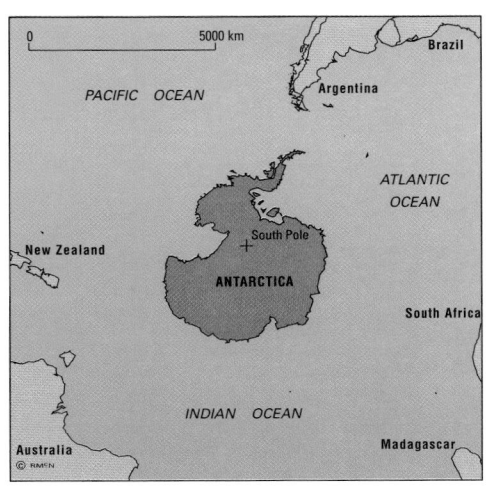

Home to the South Pole, where the average temperature is –70 degrees Fahrenheit, Antarctica (not surprisingly) has no permanent human residents. However, 45 species of birds—including seven varieties of penguins—live along its coast. The surrounding seas are home to a rich assortment of life, including tens of millions of seals and large populations of whales. More than 25 countries, including France, Russia, and the United States, have signed the Antarctic Treaty, which calls for peaceful study of the continent. Recent discoveries of holes in the ozone layer over Antartica have led to fears about global warming. *(continued)*

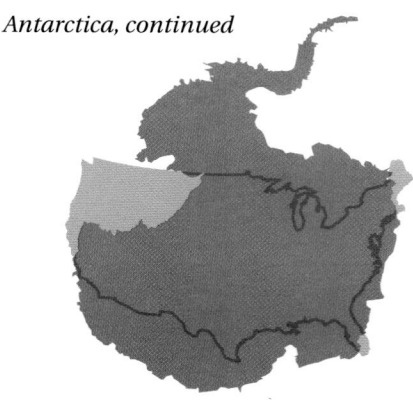

Antarctica, continued

Antarctica at a glance

Official name	Antarctica

People

Capital	None

Politics

Memberships	None

Land

Description	Continent in Southern Hemisphere
Area	5,400,000 mi² (14,000,000 km²)
Highest point	Vinson Massif, 16,066 ft (4,897 m)
Lowest point	Deep Lake, -184 ft (-56m)

People
Antarctica, which surrounds the South Pole, is the southernmost continent, the coldest place on earth, and one of the last frontiers. There are no native inhabitants, and its temporary population is made up mainly of scientists from various countries operating research stations.

Economy and the Land
Harsh climate and terrain have inhibited resource exploration and development. Antarctica's natural resources include coal, various ores, iron, offshore oil, and natural gas. Fishing for krill, a marine protein source, is another activity. Crossed by several ranges collectively known as the Transantarctic Mountains, Antarctica can be roughly divided into a mountainous western region and a larger eastern sector consisting of an icy plain rimmed by mountains. With its tip about 700 miles (1,127 km) from southern South America, the mountainous Antarctic Peninsula and its offshore islands jut northward. Nearly all of Antarctica is ice-covered, precipitation is minimal, and the continent is actually a desert.

Antarctic Peninsula

Most of Antarctica is covered by an ice sheet that contains 90 percent of the world's ice and 70 percent of its fresh water. Nearly three miles thick in some places, the ice cap has an average thickness of 7,500 feet, making Antarctica the continent with the highest mean elevation.

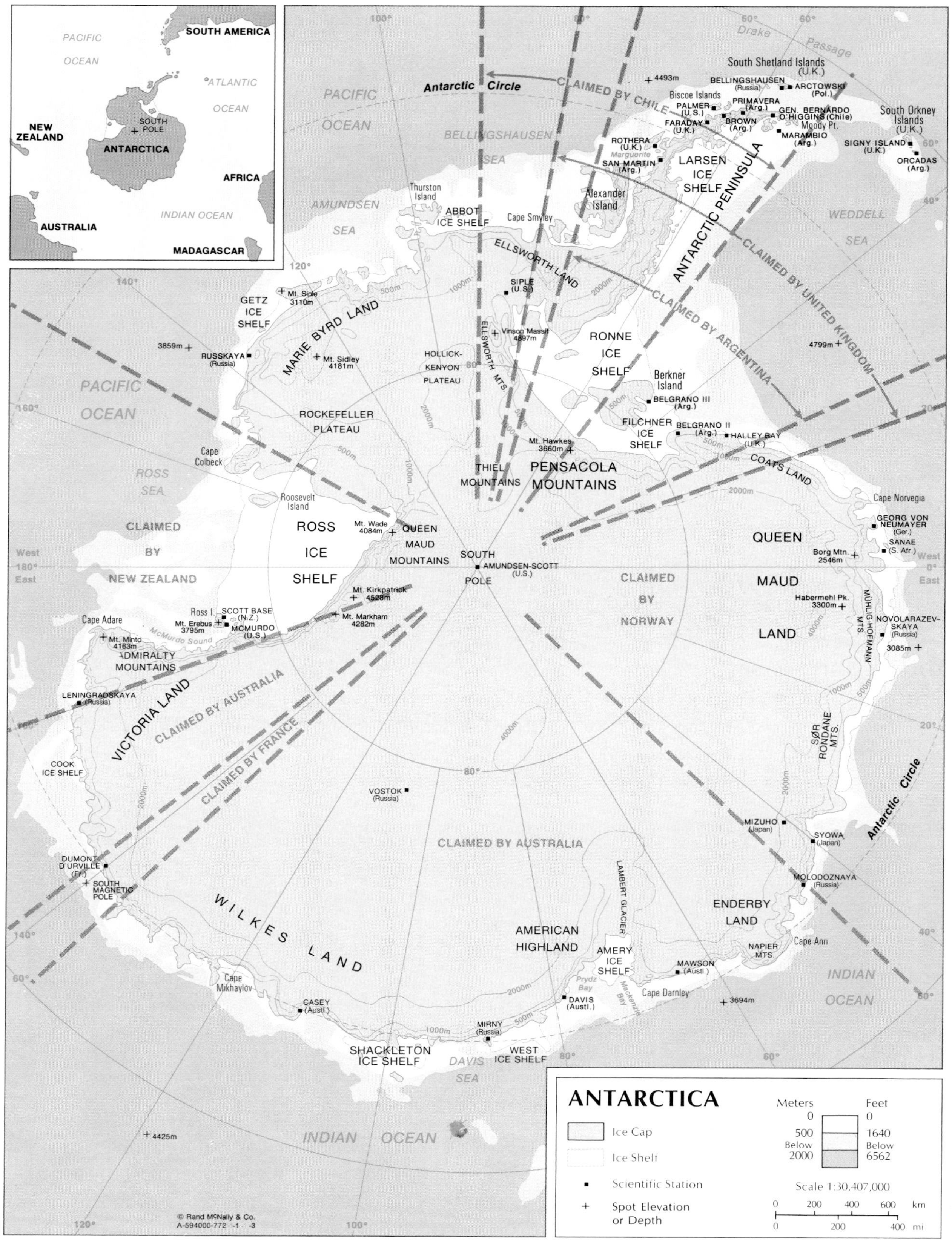

Icebergs breaking off Antarctica's coastal glaciers and ice shelves are composed of layers of snow and ice that took tens of thousands of years to form. They melt slowly as they float north into warmer ocean waters.

History and Politics
In the 1770s Captain James Cook of Britain set out in search of the southernmost continent and sailed completely around Antarctica without sighting land. Explorations beginning in 1820 resulted in sightings of the mainland or offshore islands by the British, Russians, and Americans. British explorer Sir James C. Ross conducted the first extensive explorations. After a lull of several decades, interest in Antarctica was renewed in the late nineteenth and early twentieth centuries. Captain Robert F. Scott and Ernest Shackleton of Britain and Roald Amundsen of Norway led the renewed interest. Amundsen won the race to the South Pole in 1911. An Antarctic Treaty signed in 1959 permitted only peaceful scientific research to be conducted in the region. It also delayed settlement until 1989 of overlapping claims to the territory held by Norway, Australia, France, New Zealand, Chile, Britain, and Argentina. In 1988 several countries signed agreements to allow exploitation of Antarctica's natural resources.

8

Grove of coconut palms

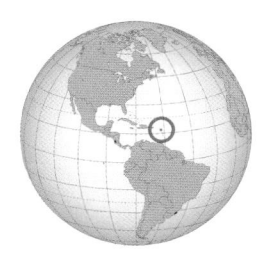

ANTIGUA AND BARBUDA

Much of the islands' coast remains untouched by humans.

Tourism is the main industry of this three-island nation, whose inhabitants are descended from slaves brought by British colonists in the 1600s. Although prone to drought, the land supports many crops including cotton and sugarcane. Debate continues between those who want to preserve the islands' natural areas and those who want to develop them for more tourism.

People
Most Antiguans are descendants of black African slaves brought by the British to work sugarcane plantations. The largest urban area is St. John's, but most Antiguans live in rural areas. British rule has left its imprint; most people are Protestant and speak English.

Economy and the Land
The dry, tropical climate and white-sand beaches attract many visitors, making tourism the economic mainstay. Once dependent on sugar cultivation, the nation has shifted to a multicrop agriculture. The country is composed of three islands: Antigua, Barbuda, and uninhabited Redondo. Formed by volcanoes, the low-lying islands are mostly flat.

History and Politics
The original inhabitants of Antigua and Barbuda were the Carib Indians. Columbus arrived at Antigua in 1493, and after unsuccessful Spanish and French attempts at colonization, the British began settlement in the 1600s. The country remained a British colony until 1967, when it became an associated state of the United Kingdom. Antigua gained independence in 1981. In March 1994, the Antigua Labour Party was returned to power for the third time, pledging a more open political system.

Antigua and Barbuda at a glance

Official name	Antigua andBarbuda

People

Population	67,000
Density	392/mi² (152/km²)
Urban	32%
Capital	St. John's, Antigua I., 24,359
Ethnic groups	Black, British, Portuguese, Lebanese, Syrian
Languages	English, local dialects
Religions	Anglican, Protestant, Roman Catholic
Life expectancy	75 female, 71 male
Literacy	89%

Politics

Government	Parliamentary state
Parties	Labour, United Progressive
Suffrage	Universal, over 18
Memberships	CW, OAS, UN
Subdivisions	7 parishes

Economy

GDP	$368,500,000
Per capita	$4,786
Monetary unit	East Caribbean dollar
Trade partners	Exports: U.S., U.K., Canada Imports: U.S., U.K., Yugoslavia
Exports	Petroleum, manufactures, food, machinery and transportation equipment
Imports	Food, machinery and transportation equipment, manufactures, chemicals

Land

Description	Caribbean islands
Area	171 mi² (442 km²)
Highest point	Boggy Pk., 1,319 ft (402 m)
Lowest point	Sea level

Some of the world's most expensive yachts call at English Harbor, Antigua's beautiful natural harbor.

Scale 1:1,000,000   One inch represents approximately 16 miles.
One centimeter represents 10 kilometers.

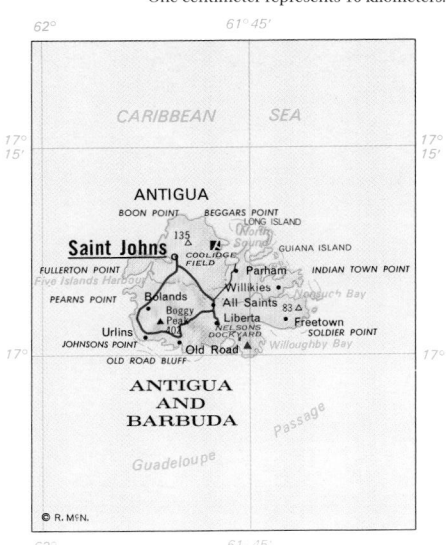

Most tourist activity is centered on Antigua, which is a popular port-of-call for cruise ships. Barbuda is relatively unvisited, but has excellent fishing and diving. Redondo is an uninhabited rock.

ARGENTINA

Argentina is a nation of diversity and contrasts; from the swamps and forests of the north, to the grassy plains west of Buenos Aires, to the barren Patagonian region of the south. The Indians who once lived there have been supplanted by Italian and Spanish immigrants and their descendants, who comprise 85 percent of the population. The government too has shown many faces. The military dictatorship which killed thousands of young people in the late 1970s was replaced by democratic rule in 1983. Today the nation is trying to stabilize and leave behind its turbulent past.

People
An indigenous Indian population, Spanish settlement, and a turn-of-the-century influx of immigrants have made Argentina an ethnically diverse nation. Today, most Argentines are descendants of Spanish and Italian immigrants. Other Europeans, mestizos of mixed Indian-Spanish blood, Indians, Middle Easterners, and Latin American immigrants diversify the population further. Spanish influence is evident in the major religion, Roman Catholicism; the official language, Spanish; and many aspects of cultural life.

Economy and the Land
Political difficulties beginning in the 1930s have resulted in economic problems and have kept this one-time economic giant from realizing its potential. The most valuable natural resource is the rich soil of the pampas, fertile plains in the east-central region. The greatest contributors to the economy, however, are manufacturing and services. The second largest country in South America, Argentina has a varied terrain, with northern lowlands, the east-central pampas, the Andes Mountains in the west, and the southern Patagonian steppe. The climate likewise varies, from subtropical in the north to subarctic in the south.

History and Politics
The earliest inhabitants of the area were Indians. In the 1500s silver-seeking Spaniards arrived, and by 1580 they had established a colony on the site of present-day Buenos Aires. In 1816 Argentina officially announced its independence from Spain. A successful struggle for independence ensued, and in 1853 a constitution was adopted and a president elected. Prosperity continued through the 1920s, and immigration and foreign investment increased. Unsatisfactory power distribution and concern over foreign investment resulted in a military coup in 1930. Thus began a series of civil and military governments; coups; the election, overthrow, and reelection of Juan Perón; and controversial human-rights violations. In 1982 Argentina lost a war with Britain over the Falkland Islands. Years of struggling with human rights transgressions followed. Since winning the election in 1989, the Perónistas have introduced austere economic reforms and rescheduled foreign debts.

The Horns are a dramatic series of peaks in the Andes Mountains that form the western border of Patagonia. Portuguese explorer Ferdinand Magellan named the region Patagones, a Spanish word meaning "big feet," after encountering a group of indigenous people who wore oversize boots.

Beach, Mar del Plata

The eighth largest country in the world in area, Argentina devotes much of its land to raising cattle and sheep. Its portion of the Andes along the border with Chile includes 30 peaks higher than 20,000 feet. Argentina continues to claim the United Kingdom's Falkland Islands as part of its territory, calling them the Islas Malvinas.

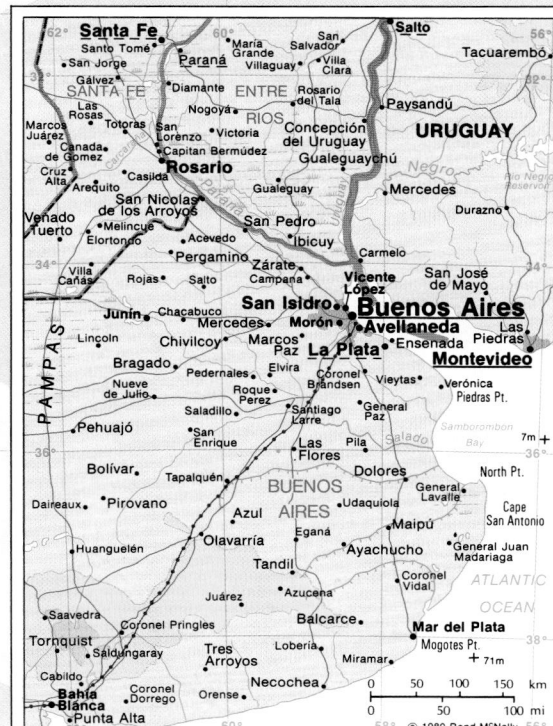

Colorful rock strata in the Andean foothills

Argentina at a glance

Official name Argentine Republic

People

Population	34,083,000
Density	32/mi² (12/km²)
Urban	86%
Capital	Buenos Aires (de facto), 2,960,976; Viedma (future) 24,346
Ethnic groups	White 85%; mestizo, Amerindian, and others 15%
Languages	Spanish, English, Italian, German, French
Religions	Roman Catholic 90%, Jewish 2%, Protestant 2%
Life expectancy	75 female, 68 male
Literacy	95%

Politics

Government	Republic
Parties	Justicialist (Peronista), Radical Civic Union, Union of the Democratic Center, others
Suffrage	Universal, over 18
Memberships	OAS, UN
Subdivisions	22 provinces, 1 district, 1 national territory

Economy

GDP	$185,000,000,000
Per capita	$5,615
Monetary unit	Peso
Trade partners	Exports: U.S., Brazil, Netherlands Imports: U.S., Brazil, Germany
Exports	Meat, wheat, corn, oilseed, hides, wool
Imports	Machinery, chemicals, metals, fuel

Land

Description	Southern South America
Area	1,073,519 mi² (2,780,400 km²)
Highest point	Aconcagua, 22,831 ft (6,959 m)
Lowest point	Salinas Chicas, -138 ft (-42 m)

Gauchos—Argentinian cowboys—have traditions as rich as their American counterparts. They work on the many cattle ranches found in the vast plains of the Pampas region of central Argentina.

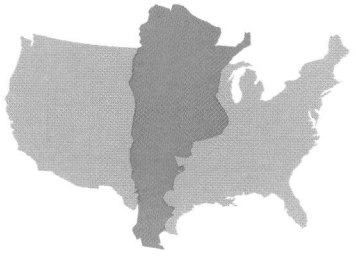

POPULATION COMPARISON
Argentina=13% of U.S.

United States

GDP COMPARISON
Argentina=3% of U.S.

United States

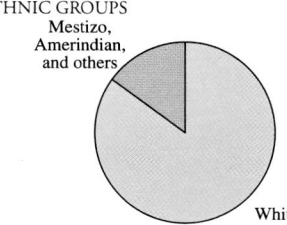

ETHNIC GROUPS
Mestizo, Amerindian, and others

White

POPULATION DISTRIBUTION
Urban — Rural

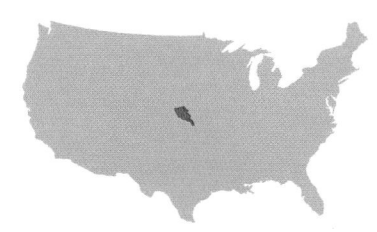

Sheep graze around a Roman temple at Garni, near the Turkish border.

ARMENIA

One of the world's oldest societies, Armenia has managed to preserve its culture despite being frequently overrun by Turks, Arabs, Russians and others through the centuries. Most recently, Armenia gained its independence from the collapsing Soviet Union in September 1991. Continuing territorial hostilities with neighboring Azerbaijan have sapped the fledgling nation's economy.

People

Two Armenians

The Armenians are among Europe's oldest and most distinct ethnic groups, having inhabited the area east and south of the Black Sea since the seventh century B.C. Both the Armenian alphabet and the Armenian church date back to the fourth century and remain substantially unchanged today. Early Armenia left a legacy of many gifted artists, writers, and philosophers.

Economy and the Land

Most of Armenia is mountainous and dry. Despite fertile soils in some of the mountain valleys, agriculture is of little importance. Armenia's great rivers have provided hydroelectric power for an important machine-building industry. Armenia is subject to severe earthquakes, and it is still rebuilding from a 1988 earthquake that killed twenty-five thousand people and destroyed one-tenth of the nation's industrial capacity and housing. Transportation is not well developed and, in recent years, blockades imposed against Armenia by neighboring Azerbaijan have crippled the economy.

History and Politics

Armenia traces its beginnings to the first millennium B.C. when the Urartu empire fell to the Armens. Alexander the Great conquered Armenia around 300 B.C., but its independence was restored one hundred years later. By the early part of the first century A.D., Armenia encompassed parts of present-day Turkey, Syria, Iraq, Iran, and the former Soviet Union. Later, various groups invaded Armenia, including the Arabs, Turks, and Persians. The Russians gained control over the nation in 1828. Continued calls for independence led to the massacre of more than two hundred thousand Armenians by the Turks in the 1890s. Armenians tried to assert their independence in 1918, but the Soviets took full control in 1920. Protests by ethnic Armenians in the enclave of Nagorno-Karabakh within Azerbaijan led to escalating violence between Armenia and Azerbaijan. The struggle fueled rising Armenian nationalism, and Armenia first declared its independence from the Soviet Union in August 1990. The country did not achieve true sovereignty until the break-up of the Soviet Union in December 1991. The Nagorno-Karabakh problem remains unsolved, although a cease-fire was signed in May 1994.

POPULATION COMPARISON
Armenia=1% of U.S.

United States

GDP COMPARISON
Armenia=0.1% of U.S.

United States

ETHNIC GROUPS

Russian
Azeri
Other
Armenian

POPULATION DISTRIBUTION
Urban | Rural

Armenia at a glance

Official name	Republic of Armenia

People

Population	3,794,000
Density	330/mi² (127/km²)
Urban	68%
Capital	Yerevan, 1,199,000
Ethnic groups	Armenian 93%, Azeri 3%, Russian 2%
Languages	Armenian, Russian
Religions	Armenian Orthodox 94%
Life expectancy	75 female, 68 male
Literacy	98%

Politics

Government	Republic
Parties	Democratic, National Democratic Union, National Movement, Revolutionary Federation, others
Suffrage	Universal, over 18
Memberships	CIS, UN
Subdivisions	None

Economy

GDP	$7,100,000,000
Per capita	$2,071
Monetary unit	Dram
Trade partners	Former Soviet republics
Exports	Machinery and transportation equipment, metals, chemicals
Imports	Machinery, energy, consumer goods

Land

Description	Southwestern Asia, landlocked
Area	11,506 mi² (29,800 km²)
Highest point	Mt. Aragats, 13,419 ft (4,090 m)
Lowest point	Along Debed River, 1,280 ft (390 m)

Shoppers search for bargains in a market hall in Yerevan. Most of Armenia's produce is imported.

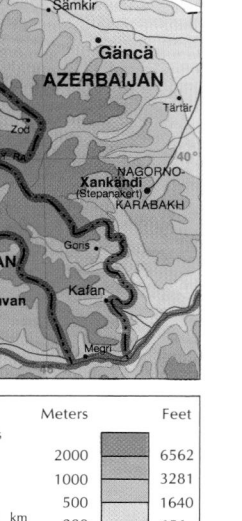

ARMENIA

	City type size indicates relative importance	Meters	Feet
——— Railroad		2000	6562
+ Spot Elevation	Scale 1:4,480,000	1000	3281
		500	1640
National capitals are underlined	0 20 40 60 80 100 km / 0 20 40 60 mi	200	656
		0	0

The Araks River valley is Armenia's primary agricultural area. Wine grapes are the primary crop; olives, figs, pomegranates, cotton, and fruits are also grown. The capital, Yerevan, has become an industrial center since the development of hydroelectric power.

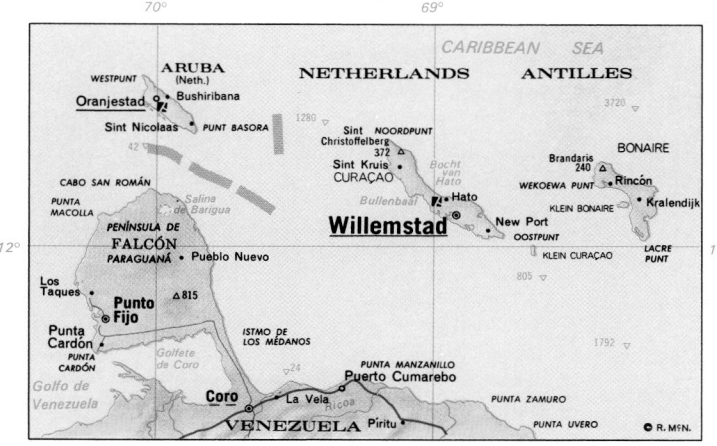

Aruba's 75 square miles are mostly flat and rock-strewn. The Bubali Bird Sanctuary is a major refuge on the north end of the island.

ARUBA

Aruba at a glance

Official name	Aruba

People

Population	67,000
Density	893/mi² (347/km²)
Urban	68%
Capital	Oranjestad, 20,045
Ethnic groups	Mixed European and West Indian 80%
Languages	Dutch, Papiamento, English, Spanish
Religions	Roman Catholic 82%, Protestant 8%
Life expectancy	80 female, 73 male
Literacy	

Politics

Government	Self-governing territory (Netherlands protection)
Parties	Electoral Movement, People's, others
Suffrage	Universal, over 18
Memberships	None
Subdivisions	None

Economy

GDP	$900,000,000
Per capita	$13,636
Monetary unit	Florin
Trade partners	U.S., European countries
Exports	Petroleum products
Imports	Food, manufactures

Land

Description	Caribbean island
Area	75 mi² (193 km²)
Highest point	Jamanota, 617 ft (188 m)
Lowest point	Sea level

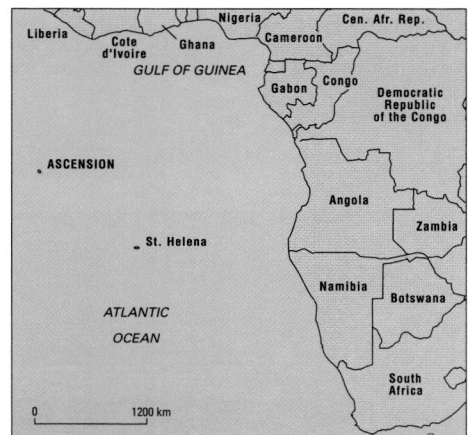

Volcanic in origin, the island of Ascension is dominated by features formed in its fiery past, including Green Mountain, an extinct crater.

Papiamento, a medley of Spanish, Dutch, Portuguese, English and Indian words, is both the principal language of Aruba and a reflection of the population of this beach-ringed island. A self-governing part of the Netherlands, Aruba was colonized by the Dutch in 1634. Tourism is supplanting oil refining as the island's main economic force, thanks to new resorts, a deep-water harbor, and an international airport.

People

Aruba's population combines descendants of the original Indian population, black Africans, Spanish invaders, and Dutch settlers. Spoken and understood almost universally here are Dutch, English, Spanish, and Papiamento—a language that combines elements of Spanish, Portuguese, English, and Dutch with Indian words.

Economy and the Land

Aruba is dry with soils unsuited for agriculture, and for many years the economy did not show much potential for development. In the twentieth century, however, nearby Venezuela began producing crude oil, and companies were attracted to Aruba as an economical and stable site to establish a refinery center. The refinery complex is now a major employer. Tourism, too, has grown, with visitors attracted by the coral reefs, white-sand beaches, and tropical climate moderated by trade winds. Aruba's land is dry and rocky, and scattered over the island are giant boulders and monoliths.

History and Politics

Early in Aruba's history, the Caribs replaced the peaceful Arawak Indians, and caves on the island are marked with signs and symbol of these early peoples. In 1499, some time after the first arrival of the Spanish, the island was claimed for the Spanish Crown. Aruba was a center of activity for pirates until the 1600s, when the Netherlands obtained possession after long years of war with the Spanish. For a brief time during the Napoleonic Wars, the British occupied Aruba, but the island remained in Dutch hands. Until 1986 Aruba was part of the Netherlands Antilles, two groups of West Indies islands that belong to the Netherlands. In 1986, in preparation for its planned 1996 independence, Aruba was made a self-governing territory equal in status to the remainder of the Netherlands Antilles. Since the island's economy has not yet recovered from the 1985 closing of its oil refinery, however, Aruba was allowed to remain a separate dependent territory beyond 1996.

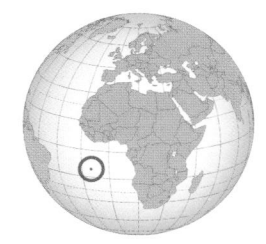

ASCENSION

Strategically located between South America and Africa, Ascension hosts a vital communications station for Great Britain and a satellite tracking station for the United States. Half of the 1,000-person population works in these two facilities. The island is administered from St. Helena, another island dependency of Great Britain, some 700 miles to the southeast.

People

Despite Ascension's sparse vegetation, subsistence farming is practiced by many people in this small island in southern Atlantic. A dependency of the British colony of St. Helena, Ascension is also home to a number of immigrants from the island, which lies about 700 miles (1,126 kilometers) to the southeast.

Economy and the Land

Agricultural activity includes raising livestock and growing vegetables and fruit. Ascension is the site of a British communication relay station and a United States satellite tracking station: thus the communications industry is a major employer. In addition, the island is known for its

wildlife: the sea turtles that come ashore to lay their eggs and the sooty terns that use Ascension as their breeding grounds. The climate of this volcanic island is mild.

History and Politics

A Portuguese explorer arrived on the island in 1501. He was followed by the British in 1701, and in 1815 Britain took possession of Ascension. In 1922 administration of Ascension was transferred to St. Helena, and along with Tristan da Cunha, Ascension remains a dependency of the colony. Mainly of strategic importance, Ascension served as a United States refueling station during World War II and played a role in the British battle with Argentina over the Falkland Islands in 1982.

Ascension at a glance

Official name	Ascension

People

Population	1,000
Density	29/mi² (11/km²)
Capital	Georgetown
Ethnic groups	St. Helenian, British, American
Languages	English
Religions	Anglican

Politics

Government	Dependency (St. Helena)
Suffrage	None
Memberships	None

Economy

Monetary unit	St. Helena pound

Land

Description	South Atlantic island
Area	34 mi² (88 km²)
Highest point	Green Mountain, 2,817 ft (859 m)
Lowest point	Sea level

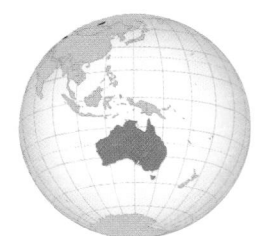

AUSTRALIA

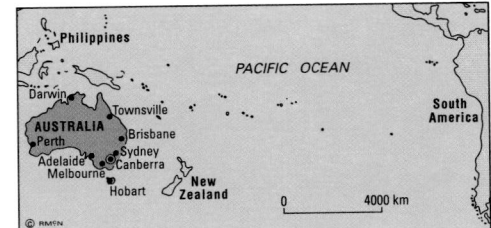

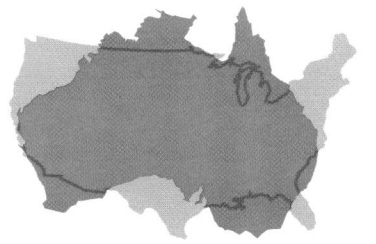

POPULATION COMPARISON
Australia=7% of U.S.

United States

GDP COMPARISON
Australia=5% of U.S.

United States

ETHNIC GROUPS

Asian

Aboriginal and other

Caucasian

POPULATION DISTRIBUTION
Urban   Rural

Ayers Rock

Since the first groups of settlers—the now legendary boatloads of convicts—arrived in Australia in 1788 from Britain, successive waves of immigrants have built a modern western society with a vibrant culture. However, this success came at severe cost to the native aboriginal peoples, who suffered severe discrimination and remain economically disadvantaged. Much of Australia's interior remains unpopulated, home only to the country's many unique animals, such as kangaroos, koalas and wombats.

Sailing is popular in Sydney, which boasts a postcard-perfect harbor and skyline.

Aboriginal dancers

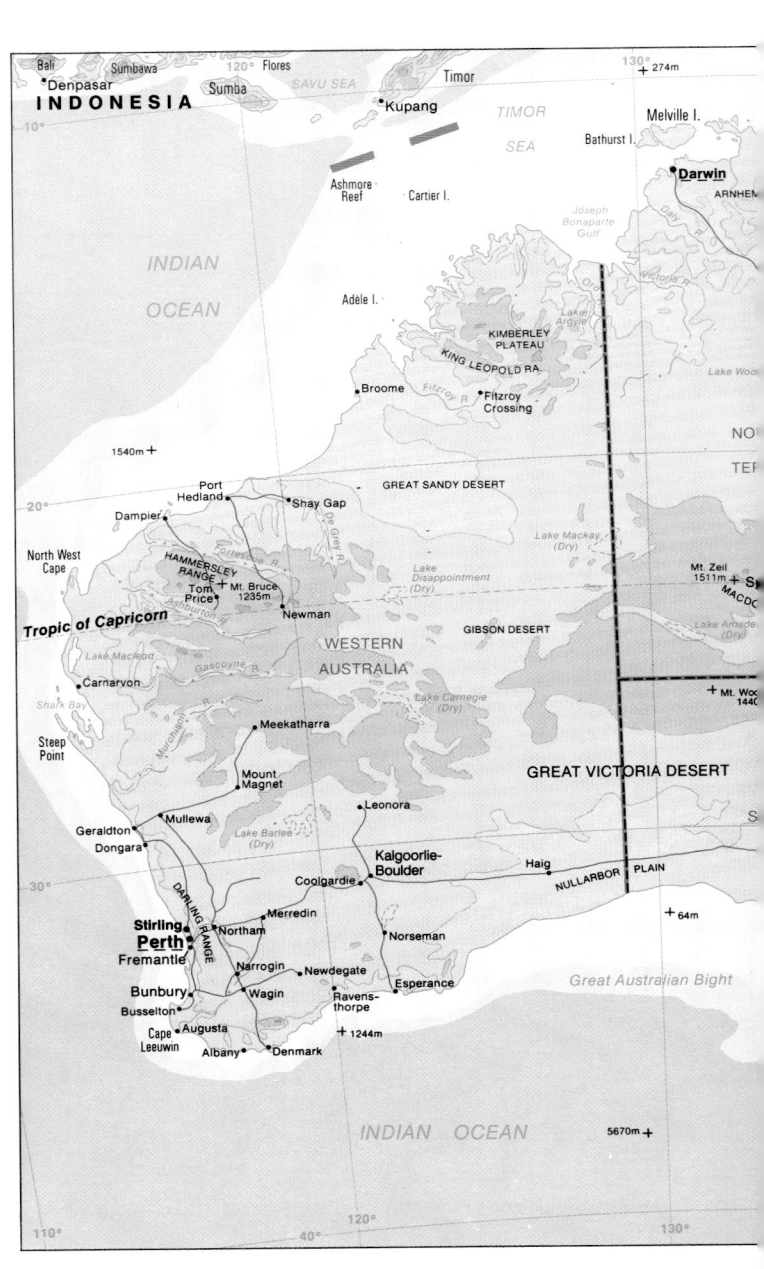

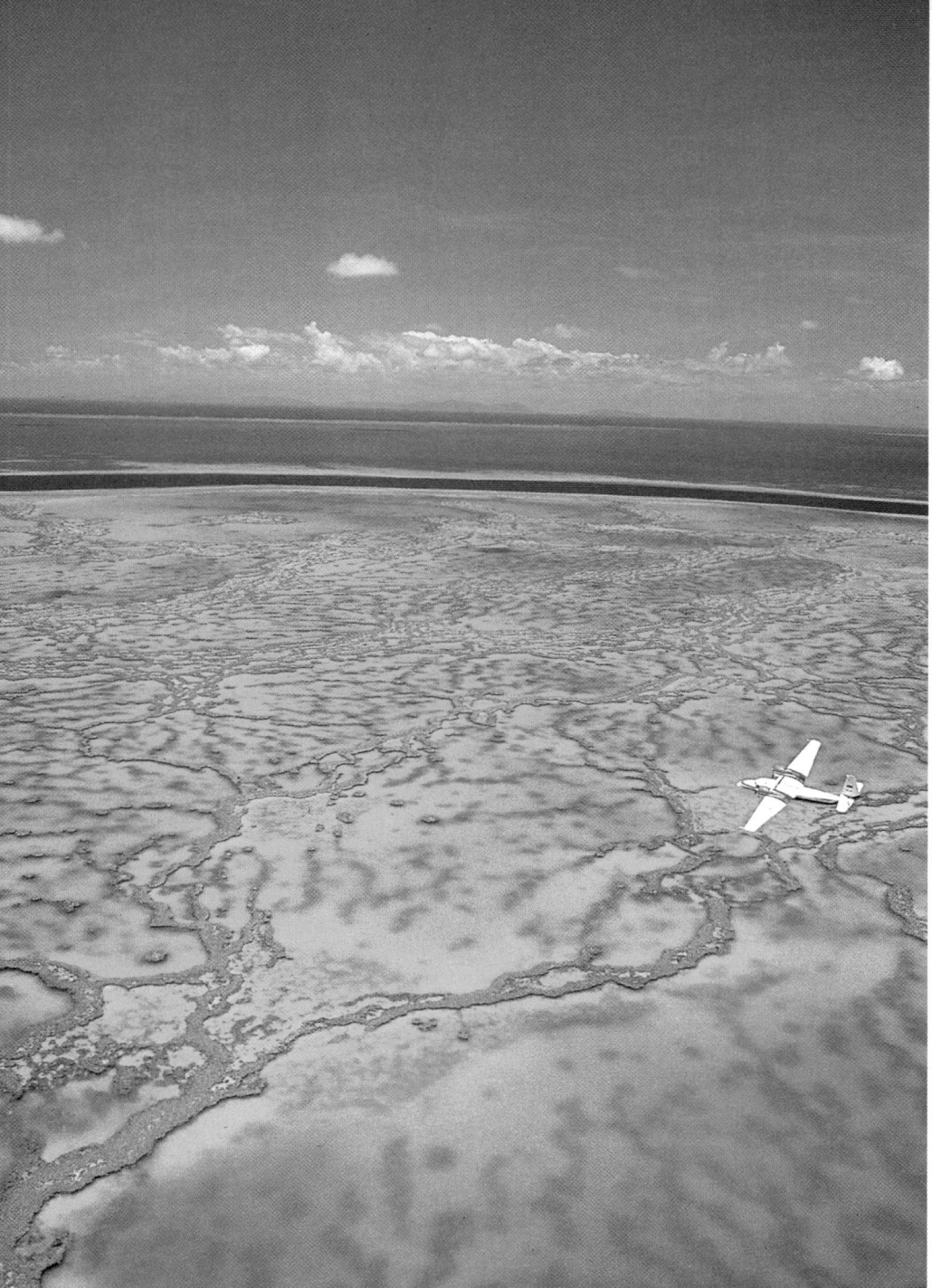

Australia at a glance

Official name	Commonwealth of Australia

People

Population	18,205,000
Density	6.1/mi² (2.4/km²)
Urban	85%
Capital	Canberra, 276,162
Ethnic groups	Caucasian 95%, Asian 4%, Aboriginal and other 1%
Languages	English, indigenous
Religions	Anglican 26%, Roman Catholic 26%, other Christian 24%
Life expectancy	80 female, 74 male
Literacy	100%

Politics

Government	Parliamentary state
Parties	Labor, Liberal, National
Suffrage	Universal, over 18
Memberships	CW, OECD, UN
Subdivisions	6 states, 2 territories

Economy

GDP	$339,700,000,000
Per capita	$20,024
Monitary unit	Dollar
Trade partners	Exports: Japan, U.S., New Zealand, Korea Imports: U.S., Japan, U.K.
Exports	Metals, minerals, coal, wool, grain, meat, manufactures
Imports	Manufactures, machinery, consumer goods

Land

Description	Continent between South Pacific and Indian oceans
Area	2,966,155 mi² (7,682,300 km²)
Highest point	Mt. Kosciusko, 7,310 ft (2,228 m)
Lowest point	Lake Eyre (North), -52 ft (-16 m)

Rock pillars along coast

Koala Bear

The unusual Olga Rocks in Uluru National Park resemble walruses on a beach.

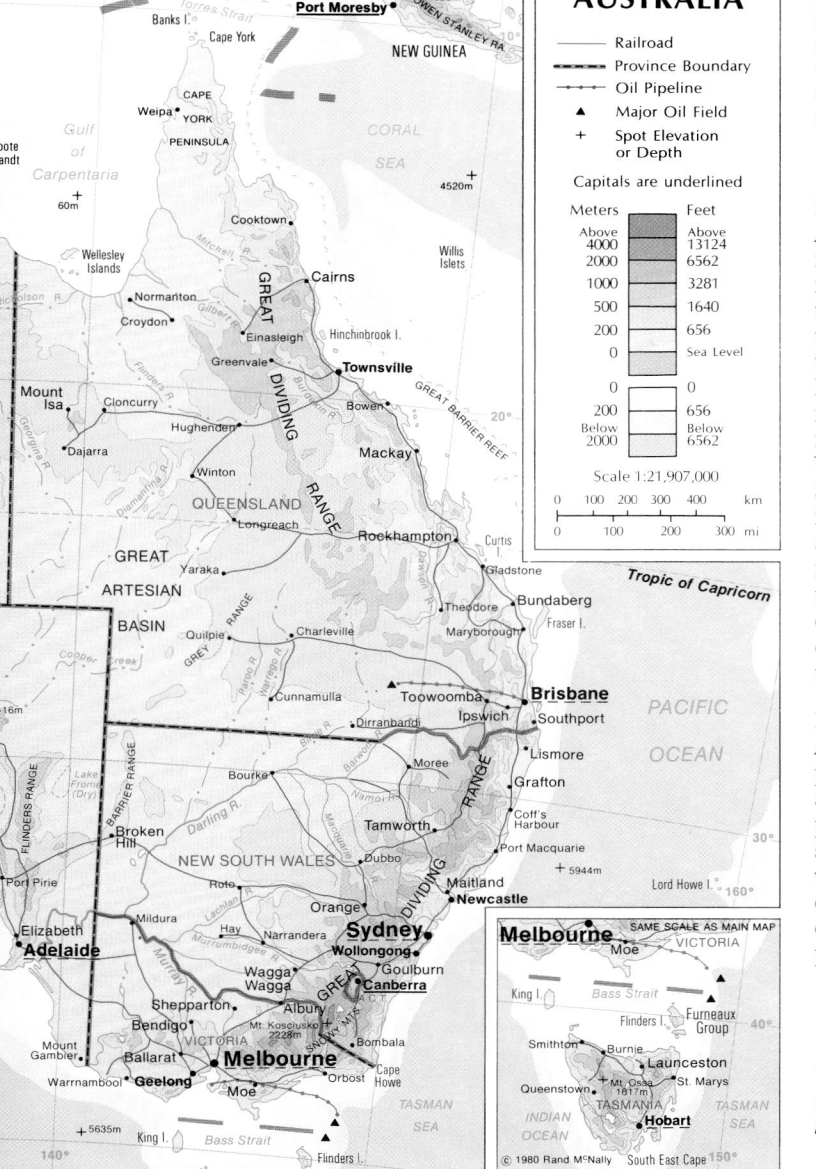

AUSTRALIA

- Railroad
- Province Boundary
- Oil Pipeline
- ▲ Major Oil Field
- + Spot Elevation or Depth

Capitals are underlined

Meters	Feet
Above 4000	Above 13124
2000	6562
1000	3281
500	1640
200	656
0	Sea Level
0	0
200	656
Below 2000	Below 6562

Scale 1:21,907,000

The Great Barrier Reef off Australia's northeast coast is the world's largest coral reef. Popular with divers, it is home to a myriad of aquatic creatures.

People

Australia's culture reflects a unique combination of British, other European, and aboriginal influences. Settlement and rule by the United Kingdom gave the country a distinctly British flavor, and many Australians trace their roots to early British settlers. Planned immigration also played a major role in Australia's development, bringing more than three million Europeans since World War II. Refugees, most recently from Southeast Asia, make up another group of incoming peoples. The country is home to a small number of aborigines. Its size and a relatively dry terrain have resulted in uneven settlement patterns, with people concentrated in the rainier southeastern coastal area. The population is mainly urban, though overall density remains low.

Economy and the Land

Australia's economy is characterized by a postwar shift from agriculture to industry and services, as well as inflation and unemployment. Wool is a major export, and livestock raising takes place on relatively flat, wide grazing lands surrounding an arid central region. Commercial crop raising is concentrated on a fertile southeastern plain. Plentiful mineral resources provide for a strong mining industry. Australia is the world's smallest continent but one of its largest countries. The climate is varied, and part of the country lies within the tropics.

History and Politics

Aboriginal peoples probably arrived about forty thousand years ago and established a hunter-gatherer society. The Dutch explored the area in the seventeenth century, but no claims were made until the eighteenth century, when British Captain James Cook found his way to the fertile east and annexed the land to Britain. The first colony, New South Wales, was founded in 1788, and many of the early settlers were British convicts. During the 1800s, a squatter movement spread the population to other parts of the island, and the discovery of gold led to a population boom. Demands for self-government soon began, and by the 1890s all the colonies were self-governing, with Britain maintaining control of foreign affairs and defense. Nationalism continued to increase, and a new nation, the Commonwealth of Australia, was created in 1901. Currently a movement is underway to declare Australia a republic and thus loosen ties with Britain.

The world's sixth-largest country is also the only country to occupy its own island continent. Despite its size, Australia is sparsely populated, with most people living around the coastal centers of Melbourne, Sydney and Brisbane.

Hallstatt is a picturesque example of the villages in the lake district near Salzburg.

Innsbruck and Hafelekarspitze Mountains

AUSTRIA

Austria was once the center of an empire that dominated Central Europe. It was reduced to its present borders after World War I, when its alliance with Germany ended in defeat. Austria emerged from German occupation during World War II to find itself caught between East and West during the Cold War. Adhering to rigid neutrality, the nation spent the post-war years building a modern and affluent society.

People

The majority of Austrians are native born, German speaking, and Roman Catholic, a homogeneity belying a history of invasions by diverse peoples. With a long cultural tradition, the country has contributed greatly to music and the arts. Vienna, the capital, is one of the great cultural centers of Europe.

Economy and the Land

Austria's economy is a blend of state and privately-owned industry. After World War II the government began nationalizing industries, returning many to the private sector as the economy stabilized. Unemployment is low, and the economy remains relatively strong. The economic mainstays are services and manufacturing. Agriculture is limited because of the overall mountainous terrain, with the Danube River basin in the east containing the most productive soils. In addition to the country's cultural heritage, the alpine landscape also attracts many tourists. The climate is generally moderate.

History and Politics

Early in its history, Austria was settled by Celts, ruled by Romans, and invaded by Germans, Slavs, Magyars, and others. Long rule by the Hapsburg family began in the thirteenth century, and in time Austria became the center of a vast empire. In 1867 Hungarian pressure resulted in the formation of the dual monarchy of Austria-Hungary. Nationalist movements against Austria culminated in the 1914 assassination of the heir to the throne, Archduke Francis Ferdinand, and set off the conflict that became World War I. In 1918 the war ended, the Hapsburg emperor was overthrown, Austria became a republic, and present-day boundaries were established. Political unrest and instability followed. In 1938 Adolf Hitler incorporated Austria into the German Reich. A period of occupation after World War II was followed by Austria's declaration of neutrality. Austria joined the European Union in June 1994.

Austria at a glance

Official name	Republic of Austria

People

Population	7,932,000
Density	245/mi² (95/km²)
Urban	58%
Capital	Vienna, 1,539,848
Ethnic groups	German 99%
Languages	German
Religions	Roman Catholic 85%, Protestant 6%
Life expectancy	79 female, 73 male
Literacy	99%

Politics

Government	Republic
Parties	Freedom, People's, Social Democratic, others
Suffrage	Universal, over 19
Memberships	OECD, UN
Subdivisions	9 states

Economy

GDP	$134,400,000,000
Per capita	$17,015
Monetary unit	Schilling
Trade partners	Exports: Germany, Italy, Switzerland Imports: Germany, Italy, Japan
Exports	Machinery and equipment, iron and steel, wood, textiles
Imports	Petroleum, food, machinery, transportation equipment, chemicals

Land

Description	Central Europe, landlocked
Area	32,377 mi² (83,856 km²)
Highest point	Grossglockner, 12,461 ft (3,798 m)
Lowest point	Neusiedler See, 377 ft (115 m)

POPULATION COMPARISON
Austria=3% of U.S.

United States

GDP COMPARISON
Austria=2% of U.S.

United States

ETHNIC GROUPS

Other

German

POPULATION DISTRIBUTION

Urban   Rural

AUSTRIA

		Meters	Feet
	Major Urban Area	4000	13124
	Railroad	2000	6562
	Glacier	1000	3281
	Spot Elevation	500	1640
		200	656
		0	0

National capitals are underlined

0   20   40   60   80 100 km
0   20   40   60 mi

Scale 1:3,755,000

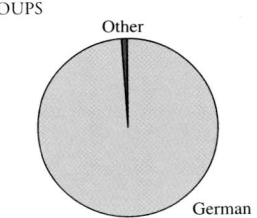

Primarily mountainous, Austria is dominated by the eastern ranges of the Alps. Winter sports such as skiing are a national passion. Innsbruck was home to the Winter Olympics in 1964 and 1976.

Parliament, Vienna

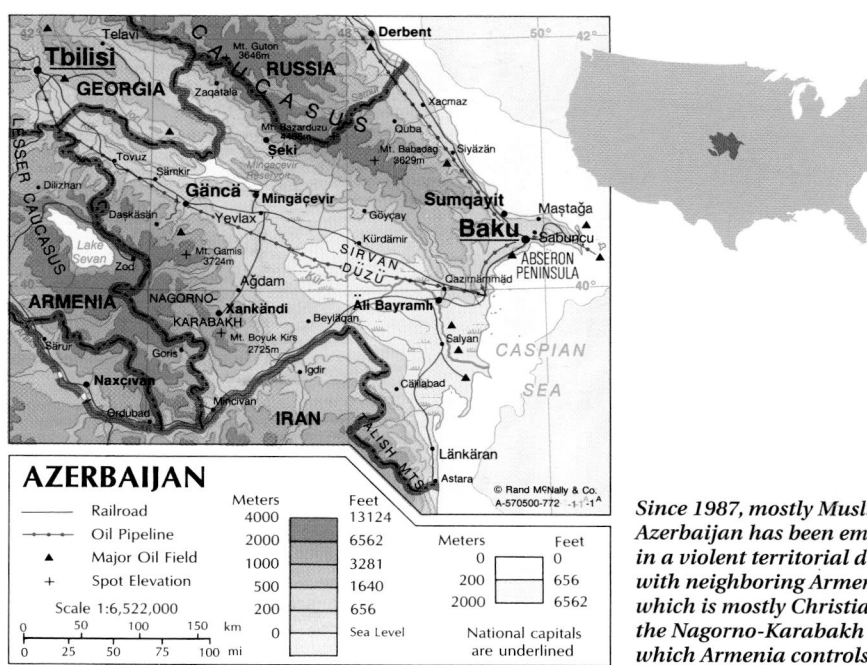

AZERBAIJAN

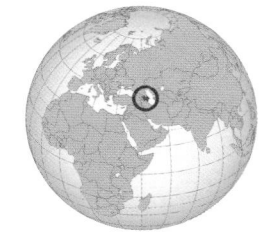

AZERBAIJAN

	Meters	Feet
Railroad	4000	13124
Oil Pipeline	2000	6562
Major Oil Field	1000	3281
Spot Elevation	500	1640
	200	656
	0	Sea Level

Scale 1:6,522,000

National capitals are underlined

Since 1987, mostly Muslim Azerbaijan has been embroiled in a violent territorial dispute with neighboring Armenia, which is mostly Christian, over the Nagorno-Karabakh region, which Armenia controls.

POPULATION COMPARISON
Azerbaijan=3% of U.S.

United States

GDP COMPARISON
Azerbaijan=0.3% of U.S.

United States

ETHNIC GROUPS

POPULATION DISTRIBUTION

Urban   Rural

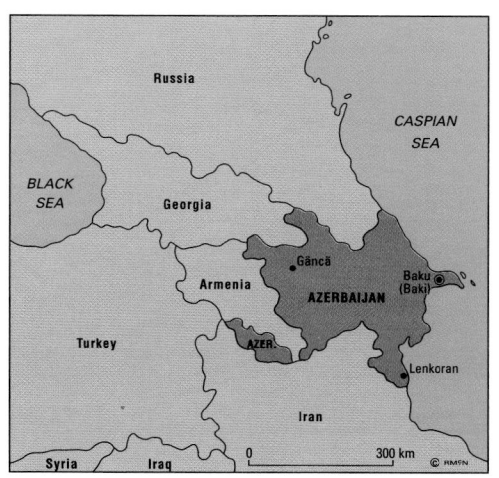

Azerbaijan had little experience as an independent country until the break-up of the Soviet Union in 1991. Like other former Soviet republics, Azerbaijan's economy has suffered during the transition to independence. One ameliorating factor has been the petroleum industry centered on the rich oil deposits near the capital of Baku.

People
The Azeris are Turkic people and account for more than 80 percent of the population. There are also small Armenian and Russian minorities. Most Azeris are Shiite Muslims, although the Armenians in the enclave of Nagorno-Karabakh are Christian. About one-half of the people live in urban areas.

Economy and the Land
Azerbaijan varies from the cool slopes of the Caucasus to flat, dry steppes. Cotton is produced in abundance. Sheep and cattle are also raised on the dry, grassy pasture of the steppes. The Lenkoran lowland in the extreme southeast part of the country is semitropical and produces many fruits and vegetables. The area around Baku is a major oil-producing and refining center, although production has been steadily declining.

History and Politics
Azerbaijan is part of a larger historical region of the same name, which includes parts of neighboring Iran. Arabs conquered the region and brought Islam in A.D. 642. Later, Mongols, Turks, and Persians invaded the region. Russian interest in the area began during the reign of Peter the Great and led to several wars with Persia. In 1828

Azerbaijan was formally divided between Russia and Persia (now Iran). The country enjoyed a brief period of independence from 1918 to 1920, when a Soviet invasion forced its incorporation into the Soviet Union. Fighting between Azerbaijan and neighboring Armenia over the Armenian enclave of Nagorno-Karabakh began in 1987, and prompted a renewed Soviet invasion of the capital city of Baku in early 1990. Azerbaijan declared its independence in August 1991. The country attained real independence after the dissolution of the Soviet Union at the end of 1991. Continuing strife with Armenia over the enclave of Nagorno-Karabakh has disrupted government functions. In June 1993, Azerbaijan's first elected president was overthrown. Political unrest continues, particularly in Nagorno-Karabakh.

Street scene in an Azerbaijani village

Azerbaijan at a glance
Official name Azerbaijani Republic

People

Population	7,491,000
Density	224/mi² (87/km²)
Urban	54%
Capital	Baku, 1,080,500
Ethnic groups	Azeri 83%, Armenian 6%, Russian 6%
Languages	Azeri, Russian, Armenian
Religions	Muslim 87%, Russian Orthodox 6%, Armenian Orthodox 6%
Life expectancy	75 female, 67 male
Literacy	98%

Politics

Government	Republic
Parties	Musavat, National Independence, Popular Front, Social Democratic, others
Suffrage	Universal, over 18
Memberships	CIS, UN
Subdivisions	1 republic

Economy

GDP	$15,500,000,000
Per capita	$2,064
Monetary unit	Manat
Trade partners	Former Soviet republics, European countries
Exports	Oil and gas, chemicals, oil-field equipment, textiles, cotton
Imports	Machinery and parts, consumer durables, food, textiles

Land

Description	Southwestern Asia, landlocked
Area	33,436 mi² (86,600 km²)
Highest point	Bazardüzü, 14,652 ft (4,466 m)
Lowest point	Caspian Sea, -92 ft (-28 m)

Despite their pollution, oil refineries are located in the heart of the Azerbaijan capital of Baku. Oil production is a vital part of the Azerbaijani economy.

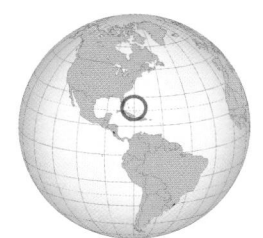

BAHAMAS

Andros Island, the largest of the islands in the Bahamas, is the only one with running fresh water. On all the rest, wells must be dug deep into the underlying rocks.

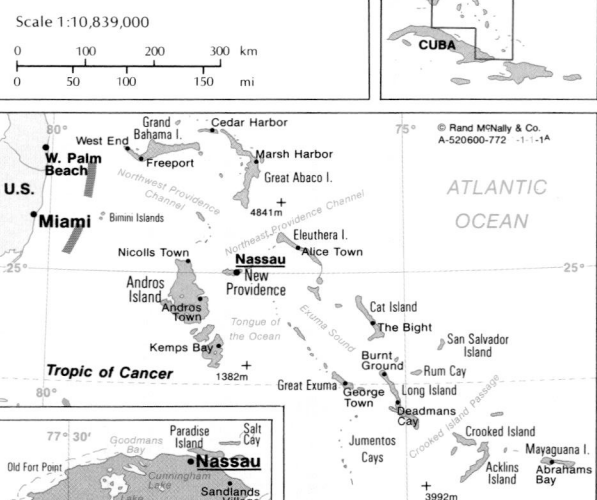

BAHAMAS
+ Spot Elevation or Depth
Scale 1:10,839,000

Bahamas at a glance
Official name   Commonwealth of the Bahamas

People

Population	270,000
Density	50/mi² (19/km²)
Urban	64%
Capital	Nassau, New Providence I., 141,000
Ethnic groups	Black 85%, white 15%
Languages	English, Creole
Religions	Baptist 32%, Anglican 20%, Roman Catholic 19%, Methodist 6%
Life expectancy	76 female, 69 male
Literacy	90%

Politics

Government	Parliamentary state
Parties	Free National Movement, Progressive Liberal
Suffrage	Universal, over 18
Memberships	CW, OAS, UN
Subdivisions	21 districts

Economy

GDP	$2,600,000,000
Per capita	$10,156
Monetary unit	Dollar
Trade partners	Exports: U.S., U.K., Japan Imports: Saudi Arabia, U.S., Nigeria
Exports	Pharmaceuticals, cement, rum, crawfish
Imports	Food, manufactures, fuel

Land

Description	Caribbean islands
Area	5,382 mi² (13,939 km²)
Highest point	Mt. Alvernia, 206 ft (63 m)
Lowest point	Sea level

Stretching 750 miles south from a point off the Florida coast, the nearly 700 islands and 2,000 islets of the Bahamas are a formidable barrier. Only three passages for large ships exist along their length. San Salvador (Watling) Island was probably Christopher Columbus's first landfall in the New World in 1492. Today the larger islands play host to legions of tourists and scores of international banks.

People
Only about 29 of the 700 Bahamian islands are inhabited, and most of the people live on Grand Bahama and New Providence. The majority blacks are mainly descendants of slaves routed through the area or brought by British Loyalists fleeing the American colonies during the revolutionary war.

Economy and the Land
Because the thin soils of these flat coral islands are not suited for agriculture, for years the country struggled to develop a strong economic base. The solution was tourism, which capitalizes on the islands' most valuable resource—a semitropical climate. Because it is a tax haven, the country is also an international finance center.

History and Politics
Christopher Columbus's first stop on his way to America in 1492, the Bahamas were originally the home of the Lucayo Indians, whom the Spaniards took for slave trade. The British arrived in the 1600s, and the islands became a British colony in 1717. The country achieved independence in 1973. In 1992 voters ended Sir Lynden Pindling's twenty-five-year tenure as Prime Minister.

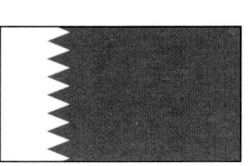

BAHRAIN

The majority of Bahrain's people live in two cities in the northeastern part of Bahrain Island. Manama, the capital, is heavily Westernized with many tall buildings. Al-Muharraq is a traditional Arab town of low stone buildings with flat roofs.

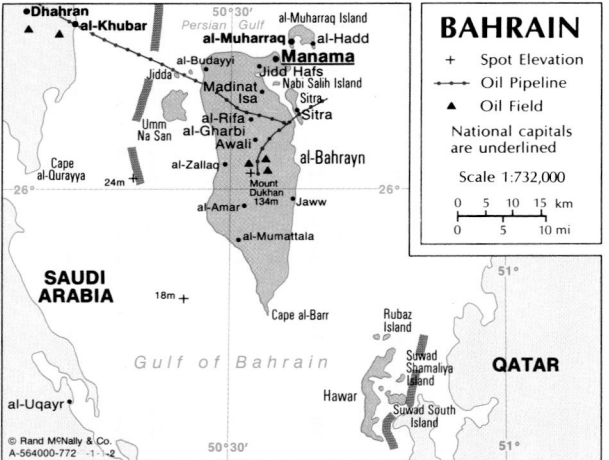

BAHRAIN
+ Spot Elevation
Oil Pipeline
▲ Oil Field
National capitals are underlined
Scale 1:732,000

Bahrain at a glance
Official name   State of Bahrain

People

Population	563,000
Density	2,109/mi² (815/km²)
Urban	83%
Capital	Manama, Bahrain I., 82,700
Ethnic groups	Bahraini 63%, Asian 13%, other Arab 10%
Languages	Arabic, English, Farsi, Urdu
Religions	Shiite Muslim 70%, Sunni Muslim 30%
Life expectancy	74 female, 69 male
Literacy	77%

Politics

Government	Monarchy
Parties	None
Suffrage	None
Memberships	AL, UN
Subdivisions	12 regions

Economy

GDP	$6,800,000,000
Per capita	$12,121
Monetary unit	Dinar
Trade partners	Exports: Saudi Arabia, Japan, United Arab Emirates Imports: Saudi Arabia, U.K., U.S.
Exports	Petroleum products, aluminum
Imports	Crude petroleum, machinery and transportation equipment, manufactures

Land

Description	Southwestern Asian islands (in Persian Gulf)
Area	267 mi² (691 km²)
Highest point	Mt. Dukhan, 440 ft (134 m)
Lowest point	Sea level

Through history, the island nation of Bahrain has shown an amazing ability to adapt. Until the 1930s, its people earned a subsistence living on pearls and shrimp. Then oil was discovered, which brought great wealth. In the 1970s, as its own oil reserves were depleted, Bahrain became a major refining center for other Persian Gulf nations' oil. In the 1980s, the country focused on becoming a major banking and trading center for the region.

People
Most residents of Bahrain are native-born Muslims, with the Sunni sect predominating in urban areas and Shiites in the countryside. Many of the country's thirty-three islands are barren, and population is concentrated in the capital city—Manama, on Bahrain Island —and on the smaller island of Muharraq. The oil economy has resulted in an influx of foreign workers and considerable westernization, and Bahrain is a Persian Gulf leader in free health care and education.

Economy and the Land
The one-time pearl-and-fish economy was reshaped by exploitation of oil and natural gas, careful management, and diversification. A major refinery processes crude oil piped from Saudi Arabia as well as the country's own oil, and Bahrain's aluminum industry is the Gulf's largest non-oil activity. Because of its location, Bahrain is able to provide Gulf countries with services such as dry docking, and the country has become a Middle Eastern banking center. Agriculture exists on northern Bahrain Island, where natural springs provide an irrigation source. The newest industry is tourism, providing a playground for Saudis and American military personnel. Much of the state is desert. Summers are hot and dry and winters are mild.

History and Politics
From about 2000 to 1800 B.C., the area of Bahrain flourished as a center for trade. After early periods of Portuguese and Iranian rule, the Al Khalifa family came to power in the eighteenth century, and it has governed ever since. Bahrain became a British protectorate in the nineteenth century, and independence was gained in 1971. Recent attempts at democratization have been quashed by the Al Khalifa family.

Carrying fish to market

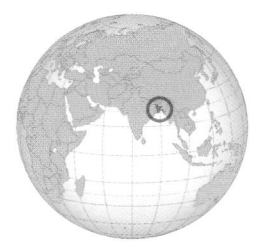

Dhaka, the capital of Bangladesh, is located near the heart of the vast delta of the Ganges and Brahmaputra rivers, one of the few two-river deltas in the world.

BANGLADESH

Bangladesh is one of the most densely populated nations on the planet, with more than 2,000 people per square mile of land. It is expected to get even more crowded. Half of its people are under age 15 and the total population is expected to soar past 140 million by the year 2000. Bangladeshis compete not just for space but also for food in an economy that has yet to recover from a 1971 civil war that left over one million dead.

People

Bangladesh's population is characterized by extremes. The people, mostly peasant farmers, are among Asia's poorest and most rural. With a relatively small area and a high birthrate, the country is also one of the world's most densely populated. Many Bangladeshis are victims of disease, floods, and ongoing medical and food shortages. Islam, the major religion, has influenced almost every aspect of life. Bangla is the official language.

Economy and the Land

Fertile flood plain soil is the chief resource of this mostly flat, river-crossed country, and farming is the main activity. Rice and jute are among the major crops. Farm output fluctuates greatly, however, subject to the frequent monsoons, floods, and droughts of a semitropical climate. Because of this and other factors, foreign aid, imports, and an emphasis on agriculture have not assuaged the continuing food shortages. In 1988 floods put 75 percent of the country under water and left twenty-five million people in dire straits.

A cyclone in 1991 killed more than one hundred thousand people and left millions at risk from lack of fresh water and food.

History and Politics

Most of Bangladesh lies in eastern Bengal, an Asian region whose western sector encompasses India's Bengal province. Early religious influences in Bengal included Buddhist rulers in the eighth century A.D. and Hindus in the eleventh. In A.D.1200 Muslim rule introduced the religion to which the majority of eastern Bengalis eventually converted, while most western Bengalis retained their Hindu beliefs. British control in India, beginning in the seventeenth century, expanded until all Bengal was part of British India by the 1850s. When British India gained independence in 1947, Muslim population centers were united into the single nation of Pakistan in an attempt to end Hindu-Muslim hostilities. More than 1,000 miles (1,600 km) separated West Pakistan, formed from northwest India, from East Pakistan, comprised mostly of eastern Bengal. The bulk of Pakistan's population resided in the eastern province and felt the west wielded political and economic power at its expense. A civil war began in 1971, and the eastern province declared itself an independent nation called Bangladesh, or "Bengal nation." That same year, West Pakistan surrendered to eastern guerrillas joined with Indian troops. The state has seen political crises since independence, including two leader assassinations and several coups. In 1982 General Ershad took control in a bloodless coup, and assumed the office

of president in 1983. Violent protests led to Ershad's resignation in December 1990 and his subsequent sentence for misappropriation of funds. Local elections in January 1994 were met with violence.

Bangladesh at a glance

Official name	People's Republic of Bangladesh

People

Population	119,370,000
Density	2,147/mi² (829/km²)
Urban	16%
Capital	Dhaka, 3,637,892
Ethnic groups	Bengali 98%
Languages	Bangla, English
Religions	Muslim 83%, Hindu 16%
Life expectancy	53 female, 53 male
Literacy	35%

Politics

Government	Republic
Parties	Awami League, Jamaat-e-Islami, Jatiyo, Nationalist, others
Suffrage	Universal, over 18
Memberships	CW, UN
Subdivisions	5 divisions

Economy

GDP	$12,200,000,000
Per capita	$101
Monetary unit	Taka
Trade partners	Exports: U.S., Italy, Japan, U.K. Imports: Japan, U.S., United Arab Emirates
Exports	Clothing, jute, leather, shrimp
Imports	Machinery, petroleum, food, textiles

Land

Description	Southern Asia
Area	55,598 mi² (143,998 km²)
Highest point	Reng Mtn., 3,141 ft (957 m)
Lowest point	Sea level

POPULATION COMPARISON
Bangladesh=46% of U.S.

Bangladesh

United States

GDP COMPARISON
Bangladesh=0.2% of U.S.

Bangladesh

United States

ETHNIC GROUPS

Other

Bengali

POPULATION DISTRIBUTION

Urban   Rural

BANGLADESH

Major Urban Area

Railroad

Scale 1:6,000,000

Meters	Feet
4000	13124
2000	6562
1000	3281
500	1640
200	656
0	0
200	656

Situated at the cusp of the Bay of Bengal in the Indian Ocean, Bangladesh has borne the brunt of numerous cyclones that have devastated the land and killed hundreds of thousands of people.

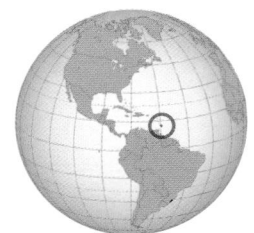

BARBADOS

Long known for its white beaches and coral reefs, Barbados has suffered from its status as a major Caribbean tourist draw. The colonial capital of Bridgetown is surrounded by scores of resorts which have taxed the island's natural resources. Away from the development, however, Barbados retains its traditional lifestyle based on sugar production.

The round House of Assembly and a monument to British Admiral Horatio Nelson form the scenic center of Bridgetown, capital of Barbados.

People

A history of British rule is reflected in the Anglican religion and English language of this easternmost West Indian island. It is one of the world's most densely populated countries, and most citizens are black descendants of African slaves.

Economy and the Land

Barbados's pleasant tropical climate and its land have determined its economic mainstays: tourism and sugar. Sunshine and year-round warmth attract thousands of visitors and, in conjunction with the soil, provide an excellent environment for sugarcane cultivation. Manufacturing consists mainly of sugar processing. The coral island's terrain is mostly flat, rising to a central ridge.

History and Politics

Originally settled by South American Arawak Indians, followed by Carib Indians, Barbados was uninhabited when the first British settlers arrived in the 1600s. More colonists followed, developing sugar plantations and bringing slaves from Africa to work them. The country remained under British control until it became independent in 1966.

Barbados at a glance

Official name	Barbados

People

Population	261,000
Density	1,572/mi^2 (607/km^2)
Urban	45%
Capital	Bridgetown, 5,928
Ethnic groups	Black 80%, mixed 16%, white 4%
Languages	English
Religions	Anglican 40%, Pentecostal 8%, Methodist 7%, Roman Catholic 4%
Life expectancy	78 female, 73 male
Literacy	99%

Politics

Government	Parliamentary state
Parties	Democratic Labor, Labor, National Democratic
Suffrage	Universal, over 18
Memberships	CW, OAS, UN
Subdivisions	11 parishes

Economy

GDP	$2,200,000,000
Per capita	$8,527
Monetary unit	Dollar
Trade partners	Exports: U.S., U.K., Trinidad and Tobago
	Imports: U.S., Trinidad and Tobago, U.K.
Exports	Sugar and molasses, chemicals, electrical equipment, clothing, rum
Imports	Food, consumer goods, raw materials, machinery, petroleum

Land

Description	Caribbean island
Area	166 mi^2 (430 km^2)
Highest point	Mt. Hillaby, 1,115 ft (340 m)
Lowest point	Sea level

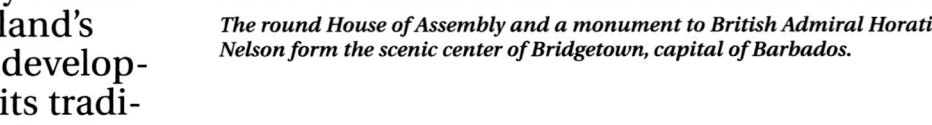

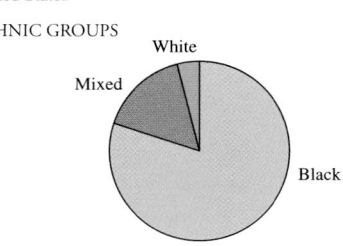

POPULATION COMPARISON
Barbados=0.1% of U.S.

United States

GDP COMPARISON
Barbados=0.03% of U.S.

United States

ETHNIC GROUPS

White

Mixed

Black

POPULATION DISTRIBUTION
Urban — Rural

The ruins of an ancient mansion overlook the coastline near the fishing village of Bathsheba.

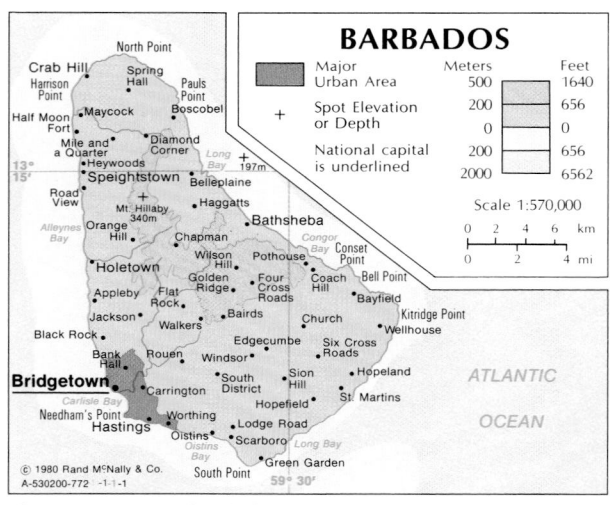

BARBADOS

	Meters	Feet
Major Urban Area	500	1640
Spot Elevation or Depth	200	656
	0	0
National capital is underlined	200	656
	2000	6562

Scale 1:570,000

0 2 4 6 km
0 2 4 mi

© 1980 Rand McNally & Co.
A-530200-772 -1-1-1

The easternmost island of the West Indies, Barbados lies more than 100 miles from the nearest island. Alone in the Atlantic Ocean, it is frequently hit by hurricanes.

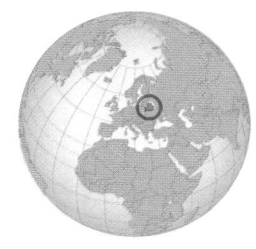

Minsk, the capital of Belarus, was almost leveled during World War II. Today the city is composed of modern buildings built during the Soviet era. It boasts numerous cultural amenities, including 200 libraries.

BELARUS

Situated between Poland and Russia, Belarus has been ruled by both nations and has suffered numerous invasions through the centuries. It was given its present borders after World War II. Independence followed the 1991 break-up of the Soviet Union. Despite the upheavals, many Belarussians continue the farming traditions of earlier generations.

People
Most people speak Belarussian, a Slavic language closely related to Russian and Ukrainian, and belong to the Orthodox church. There is also a substantial Roman Catholic minority. Belarussian people also predominate in a large area of surrounding Russian territory.

Economy and the Land
Most of the land is either forest or swamp, and the terrain is flat. The country is a net exporter of food, including meat, milk, eggs, flour, and potatoes. Peat is the major mineral resource, and is used to fuel several major electrical power plants.

History and Politics
The Belarussians are descendants of Slavic peoples who came to the area around the seventh century. The area was conquered first by Kiev, then by Lithuania, and later by

Poland. Russia gained control of Belorussia in the late 1700s. Emancipation of the serfs did not come until 1861, while the area remained backward and poor. Following the Bolshevik Revolution, Belorussia enjoyed a short period of independence before joining the Soviet Union in 1922. Despite its status as part of the Soviet Union, Belorussia retained its seat in the United Nations. Poland controlled part of Belorussia from 1921 until 1939, and the country suffered vast devastation under German occupation during World War II. Belorussia became known as Belarus after it gained its independence following the demise of the Soviet Union in 1991. The new country is struggling to create a stable market economy in the face of rampant inflation and economic chaos. In 1994 an anti-corruption candidate was elected. The country maintains close ties with Russia.

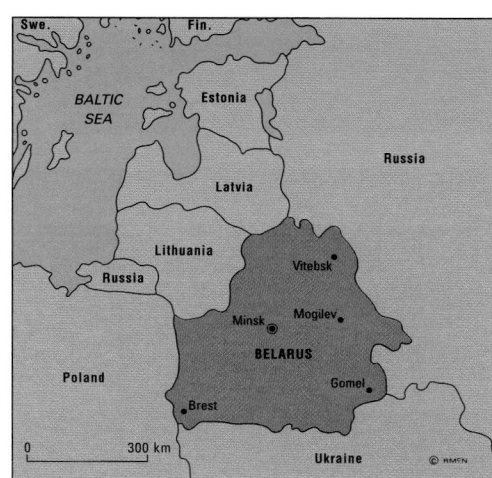

Farm in the Belarussian countryside

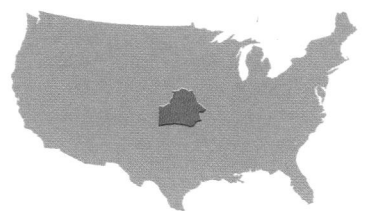

Belarus at a glance

Official name	Republic of Belarus

People

Population	10,425,000
Density	130/mi² (50/km²)
Urban	65%
Capital	Minsk, 1,633,600
Ethnic groups	Belarussian 78%, Russian 13%, Polish 4%, Ukrainian 3%
Languages	Belarussian, Russian
Religions	Russian Orthodox
Life expectancy	76 female, 66 male
Literacy	99%

Politics

Government	Republic
Parties	Popular Front, Social Democratic, United Democratic, Workers Union
Suffrage	Universal, over 18
Memberships	CIS, UN
Subdivisions	6 oblasts

Economy

GDP	$61,000,000,000
Per capita	$5,865
Monetary unit	Rubel
Trade partners	Former Soviet republics
Exports	Food, textiles, agricultural machinery
Imports	Steel, industrial raw materials

Land

Description	Eastern Europe, landlocked
Area	80,155 mi² (207,600 km²)
Highest point	Mt. Dzerzhinskaya, 1,132 ft (345 m)
Lowest point	Along Neman River, 279 ft (85 m)

Much of Belarus is flat and fertile, part of the vast East European Plain that stretches from Poland to the Ural Mountains. About one-quarter of the country is covered with forests.

21

BELGIUM

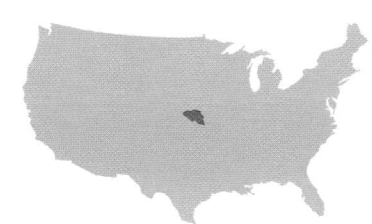

After decades of relative obscurity in comparison to its neighbors France and Germany, Belgium is now in the forefront, thanks to Brussels' role as the headquarters of the European Union. This role has been an economic boon to the capital; meanwhile, the rest of the country continues to enjoy an affluent mix of farms and industry. Although two World Wars heavily damaged many of Belgium's historic cities, Bruges in the west is the best-preserved medieval town in Europe.

POPULATION COMPARISON
Belgium=4% of U.S.
United States

GDP COMPARISON
Belgium=3% of U.S.
United States

ETHNIC GROUPS
Mixed and other
Walloon
Fleming

POPULATION DISTRIBUTION
Urban — Rural

People

Language separates Belgium into two main regions. Northern Belgium, known as Flanders, is dominated by Flemings, or Flemish-speaking descendants of Germanic Franks. French-speaking Walloons, descendants of the Celts, inhabit southern Belgium, or Wallonia. Both groups are found in centrally located Brussels. In addition, a small German-speaking population is concentrated in the east. Flemish and French divisions often result in discord, but diversity has also been a source of cultural richness. Belgium has often been at the hub of European cultural movements.

Economy and the Land

Grote Market and Cathedral, Antwerp

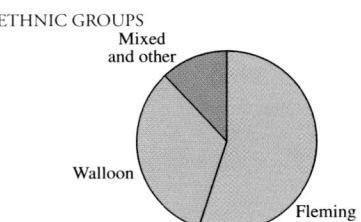

The economy, as well as the population, was affected by Belgium's location at the center of European activity. Flanders, formerly a poor, rural area, is now more prosperous than the southern Wallonia. Industry was early established as the economic base, and today the country is heavily industrialized. Although agriculture plays a minor economic role, Belgium is nearly self-sufficient in food production. The north and west are dominated by a flat fertile plain, the central region by rolling hills, and the south by the Ardennes Forest, often a tourist destination. The climate is cool and temperate.

History and Politics

Belgium's history began with the settlement of the Belgae tribe in the second century B.C. The Romans invaded the area around 50 B.C. and were overthrown by Germanic Franks in the A.D. 400s. Trade, manufacturing, and art prospered as various peoples invaded, passed through, and ruled the area. In 1794 Napoleon annexed Belgium to France. He was defeated at Waterloo in Belgium in 1815, and the country passed into Dutch hands. Dissatisfaction under Netherlands rule led to revolt and, in 1830, the formation of the independent country of Belgium. Linguistic divisions mark nearly all political activity, from parties split by language to government decisions based on linguistic rivalries.

BELGIUM

	Meters	Feet
Major Urban Area	1000	3281
Canal or Waterway	500	1640
Railroad	200	656
Spot Elevation	0	0
	200	656

National capitals are underlined

City type size indicates relative importance

Scale 1:1,913,000

0 10 20 30 40 50 km
0 10 20 30 mi

© 1980, 1991 Rand McNally & Co.
A-550300-772 -1-1-2

Belgium is divided linguistically: North of Brussels in the Flemish region, the language is Dutch; south, in the Walloon region, the language is French.

Belgium at a glance

Official name — Kingdom of Belgium

People

Population	10,075,000
Density	855/mi² (330/km²)
Urban	96%
Capital	Brussels, 136,424
Ethnic groups	Fleming 55%, Walloon 33%, mixed and others 12%
Languages	Dutch (Flemish), French, German
Religions	Roman Catholic 75%
Life expectancy	79 female, 73 male
Literacy	99%

Politics

Government	Constitutional monarchy
Parties	Flemish: Liberal, Social Christian, Socialist. Walloon: Liberal, Social Christian, Socialist, others
Suffrage	Universal, over 18
Memberships	EU, NATO, OECD, UN
Subdivisions	9 provinces

Economy

GDP	$177,500,000,000
Per capita	$17,697
Monetary unit	Franc
Trade partners	Exports: France, Germany, Netherlands. Imports: Germany, Netherlands, France
Exports	Iron and steel, transportation equipment, tractors, diamonds, petroleum
Imports	Fuel, grains, chemicals, food

Land

Description	Western Europe
Area	1,783 mi² (30,518 km²)
Highest point	Botrange, 2,277 ft (694 m)
Lowest point	Sea level

People

With the lowest population of any Central American country, Belize has a mixed populace, including descendants of black Africans, mestizos of Spanish-Indian ancestry, and Indians. Population is concentrated in six urban areas along the coast. Most people are poor, but participation in the educational system has led to a high literacy rate.

Economy and the Land

An abundance of timberland resulted in an economy based on forestry until woodlands began to be depleted in the twentieth century. Today the economy focuses on agriculture, with sugar the major crop and export. Arable land is the primary resource, but only a small portion has been cultivated. Industrial activity is limited. The recipient of much foreign aid, Belize hopes to expand export of agricultural surpluses and to develop a tourist industry based on its climate and sandy beaches. The coastal region consists of swampy lowlands rising to the Maya Mountains inland. The hot, humid climate is offset by sea breezes.

History and Politics

Until about the eleventh century A.D., Belize was the site of a flourishing Mayan civilization. Spain claimed the region in the sixteenth century. A British shipwreck in 1638 resulted in the first European settlement and began a process of British colonization, accompanied by extensive logging, piracy, and occasional Spanish and Indian attacks. In 1862 the area officially became the crown colony of British Honduras. Its name was changed to Belize in 1973, and independence was achieved in 1981. A July 1993 election resulted in an upset victory for the opposition United Democratic Party.

Belize at a glance

Official name	Belize

People

Population	212,000
Density	24/mi² (9.2/km²)
Urban	51%
Capital	Belmopan, 5,256
Ethnic groups	Mestizo 44%, Creole 30%, Mayan 11%, Garifuna 7%
Languages	English, Spanish, Mayan, Garifuna
Religions	Roman Catholic 62%, Anglican 12%, Methodist 6%, Mennonite 4%
Life expectancy	70 female, 66 male
Literacy	91%

Politics

Government	Parliamentary state
Parties	National Alliance, People's United, United Democratic
Suffrage	Universal, over 18
Memberships	CW, OAS, UN
Subdivisions	6 districts

Economy

GDP	$550,000,000
Per capita	$2,957
Monetary unit	Dollar
Trade partners	U.S., U.K., Mexico
Exports	Sugar, clothing, seafood, molasses, citrus, wood
Imports	Machinery and transportation equipment, food, manufactures, fuels

Land

Description	Central America
Area	8,866 mi² (22,963 km²)
Highest point	Victoria Pk., 3,675 ft (1,120 m)
Lowest point	Sea level

In 1970, Belize's capital was moved to Belmopan, a town 50 miles inland, from its previous location of Belize City, which was prone to hurricane damage.

BELIZE

BELIZE
— Railroad
+ Spot Elevation
National capitals are underlined

Meters	Feet
2000	6562
1000	3281
500	1640
200	656
0	0
200	656
Below 2000	Below 6562

Scale 1:3,409,000

People

Numerous peoples comprise the mostly black population of Benin. The main groups are the Fon, the Adja, the Yoruba, and the Bariba. The nation's linguistic diversity reflects its ethnic variety; French is the official language, a result of former French rule. Most Beninese are farmers, although urban migration is increasing. Indigenous beliefs predominate, but there are also Christians, especially in the south, and Muslims in the north.

Economy and the Land

Political instability has been both the cause and effect of Benin's economic problems. The agricultural economy is largely undeveloped, and palm trees and their by-products provide the chief source of income and activity for both farming and industry. Some economic relief may be found in the exploitation of offshore oil. The predominately flat terrain features coastal lagoons and dense forests, with mountains in the northwest. Heat and humidity characterize the coast, with less humidity and varied temperatures in the north.

History and Politics

In the 1500s, Dahomey, a Fon kingdom, became the power center of the Benin area. European slave traders came to the coast in the seventeenth and eighteenth centuries, establishing posts and bartering with Dahomey royalty for slaves. As the slave trade prospered, the area became known as the Slave Coast. France defeated Dahomey's army in the 1890s and subsequently made the area a territory of French West Africa. In 1960 the country gained independence, which was followed by political turmoil, various coups, and a military overthrow that installed a socialist government in 1972. In 1975 the nation changed its name from Dahomey to Benin.

Economic difficulties in the late 1980s have led the country away from socialism and towards private enterprise. Elections in March 1991 resulted in the first popularly elected president. The present government is attempting to pay off all debts.

Benin at a glance

Official name	Republic of Benin

People

Population	5,433,000
Density	125/mi² (48/km²)
Urban	38%
Capital	Porto-Novo (designated), 164,000; Cotonou (de facto), 533,212
Ethnic groups	Fon 39%, Yoruba 12%, Adja 10%, others
Languages	French, Fon, Yoruba
Religions	Voodoo and other African religions 70%, Muslim 15%, Christian 15%
Life expectancy	48 female, 45 male
Literacy	23%

Politics

Government	Republic
Parties	Democratic Union for the Forces of Progress, Movement for Democracy and Social Progress, others
Suffrage	Universal, over 18
Memberships	OAU, UN
Subdivisions	6 provinces

Economy

GDP	$6,200,000,000
Per capita	$1,220
Monetary unit	CFA franc
Trade partners	Exports: Netherlands, U.S., Spain Imports: France, U.K., Netherlands
Exports	Oil, cotton, palm products, cocoa
Imports	Food, beverages, tobacco, petroleum, manufactures

Land

Description	Western Africa
Area	43,475 mi² (112,600 km²)
Highest point	Unnamed, 2,235 ft (681 m)
Lowest point	Sea level

Like many African nations, Benin is beset by environmental problems. Deforestation is ongoing in the humid south, while desertification is claiming once-fertile land in the semi-arid north.

BENIN

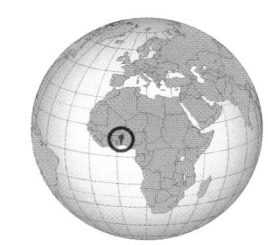

BENIN
— Railroad
+ Spot Elevation

Meters	Feet
1000	3281
500	1640
200	656
0	0
200	656

Scale 1:7,109,000

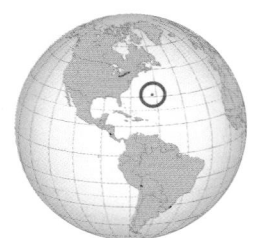

BERMUDA

Bermuda at a glance

Official name	Bermuda

People

Population	61,000
Density	2,905/mi² (1,130/km²)
Urban	100%
Capital	Hamilton, Bermuda I., 1,100
Ethnic groups	Black 58%, white 36%
Languages	English
Religions	Anglican 28%, Roman Catholic 15%, African Methodist Episcopal 12%
Life expectancy	77 female, 73 male
Literacy	98%

Politics

Government	Dependent territory (U.K.)
Parties	National Liberal, Progressive Labor, United
Suffrage	Universal, over 21
Memberships	None
Subdivisions	9 parishes, 2 municipalities

Economy

GDP	$1,300,000,000
Per capita	$21,667
Monetary unit	Dollar
Trade partners	Exports: U.S., Italy, Canada Imports: U.S., U.K., Canada
Exports	Food, manufactures
Imports	Fuel, food, machinery

Land

Description	North Atlantic islands (east of North Carolina)
Area	21 mi² (54 km²)
Highest point	Town Hill, 259 ft (79 m)
Lowest point	Sea level

One of the wealthiest countries in the world, Bermuda each year attracts scores of tourists to its golf courses and beaches. Unlike many island resorts, the atmosphere is more formal than casual, a legacy of its British background. Ties to England are strong, with the Queen's birthday celebrated as a major national holiday.

People
The people of this British colony are mainly black descendants of African slaves. Descendants of British settlers and Portuguese indentured workers—plus immigrants from Canada, the West Indies, Asia, and Europe—make up minorities. In addition, there are a number of American military personnel living here.

Economy and the Land
A mild climate, beautiful beaches, and a scenic, hilly terrain make tourism Bermuda's economic mainstay. Foreign businesses, attracted by tax exemptions, provide additional economic contributions. There is limited light manufacturing, agriculture, and fishing, and no heavy industry. Situated about 650 miles (1,046 kilometers) east of the U.S. state of North Carolina, the archipelago consists of many small islands and islets. About twenty are inhabited.

History and Politics
The colony received its name from Juan de Bermudas, a Spanish explorer who sailed past the islands in 1503, not landing because of the dangerous coral reefs. Spain showed no real interest in the islands, and Britain seemed likewise apathetic following the visit of an Englishman in 1593. In 1690 a British ship carrying colonists found the soil fertile and land scenic, and soon Britain had settled the islands. Bermuda continues as a British colony, recognizing Great Britain's queen as the head of state, but has been internally self-governing since 1968.

BHUTAN

Bhutan at a glance

Official name	Kingdom of Bhutan

People

Population	1,758,000
Density	98/mi² (38/km²)
Urban	5%
Capital	Thimphu, 12,000
Ethnic groups	Bhotia 60%, Nepalese 25%, indigenous 15%
Languages	Dzongkha, Tibetan and Nepalese dialects
Religions	Buddhist 75%, Hindu 25%
Life expectancy	49 female, 48 male

Politics

Government	Monarchy (Indian protection)
Parties	None
Suffrage	One vote per family
Memberships	UN
Subdivisions	18 districts

Economy

GDP	$500,000,000
Per capita	$298
Monetary unit	Ngultrum, Indian rupee
Trade partners	India
Exports	Cardamom, gypsum, timber, handicrafts, cement, fruit
Imports	Fuel, grain, machinery, transportation equipment, textiles

Land

Description	Southern Asia, landlocked
Area	17,954 mi² (46,500 km²)
Highest point	Kula Kangri, 24,784 ft (7,554 m)
Lowest point	Along Manās River, 318 ft (97 m)

Lying between India and Tibet, Bhutan is a peaceful land deeply influenced by Buddhism and Hinduism. The country has developed close political ties to India since gaining independence from Britain in 1949.

People
A mountainous terrain long isolated Bhutan from the outside world and limited internal mingling of its peoples. The population is ethnically divided into the Bhotia, Nepalese, and various tribes. Of Tibetan ancestry, the Bhotes are a majority and as such have determined the major religion, Buddhism, and language, Dzongkha, a Tibetan dialect. The Nepalese are mostly Hindu and speak Nepalese; tribal dialects diversify language further. A largely rural population, many villages grew up around *dzongs*, or monastery fortresses, built in strategic valley locations during Bhutan's past. In 1989 a controversial program began in which settlers who could not prove Bhutanese descent were evicted.

Economy and the Land
Partially due to physical isolation, Bhutan has one of the world's least developed economies and remains dependent on foreign aid. There is potential for success, however. Forests cover much of the land, limiting agricultural area but offering opportunity for the expansion of forestry. Farming is concentrated in the more densely populated, fertile valleys of the Himalayas, and the country is self-sufficient in food production. The climate varies with altitude, the icy Himalayas in the north give way to temperate central valleys and a subtropical south.

History and Politics
Bhutan's early history remains mostly unknown, but it is thought that by the early sixteenth century, descendants of Tibetan invaders were ruling their lands from strategically located dzongs. In the 1600s a Tibetan lama consolidated the area and became the political and religious leader. Proximity to and interaction with British India resulted in British control of Bhutan's foreign affairs in the nineteenth and early twentieth centuries. In 1907 the current hereditary monarchy was established. India gained independence from Britain in 1947 and soon assumed the role of adviser in Bhutan's foreign affairs. Bhutan became independent in 1949, but ties with India were strengthened in the late 1950s to counter Chinese influence. In recent years the King has instituted a policy of expelling people he considers refugees, which has caused widespread hardship.

Corn dries in a farming settlement near La Paz, capital of Bolivia. At this high altitude—over 10,000 feet—crops are limited to those which can thrive in the thin air. In addition to corn, this includes such staples as wheat, rye, and oats.

BOLIVIA

Bolivia is a land of mountains and high plateaus; a majority of its people live at elevations higher than 12,000 feet. Many work as miners of the rich deposits of silver which are found high up in the Andes, at elevations between 13,000 and 15,000 feet. It is a hard life and people from the lowlands have difficulty adjusting to the altitude. Despite its mineral riches, Bolivia is poor, owing mainly to its isolated location. The country lost access to the Pacific Ocean after a series of wars earlier in this century.

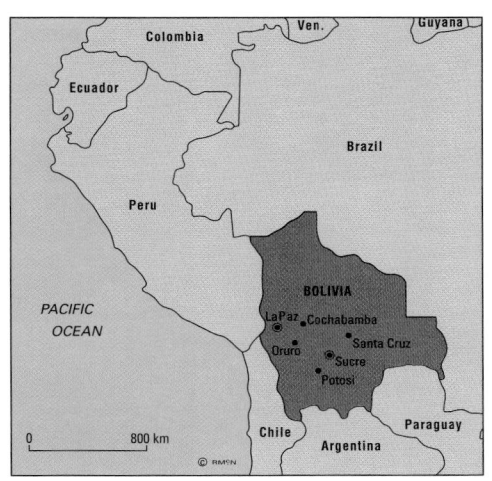

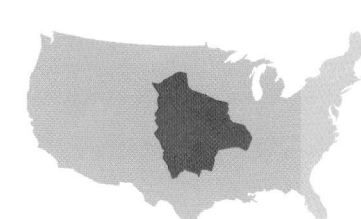

Rugged landscape near Villazón

People

Indians compose the majority of Bolivia's population, while minorities include mestizos, of Spanish-Indian descent, and Europeans. Although most people live at a subsistence level, Bolivia has a rich cultural heritage, evidenced by early Aymaran and Quechuan artifacts; Spanish-influenced Indian and mestizo art; and twentieth-century achievements. Roman Catholicism is the major religion, and is frequently combined with Indian beliefs.

Economy and the Land

Although the underdeveloped Bolivia is among South America's poorest nations, it is rich in natural resources. While farming is the main activity, mining makes the largest contribution to the gross national product. Population, industry, and major cities are concentrated on the western altiplano, an Andean high plateau where many continue to practice agriculture according to ancestral methods. The eastern llano, or lowland plain, contains fuel deposits and is the site of commercial farming. The _yungas_ (hills and valleys) between the altiplano and the llano form the most developed agricultural region. Successful development of Bolivia's rich resources is partially dependent upon political stability. The climate varies from tropical to semiarid and cool, depending on altitude.

History and Politics

The Aymara Indian culture flourished in the area that is now Bolivia, between the seventh and tenth centuries. In the mid-1400s the area was absorbed into the expanding empire of the Incas, who controlled the region until ousted by the Spanish in 1535. Simón Bolívar, the Venezuelan organizer of the South American movement to free Spanish colonies, helped lead the way to independence, which was gained in 1825. As Bolivia developed economically, the Indian population remained ensconced in poverty and enjoyed few rights. After years of turmoil, a 1952 revolution installed a government that introduced suffrage, land and educational reforms. Several military coups followed, and civilian control was re-established in 1982. The government elected in 1993 has created stability and reduced foreign debt.

Bolivia at a glance

Official name	Republic of Bolivia

People

Population	6,790,000
Density	16/mi² (6.2/km²)
Urban	51%
Capital	La Paz (seat of government), 713, 378; Sucre (legal capital), 131,769
Ethnic groups	Quechua 30%, Aymara 25%, mixed 25-30%, European 5-15%
Languages	Aymara, Quechua, Spanish
Religions	Roman Catholic 95%, Methodist and other Protestant
Life expectancy	64 female, 59 male
Literacy	78%

Politics

Government	Republic
Parties	Civic Solidarity Union, Condepa, Nationalist Revolutionary Movement, Patriotic Accord
Suffrage	Universal adult (married, 18; single, 21)
Memberships	OAS, UN
Subdivisions	9 departments

Economy

GDP	$15,800,000,000
Per capita	$2,132
Monetary unit	Boliviano
Trade partners	Exports: Argentina, U.S., U.K. Imports: U.S., Brazil, Argentina
Exports	Metals, natural gas, coffee, soybeans, sugar, cotton, lumber
Imports	Food, petroleum, consumer goods, capital goods

Land

Description	Central South America, landlocked
Area	424,165 mi² (1,098,581 km²)
Highest point	Volcan Sajama, 21,463 ft (6,542 m)
Lowest point	Along Paraguay River, 226 ft (69 m)

Lake Titicaca straddles the border between Bolivia and Peru. At 12,500 feet, it is the highest large body of navigable water in the world.

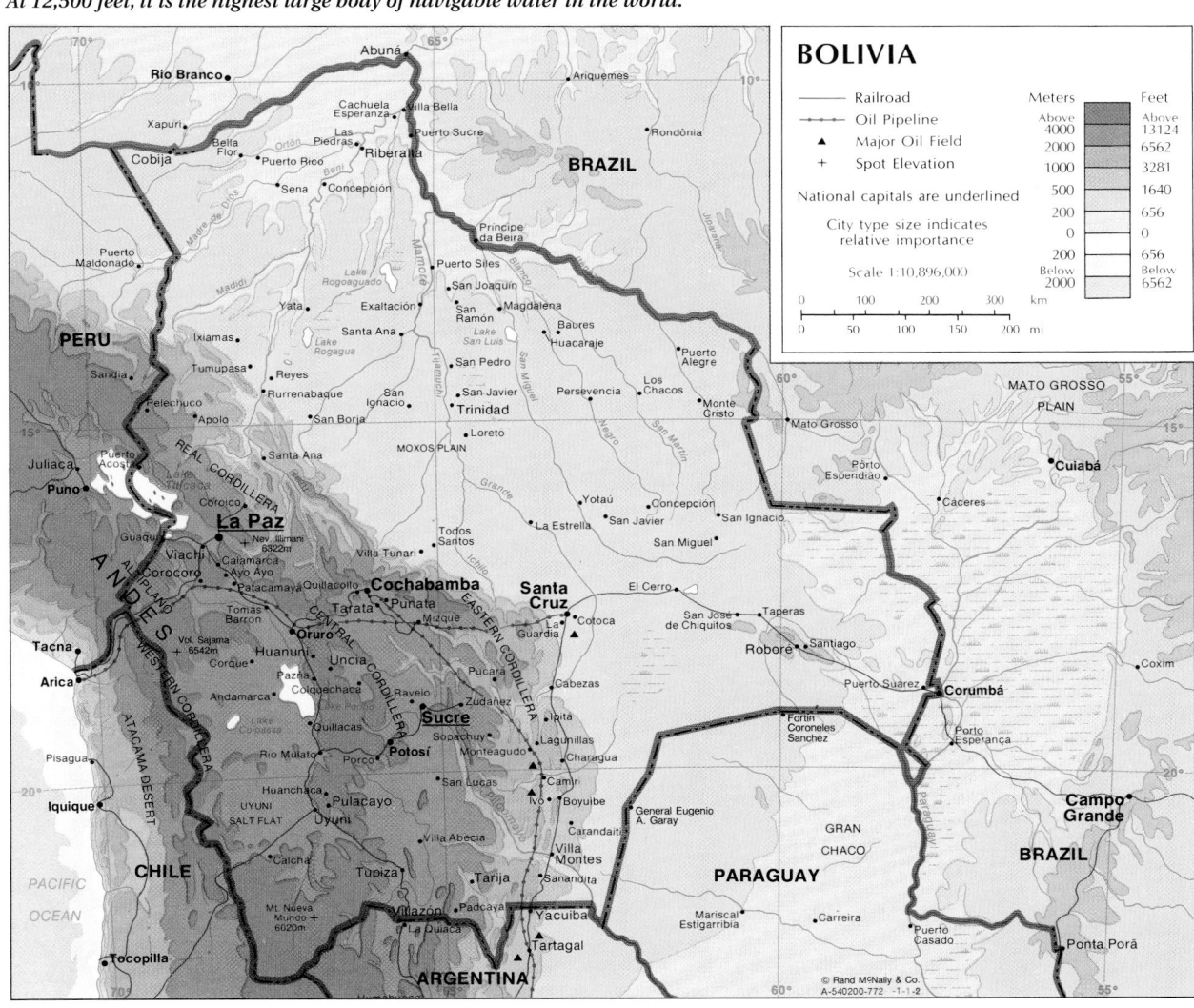

BOLIVIA

	Meters	Feet
Railroad	Above 4000	Above 13124
Oil Pipeline	2000	6562
▲ Major Oil Field	1000	3281
+ Spot Elevation	500	1640
National capitals are underlined	200	656
City type size indicates relative importance	0	0
	200	656
Scale 1:10,896,000	Below 2000	Below 6562

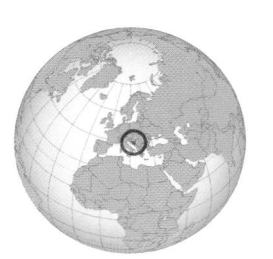

A farmer tends to his sheep in war-torn Bosnia and Herzegovina. Guarding the bridge in the background are British troops, part of the United Nations force.

BOSNIA AND HERZEGOVINA

After decades of peace, Bosnia and Herzegovina has been shattered by violent ethnic strife since independence was declared from Yugoslavia in 1992. The fighting between ethnic Serbs and ethnic Croats and Muslims has frustrated all efforts at mediation by the United Nations and other international organizations. Images of a shattered Sarajevo have shocked the world. Similar scenes are repeated throughout the country, and more than half the population has been displaced by fighting.

Soldiers walk through a village destroyed by the fighting.

People
Before the outbreak of war in 1992, Muslims accounted for about 40 percent of the population, and Serbians comprised about 30 percent. Subsequent war-related refugee movements and ethnic cleansing have had a profound effect on the population structure.

Economy and the Land
The main activity is agriculture, and there is limited industrial development. The country has ample mineral and hydroelectric resources. The region was one of the poorer of the former Yugoslavian republics. Bosnia, in the north, is a land of mountains and dense forests, while the Herzegovina region, in the south, is a rocky plateau. Bosnia and Herzegovina has many spas, which have historically been popular tourist destinations.

History and Politics
The Serbs and the Croats settled Bosnia in the seventh century, and the country later became part of the Roman Empire. Bosnia established itself as a self-governing country under Hungarian rule in the 1100s. Bosnia and Herzegovina were joined when they were conquered by the Ottoman Turks in the fifteenth century. Bosnia and Herzegovina was one of the few areas of Europe that converted to Islam during this period. In 1878 the region was relinquished to Austro-Hungarian rule, and was annexed by Austria-Hungary in 1908. Following World War I, both Bosnia and Herzegovina were incorporated into Serbia, and later into Yugoslavia. When Yugoslavia began to break up in the early 1990s, ethnic Muslims and Croatians overwhelmingly favored independence, but most of the region's ethnic Serbians resisted the notion and boycotted the referendum. Fighting over independence broke out following the country's secession from Yugoslavia in 1992. The bitter war and its many broken cease-fire agreements have left the survival of the nation in doubt.

Bosnia and Herzegovina at a glance

Official name	Republic of Bosnia and Herzegovina

People

Population	4,481,000
Density	227/mi² (88/km²)
Urban	36%
Capital	Sarajevo, 341,200
Ethnic groups	Muslim 44%, Serb 31%, Croat 17%
Languages	Serbo-Croatian
Religions	Muslim 40%, Orthodox 31%, Roman Catholic 15%
Life expectancy	78 female, 72 male
Literacy	86%

Politics

Government	Republic
Parties	Croation Democratic Union, Democratic Action, Muslim-Bosnian Organization, Serbian Democratic, others
Suffrage	Universal, over 18; over 16 if employed
Memberships	UN
Subdivisions	None

Economy

GDP	$14,000,000,000
Per capita	$3,098
Monetary unit	Yugoslavian dinar, Croatian dinar
Trade partners	Former Yugoslavian republics
Exports	Manufactures, machinery and transportation equipment, raw materials
Imports	Fuels, machinery and transportation equipment, chemicals, raw materials, food

Land

Description	Eastern Europe
Area	19,741 mi² (51,129 km²)
Highest point	Magli´c, 7,828 ft (2,386 m)
Lowest point	Sea level

POPULATION COMPARISON
Bosnia and Herzegovina=2% of U.S.

United States

GDP COMPARISON
Bosnia and Herzegovina=2% of U.S.

United States

ETHNIC GROUPS

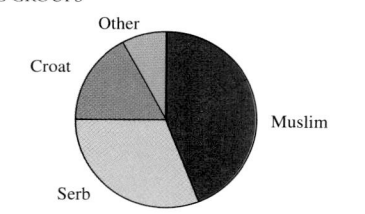

POPULATION DISTRIBUTION

Urban — Rural

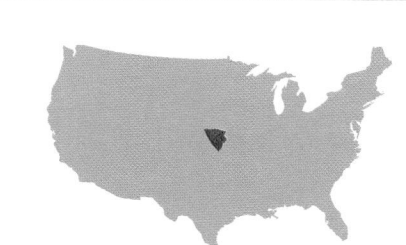

BOSNIA AND HERZEGOVINA

Meters	Feet
4000	13124
2000	6562
1000	3281
500	1640
200	656
0	0
200	656
2000	6562

Major Urban Area
Railroad
Canal or Waterway
+ Spot Elevation
City type size indicates relative importance

Scale 1:4,000,000

Despite Bosnia and Herzegovina's proximity to the Adriatic Sea, it is cut off from the coast by the long, narrow strip of Croatia. Its sole access is a thin corridor less than five miles long.

BOTSWANA

The gemsbok is just one of the many species of large antelope that thrive on the vast plains of Botswana. A series of national parks helps protect the wildlife from poachers.

Botswana is a land of drama and stark beauty. The Kalahari Desert covers the south and west. The Okavango Swamp and the salt pans of the Makgadikgadi area dominate the north. Sparsely populated by humans, the land is home to large numbers of the animals commonly associated with Africa, such as lions, elephants, and giraffes.

People
The population of this sparsely-populated country is composed mostly of Tswana, Bantu peoples of various groups. Following settlement patterns laid down centuries ago, Tswana predominate in the more fertile eastern region, and the minority Bushmen are concentrated in the Kalahari Desert. There is also a white minority population. English is an official language, reflecting years of British rule, but the majority speak Tswana. Half of the people follow traditional beliefs, while the rest are Christian.

Economy and the Land
Agriculture and livestock raising are the primary activities, although they are limited by the southwestern Kalahari Desert. The most productive farmland lies in the east and north, where rainfall is higher and grazing lands are plentiful. Since the early 1970s, when increased exploitation of natural resources began, the economy has developed rapidly. Diamond mining is the main focus of this growth, together with development of copper, nickel, and coal. The climate is mostly subtropical.

History and Politics
In Botswana's early history, Bushmen, the original inhabitants, retreated into the Kalahari region when the Tswana invaded and established their settlements in the more fertile east. Intertribal wars in the early nineteenth century were followed by conflicts with the Boers, settlers of Dutch or Huguenot descent. These conflicts led the Tswana to seek British assistance, and the area of present-day Botswana became part of the British protectorate of Bechuanaland. When the Union of South Africa was created in 1910, those living in Bechuanaland (later Botswana), Basutoland (later Lesotho), and Swaziland requested and were granted exclusion from the Union. British rule continued until 1966, when the protectorate of Bechuanaland became the Republic of Botswana. With outstanding leadership and a tribal history of democracy, Botswana has developed into Africa's oldest and most prosperous democracy.

Botswana at a glance

Official name	Republic of Botswana

People
Population	1,438,000
Density	6.4/mi^2 (2.5/km^2)
Urban	25%
Capital	Gaborone, 133,468
Ethnic groups	Tswana 95%; Kalanga, Baswara, and Kgalagadi 4%; white 1%
Languages	English, Tswana
Religions	Khoisan 50%, Roman Catholic and other Christian 50%
Life expectancy	64 female, 58 male
Literacy	72%

Politics
Government	Republic
Parties	Democratic, National Front
Suffrage	Universal, over 21
Memberships	CW, OAU, UN
Subdivisions	10 districts

Economy
GDP	$6,000,000,000
Per capita	$4,351
Monetary unit	Pula
Trade partners	Switzerland, U.K., Southern African countries
Exports	Diamonds, copper, nickel, meat
Imports	Food, motor vehicles, textiles, petroleum

Land
Description	Southern Africa, landlocked
Area	224,711 mi^2 (582,000 km^2)
Highest point	Unnamed, 4,969 ft (1,515 m)
Lowest point	Confluence of Shashi and Limpopo rivers, 1,684 ft (513 m)

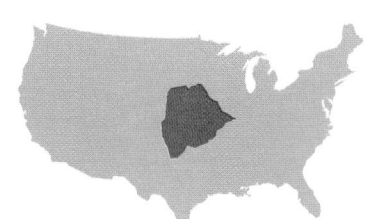

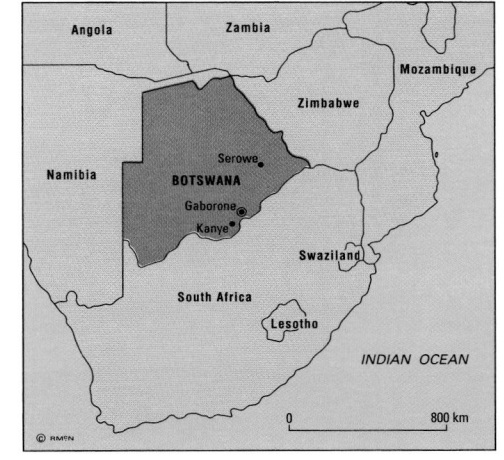

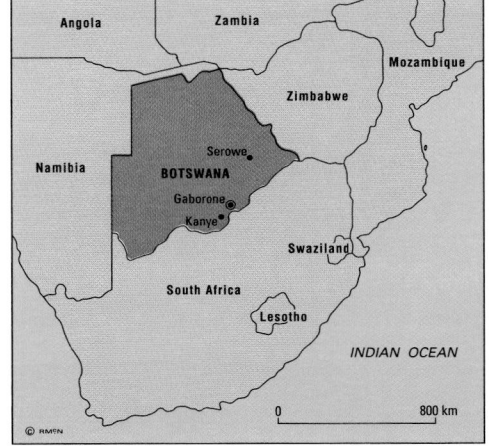

Salt pan, Makgadikgadi

Okavango Swamp

POPULATION COMPARISON
Botswana=0.5% of U.S.

United States

GDP COMPARISON
Botswana=0.09% of U.S.

United States

ETHNIC GROUPS

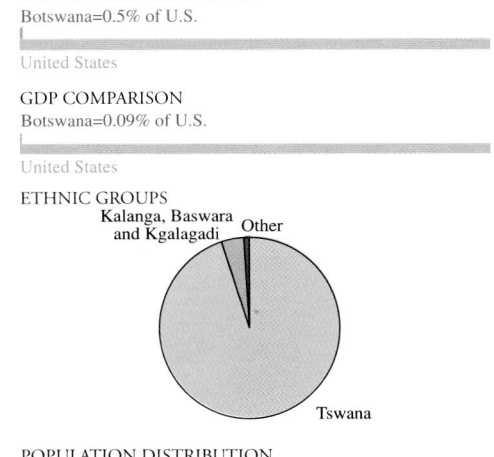

Kalanga, Baswara and Kgalagadi / Other / Tswana

POPULATION DISTRIBUTION
Urban — Rural

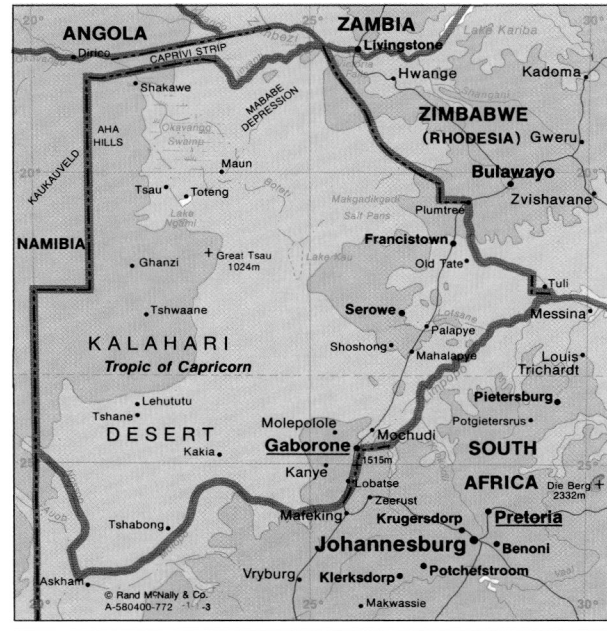

BOTSWANA

	Meters	Feet
	4000	13124
	2000	6562
	1000	3281
	500	1640
	200	656

City type size indicates relative importance
Railroad
+ Spot Elevation
Scale 1:14,333,000
National capitals are underlined

0 50 100 150 200 250 km
0 50 100 150 mi

Botswana shares a long border with South Africa, and its economy is closely tied to its larger neighbor to the south.

BRAZIL

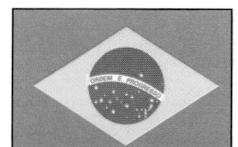

Vast and verdant, the rain forest that covers half of Brazil is a source of both tremendous resources and great controversy. A growing population and rampant development have placed Brazil at odds internationally with those concerned about the future of the rain forest and its myriad of species and indigenous peoples. Crafting long-term policy has been complicated by the nation's chaotic political life; government by democracy has been as turbulent as it was previously under a series of dictatorships.

People

The largest South American nation, Brazil is also the most populous. Indigenous Indians, Portuguese colonists, black African slaves, and European and Japanese immigrants shaped the mixed population. Today, native Indians compose less than 1% of the population, and the group is disappearing rapidly due to contact with modern cultures and other factors. Brazil is the only Portuguese-speaking nation in the Americas, and Roman Catholicism is the major religion.

Economy and the Land

Brazil's prosperous economy stems from a diversified base of agriculture, mining, and industry. Most commercial farms and ranches lie in the southern plateau region, and coffee, cocoa, soybeans, and beef are important products. Mineral resources include iron ore deposits, many found in the central and southern plateau regions. Additional mineral deposits have recently been discovered in the Amazon area. During and after World War II, the country focused on industrial expansion in the southeast, and in 1960 it moved the capital from Rio de Janeiro to Brasília to redistribute activity. Undeveloped states have been targeted for development, but such programs may require displacement of the Indian population. Forests cover about half the country, and the Amazon River basin is the site of the world's largest rain forest. The northeast consists of semiarid grasslands, and the central west and south are marked by hills, mountains, and rolling plains. Overall the climate is semitropical to tropical, with heavy rains.

History and Politics

Portugal obtained rights to the region in a 1494 treaty with Spain and claimed Brazil in 1500. As the native Indian population died out, blacks were brought from Africa to work the plantations. In the 1800s, during the Napoleonic Wars, the Portuguese royal family fled to Rio de Janeiro, and in 1815 the colony became a kingdom. In 1821 the Portuguese king departed for Portugal, leaving Brazil's rule to his son, who declared Brazil an independent country and himself emperor in 1822. Economic development in the mid-1800s brought an influx of Europeans. Following a military takeover in 1889, Brazil became a republic. In recent years key political issues have been the massive foreign debt and worldwide concern over the destruction of the rain forest. Corruption at high government levels has been extensive. October 1994 elections were won by the Social Democratic party.

Brazil at a glance

Official name	Federative Republic of Brazil

People

Population	159,690,000
Density	49/mi² (19/km²)
Urban	75%
Capital	Brasília, 1,513,470
Ethnic groups	White 55%, mixed 38%, black 6%
Languages	Portuguese, Spanish, English, French
Religions	Roman Catholic 90%
Life expectancy	69 female, 64 male
Literacy	81%

Politics

Government	Republic
Parties	Democratic Movement, Liberal Front, National Reconstruction, Social Democrat, Workers', others
Suffrage	Universal, over 16
Memberships	OAS, UN
Subdivisions	26 states, 1 federal district

Economy

GDP	$785,000,000,000
Per capita	$4,918
Monetary unit	Real
Trade partners	Exports: U.S., Netherlands, Japan Imports: U.S., Germany, Argentina, Iraq
Exports	Iron ore, soybeans, orange juice, shoes, coffee
Imports	Petroleum, machinery, chemicals, food, coal

Land

Description	Eastern South America
Area	3,286,500 mi² (8,511,996 km²)
Highest point	Neblina Peak, 9,888 ft (3,014 m)
Lowest point	Sea level

(above) Macaw; (right) giant waterlilies

The Iguacu Falls form part of the border between Brazil and Argentina. Over two miles wide and averaging 260 feet in height, the falls are among the most splendid sights in South America.

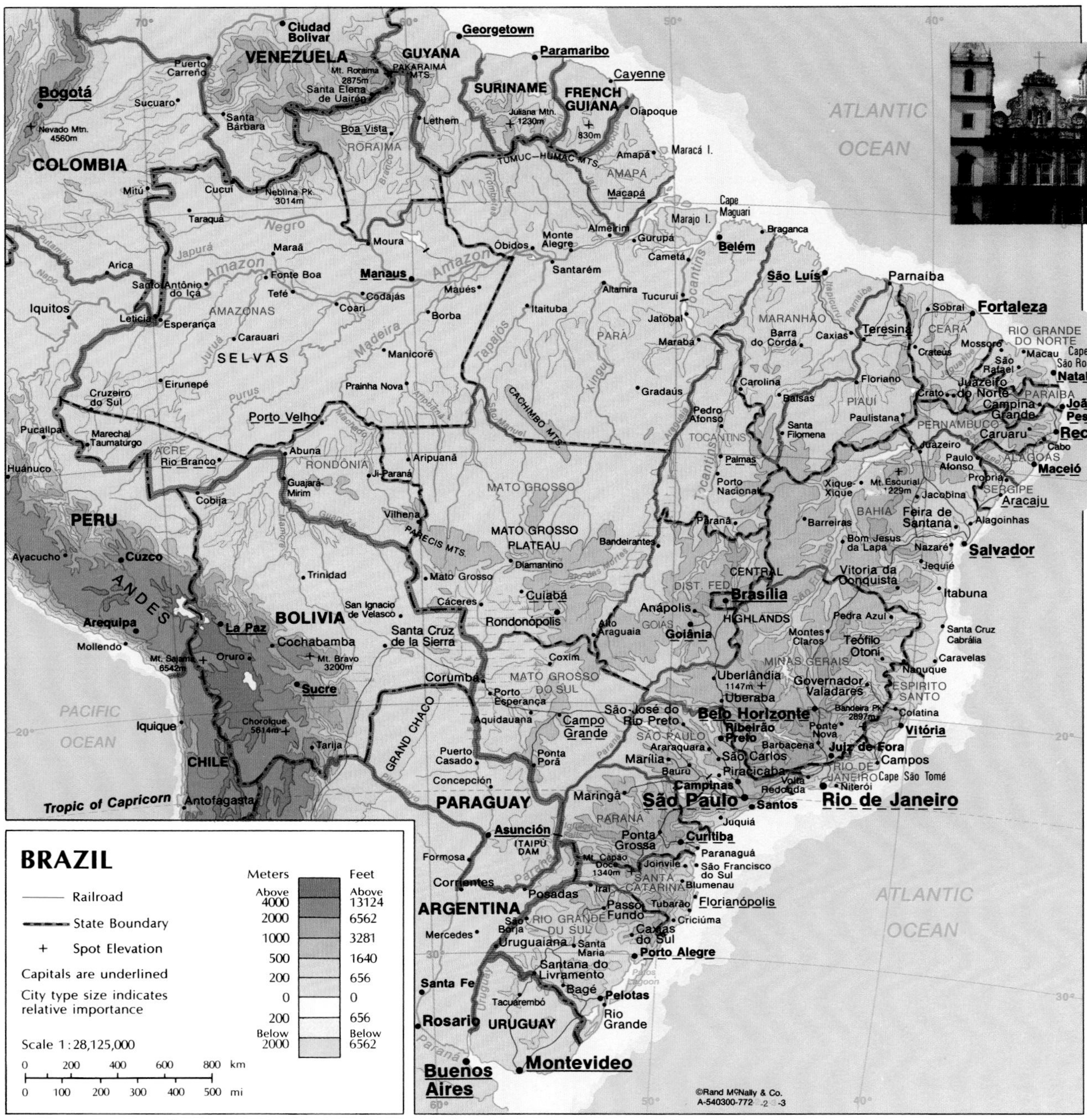

The Amazon River drains one-third of South America and has tributaries in Bolivia, Colombia, Ecuador, Guyana, Peru, and Venezuela. More than 150 miles wide at its mouth, the river pours 58 billion gallons of water into the Atlantic Ocean each second.

Cathedral of Salvador de Bahia

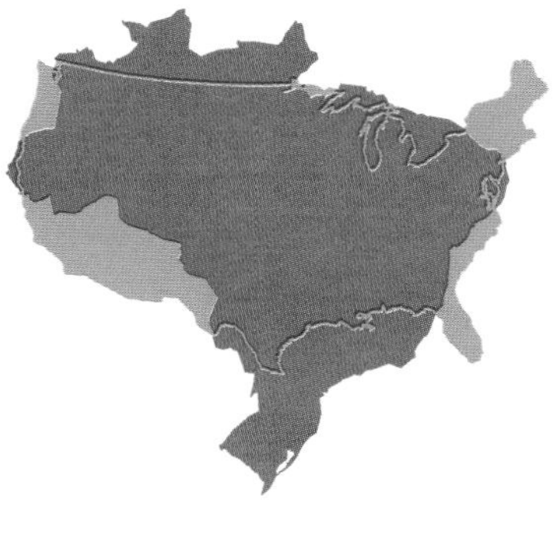

POPULATION COMPARISON

Brazil=61% of U.S.

United States

GDP COMPARISON

Brazil=12% of U.S.

United States

ETHNIC GROUPS

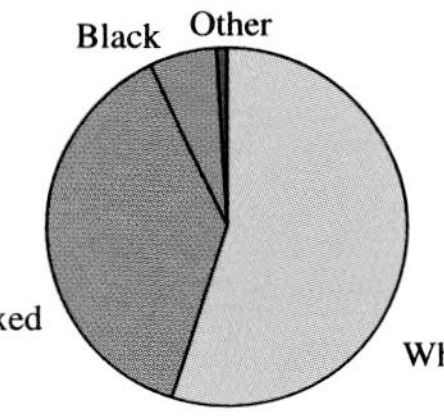

POPULATION DISTRIBUTION

Urban Rural

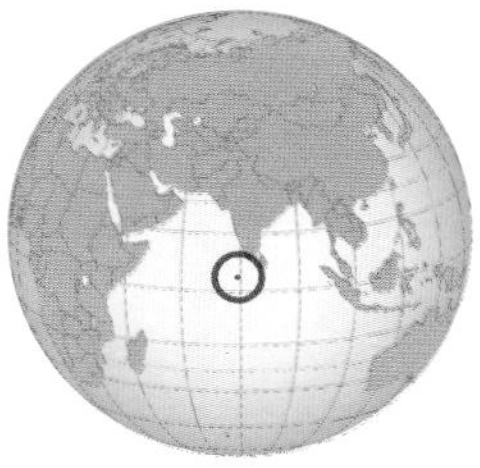

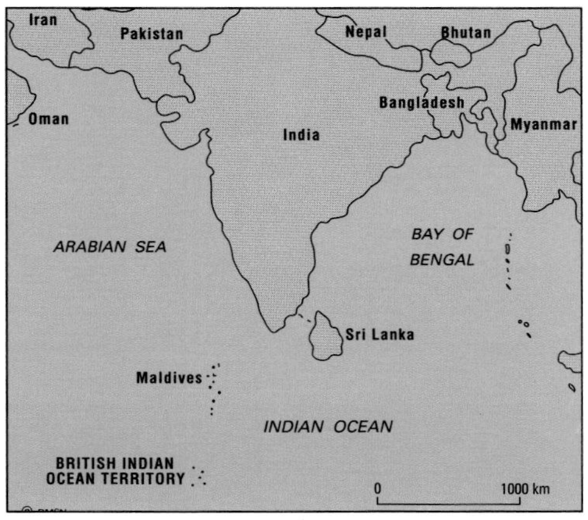

Diego Garcia's strategic location near Africa, the Middle East and India has made the island a vital link in the United States's worldwide network of military bases.

British Indian Ocean Territory

British Indian Ocean Territory at a glance

Official name	British Indian Ocean Territory
People	
Ethnic groups	American and British
Languages	English
Politics	
Government	Dependent territory (U.K.)
Economy	
Monetary unit	U.K. pound sterling, U.S. dollar
Land	
Description	Indian Ocean islands
Area	23 mi^2 (60 km^2)
Highest point	46 ft (14 m)
Lowest point	Sea level

People

Up until the early 1970s, the Chagos Islands, which make up the British Indian Ocean Territory, were inhabited by the Ilois, descendants of slaves who had worked the islands' coconut plantations. Between 1967 and 1973, about 3,000 Ilois were removed and resettled in Mauritius and Seychelles to make way for British and United States military development. There are about 2,500 temporary residents, including about 2,000 military personnel working for a joint British-United States military operation.

Economy and the Land

Because of its proximity to the Persian Gulf, the British Indian Ocean Territory is of strategic importance, and the island of Diego Garcia is the site of a United States naval facility. Diego Garcia, the largest island of the Chagos archipelago, has a lagoon with natural anchorages and a V shape well suited for a runway construction. Other major island groups in the archipelago include Peros Banhos and Salomon. In total, the British Indian Ocean Territory comprises about 2,300 islands. The overall terrain is flat and low, and the climate is tropical, with heat and humidity moderated by trade winds.

History and Politics

European rivalry for the spice trade and routes to India and the Far East centered in the coastal lands and islands of the Indian Ocean in the 1700s. An economy based on the production of copra, or coconut meat, soon developed, and slaves were brought to work the plantations. With the end of slavery in the nineteenth century, the slaves became contract employees, and work on the plantations continued. These former slaves and their descendants became known as the Ilois. Following the Napoleonic Wars, in the 1814 Treaty of Paris, France ceded to Britain the colony of Mauritius and its dependencies, which included Seychelles and Chagos Islands. These islands were administered from Mauritius until 1903, when Seychelles became a separate colony. In 1965 Britain separated the Chagos Islands, along with the islands of Aldabra, Desroches, and Farquhar, from Mauritius to create the British Indian Ocean Territory. The United States and Britain agreed to develop the islands as a joint military project. The copra plantations were dissolved and operations began in 1973. When Seychelles gained independence in 1976, Britain ceded Aldabra, Desroches, and Farquhar to the new country. The current United States lease on the island of Diego Garcia extends to the year 2025.

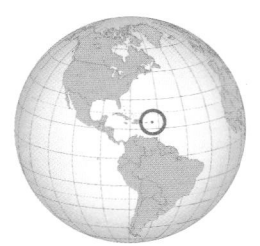

Tourism has brought affluence to the British Virgin Islands: they are among the wealthiest islands in the Caribbean. The most populous island, Tortola, boasts dramatic mountain scenery and a rain forest in a protected preserve. Since 1985, the islands' economy has been boosted by the incorporation fees paid by off-shore companies taking advantage of the liberal regulatory climate.

BRITISH VIRGIN ISLANDS

Virgin Islands, British at a glance

Official name	British Virgin Islands

People

Population	13,000
Density	220/mi² (85/km²)
Urban	12%
Capital	Road Town, Tortola Island, 2,479
Ethnic groups	Black 89%, white 7%, mixed 2%
Languages	English
Religions	Methodist 45%, Anglican 21%, Church of God 7%, Roman Catholic 6%
Life expectancy	75 female, 71 male
Literacy	98%

Politics

Government	Dependent territory (U.K.)
Parties	Independent Progressive, United, Virgin Islands
Suffrage	Universal, over 18
Memberships	None
Subdivisions	None

Economy

GDP	$133,000,000
Per capita	$9,500
Monetary unit	U.S. dollar
Trade partners	U.S., Virgin Islands (U.S.)
Exports	Rum, fish, sand and gravel, fruit
Imports	Building materials, automobiles, food, machinery

Land

Description	Caribbean islands
Area	59 mi² (153 km²)
Highest point	Sage Mountain, 1,710 ft (521 m)
Lowest point	Sea level

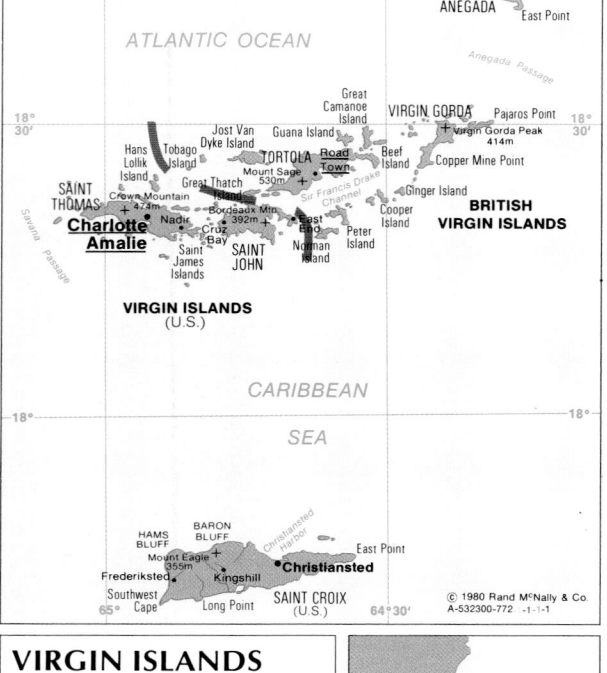

Altogether, the British Virgin Islands have a land size equal to only four-fifths of Washington D.C.

VIRGIN ISLANDS

+ Spot Elevation

Scale 1:1,381,000

0 10 20 30 40 km
0 10 20 mi

© 1980 Rand McNally & Co.
A-532300-772 -1-1-1

BRUNEI

Roads are few in the two parts of land comprising Brunei. Most transportation is by boat along the many rivers.

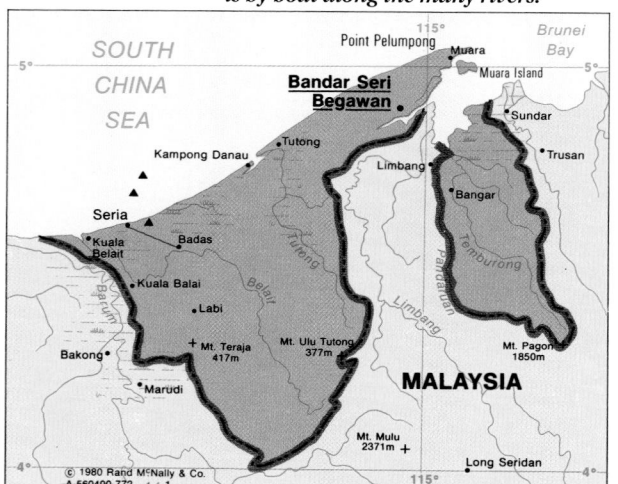

BRUNEI

— Railroad
▲ Major Oil Field
+ Spot Elevation

National capitals are underlined

Scale 1:2,000,000

0 10 20 30 40 50 km
0 10 20 30 mi

Brunei is an anomaly. Enriched by its oil reserves, the small country is ruled by a sultan who has decreed that there be no income tax, and who has invested the petroleum revenues in education and health care.

People
The majority of Brunei's population is Malay, with minorities of Chinese and indigenous peoples. Most Malays are Muslim, and the Chinese are mainly Christian or Buddhist. Many Chinese, although wealthy, are unable to become citizens due to language-proficiency exams and strict residency requirements. The standard of living is high because of Brunei's oil-based economy, yet wealth is not equally distributed.

Economy and the Land
Oil and natural gas are the economic mainstays, giving Brunei a high per capita gross domestic product. Much food is imported, however, and the country has failed to diversify. Situated on northeastern Borneo, Brunei is generally flat and covered with dense rain forests. The climate is tropical.

History and Politics
Historical records of Brunei date back to the seventh century. The country was an important trading center, and by the sixteenth century the sultan of Brunei ruled Borneo and parts of nearby islands. In 1888 Brunei became a British protectorate, and in 1984 it gained independence from Great Britain. The nation is ruled by a sultan who has been on the throne since 1967.

Brunei at a glance

Official name	Negara Brunei Darussalam

People

Population	289,000
Density	130/mi² (50/km²)
Urban	58%
Capital	Bandar Seri Begawan, 22,777
Ethnic groups	Malay 64%, Chinese 20%, indigenous 8%, Tamil 3%
Languages	Malay, English, Chinese
Religions	Muslim 63%, Buddhist 14%, Roman Catholic and other Christian 8%
Life expectancy	76 female, 73 male
Literacy	77%

Politics

Government	Monarchy
Parties	None
Suffrage	None
Memberships	ASEAN, CW, UN
Subdivisions	4 districts.

Economy

GDP	$2,500,000,000
Per capita	$9,579
Monetary unit	Dollar
Trade partners	Exports: Japan, Thailand, Korea Imports: Singapore, Japan, U.S.
Exports	Petroleum, natural gas
Imports	Machinery and transportation equipment, manufactures, food, chemicals

Land

Description	Southeastern Asia (island of Borneo)
Area	2,226 mi² (5,765 km²)
Highest point	Mt. Pagon, 6,070 ft (1,850 m)
Lowest point	Sea level

Houses on hillside, Veliko Tarnovo

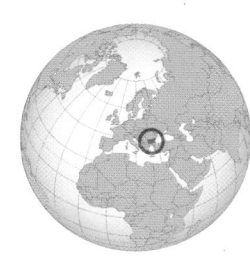

BULGARIA

The ruins of the Tsarevets Citadel in Veliko Tarnovo date from the 12th Century.

POPULATION COMPARISON
Bulgaria=3% of U.S.

United States

GDP COMPARISON
Bulgaria=0.5% of U.S.

United States

ETHNIC GROUPS

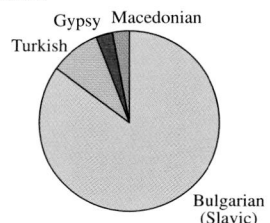

Gypsy Macedonian
Turkish

Bulgarian
(Slavic)

POPULATION DISTRIBUTION
Urban   Rural

Bulgaria at a glance

Official name	Republic of Bulgaria

People

Population	8,787,000
Density	205/mi² (79/km²)
Urban	68%
Capital	Sofia, 1,136,875
Ethnic groups	Bulgarian (Slavic) 85%, Turkish 9%, Gypsy 3%, Macedonian 3%
Languages	Bulgarian, Turkish
Religions	Bulgarian Orthodox 85%, Muslim 13%
Life expectancy	75 female, 69 male
Literacy	93%

Politics

Government	Republic
Parties	Movements for Rights and Freedoms, New Union for Democracy, Socialist, Union of Democratic Forces
Suffrage	Universal, over 18
Memberships	UN
Subdivisions	9 regions

Economy

GDP	$33,900,000,000
Per capita	$3,834
Monetary unit	Lev
Trade partners	Exports: Former Soviet republics, Czechoslovakia, Poland Imports: Former Soviet republics, Germany, Poland.
Exports	Machinery, agricultural products, manufactures
Imports	Fuel and minerals, machinery and equipment, manufactures, food

Land

Description	Eastern Europe
Area	42,855 mi² (110,994 km²)
Highest point	Musala, 9,596 ft (2,925 m)
Lowest point	Sea level

Bulgaria's influence on the Balkan Peninsula has waxed and waned through the centuries. The country was reduced to its present size after it sided with Germany in World War I. Currently, Bulgaria, like other former communist states, is struggling to adapt to a market economy. Many people have left the fertile countryside in hopes of securing higher-paying industrial jobs in the cities.

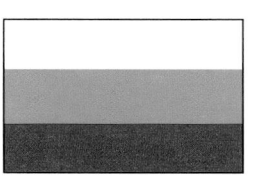

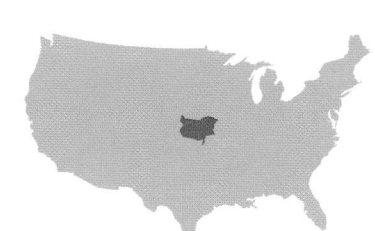

People

Bulgaria's ethnic composition was determined early in its history when Bulgar tribes conquered the area's Slavic inhabitants. Bulgarians, descendants of these peoples, are a majority today, while Turks, Gypsies, and Macedonians compose the main minority groups. Postwar development is reflected in an agriculture-to-industry shift in employment and a resultant rural-to-urban population movement.

Economy and the Land

A market economy is the declared goal of the post-Soviet government. However, the pace of reform is slow, with 90% of the economy still under the control of the state. Rich soils in river valleys, as well as a climate similar to that of the American Midwest, make the area well-suited for raising livestock, growing grain and other crops. The overall terrain is mountainous.

History and Politics

The area of modern Bulgaria was absorbed by the Roman Empire by A.D. 15, and was subsequently invaded by the Slavs. In the seventh century Bulgars conquered the region and settled alongside Slavic inhabitants. Rule by the Ottoman Turks began in the late fourteenth century and lasted until 1878, when the Bulgarians defeated the Turks with the aid of Russia and Romania. The Principality of Bulgaria emerged in

1885, with boundaries approximating those of today, and in 1908 Bulgaria was declared an independent kingdom. Increased territory and a desire for access to the Aegean Sea were partially responsible for Bulgaria's involvement in the Balkan Wars of 1912 and 1913, and alliances with Germany during both World Wars. Following Bulgaria's declaration of war on the United States and Britain in World War II, the Soviet Union declared war on Bulgaria. Defeat came in 1944, when the monarchy was overthrown and a Communist government was established shortly thereafter. In 1989 pressure from the people for more participation in the government resulted in the resignation of General Zhivkov, Bulgaria's leader for thirty-five years. A severe economic downturn forced multiparty elections in 1990, with the Bulgarian Socialist (formerly Communist) Party retaining control. Worsening economic conditions in late 1990 led to the collapse of the governing party. Elections in late 1991 were won by the Union of Democratic Forces, in forced coalition with the Muslim Turkish minority. The Bulgarian Socialist Party regained control in 1994 after the country had endured years of economic hardship.

The rounded peaks of the Balkan Mountains dominate Bulgaria's terrain. The government has been working to improve road and rail communication to many isolated regions, where the people work the land as they have for centuries.

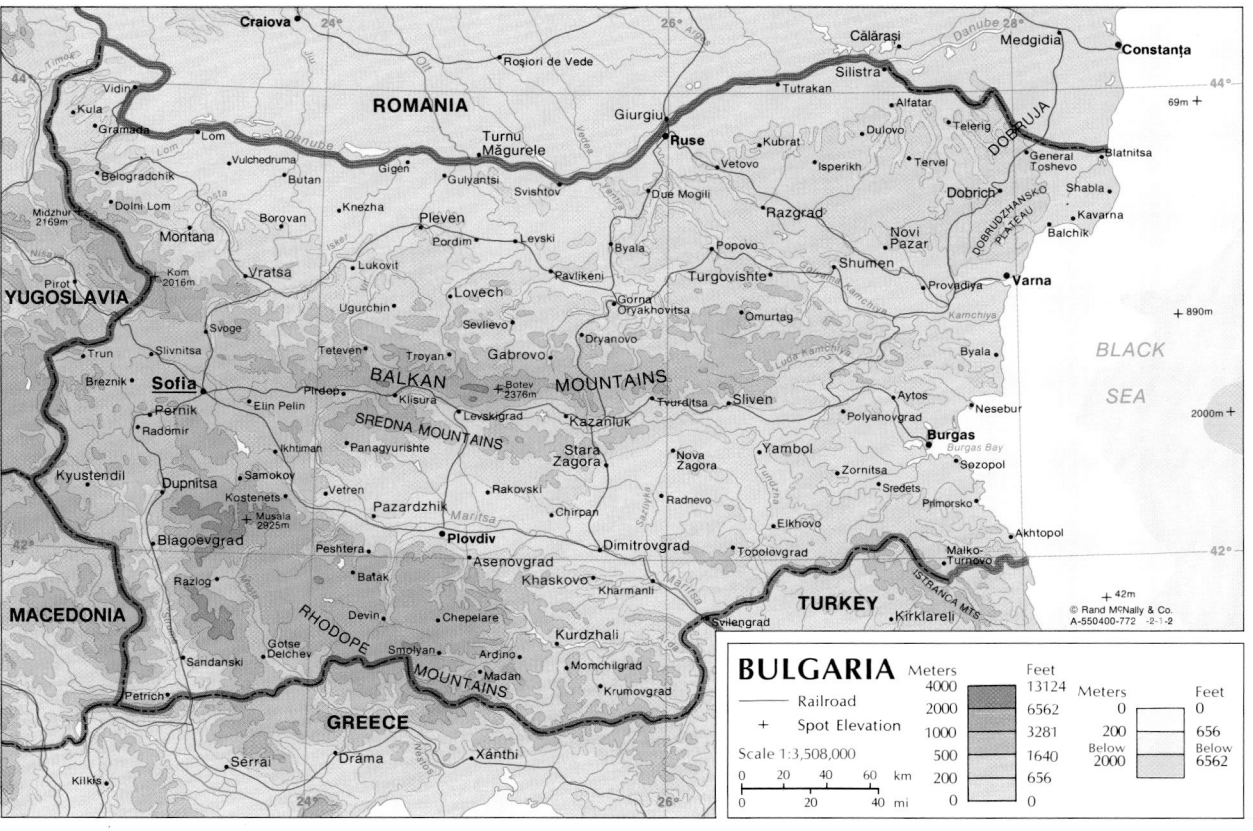

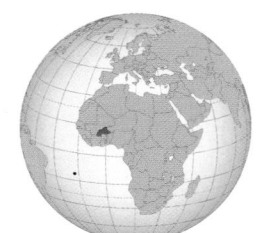

Burkina Faso was known as Upper Volta until 1984. It is a landlocked and poor country. Drought, deforestation, and few natural resources have made life hard for its people. Life expectancy for men is only 47 years, and few people are literate. The government is heavily dependent on foreign aid in its efforts to combat high levels of infant mortality and disease.

BURKINA FASO

A village of mud and thatch huts near the Niger border is typical of the primitive conditions under which most of the people of Burkina Faso live.

Fulani girl

People
The agricultural Mossi, descendants of warrior migrants, are Burkina Faso's majority population. Other groups include the Fulani, Lobi, Malinke, Bobo, Senufo, and Gurunsi. Ethnic languages vary, although French is the official language.

Economy and the Land
Burkina Faso's agricultural economy suffers from frequent droughts and an underdeveloped transportation system. Most people engage in subsistence farming or livestock raising, and industrialization is minimal. Resources are limited but include gold and manganese. The country remains dependent on foreign aid, much of it from France. The land is marked by northern desert, central savanna, and southern forests, while the climate is generally tropical.

History and Politics
The Mossi arrived from central or eastern Africa during the eleventh century and established their kingdom in the area of Burkina Faso. The French came in the late nineteenth century. In 1919 France united various provinces and created the colony of Upper Volta. The colony was divided among other French colonies in 1932, reinstituted in 1937 as an administrative unit called the Upper Coast, and returned to territorial status as Upper Volta in 1947. It gained independence in 1960. Economic problems and accusations of government corruption led to leadership changes and military rule, including numerous coups. In 1984 the country changed its name from Upper Volta to Burkina Faso. It has since functioned under a civilian, multiparty government.

POPULATION COMPARISON
Burkina Faso=4% of U.S.

United States

GDP COMPARISON
Burkina Faso=0.1% of U.S.

United States

ETHNIC GROUPS

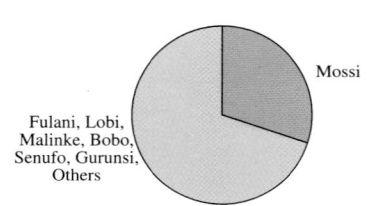

Mossi

Fulani, Lobi, Malinke, Bobo, Senufo, Gurunsi, Others

POPULATION DISTRIBUTION
Urban   Rural

Burkina Faso at a glance

Official name	Burkina Faso

People

Population	10,275,000
Density	97/mi² (38/km²)
Urban	15%
Capital	Ouagadougou, 441,514
Ethnic groups	Mossi 30%, Fulani, Lobi, Malinke, Bobo, Senufo, Gurunsi, others
Languages	French, indigenous
Religions	Animist 65%, Muslim 25%, Roman Catholic and other Christian 10%
Life expectancy	50 female, 47 male
Literacy	18%

People

Government	Republic
Parties	National Convention of Progressive Patriots, Organization for Popular Democracy-Labor Movement, others
Suffrage	Universal adult
Memberships	OAU, UN
Subdivisions	30 provinces

Economy

GDP	$7,000,000,000
Per capita	$714
Monetary unit	CFA franc
Trade partners	Exports: France, Cote d' Ivoire, Switzerland Imports: France, Cote d'Ivoire, U.S.
Exports	Oilseed, cotton, live animals, gold
Imports	Grain and other food, petroleum, machinery

Land

Description	Western Africa, landlocked
Area	105,869 mi² (274,200 km²)
Highest point	Téna Kourou, 2,451 ft (747 m)
Lowest point	Along Pendjari River, 443 ft (135 m)

Baobab trees in dry season

Burkina Faso was originally named Upper Volta for the three upper branches of the Volta River that flow through it. These are the Black Volta, the White Volta, and the Red Volta.

BURKINA FASO

——	Railroad
+	Spot Elevation

National capitals are underlined

Scale 1:10,839,000

Meters	Feet
1000	3281
500	1640
200	656
0	0

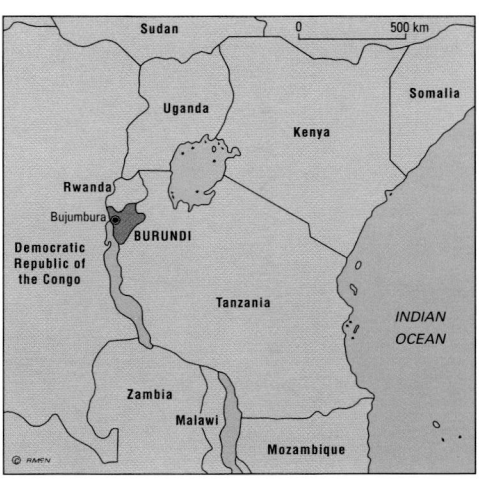

Burundi at a glance

Official name	Republic of Burundi

People

Population	6,192,000
Density	576/mi² (222/km²)
Urban	5%
Capital	Bujumbura, 226,628
Ethnic groups	Hutu 85%, Tutsi 14%, Twa (Pygmy) 1%
Languages	French, Kirundi, Swahili
Religions	Roman Catholic 62%, Animist 32%, Protestant 5%, Muslim 1%
Life expectancy	50 female, 46 male
Literacy	50%

Politics

Government	Republic
Parties	Front for Democracy, People's, Reconciliation of the People, Unity and Progress
Suffrage	Universal adult
Memberships	OAU, UN
Subdivisions	15 provinces

Economy

GDP	$4,400,000,000
Per capita	$719
Monetary unit	Franc
Trade partners	Exports: Germany, Finland Imports: Belgium, Germany, Iran, France
Exports	Coffee, tea, hides and skins
Imports	Machinery, petroleum, food, manufactures

Land

Description	Eastern Africa, landlocked
Area	10,745 mi² (27,830 km²)
Highest point	Mt. Heha, 8,760 ft (2,670 m)
Lowest point	Lake Tanganyika, 2,534 ft (772 m)

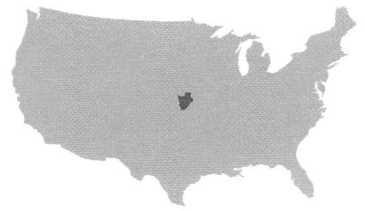

POPULATION COMPARISON
Burundi=2% of U.S.

United States

GDP COMPARISON
Burundi=0.07% of U.S.

United States

ETHNIC GROUPS

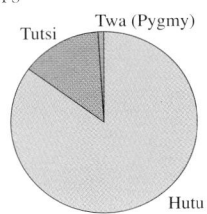

Tutsi — Twa (Pygmy) — Hutu

POPULATION DISTRIBUTION

Urban — Rural

Most Burundians engage in subsistence agriculture, scratching out an existence on small plots of land.

BURUNDI

Although temperate and fertile, Burundi is a land of tragedy. Tribal warfare between the two dominant groups, the Hutu and the Tutsi, has left hundreds of thousands of people dead in both Burundi and neighboring Rwanda.

People

One of Africa's most densely populated nations, Burundi has a populace composed mainly of three Bantu groups. The Hutu are a majority, while the Tutsi, descendants of invaders from Ethiopia, wield most of the power. The Twa are Pygmy hunters, probably descended from the area's inhabitants prior to the influx of the Hutu. Most Burundians are subsistence farmers and Roman Catholic, evidence of foreign influence and rule.

Economy and the Land

An undeveloped country, Burundi relies mainly on agriculture, although undependable rainfall, depleted soil, and erosion occasionally combine for famine. Coffee is a major export. Exploitation of nickel deposits, industrial development through foreign investment, and expansion of tourism offer potential for growth. Although the country is situated near the equator, its high altitude and hilly terrain result in a pleasant climate.

History and Politics

In the 14th century, invading pastoral Tutsi warriors conquered the Hutus and Pygmy Twa and established themselves as the region's power base. The areas of modern Burundi and Rwanda were absorbed into German East Africa in the 1890s. Following Belgian occupation during World War I, in 1919 the League of Nations placed present-day Burundi and Rwanda under Belgian rule as part of Ruanda-Urundi. After World War II Ruanda-Urundi was made a UN trust territory under Belgian administration. In 1962 Urundi became Burundi, an independent monarchy, and political turmoil soon followed. A Tutsi-dominated government replaced the monarchy in 1966. The country's first multiparty elections were held in 1993. The new president, a member of the majority Hutu, was assassinated four months later. Violence ensued between the Hutu and the Tutsi, causing more than 100,000 deaths and creating 500,000 refugees. In 1996 a Tutsi military coup reinstated a former president. Neighboring countries imposed an embargo on Burundi, but sporadic violence continues in rural areas.

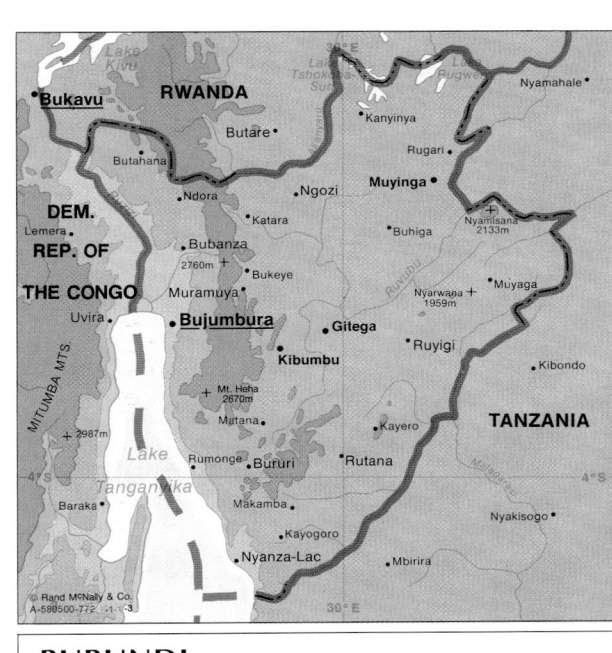

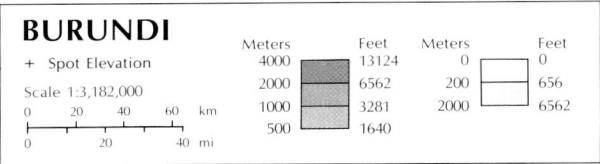

BURUNDI

+ Spot Elevation

Scale 1:3,182,000

0 20 40 60 80 km
0   20   40 mi

Meters	Feet	Meters	Feet
4000	13124	0	0
2000	6562	200	656
1000	3281	2000	6562
500	1640		

The mountainous region in the middle of Burundi divides the tributaries and drainage areas of the Nile and Congo Rivers.

Fugitives from the bloodshed of Burundi and Rwanda take shelter at the crowded Ngara Refugee Camp just across the border from Burundi in Tanzania.

Hutu and Tutsi refugees in food queue, Bujumbura

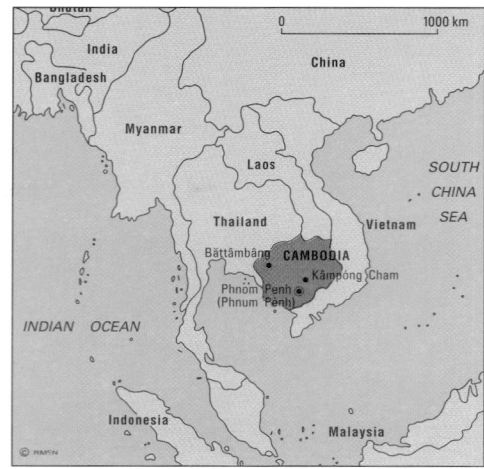

CAMBODIA

C ambodia is a remnant of the Khmer Empire, which ruled Southeast Asia during the ninth through fifteenth centuries. The Empire's legacy includes the magnificent stone temples of Angkor Wat. Cambodia's recent history has been marked by catastrophe. Millions were killed in the Vietnam War and in the genocide wrought by the Khmer Rouge government.

Using their great wealth and huge labor force, Khmer kings built Angkor Wat between the 9th and 13th centuries. The monumental complex covers several square miles and includes some of the most magnificent architectural creations ever conceived by humans.

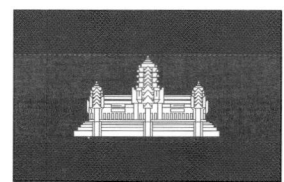

Floating houses

People

The Khmer, one of the oldest peoples in Southeast Asia, constitute the major ethnic group in Cambodia. The population has declined significantly since the mid-1970s due to war, famine, human-rights abuses, and emigration. Because of an urban-evacuation campaign initiated by the Khmer Rouge, Cambodia's previous regime, most Cambodians live in rural areas, working as farmers or laborers. Although religious activity was often punished by death during the Khmer Rouge era and discouraged by the communists, the practice of Buddhism, the main religion, is on the rise.

Economy and the Land

Cambodia's flat central region and wet climate make it well suited for rice production. Along with rubber, rice was the mainstay of the economy before the 1970s, but the Vietnam and civil wars all but destroyed agriculture. This sector of the economy has begun to recover recently, but a shortage of skilled labor, combined with the effects of war, have held back development. The terrain is marked by the central plain, forests, and mountains in the south, west, and along the Thai border. The climate is tropical, with high rainfall and humidity.

History and Politics

Cambodia traces its roots to the Hindu kingdoms of Funan and Chenla, which reigned in the early centuries A.D. The Khmer Empire dominated until the fifteenth century, incorporating much of present-day Laos, Thailand, and Vietnam and constructing the

stone temples of Angkor Wat, considered one of Southeast Asia's greatest architectural achievements. By 1431 the Siamese had overrun the region, and subsequent years saw the rise of the Siamese, Vietnamese, and Lao. By the mid-1700s Cambodia's boundaries approximated those of today. During the 1800s, as French control in Indochina expanded, the area became a French protectorate. Cambodia gained independence in 1953 under King Sihanouk, who, after changing his title to "prince," became prime minister in 1955 and head of state in 1960. In 1970, after Sihanouk was ousted, Lon Nol was installed as prime minister, and the monarchy of Cambodia changed to the Khmer Republic. During this time the Vietnam War spilled over the Khmer Republic's borders, as United States forces made bombing raids against what they claimed were North Vietnamese bases. Resulting anti-American sentiment gave rise to discontent with Lon Nol's pro-United States regime. The Khmer Communists, or Khmer Rouge, seized power in 1975 and, led by Pol Pot, exiled most Cambodians to the countryside. An estimated three million died under the Khmer Rouge; many were executed because they were educated or had links to the former government. Vietnamese troops supported by some Cambodian Communists invaded Cambodia in late 1978, and by early 1979 they had overthrown the Khmer Rouge. While 1993 elections and a new constitution resulted in Prince Sihanouk again becoming King of Cambodia, the Khmer Rouge have regained much of their former power.

Cambodia at a glance

Official name	Kingdom of Cambodia

People

Population	9,713,000
Density	139/mi² (54/km²)
Urban	12%
Capital	Phnom Penh, 620,000
Ethnic groups	Khmer 90%, Vietnamese 5%
Languages	Khmer, French
Religions	Buddhist 95%
Life expectancy	52 female, 50 male
Literacy	35%

Politics

Government	Constitutional Monarchy
Parties	Buddhist Liberal Democratic, FUNCINPEC, People's
Suffrage	Universal, over 18
Memberships	UN
Subdivisions	20 provinces

Economy

GDP	$6,000,000,000
Per capita	$672
Monetary unit	Riel
Trade partners	Vietnam, former Soviet republics, Eastern European countries
Exports	Rubber, rice, pepper, wood
Imports	Fuel, consumer goods, machinery

Land

Description	Southeastern Asia
Area	69,898 mi² (181,035 km²)
Highest point	Mt. Aoral, 5,948 ft (1,813 m)
Lowest point	Sea level

Despite efforts to remain at peace, Cambodia's proximity to Vietnam and Laos drew it into the wars in those countries during the 1960s and 1970s.

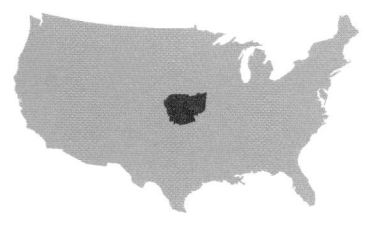

Cultivating rice

POPULATION COMPARISON
Cameroon=5% of U.S.

United States

GDP COMPARISON
Cameroon=0.3% of U.S.

United States

ETHNIC GROUPS

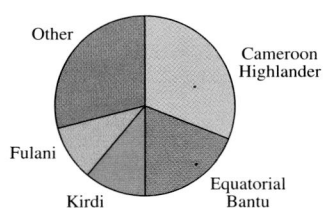

Other
Cameroon Highlander
Fulani
Kirdi
Equatorial Bantu

POPULATION DISTRIBUTION

Urban — Rural

Cameroon at a glance

Official name	Republic of Cameroon

People

Population	13,330,000
Density	73/mi^2 (28/km^2)
Urban	40%
Capital	Yaoundé, 560,785
Ethnic groups	Cameroon Highlander 31%, Equatorial Bantu 19%, Kirdi 11%, Fulani 10%
Languages	English, French, indigenous.
Religions	Bangwa and other African religions 51%, Christian 33%, Muslim 16%
Life expectancy	58 female, 55 male
Literacy	54%

Politics

Government	Republic
Parties	National Union for Democracy and Progress, People's Democratic Movement, Union of the Peoples
Suffrage	Universal, over 20
Memberships	OAU, UN
Subdivisions	10 provinces

Economy

GDP	$19,100,000,000
Per capita	$1,483
Monetary unit	CFA franc
Trade partners	Exports: France, Belgium, U.S. Imports: France, Netherlands, Japan, Germany
Exports	Petroleum, coffee, cocoa, lumber, manufactures
Imports	Machinery and electrical equipment, transportation equipment, chemicals

Land

Description	Central Africa
Area	183,568 mi^2 (475,440 km^2)
Highest point	Cameroon Mtn., 13,451 ft (4,100 m)
Lowest point	Sea level

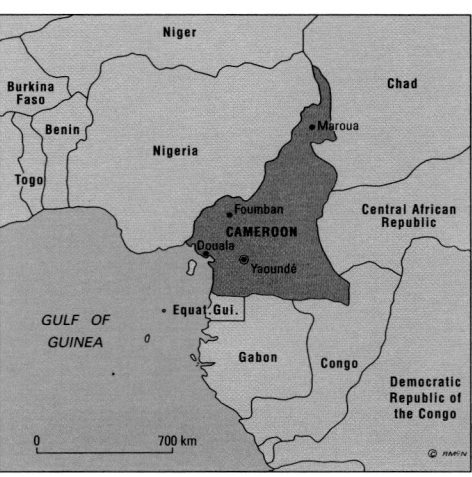

CAMEROON

C ameroon's more than 200 ethnic groups have benefited from decades of peace. Offshore oil reserves and a thriving agricultural sector have given the country one of the most successful economies in sub-Saharan Africa. More than 80 percent of the people live on small farms.

(photo at top) Rain forest near the town of Mamfe, close to the Nigerian border

People

Immigration and foreign rule shaped Cameroon's diverse population, composed of some two hundred groups speaking twenty-four major African languages. Both English and French are official languages, resulting from the merging of former French-ruled eastern and British-ruled western territories. Population is concentrated in the French-speaking eastern region. The majority of people practice indigenous beliefs that often influence Islamic and Christian practices as well.

Economy and the Land

Recent economic plans have focused on agriculture, industry, and the development of oil deposits. Agriculture is still the country's economic base, but oil is a major export. A varied terrain features southern coastal plains and rain forests, central plateaus, mountainous western forests, and northern savanna and marshes. Although this has hindered transportation development and thus slowed economic growth, improvements are being made. Climate varies from a hot, humid coastal region to fluctuating temperatures and less humidity northward.

History and Politics

The Sao people reached the Cameroon area in the tenth century. The Portuguese arrived in the 1500s, and the following three centuries saw an influx of European and African peoples and an active slave trade along the coast. In 1884 Germany set up a protectorate that included modern Cameroon by 1914. During World War I British and French troops occupied the area, and in 1919, following the war, the League of Nations divided Cameroon into eastern French and western British mandates. The Cameroons became trust territories in 1946, and French Cameroon became an independent republic in 1960. In 1961 the northern region of British Cameroon elected to join Nigeria, and the southern area chose to unite with the eastern Republic of Cameroon. This resulted in a two-state Federal Republic of Cameroon. A 1972 referendum combined the states into the United Republic of Cameroon and, in 1984, the official name became the Republic of Cameroon. An election in October 1992 returned an authoritarian government to power despite widespread claims of electoral fraud by foreign observers. Rioting and mass arrests ensued.

Coast near Kribi

Cameroonian boy

Kirdi village in the Kapsikis mountains.

CAMEROON

— Railroad

+ Spot Elevation

National capitals are underlined

City type size indicates relative importance

Scale 1:12,000,000

0 50 100 150 200 km
0 50 100 150 mi

Meters	Feet
4000	13124
2000	6562
1000	3281
500	1640
200	656
0	0
200	656
2000	6562

Cameroon has three distinct areas. The south features dense tropical rain forests. The central region supports a mixed forest of evergreens and deciduous trees. The semi-arid north has vast areas of savanna.

35

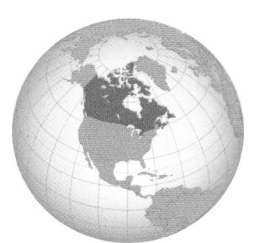

The tiny fishing village of Prospect is typical of many small towns scattered along the rocky coast of Nova Scotia.

Cross-country skiers, Baffin Island

Vermilion Lake and Mount Rundle

CANADA

Much of Canada, the largest country in the western hemisphere, is largely unchanged since it was explored by fur traders over 200 years ago. The majority of Canadians live in cities and towns located within 100 miles of the border with the United States. The land teems with wildlife and is endowed with natural riches of forests, minerals, and fertile fields. Canada is sometimes thought of as less a nation than an alliance of territories. Indeed, French-speaking Quebec continues to debate whether to declare its own independence.

Waterfront, Lunenberg, Nova Scotia

Canada has a population density of only about seven persons per square mile. This contrasts sharply with China, which is nearly as large but has a density of 324 people per square mile.

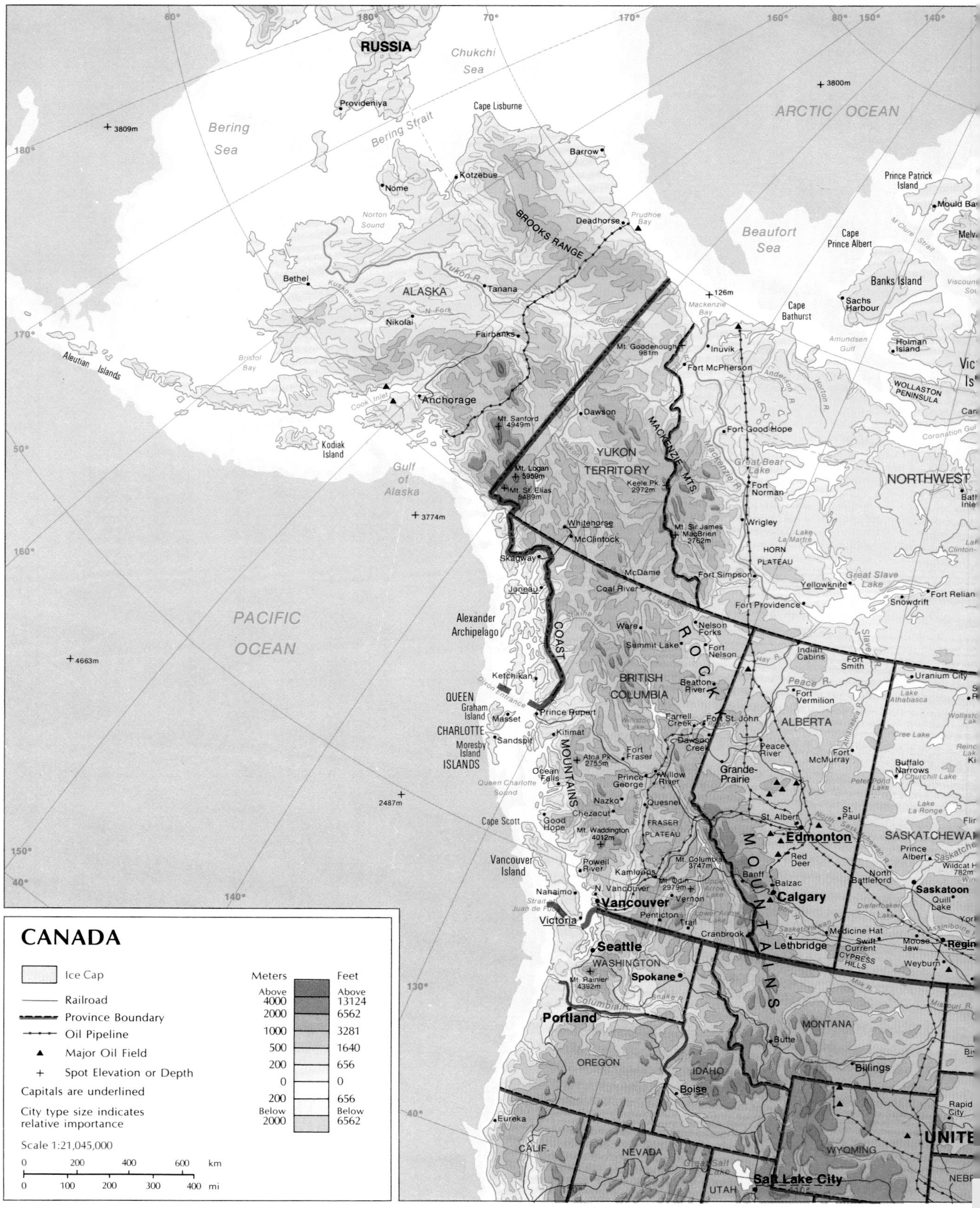

Canada at a glance

Official name   Canada

People

Population	28,285,000
Density	7.3/mi² (2.8/km²)
Urban	77%
Capital	Ottawa, 313,987
Ethnic groups	British origin 40%, French origin 27%, other European 23%, native Canadian 2%
Languages	English, French
Religions	Roman Catholic 47%, United Church 16%, Anglican 10%, other Christian
Life expectancy	81 female, 74 male
Literacy	99%

Politics

Government	Parliamentary state
Parties	Bloc Quebecios, Liberal, New Democratic, Progressive Conservative, Reform
Suffrage	Universal, over 18
Memberships	CW, NATO, OAS, OECD, UN
Subdivisions	10 provinces, 2 territories

Economy

GDP	$617,700,000,000
Per capita	$20,233
Monetary unit	Dollar
Trade partners	U.S., Japan, U.K.
Exports	Newsprint, wood pulp, timber, petroleum, machinery, natural gas, aluminum
Imports	Petroleum, chemicals, transportation equipment, manufactures, computers

Land

Description	Northern North America
Area	3,849,674 mi² (9,970,610 km²)
Highest point	Mt. Logan, 19,551 ft (5,959 m)

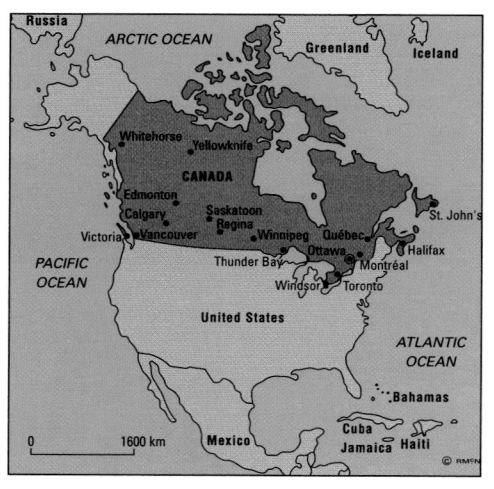

CANADA

Ice Cap
Railroad
Province Boundary
Oil Pipeline
▲ Major Oil Field
+ Spot Elevation or Depth
Capitals are underlined
City type size indicates relative importance

Meters	Feet
Above 4000	Above 13124
2000	6562
1000	3281
500	1640
200	656
0	0
200	656
Below 2000	Below 6562

Scale 1:21,045,000

0 200 400 600 km
0 100 200 300 400 mi

People

Canada was greatly influenced by French and British rule, and its culture reflects this dual nature. Descendants of British and French settlers compose the two main population groups, and languages include both English and French. French-speaking inhabitants are concentrated in the Province of Québec. Minorities include descendants of various European groups, indigenous Indians, and Inuit. Because of the rugged terrain and harsh climate of northern Canada, population is concentrated near the United States border.

Economy and the Land

Rich natural resources—including extensive mineral deposits, fertile land, forests, and lakes—helped shape Canada's diversified economy, which ranks among the world's most prosperous. Economic problems are those common to most modern industrial nations. Agriculture, mining, and industry are highly developed. Canada is a major wheat producer; mineral output includes asbestos, zinc, silver, and nickel; and crude petroleum is an important export. The service sector is also active. Second only to Russia in land area, Canada has a terrain that varies from eastern rolling hills and plains to mountains in the west. The Canadian Shield consists of ancient rock and extends from Labrador to the Arctic Islands. It is covered by thick forests in the south and tundra in the north. Overall, summers are moderate and winters long and cold.

History and Politics

Canada's first inhabitants were Asian Indians and Inuit, an Arctic people. Around the year 1000, Vikings were the first Europeans to reach North America, and in 1497 John Cabot claimed the Newfoundland coastal area for Britain. Jacques Cartier established French claim when he landed at the Gaspé Peninsula in the 1500s. Subsequent French and British rivalry culminated in several wars during the late seventeenth and eighteenth centuries. The wars ended with the 1763 Treaty of Paris, by which France lost Canada and other North American territory to Britain. To aid in resolving the continued conflict between French and English residents, the British North America Act of 1867 united the colonies into the Dominion of Canada. Canada fought on the side of the British during World War I. In 1926, along with other dominions, Canada declared itself an independent member of the British Commonwealth and, in 1931, Britain recognized the declaration through the Statute of Westminster. Canada once again allied itself with Britain during World War II. In 1988 Canada saw vigorous debate over a free trade pact with the United States, which narrowly won approval. The Quebec separatist movement is striving for independent status for French-speaking Quebec.

The Selwyn Mountains divide the Yukon Territory and the Northwest Territories. This sparsely populated part of Canada is rich in timber and other natural resources.

POPULATION COMPARISON
Canada=11% of U.S.

United States

GDP COMPARISON
Canada=10% of U.S.

United States

ETHNIC GROUPS

Native Canadian
Other
Other European
British Origin
French Origin

POPULATION DISTRIBUTION
Urban   Rural

The CN Tower, the world's tallest free-standing structure, is a point of civic pride in Toronto, Canada's most populous city. The nearby Sky-Dome, which boasts a retractable roof, is home to baseball's Toronto Blue Jays.

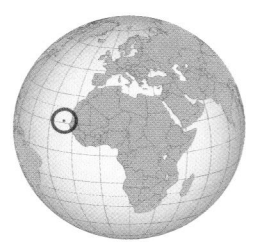

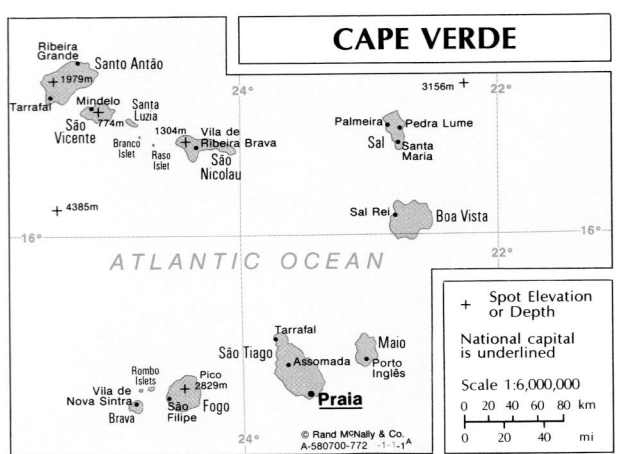

Located on the trade routes to and from Africa, Cape Verde is a busy refueling point for both ships and airplanes.

CAPE VERDE

The people of Cape Verde are descendants of Portuguese colonists and the slaves they brought with them 500 years ago. Although the islands are prone to long-term drought, some crops, such as bananas, are grown successfully. But most food must be imported, and the country relies heavily on foreign aid.

People
The Portuguese-African heritage of Cape Verde's population is a result of Portuguese rule and the forced transmigration of Africans for slavery. Although Portuguese is an official language, the majority speaks Crioulo, a creole dialect. Most people are Roman Catholic, but indigenous practices exist, sometimes in combination with Catholicism. The mainly poor population is largely undernourished and plagued by unemployment. The country consists of five islets and ten main islands, and all but one are inhabited.

Economy and the Land
The volcanic, mountainous islands have few natural resources and low rainfall; thus the country's economy remains underdeveloped. Fishing and agriculture are important for both subsistence and commercial purposes. Much of the land is too dry for farming, and drought is a frequent problem. Cape Verde's location on air and sea

routes and its tropical climate offer potential for expansion into services and tourism. However, Cape Verde will most likely continue to rely on foreign aid for some time.

History and Politics
The islands that make up Cape Verde were uninhabited when the Portuguese arrived around 1460. Settlement began in 1462, and by the sixteenth century Cape Verde had become a shipping center for the African slave trade. Until 1879 Portugal ruled Cape Verde and present-day Guinea-Bissau as a single colony. A movement for the independence of Cape Verde and Guinea-Bissau began in the 1950s, and a 1974 coup in Portugal ultimately resulted in autonomy for both countries, with Cape Verde proclaiming independence in 1975. Plans to unify Cape Verde and Guinea-Bissau were abandoned following a 1980 coup in Guinea-Bissau.

Cape Verde at a glance
Official name	Republic of Cape Verde

People
Population	429,000
Density	276/mi² (106/km²)
Urban	29%
Capital	Praia, São Tiago I., 61,644
Ethnic groups	Creole (mulatto) 71%, African 28%, European 1%
Languages	Portuguese, Crioulo
Religions	Roman Catholic, Nazarene and other Protestant
Life expectancy	69 female, 67 male
Literacy	66%

Politics
Government	Republic
Parties	African Party for Independence, Movement for Democracy
Suffrage	Universal, over 18
Memberships	OAU, UN
Subdivisions	14 districts

Economy
GDP	$415,000,000
Per capita	$1,089
Monetary unit	Escudo
Trade partners	Exports: Algeria, Portugal Imports: Portugal, Netherlands, Japan
Exports	Bananas, fish, salt
Imports	Petroleum, food, manufactures, industrial products

Land
Description	Western African islands
Area	1,557 mi² (4,033 km²)
Highest point	Pico, 9,281 ft (2,829 m)
Lowest point	Sea level

CAYMAN ISLANDS

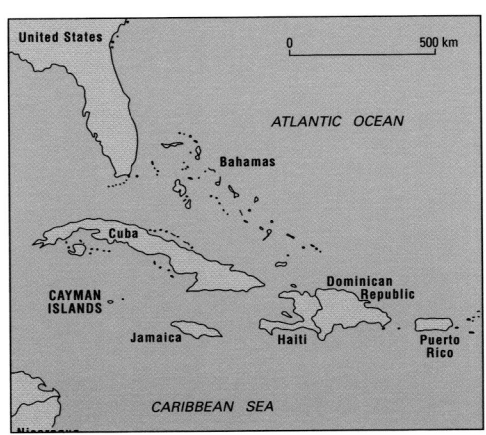

The Cayman Islands have successfully created one of the most profitable tourism-based economies in the Caribbean. A British dependency, the three small islands are visited by scores of wealthy North Americans each year who relax on the long, white beaches and dive among the spectacular reefs.

People
The population of the Caymans combines descendants of African slaves, Jamaican and North American immigrants, and people of European ancestry. Most live on Grand Cayman Island. The standard of living is relatively high, mainly because of the proliferation of offshore banking.

Economy and the Land
In the 1960s the government created a board of tourism and established tax laws favorable to financial services, and today tourism and banking are the economic leaders. Fishing, especially for turtles, also contributes to the economy. The Caymans consist of the coral islands of Grand Cayman, the largest and most populated; Little Cayman; and Cayman Brac. The climate is tropical, with cooling trade winds.

History and Politics
Christopher Columbus arrived at the Cayman Islands in 1503. In 1670 Spain

ceded the Caymans and Jamaica to Britain. True settlement began in 1734 on Grand Cayman, and Cayman Brac and Little Cayman were settled in 1833. In 1959 administration of the Cayman Islands was separated from that of Jamaica, but the Cayman Islands remained under British rule. A governor appointed by the British Crown is head of government.

Cayman Islands at a glance
Official name	Cayman Islands

People
Population	33,000
Density	330/mi² (127/km²)
Urban	100%
Capital	Georgetown, Grand Cayman I., 12,921
Ethnic groups	Mixed 40%, black 20%, white 20%
Languages	English
Religions	United church, Anglican, Baptist, Roman Catholic, Church of God
Life expectancy	79 female, 75 male
Literacy	98%

Politics
Government	Dependent territory (U.K.)
Parties	None
Suffrage	Universal, over 18
Memberships	None
Subdivisions	8 districts

Economy
GDP	$670,000,000
Per capita	$25,769
Monetary unit	Dollar
Trade partners	Exports: U.S. Imports: U.S., Netherlands Antilles, Japan
Exports	Turtle products, manufactures
Imports	Food, manufactures

Land
Description	Caribbean islands
Area	100 mi² (259 km²)
Highest point	140 ft (43 m)
Lowest point	Sea level

The Ubangi River forms part of the border between the Central African Republic and Democratic Republic of the Congo. Because of a series of rapids, the river is not navigable above Bangui.

CENTRAL AFRICAN REPUBLIC

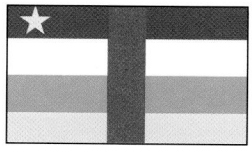

The **Central African Republic** is one of the last great wildlife refuges in Africa. Rampant poverty has led to poaching, and the politically unstable government has been unable to intervene. A former colony of France, the country relies heavily on foreign aid to keep its weak economy afloat.

People

Lying near Africa's geographical center, the Central African Republic was the stopping point for many pre-colonial nomadic groups. The resultant multiethnic populace was further diversified by migrations during the slave-trade era. Of the country's many languages, Sango is most widely used. Overall, the population is rural and suffers from poverty and a low literacy rate.

Economy and the Land

Fertile land, extensive forests, and mineral deposits provide adequate bases for agriculture, forestry, and mining. Economic development remains minimal, however, impeded by poor transportation routes, a landlocked location, lack of skilled labor, and political instability. Subsistence farming continues as the major activity, and agriculture is the chief contributor to the economy. The country consists of a plateau region with southern rain forests and a northeastern semidesert. The climate is temperate, and ample rainfall sometimes results in impassable roads.

History and Politics

Little is known of the area's early history except that it was the site of many migrations. European slave trade in the nineteenth century led to the 1894 creation of a French territory called the Ubangi-Chari. This in turn combined with the areas of the present-day Congo, Chad, and Gabon in 1910 to form French Equatorial Africa. The Central African Republic gained independence in 1960. A 1966 military coup installed military chief Jean-Bedel Bokassa, who in 1976 assumed the title of emperor, changed the republic to a monarchy, and renamed the nation the Central African Empire. A 1979 coup ended the monarchy and reinstated the name Central African Republic. The country enacted a new constitution in 1986 and held its first free elections in August 1993. Voters overwhelmingly rejected the incumbent dictator in favor of reform candidates.

POPULATION COMPARISON
Central African Republic=1% of U.S.

United States

GDP COMPARISON
Central African Republic=0.02% of U.S.

United States

ETHNIC GROUPS

Other
Sara — Baya
Mandjia
Banda

POPULATION DISTRIBUTION
Urban — Rural

A woman and her children sell their produce at market.

Central African Republic at a glance

Official name	Central African Republic

People

Population	3,177,000
Density	13/mi² (5.1/km²)
Urban	47%
Capital	Bangui, 596,800
Ethnic groups	Baya 34%, Banda 27%, Mandjia 21%, Sara 10%
Languages	French, Sango, Arabic, indigenous
Religions	Protestant 24%, Roman Catholic 25%, Muslim 15%
Life expectancy	49 female, 45 male
Literacy	27%

Politics

Government	Republic
Parties	Democratic Rally, People's Liberation, others
Suffrage	Universal, over 21
Memberships	OAU, UN
Subdivisions	16 prefectures, 1 autonomous commune

Economy

GDP	$2,500,000,000
Per capita	$815
Monetary unit	CFA franc
Trade partners	Exports: Belgium, France, Switzerland Imports: France, Cameroon, Japan
Exports	Diamonds, cotton, coffee, lumber, tobacco
Imports	Food, textiles, petroleum, machinery, electrical equipment

Land

Description	Central Africa, landlocked
Area	240,535 mi² (622,984 km²)
Highest point	Mont Ngaoui, 4,626 ft (1,410 m)
Lowest point	Along Ubangi River, 1,100 ft (335 m)

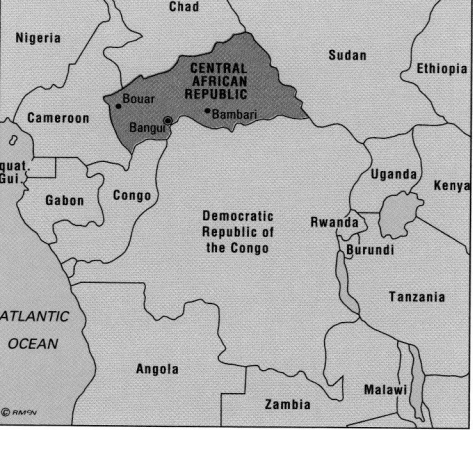

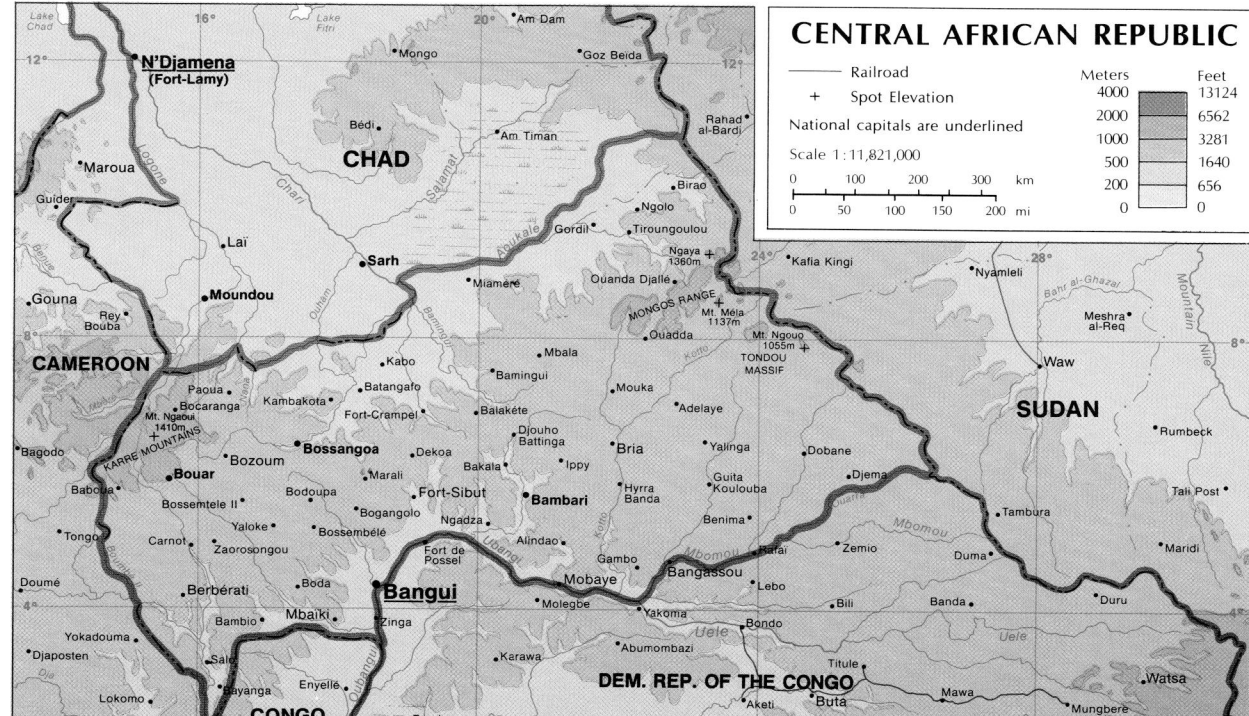

CENTRAL AFRICAN REPUBLIC

— Railroad
+ Spot Elevation
National capitals are underlined
Scale 1:11,821,000

Meters	Feet
4000	13124
2000	6562
1000	3281
500	1640
200	656
0	0

The dense rain forests that cover the southwest portion of the Central African Republic have been spared from logging because of the country's landlocked location and lack of transportation.

The northern two-thirds of Chad is in the Sahara Desert, where rainfall averages less than one inch per year. It is home to nomadic tribes who eke out an existence raising livestock.

CHAD

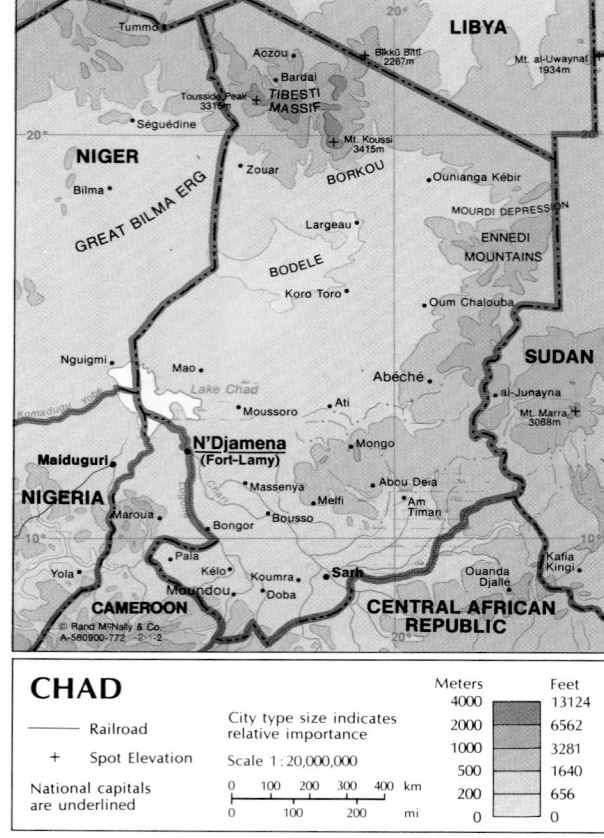

CHAD

——	Railroad
+	Spot Elevation

City type size indicates relative importance

Scale 1 : 20,000,000

National capitals are underlined

	Meters	Feet
	4000	13124
	2000	6562
	1000	3281
	500	1640
	200	656
	0	0

© Rand McNally & Co.
A-560900-772

Chad at a glance
Official name   Republic of Chad

People
Population	6,396,000
Density	13/mi² (5.0/km²)
Urban	32%
Capital	N'Djamena, 500,000
Ethnic groups	Sara and other African, Arab
Languages	Arabic, French, indigenous
Religions	Muslim 44%, Christian 33%, Animist 23%
Life expectancy	49 female, 46 male
Literacy	30%

Politics
Government	Republic
Parties	National Recovery, Patriotic Salvation Movement
Suffrage	Universal adult
Memberships	OAU, UN
Subdivisions	14 prefectures

Economy
GDP	$2,700,000,000
Per capita	$510
Monetary unit	CFA franc
Trade partners	Exports: France, Nigeria, Cameroon
	Imports: U.S., France, Nigeria
Exports	Cotton, cattle, textiles, fish
Imports	Machinery and transportation equipment, industrial goods, petroleum, food

Land
Description	Central Africa, landlocked
Area	495,755 mi² (1,284,000 km²)
Highest point	Mt. Koussi, 11,204 ft (3,415 m)
Lowest point	Bodélé Depression, 525 ft (160 m)

People
Centuries ago, Islamic Arabs mixed with indigenous black Africans and established Chad's diverse population. This variety has led to a rich but often troubled culture. Descendants of Arab invaders mainly inhabit the north, where Islam predominates and nomadic farming is the major activity. In the south—traditionally the economic and political center—the black Sara predominate, operating small farms and practicing indigenous or Christian beliefs. Chad's many languages also reflect its ethnic variety.

Economy and the Land
Natural features and instability arising from ethnic and regional conflict have combined to prevent Chad from prospering. Agriculture and fishing are economic mainstays and are often conducted at subsistence levels. The Sahara extends into Chad's northern region, and the southern grasslands with their heavy rains compose the primary agricultural area. The relative prosperity of the region, in conjunction with its predominantly Sara population, has fueled much of the political conflict. Future growth is greatly dependent on political equilibrium. Climate varies from the hot, dry northern desert to the semiarid central region and rainier south.

History and Politics
African and Arab societies began prospering in the Lake Chad region around the eighth century A.D. Subsequent centuries saw the landlocked area become an ethnic crossroads for Muslim nomads and African groups. European traders arrived in the late 1800s, and by 1900 France had gained control. When created in 1910, French Equatorial Africa's boundaries included modern Chad, Gabon, the Congo, and the Central African Republic. Following Chad's independence in 1960, the southern Sara gained dominance over the government. A northern rebel group has emerged and government-rebel conflict has continued. Libyan troops entered Chad in 1980, and conflict continued until a cease-fire was implemented in 1987. Isolated incursions continue. The pro-Western government fell to rebel forces in December 1990. A 1993 national conference established an interim constitution and a transitional government.

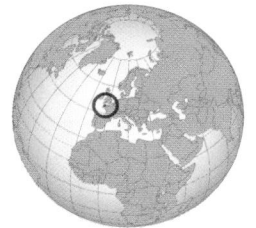

CHANNEL ISLANDS

People
Most of the inhabitants of the Channel Islands are French and British, thus mostly Roman Catholic and Anglican. English is the main language, and Norman-French dialect is spoken in some areas.

Economy and the Land
The mild climate has encouraged tourism and agriculture. However, in recent years financial services have become very important to the economy. The Channel Islands consist of the main islands of Jersey, Guernsey, Alderney, and Sark, plus several smaller islands.

History and Politics
In the tenth century, the Channel Islands came under the duke of Normandy, and in 1066 the Norman Conquest tied them to Britain. The islands continue as a British dependency.

Channel Islands at a glance
Official name   Channel Islands

People
Population	150,000
Density	2,000/mi² (773/km²)
Urban	31%
Capital	St. Peter Port, Guernsey Island, 16,648; St. Helier, Jersey Island, 28,123
Ethnic groups	Channel Islander (mixed British and French)
Languages	English, French
Religions	Anglican, Roman Catholic, Methodist
Life expectancy	74 female, 67 male

Politics
Government	Dependent territory (U.K.)
Suffrage	Universal adult
Memberships	None

Economy
Monetary unit	U.K. pound sterling

Land
Description	Northwestern European Islands
Area	75 mi² (194 km²)
Highest point	460 ft (140 m)
Lowest point	Sea level

Scale 1:1,000,000   One inch represents approximately 16 miles. One centimeter represents 10 kilometers.

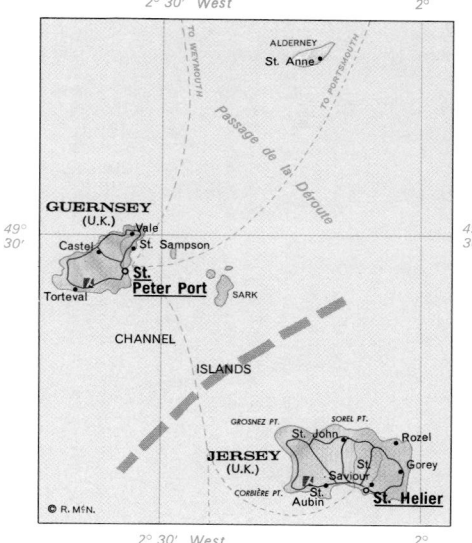

The Channel Islands are two distinct entities—Guernsey and Jersey—each with its own constitution and local laws and customs. Guernsey's dependencies include Alderney, Sark, Herm, Jethou, Lihou, and Brecqhou, while the Ecrehous rocks and Les Minquiers belong to Jersey.

Magnificent desolation is a term that applies to Chile's far south. Torres del Paine National Park, shown here, is part of a region of unspoiled mountains, lakes, forests, and glaciers.

Rocky beach near Punta Arenas

CHILE

Chile is rapidly becoming the economic success of South America. Wealth generated by the world's largest known copper deposits has been supplemented by booming agricultural exports from the country's fertile central region. Chile's southern hemisphere location has allowed it to become a major source of fruits and vegetables during the winter for the United States.

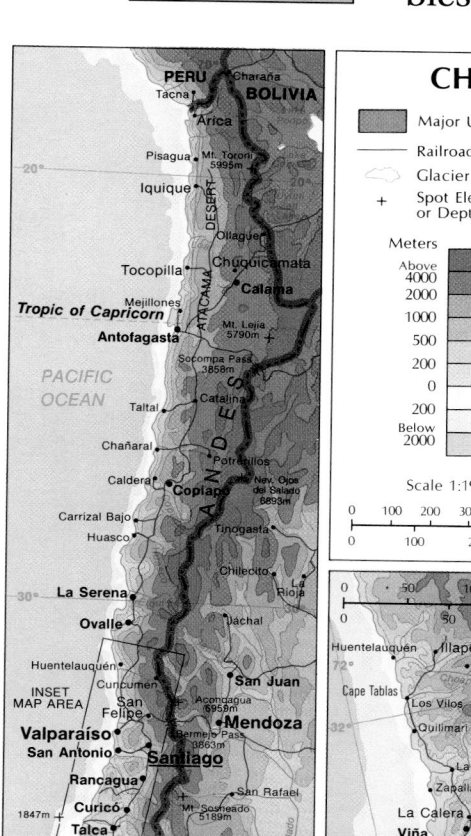

CHILE

- Major Urban Area
- Railroad
- Glacier
- + Spot Elevation or Depth

Meters	Feet
Above 4000	Above 13124
2000	6562
1000	3281
500	1640
200	656
0	0
200	656
Below 2000	Below 6562

Scale 1:19,031,000

0 100 200 300 400 500 km
0 100 200 300 mi

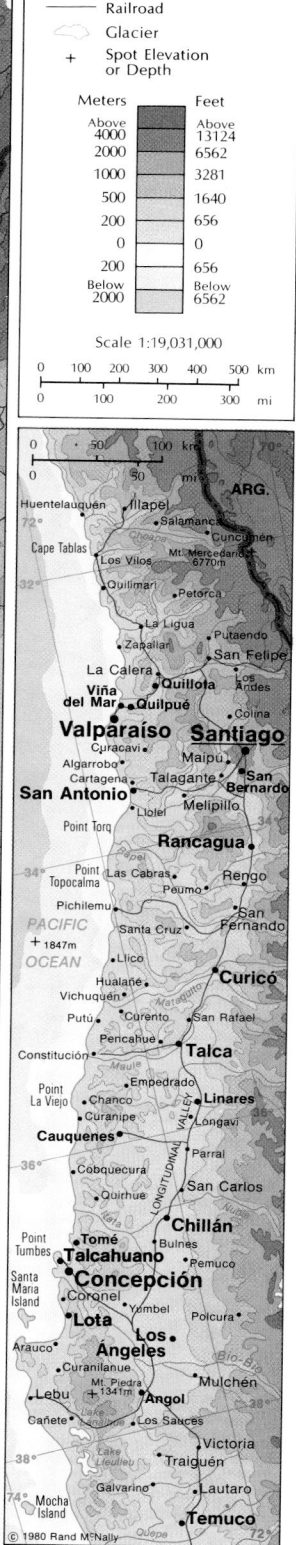

People
Chile's land barriers—the eastern Andes, western coastal range, and northern desert—have resulted in a mostly urban population concentrated in a central valley. Mestizos, of Spanish-Indian heritage, and descendants of Spanish immigrants predominate. In addition to an Indian minority, the population includes those who trace their roots to Irish and English colonists or nineteenth-century German immigrants. The country enjoys a relatively high literacy rate, but poverty remains a problem.

Economy and the Land
Chile's land provides the natural resources necessary for a successful economy, and growth has been high in the post-Pinochet era. However, there is concern about the increasing gap between the rich and the poor. The northern desert region is the site of mineral deposits, and mining is a major component of trade, making Chile vulnerable to outside market forces. An agricultural zone lies in the central valley, while the South offers forests, grazing land, and some petroleum deposits. The climate varies from region to region but is generally mild.

History and Politics
Upon their arrival in the 1500s, the Spanish defeated the northern Inca Indians, although many years were spent in conflict with Araucanian Indians of the central and southern regions. From the sixteenth through nineteenth centuries, Chile received little attention from ruling Spain, and colonists established a successful agriculture. In 1818 Bernardo O'Higgins led the way to victory over the Spanish and became ruler of independent Chile. By the 1920s, dissent arising from unequal power and land distribution united the middle and working classes, but social welfare, education, and economic programs were unable to eliminate inequalities rooted in the past. A 1960 earthquake and tidal wave added to the country's problems. Leftist Salvador Allende Gossens was elected to power in 1970, governing until his death in 1973 in a military coup, which installed Augusto Pinochet. Civil disturbances and grave human-rights abuses marked his right-wing government. This dictatorship ended in 1989, although Pinochet continued to be the army's commander-in-chief.

Chile is a place of weather extremes. Some parts of the Atacama Desert in the north have never seen rain, while the frequent, violent storms at Cape Horn at the country's southern tip have claimed countless ships.

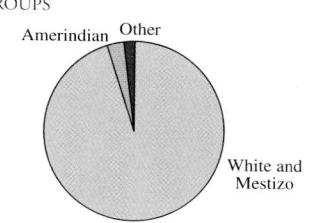

POPULATION COMPARISON
Chile=5% of U.S.

United States

GDP COMPARISON
Chile=1% of U.S.

United States

ETHNIC GROUPS

Amerindian Other

White and Mestizo

POPULATION DISTRIBUTION
Urban   Rural

Chile at a glance
Official name   Republic of Chile

People

Population	14,050,000
Density	48/mi² (19/km²)
Urban	85%
Capital	Santiago, 232,667
Ethnic groups	White and mestizo 95%, Amerindian 3%
Languages	Spanish
Religions	Roman Catholic 89%, Pentecostal and other Protestant 11%
Life expectancy	76 female, 69 male
Literacy	93%

Politics

Government	Republic
Parties	Christian Democratic, Democracy, National Renewal, Radical, others
Suffrage	Universal, over 18
Memberships	OAS, UN
Subdivisions	13 regions

Economy

GDP	$96,000,000,000
Per capita	$7,041
Monetary unit	Peso
Trade partners	Exports: U.S., Japan, Germany Imports: U.S., Japan, Brazil, Germany
Exports	Copper and other metals, lumber, fish, fruit
Imports	Petroleum, wheat, manufactures, raw materials

Land

Description	Southern South America
Area	292,135 mi² (756,626 km²)
Highest point	Nevado Ojos del Salado, 22,615 ft (6,893 m)
Lowest point	Sea level

CHINA

A nation of superlatives—the world's most populous country, the third-largest country in area, a 4,000-year-old culture—China is also an almost boundless patchwork of peoples and lands that defies generalization. From the peasants farming their small plots in the countryside to the exploding populations of the booming coastal cities, the Chinese are united by close-knit families. Efforts by the Communist government to limit couples to one child are widely flaunted, and as economic growth enriches more Chinese, other government strictures are being ignored as well.

People

China is the world's most populous nation. Its population is concentrated in the east, and Han Chinese are the majority group. Zhuang, Hui, Uygur, Yi, Miao, Manchu, and Tibetan peoples compose minorities. Many Chinese languages are spoken, but the national language is Modern Standard Chinese, or Mandarin, based on a northern dialect. Following a Communist revolution in 1949, religious activity was discouraged. It is now on the increase, and religions include Taoism and Buddhism, as well as Islam and Christianity. China's population has soared to over 1.1 billion, and family-planning programs have been implemented to aid population control. With a recorded civilization going back about 3,500 years, China has contributed much to world culture.

The Great Wall

Giant Panda

Despite the exodus of rural dwellers to the rapidly developing cities, more than three out of four Chinese still work in agriculture. Here a man stacks harvested rice near Guilin in the Guangxi autonomous region.

No region of China can be considered typically "Chinese." Among the nation's many features are the fertile river deltas of the east, the Himalayas of the west, and the Gobi Desert of the north.

Courtyard, the Forbidden City, Beijing

Economy and the Land
Economic progress dates from 1949, when the new People's Republic of China faced a starving, war-torn, and unemployed population. As of 1993, the Chinese economy was the third-largest in the world. Industry is expanding, but agriculture continues as the major activity. Natural resources include coal, oil, natural gas, and minerals, many of which remain to be explored. A current economic plan focuses on growth in agriculture, industry, science and technology, and national defense. China's terrain is varied: two-thirds consists of mountainous or semiarid land, with fertile plains and deltas in the east. The climate is marked by hot, humid summers, while the dry winters are often cold.

A stark landscape of rock outcroppings lends an air of mystery to the Green (Yu) River at dawn. Flowing through the subtropical Guangxi region, the river supplies water for numerous sugarcane plantations.

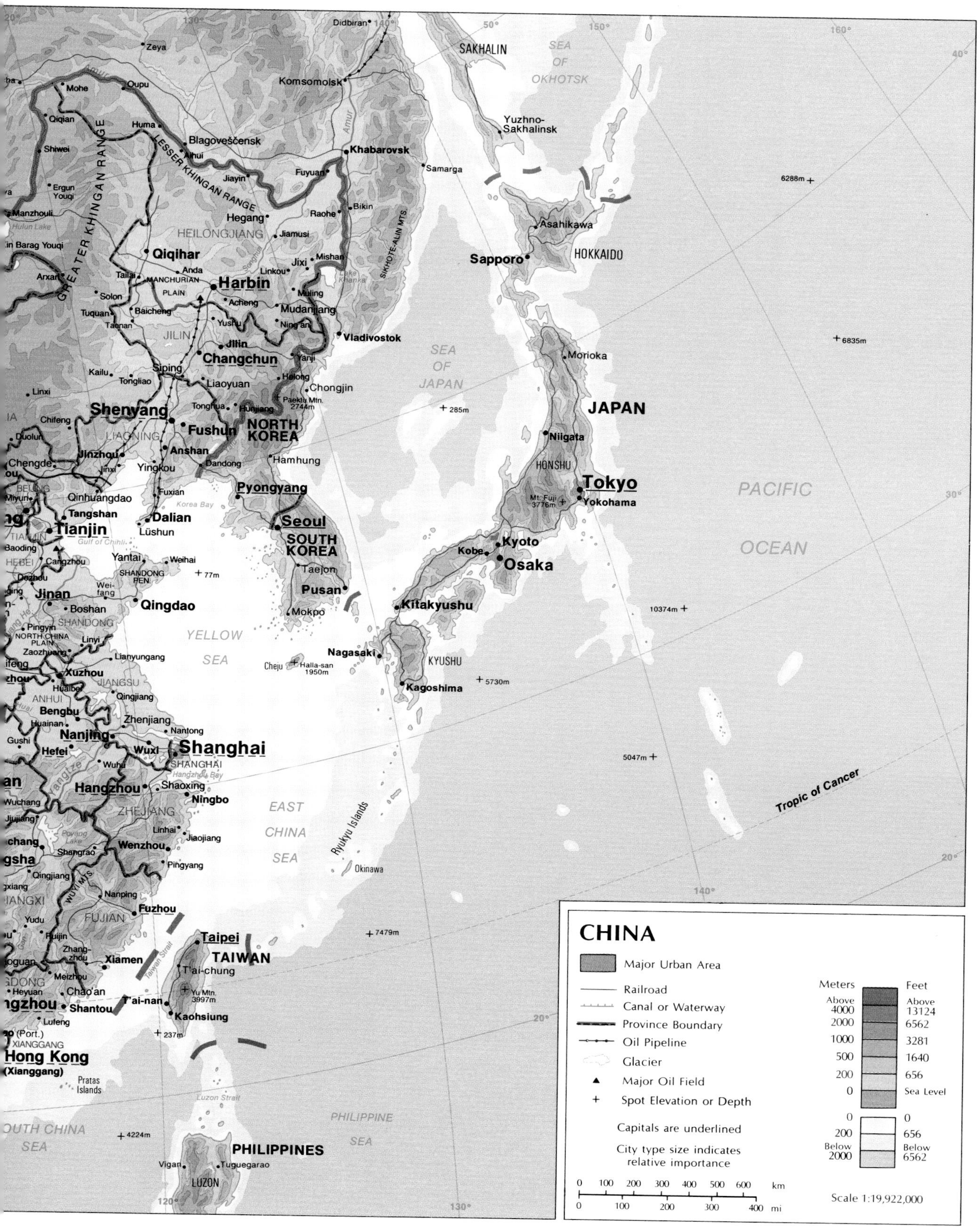

History and Politics
China's civilization ranks among the world's oldest. The first dynasty, the Shang, began sometime during the second millennium B.C. Kublai Khan's thirteenth-century invasion brought China the first of its various foreign rulers. In the nineteenth century, despite government efforts to the contrary, foreign influence and intervention grew. The government was weakened by the Opium War with Britain in the 1840s; the Taiping Rebellion, a civil war; and a war with Japan from 1894 to 1895. Opposition to foreign influences erupted in the anti-foreign and anti-Christian Boxer Rebellion of 1900. After China became a republic in 1912, the death of the president in 1916 triggered the warlord period, in which conflicts were widespread and power was concentrated among military leaders. Attempts to unite the nation began in the 1920s with Sun Yat-sen's Nationalist party, initially allied with the Communist party. Under the leadership of Chiang Kai-shek, the Nationalist party overcame the warlords, captured Beijing, and executed many Communists. Remaining Communists reorganized under Mao Zedong, and the Communist-Nationalist conflict continued, along with Japanese invasion and occupation. By 1949 the Communists controlled most of the country, and the People's Republic of China was proclaimed. Chiang Kai-shek fled to Taiwan, proclaiming T'aipei as China's provisional capital. After Mao's death in 1976, Deng Xiaoping encouraged greater contact with the outside world and the development of increased foreign trade. The United States rewarded China's efforts to become part of the international community by recognizing Beijing, rather than T'aipei, as China's capital. In 1989, pro-democracy student demonstrations in Beijing's Tiananmen Square erupted into violence, and many people were arrested or killed. Although the political situation remained repressive at the time of Deng's death in 1997, the country is experiencing rapid economic growth.

CHINA

- Major Urban Area
- Railroad
- Canal or Waterway
- Province Boundary
- Oil Pipeline
- Glacier
- ▲ Major Oil Field
- + Spot Elevation or Depth

Capitals are underlined

City type size indicates relative importance

Meters	Feet
Above 4000	Above 13124
2000	6562
1000	3281
500	1640
200	656
0	Sea Level
0	0
200	656
Below 2000	Below 6562

Scale 1:19,922,000

0 100 200 300 400 500 600 km
0 100 200 300 400 mi

Plowing with water buffalo

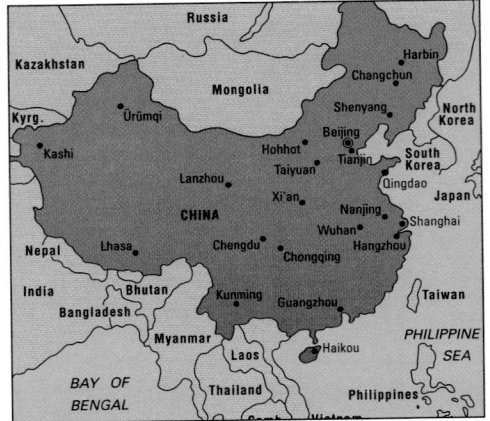

China at a glance

Official name	People's Republic of China

People

Population	1,196,980,000
Density	324/mi² (125/km²)
Urban	26%
Capital	Beijing (Peking), 6,710,000
Ethnic groups	Han Chinese 93%, Zhuang, Uygur, Hui, Yi, Tibetan, Miao, Manchu, others
Languages	Chinese dialects
Religions	Taoist, Buddhist, and Muslim 3%
Life expectancy	73 female, 69 male
Literacy	73%

Politics

Government	Socialist republic
Parties	Communist
Suffrage	Universal, over 18
Memberships	UN
Subdivisions	22 provinces, 5 autonomous regions, 3 municipalities

Economy

GDP	$2,610,000,000,000
Per capita	$2,214
Monetary unit	Yuan
Trade partners	Japan, U.S.
Exports	Textiles, clothing, telecommunications and recording equipment, petroleum
Imports	Machinery, chemicals, manufactures, steel, textile yarn, fertilizer.

Land

Description	Eastern Asia
Area	3,689,631 mi² (9,556,100 km²)
Highest point	Mt. Everest, 29,028 ft (8,848 m)
Lowest point	Turfan Depression, -505 ft (-154 m)

The above information excludes Taiwan.

Bicyclists vie with trucks and buses for road space in Kunming. Bicycles are ubiquitous in China, where cars are a luxury few can afford.

At 3,900 miles in length, the Yangtze River is the longest river in Asia and the fourth-longest in the world. It spans 10 of China's provinces and autonomous regions and is the country's main inland waterway.

POPULATION COMPARISON
China=456% of U.S.

United States

GDP COMPARISON
China=41% of U.S.

United States

ETHNIC GROUPS

Zhuang, Uygur, Hui, Yi, Tibetan, Miao, Manchu, and others

Han Chinese

POPULATION DISTRIBUTION

Urban   Rural

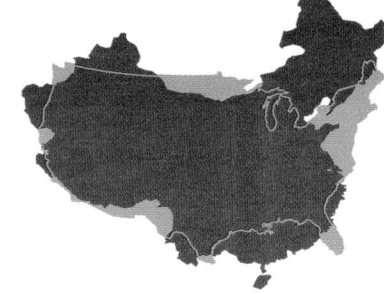

Tea cultivation

A group of Kirgiz men pose near the Pamir mountains, which are just across the border in Tajikistan. Many diverse ethnic groups call China home.

Bogotá, Colombia's capital, lies in a basin in the Eastern Cordillera of the Andes, at an elevation of 8,500 feet.

COLOMBIA

People

Colombia's mixed population traces its roots to indigenous Indians, Spanish colonists, and black African slaves. Most numerous today are mestizos, those of Spanish-Indian descent. Roman Catholicism, the Spanish language, and Colombia's overall culture evidence the long-lasting effect of Spanish rule. Over the past decades the population has shifted from mainly rural to urban as the economy has expanded into industry.

Economy and the Land

Industry now keeps pace with traditional agriculture in economic contributions, and mining is also important. Natural resources include oil, coal, natural gas, most of the world's emeralds, plus fertile soils. The traditional coffee crop also remains important for Colombia, a leading coffee producer. The terrain features a flat coastal region, central highlands, and wide eastern llanos, or plains. The climate is tropical on the coast and in the west, with cooler temperatures in the highlands.

History and Politics

In the 1500s Spaniards conquered the native Indian groups and established the area as a Spanish colony. In the early 1700s Bogotá became the capital of the viceroyalty of New Granada, which included modern Colombia, Venezuela, Ecuador, and Panama. Rebellion in Venezuela in 1796 sparked revolts elsewhere in New Granada, including Colombia, and in 1813 independence was declared. In 1819 the Republic of Greater Colombia was formed and included all the former members of the Spanish viceroyalty. Independence leader Simón Bolívar became president. By 1830 Venezuela and Ecuador had seceded from the republic, followed by Panama in 1903. The Conservative and Liberal parties, dominating forces in Colombia's political history, arose from differences between supporters of Bolívar and Santander. Conservative-Liberal conflict led to a violent civil war from 1899 to 1902, as well as to *La Violencia*,

Like the people in many developing countries, large numbers of Colombians are forsaking rural lives on the land for the economic hope of the cities. Coffee has been joined as an important export by petroleum and coal. Colombia's place as one of Latin America's democracies continues to be threatened by widespread lawlessness, especially that of its notorious drug lords.

The Violence, a civil disorder that continued from the 1940s to the 1960s and resulted in about three hundred thousand deaths. From the late 1950s through the 1970s, the government alternated between conservative and liberal rule. Political unrest reduced the effectiveness of both parties. By the 1980s growing drug traffic presented Colombia with new problems. The government is now faced with widespread corruption and increasing violence.

Colonial buildings, Bogotá

Colombia at a glance

Official name	Republic of Colombia

People

Population	34,870,000
Density	79/mi² (31/km²)
Urban	70%
Capital	Bogotá, 3,982,941
Ethnic groups	Mestizo 58%, white 20%, mulatto 14%, black 4%
Languages	Spanish
Religions	Roman Catholic 95%
Life expectancy	72 female, 66 male
Literacy	87%

Politics

Government	Republic
Parties	Conservative, Liberal, others
Suffrage	Universal, over 18
Memberships	OAS, UN
Subdivisions	32 departments, 1 capital district

Economy

GDP	$51,000,000,000
Per capita	$1,538
Monetary unit	Peso
Trade partners	Exports: U.S., Germany, Netherlands Imports: U.S., Japan, Germany
Exports	Petroleum, coffee, coal, bananas, flowers
Imports	Machinery and transportation equipment, food, chemicals, paper products

Land

Description	Northern South America
Area	440,831 mi² (1,141,748 km²)
Highest point	Cristóbal Colón Peak, 19,029 ft (5,800 m)
Lowest point	Sea level

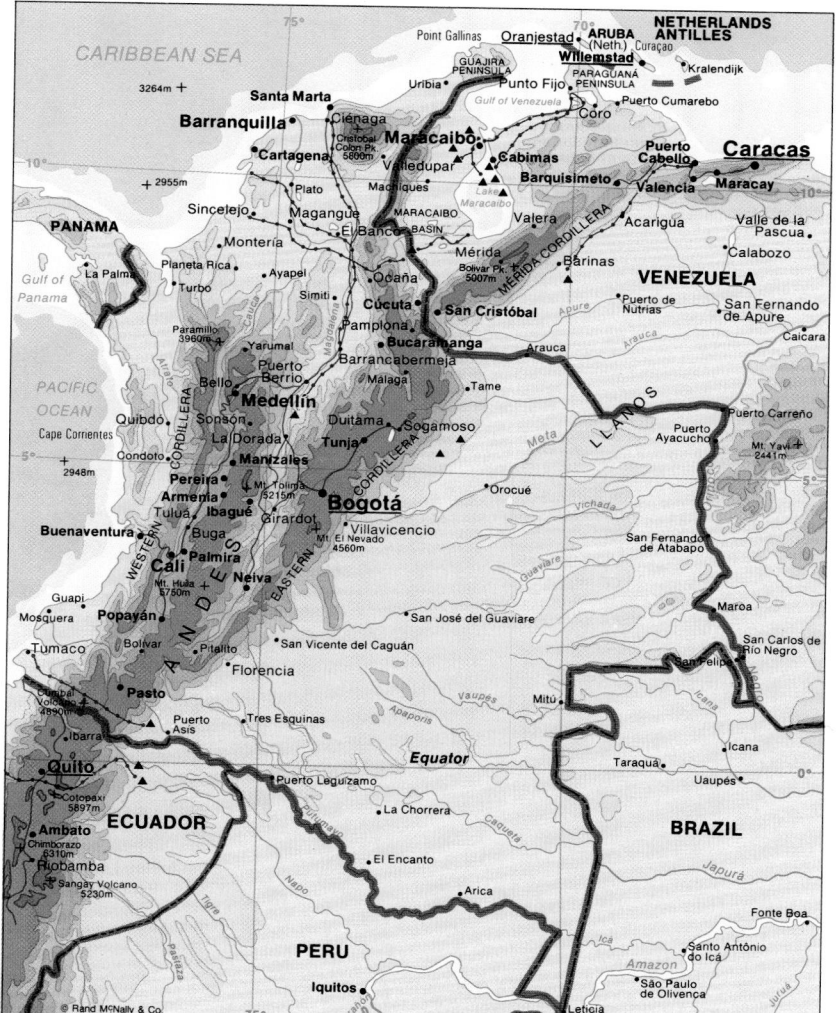

COLOMBIA

| Railroad |
| Oil Pipeline |
| ▲ Major Oil Field |
| + Spot Elevation or Depth |

National capitals are underlined

Scale 1:13,519,000

Meters	Feet
Above 4000	Above 13124
2000	6562
1000	3281
500	1640
200	656
0	0

Meters	Feet
0	0
200	656
Below 2000	Below 6562

© Rand McNally & Co.
A-540500-772 -1-1-3

Colombia's vast Llanos plain in the east has historically been sparsely populated, its poor soil good for little more than cattle grazing. But this is changing since the recent discovery of rich oil deposits.

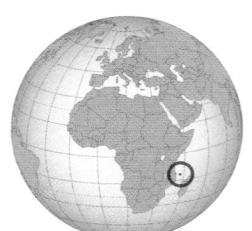

Comoros claims the island of Mayotte as part of its territory, but the latter voted against independence from France in 1974 and remains under French administration.

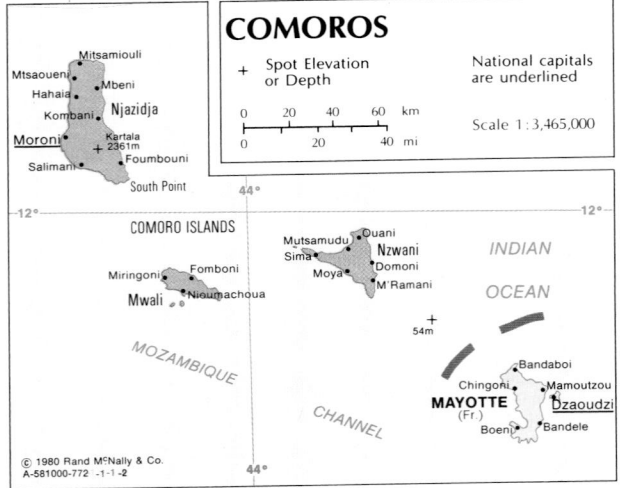

COMOROS

+ Spot Elevation or Depth

National capitals are underlined

0 20 40 60 km
0   20   40 mi

Scale 1 : 3,465,000

© 1980 Rand McNally & Co.
A-581000-772 -1-1 -2

COMOROS

People

The ethnic groups of Comoros' Njazidja, Nzwani, and Mwali islands are mainly of Arab-African descent, practice Islam, and speak Comoran, a Swahili dialect. Arab culture, however, predominates throughout the island group. Poverty, disease, a shortage of medical care, and low literacy continue to plague the nation.

Economy and the Land

Comoros' economic mainstay is agriculture, and most Comorans practice subsistence farming and fishing. Plantations employ workers to produce the main cash crops, which include spices and essential (perfume) oils. Of volcanic origin, the islands have soils of varying quality, and some are unsuited for farming. Terrain varies from the mountains of Njazidja to

the hills and valleys of Mwali. The climate is cool and dry, with a winter rainy season.

History and Politics

The Comoro Islands have been invaded by coastal African, Persian Gulf, Indonesian, and Malagasy peoples. Portuguese explorers landed in the 1500s, around the same time Arab Shirazis, most likely from Persia, introduced Islam. The French took Mayotte in 1840 and had established colonial rule over the four main islands by 1912. Comoros declared unilateral independence in 1975. Mayotte, however, voted to remain under French administration. In 1997 two separate secessionist rebellions occurred on the islands of Anjouan and Mohéli. The islands are currently negotiating with the Comoran government.

Comoros at a glance

Official name	Federal Islamic Republic of the Comoros

People

Population	540,000
Density	626/mi² (242/km²)
Urban	28%
Capital	Moroni, Njazidja I., 23,432
Ethnic groups	African-Arab descent (Antalote, Cafre, Makoa, Oimatsaha, Sakalava)
Languages	Arabic, French, Comoran
Religions	Sunni Muslim 86%, Roman Catholic 14%
Life expectancy	57 female, 56 male
Literacy	48%

Politics

Government	Islamic republic
Parties	Rally for Democracy and Renewal, Union for Democracy and Decentralization, Union for Progress, others
Suffrage	Universal, over 18
Memberships	OAU, UN
Subdivisions	3 islands

Economy

GDP	$360,000,000
Per capita	$716
Monetary unit	Franc
Trade partners	Exports: France, U.S., Mauritius Imports: France and other European countries
Exports	Vanilla, cloves, perfume oils, copra
Imports	Rice and other food, cement, petroleum, manufactures

Land

Description	Southeastern African islands
Area	863 mi² (2,235 km²)
Highest point	Kartala, 7,746 ft (2,361 m)
Lowest point	Sea level

The above information excludes Mayotte.

The Ubangi River and the northern portion of the Congo River are vital highways for transporting goods such as cocoa and coffee. But rapids and falls at Brazzaville necessitate the transfer of goods to railroad cars for the journey to the port town of Pointe Noire.

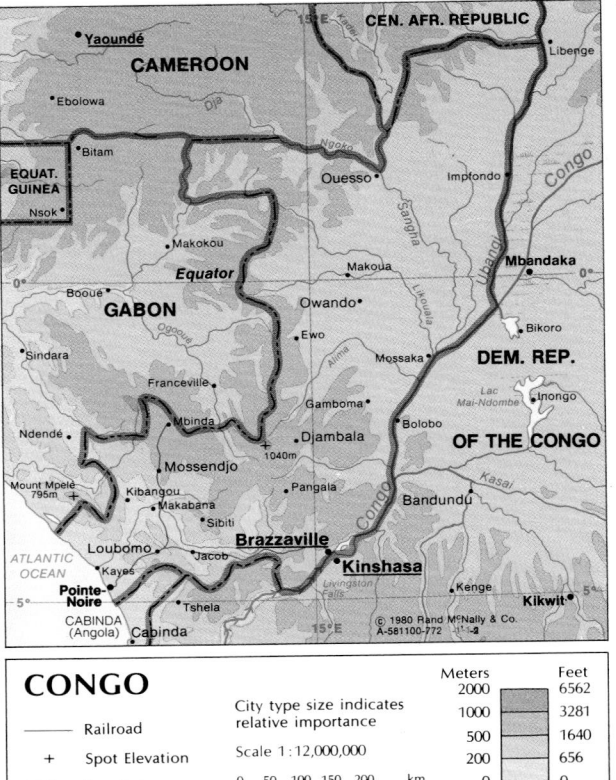

CONGO

CONGO

	Meters	Feet
	2000	6562
	1000	3281
	500	1640
	200	656
	0	0
	200	656

City type size indicates relative importance

—— Railroad

+ Spot Elevation

Scale 1 : 12,000,000

National capitals are underlined

0 50 100 150 200 km
0   50   100   150 mi

© 1980 Rand McNally & Co.
A-581100-772 -1-1-4

People

The Congo's main groups, the Kongo, Sangho, Bateke, and Mbochi create an ethnically and linguistically diverse populace. The official language, French, reflects former colonial rule. Population is concentrated in the south, away from the dense forests, heavy rainfall, and hot climate of the north. Educational programs have improved, although rural inhabitants remain relatively isolated.

Economy and the Land

Brazzaville was the commercial center of the former colony called French Equatorial Africa. The Congo now benefits from the early groundwork laid for service and transport industries. Subsistence farming occu-

pies most Congolese, however, and takes most of the cultivated land. Low productivity and a growing populace create a need for foreign aid, much of it from France. Offshore petroleum is the most valuable mineral resource and a major economic contributor. The land is marked by coastal plains, a south-central valley, a central plateau, and the Congo River basin in the north. The climate is tropical.

History and Politics

Several tribal kingdoms existed in the area during its early history. The Portuguese arrived on the coast in the 1400s, and slave trade flourished until it was banned in the 1800s. A Teke king then signed a treaty placing the area, known as Middle Congo, under

French protection. In 1910 Middle Congo, the present-day Central African Republic, Gabon, and Chad were joined to form French Equatorial Africa. The Republic of the Congo became independent in 1960. Subsequent years saw unrest, including coups, a presidential assassination, and accusations of corruption and human rights violations. Democratic reforms and the legalization of opposition parties have unleashed intense ethnic and regional rivalries that threaten the nation's stability.

Congo at a glance

Official name	Republic of the Congo

People

Population	2,474,000
Density	19/mi² (7.2/km²)
Urban	41%
Capital	Brazzaville, 693,712
Ethnic groups	Kongo 48%, Sangho 20%, Bateke 17%, Mbochi 12%
Languages	French, Lingala, Kikongo, indigenous
Religions	Christian 50%, Animist 48%, Muslim 2%
Life expectancy	54 female, 49 male
Literacy	57%

Politics

Government	Republic
Parties	Labor, Movement for Democracy and Integral Development, Pan-African Union for Social Democracy, others
Suffrage	Universal, over 18
Memberships	OAU, UN
Subdivisions	9 regions, 1 federal district

Economy

GDP	$7,000,000,000
Per capita	$2,901
Monetary unit	CFA franc
Trade partners	Exports: U.S., Spain, France Imports: France, Spain, U.S.
Exports	Petroleum, lumber, coffee, cocoa, sugar, diamonds
Imports	Food, manufactures, machinery

Land

Description	Central Africa
Area	132,047 mi² (342,000 km²)
Highest point	Mt. Nabeba, 3,219 ft (981 m)
Lowest point	Sea level

Nyamulagira Volcano in the eastern Democratic Republic of the Congo

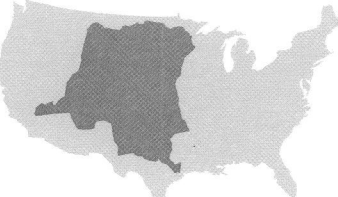

Boys paddle their dugouts on the Ngiri River, part of the web of Congo River tributaries.

CONGO,
DEMOCRATIC REPUBLIC OF THE

People

The diverse population of Democratic Republic of the Congo is composed of more than 200 African ethnic groups, with Bantu peoples in the majority. Belgian settlers introduced French, but hundreds of indigenous languages are more widely spoken. Much of the population is Christian, another result of former European rule. Many non-Christians practice traditional or syncretic faiths, such as Kimbanguism. The majority of Congolese are rural farmers.

Economy and the Land

D.R.C. is rich in mineral resources, particularly copper, cobalt, diamonds, and petroleum; mining has supplanted agriculture in economic importance and now dominates the economy. Agriculture continues to employ most Congolese, however, and subsistence farming is practiced in nearly every region. Industrial activity—especially petroleum refining and hydroelectric production—was once a growing part of the economy, but suffered during the recent civil war. D.R.C.'s terrain is composed of mountains and plateaus. The climate is equatorial, with hot and humid weather in the north and west, and cooler and drier conditions in the south and east.

History and Politics

The earliest inhabitants of the modern D.R.C. were probably Pygmies who settled in the area thousands of years ago. By the A.D. 700s, sophisticated civilizations had developed in what is now southeastern D.R.C. In the early 1500s, the Portuguese began the forced emigration of black Africans for slavery. Other Europeans came to the area as the slave trade grew, but the interior remained relatively unexplored until the 1870s. Belgian King Leopold II realized the potential value of the region, and in 1885 his claim was recognized. Belgium took control from Leopold in 1908, renaming the colony the Belgian Congo. Nationalist sentiment grew until rioting broke out in 1959. The country, which was then called the Congo, gained independence in 1960, and a weak government assumed control. Violent civil disorder, provincial secession, and a political assassination characterized the next five years. The country stabilized under the rule of President Mobutu Sese Seko, a former army general, who changed its name to Zaire. Later, a rebel movement arose in response to government corruption and human rights abuses. In 1997 Laurent Kabila, a rebel leader, took control, assumed the presidency, and changed the name of the country to the Democratic Republic of the Congo. Despite his earlier promises to install a democratic government, Kabila has proven to be a dictator.

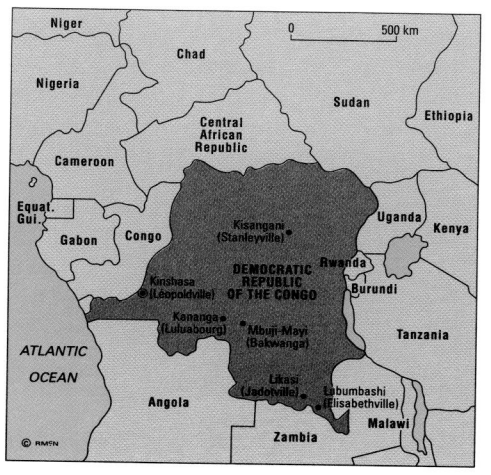

Lbinza tribespeople with grubs they have gathered for food

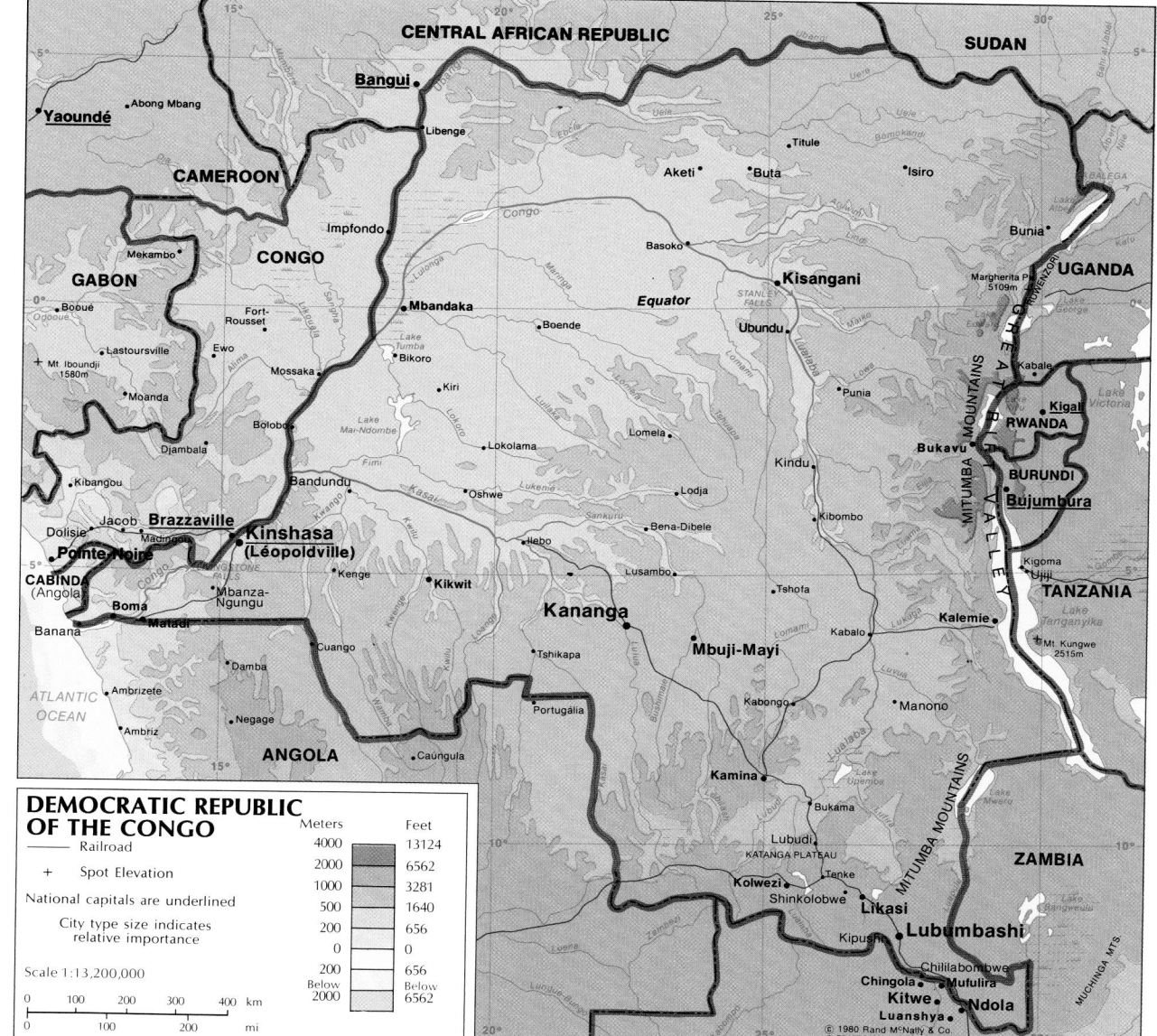

DEMOCRATIC REPUBLIC OF THE CONGO

—— Railroad

+ Spot Elevation

National capitals are underlined

City type size indicates relative importance

Scale 1:13,200,000

Meters	Feet
4000	13124
2000	6562
1000	3281
500	1640
200	656
0	0
200 Below 2000	656 Below 6562

0   100   200   300   400 km
0   100   200 mi

© 1980 Rand McNally & Co.
A-581200-772 .-1--2

Democratic Republic of the Congo at a glance

(These figures are from latest available data, prior to the 1997 civil war.)

Official name	Democratic Republic of the Congo

People

Population	43,365,000
Density	48/mi² (18/km²)
Urban	28%
Capital	Kinshasa, 3,000,000
Ethnic groups	Kongo, Luba, Mongo, Mangbetu-Azande, others
Languages	French, Kikongo, Lingala, Swahili, Tshiluba, Kingwana
Religions	Roman Catholic 50%, Protestant 20%, Kimbanguist 10%, Muslim 10%
Life expectancy	53 female, 50 male
Literacy	72%

Politics

Government	Military
Parties	Popular Movement of the Revolution, others
Suffrage	Universal, over 18
Memberships	OAS, UN
Subdivisions	10 regions, 1 independent town

Economy

GDP	$21,000,000,000
Per capita	$528
Monetary unit	Zaire
Trade partners	Exports: U.S., Belgium, Germany Imports: Belgium, Brazil, France
Exports	Copper, coffee, diamonds, cobalt, petroleum
Imports	Manufactures, food, machinery, transportation equipment, fuel

Land

Description	Central Africa
Area	905,355 mi² (2,344,858 km²)
Highest point	Margherita Pk., 16,763 ft (5,109 m)
Lowest point	Sea level

The vast basin of the Congo River covers much of the Democratic Republic of the Congo. In fact, the country took its former name from the Congo: "Zaire" derives from an African word meaning "river."

47

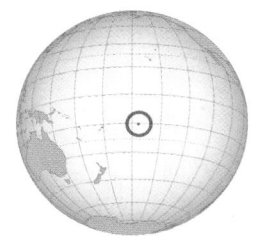

A t the heart of Polynesia, the Cook Islands are striving to make a place for themselves in the modern world. Their relative isolation has made economic development difficult and has kept their natural beauty from being discovered by many tourists. Although internally self-governing, the islands are heavily dependent on aid from New Zealand.

COOK ISLANDS

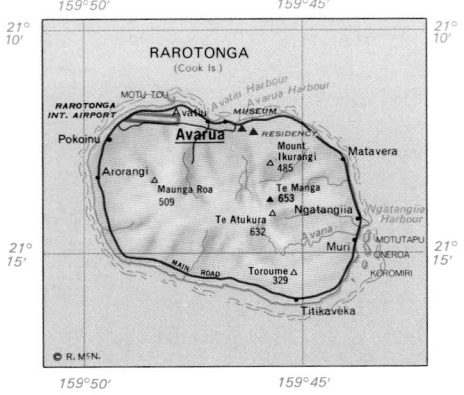

Scale 1:300,000   One inch represents approximately 4.7 miles. One centimeter represents 3 kilometers.

The Cook Islands were one of many places settled by the Polynesians as they explored the South Pacific, from South America to Australia, many thousands of years ago.

People
Scattered over a very wide area, the Cook Islands have one of the most dispersed populations in the Pacific. Of the fifteen islands, Rarotonga is the largest and most populated. Many of the islands' Polynesians are of Maori ancestry.

Economy and the Land
The economy is agricultural. In the north are coral islands; in the south, volcanic islands. The climate is warm, with occasional hurricanes.

History and Politics
Captain James Cook arrived in the area in 1773. In 1888 the islands came under British protection, and in 1901 they were annexed to New Zealand. The islands can unilaterally declare independence from New Zealand at any time.

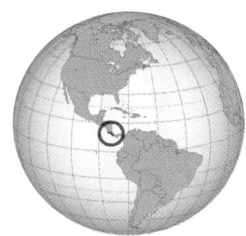

North of Limón, Costa Rica's Caribbean coast is sparsely populated swampland. The southern coast is dominated by banana plantations.

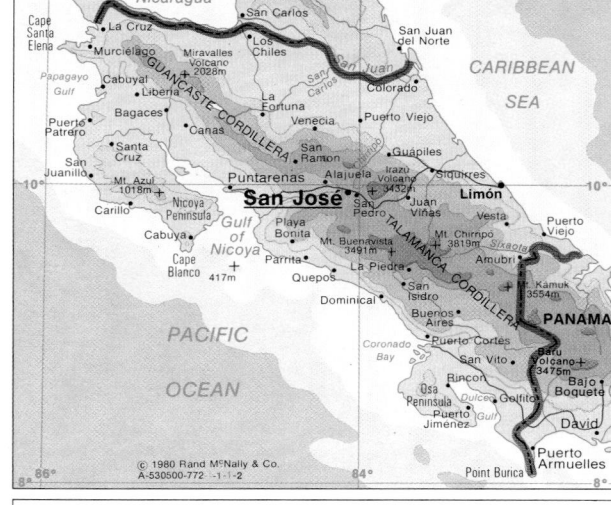

COSTA RICA

People
Compared with most other Central American countries, Costa Rica has a relatively large population of European descent, mostly Spanish with minorities of German, Dutch, and Swiss ancestry. Together with mestizos, people of Spanish-Indian heritage, they compose the bulk of the population. Descendants of black Jamaican immigrants inhabit mainly the Caribbean coastal region. Indigenous Indians in scattered enclaves continue traditional lifestyles; some, however, have been assimilated into the country's majority culture.

Economy and the Land
Costa Rica's economy, one of the most prosperous in Central America, has not been without problems, some resulting from falling coffee prices and rising oil costs. Agriculture remains important, producing traditional coffee and banana crops, while the country attempts to expand industry. Population and agriculture are concentrated in the central highlands. Much of the country is forested, and the mountainous central area is bordered by coastal plains on the east and west. The climate is semitropical to tropical.

History and Politics
In 1502 Christopher Columbus arrived and claimed the area for Spain. Spaniards named the region Rich Coast, and settlers soon flocked to the new land to seek their fortune. Rather than riches, they found an Indian population unwilling to surrender its land. But many Spaniards remained, establishing farms in the central area. In 1821 the Central American provinces of Costa Rica, Guatemala, El Salvador, Honduras, and Nicaragua declared themselves independent from Spain, and by 1823 they had formed the Federation of Central America. Despite efforts to sustain it, the federation was in a state of virtual collapse by 1838, and Costa Rica became an independent republic. Since the first free elections in 1889, Costa Rica has experienced a presidential overthrow in 1919 and a civil war in 1948, which arose over a disputed election. In the 1980s the country worked to promote peaceful solutions to armed conflicts in the region. It is Central America's oldest and most stable democracy.

COSTA RICA

	Meters	Feet
Railroad		
Spot Elevation or Depth		
	4000	13124
	2000	6562
	1000	3281
	500	1640
	200	656
	0	0

Meters	Feet
0	0
200	656
Below 2000	Below 6562

Scale 1:5,460,000

A chief is surrounded by members of his tribe near the coastal city of Grand-Bassam. More than sixty different tribes live in Cote d'Ivoire.

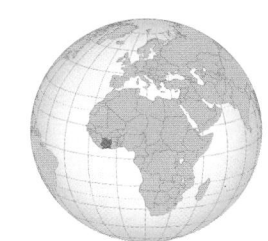

COTE D'IVOIRE

People

Cote d'Ivoire is composed almost entirely of black Africans from more than sixty ethnic groups. French is the nation's official language, a result of former French rule, but many indigenous languages are spoken as well. Indigenous religions predominate, though a significant number of Ivorians are Muslim or Christian. Most Ivorians live in huts in small villages, but increased numbers have moved to the cities to find work. Overcrowding is a major problem in the cities.

Economy and the Land

Once solely dependent upon the export of cocoa and coffee, Cote d'Ivoire now produces and exports a variety of agricultural goods. Forest land, when cleared, provides rich soil for agriculture—still the country's main activity. Petroleum, textile, and apparel industries also contribute to the strong economy. Cote d'Ivoire pursues a policy of economic liberalism in which foreign investment is encouraged. As a result, foreigners hold high-level positions in most Cote d'Ivoire industries. The hot, humid coastal region gives way to inland tropical forest. Beyond the forest lies savanna, and to the northwest are highlands.

History and Politics

Cote d'Ivoire once consisted of many African kingdoms. French sailors gave the region its present name when they began

Cote d'Ivoire's recent history can be found in its name, which is French for "ivory coast." The country was a center of the lucrative trade in elephant tusks through most of this century. Today, it profits not from ivory but from exporting coffee and cocoa. Cote d'Ivoire is the most prosperous country in tropical Africa.

trading for ivory and other goods in 1483. Missionaries arrived in 1637, but European settlement was hindered by the rugged coastline and intertribal conflicts. Cote d'Ivoire became a French colony in 1893. Movements toward autonomy began after World War II, and in 1960 Cote d'Ivoire declared itself an independent republic. The nation has enjoyed political stability since independence and has maintained close economic ties with France. The nation enjoyed many years of political stability under the rule of President Houphouet-Boigny. However, protests against the government and against one-party rule led to Cote d'Ivoire's first multi-party election in 1990. The ruling party won an overwhelming victory, leading to charges of fraud by the opposition. Houphouet-Boigny's death in 1993 was followed by a smooth transition of power.

Cote d'Ivoire at a glance

Official name	Republic of Cote d'Ivoire

People

Population	14,540,000
Density	117/mi² (45/km²)
Urban	40%
Capital	Abidjan (de facto), 1,929,079; Yamoussoukro (future), 106,786
Ethnic groups	Baule 23%, Bete 18%, Senoufou 15%, Malinke 11%, other African
Languages	French, Dioula and other indigenous
Religions	Animist 63%, Muslim 25%, Christian 12%
Life expectancy	53 female, 50 male
Literacy	54%

Politics

Government	Republic
Parties	Democratic, Popular Front
Suffrage	Universal, over 21
Memberships	OAU, UN
Subdivisions	49 departments

Economy

GDP	$21,000,000,000
Per capita	$1,526
Monetary unit	CFA franc
Trade partners	Exports: Netherlands, France, U.S. Imports: France, Nigeria
Exports	Cocoa, coffee, wood, cotton, bananas, pineapples, palm oil
Imports	Manufactures, raw materials and fuel

Land

Description	Western Africa
Area	124,518 mi² (322,500 km²)
Highest point	Mont Nimba, 5,748 ft (1,752 m)
Lowest point	Sea level

Camel and villagers, northern Cote d'Ivoire

Away from the coastal swamps and mangroves, Cote d'Ivoire has one of the densest tropical forests in Africa. The forest covers one-third of the country.

COTE D'IVOIRE

Railroad
+ Spot Elevation
Scale 1:9,267,000

Meters	Feet
2000	6562
1000	3281
500	1640
200	656
0	0

Meters	Feet
0	0
200	656
Below 2000	Below 6562

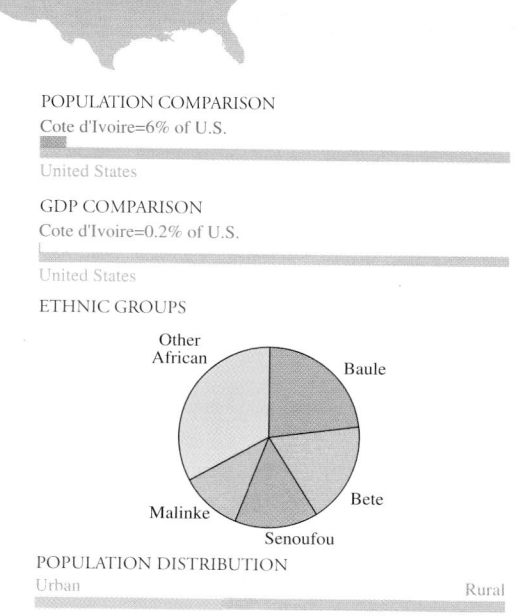

POPULATION COMPARISON
Cote d'Ivoire=6% of U.S.

United States

GDP COMPARISON
Cote d'Ivoire=0.2% of U.S.

United States

ETHNIC GROUPS

Other African / Baule / Bete / Senoufou / Malinke

POPULATION DISTRIBUTION
Urban   Rural

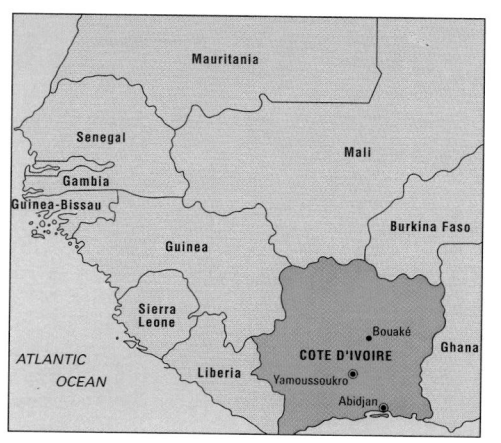

CROATIA

When Croatia declared independence from Yugoslavia in 1991, it sparked the bloodshed which continues to plague the region. The Adriatic coast, home to some of Europe's most popular tourist destinations, such as Dubrovnik, has been reduced to shambles by the fighting. Various efforts to mediate peace have failed.

The beautifully preserved town of Dubrovnik was the jewel of Croatia's Dalmatian Coast before it was heavily damaged by shelling during the recent strife in the former Yugoslavia. Efforts are being made to repair the damage to the Renaissance-era Old Town, but peace will have to return before Dubrovnik can again cast its spell on visitors.

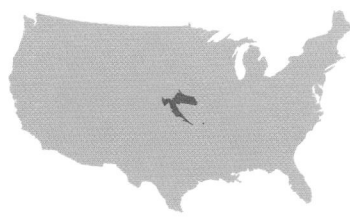

People

Despite a common heritage with the Serbian people of Yugoslavia, the Croats have their own distinct culture and traditions. The basis of the continuing friction between the Croats and Serbs is religious in origin: the Croats are Roman Catholic, while the Serbs are mainly Orthodox. The religious difference resulted in a more Western European cultural orientation for the Croats and an eastern affiliation for the Serbs. Most of Croatia's Serbian minority lives in northwestern Croatia.

Economy and the Land

Croatia is a land of extremely varied terrain, and includes the historic regions of Croatia, Dalmatia, Slavonia, and part of Istria. Croatia's fertile plains produce ample supplies of grains. Grapes, olives, and citrus fruits are grown along the mountainous coast. Croatia has a well-developed industrial sector, and leading industries include

Roman amphitheater, Pula

petrochemicals, food processing, and shipbuilding. The Adriatic coast attracts tourists from all over the world.

History and Politics

Slavic people settled in Croatia in the seventh century and established their own independent state. The original tribal organization of the people was eventually replaced by a feudal one. In 1102 the country chose to merge with Hungary. Turkey invaded Croatia in 1463, but in 1699, Croatia was reclaimed by the Austro-Hungarian Hapsburg Empire. Tiring of foreign rule, the Croats began to agitate for independence in the mid-1800s, but Croatia nevertheless joined the Serbs and Slovenes in the new state of Yugoslavia in 1918. In 1941 Germany invaded Yugoslavia, and Croatia was set up as an independent state. Allied with the Nazis, this government was responsible for the deaths of thousands of Serbs and Jews. The end of World War II marked the end of

Croatian independence and, in 1946, Croatia became a state of the new Yugoslavia, united under the dictator Tito. Enmity between the Croats and Serbs continued to simmer in the postwar period, and terrorism was common. Tito's death in 1980 plunged the country into a political and economic crisis, and Croats began to demand greater autonomy. Croatia claimed home rule in February 1991, and fighting between the Croats and the Yugoslavian army began shortly thereafter. Along with neighboring Slovenia, Croatia declared its independence on June 25, 1991. The war between Croatia and Serbian Yugoslavia continued to escalate throughout 1991. More than ten thousand people were killed by the time a cease-fire was reached in early 1992, when a United Nations peacekeeping force was sent in. Ethnic Serbs in western Croatia have declared the independence of their homeland, Krajina, and tensions remain high.

Croatia at a glance

Official name	Republic of Croatia

People

Population	4,801,000
Density	220/mi² (85/km²)
Urban	51%
Capital	Zagreb, 697,925
Ethnic groups	Croat 78%, Serb 12%, Muslim 1%
Languages	Serbo-Croatian
Religions	Roman Catholic 77%, Orthodox 11%, Muslim 1%
Life expectancy	77 female, 70 male
Literacy	97%

Politics

Government	Republic
Parties	Democratic Change, Democratic Union, Peasant, Social Democratic, Social Liberal, others
Suffrage	Universal, over 18; over 16 if employed
Memberships	UN
Subdivisions	21 counties

Economy

GDP	$21,800,000,000
Per capita	$4,542
Monetary unit	Kuna
Trade partners	Former Yugoslav republics
Exports	Machinery and transportation equipment, manufactures, food, raw materials
Imports	Machinery and transportation equipment, fuel and lubricants, food, chemicals

Land

Description	Eastern Europe
Area	21,829 mi² (56,538 km²)
Highest point	Troglav, 6,276 ft (1,913 m)
Lowest point	Sea level

CROATIA

Meters	Feet	
4000	13124	
2000	6562	
1000	3281	
500	1640	
200	656	
0	0	
200	656	
2000	6562	

- Major Urban Area
- Railroad
- Canal or Waterway
- + Spot Elevation
- City type size indicates relative importance

Scale 1:4,000,000

Croatia's tradition of growing olives and grapes is made possible by the Mediterranean climate along the coast. Inland, around Zagreb, the weather is seasonal, with hot summers and cold winters.

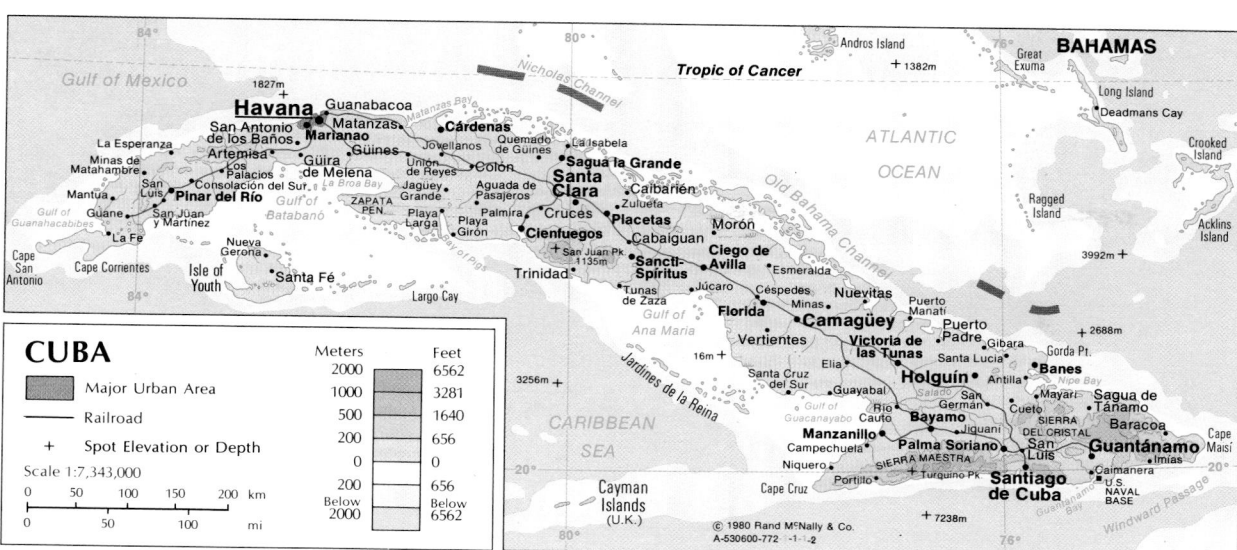

CUBA

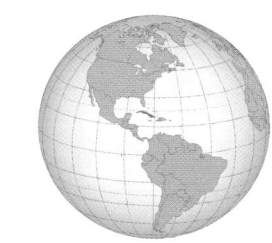

Cuba is the largest island of the West Indies. It is one of four islands—with Jamaica, Hispaniola, and Puerto Rico—that make up the Greater Antilles archipelago.

CUBA

	Meters	Feet
Major Urban Area	2000	6562
Railroad	1000	3281
Spot Elevation or Depth	500	1640
	200	656
Scale 1:7,343,000	0	0
	200 Below 2000	656 Below 6562

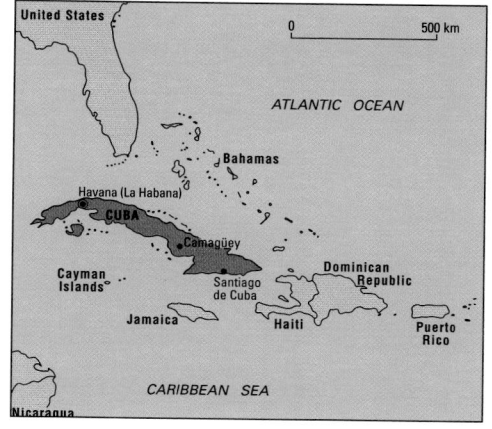

A lmost 35 years of communist rule and economic isolation by the United States have kept Cuba undeveloped. Havana is little changed since the 1950s, while sugarcane remains the lifeblood of the countryside. The close proximity of Florida to Cuba has proved to be an irresistible lure for thousands of Cubans who have made the 90-mile journey in all manner of rafts and boats.

People
Most Cubans are descendants of Spanish colonists, African slaves, or a blend of the two. The government provides free education and health care. Although religious practices are discouraged, most people belong to the Roman Catholic church. Personal income, health, education, and housing have improved since the 1959 revolution, but most food products and consumer goods remain in short supply.

Economy and the Land
Cuba's economy is largely dependent on sugar, although other forms of agriculture are also important. The most fertile soils lie in the central region between mountain ranges, while mineral deposits, including oil and nickel, are found in the northeast. In addition to agriculture and mining, industry is an economic contributor. Most economic activity is nationalized, and has, until recently, been dependent on aid from the former Soviet Union. Mountains, plains, and a scenic coastline make Cuba one of the most beautiful islands in the West Indies. The climate is tropical.

History and Politics
Christopher Columbus claimed Cuba for Spain in 1492, and Spanish settlement began in 1511. When the native Indian population died out, African slaves were brought to work plantations. The United States joined with Cuba against Spain in the Spanish-American War in 1898. Cuba gained full independence in 1902. Unrest continued, however, and the United States again intervened from 1906 to 1909 and in 1917. A 1933 coup ousted a nine-year dictatorship, and a subsequent government overthrow in 1934 ushered in an era dominated by Sergeant Fulgencio Batista. After ruling through other presidents and serving an elected term himself, Batista seized power in a 1952 coup that established an unpopular and oppressive regime. Led by lawyer Fidel Castro, a revolutionary group opposed to Batista gained quick support, and Batista fled the country on January 1, 1959, leaving the government to Castro. Early United States support of Castro soured when nationalization of American businesses began. American aid soon ceased, and Cuba looked to the Soviet Union for assistance. The United States ended diplomatic relations with Cuba in 1961. In 1962 the United States and the Soviet Union became embroiled in a dispute over Soviet missile bases in Cuba that ended with removal of the missiles. Fidel Castro remains in power despite a weakened economy following the withdrawal of Soviet support. Political and economic sanctions, as well as massive illegal emigration, continue to sour relations with the U.S.

Beach, Matanzas Bay

Old buildings, Havana

Cuba at a glance

Official name Republic of Cuba

People
Population	11,015,000
Density	257/mi² (99/km²)
Urban	74%
Capital	Havana, 2,119,059
Ethnic groups	Mulatto 51%, white 37%, black 11%, Chinese 1%
Languages	Spanish
Religions	Roman Catholic, Pentecostal, Baptist
Life expectancy	78 female, 74 male
Literacy	94%

Politics
Government	Socialist republic
Parties	Communist
Suffrage	Universal, over 16
Memberships	UN
Subdivisions	13 provinces, 1 city, 1 municipality

Economy
GDP	$14,900,000,000
Per capita	$1,382
Monetary unit	Peso
Trade partners	Former Soviet republics, Germany
Exports	Sugar, nickel, medical supplies, shellfish, fruit, tobacco, coffee
Imports	Petroleum, machinery, raw materials, food

Land
Description	Caribbean island
Area	42,804 mi² (110,861 km²)
Highest point	Turquino Peak, 6,470 ft (1,972 m)
Lowest point	Sea level

Havana surrounds a small bay on the north coast of Cuba. Castillo del Morro on the eastern point was one of a series of fortifications built by the Spaniards in the 17th century for protection from pirates.

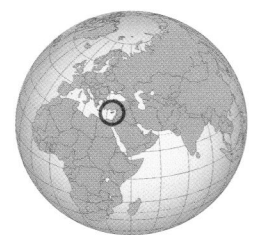

Having endured countless invasions during its long history, Cyprus turned on itself after World War II. The island's Greek and Turkish communities became increasingly hostile until a 1974 Greek-led coup precipitated an invasion by Turkey. Today the island is divided, and an uneasy peace is enforced by United Nations troops.

CYPRUS

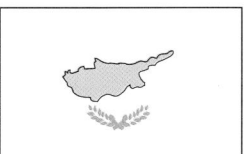

People
Most Cypriots occupying the southern two thirds of the island are of Greek ancestry, and their religion, language, and general culture reflect this heritage. Family and religion are a dominant influence in the community. Decades of British rule had little impact.

Economy and the Land
Conflict between the Greek and Turkish Cypriots has severely disrupted the economy of the island. With foreign assistance, Greek Cypriots have made considerable progress, expanding traditional southern agriculture to light manufacturing and tourism. Known for its scenic beauty and tourist appeal, southern Cyprus is marked by a fertile southern plain bordered by the rugged Troodos Mountains to the southwest. Sandy beaches dot the coastline. The Mediterranean climate brings hot, dry summers and damp, cool winters.

History and Politics
History of Cyprus and North Cyprus follows NORTH CYPRUS.

Cyprus at a glance
Official name	Republic of Cyprus

People
Population	551,000
Density	242/mi² (93/km²)
Urban	53%
Capital	Nicosia (Levkosía), 48,221
Ethnic groups	Greek
Languages	Greek, English
Religions	Greek Orthodox
Life expectancy	79 female, 75 male
Literacy	94%

Politics
Government	Republic
Parties	Democratic, Democratic Rally, Progressive Party of the Working People
Suffrage	Universal, over 18
Memberships	CW, UN
Subdivisions	6 districts

Economy
GDP	$6,700,000,000
Per capita	$9,397
Monetary unit	Pound
Trade partners	Exports: U.K., Greece, Lebanon Imports: U.K., Japan, Italy
Exports	Fruit, potatoes, grapes, wine, cement, clothing and shoes
Imports	Manufactures, petroleum, food, machinery

Land
Description	Southern part of the island of Cyprus
Area	2,276 mi² (5,896 km²)
Highest point	Ólimbos, 6,401 ft (1,951 m)
Lowest point	Sea level

Grapes ripen on vines growing in the Troodos Mountains, which dominate the center of Cyprus.

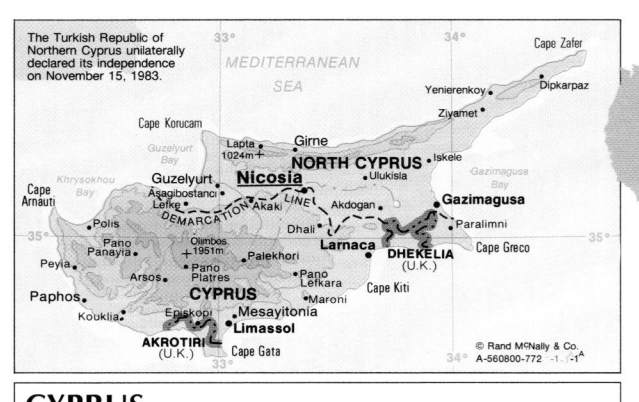

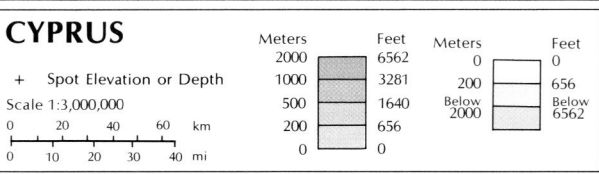

Cyprus suffers from frequent droughts because most of the sources of fresh water lie in the Turkish-controlled area. The fertile central plain is almost evenly divided between the two sides. It supports olive plantations which date back to ancient times.

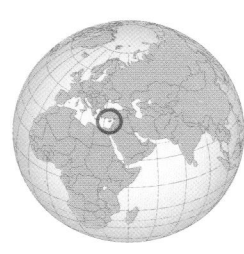

Since the island became divided in 1974, 200,000 ethnic Greeks have been expelled from Turkish-controlled North Cyprus. Thousands of Turkish immigrants have poured into the country. At present, North Cyprus is not internationally recognized.

NORTH CYPRUS

People
The northern part of the island is occupied by Cypriots of Turkish ancestry who speak Turkish and are Sunni Muslims. The 1974 Turkish invasion resulted in a formal segregation of this settlement pattern. The Turkish Cypriot ancestors arrived on the island during the three centuries of Ottoman rule.

Economy and the Land
Since the partition of the island, North Cyprus has become somewhat isolated. Lacking in capital, foreign aid, and official recognition, it remains agriculturally based and dependent upon Turkey for tourism, trade, and assistance. The mostly barren Kyrenia Range dominates North Cyprus.

History and Politics
In the Late Bronze Age—from 1600 to 1050 B.C.—a Greek culture flourished in Cyprus. Rule by various peoples followed, including Assyrians, Egyptians, Persians, Romans, Byzantines, French, and Venetians. The Ottoman Turks invaded in 1571. In the nineteenth century, Turkey ceded the island to the British as security for a loan. Although many Turks remained on Cyprus, the British declared it a crown colony in 1925. A growing desire for *enosis,* or union, with Greece led to rioting and guerrilla activity by Greek Cypriots. The Turkish government, opposed to absorption by Greece, desired separation into Greek and Turkish sectors. Cyprus became independent in 1960, with treaties forbidding either enosis or partition, but Greek-Turkish conflicts continued. A 1974 coup by pro-enosis forces led to an invasion by Turkey. The resulting partition runs east-west across the island dividing Nicosia, which serves as a capital for both countries. North Cyprus, which is not recognized internationally, maintains a separate government with a prime minister and a president. The United Nations, in an attempt to force a resolution of the continuing conflict, is threatening withdrawal of its peacekeeping forces.

North Cyprus at a glance
Official name	Turkish Republic of Northern Cyprus

People
Population	182,000
Density	141/mi² (54/km²)
Capital	Nicosia (Lefko̧sa), 37,400
Ethnic groups	Turkish 99%, Greek, Maronite, and others 1%
Languages	Turkish
Religions	Sunni Muslim

Politics
Government	Republic
Parties	Democratic Struggle, National Unity
Memberships	None
Subdivisions	3 districts

Economy
GDP	$550,000,000
Per capita	$2,865
Monetary unit	Turkish lira
Trade partners	Turkey, U.K., Germany
Exports	Food and livestock, manufactures, crude materials
Imports	Manufactures, machinery and transportation equipment, mineral fuels

Land
Description	Northern part of the island of Cyprus
Area	1,295 mi² (3,355 km²)
Highest point	Unnamed, 3,360 ft (1,024 m)
Lowest point	Sea level

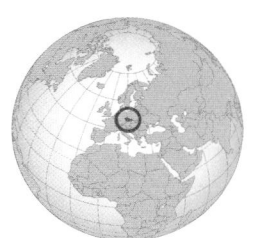

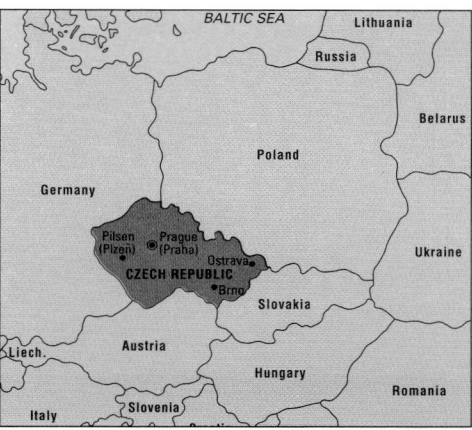

The Moravská Sázava River flows through gently rolling countryside dotted with farms.

Czech Republic at a glance

Official name   Czech Republic

People

Population	10,430,000
Density	343/mi² (132/km²)
Capital	Prague, 1,212,010
Ethnic groups	Czech 94%, Slovak 3%
Languages	Czech, Slovak
Religions	Roman Catholic 39%, Protestant 5%, Orthodox 3%
Life expectancy	77 female, 69 male

Politics

Government	Republic
Parties	Civic Democratic, Left Bloc, Liberal National Socialist, Liberal Social Union, Social Democracy, others
Suffrage	Universal, over 18
Memberships	UN
Subdivisions	8 regions

Economy

GDP	$75,000,000,000
Per capita	$7,257
Monetary unit	Koruna
Trade partners	Exports: Slovakia, Germany, Poland Imports: Slovakia, former Soviet republics, Germany
Exports	Manufactures, machinery and transportation equipment, chemicals, fuels, minerals
Imports	Machinery and transportation equipment, fuel, manufactures, raw materials

Land

Description	Eastern Europe, landlocked
Area	30,450 mi² (78,864 km²)
Highest point	Sněžka, 5,256 ft (1,602 m)
Lowest point	Along Elbe River, 377 ft (115 m)

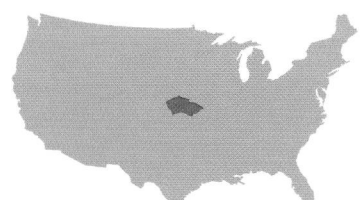

Prague's beautiful Old Town has been untouched by war since the Middle Ages. With the fall of communism, the city has begun to reclaim its role as a center of culture in Central Europe.

CZECH REPUBLIC

Freed in 1989 from domination by the Soviet Union, Czechoslovakia knew only four years as a democratic republic until it peacefully split in what became known as "the velvet divorce." Ironically, the Czech Republic, which resisted the split, has prospered, while Slovakia, the enthusiastic instigator, has languished. Its economy booming, the Czech Republic will likely be highly integrated with Western Europe by the end of the century.

People

Although the Czechs are Slavic in origin, their culture has been profoundly influenced by the Germans as a result of centuries of Austrian rule. By eastern European standards, the people are well educated and highly skilled. The language is Czech, and the predominate religion is Roman Catholic. There is a small Slovak minority.

Economy and the Land

An industrial nation, the Czech Republic has moved aggressively since 1991 to establish a free market economy. Unlike other eastern European nations, the Czech Republic has managed to keep unemployment and government spending in check during the transition from communism to capitalism. Coal deposits have traditionally formed the base for the development of glass, chemical, and machine industries.

POPULATION COMPARISON
Czech Republic=4% of U.S.

United States

GDP COMPARISON
Czech Republic=1% of U.S.

United States

ETHNIC GROUPS

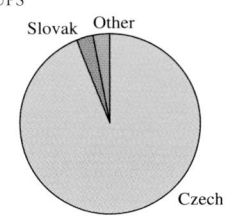

Slovak   Other

Czech

Most of the land is low hills and plateaus bounded on three sides by mountain ranges. The climate is temperate.

History and Politics

Slavic tribes were established in the region by the fifth century, and the area fell under the rule of the Roman Empire. An important Moravian state rose in the ninth century, followed by the advent of a strong Bohemian kingdom that reached its zenith in the thirteenth century. Austria gained control of the area in the 1500s, and sovereignty later passed to Austria-Hungary. With the collapse of Austria-Hungary at the end of World War I, an independent Czechoslovakia, consisting of Bohemia, Moravia, Silesia, and Slovakia, was formed. Nazi Germany invaded Czechoslovakia in 1939, and the Soviet Union liberated the nation from German occupation during 1944 and 1945. By 1948 Communists controlled the government, and political purges continued from 1949 to 1952. A 1968 invasion by the Soviet Union, Bulgaria, Hungary, Poland, and East Germany resulted when the Czechoslovakian Communist party leader introduced liberal reforms. Demonstrations forced the Communist party to relinquish its hold on power in 1989. Growing economic differences between the rural east and the industrialized west led to the breakup of Czechoslovakia into the Czech Republic and Slovakia in 1993.

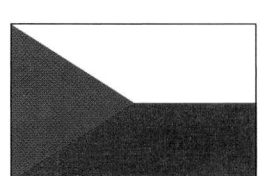

(top) Church outside of Olomouc

(bottom) Rural home

Unlike the rest of Central Europe, Prague has survived centuries of war untouched. It is one of Europe's centers of historic architecture and culture.

CZECH REPUBLIC

		Meters	Feet
▨	Major Urban Area	4000	13124
—	Railroad	2000	6562
┄	Canal	1000	3281
		500	1640
Capitals are underlined		200	656
		0	0

0   20   40   60   80   100 km

0   20   40   60   mi

Scale 1:4,938,000

©Rand McNally & Co.
A-550500-772

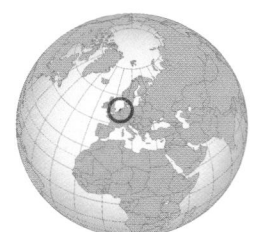

For centuries people have been drawn to Nyhavn Canal in Copenhagen. In the early 1800s, Hans Christian Andersen wrote his first fairy tale in one of the colorful houses lining the docks.

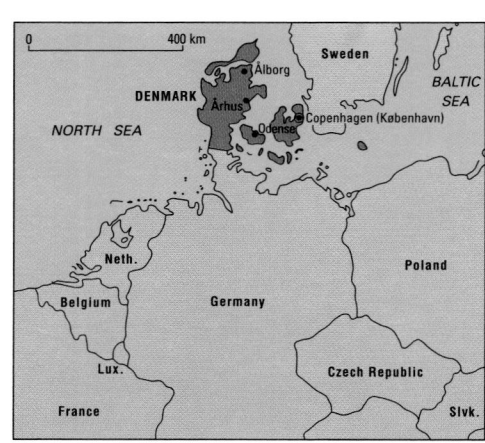

DENMARK

Once the home of Vikings and their marauding hordes, Denmark is today a prosperous nation of towns and farms known for their tidy order. The Danes share the modern Scandinavian predilection for the welfare state that provides for most needs from cradle to grave. Such beneficence extends to others as well: the Danes devote a high percentage of their gross national product to Third World aid programs.

Tivoli Gardens, Copenhagen

People
Denmark is made up of the Jutland Peninsula and more than four hundred islands, about one hundred of which are inhabited. Greenland, which is situated northeast of Canada, and the Faeroe Islands, which are located between Scotland and Iceland in the North Atlantic, are also part of Denmark. Lutheran, Danish-speaking Scandinavians constitute the homogenous population of the peninsula and surrounding islands, although a German minority is concentrated near the German border.

Economy and the Land
Despite limited natural resources, Denmark has a diversified economy. Agriculture contributes to trade, and pork and bacon are important products. Postwar expansion

focused on industry, and the country now imports the raw materials it lacks and exports finished products. The North Sea is the site of oil and natural gas deposits. On the Faeroe Islands, traditional fishing continues as the economic mainstay. Most of Denmark's terrain is rolling, with hills covering much of the peninsula and the nearby islands. Coastal regions are marked by fjords and sandy beaches, especially in the west. The climate is temperate, with North Sea winds moderating temperatures. The rugged Faeroe Islands are damp, cloudy, and windy.

History and Politics
By the first century, access to the sea had brought contact with other civilizations. This led to the Viking era, which lasted from the ninth to eleventh centuries and

resulted in temporary Danish rule of England. In the fourteenth century, Sweden, Norway, Finland, Iceland, the Faeroe Islands, and Greenland were united under Danish rule. Sweden and Finland withdrew from the union in the 1500s, and Denmark lost Norway to Sweden in 1814. A constitutional monarchy was instituted in 1849. Late nineteenth-century social reform, reflected in a new constitution in 1915, laid the groundwork for Denmark's current welfare state. The country remained neutral in World War I. Iceland gained independence following the war but maintained its union with Denmark until 1944. Despite declared neutrality in World War II, Denmark was invaded and occupied by Germany from 1940 to 1945.

Denmark at a glance

Official name	Kingdom of Denmark

People

Population	5,207,000
Density	313/mi² (121/km²)
Urban	85%
Capital	Copenhagen, 464,566
Ethnic groups	Danish (Scandinavian), German
Languages	Danish
Religions	Lutheran 91%
Life expectancy	79 female, 73 male
Literacy	99%

Politics

Government	Constitutional monarchy
Parties	Conservative, Liberal, Social Democratic, Socialist People's, others
Suffrage	Universal, over 18
Memberships	EU, NATO, OECD, UN
Subdivisions	14 counties, 2 cities

Economy

GDP	$95,600,000,000
Per capita	$18,495
Monetary unit	Krone
Trade partners	Germany, Sweden, U.K.
Exports	Meat, dairy products, ships, fish, chemicals, machinery
Imports	Petroleum, machinery, chemicals, food, textiles, paper

Land

Description	Northern Europe
Area	16,639 mi² (43,094 km²)
Highest point	Yding Skovhoj, 568 ft (173 m)
Lowest point	Lammefjord, -23 ft (-7 m)

The above information excludes Greenland and the Faeroe Islands

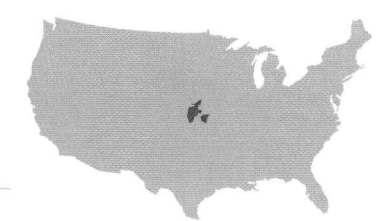

The main peninsula of Denmark, Jutland, literally juts up from Europe to divide the North and Baltic Seas. The rest of the country consists of 485 islands, many linked only by ferries.

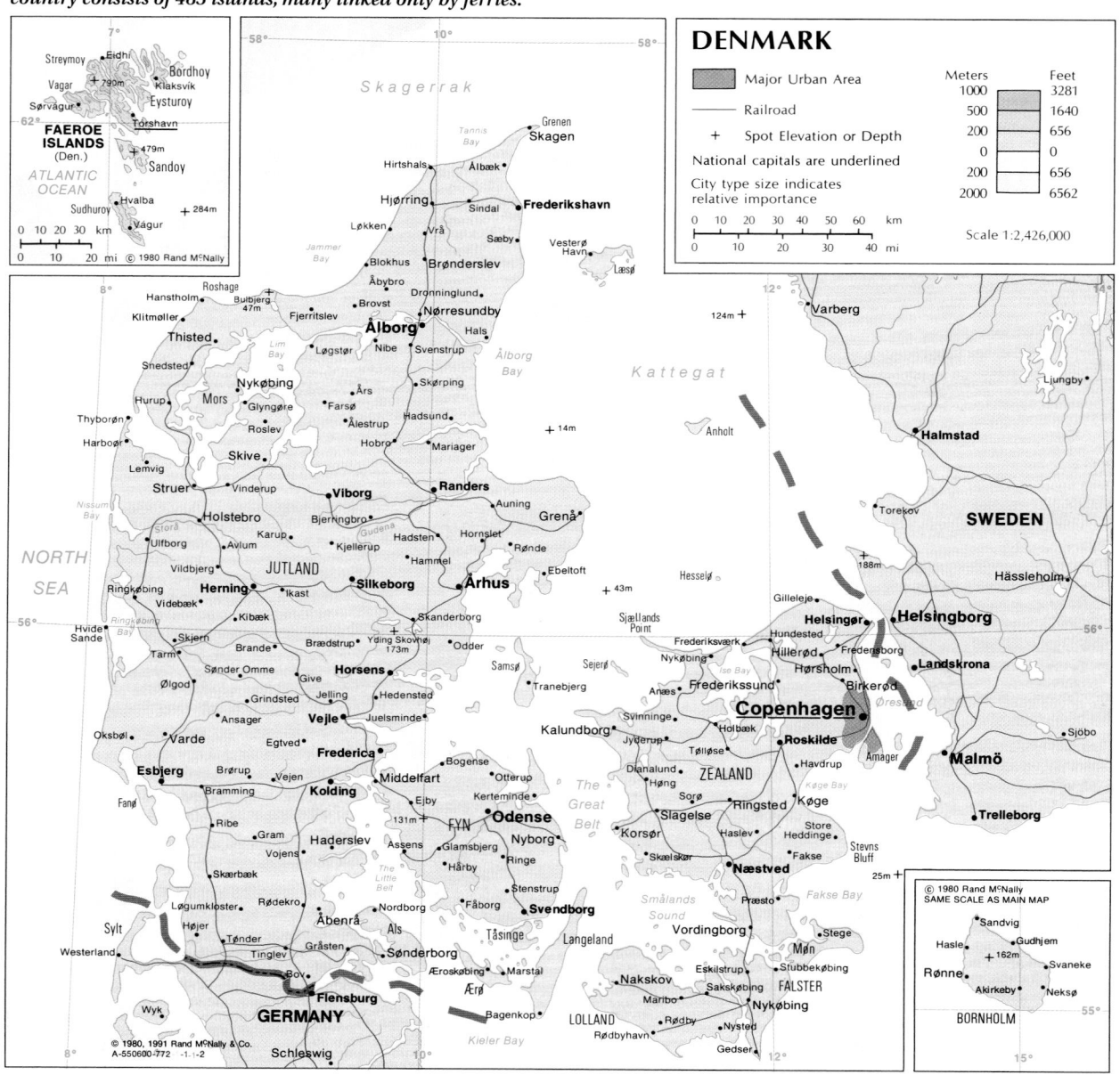

DENMARK

Major Urban Area
Railroad
Spot Elevation or Depth
National capitals are underlined
City type size indicates relative importance

Scale 1:2,426,000

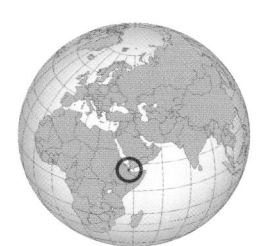

Djibouti has little in the way of resources beyond its deep-water port in the capital of Djibouti City. As such, it is the main shipping center for the entire region, including Ethiopia. Revenues from commerce do not supply sufficient funds to feed the people, and as a consequence, Djibouti relies heavily on foreign aid from France and the United States, which are mindful of the country's strategic location.

DJIBOUTI

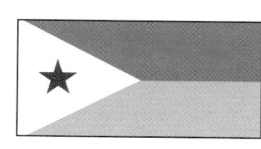

Djibouti at a glance

Official name	Republic of Djibouti

People

Population	557,000
Density	62/mi² (24/km²)
Urban	81%
Capital	Djibouti, 329,337
Ethnic groups	Somali 60%, Afar 35%
Languages	French, Arabic, Somali, Afar
Religions	Muslim 94%, Christian 6%
Life expectancy	51 female, 47 male
Literacy	48%

Politics

Government	Republic
Parties	Democratic Renewal, National Democratic, People's Progress Assembly, others
Suffrage	Universal adult
Memberships	AL, OAU, UN
Subdivisions	5 districts

Economy

GDP	$500,000,000
Per capita	$1,263
Monetary unit	Franc
Trade partners	Exports: France, Yemen, Somalia Imports: France, Ethiopia, Italy
Exports	Hides and skins, coffee
Imports	Food, beverages, transportation equipment, chemicals, petroleum

Land

Description	Eastern Africa
Area	8,958 mi² (23,200 km²)
Highest point	Moussa 'Ali, 6,631 ft (2,021 m)
Lowest point	Lake Assal, -515 ft (-157 m)

People
Characterized by strong cultural unity, Islam, and ethnic ties to Somalia, Somali Issas compose Djibouti's majority. Afars, who make up another main group, are also mostly Muslim and are linked ethnically with Afars in Ethiopia. Rivalry between the two groups has marked the nation's history. Because of unproductive land, much of the population is concentrated in the capital city of Djibouti.

Economy and the Land
Traditional nomadic herding continues as a way of life for many Djiboutians, despite heat, aridity, and limited grazing area. Several assets promote Djibouti as a port and trade center: a strategic position on the Gulf of Aden, an improved harbor, and a railway linking the city of Djibouti with Addis Ababa in Ethiopia. Marked by mountains that divide a coastal plain from a plateau region, the terrain is mostly desert. The climate is extremely hot and dry.

History and Politics
In the ninth century Arab missionaries introduced Islam to the population, and by the 1800s a pattern of conflict between the Issas and Afars had developed. The French purchased the port of Obcock from Afar sultans in 1862, and their territorial control expanded until the region became French Somaliland. The goal of the pro-independence Issas was defeated in elections in 1958 and 1967 when the majority voted for continued French control. The country became the French Territory of Afars and Issas in 1967, and as the Issa population grew, so did demands for independence. A 1977 referendum created the independent Republic of Djibouti. The country has been involved in ethnic conflict since 1991.

The busy rail line from Djibouti City to Addis Ababa in Ethiopia carries great amounts of goods. It passes through an endless desert populated only by a few nomads.

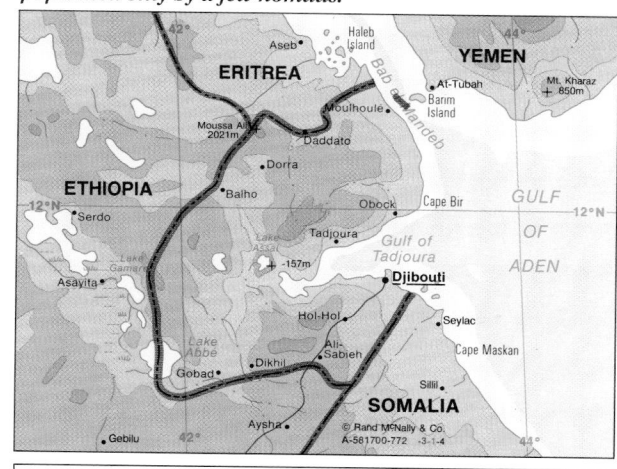

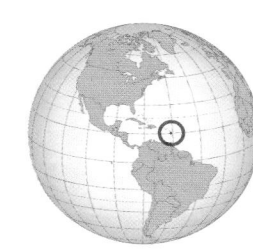

Unlike the common perception of Caribbean islands, Dominica is not ringed by beaches and resorts. But it does possess many natural wonders uniquely its own: rain forests, volcanic lakes, and national parks, as well as the sole surviving group of Carib Indians, the people who once populated the region. Translating these assets into revenue has not been easy, and Dominica remains very poor.

DOMINICA

Dominica at a glance

Official name	Commonwealth of Dominica

People

Population	89,000
Density	292/mi² (113/km²)
Urban	27%
Capital	Roseau, 9,348
Ethnic groups	Black 91%, mixed 6%, West Indian 2%
Languages	English, French
Religions	Roman Catholic 77%, Methodist 5%, Pentecostal 3%
Life expectancy	80 female, 74 male
Literacy	83%

Politics

Government	Republic
Parties	Freedom, Labor
Suffrage	Universal, over 18
Memberships	CW, OAS, UN
Subdivisions	10 parishes

Economy

GDP	$185,000,000
Per capita	$2,126
Monetary unit	East Caribbean dollar
Trade partners	Exports: U.K., Jamaica, U.S. Imports: U.S., U.K., Trinidad and Tobago
Exports	Bananas, coconuts, grapefruit, soap, galvanized sheets
Imports	Food, oils and fats, chemicals, fuels and lubricants, manufactures

Land

Description	Caribbean island
Area	305 mi² (790 km²)
Highest point	Morne Diablotins, 4,747 ft (1,447 m)
Lowest point	Sea level

People
Dominica's population consists of descendants of black Africans, brought to the island as slaves, and Carib Indians descended from early inhabitants. The Carib population is concentrated in the northeastern part of the island, and maintains its own customs and lifestyle. English is widely spoken in urban areas, but villagers, who compose a majority, speak mainly a French-African blend, resulting from French rule and the importation of Africans.

Economy and the Land
Of volcanic origin, the island has soils suitable for farming, but a mountainous and densely-forested terrain limits land accessible to cultivation. Agriculture is the economic mainstay, although hurricanes have hindered production. Forestry and fishing offer potential for expansion, and a tropical climate and scenic landscape create a basis for tourism.

History and Politics
In the fourteenth century Carib Indians conquered the Arawak, who originally inhabited the island. Although Christopher Columbus arrived at Dominica in 1493, Carib hostilities discouraged Spanish settlement. French and British rivalry for control of the island followed, and British possession was recognized in 1783. Dominica gained independence in 1978.

Scale 1:1,000,000   One inch represents approximately 16 miles. One centimeter represents 10 kilometers.

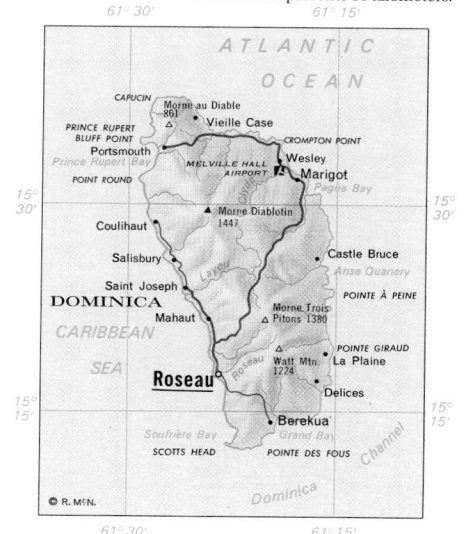

The many rivers of Dominica are choked by dense rain forest vegetation, making them unsuitable for boats larger than canoes.

B y almost every political and economic measure, the Dominican Republic looks better than its neighbor, Haiti. However, the country is beset by its own set of problems: political unrest, deforestation, and rampant poverty. Its main export, sugar, has been hurt by diminished prices worldwide.

DOMINICAN REPUBLIC

People

Occupying eastern Hispaniola Island, the Dominican Republic borders Haiti and has a population of mixed ancestry. Haitians, other blacks, Spaniards, and European Jews compose minority groups. Population growth has resulted in unemployment and made it difficult for the government to meet food and service needs.

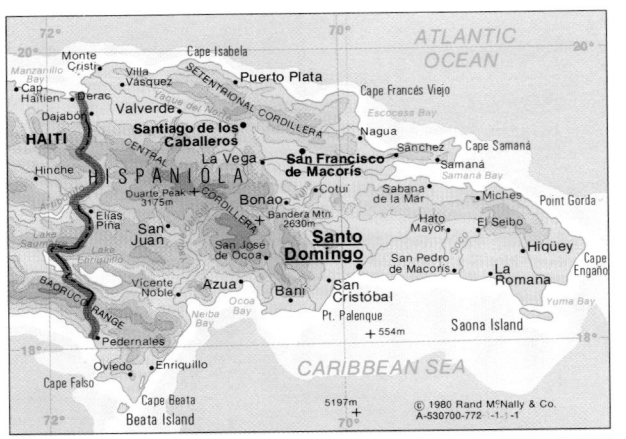

Founded by Christopher Columbus's brother, Bartholomew, in 1496, Santo Domingo has been continuously inhabited by Europeans longer than any other town in the Western Hemisphere.

DOMINICAN REPUBLIC

	Meters	Feet		
Railroad	4000	13124		
+ Spot Elevation or Depth	2000	6562	Meters	Feet
National capitals are underlined	1000	3281	0	0
	500	1640	200	656
Scale 1:5,458,000	200	656	Below 2000	Below 6562
0 25 50 75 100 125 km	0	Sea Level		
0 25 50 75 mi				

Economy and the Land

Agriculture remains important, with sugar a main component of trade, and sugar refining a major manufacturing activity. Farmland is limited, however, by a northwest-to-southeast mountain range and an arid region west of the range. Mineral exploitation and iron exports contribute to trade, and a number of American firms have subsidiaries here. Tourism is growing, aided by the warm, tropical climate.

History and Politics

In 1492 Christopher Columbus arrived at Hispaniola Island. Spanish colonists followed, and the Indian population was virtually wiped out, although some intermingling with Spanish probably occurred. In 1697 the western region of the island, which would become Haiti, was ceded to France. The entire island came under Haitian control as the Republic of Haiti in 1822, and an 1844 revolution established the independent Dominican Republic. Since independence the country has experienced periods of instability, evidenced by military coups, United States military intervention, and human rights abuses. In May 1994 an aged and ill President Balaguer was re-elected for a seventh term. Election monitors reported massive fraud and disenfranchisement, and an international commission was established to review the results.

Dominican Republic at a glance

Official name	Dominican Republic

People

Population	7,896,000
Density	422/mi² (163/km²)
Urban	60%
Capital	Santo Domingo, 2,411,900
Ethnic groups	Mulatto 73%, white 16%, black 11%
Languages	Spanish
Religions	Roman Catholic 95%
Life expectancy	70 female, 65 male
Literacy	83%

Politics

Government	Republic
Parties	Liberation, Revolutionary, Social Christian Reformist, others
Suffrage	Universal, over 18 or married
Memberships	OAS, UN
Subdivisions	29 provinces, 1 district

Economy

GDP	$23,000,000,000
Per capita	$3,030
Monetary unit	Peso
Trade partners	Exports: U.S., Netherlands Imports: U.S., western European countries
Exports	Sugar, coffee, cocoa, gold, ferronickel
Imports	Food, petroleum, cotton and fabrics, chemicals and pharmaceuticals

Land

Description	Caribbean island (eastern Hispaniola)
Area	18,704 mi² (48,442 km²)
Highest point	Duarte Peak, 10,417 ft (3,175 m)
Lowest point	Lago Enriquillo, -131 ft (-40 m)

Quito, Ecuador's capital, sits within 20 miles of the equator. Nevertheless, it enjoys a temperate climate, thanks to its high altitude. Built on the slopes of dormant volcano Pichincha, Quito has been severely damaged by earthquakes many times. Because of this, it has few tall buildings.

ECUADOR

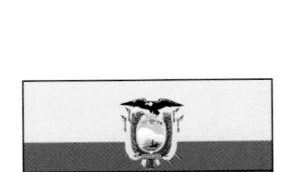

E cuador is a country of modest means that has benefited during the last 20 years from its oil deposits. As the exports have dwindled, so has the economy. Complicating matters are border disputes with Peru that often flare up into fighting. Ecuador's large Indian population has staged many protests demanding greater rights from the government, which is dominated by descendants of Spanish colonists.

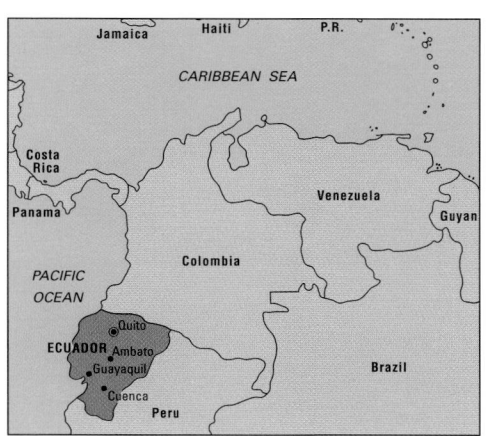

People

Ecuador's ethnicity was established by an indigenous Indian population and Spanish colonists. Minority whites, of Spanish or other European descent, live mainly in urban areas or operate large farms called haciendas. Of mixed Spanish-Indian blood, mestizos compose over half the population, although economic and political power is concentrated among whites. Minority Indians speak Quechua or other Indian languages and maintain traditional customs in Andean villages or nomadic jungle tribes. Blacks are concentrated on the northern coastal plain. Recent trends show a movement from the interior highlands to the fertile coastal plain and a rural-to-urban shift. A history of economic inequality has produced a literary and artistic tradition that has focused on social reform.

Economy and the Land

Despite an oil boom in the 1970s, Ecuador remains underdeveloped. Minor oil production began in 1911, but since a 1967 petroleum discovery in the oriente, a jungle region east of the Andes, Ecuador has become an oil exporter. Agriculture remains important for much of the population, although primitive and inefficient practices continue among the poor. Rich soils of the costa, extending from the Pacific to the Andes, support most of the export crops. Forestry and fishing have growth potential, and the waters around the Galapagos Islands are rich in tuna. Manufacturing is mainly devoted to meeting domestic needs. The *oriente* and *costa* lie on either side of the sierra, a region of highland plateaus between the two Andean chains. Varied altitudes result in a climate ranging from tropical in the lowlands to temperate in the plateaus and cold in the high mountains. A variety of wildlife inhabits the Galapagos Islands, five large

and nine small islands about 600 miles (966 km) off Ecuador's coast in the Pacific Ocean.

History and Politics

In the fifteenth century Incas conquered and subsequently united the area's various tribes. In the 1500s the Spanish gained control, using Indians and African slaves to work the plantations. Weakened by the Napoleonic Wars, Spain lost control of Ecuador in 1822, and Simón Bolívar united the independent state with the Republic of Greater Colombia. Ecuador left the union as a separate republic in 1830, and subsequent years saw instability and rule by presidents, dictators, and juntas. From 1925 to 1948 no leader was able to complete a full term in office. A new constitution was established in 1978. Elections in 1992 were won by the right-wing United Republican Party committed to a privatization policy. The fall in world crude oil prices in 1993 caused an economic crisis and riots over the increase in gasoline prices.

The southern province of Morona-Santiago is heavily forested.

(top) Salasca Indian woman, Rio Bamba

(bottom) Cotopaxi, an active volcano

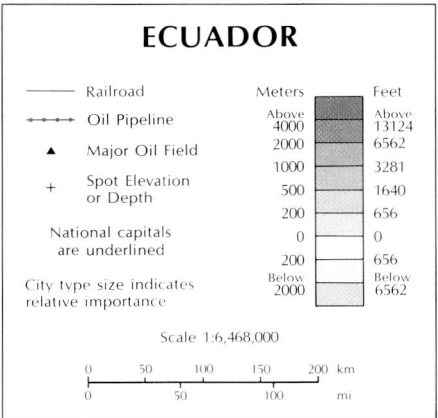

ECUADOR

Railroad	Meters	Feet
Oil Pipeline	Above 4000	Above 13124
Major Oil Field	2000	6562
Spot Elevation or Depth	1000	3281
	500	1640
National capitals are underlined	200	656
	0	0
City type size indicates relative importance	200	656
	Below 2000	Below 6562

Scale 1:6,468,000

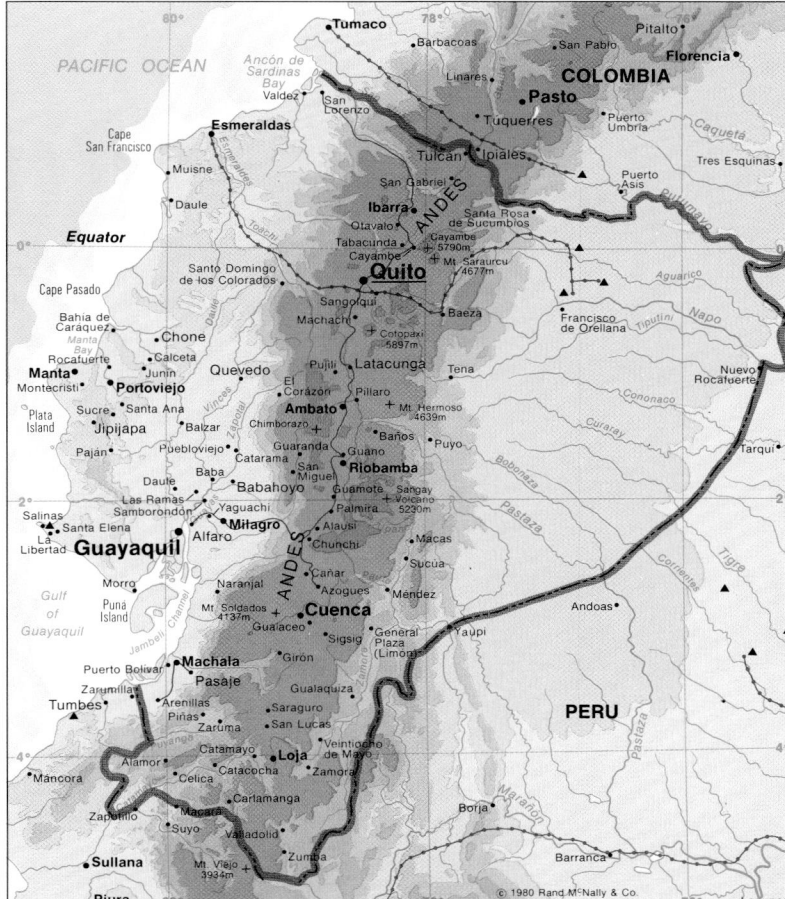

Ecuador at a glance

Official name Republic of Ecuador

People

Population	10,515,000
Density	100/mi² (39/km²)
Urban	56%
Capital	Quito, 1,100,847
Ethnic groups	Mestizo 55%, Amerindian 25%, white 10%, black 10%
Languages	Spanish, Quechua, indigenous
Religions	Roman Catholic 95%
Life expectancy	69 female, 65 male
Literacy	86%

Politics

Government	Republic
Parties	Democratic Left, Republican Unity, Roldosist, Socialist, Social Christian, others
Suffrage	Universal, over 18
Memberships	OAS, OPEC, UN
Subdivisions	21 provinces

Economy

GDP	$11,800,000,000
Per capita	$1,085
Monetary unit	Sucre
Trade partners	Exports: U.S., Peru, Chile Imports: U.S., Japan, Germany
Exports	Petroleum, coffee, bananas, cocoa, shrimp, fish
Imports	Transportation equipment, vehicles, machinery, chemicals

Land

Description	Western South America
Area	105,037 mi² (272,045 km²)
Highest point	Chimborazo, 20,702 ft (6,310 m)
Lowest point	Sea level

The Galapagos Islands, 600 miles west of the mainland, are home to many unusual plant and animal species, including the famous huge tortoises. The study of these creatures helped Charles Darwin formulate his theories about evolution in the nineteenth century.

Archeological records trace Egyptian history back 6,000 years. The pyramids and many other monuments date back 4,500 years. Today, much of Egypt's population still lives near the Nile River, as it always has, but nearly everything else about Egyptian life has changed. The population has mushroomed: Cairo is now a city of over nine million people. This growth has strained the country's economy. Widespread poverty has fueled Islamic fundamentalists who seek to bring down Egypt's secular government.

EGYPT

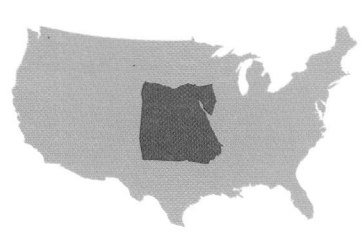

People
Egypt's population is relatively homogeneous, and Egyptians compose the largest group. Descended from ancient Nile Valley inhabitants, Egyptians have intermixed somewhat with Mediterranean and Asiatic peoples in the north and with black Africans in the south. Minorities include Bedouins, Arabic-speaking desert nomads; Nubians, black descendants of migrants from the Sudan; and Copts, a Christian group. Islam, the major religion, is also a cultural force; many Christians and Muslims follow Islamic lifestyles. A desert terrain confines about 99 percent of the population to less than four percent of the land, in the fertile Nile River valley and along the Suez Canal.

Economy and the Land
Egypt's economy has suffered from wars, shifting alliances, and limited natural resources. Government-sponsored expansion and reform in the 1950s concentrated on manufacturing, and most industry was nationalized during the 1960s. Agriculture, centered in the Nile Valley, remains an economic mainstay, and cotton, a principal crop, is both exported and processed. Petroleum is found, mainly in the Gulf of Suez. Tourism is one of the nation's most important economic activities. Much of Egypt is desert, with hills and mountains in the east and along the Nile River, while the climate is warm and dry.

History and Politics
Egypt's recorded history began when King Menes united the region in about 3100 B.C., beginning a series of Egyptian dynasties. Art and architecture flourished during the Age of the Pyramids, from 2700 to 2200 B.C. In time native dynasties gave way to foreign conquerors, including Alexander the Great in the fourth century B.C. The Coptic Christian church emerged between the fourth and sixth centuries A.D., but in the 600s Arabs conquered the area and established Islam as the main religion. Ruling parties changed frequently, and in 1517 the Ottoman Turks added Egypt to their empire. Upon completion of the strategically important Suez Canal in 1869, foreign interest in Egypt increased. In 1875 Egypt sold its share of the canal to Britain, and a rebellion against foreign intervention ended with British occupation in 1882. Turkey sided with Germany in World War I, and the United Kingdom made Egypt a British protectorate in 1914. The country became an independent monarchy in 1922, but the British presence remained. In 1945 Egypt and six other nations formed the Arab League. The founding of Israel in 1948 initiated an era of Arab-Israeli hostilities, including periodic warfare in which Egypt often had a major role. Dissatisfaction over dealings with Israel and continued British occupation of the Suez Canal led to the overthrow of the king, and Egypt became a republic in 1953. Following a power struggle, Gamal Abdel Nasser was elected president in 1956, and the British agreed to remove their troops. Upon the death of Nasser in 1970, Vice President Anwar Sadat came to power. Negotiations between Egyptian president Sadat and Israeli prime minister Menachem Begin began in 1977, and in 1979 the leaders signed a peace treaty ending conflicts between Egypt and Israel. As a result, Egypt was suspended from the Arab League until 1989. In 1981 President Sadat was assassinated and was succeeded by Hosni Mubarek, who is faced with a growing fundamentalist Muslim campaign of violence targeting tourists and government officers.

The Aswan High Dam, built in the 1960s, has had a disastrous effect on the agricultural land of the Nile Valley. The dam has greatly reduced the annual flooding which used to enrich the land with nutrients.

Egypt at a glance

Official name	Arab Republic of Egypt

People

Population	58,100,000
Density	150/mi² (58/km²)
Urban	44%
Capital	Cairo, 6,068,695
Ethnic groups	Egyptian (Eastern Hamitic) 90%
Languages	Arabic
Religions	Muslim 94%, Coptic Christian and others 6%
Life expectancy	63 female, 60 male
Literacy	48%

Politics

Government	Socialist republic
Parties	National Democratic, National Progressive Unionist Grouping, others
Suffrage	Universal, over 18
Memberships	AL, OAU, UN
Subdivisions	26 governorates

Economy

GDP	$139,000,000,000
Per capita	$2,436
Monetary unit	Pound
Trade partners	Exports: Italy, former Soviet republics, France. Imports: U.S., Germany, France
Exports	Petroleum, cotton, textiles, metals, chemicals
Imports	Machinery, food, fertilizer, wood products, manufactures

Land

Description	Northeastern Africa
Area	386,662 mi² (1,001,449 km²)
Highest point	Mt. Katrina, 8,668 ft (2,642 m)
Lowest point	Qattara Depression, -436 ft (-133 m)

Photos at right:
(top) The Nile is a highway of commerce, traversed by scores of traditional sail-powered felukkas

(bottom) Great Pyramid and Sphinx at night

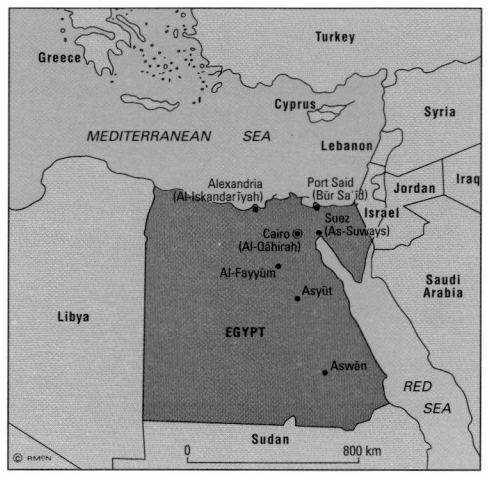

El Salvador at a glance

Official name Republic of El Salvador

People

Population	5,280,000
Density	650/mi² (251/km²)
Urban	44%
Capital	San Salvador, 462,652
Ethnic groups	Mestizo 94%, Amerindian 5%, white 1%
Languages	Spanish, Nahua
Religions	Roman Catholic 75%
Life expectancy	69 female, 64 male
Literacy	73%

Politics

Government	Republic
Parties	Authentic Christian Movement, Christian Democratic, National Republican Alliance, others
Suffrage	Universal, over 18
Memberships	OAS, UN
Subdivisions	14 departments

Economy

GDP	$14,200,000,000
Per capita	$2,520
Monetary unit	Colon
Trade partners	Exports: U.S., Guatemala, Germany Imports: U.S., Guatemala, Mexico
Exports	Coffee, sugar, cotton, shrimp
Imports	Petroleum, manufactures, food, machinery, construction materials, fertilizer

Land

Description	Central America
Area	8,124 mi² (21,041 km²)
Highest point	Cerro El Pital, 8,957 ft (2,730 m)
Lowest point	Sea level

People

Most Salvadorans are Spanish-speaking mestizos, people of Spanish-Indian descent. An Indian minority is mainly descended from the Pipil, a Nahuatl group related to the Aztecs. The Nahuatl dialect is still spoken among some Indians. El Salvador, the smallest Central American country in area, has the highest population density in mainland Latin America, with inhabitants concentrated in a central valley-and-plateau region.

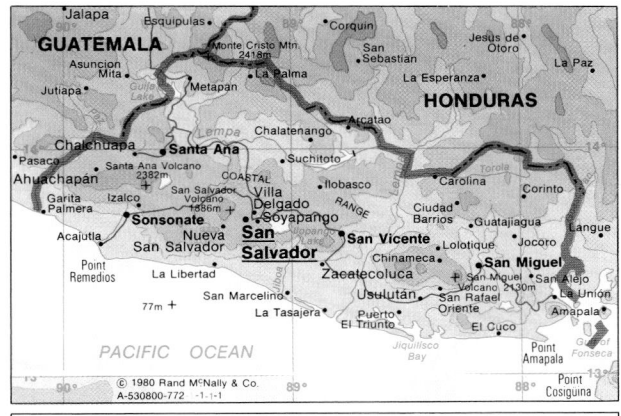

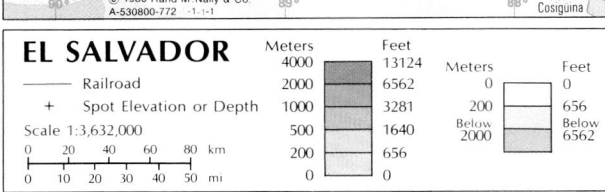

Unlike its neighbors, El Salvador has no undeveloped land left for cultivation. As the population has grown, many Salvadorans have crossed the borders into Guatemala and Honduras in search of livelihoods.

EL SALVADOR

Economy and the Land

El Salvador's economy has been plagued by political instability, low literacy, high population density, and high unemployment. Agriculture remains the economic mainstay, and most arable land has been cultivated. Coffee, cotton, and sugar are produced on large commercial plantations, while subsistence farmers rely on corn, bean, and sorghum crops. East-to-west mountain ranges divide El Salvador into a southern coastal region, central valleys and plateaus, and northern mountains. The climate is subtropical.

History and Politics

Maya and Pipil predominated in the area of El Salvador prior to Spanish arrival. In the 1500s Pipil defeated invading Spaniards but were conquered in a subsequent invasion. In 1821 the Spanish-controlled Central American colonies declared independence, and in 1823 they united as the Federation of Central America. By 1838 the problem-ridden federation was in a state of collapse, and as the union dissolved, El Salvador became independent. Instability and revolution soon followed. The expansion of the coffee economy in the late 1800s exacerbated problems by further concentrating wealth and power among large-estate holders. A dictatorship from 1931 to 1944 was followed by instability under various military rulers. In 1969 a brief war with Honduras arose from resentment toward land-ownership laws, border disputes, and nationalistic feelings following a series of soccer games between the two countries. During the 1980s, the United States provided extensive military and economic aid in an attempt to moderate the government. A twelve-year civil war erupted which did not end until 1992. Elections in 1994 were won by the National Republican Alliance (ARENA), the ruling rightist party. Their economic reform plan is strongly opposed by labor unions.

Equatorial New Guinea at a glance

Official name Republic of Equatorial Guinea

People

Population	394,000
Density	36/mi² (14/km²)
Urban	29%
Capital	Malabo, Bioko I., 31,630
Ethnic groups	Fang 80%, Bubi 15%
Languages	Spanish, indigenous, English
Religions	Roman Catholic 83%, other Christian, tribal religionist
Life expectancy	50 female, 46 male
Literacy	50%

Politics

Government	Republic
Parties	Democratic
Suffrage	Universal adult
Memberships	OAS, UN
Subdivisions	7 provinces

Economy

GDP	$280,000,000
Per capita	$711
Monetary unit	CFA franc
Trade partners	Exports: Spain, Italy, Netherlands Imports: France, Spain, Italy
Exports	Coffee, wood, cocoa
Imports	Petroleum, food, beverages, clothing, machinery

Land

Description	Central Africa
Area	10,831 mi² (28,051 km²)
Highest point	Santa Isabel Peak, 9,869 ft (3,008 m)
Lowest point	Sea level

People

Several ethnic groups inhabit Equatorial Guinea's five islands, as well as the mainland region of Río Muni. Although the majority Fang, a Bantu people, are concentrated in Río Muni, they also inhabit Bioko, the largest island. Found mainly on Bioko Island are the minority Bubi, also a Bantu people. Coastal groups known as *playeros*, or "those who live on the beach," live on both the mainland and the small islands. The Fernandino, of mixed African heritage, are concentrated on Bioko.

EQUATORIAL GUINEA

Economy and the Land

Equatorial Guinea's economy is based on agriculture and forestry; cocoa, coffee, and wood are the main products. Cocoa production is centered on fertile Bioko Island, and coffee in Río Muni. The mainland's rain forests also provide for forestry. Mineral exploration has revealed petroleum and natural gas in the waters north of Bioko, and petroleum, iron ore, and radioactive materials in Río Muni. Bioko is of volcanic origin, and Río Muni consists of a coastal plain and interior hills. The climate is tropical, with high temperatures and humidity.

History and Politics

Pygmies most likely inhabited the Río Muni area prior to the thirteenth century, when mainland Bubi came to Bioko. From the seventeenth to the nineteenth centuries, Bantu migrations brought first the coastal tribes and then the Fang. Portugal claimed Bioko and part of the mainland in the 1400s, then ceded them to Spain in 1778. From 1827 to 1843, British antislavery activities were based on Bioko, which became the home of many former slaves, the ancestors of the Fernandino population. In 1959 the area became the Spanish Territory of the Gulf of Guinea, and the name was changed to Equatorial Guinea in 1963. Independence was achieved in 1968.

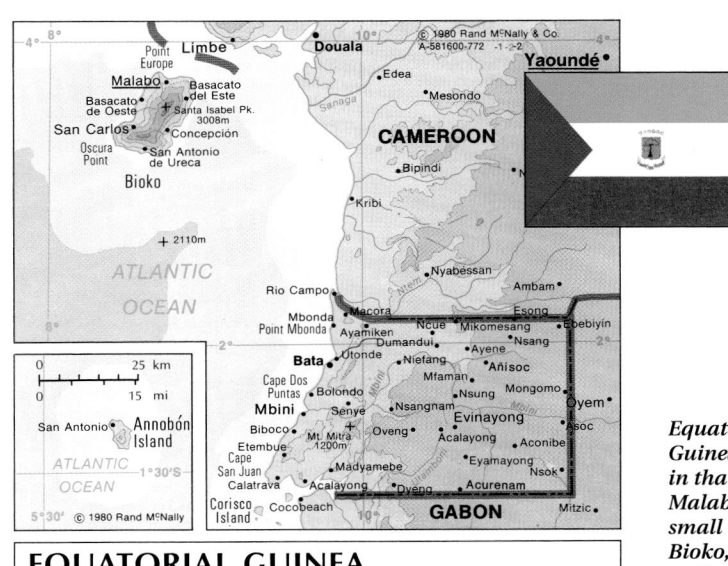

Equatorial Guinea is unusual in that the capital, Malabo, is on the small island of Bioko, which is well-removed from the much larger mainland.

Eritrea has appropriated all of Ethiopia's former coastline, leaving that nation landlocked. Eritrea has a commanding presence on the Red Sea, course of the world's busiest shipping routes.

ERITREA

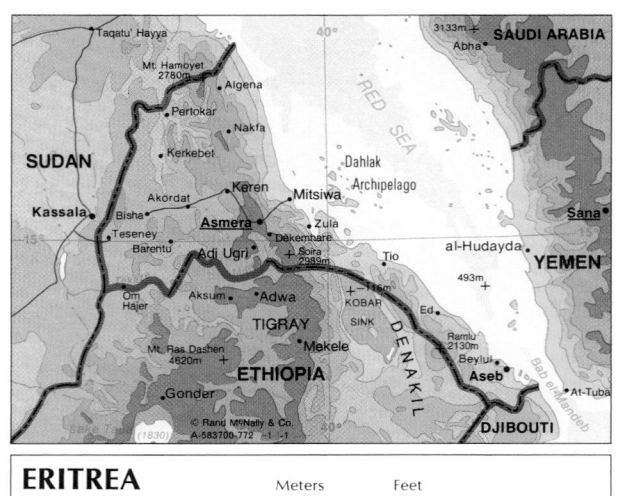

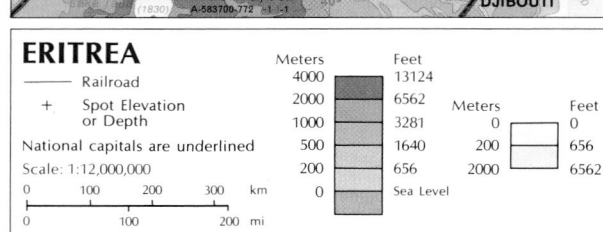

ERITREA

	Meters	Feet
Railroad	4000	13124
Spot Elevation or Depth	2000	6562
	1000	3281
National capitals are underlined	500	1640
Scale: 1:12,000,000	200	656

Eritrea at a glance

Official name	State of Eritrea

People

Population	3,458,000
Density	96/mi² (37/km²)
Urban	15%
Capital	Asmera, 358,100
Ethnic groups	Tigray 50%, Tigre and Kunama 30%, Afar 4%, Saho 3%
Languages	Tigre, Kunama, Cushitic dialects, Nora Bana, Arabic
Religions	Muslim, Coptic Christian, Roman Catholic, Protestant

Politics

Government	Republic
Parties	Liberation Front, Liberation Front-United Organization, People's Liberation Front
Memberships	OAU, UN
Subdivisions	3 administrative regions

Economy

GDP	$1,700,000,000
Per capita	$496

Economy

Description	Eastern Africa
Area	36,170 mi² (93,679 km²)
Highest point	Soira, 9,806 ft (2,989 m)
Lowest point	Unnamed, -515 ft (-157 m)

People

Eritrea is a land of diverse languages and religions. The main ethnic groups are the Tigre and Afar, although there are also Kunama, Saho, Agau, and others. Tigre and Kunama are two of the predominant languages, along with Arabic and others. About half of the population is Coptic Christian, and the other half practices Islam.

Economy and the Land

Eritrea's climate is dry and the region suffers from chronic drought. Some cotton and oilseed crops are grown, but fish provide the major source of food. Crop failure resulted in severe food shortages in 1994. Thirty years of war with Ethiopia left the country's infrastructure in disrepair, but the rebuilding process has been swift. Despite many advances, the country is still dependent on foreign aid. Eritrea hopes to develop its Red Sea coastline as a tourist attraction.

History and Politics

Eritrea was originally settled by people who migrated across the Red Sea from Yemen. In A.D. 950 the region now known as Eritrea was part of the Ethiopian empire. In 1557 the city of Massawa and surrounding areas were captured by the Ottoman Turks, who established loose control of the region until it was overtaken by the Egyptians in 1846. Sovereignty shifted between Turkey and Egypt until 1890, when the Italians invaded the region and established the colony of Eritrea in 1890. Fifty years of Italian rule left Eritrea with sound industrial, educational, governmental, and transportation systems that were rare elsewhere in Africa. It also left the Eritreans with a strong sense of national identity, despite their cultural diversity.

After the British captured the region from the Italians in World War II, the United Nations handed it over to Ethiopia in 1952, despite claims by some that Eritrea should be granted its independence. The Ethiopians were instructed to administer Eritrea as a self-governing territory within Ethiopia, but they violated the arrangement by annexing Eritrea in 1962. This action ignited a civil war which lasted for more than thirty years. After defeating the Marxist regime in 1991, the Eritreans agreed to wait almost two years before legalizing their status as an independent nation. In May 1993 Eritrea became independent and a transitional government was elected to function until a constitution is drafted. Disastrous crop failures following independence failed to rock the stability or dampen the spirit of this hard-working new country.

ESTONIA

Estonia includes 1,520 islands in the Baltic Sea. Most are unpopulated and many are little more than rocks jutting above the water.

ESTONIA

		Meters	Feet
Railroad	National capitals are underlined	200	656
Spot Elevation	City type size indicates relative importance	0	0
Scale 1:5,200,000		200	656

Estonia at a glance

Official name	Republic of Estonia

People

Population	1,515,000
Density	87/mi² (34/km²)
Urban	72%
Capital	Tallinn, 481,500
Ethnic groups	Estonian 62%, Russian 30%, Ukrainian 3%
Languages	Estonian, Latvian, Lithuanian, Russian
Religions	Lutheran
Life expectancy	76 female, 67 male
Literacy	99%

Politics

Government	Republic
Parties	Fatherland, Moderates, National Independence, Popular Front, Safe Home
Suffrage	Universal, over 18
Memberships	UN
Subdivisions	15 counties, 6 municipalities

Economy

GDP	$8,800,000,000
Per capita	$5,456
Monetary unit	Kroon
Trade partners	Former Soviet republics
Exports	Machinery, food, chemicals, electricity
Imports	Machinery, oil, chemicals

Land

Description	Eastern Europe
Area	17,413 mi² (45,100 km²)
Highest point	Suur Munamägi, 1,043 ft (318 m)
Lowest point	Sea level

People

The Estonians have retained their own unique language and culture for centuries, despite almost continuous foreign intervention. Before the Soviet invasion in 1940, the Estonians, who are related to the Finns, accounted for almost all of the population. Since then, massive immigration has increased the Russians' share of the population to almost one-third. Estonia has a relatively high urban population, and most people are engaged in industry.

Economy and the Land

Most of Estonia's industry is centered on shale oil, its only major industrial raw material. Shale oil has permitted Estonia to develop a sound manufacturing base. Agriculture is based on livestock and dairy products, and most crops are grown to supply animal feed. Estonia's natural landscape is plains and poorly drained marshes, although much of the land has been drained for agriculture. More than a third of the land is forested.

History and Politics

Prior to incorporation into the Soviet Union, Estonia enjoyed only twenty years of independence during its long history. Danes conquered the territory in 1219 and sold it to the Teutonic Knights in 1346. The Swedes invaded in 1561 and domination alternated between Sweden and Poland until Peter the Great of Russia conquered it in 1721. The country was granted independence in 1918, but freedom lasted only until the Soviet invasion of 1940, after which Estonia was forced to become a Soviet Socialist Republic. Estonians enjoyed the highest overall standard of living in the Soviet Union. Estonia's "home rule" legislation led the Baltic states' drive for independence following the introduction of glasnost in the Soviet Union. International recognition as an independent nation was achieved in 1991, several months before the breakup of the Soviet Union. The first free elections in any former Soviet Union country were held in late 1992. Tensions exist between Estonians and ethnic Russians over discrimination and language laws.

A nation with roots going back to the ancient Egyptians and Romans, Ethiopia has fared poorly in the 20th Century. Drought, coupled with guerrilla insurgencies that hampered relief efforts, resulted in reoccurring widespread starvation beginning in the 1970s. The independence of Eritrea in 1993 deprived Ethiopia of its access to shipping, leaving the country more dependent upon its neighbors.

ETHIOPIA

People

Ethiopia is ethnically, linguistically, and religiously diverse, but the Oromo, Amhara, and Tigre predominate. The Oromo include agricultural Muslims, Christians, and nomadic herders with traditional religions. Mainly Christian and agricultural, the Amhara have dominated the country politically. The official language is Amharic; Arabic and indigenous languages are also spoken. Ethiopia's boundaries encompass over forty ethnic groups.

Economy and the Land

In addition to problems caused by political instability, drought has plagued Ethiopia's agricultural economy. Existing problems of soil erosion and deforestation resulted in disaster in 1982 when planting-season rains failed to fall in much of the country. The consequences of drought are especially severe in the north and west. A grain shortfall in 1993 produced widespread famine. Subsistence farming remains a major activity, and much arable land is uncultivated. Mines produce gold, copper, and platinum, and there is potential for expansion. A central plateau is split diagonally by the Great Rift Valley, with lowlands on the west and plains in the southeast.

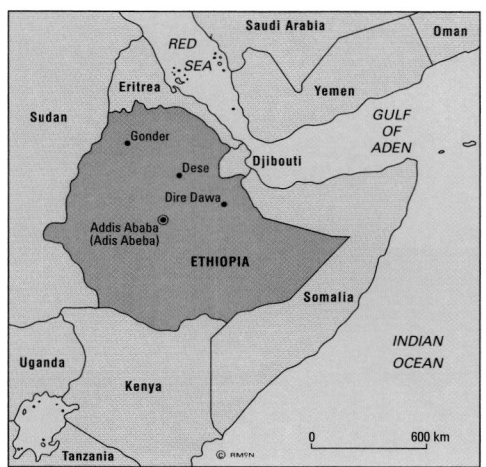

The climate is temperate on the plateau and hot in the lowlands.

History and Politics

Ethiopia's history is one of the oldest in the world. Its ethnic patterns were established by indigenous Cushites and Semite settlers, who probably arrived from Arabia about 3,000 years ago. Christianity was introduced in the early fourth century. During the 1800s modern Ethiopia began to develop under Emperor Menelik II. Ras Tafari Makonnen became emperor in 1930, taking the name Haile Selassie. Italians invaded in the 1930s and occupied the country until 1941, when Selassie returned to the throne. Discontent with the feudal society increased until Selassie was ousted by the military in 1974. Reform programs and the change in leadership did little to ease political tensions, which sometimes erupted in governmental and civilian violence. Government troops continued their battle with separatists in Eritrea, a former Italian colony and autonomous province incorporated into Ethiopia in 1962. Since the 1980s, widespread famine and drought aggravated political problems. Civil war hampered worldwide relief efforts. Over 250,000 people died in the war which ended in 1991 when the country's Marxist regime fell to Eritrean and Tigrean rebels. Eritrea gained full independence in 1993, leaving Ethiopia a landlocked country. A new constitution adopted in December 1994 establishes a federal system of government. The country's first multiparty election was held in May 1995.

Much of Ethiopia belies the images of a stark landscape broadcast to the world during the famines of the 1980s. A quarter of the country is wooded, and the many river valleys are green and have rich soils. Poor transportation and war have kept food from one area from reaching another.

POPULATION COMPARISON
Ethiopia=21% of U.S.
United States

GDP COMPARISON
Ethiopia=0.4% of U.S.
United States

ETHNIC GROUPS

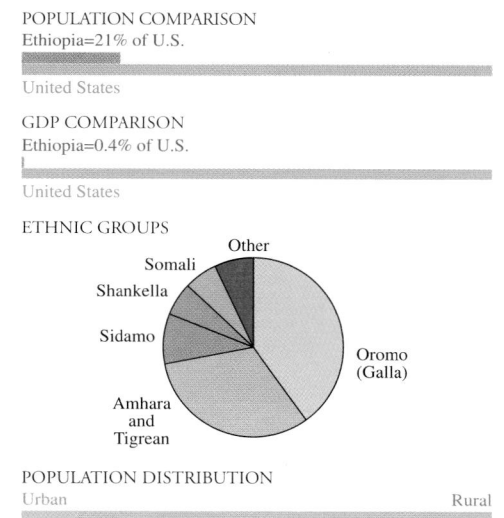

Other
Somali
Shankella
Sidamo
Oromo (Galla)
Amhara and Tigrean

POPULATION DISTRIBUTION
Urban — Rural

Although most Ethiopians live off the land, working as farmers or shepherds, the populace shares few other unifying traits. Ethiopia is characterized by a remarkable diversity of languages and cultures.

Ethiopia at a glance

Official name	Ethiopia

People

Population	55,070,000
Density	123/mi² (48/km²)
Urban	12%
Capital	Addis Ababa, 1,912,500
Ethnic groups	Oromo (Galla) 40%, Amhara and Tigrean 32%, Sidamo 9%, Shankella 6%, Somali 6%
Languages	Amharic, Tigrinya, Orominga, Guaraginga, Somali, Arabic
Religions	Muslim 40-50%, Ethiopian Orthodox 35-40%, Animist 12%
Life expectancy	49 female, 45 male
Literacy	62%

Politics

Government	Provisional military government
Parties	Ethiopian People's Revolutionary Party, Oromo Liberation Front, others
Suffrage	Universal, over 18
Memberships	OAU, UN
Subdivisions	14 administrative regions

Economy

GDP	$22,700,000,000
Per capita	$412
Monetary unit	Birr
Trade partners	Exports: Germany, Japan, U.S. Imports: Italy, former Soviet republics, U.S.
Exports	Coffee, animal hides
Imports	Food, fuel, manufacture

Land

Description	Eastern Africa, landlocked
Area	446,953 mi² (1,157,603 km²)
Highest point	Mt. Ras Dashen, 15,158 ft (4,620 m)
Lowest point	Asälē, -410 ft (-125 m)

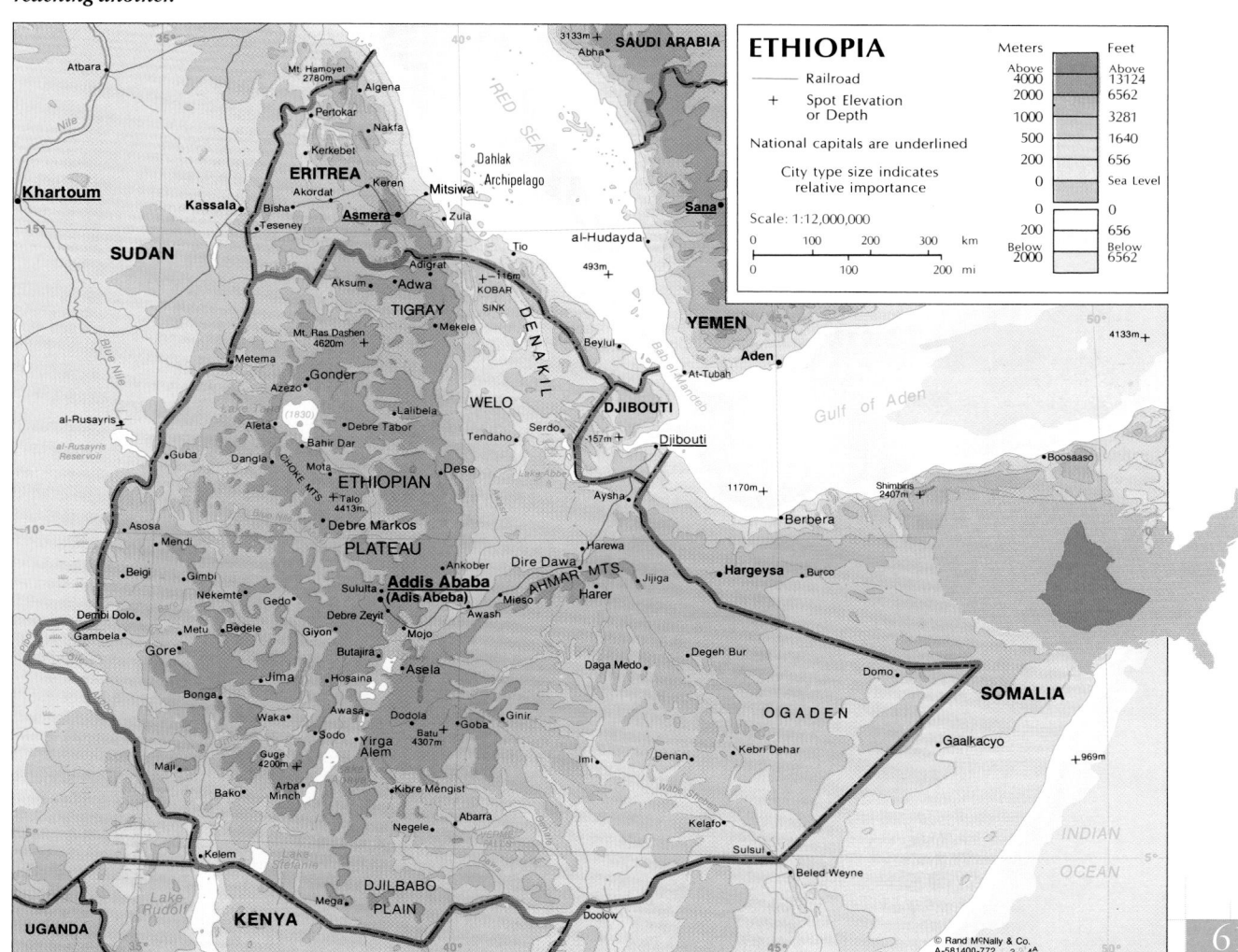

ETHIOPIA

		Meters	Feet
	Railroad	Above 4000	Above 13124
+	Spot Elevation or Depth	2000	6562
		1000	3281
	National capitals are underlined	500	1640
		200	656
	City type size indicates relative importance	0	Sea Level
		0	0
	Scale: 1:12,000,000	200	656
		Below 2000	Below 6562

Scale 0 100 200 300 km / 0 100 200 mi

© Rand McNally & Co.
A-581400-772

T**he people of the Faeroe Islands** lead a wet and windy existence in the cold North Atlantic between Scotland and Iceland. A self-governing part of Denmark, the islands are culturally close to Iceland. Rich fishing stocks afford the inhabitants a high standard of living.

FAEROE ISLANDS

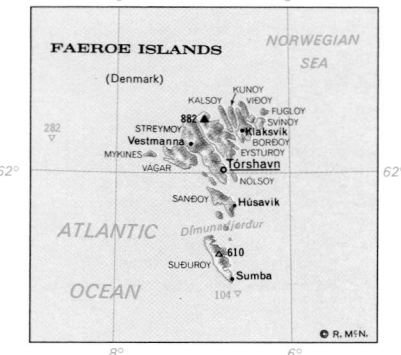

Scale 1:4,500,000 One inch represents approximately 71 miles.
One centimeter represents 45 kilometers.

Ferry service from Scandinavia and Scotland to the Faeroes runs only in summer. The rest of the year the islands are accessible only by air.

Faeroe Islands at a glance

Official name	Faeroe Islands

People

Population	49,000
Density	91/mi² (35/km²)
Urban	31%
Capital	Tórshavn, Streymoy I., 14,767
Ethnic groups	Faeroese (Scandinavian)
Languages	Danish, Faeroese
Religions	Evangelical Lutheran
Life expectancy	91 female, 75 male

Politics

Government	Self-governing territory (Danish protection)
Parties	Cooperative Coalition, People's, Republican, Social Democrat
Suffrage	Universal, over 20
Memberships	None
Subdivisions	None

Economy

GDP	$662,000,000
Per capita	$13,792
Monetary unit	Danish krone
Trade partners	Exports: Denmark, Germany, U.K. Imports: Denmark, Norway
Exports	Fish and shellfish, transportation equipment
Imports	Machinery and transportation equipment, manufactures, food and livestock

Land

Description	North Atlantic islands
Area	540 mi² (1,399 km²)
Highest point	Slættaratindur, 2,894 ft (882 m)
Lowest point	Sea level

People

Most of the inhabitants of the Faeroe Islands are of Norse descent. Their language, Faeroese, is related to the Old Norse language, and many islanders feel strongly about preserving their linguistic heritage. Danish is taught in schools, however. Eighteen of the more than twenty islands are inhabited, but over one-third of the population lives on Streymoy, the largest island of the group.

Economy and the Land

Today, as in the past, the Faeroe Islands' economy is dependent upon a fishing industry subsidized by Denmark. Only about 6 percent of the land is cultivated, and besides potatoes and some vegetables, this area provides grass for sheep-raising. Coal is mined on the island of Suduroy, and throughout the island group people make and sell handicrafts. In addition, some islanders collect and sell the eggs and feathers of the birds that inhabit the cliffs along the coast. The main islands in this volcanic chain are Streymoy, Eysturoy, Vágar, Suduroy, and Sandoy. Many islands rise to steep cliffs from a rugged and uneven coastline. Winters are mild, and summers cool.

History and Politics

Norse settlers arrived in the eighth century, but the islands didn't officially become part of Norway until the eleventh century. In the 1300s, along with Norway, Sweden, Finland, Iceland, and Greenland, the Faeroe Islands came under Danish rule. During World War II, when the Germans invaded Denmark, the British occupied the islands. In 1946 the people participated in a plebiscite, and the result was a declaration of the islands' independence from Denmark. But when the island of Sudero remained in favor of Danish rule, the Danish King announced the result was not conclusive, and the islands continued under Danish control. Two years later, however, the Faeroe Islands became self-governing.

The Falkland Islands are barren, cold, and swept by frequent storms. Recent efforts to boost tourism by marketing the excellent trout fishing have met with limited success owing to the islands' isolated location.

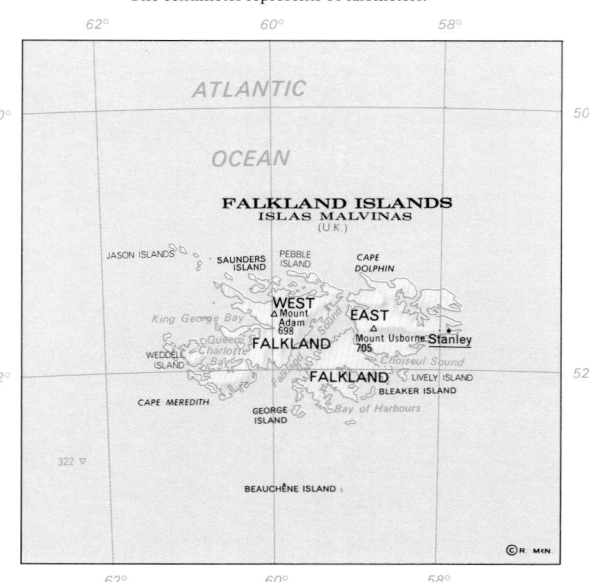

Scale 1:6,000,000 One inch represents approximately 95 miles.
One centimeter represents 60 kilometers.

FALKLAND ISLANDS

A**rgentina's 1982 invasion of the Falkland Islands** (which Argentineans call the Islas Malvinas) resulted in over 1,000 deaths and ended in failure. Since then, the British have kept a large garrison on the island. The troops protect the mostly British inhabitants who work at the islands' only industries: sheepherding and wool production.

Falkland Islands at a glance

Official name	Colony of the Falkland Islands

People

Population	2,100
Density	0.4/mi² (0.2/km²)
Urban	59%
Capital	Stanley, East Falkland I., 1,557
Ethnic groups	British descent
Languages	English
Religions	Anglican, Roman Catholic, United Free Church

Politics

Government	Dependent territory (U.K.)
Suffrage	Universal, over 18
Memberships	None
Subdivisions	None

Economy

Monetary unit	Pound
Trade partners	Exports: U.K., Netherlands, Japan Imports: U.K., Netherlands Antilles, Japan
Exports	Wool, animal hides
Imports	Food, clothing, fuel, machinery

Land

Description	South Atlantic islands (east of Argentina)
Area	4,700 mi² (12,173 km²)
Highest point	Mt. Usborne, 2,312 ft (705 m)
Lowest point	Sea level

People

Most Falkland Island inhabitants are of British descent, an ancestry reflected in their official language, English, and majority Anglican religion.

Economy and the Land

Sheep raising is the main activity, supplemented by fishing. In 1982 Britain funded the Falkland Islands Development Corporation, which began operation in 1984. Situated about 300 miles (482 km) east of southern Argentina, East and West Falkland compose the main and largest islands. Numerous small islands are also part of the Falklands. The climate is cool, damp, and windy.

History and Politics

Although the British sighted the islands in 1592, the French established the first settlement in 1764, on East Falkland. The British settled on West Falkland the next year. Spain, which ruled the Argentinean territories to the west, purchased the French area and drove out the British in 1770. When Argentina gained independence from Spain in 1816, it claimed Spain's right to the islands. Britain reasserted its rule over the islands in the 1830s. The Falklands became a British colony in 1892, with dependencies annexed in 1908. Continued Argentinean claims resulted in a 1982 Argentinean invasion and occupation. The British won the subsequent battle and continue to govern the Falklands. The dependencies of South Georgia and the South Sandwich Islands became a separate British colony in 1985.

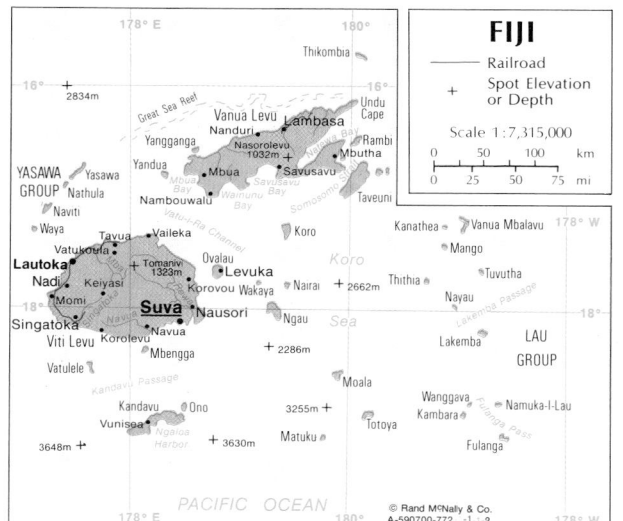

FIJI
— Railroad
+ Spot Elevation or Depth
Scale 1:7,315,000

Although Fiji consists of over 300 islands, the vast majority of Fijians live on the two largest volcanic islands, Viti Levu and Vanua Levu.

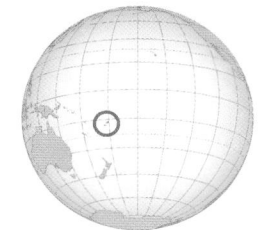

Fiji at a glance

Official name	Republic of Fiji

People

Population	775,000
Density	110/mi² (42/km²)
Urban	39%
Capital	Suva, Viti Levu I., 69,665
Ethnic groups	Fijian 49%, Indian 46%
Languages	English, Fijian, Hindustani
Religions	Methodist and other Christian 52%, Hindu 38%, Muslim 8%
Life expectancy	74 female, 70 male
Literacy	86%

Politics

Government	Republic
Parties	Alliance, Labor, National Federation
Suffrage	None
Memberships	UN
Subdivisions	4 divisions

Economy

GDP	$3,000,000,000
Per capita	$3,979
Monetary unit	Dollar
Trade partners	Exports: U.K., Malaysia, New Zealand Imports: Australia, New Zealand, Japan, Singapore
Exports	Sugar, gold, clothing, copra, fish, lumber
Imports	Machinery and transportation equipment, food, petroleum products

Land

Description	South Pacific islands
Area	7,056 mi² (18,274 km²)
Highest point	Tomanivi (Victoria), 4,341 ft (1,323 m)
Lowest point	Sea level

A tropical paradise of 330 islands, Fiji's political life has been in turmoil since a 1987 coup. Relations are tense between native Fijians and Indians, who each account for approximately half of the population. The economy is based on sugar exports and tourism.

People

Almost half of Fiji's population is descended from laborers brought from British India between 1879 and 1916. Most Indians are Hindu, but a Muslim minority also exists. Native Fijians are of Melanesian and Polynesian heritage, and most are Christian. English is the official language, a result of British rule; but Indians speak Hindustani, and the main Fijian dialect is Bauan. Tensions between the two groups occasionally arise because plantation owners, who are mainly Indian, must often lease their land from Fijians, the major landowners. About 100 of the 330 islands are inhabited.

Economy and the Land

The traditional sugarcane crop continues to be the basis of Fiji's economy, and agri-cultural diversification is a current goal. Tourism is another economic contributor, and expansion of forestry is planned. Terrain varies from island to island and is characterized by mountains, valleys, rain forests, and fertile plains. The tropical islands are cooled by ocean breezes.

History and Politics

Little is known of Fiji's history prior to the arrival of Europeans. Melanesians probably migrated from Indonesia, followed by Polynesian settlers in the second century. After a Dutch navigator sighted Fiji in 1643, Captain James Cook of Britain visited the island in the eighteenth century. The nine-teenth century saw the arrival of European missionaries, traders, whalers, and several native wars. In 1874 tribal chiefs ceded Fiji to the British, who established sugar plan-tations and brought indentured Indian laborers. The country became independent in 1970. Fiji was ejected from the British Commonwealth in 1987 after declaring itself a republic and limiting participation by Indians in the government. A new con-stitution in 1990 institutionalized the dom-ination of ethnic Fijians.

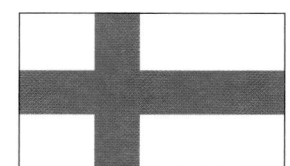

Finland's expansive Lake District is a medley of crystal lakes, rolling mead-ows, and deep forests. Whether canoeing, hiking, or cross-country skiing, Finns find a way to enjoy the District's sylvan charms in all seasons.

A fter decades of uneasy coexistence with the Soviet Union, Finland now openly embraces the Western European society it has quietly been a part of all along. It joined the European Union in 1995. The modern culture is distinguished by its unique language, whose roots are in the Ural Mountains, far to the east in Russia. *(continued)*

Fish are an important part of the Finnish diet. Fish vendors, such as this woman in Helsinki, can be found throughout the country. The Baltic Sea yields herring; the northern waters team with salmon, trout, and whitefish; and the southern lakes are filled with perch and pike. A popular snack is kalakukko, bread with fish in the middle.

POPULATION COMPARISON
Finland=2% of U.S.

United States

GDP COMPARISON
Finland=1% of U.S.

United States

POPULATION DISTRIBUTION
Urban   Rural

The sub-Arctic climate is moderated somewhat by the mild influences of North Atlantic currents, the Baltic Sea, and 60,000 lakes. Nevertheless, winters are long and cold.

People

The mainly Finnish population includes minorities of Swedes—a result of past Swedish rule—and indigenous Lapps. As part of northern Finland lies within the Arctic Circle, population is concentrated in the south. Finland's rich cultural tradition has contributed much to the arts. Its highly developed social welfare programs provide free education through the university level, as well as national health insurance.

Economy and the Land

Much of Finland's economy is based on its rich forests, which support trade and manufacturing activities. The steel industry is also important. Agriculture focuses on dairy farming and livestock raising; hence many fruits and vegetables must be imported. Coastal islands and lowlands, a central lake region, and northern hills mark Finland's scenic terrain. Summers in the south and central regions are warm, and winters long and cold. Northern Finland—located in the "Land of the Midnight Sun"—has periods of uninterrupted daylight in the summer and darkness in the winter.

History and Politics

The indigenous nomadic Lapps migrated north in the first century when the Finns arrived, probably from west-central Russia. A Russian-Swedish struggle for control of the area ended with Swedish rule in the 1100s. Finland was united with Denmark from the fourteenth through the sixteenth centuries. Russia and Sweden fought several wars for control of the country. In 1809 Finland became an autonomous grand duchy within the Russian Empire. After the Russian czar was overthrown in the 1917 Bolshevik Revolution, the new Russian government recognized Finland's declaration of independence. During World War II, Finland fought against the Soviets and, by the peace treaty signed in 1947, lost a portion of its land to the Soviet Union. During the postwar years, Finland and the Soviet Union developed strong economic ties that resulted in prosperity for Finland. The dissolution of the Soviet Union and a worldwide recession have threatened its economic stability.

Fruit market, Turku

Boats in bay, Helsinki

Finland at a glance

Official name	Republic of Finland

People

Population	5,098,000
Density	39/mi^2 (15/km^2)
Urban	60%
Capital	Helsinki, 501,514
Ethnic groups	Finnish (mixed Scandinavian and Baltic), Swedish, Lappic, Gypsy, Tatar
Languages	Finnish, Swedish, Lapp, Russian
Religions	Jehovah's Witness, Free Church, Adventist, Confessional Lutheran
Life expectancy	80 female, 72 male
Literacy	100%

Politics

Government	Republic
Parties	Center, Leftist Alliance, National Coalition, Social Democratic, others
Suffrage	Universal, over 18
Memberships	EU, NATO, OECD, UN
Subdivisions	12 provinces

Economy

GDP	$81,100,000,000
Per capita	$15,983
Monetary unit	Markkaa
Trade partners	Exports: Former Soviet republics, Sweden, Germany Imports: Germany, Sweden, former Soviet republics
Exports	Lumber, paper and pulp, ships, machinery, clothing and footwear
Imports	Food, petroleum, chemicals, transportation equipment, iron and steel

Land

Description	Northern Europe
Area	130,559 mi^2 (338,145 km^2)
Highest point	Haltia Mtn., 4,357 ft (1,328 m)
Lowest point	Sea level

Helsinki's Market Square is dominated by City Hall and the Senate. Most of the city has been built since 1812 when the capital was moved from Turku.

FINLAND

	Meters	Feet		Meters	Feet
Railroad	2000	6562			
+ Spot Elevation	1000	3281		0	0
Scale 1:8,634,000	500	1640		200	656
	200	656		2000	6562
	0	0			

© 1980 Rand McNally & Co.
A-550800-772

FRANCE

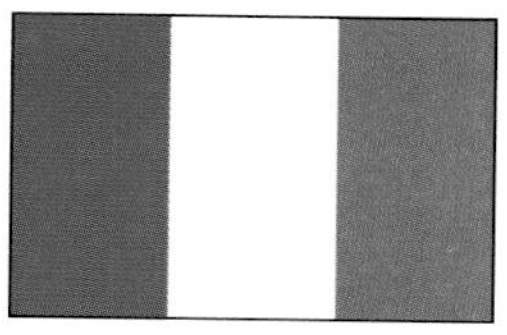

Grapes ripen on the vines under autumn skies in the Champagne region. To people the world over, the names of certain French regions and cities, such as Burgundy, Bordeaux, and Chablis, are synonymous with fine wine.

Renowned for its beauty and culture, France is a country filled with splendor: from the graceful magnificence of Paris, to the countryside of Normandy so popular with impressionist painters, to the sun-drenched glow of Provence. Although gritty industrial areas mar some regions, they are part of a modern economy that has produced such innovations as Europe's first high-speed train network. Preserving all that is French has led to darker traits, such as xenophobic discrimination against immigrants from former French colonies.

France at a glance

People

Official name	French Republic
Population	58,010,000
Density	275/mi² (106/km²)
Urban	73%
Capital	Paris, 2,152,423
Ethnic groups	French (mixed Celtic, Latin, and Teutonic)
Languages	French
Religions	Roman Catholic 90%, Protestant 2%, Jewish 1%, Muslim 1%
Life expectancy	81 female, 73 male
Literacy	99%

Politics

Government	Republic
Parties	Left Radical Movement, Rally for the Republic, Socialist, Union for Democracy, others
Suffrage	Universal, over 18
Memberships	EU, NATO, OECD, UN
Subdivisions	96 departments

Economy

GDP	$1,050,000,000,000
Per capita	$18,239
Monetary unit	Franc
Trade partners	Germany, Italy, Belgium
Exports	Machinery and transportation equipment, chemicals, food
Imports	Petroleum, machinery, agricultural products, chemicals, iron and steel

Land

Description	Western Europe
Area	211,208 mi² (547,026 km²)
Highest point	Mt. Blanc, (Monte Bianco), 15,771 ft (4,807 m)
Lowest point	Lac de Cazaux et de Sanguinet, -10 ft (-3 m)

The above information excludes French overseas departments.

Outdoor café, Nice

People
Many centuries ago, Celtic and Teutonic tribes and Latins established France's current ethnic patterns. The French language developed from the Latin of invading Romans but includes Celtic and Germanic influences as well. Language and customs vary somewhat from region to region, but most people who speak dialects also speak French. France has long contributed to learning and the arts, and Paris is a world cultural center. In addition to mainland divisions, the country has overseas departments and territories.

Economy and the Land
The French economy is highly developed. The nation is a leader in agriculture and industry; its problems of inflation and unemployment are common to other modern countries. Soils in the north and northeast are especially productive, and grapes are grown in the south. Minerals include iron ore and bauxite. Industry is diversified, centered in the Paris manufacturing area, and tourism is important. About two-thirds of the country is flat to rolling, and about one-third is mountainous, including the Pyrenees in the South and the Alps in the east. In the west and north, winters are cool and summers mild. Climate varies with altitude. The southern coast has a Mediterranean climate with hot summers and mild winters. *(continued)*

Normandy's fishing villages provide a serene respite from life's harried pace. Twice Normandy has seen invasions that changed the course of history: In 1066 William of Normandy embarked from its shores to conquer England; in 1944 the Allies' landings launched the liberation of Europe.

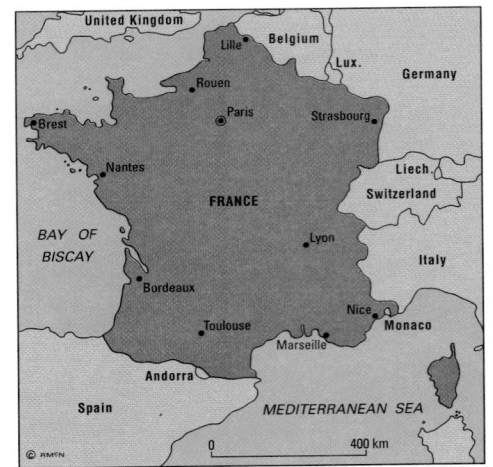

Bridge over the Dordogne

Eiffel Tower at night

France, continued

History and Politics

In ancient times Celtic tribes inhabited the area that encompasses present-day France. The Romans, who called the region Gaul, began to invade about 200 B.C., and by the 50s B.C. the entire region had come under Roman rule. Northern Germanic tribes—including the Franks, Visigoths, and Burgundians—spread throughout the region as Roman control weakened. The Franks defeated the Romans in A.D. 486. In the 800s Charlemagne greatly expanded Frankish-controlled territory, which was subsequently divided into three kingdoms. The western kingdom and part of the central kingdom included modern France. In 987 the Capetian dynasty began when Hugh Capet came to the throne, an event which is often considered the start of the French nation. During subsequent centuries, the power of the kings increased and France became a leading world power. Ambitious projects, such as the palace built by Louis XIV at Versailles, and several military campaigns, resulted in financial difficulties. The failing economy and divisions between rich and poor led to the French Revolution in 1789 and the First French Republic in 1792. Napoleon Bonaparte, who had gained prominence during the revolution, overthrew the government in 1799 and established the First Empire, which ended in 1815 with his defeat at Waterloo in Belgium. The subsequent monarchy resulted in discontent, and an 1848 revolution established the Second French Republic with an elected president, who in turn proclaimed himself emperor and set up the Second Empire in 1852. Following a war with Prussia in 1870, the emperor was ousted, and the Third Republic began. This republic repulsed Germany's invasion in World War I but ended in 1940 when invading Germans defeated the French. By 1942 the Nazis had control of the entire country. The Allies liberated France in 1944, and General Charles de Gaulle headed a provisional government until 1946, when the Fourth Republic was established. Colonial revolts in Africa and French Indochina took their toll on the economy during the 1950s. Controversy over a continuing Algerian war for independence brought de Gaulle

to power once more and resulted in the Fifth Republic in 1958. Dissension and national strikes erupted during the 1960s, a result of dissatisfaction with the government, and de Gaulle resigned in 1969. In 1987 François Mitterand was re-elected, giving the Socialists a plurality until 1993. Since then the country has moved steadily to the right. France's increasingly complex social problems are forcing wider representation in the government.

FRANCE

Major Urban Area

Railroad

Canal or Waterway

+ Spot Elevation or Depth

National capitals are underlined

City type size indicates relative importance

Meters	Feet
Above 4000	Above 13124
2000	6562
1000	3281
500	1640
200	656
0	0
200	656
Below 2000	Below 6562

Scale 1:6,892,000

© 1980, 1991 Rand McNally & Co.
A-550900-772 -2-1-2

For a moderate-size country, France contains an astonishing variety of topographic features, including rugged mountains, uplands, lowlands, plains, plateaus, and river valleys.

POPULATION COMPARISON
France=22% of U.S.

United States

GDP COMPARISON
France=17% of U.S.

United States

POPULATION DISTRIBUTION
Urban   Rural

The cathedral of Sacre Couer has a powerful presence on the Paris skyline, thanks to its grand location atop Montmarte. The surrounding warren of streets and quaint squares was popular with artists earlier in the century.

French Guiana at a glance

Official name   Department of Guiana

People

Population	134,000
Density	3.8/mi² (1.5/km²)
Urban	75%
Capital	Cayenne, 38,091
Ethnic groups	Black or mulatto 66%; white 12%; East Indian, Chinese, and Amerindian 12%
Languages	French
Religions	Roman Catholic
Life expectancy	78 female, 72 male
Literacy	82%

Politics

Government	Overseas department (France)
Parties	Democratic Action, Rally for the Republic, Socialist, Union for French Democracy
Suffrage	Universal, over 18
Memberships	None
Subdivisions	2 arrondissements

Economy

GDP	$421,000,000
Per capita	$5,198
Monetary unit	French franc
Trade partners	Exports: France, Guadeloupe, Spain Imports: France, Trinidad and Tobago, Germany
Exports	Shrimp, timber, rum, rosewood essence
Imports	Food, manufactures, petroleum

Land

Description	Northeastern South America
Area	35,135 mi² (91,000 km²)
Highest point	Unnamed, 2,723 ft (830 m)
Lowest point	Sea level

People

French Guiana has a majority population of black descendants of African slaves and people of mixed African-European ancestry. Population is concentrated in the more accessible coastal area, but the interior wilderness is home to minority Indians and the descendants of slaves who fled to pursue traditional African lifestyles. French is the predominant language, but a French-English creole is also spoken. Two

An overseas department of France,

An overseas department of France, French Guiana serves as the launch site for the French Arienne rockets. The land is sparsely populated, and nine-tenths of it is still covered by dense tropical forest.

FRENCH GUIANA

Indo-Chinese refugee settlements were established in 1977 and 1979.

Economy and the Land

Shrimp production and a growing timber industry are French Guiana's economic mainstays. The land remains largely undeveloped, however, and reliance on French aid continues. Agriculture is limited by wilderness, but mineral deposits offer potential for mining. The fertile coastal plains of the north give way to hills and mountains along the Brazilian border. Rain forests cover much of the landscape, which features a tropical climate.

History and Politics

Indigenous Indians and a hot climate defeated France's attempt at settlement in the early 1600s. The first permanent French settlement was established in 1634, and the area became a French colony in 1667. For almost one hundred years, beginning in the 1850s, penal colonies such as Devil's Island brought an influx of European prisoners. The region became a French overseas department in 1946. A minority nationalist group strives for greater autonomy.

FRENCH GUIANA

+ Spot Elevation
National capitals are underlined
Scale 1:5,280,000

	Meters	Feet	Meters	Feet
	1000	3281	0	0
	500	1640	200	656
	200	656	Below 2000	Below 6562
	0	0		

The infamous penal colony of Devil's Island lies 10 miles off French Guiana's coast. Before its closure in 1951, it was France's repository of political prisoners and wartime traitors.

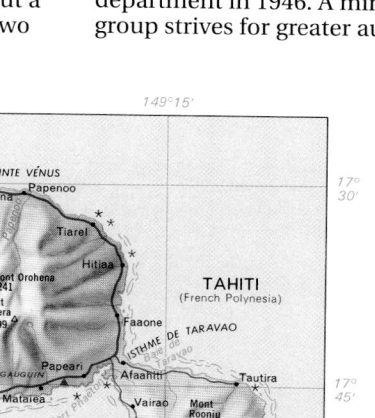

Contrary to popular belief, the French Polynesian island of Tahiti isn't surrounded by palm-fringed beaches. Most of the coastline is rocky. Beachcombing tourists take a ferry to nearby Moorea.

Scale 1:1,000,000   One inch represents approximately 16 miles.
One centimeter represents 10 kilometers.

French Polynesia at a glance

Official name   Territory of French Polynesia

People

Population	217,000
Density	160/mi² (62/km²)
Urban	65%
Capital	Papeete, Tahiti I., 23,555
Ethnic groups	Polynesian 78%, Chinese 12%, French descent 6%
Languages	French, Tahitian
Religions	Evangelical and other Protestant 54%, Roman Catholic 30%
Life expectancy	73 female, 68 male
Literacy	98%

Politics

Government	Overseas territory (France)
Parties	Amuitahiraa Mo Porinesia, Ia Mana, Pupu Here Ai'a, Tahoeraa Huiraatira
Suffrage	Universal, over 18
Memberships	None
Subdivisions	5 circumscriptions

Economy

GDP	$1,500,000,000
Per capita	$7,212
Monetary unit	CFP franc
Trade partners	Exports: France, Japan, U.S. Imports: France, U.S., Greece
Exports	Coconut products, mother-of-pearl, vanilla, shark meat
Imports	Fuel, food, machinery

Land

Description	South Pacific islands
Area	1,359 mi² (3,521 km²)
Highest point	Mont Orohena, 7,352 ft (2,241 m)
Lowest point	Sea level

People

Most inhabitants are Polynesian, with minorities including Chinese and French. More than one hundred islands compose the five archipelagoes, and population and commercial activity are concentrated in Papeete on Tahiti. Although per capita income is relatively high, wealth is not equally distributed. Emigration from the poorer islands to Tahiti is common. Polynesia's reputation as a tropical paradise has attracted many European and American writers and artists, including French painter Paul Gauguin.

Economy and the Land

The islands' economy is based on natural resources; coconut, mother-of-pearl, and tourism contribute. This South Pacific territory, located south of the equator and midway between South America and Australia, is spread over roughly 1.5 million square miles (3.9 million sq km) and is made up of the Marquesas Islands, the Society Islands, the Tuamotu Archipelago, the Gambier Islands, and the Austral Islands. The Marquesas, known for their beauty, form the northernmost group. The Society Islands, southwest of the Marquesas, include Tahiti and Bora-Bora, both popular tourist spots. The Tuamoto Archipelago lies south of the Marquesas and east of the Society Islands, the Gambier Islands are situated at the

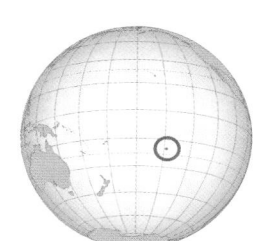

FRENCH POLYNESIA

southern tip of the Tuamotu group, and the Austral Islands lie to the southwest. The region includes both volcanic and coral islands, and the climate is tropical, with a rainy season extending from November to April.

History and Politics

The original settlers probably came from Micronesia and Melanesia in the east. Europeans began arriving around the sixteenth century. By the late 1700s they had reached the five major island groups, and visitors to the area included mutineers from the British vessel *Bounty*. By the 1880s the islands had come under French rule, although they did not become an overseas territory until 1946. The country has since moved toward internal autonomy, with discussion of eventual independence.

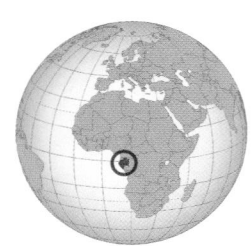

GABON

Gabon at a glance

Official name   Gabonese Republic

People

Population	1,035,000
Density	10/mi² (3.9/km²)
Urban	46%
Capital	Libreville, 235,700
Ethnic groups	Fang, Eshira, Bapounou, Bateke
Languages	French, Fang, indigenous
Religions	Roman Catholic and other Christian 55-75%, Muslim
Life expectancy	55 female, 52 male
Literacy	61%

Politics

Government	Republic
Parties	Democratic, National Recovery Movement-Lumberjacks, Party for Progress
Suffrage	Universal, over 21
Memberships	OAU, OPEC, UN
Subdivisions	9 provinces

Economy

GDP	$5,400,000,000
Per capita	$4,843
Monetary unit	CFA franc
Trade partners	Exports: France, U.S., Spain Imports: France, U.S., Japan
Exports	Petroleum, manganese, wood, uranium
Imports	Food, chemicals, petroleum, construction materials, manufactures

Land

Description	Central Africa
Area	103,347 mi² (267,667 km²)
Highest point	Unnamed, 3,360 ft (1,024 m)
Lowest point	Sea level

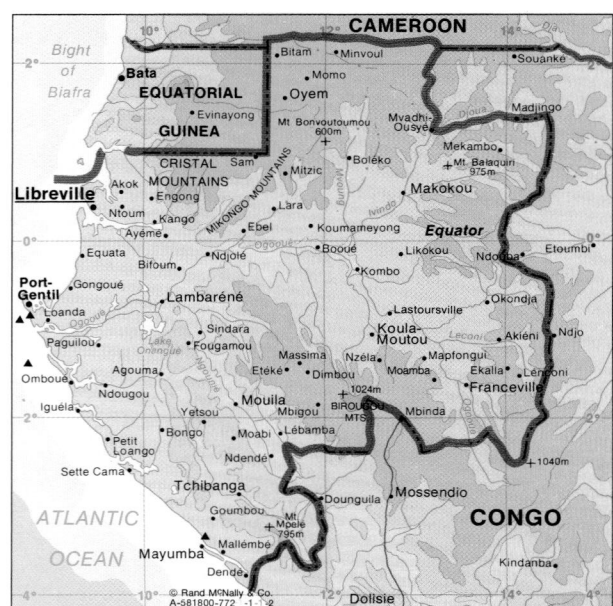

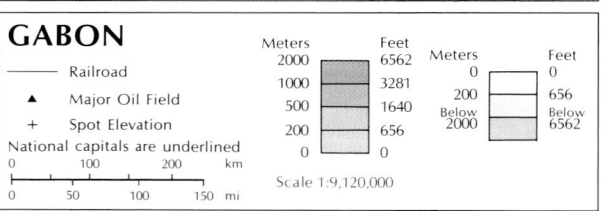

GABON

		Meters	Feet	Meters	Feet
——	Railroad	2000	6562		
▲	Major Oil Field	1000	3281	200	656
+	Spot Elevation	500	1640	Below	Below
	National capitals are underlined	200	656	2000	6562
		Below	0	0	0

0 100 200 km
0 50 100 150 mi
Scale 1:9,120,000

Albert Schweitzer, the 20th century's most famous medical missionary, established a hospital at the river city of Lambaréné to combat the many sicknesses endemic in equatorial Africa.

People

Of Gabon's more than forty ethnic groups, the Fang are a majority and inhabit the area north of the Ogooué River. Other major groups include the Eshira, Bapounou, and Bateke. The French, who colonized the area, compose a larger group today than during colonial times. Each of the groups has its own distinct language and culture, but French remains the official language.

Economy and the Land

Gabon is located astride the equator, and its many resources include petroleum, manganese, uranium, and dense rain forests. The most important activities are oil production, forestry, and mining. The economy depends greatly on foreign investment and imported labor, however, and many native Gabonese continue as subsistence farmers. While the labor short-age hinders economic development, the country has a high per capita income. The terrain is marked by a coastal plain, inland forested hills, and savanna in the east and south. The climate is hot and humid.

History and Politics

First inhabited by Pygmies, Gabon was the site of migrations by numerous Bantu peoples during its early history. The thick rain forests isolated the migrant groups from one another and thus preserved their individual cultures. The Portuguese arrived in the fifteenth century, followed by the Dutch, British, and French in the 1700s. The slave and ivory trades flourished, and the Fang, drawn by the prosperity, migrated to the coast in the 1800s. A group of freed slaves founded Libreville, which later became the capital. By 1885 France had gained control of the area, and in 1910 it was united with present-day Chad, the Congo, and the Central African Republic as French Equatorial Africa. Gabon became independent in 1960, and in 1964 French assistance thwarted a military takeover. After anti-government protests in 1990, opposition parties were legalized.

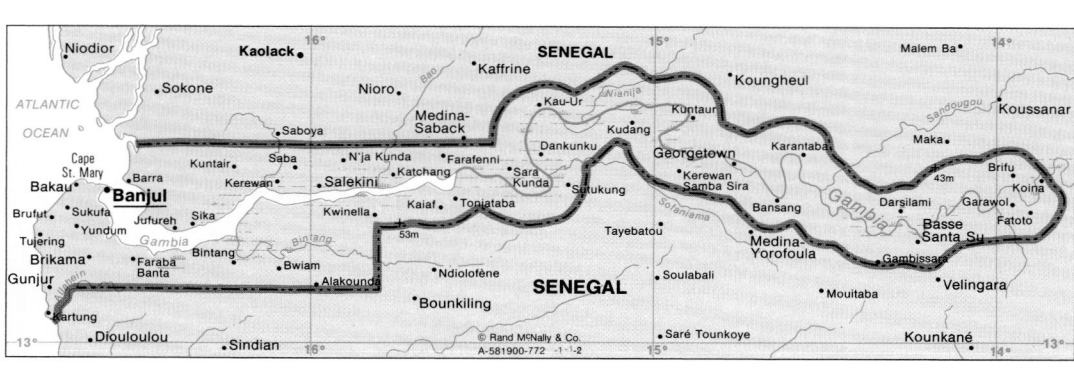

Agriculture is limited by Gambia's size. Rice is grown in the swamps close to the river, and peanuts are grown in the sandy soil away from the banks.

GAMBIA

+	Spot Elevation
	National capital is underlined

Meters	Feet
500	1640
200	656
0	0
200	656

Scale 1:2,280,000
0 10 20 30 km
0 10 20 mi

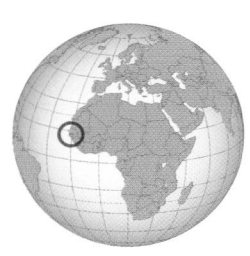

GAMBIA

People

Gambia's population includes the Mandingo, or Malinke; Fulani; Wolof; Jola; and Serahuli. Most people are Muslim, and language differs from group to group, although the official language is English. Gambians are mainly rural farmers, and literacy is low, with educational opportunities focused in the Banjul area. The population's size varies with the arrival and departure of seasonal Senegalese farm laborers.

Economy and the Land

Gambia's economy relies on peanut production, and crop diversification is a current goal. Subsistence crops include rice, and the government hopes increased rice production will decrease dependence on imports and foreign aid. Fishing and tourism have expanded in the past years. In addition, the Gambia River, which provides a route to the African interior, offers potential for an increased role in trade. Dense mangrove swamps border the river, giving way to flat ground that floods in the rainy season. Behind this lie sand hills and plateaus. Low-lying Gambia, with its subtropical climate, is virtually an enclave within Senegal.

History and Politics

From the thirteenth to the fifteenth centuries the flourishing Mali Empire included the Gambia area. The Portuguese arrived in the fifteenth century, established slave trading posts, and sold trade rights to Britain in 1588. During the seventeenth and eighteenth centuries France and Britain competed for control of the river trade. By the late 1800s the Banjul area had become a British colony and the interior a British protectorate. Gambia achieved independence as a monarchy in 1965 and became a republic in 1970. Many years of electoral democracy were interrupted by a bloodless coup in July 1994. The new regime promised reforms, including a new constitution, followed by free elections.

Gambia at a glance

Official name   Republic of the Gambia

People

Population	1,082,000
Density	262/mi² (101/km²)
Urban	23%
Capital	Banjul, 44,188
Ethnic groups	Malinke 42%, Fulani 18%, Wolof 16%, Jola 10%, Serahuli 9%
Languages	English, Malinke, Wolof, Fula, indigenous
Religions	Muslim 90%, Christian 9%, tribal religionist 1%
Life expectancy	47 female, 43 male
Literacy	27%

Politics

Government	Provisional military government
Parties	National Convention, People's, People's Progressive
Suffrage	Universal, over 21
Memberships	CW, OAU, UN
Subdivisions	5 divisions, 1 city

Economy

GDP	$740,000,000
Per capita	$808
Monetary unit	Dalasi
Trade partners	Exports: Japan, European countries, African countries. Imports: European countries, Asian countries
Exports	Peanuts, fish, cotton, palm kernels. Imports Food, manufactures, raw materials, fuel

Land

Description	Western Africa
Area	4,127 mi² (10,689 km²)
Highest point	Unnamed, 174 ft (53 m)
Lowest point	Sea level

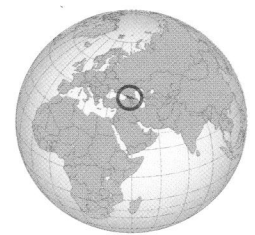

Church and village on the road from Tbilisi, Georgia's capital, to the ski resort of Guduari

GEORGIA

G eorgia has seen the same bloody ethnic fighting all too common to the southern parts of the former Soviet Union since its demise. The violence has disrupted imports of energy supplies, resulting in massive power shortages and a crippling of the economy. Until peace is restored and a stable government in place, Georgia will remain impoverished.

People
Georgians are the descendants of the original inhabitants of the Caucasus region, and are proud of their ancient culture and language. Georgians have been Christians since the fourth century, and are world renowned for their many important contributions to the arts. Georgia is also home to Armenian, Russian, Abkhazian, and Ossetian minorities.

Economy and the Land
Despite its small size, Georgia has a variety of climates and terrains. Most of Georgia is mountainous or forested, but there are also fertile plains and valleys that are highly suitable for agriculture. Vineyards and orchards are scattered throughout the country. The area on the shores of the Black Sea is subtropical and is used for growing tea and citrus fruit. Georgia also has a well-developed industrial base as a result of its enormous hydroelectric power resources. The country has abundant mineral deposits, including coal and manganese. Georgia also has an active tourism industry that has been recently weakened by political instability.

History and Politics
Civilization has flourished in the Georgian region since 3000 B.C. The country's great wealth attracted a variety of invaders, including the Roman, Byzantine, and Persian empires. Arabs invaded the region in the seventh century. The early thirteenth century marked a high point in Georgia's cultural influence throughout the region, but this era was brought to a sudden end by the invasion of the Mongols. The country was later divided between the Turks and the Persians before it was annexed by Russia in 1801. Georgia, the birthplace of Joseph Stalin, played an important role in the Russian revolution of 1917. After the revolution, Georgia declared its independence, but Soviet troops invaded the country and forced its surrender in 1921. Resistance continued until great purges in the late 1930s eliminated Georgia's enemies of communism. After Soviet troops attacked Georgian demonstrators with poison gas in 1990, Georgia declared its independence in April 1991. It achieved full independence after the Soviet Union fell the following December, but freedom did not bring peace. Fighting immediately resumed as pro-democracy elements battled to force the resignation of the country's first-elected president, the controversial Zviad Gamsakhurdia. In 1992 the former Soviet foreign minister Eduard Shevardnadze was elected head of state. Georgia has been troubled by secessionist wars ignited by ethnic minorities in the Georgian territory of Abkhazia. Russia aided the government after Georgia agreed to join the Commonwealth of Independent States in 1994.

11th-century cathedral

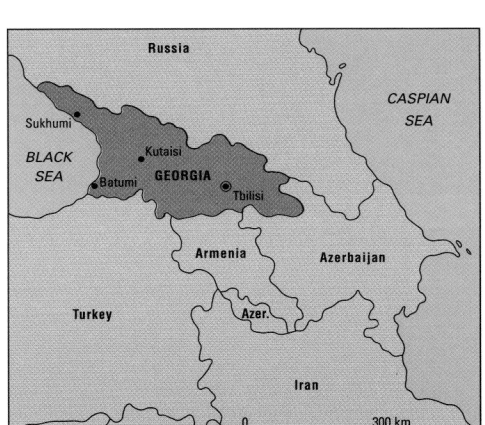

Rustaveli Boulevard, Tbilisi

Georgia at a glance

Official name	Republic of Georgia

People

Population	5,704,000
Density	212/mi² (82/km²)
Urban	56%
Capital	Tbilisi, 1,279,000
Ethnic groups	Georgian 70%, Armenian 8%, Russian 6%, Azeri 6%, Ossetian 3%, Abkhaz 2%
Languages	Georgian, Russian, Armenian, Azeri
Religions	Georgian Orthodox 65%, Muslim 11%, Russian Orthodox 10%
Life expectancy	76 female, 69 male
Literacy	99%

Politics

Government	Republic
Parties	Round Table-Free Georgia, others
Suffrage	Universal, over 18
Memberships	CIS, UN
Subdivisions	2 republics

Economy

GDP	$7,800,000,000
Per capita	$1,148
Monetary unit	Coupon
Trade partners	Former Soviet republics
Exports	Fruit, tea, machinery, metals, textiles
Imports	Machinery, fuel, transportation equipment, textiles

Land

Description	Southwestern Asia
Area	26,911 mi² (69,700 km²)
Highest point	Mt. Shkhara, 16,627 ft (5,068 m)
Lowest point	Sea level

POPULATION COMPARISON
Georgia=2% of U.S.

United States

ETHNIC GROUPS

Other
Abkhaz
Ossetian
Azeri
Russian
Armenian
Georgian

POPULATION DISTRIBUTION

Urban _____ Rural

Along the Black Sea, Georgia has a subtropical climate favorable for grape-growing and citrus orchards. Once popular with Russian vacationers, the region's beach resorts have been empty since fighting began.

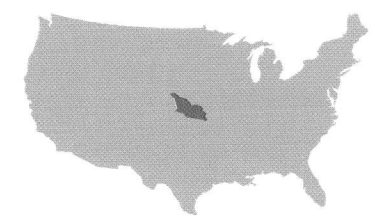

GEORGIA

| Railroad |
| Oil Pipeline |
| Major Oil Field |

Glacier
Spot Elevation
National capitals are underlined

Scale 1:7,143,000

GERMANY

The Bavarian Alps are filled with the kind of quaint scenes people often associate with Germany: flower-bedecked houses set in green valleys backed by soaring snow-capped peaks.

Twice defeated in World Wars in the first half of the century, Germany has become one of the world's economic and industrial powerhouses in the second half. Four decades of Soviet domination of the eastern portion of the country ended in 1989 with the fall of both the Berlin Wall and communism. The heady rejoicing following reunification has been tempered by resentment on both sides. Westerners resent the vast sums of money needed to rebuild the east, while easterners resent the patronizing attitudes of the west.

People
Germany has a homogeneous, German-speaking population with a very small Turkish minority. Roman Catholics, Evangelicals, and other Protestants are the largest religious groups. Germans are well-educated and boast a rich cultural heritage of achievements in music, literature, philosophy, and science. Germany has the largest population of any European nation, excluding Russia.

Economy and the Land
Despite the devastating effects of World War II and Germany's 45-year division into two countries, the country has one of the world's strongest economies. Industry is the basis of its prosperity, with mining, manufacturing, construction, and utilities as important contributors. The Ruhr district, which is the nation's most important industrial region, is located near the Rhine River in west-central Germany and includes cities such as Essen and Dortmund. Agriculture remains important in the southern and central regions. Germany's terrain varies from northern plains to central uplands and hills that rise to the southern Bavarian Alps. A mild climate is tempered by the sea in the north; in the south the winters are colder because of the Alps.

History and Politics
In ancient times Germanic tribes overcame Celtic inhabitants in the area of Germany and established a northern stronghold against Roman expansion of Gaul. As the Roman Empire weakened, the Germanic peoples invaded, deposing the Roman governor of Gaul in the fifth century A.D. The Franks composed the strongest tribe, and in the ninth century Frankish-controlled territory was expanded and united under Charlemagne. Unity did not last, however, and Germany remained a disjointed territory of warring feudal states, duchies, and independent cities. The Reformation, a movement led by German monk Martin Luther, began in 1517 and evolved into the Protestant branch of Christianity. The rise of Prussian power and growing nationalism eventually united the German states into the German Empire in 1871, and Prussian chancellor Otto von Bismarck installed Prussian King Wilhelm I as emperor. In a few short years, Germany rose to become Europe's foremost industrial and military power. In 1914 Germany allied with Austria; their subsequent invasions of France and Russia led to World War I. Hardships imposed by the victors against Germany led to instability and economic collapse. Promising prosperity, Adolf Hitler and his National Socialist, or Nazi, party rose to power in 1933. Hitler's ruthless nationalist policies included a genocidal program to eliminate Jews and many other peoples, and his ambitions to conquer all of Europe led to World War II. The Allied Forces defeated Germany in 1945 only after enormous casualties had been inflicted on both sides. The United States, Britain, the Soviet Union, and France subsequently divided Germany into four zones of occupation. The eastern, Soviet-occupied zone became a Communist country called the German Democratic Republic, or East Germany. The three remaining zones of Germany were combined to form the capitalist Federal Republic of Germany, or West Germany. Berlin, not included in occupation zones, was divided between the east and west. The Berlin Wall became a symbol of the cold war between the United States and the Soviet Union. In the late 1980s the Soviet Union began to loosen its grip on its satellite nations, and in 1989 East Germans began a mass exodus to West Germany. In October 1990 East Germany was officially absorbed into West Germany. Elation over reunification has been followed by unforeseen economic problems and rising political violence.

(top) The old walled city of Rothenburg

(middle) Eastern German factories

(bottom) Spree River, Berlin

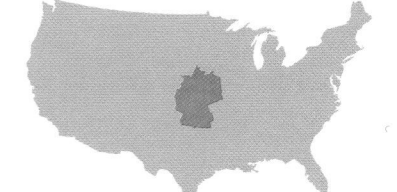

POPULATION COMPARISON
Germany=31% of U.S.

United States

GDP COMPARISON
Germany=21% of U.S.

United States

ETHNIC GROUPS

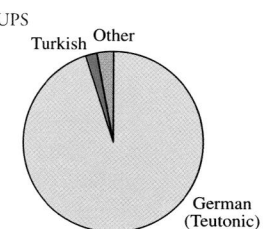

Turkish Other

German (Teutonic)

POPULATION DISTRIBUTION
Urban   Rural

In the north, Germany is a featureless plain meeting the sea. South, in Bavaria, it is a series of peaks bordering the Swiss and Austrian Alps. In between are dramatic features such as the castle-lined Rhine Valley and the fog-shrouded forests east of Berlin.

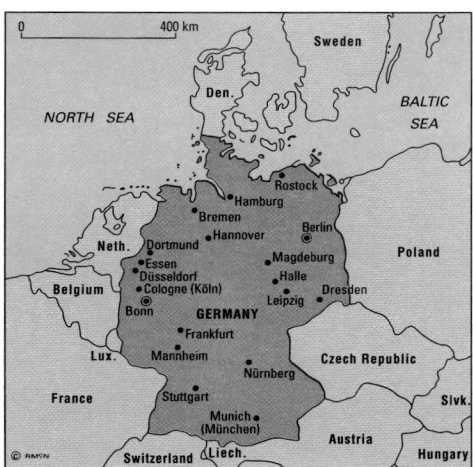

Germany at a glance

Official name	Federal Republic of Germany

People

Population	81,710,000
Density	593/mi^2 (229/km^2)
Urban	85%
Capital	Berlin (designated), 3,433,695; Bonn (de facto), 292,234
Ethnic groups	German (Teutonic) 95%, Turkish 2%
Languages	German
Religions	Evangelical and other Protestant 45%, Roman Catholic 37%
Life expectancy	79 female, 73 male
Literacy	99%

Politics

Government	Republic
Parties	Christian Democratic Union, Christian Social Union, Free Democratic, Social Democratic, others
Suffrage	Universal, over 18
Memberships	EU, NATO, OECD, UN
Subdivisions	16 states

Economy

GDP	$1,331,000,000,000
Per capita	$16,516
Monetary unit	Mark
Trade partners	Exports: France, Italy, Netherlands, U.K. Imports: France, Netherlands, Italy, Belgium
Exports	Machinery, chemicals, transportation equipment, iron and steel
Imports	Manufactures, agricultural products, raw materials, fuel

Land

Description	Northern Europe
Area	137,822 mi^2 (356,955 km^2)
Highest point	Zugspitze, 9,718 ft (2,962 m)
Lowest point	Freepsum Lake, -7 ft (-2 m)

GERMANY

Major Urban Area
Railroad
Canal or Waterway
Spot Elevation or Depth
State Boundary
Capitals are underlined
City type size indicates relative importance

Scale 1:4,413,000

The Kurfurstendamn is Berlin's main avenue of shopping and nightlife. A major feature is the Kaiser Wilhelm Church; destroyed in World War II, its ruins house a peace museum.

Brandenburg Gate, Berlin

Shepherd and flock in eastern Germany

Frankfurt grew to become Germany's economic capital after World War II. Primarily composed of modern structures, the city contains little of historical interest. It is bisected by the Main River.

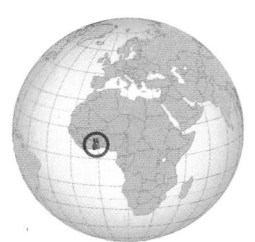

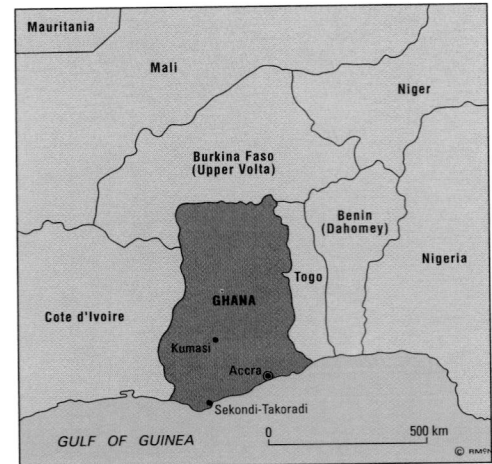

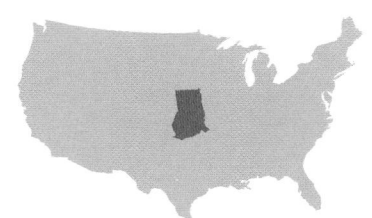

GHANA

The first of Britain's African colonies granted independence, Ghana hoped to be a model for the others to follow. Sadly, it became an example of how badly things can go wrong. Rule by a series of dictators was interspersed with bloody coups, and scores of people died in ethnic clashes. Recent efforts to mend the economy and allow for democratic elections offer some hope that Ghana may finally be on the right course.

POPULATION COMPARISON
Ghana=7% of U.S.

United States

GDP COMPARISON
Ghana=0.4% of U.S.

United States

ETHNIC GROUPS

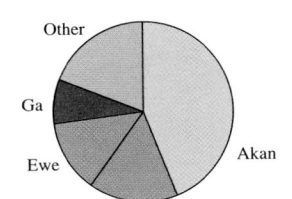

POPULATION DISTRIBUTION
Urban   Rural

Lake Volta, created by a hydroelectric dam on the Volta River, is the world's largest artificial lake.

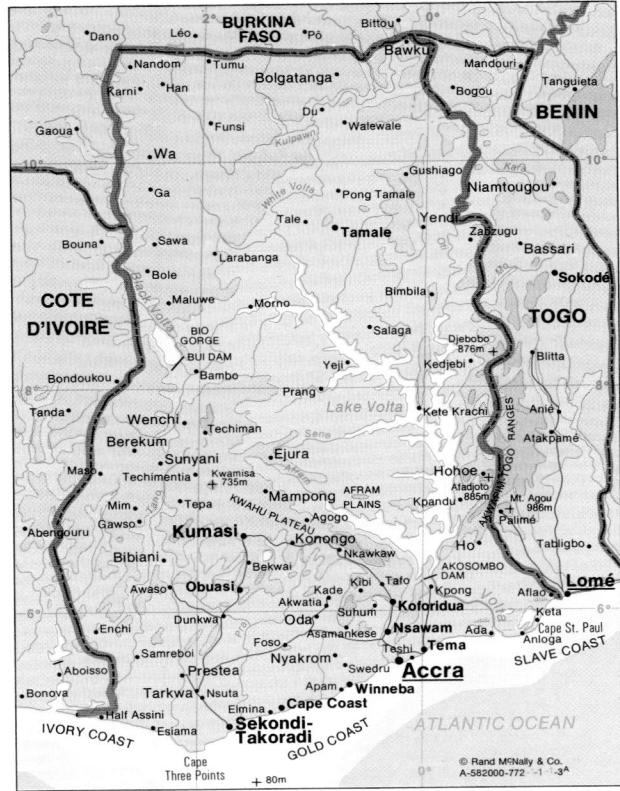

GHANA

	Meters	Feet
	1000	3281
	500	1640
	200	656
	0	0
	200	656
	Below 2000	Below 6562

— Railroad

+ Spot Elevation or Depth

National capitals are underlined

City type size indicates relative importance

Scale 1:7,238,000

0   50   100   150 km

0   50   100 mi

People

Nearly all Ghanaians are black Africans. The Akan, the majority group, are further divided into the Fanti, who live mainly along the coast, and the Ashanti, who inhabit the forests north of the coast. The Ewe and Ga live in the south and southeast. Other groups include the Guan, living on the Volta River plains, and the Moshi-Dagomba in the North. Ghana's more than fifty languages and dialects reflect this ethnic diversity, and English, the official language, is spoken by a minority. Islam and traditional African religions predominate, but a Christian minority also exists. Most people live in rural areas, and the literacy rate is low.

Economy and the Land

Agriculture is the economic base, but Ghana's natural resources are diverse. Production of cocoa, the most important export, is concentrated in the Ashanti region, a belt of tropical rain forest extending north from the coastal plain. Resources include forests and mineral deposits, and exploitation of bauxite, gold, diamonds, and manganese ore is currently underway. Ghana has enjoyed steady economic growth since the 1980s. Its coastal lowlands give way to scrub and plains, the Ashanti rain forest, and northern savanna. A dam on the Volta River has created the world's largest reservoir. The climate is tropical.

History and Politics

The ancestors of today's Ghanaians probably migrated from the northern areas of Mauritania and Mali in the thirteenth century. The Portuguese reached the shore around 1470 and called the area the Gold Coast. Many countries competed for the region, but in 1874 the Gold Coast was made a British colony. By 1901 Britain had extended its control to the inland Ashanti area, which became a colony, and the northern territories, which became a protectorate. The three regions were merged with British Togoland, a onetime German colony under British administration since 1922. In 1957 the four regions united as independent Ghana. Instability resulted, arising from a history of disunity and economic problems. The parliamentary state became a republic in 1960, and civilian rule has alternated with military governments. The leader of the 1981 military coup was elected as a civilian president in 1992 and has overseen a successful economic recovery program.

Ghana at a glance
Official name   Republic of Ghana

People

Population	17,210,000
Density	187/mi² (72/km²)
Urban	34%
Capital	Accra, 949,113
Ethnic groups	Akan 44%, Moshi-Dagomba 16%, Ewe 13%, Ga 8%
Languages	English, Akan and other indigenous
Religions	Tribal religionist 38%, Muslim 30%, Christian 24%
Life expectancy	58 female, 54 male
Literacy	60%

Politics

Government	Republic
Parties	None
Suffrage	Universal, over 18
Memberships	CW, OAU, UN
Subdivisions	10 regions

Economy

GDP	$25,000,000,000
Per capita	$1,520
Monetary unit	Cedi
Trade partners	Exports: Switzerland, U.S. Imports: Nigeria, U.S., Germany
Exports	Cocoa, gold, timber, tuna, bauxite, aluminum
Imports	Petroleum, manufactures, food, machinery

Land

Description	Western Africa
Area	92,098 mi² (238,533 km²)
Highest point	Afadjoto, 2,905 ft (885 m)
Lowest point	Sea level

People and boats on beach, Winneba

Corn grows at a village near the town of Tamale in north Ghana. Like the rest of Central Africa's people, most Ghanaians are subsistence farmers.

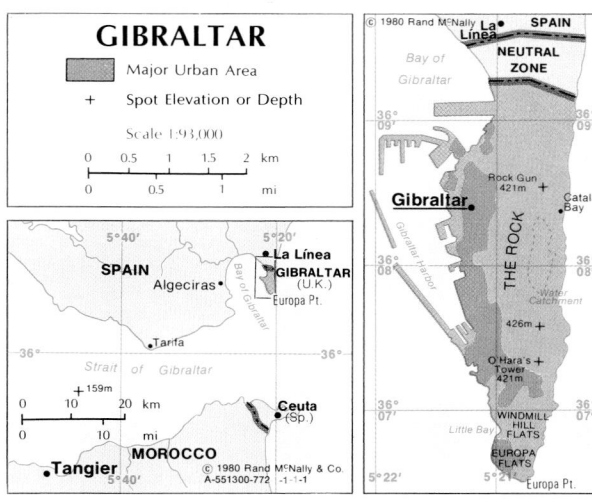

GIBRALTAR
- Major Urban Area
- + Spot Elevation or Depth
- Scale 1:93,000

The border on the narrow isthmus connecting Gibraltar to the mainland was closed by Spain from 1969 to 1985. Its opening was a boon to tourism, the primary component of the Rock's economy.

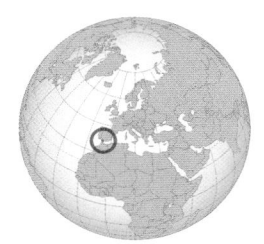

GIBRALTAR

Gibraltar at a glance

Official name	Gibraltar

People

Population	32,000
Density	13,913/mi² (5,333/km²)
Urban	100%
Capital	Gibraltar, 32,000
Ethnic groups	Gibraltarian (mixed Italian, English, Maltese, Portuguese, and Spanish) 75%, British 14%
Languages	English, Spanish, Italian, Portuguese, Russian
Religions	Roman Catholic 74%, Anglican 8%, Muslim 8%, Jewish 2%, Hindu 1%
Life expectancy	79 female, 73 male
Literacy	

Politics

Government	Dependent territory (U.K.)
Parties	National, Social Democratic, Socialist Labor
Suffrage	Universal, over 18
Memberships	None
Subdivisions	None

Economy

GNP	$182,000,000
Per capita	$5,871
Monetary unit	Pound
Trade partners	Exports: U.K., Morocco, Portugal Imports: U.K., Spain, Japan
Exports	Petroleum, manufactures
Imports	Fuel, manufactures, food

Land

Description	Southwestern Europe (peninsula on Spain's southern coast)
Area	2.3 mi² (6.0 km²)
Highest point	1,398 ft (426 m)
Lowest point	Sea level

Commanding the entrance to the Mediterranean, Gibraltar is a colonial remnant of the time when Britain's empire spanned the globe and its navy ruled the sea. The inhabitants are almost universally British and regularly indicate their desire to remain under British rule. This has complicated relations with Spain, which would like to assume control.

People

Occupying a narrow peninsula on Spain's southern coast, the British colony of Gibraltar has a mixed population of Italian, Maltese, Portuguese, and Spanish descent. A large number of British residents are also present, many of them military personnel. Most are bilingual, speaking English and Spanish

Economy and the Land

With land unsuited for agriculture and a lack of mineral resources, Gibraltar depends mainly on the British military presence and tourism. More than half of Gibraltar's male population works for British departments or the Gibraltar government. The private sector provides jobs as well, and shipping-related activities, construction, hotels, food services, and retail distributors are employers. The bottling industry provides for earnings in manufacturing. Connected to Spain by an isthmus, Gibraltar consists mainly of the limestone-and-shale ridge known as the Rock of Gibraltar. The climate is mild.

History and Politics

Drawn by Gibraltar's strategic location at the Atlantic entrance to the Mediterranean, Phoenicians, Carthaginians, Romans, Vandals, Visigoths, and Moors all played a role in the land's history. After nearly three hundred years under Spanish control, Gibraltar was captured by Britain in 1704, during the War of the Spanish Succession. It was officially ceded to the British in the 1713 Peace of Utrecht. In a 1967 referendum, residents voted to remain under British control. British-Spanish competition for the colony has continued, however, and the border between Spain and Gibraltar was closed by the Spanish government in 1969 and did not reopen until 1985.

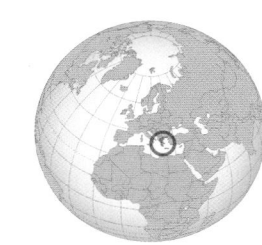

Greece, the birthplace of Western civilization, is today a land of contrasts, where treasured buildings of the ancient world exist next to ugly modernity. The cradle of democracy is now beset with a host of political problems. Still, Greece remains extremely popular with tourists, especially European sunseekers. But while some parts of the country are overrun with visitors, others are all but undiscovered. *(continued)*

GREECE

A hundred years ago, Athens was a small town, home to only 30,000 people and surrounded by olive groves. Today it is a fast-growing metropolis of more than three million. To combat the smog which is destroying Athens' ancient monuments, cars have been banned from the city center.

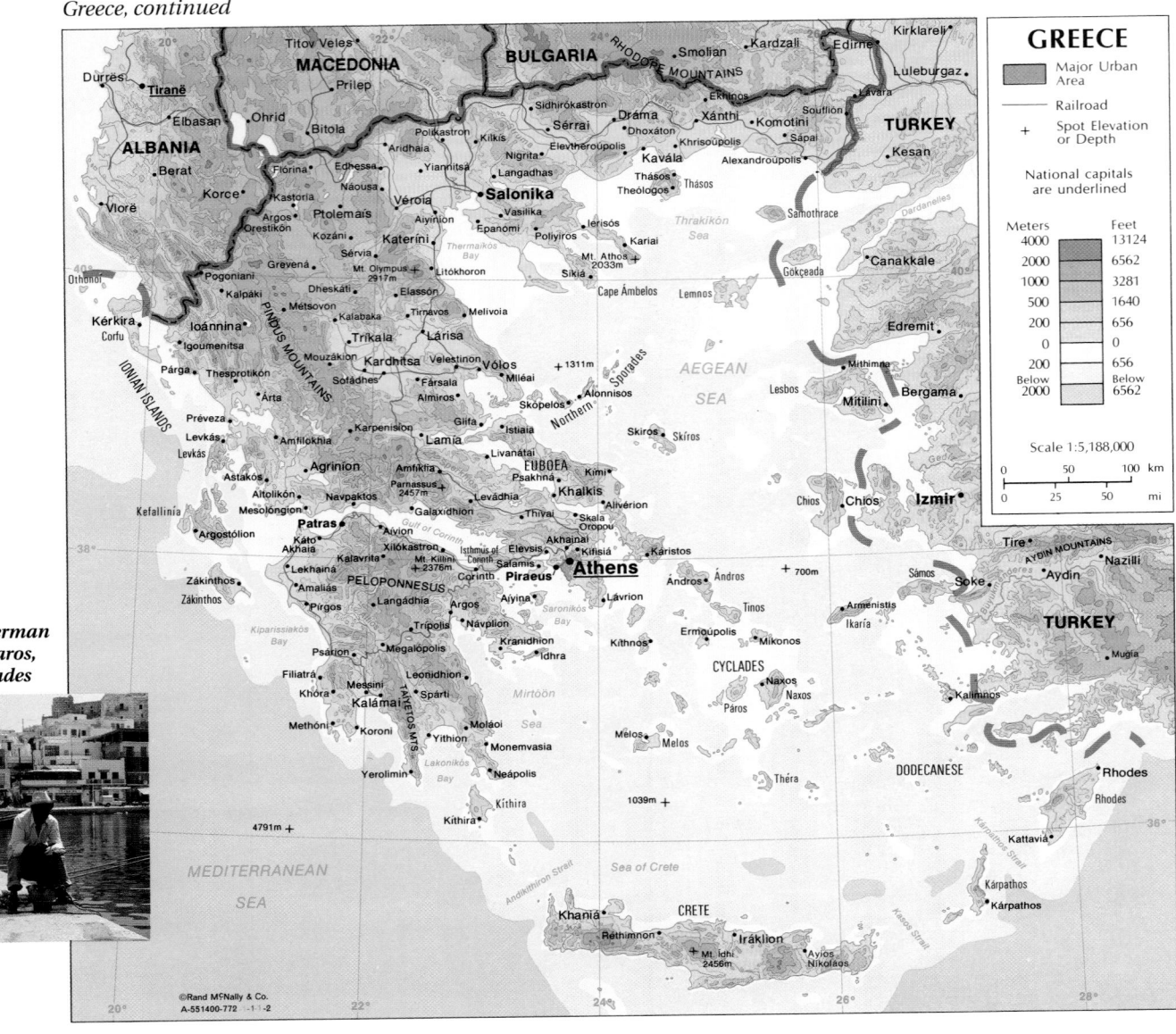

GREECE

Major Urban Area

Railroad

+ Spot Elevation or Depth

National capitals are underlined

Meters		Feet
4000		13124
2000		6562
1000		3281
500		1640
200		656
0		0
200		656
Below 2000		Below 6562

Scale 1:5,188,000

0   50   100 km

0   25   50 mi

Fisherman on Paros, Cyclades

Of the more than 2,000 Greek islands, only 169 are inhabited. Some, such as Crete and Rhodes, were as important a part of the ancient world as was Athens. Today, the islands and their white-washed villages sit serenely in the sun surrounded by blue Mediterranean waters.

Fresco, Knossos ruins, Crete

People

Greece has played a central role in European, African, and Asian cultures for thousands of years, but today its population is almost homogeneous. Native Greek inhabitants are united by a language that dates back 3,000 years and a religion that influences many aspects of everyday life. Athens, the capital, was the cultural center of an ancient civilization that produced masterpieces of art and literature and broke ground in philosophy, political thought, and science.

Economy and the Land

The economy of Greece takes its shape from terrain and location. Dominated by the sea and long a maritime trading power, Greece has one of the largest merchant fleets in the world and depends greatly on commerce. The mountainous terrain and poor soil limit agriculture, although Greece is a leading producer of lemons and olives. The service sector, including tourism, provides most of Greece's national income. Inhabitants enjoy a temperate climate, with mild, wet winters, and hot, dry summers.

Waterfront homes face the Aegean Sea on Mikonos, Greece's most famous and most-visited small island.

A Byzantine church sits serenely on a hill on the south coast of Crete, the southernmost part of Europe. The rugged island was once home to the Minoans, whose rich culture flourished 5,000 years ago.

A characteristically white-washed church contrasts with the azure waters surrounding Santorini, another picture-perfect Greek island. The island of Akrotiri in the distance is a major archeological site.

History and Politics

Greece's history begins with the early Bronze Age cultures of the Minoans and the Mycenaeans. The city-state, or *polis*, began to develop around the tenth century B.C., and Athens, a democracy, and Sparta, an oligarchy, gradually emerged as Greece's leaders. The Persian Wars, in which the city-states united to repel a vastly superior army, ushered in the Golden Age of Athens, a cultural explosion in the fifth century B.C. The Parthenon, perhaps Greece's most famous building, was built at this time. Athens was defeated by Sparta in the Peloponnesian War, and by 338 B.C. Philip II of Macedon had conquered all of Greece. His son, Alexander the Great, defeated the Persians and spread Greek civilization and language all over the known world. Greece became a Roman province in 146 B.C. and part of the Byzantine Empire in A.D. 395, but its traditions had a marked influence on these empires. Absorbed into the Ottoman Empire in the 1450s, Greece had gained independence by 1830 and became a constitutional monarchy about fifteen years later. For much of the twentieth century the nation was divided between republicans and monarchists. During World War II Germany occupied Greece, and postwar instability led to a civil war, which Communist rebels eventually lost. A repressive military junta ruled Greece from 1967 until 1974, followed by a civilian government. The Greeks voted for a republic, over a monarchy, and in 1993 Socialists regained power.

Greece at a glance

Official name	Hellenic Republic

People

Population	10,475,000
Density	206/mi² (79/km²)
Urban	63%
Capital	Athens, 748,110
Ethnic groups	Greek 98%
Languages	Greek, English, French
Religions	Greek Orthodox 98%, Muslim 1%
Life expectancy	80 female, 75 male
Literacy	93%

Politics

Government	Republic
Parties	New Democracy, Left Alliance, Panhellenic Socialist Movement, others
Suffrage	Universal, over 18
Memberships	EU, NATO, OECD, UN
Subdivisions	13 regions

Economy

GDP	$93,200,000,000
Per capita	$9,251
Monetary unit	Drachma
Trade partners	Germany, Italy, France
Exports	Manufactures, food and beverages, fuel and lubricants
Imports	Manufactures, machinery, food, fuels and lubricants

Land

Description	Southeastern Europe
Area	50,949 mi² (131,957 km²)
Highest point	Mt. Olympus, 9,570 ft (2,917 m)
Lowest point	Sea level

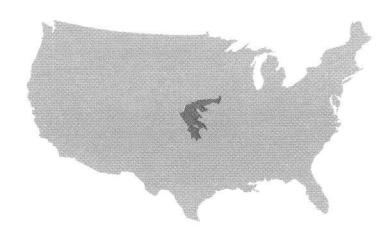

POPULATION COMPARISON
Greece=4% of U.S.

United States

GDP COMPARISON
Greece=2% of U.S.

United States

ETHNIC GROUPS

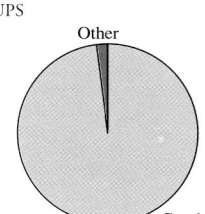

Other

Greek

POPULATION DISTRIBUTION

Urban   Rural

(top) Cliffs of Thera

(bottom) Relief sculpture, Delphi

Corinthian columns near Corinth

The Parthenon, Athens

Three columns are all that remain of Tholos, an important part of the ancient Greek ruins at Delphi. Ancient legend held that the city, in the center of Greece, was also the center of the world.

GREENLAND

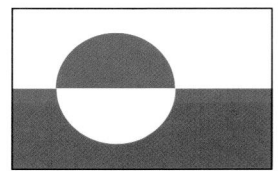

People

Most Greenlanders are native-born descendants of mixed Inuit-Danish ancestry. Lutheranism, the predominant religion, reflects Danish ties. Descended from an indigenous Arctic people, pure Inuit are a minority and usually follow traditional lifestyles. Most of the island lies within the Arctic Circle, and population is concentrated along the southern coast.

Economy and the Land

Fishing is the state's economic backbone. Despite a difficult arctic environment, mining of zinc and lead continues; but iron, coal, uranium, and molybdenum deposits remain undeveloped. The largest island in the world, Greenland is composed of an inland plateau, coastal mountains and fjords, and offshore islands. More than 80 percent of the island lies under permanent ice cap. Greenland is situated in the "Land of the Midnight Sun," and certain areas have twenty-four consecutive hours of daylight in summer and darkness in winter. The climate is cold, with warmer temperatures and more precipitation in the southwest.

Greenland at a glance

Official name	Greenland

People

Population	57,000
Density	0.07/mi^2 (0.03/km^2)
Urban	78%
Capital	Godthåb, 12,217
Ethnic groups	Greenlander (Inuit and native-born whites) 86%, Danish 14%
Languages	Danish, Greenlandic, Inuit dialects
Religions	Lutheran
Life expectancy	71 female, 62 male

Politics

Government	Self-governing territory (Danish protection)
Parties	Forward (Siumut), Inuit Movement, Polar (Issittrup), Unity (Atassut)
Suffrage	Universal, over 18
Memberships	None
Subdivisions	3 municipalities

Economy

GNP	$500,000,000
Per capita	$9,091
Monetary unit	Danish krone
Trade partners	Exports: Denmark, U.K., Germany
	Imports: Denmark, Norway, U.S.
Exports	Fish, minerals
Imports	Manufactures, machinery and transportation equipment, food, petroleum

Land

Description	North Atlantic island
Area	840,004 mi^2 (2,175,600 km^2)
Highest point	Gunnbjorn Mtn., 12,139 ft (3,700 m)
Lowest point	Sea level

History and Politics

Following early migration of Arctic Inuit, Norwegian Vikings sighted Greenland in the ninth century, and in the tenth century Erik the Red brought the first settlers from Iceland. Greenland united with Norway in the 1200s, and the two regions, along with several others, came under Danish rule in the 1300s. Denmark retained control of Greenland when Norway left the union in 1814. American troops defended the island during World War II. In 1953 the island became a province of Denmark, and in 1979 it gained home rule.

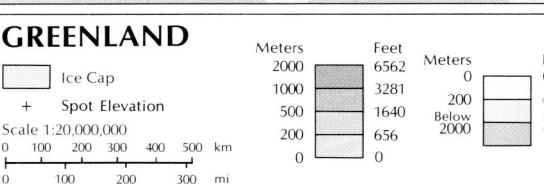

GREENLAND

		Meters	Feet		Meters
	Ice Cap	2000	6562		0
+	Spot Elevation	1000	3281		200
		500	1640		Below
		200	656		2000
		0			

Scale 1:20,000,000
0 100 200 300 400 500 km
0 100 200 300 mi

Greenland is green in name only. The island, except for its coastal areas, lies under an enormous ice cap that averages close to one mile in depth.

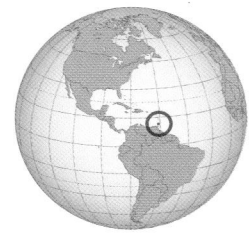

Once known as the Isle of Spice, Grenada continues to cultivate ginger, cloves, and cinnamon on its coastal plains. Inland, a nature preserve contains lakes, a rain forest, and volcanic mountains.

GRENADA

+ Spot Elevation or Depth

National capital is underlined

Scale 1:787,000

0 4 8 12 km
0 2 4 6 8 mi

© 1980 Rand McNally & Co.
A-532600-772 -1-1-1

GRENADA

People

Grenada's culture bears the influences of former British and French rule. The most widely spoken language is English, although a French patois is also spoken, and the majority of the population is Roman Catholic. Most Grenadians are black, descended from African slaves brought to the island by the British, but there are small East Indian and European populations.

Economy and the Land

Rich volcanic soils and heavy rainfall have made agriculture the chief economic activity. Also known as the Isle of Spice, Grenada is one of the world's leading producers of nutmeg and mace. Many tropical fruits are also raised, and the small plots of peasant farmers dot the hilly terrain. Another mainstay of the economy is tourism, with visitors drawn by the beaches and tropical climate. Grenada has little industry; high unemployment has plagued the nation in recent years.

History and Politics

The Carib Indians resisted European attempts to colonize Grenada for more than 100 years after Christopher Columbus discovered the island in 1498. The French established the first settlement in 1650 and slaughtered the Caribs, but the British finally gained control in 1783. In 1974 Grenada achieved full independence under Prime Minister Eric Gairy, despite widespread opposition to his policies. In 1979 foes of the regime staged a coup and installed a Marxist government headed by Maurice Bishop. Power struggles resulted, and a military branch of the government seized power in 1983 and executed Bishop, along with several of his ministers. The United States led a subsequent invasion that deposed the Marxists. A centrist government has ruled since 1984.

Grenada at a glance

Official name	Grenada

People

Population	92,000
Density	692/mi^2 (267/km^2)
Urban	15%
Capital	St. George's, 4,439
Ethnic groups	Black 82%, mixed 13%, East Indian 3%
Languages	English, French
Religions	Roman Catholic 59%, Anglican 17%, Seventh Day Adventist 6%
Life expectancy	73 female, 68 male
Literacy	98%

Politics

Government	Parliamentary state
Parties	National, Nat'l Democratic Congress, New Nat'l, United Labor
Suffrage	Universal, over 18
Memberships	CW, OAS, UN
Subdivisions	7 parishes

Economy

GDP	$250,000,000
Per capita	$2,551
Monetary unit	East Caribbean dollar
Trade partners	Exports: U.K., Netherlands, Germany
	Imports: U.S., U.K., Trinidad and Tobago
Exports	Nutmeg, cocoa beans, bananas, mace, textiles
Imports	Food, manufactures, machinery, chemicals, fuel

Land

Description	Caribbean island
Area	133 mi^2 (344 km^2)
Highest point	Mt. St. Catherine, 2,757 ft (840 m)
Lowest point	Sea level

The two main islands of Guadeloupe—mountainous Basse-Terre and flat Grande-Terre— are connected by a drawbridge.

GUADELOUPE

A French possession since 1635, Guadeloupe is home to Creole, one of the most vibrant cultures of the Caribbean. Heavily dependent on French subsidies, the islands also gain income from the export of bananas, sugar and rum, and from tourism.

People
Most of the people of these French islands in the Caribbean are black or of mixed black and white ancestry. A white community in the Îles des Saintes island group is descended from the original French settlers.

Economy and the Land
Important economic contributors include tourism, agriculture, sugar refining, and rum distilling. A drawbridge crossing a narrow strait connects the volcanic island of Basse-Terre, or Guadeloupe proper, to Grande-Terre, part of a limestone island chain. Together, these two islands are known as Guadeloupe. Other islands include the Îles des Saintes group, Marie-

Galante, La Désirade, St. Barthélemy, the northern section of St. Martin, and Îles de la Petite Terre. The climate is warm with moderating trade winds.

History and Politics
Around A.D. 1000 the Carib Indians took the main island from the Arawaks. In 1493 Christopher Columbus arrived, but the first French settlers did not come to the islands until 1635. About ten years later the sugar economy was underway, and slaves were imported from Africa to work the plantations. In 1946 France changed Guadeloupe's status from colony to overseas department.

Guadeloupe at a glance
Official name	Department of Guadeloupe

People
Population	432,000
Density	629/mi² (243/km²)
Urban	49%
Capital	Basse-Terre, Basse-Terre Island, 13,656
Ethnic groups	Black or mulatto 90%, white 5%
Languages	French, Creole
Religions	Roman Catholic 95%
Life expectancy	78 female, 71 male
Literacy	90%

Politics
Government	Overseas department (France)
Parties	Communist, Rally for the Republic, Socialist
Suffrage	Universal, over 18
Memberships	None
Subdivisions	3 arrondissements

Economy
GDP	$1,500,000,000
Per capita	$4,412
Monetary unit	French franc
Trade partners	Exports: France, Martinique. Imports: France, U.S., Italy
Exports	Bananas, sugar, rum
Imports	Transportation equipment, food, clothing, manufactures, petroleum

Land
Description	Caribbean islands
Area	687 mi² (1,780 km²)
Highest point	Soufrière, 4,813 ft (1,467 m)
Lowest point	Sea level

Scene of fierce combat in 1944 when the United States fought to liberate the island from Japan, Guam is now a popular destination for Japanese tourists. Strategically located in the western Pacific Ocean, Guam depends upon U.S. military spending for its economic well-being.

Guam at a glance
Official name	Territory of Guam

People
Population	152,000
Density	727/mi² (281/km²)
Urban	53%
Capital	Agana, 1,139
Ethnic groups	Chamorro 47%, Filipino 25%, Caucasian 10%
Languages	English, Chamorro, Japanese
Religions	Roman Catholic 98%
Life expectancy	79 female, 73 male
Literacy	96%

Politics
Government	Unincorporated territory (U.S.)
Parties	Democratic, Republican
Suffrage	Universal, over 18
Memberships	None
Subdivisions	19 municipalities

Economy
GDP	$2,000,000,000
Per capita	$13,889
Monetary unit	U.S. dollar
Trade partners	Exports: U.S., Pacific islands. Imports: U.S., Japan
Exports	Building materials, fish, food
Imports	Petroleum, food, manufactures

Land
Description	North Pacific island
Area	209 mi² (541 km²)
Highest point	Mt. Lamlam, 1,332 ft (406 m)
Lowest point	Sea level

People
The main ethnic group in Guam is the Chamorros, who are of mixed Micronesian, Filipino, and Spanish ancestry. Because of the United States military base and its fluctuating personnel, the size and nature of the population vary.

Economy and the Land
The United States military and a growing tourist industry provide employment for the islanders, and there is some light industry as well. Many residents, however, continue to practice subsistence farming. The largest island in the Mariana Islands, Guam has hills and mountains in the south and a flat plateau in the north. The climate is tropical.

History and Politics
Magellan arrived on Guam in 1521, and in 1565 Spain took formal possession of the island. In 1898, following the Spanish-American War, Spain ceded the island to the United States. It became a major United States military base, and during World War II the Japanese occupied the island. The people of Guam were granted United States citizenship in 1950; however, they do not vote in national elections.

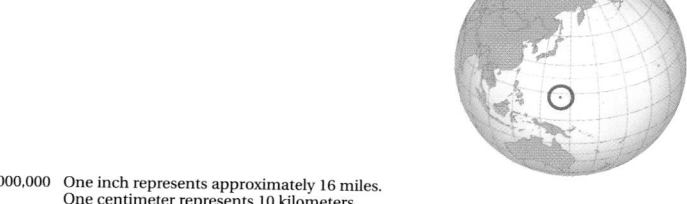

GUAM

The largest and southernmost island in the Mariana Island archipelago, Guam is a classic Pacific volcanic island surrounded by coral reef.

Lake Atitlan

GUATEMALA

As the center of Mayan culture, Guatemala was one of the most important lands in Central America for 1,000 years before the Spanish arrived in the 16th Century. Today, that is still true. In spite of decades of political turmoil and repression, it has the region's strongest economy and greatest population. Each year, archeologists unearth more Mayan treasures. Nobody knows how many more are hidden in the vast tropical forests.

The great Mayan city of Tikal flourished more than 1,000 years ago in northern Guatemala. Ruins of its 200-foot-tall temples still soar above the surrounding jungle.

People

Guatemala's population is made up of majority ladinos and minority Indians. Ladinos include both mestizos, those of Spanish-Indian origin, and westernized Indians of Mayan descent. Classified on the basis of culture rather than race, ladinos follow a Spanish-American lifestyle and speak Spanish. Non-ladino Indians are of Mayan descent and speak several Mayan dialects. Many are poor, uneducated, and suffer from persecution. Roman Catholicism often combines with traditional Mayan religious practice. Population is concentrated in the central highlands.

Colorful cloth at outdoor market

Economy and the Land

Most Guatemalans practice agriculture in some form. Indians generally operate small,

unproductive subsistence farms. Export crops are mainly produced on large plantations on the fertile southern plain that borders the Pacific. Although light industry is growing, it is unable to absorb rural immigrants seeking employment in the cities. Much of the landscape is mountainous, with the Pacific plain and Caribbean lowlands bordering central highlands. Northern rain forests and grasslands are sparsely populated and largely undeveloped. The climate is tropical in low areas and temperate in the highlands.

History and Politics

Indians in the region were absorbed into the Mayan civilization that flourished in Central America by the fourth century. In 1523 the Spanish defeated the indigenous Indians and went on to establish one of the most influential colonies in Central America. Guatemala joined Costa Rica, El Salvador, Nicaragua, and Honduras in 1821 to declare independence from Spain, and the former Spanish colonies formed the Federation of Central America in 1823. Almost from the start, the federation was marked by dissension, and by 1838 it had, in effect, been dissolved. Following a series of dictatorships, social and economic reform began in 1944 and continued under two successive presidents. The government was ousted in a United States-backed 1954 coup, and military rule was established. In 1985 the country returned to a civilian government. The years since have been filled with corruption and some of the worst human rights abuses in Central America. Peace talks between the government and many dissident groups, including that of Nobel Peace Prize winner Rigoberta Menchú, are ongoing.

Guatemala at a glance

Official name	Republic of Guatemala

People

Population	10,420,000
Density	248/mi² (96/km²)
Urban	39%
Capital	Guatemala, 1,057,210
Ethnic groups	Ladino (mestizo) 56%, Amerindian 44%
Languages	Spanish, Amerindian
Religions	Roman Catholic, Protestant, tribal religionist
Life expectancy	67 female, 62 male
Literacy	55%

Politics

Government	Republic
Parties	Christian Democratic, Democratic Party of National Cooperation, National Centrist Union, Revolutionary, others
Suffrage	Universal, over 18
Memberships	OAS, UN
Subdivisions	22 departments

Economy

GDP	$31,300,000,000
Per capita	$3,225
Monetary unit	Quetzal
Trade partners	Exports: U.S., El Salvador, Germany Imports: U.S., Venezuela, Germany, Japan
Exports	Coffee, sugar, bananas, beef
Imports	Fuel, machinery, grain, fertilizer, transportation equipment

Land

Description	Central America
Area	42,042 mi² (108,889 km²)
Highest point	Volcán Tajumulco, 13,845 ft (4,220 m)
Lowest point	Sea level

POPULATION COMPARISON
Guatemala=4% of U.S.

United States

GDP COMPARISON
Guatemala=0.5% of U.S.

United States

ETHNIC GROUPS

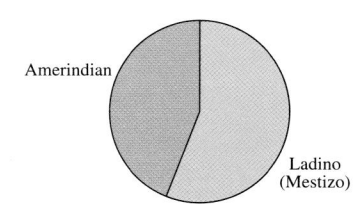

Amerindian

Ladino (Mestizo)

POPULATION DISTRIBUTION

Urban   Rural

GUATEMALA

— Railroad

+ Spot Elevation or Depth

National capitals are underlined

City type size indicates relative importance

Scale 1:4,318,000

Meters	Feet
Above 4000	Above 13124
2000	6562
1000	3281
500	1640
200	656
0	0

Meters	Feet
0	0
200	656
Below 2000	Below 6562

© Rand McNally & Co.
A-531000-772

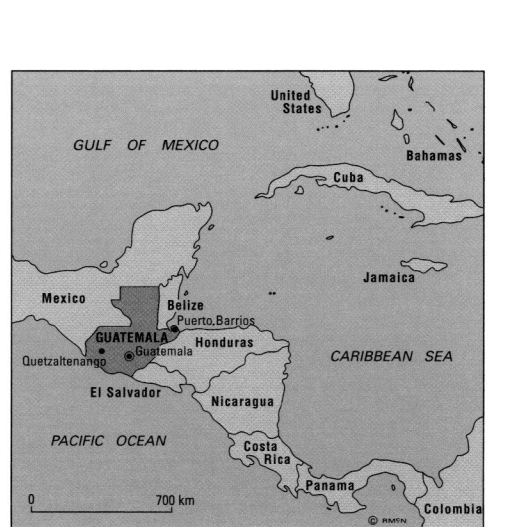

Guatemala is unable to reap full economic benefit from its Pacific Coast, owing to the lack of a deepwater port.

Guinea at a glance

Official name   Republic of Guinea

People

Population	6,469,000
Density	68/mi² (26/km²)
Urban	26%
Capital	Conakry, 800,000
Ethnic groups	Fulani 35%, Malinke 30%, Susu 20%, others
Languages	French, indigenous
Religions	Muslim 85%, Christian 8%, Animist 7%
Life expectancy	45 female, 44 male
Literacy	24%

Politics

Government	Provisional military government
Parties	Party of Unity and Progress, Rally of the People, Union for the New Republic, others
Suffrage	Universal, adult
Memberships	OAU, UN
Subdivisions	33 administrative regions

Economy

GDP	$3,100,000,000
Per capita	$406
Monetary unit	Franc
Trade partners	Exports: U.S., European countries, former Soviet republics Imports: U.S., France, Brazil
Exports	Alumina, bauxite, diamonds, coffee, pineapples, bananas, palm kernels
Imports	Petroleum, metals, machinery and transportation equipment, food

Land

Description	Western Africa
Area	94,926 mi² (245,857 km²)
Highest point	Mont Nimba, 5,748 ft (1,752 m)
Lowest point	Sea level

People

Guinea's population is composed of several ethnic groups, with three—the Fulani, Malinke, and Susu—forming the majority. Most Guineans are rural farmers, living in hamlets, and the only true urban center is Conakry. Mortality as well as emigration rates are high. Eight languages besides French, the language of the colonial power, are taught in the schools.

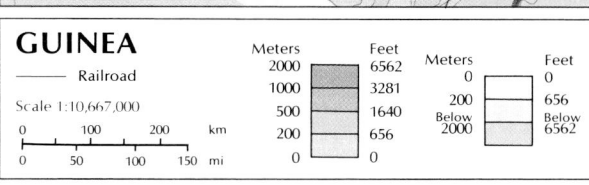

GUINEA

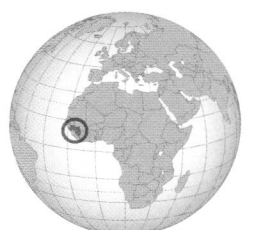

Guinea's coastal plains are very fertile and its eastern mountains have great hydropower potential. Under the land there are rich deposits of diamonds, gold, and uranium.

Economy and the Land

Rich soil and a varied terrain suited for diverse crop production have made agriculture an important economic activity. Guinea also has vast mineral reserves, including one of the world's largest bauxite deposits. Centralized economic planning and state enterprise have characterized the republic, but Guinea now encourages private and foreign investments. The terrain is mostly flat along the coast and mountainous in the interior. The climate is tropical on the coast, hot and dry in the north and northeast, and cooler with less humidity in the highlands.

History and Politics

As part of the Ghana, Mali, and Songhai empires that flourished in West Africa between the fourth and fifteenth centuries, Guinea was a trading center for gold and slaves. The Portuguese arrived on the coast in the 1400s, and European competition for Guinean trade soon began. In the 1890s France declared the area a colony and named it French Guinea. A movement for autonomy began after World War II with a series of reforms by the French and the growth of a labor movement headed by Sékou Touré, later the nation's first president. The first of the French colonies in West Africa to attain independence, in 1958 Guinea was also the only colony to reject membership in the French Community. The country's first multiparty elections were held in December 1993 amid violence and confusion. The results were not accepted by opposition leaders, and the winner, Presidente Conte, has since resumed a military title.

Guinea-Bissau at a glance

Official name   Republic of Guinea-Bissau

People

Population	1,111,000
Density	80/mi² (31/km²)
Urban	20%
Capital	Bissau, 125,000
Ethnic groups	Balanta 30%, Fulani 20%, Manjaca 14%, Malinke 13%, Papel 7%
Languages	Portuguese, Crioulo, indigenous
Religions	Tribal religionist 65%, Muslim 30%, Christian 5%
Life expectancy	45 female, 42 male
Literacy	36%

Politics

Government	Republic
Parties	African Party for Independence, Democratic Front, Democratic Social Front
Suffrage	Universal, over 15
Memberships	OAU, UN
Subdivisions	9 regions

Economy

GDP	$860,000,000
Per capita	$811
Monetary unit	Peso
Trade partners	Exports: Portugal, Senegal, France Imports: Portugal, Netherlands, Senegal
Exports	Cashews, fish, peanuts, palm kernels
Imports	Manufactures, food, petroleum

Land

Description	Western Africa
Area	13,948 mi² (36,125 km²)
Highest point	Unnamed, 860 ft (262 m)
Lowest point	Sea level

People

Guinea-Bissau's largest ethnic group, the Balanta, mainly inhabit the coastal area. Most practice traditional beliefs, although some are Christian. Predominately Muslim peoples, the Fulani and Malinke are concentrated in the northwest. The Manjaca inhabit the northern and central coastal regions. Although the official language is Portuguese, many speak Crioulo, a creole dialect also spoken in Cape Verde.

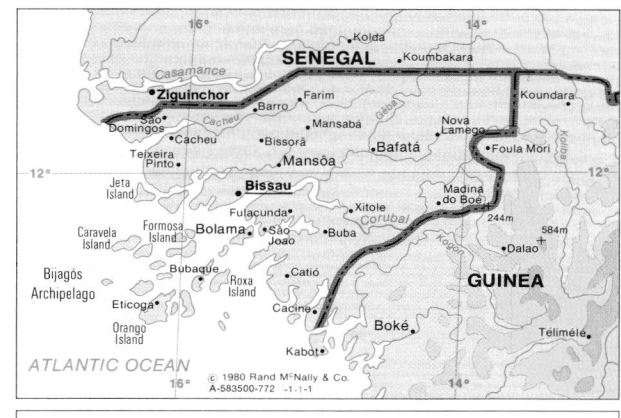
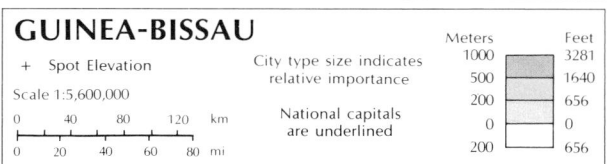

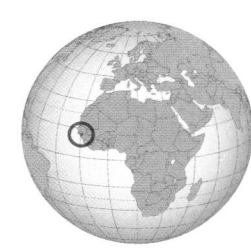

Guinea-Bissau has two distinct regions: coastal lowlands and the northeastern highlands. Rainfall is highest along the coast, averaging 100 inches per year.

GUINEA-BISSAU

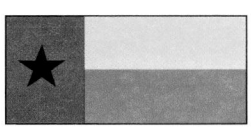

Economy and the Land

Guinea-Bissau's economy is underdeveloped and dependent upon agriculture. Peanuts, cotton, corn, and sorghum are grown in the north, and palm-oil production is concentrated along the coast. Timber is produced primarily in the south. Fishing, especially shrimp production, has increased since 1976. Bauxite deposits have been located, and exploration for additional resources continues. Mineral exploitation is hindered by a lack of transportation routes, however. A swamp-covered coastal plain rises to an eastern savanna. The climate is tropical. The country includes the Bijagos Archipelago, which lies just off the coast.

History and Politics

The area of Guinea-Bissau was inhabited by diverse peoples prior to the arrival of the Portuguese in 1446. Ruled as a single colony with Cape Verde, the region soon developed into a base for the Portuguese slave trade. In 1879 it was separated from Cape Verde as Portuguese Guinea, and its status changed to overseas province in 1951. A movement for the independence of Guinea-Bissau and Cape Verde developed in the 1950s, and a coup in Portugal in 1974 resulted in independence the same year. Attempts to unite Guinea-Bissau and Cape Verde were unsuccessful, and a 1980 coup installed an anti-unification government. The country's first multiparty presidential elections were held in July 1994.

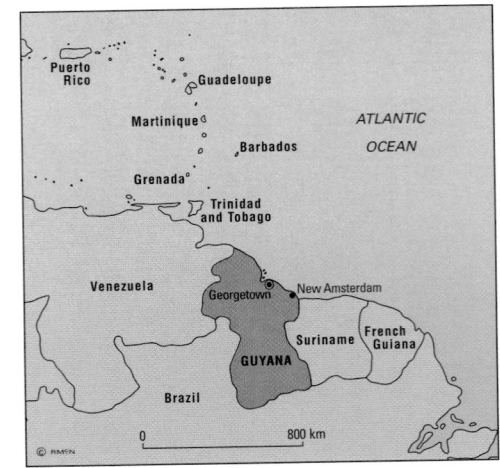

GUYANA

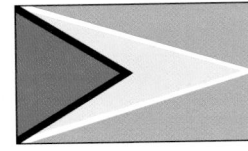

Official name	Co-operative Republic of Guyana

People

Population	726,000
Density	8.7/mi² (3.4/km²)
Urban	33%
Capital	Georgetown, 78,500
Ethnic groups	East Indian 51%, black 30%, mixed 11%, Amerindian 5%.
Languages	English, indigenous
Religions	Anglican and other Christian 57%, Hindu 33%, Muslim 9%
Life expectancy	68 female, 62 male
Literacy	95%

Politics

Government	Republic
Parties	People's National Congress, People's Progressive, others
Suffrage	Universal, over 18
Memberships	CW, OAS, UN
Subdivisions	10 regions

Economy

GDP	$1,400,000,000
Per capita	$1,900
Monetary unit	Dollar
Trade partners	Exports: U.K., U.S., Trinidad and Tobago Imports: Trinidad and Tobago, U.S., U.K.
Exports	Bauxite, sugar, gold, rice, shrimp, molasses, timber, rum
Imports	Manufactures, machinery, food, petroleum

Land

Description	Northeastern South America
Area	83,000 mi² (214,969 km²)
Highest point	Mt. Roraima, 9,432 ft (2,875 m)
Lowest point	Sea level

Formerly British Guiana, this small nation shares many traditions with Britain's other former holdings in the Caribbean. Events after independence in 1966 were mostly tragic. After the government nationalized Guyana's two main industries—bauxite in 1971 and sugar in 1976—mismanagement bankrupted both and plunged the country into a deep depression. However, recent economic reforms have shown some positive results.

People

Guyana's population includes descendants of black African slaves and East Indian, Chinese, and Portuguese laborers who were brought to work sugar plantations. Amerindians, the indigenous peoples of Guyana, are a minority. Ninety percent of the people live along the fertile coastal plain, where farming and manufacturing are concentrated.

Economy and the Land

Agriculture and mining compose the backbone of the Guyanese economy. Sugar and rice continue to be important crops, and mines produce bauxite, manganese, diamonds, and gold. Guyana's inland forests give way to savanna and a coastal plain. The climate is tropical.

Woman in Georgetown

History and Politics

First gaining European notice in 1498 with the voyages of Christopher Columbus, Guyana was the stage for competing colonial interests—British, French, and Dutch—until it officially became British Guiana in 1831. Slavery was abolished several years later, causing the British to import indentured

laborers, the ancestors of today's majority group. A constitution, adopted in 1953, was suspended when Britain feared a Communist victory at the polls. In the early 1960s racial tensions erupted into riots between East Indians and blacks. In 1966 the country gained independence, and adopted the name Guyana. Guyana became a republic in 1970 and has pursued socialist policies. The two main political parties continue to reflect its ethnic divisions: the People's National Congress (PNC) is supported by blacks, and the People's Progressive Party (PPP) by East Indians. A 1992 election was won by the PPP.

POPULATION COMPARISON
Guyana=0.3% of U.S.

United States

GDP COMPARISON
Guyana=0.02% of U.S.

United States

ETHNIC GROUPS

POPULATION DISTRIBUTION
Urban   Rural

The spectacular Kaieteur Gorge in Guyana's interior boasts an impressive waterfall. Because its location is almost completely inaccessible, the gorge is visited by few people.

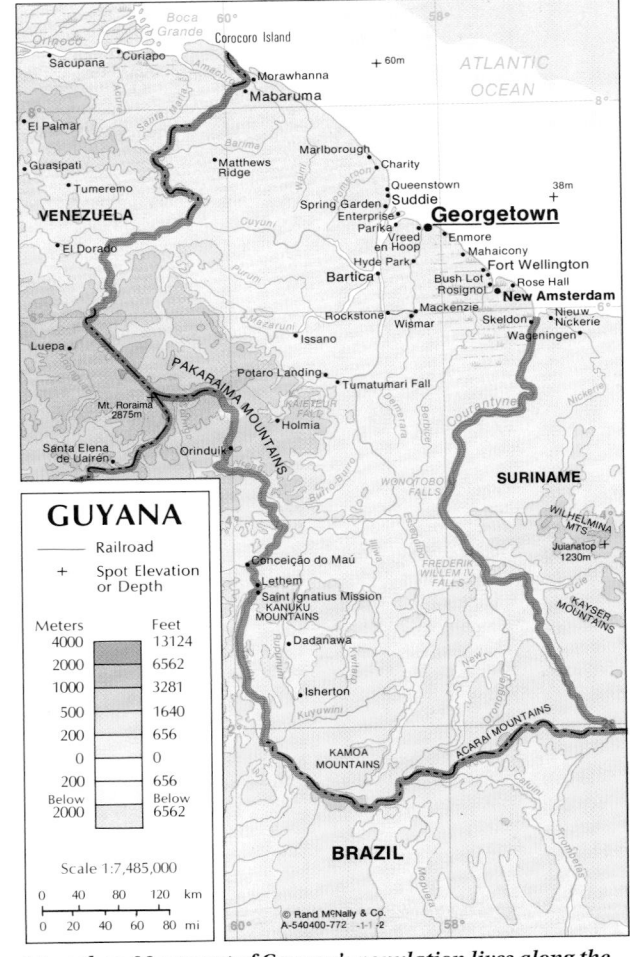

GUYANA

— Railroad

+ Spot Elevation or Depth

Meters	Feet
4000	13124
2000	6562
1000	3281
500	1640
200	656
0	0
200	656
Below 2000	Below 6562

Scale 1:7,485,000

© Rand McNally & Co.
A-540400-772

More than 90 percent of Guyana's population lives along the humid, muddy coast, where concrete barriers protect the low-lying area from tidal surges.

Port-au-Prince, the capital of Haiti, has seen little modern development, due to the country's political turmoil. Its streets are still graced with many buildings from the French colonial period.

HAITI

By every account, Haiti is a mess. The poorest nation in the Western Hemisphere, it has suffered under generations of rulers more interested in lining their pockets than governing the country. Malnutrition, disease and political killings have made Haiti a very difficult place to live.

People
The world's oldest black republic, Haiti has a population composed mainly of descendants of African slaves. Most people are poor and rural. Although French is an official language, Haitian Creole, a combination of French and West African languages, is more widely spoken. Roman Catholicism is the major religion. Voodooism, which blends Christian and African beliefs, is also practiced.

Economy and the Land
Haiti's economy remains underdeveloped. Most people rely on subsistence farming, though productivity is hampered by high population density in productive regions. Coffee is a main commercial crop and export. Recent growth of light industry is partially attributable to tax exemptions and low labor costs. Occupying the western third of Hispaniola Island, Haiti has an overall mountainous terrain and a tropical climate.

History and Politics
Christopher Columbus reached Hispaniola in 1492, and the indigenous Arawak Indians almost completely died out during subsequent Spanish settlement. Most Spanish settlers had gone to seek their fortunes in other colonies by the 1600s, and western Hispaniola came under

French control in 1697. Slave importation increased rapidly, and in less than a hundred years black Africans far outnumbered the French. In a 1791 revolution led by Toussaint L'Ouverture, Jean Jacques Dessalines, and Henri Christophe, the slaves rose against the French. By 1804 the country achieved independence from France, and the area was renamed Haiti. In the 1820s Haitians conquered the eastern region of the island, now the Dominican Republic, and it remained part of Haiti until 1844. Instability increased under various dictatorships from 1843 to 1915, and United States marines occupied the country from 1915 to 1934. After a time of alternating military and civilian rule, François Duvalier came to office in 1957, declaring himself president-for-life in 1964. His rule was marked by repression, corruption, and human-rights abuses. His son, Jean-Claude, succeeded him as president-for-life in 1971. The Duvalier dictatorship ended in 1986 when Jean-Claude fled the country. Continued unrest resulted in six different governments between 1987 and 1990. There were hopes that an internationally monitored election in 1990 would bring peace and democracy. However, a coup in September 1991 forced the winner, Jean-Bertrand Aristide, into exile. International pressure and sanctions resulted in his return in 1994.

Woman at market, Port-au-Prince

Haiti at a glance

Official name   Republic of Haiti

People

Population	7,069,000
Density	660/mi² (255/km²)
Urban	29%
Capital	Port-au-Prince, 797,000
Ethnic groups	Black 95%, mulatto and white 5%
Languages	Creole, French
Religions	Roman Catholic 80%, Baptist 10%, Pentecostal 4%
Life expectancy	58 female, 55 male
Literacy	53%

Politics

Government	Provisional military government
Parties	Christian Democratic, Movement to Install Democracy, National Alliance Front, Social Christian
Suffrage	Universal, over 18
Memberships	OAS, UN
Subdivisions	9 departments

Economy

GDP	$5,220,000,000
Per capita	$948
Monetary unit	Gourde
Trade partners	Exports: U.S., Italy Imports: U.S., Canada, Japan
Exports	Manufactures, coffee and other food
Imports	Machinery and manufactures, food, petroleum, chemicals, fats and oils

Land

Description	Caribbean island (western Hispaniola)
Area	10,714 mi² (27,750 km²)
Highest point	La Selle Peak, 8,773 ft (2,674 m)
Lowest point	Sea level

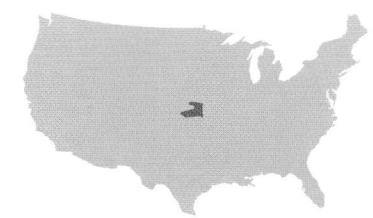

POPULATION COMPARISON
Haiti=3% of U.S.

United States

GDP COMPARISON
Haiti=0.08% of U.S.

United States

ETHNIC GROUPS

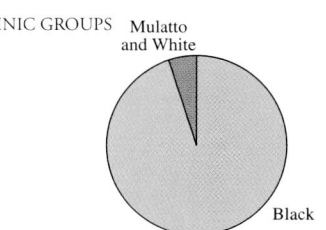

Mulatto and White

Black

POPULATION DISTRIBUTION
Urban   Rural

Once covered with trees, Haiti has stripped bare its portion of the island of Hispaniola.

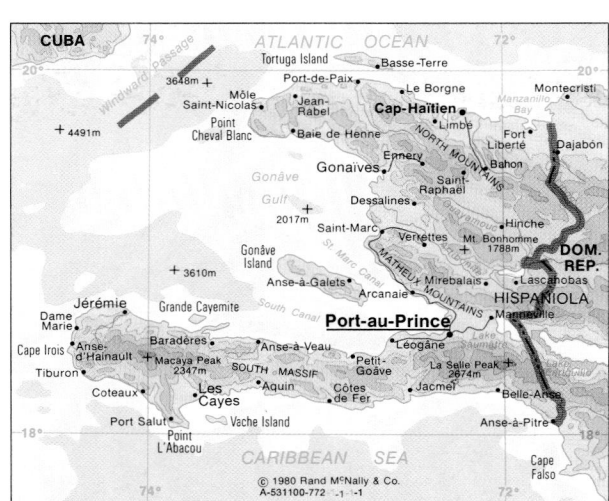

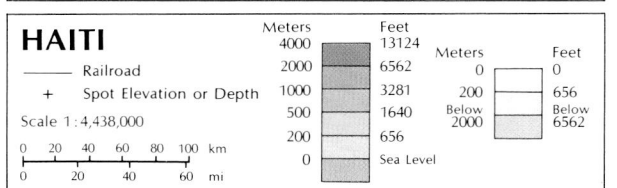

HAITI	Meters	Feet			
—— Railroad	4000	13124	Meters		Feet
+ Spot Elevation or Depth	2000	6562	0		0
	1000	3281	200		656
Scale 1: 4,438,000	500	1640	Below 2000		Below 6562
0 20 40 60 80 100 km	200	656			
0 20 40 60 mi	0	Sea Level			

HONDURAS

Recent efforts at land reform have done little to improve the lives of Hondurans, who are very poor and whose numbers are growing fast. The economy is unstable because it is tied to coffee and banana exports, two crops subject to significant price fluctuations.

Swimming at Caribbean beach, Roatán Island

People

Most Hondurans are mestizos—people of Spanish-Indian descent. Other groups include Indians and descendants of black Africans and Europeans. Most Indians have been assimilated into the majority culture, but a minority continues to practice a traditional Indian lifestyle. The Spanish language predominates, and English is spoken by a small population of British descent on the northern coast and Bay Islands. Poverty is an ongoing problem for the mainly rural population, and economic and educational improvements mostly affect urban inhabitants.

Economy and the Land

Honduras has an underdeveloped economy based on banana cultivation. Other activities include livestock raising, coffee production, forestry, and some mining. Honduras's terrain is mostly mountainous, with lowlands along some coastal regions. The climate varies from tropical in the lowlands to temperate in the mountains.

History and Politics

Early in its history Honduras was part of the Mayan Empire. By 1502, when Christopher Columbus arrived to claim the region for Spain, the decline of the Maya had rendered the Indians weak and unable to stave off Spanish settlement. The Spanish colonial period introduced gold and silver mines, cattle ranches, and African slaves. In 1821 Honduras, El Salvador, Nicaragua, Costa Rica, and Guatemala declared independence from Spain and, in 1823, formed the Federation of Central America. The unstable union had virtually collapsed by 1838, and the member states became independent as the federation dissolved. Instability, Guatemalan political influence, and the development of a banana economy based on United States-owned plantations marked the 1800s and early 1900s. Frequent revolutions have characterized the twentieth century, and a dictator governed from 1933 to 1948. Since the 1950s civilian governments have alternated with military coups and rule. Controversies focus on issues of poverty and land distribution. Amnesty International continues to report extensive human rights abuses. Presidential elections in 1993 brought reformers to power who promise to confront the military and to stop abuses.

Honduras at a glance

Official name	Republic of Honduras

People

Population	5,822,000
Density	135/mi² (52/km²)
Urban	44%
Capital	Tegucigalpa, 576,661
Ethnic groups	Mestizo 90%, Amerindian 7%, black 2%, white 1%
Languages	Spanish, indigenous
Religions	Roman Catholic 97%
Life expectancy	68 female, 64 male
Literacy	73%

Politics

Government	Republic
Parties	Liberal, National, others
Suffrage	Universal, over 18
Memberships	OAS, UN
Subdivisions	18 departments

Economy

GDP	$10,000,000,000
Per capita	$1,936
Monetary unit	Lempira
Trade partners	Exports: U.S., Germany, Japan Imports: U.S., Japan, Mexico
Exports	Bananas, coffee, shrimp, lobster, minerals, lumber
Imports	Machinery and transportation equipment, chemicals, manufactures, fuel

Land

Description	Central America
Area	43,277 mi² (112,088 km²)
Highest point	Las Minas Mtn., 9,347 ft (2,849 m)
Lowest point	Sea level

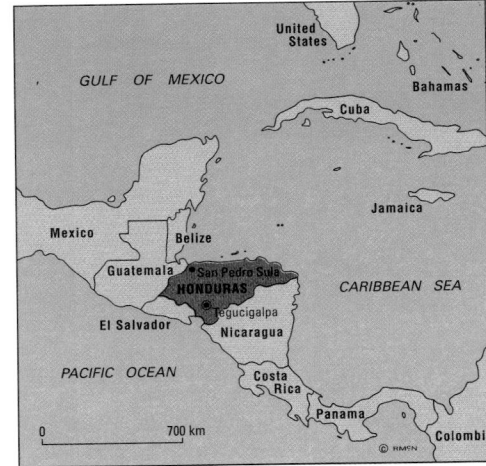

POPULATION COMPARISON
Honduras=2% of U.S.

United States

GDP COMPARISON
Honduras=0.08% of U.S.

United States

ETHNIC GROUPS

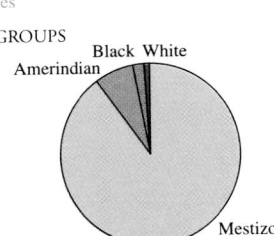

POPULATION DISTRIBUTION
Urban   Rural

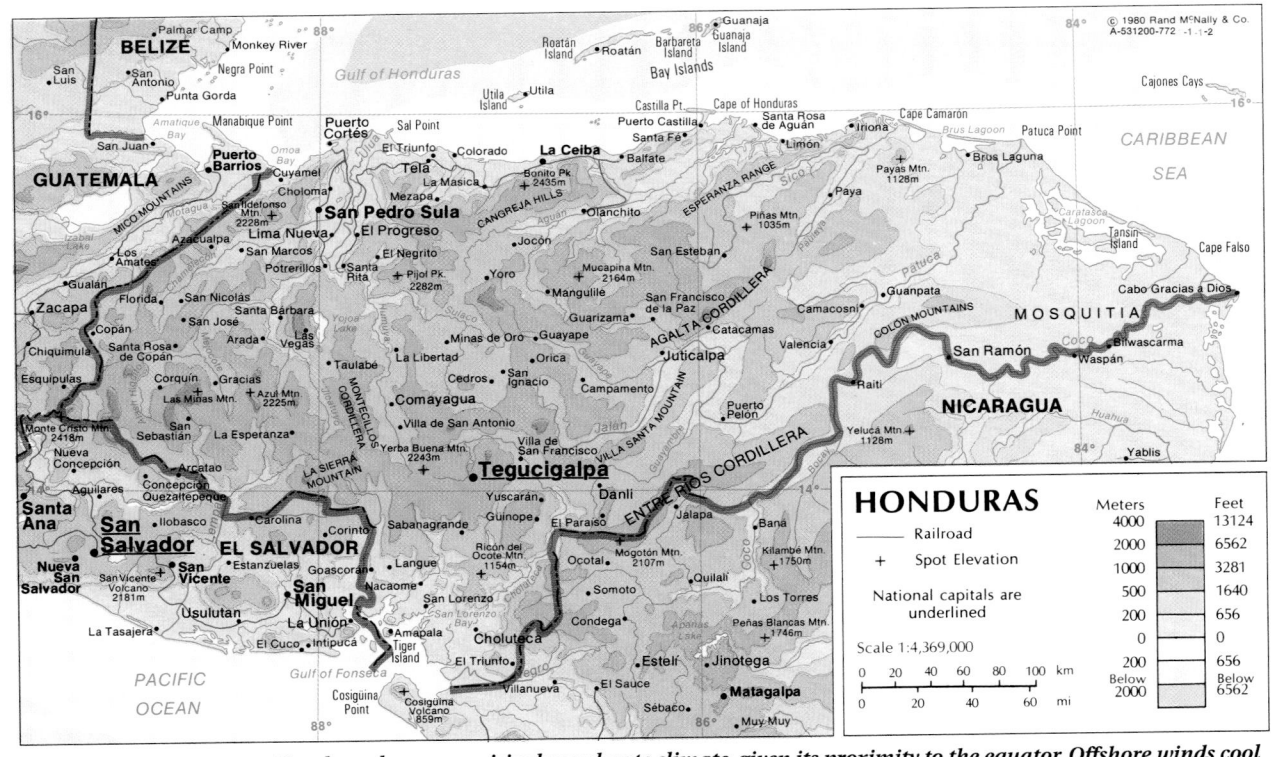

Honduras has a surprisingly moderate climate, given its proximity to the equator. Offshore winds cool the coastal plains, while the mountainous interior is temperate owing to its high elevation.

W hen Britain acquired the tiny island of Hong Kong in the mid 1840s, one British official described it as "a barren rock with hardly a house upon it." Since then, that "barren rock" and neighboring lands have developed into a great international business and manufacturing center. The world now waits to see what Chinese rule will mean for Hong Kong.

People

Hong Kong has a majority Chinese population. Cantonese, a Chinese dialect, is spoken by most of the people, and English and Chinese are the official languages. Major religions are Taoism, Christianity, and Buddhism. Hong Kong is one of the world's most densely populated areas.

Economy and the Land

Low taxes, duty-free status, an accessible location, and an excellent natural harbor have helped make Hong Kong an Asian center of trade, finance, manufacturing, and transportation. Situated on the coast of China, Hong Kong borders Guangdong province. It consists of the islands of Hong Kong and Lantau, the Kowloon Peninsula, and the New Territories, which include a mainland area and many islands. In addition to mountains, the New Territories contain some level areas suitable for agriculture, while the islands are hilly. The climate is tropical, with hot, rainy summers and cool, humid winters.

History and Politics

Inhabited since ancient times, Hong Kong came under Chinese rule around the third century B.C. In 1839 British opium smuggling led to the Opium War between Britain and China, and a victorious Britain received the island of Hong Kong in an 1842 treaty. In 1860 the British gained control of the Kowloon Peninsula, and in 1898 the New Territories came under British rule through a 99-year lease with China. Democratic institutions were introduced to Hong Kong by the British shortly before the expiration of the lease, an action that infuriated Chinese rulers and tempted them to rescind their promise not to interfere with Hong Kong's thriving economy for at least 50 years. On July 1, 1997, Hong Kong returned to Chinese rule as a special administrative region.

HONG KONG

Hong Kong's breathtaking growth is on vivid display in this view from atop Victoria Peak on Hong Kong Island. A constant parade of ferries links the island with the Kowloon Peninsula. With its myriad high-rise buildings, Hong Kong has one of the highest population densities in the world.

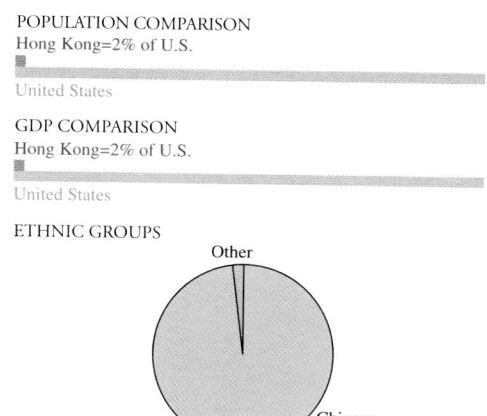

POPULATION COMPARISON
Hong Kong=2% of U.S.

United States

GDP COMPARISON
Hong Kong=2% of U.S.

United States

ETHNIC GROUPS

Other

Chinese

POPULATION DISTRIBUTION

Urban   Rural

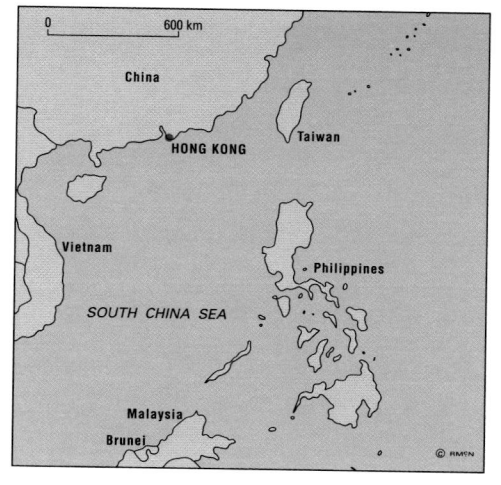

Fishing houseboats docked at Aberdeen

Hong Kong at a glance

Official name Hong Kong

People

Population	5,927,000
Density	14,316/mi² (5,529/km²)
Urban	94%
Capital	Xianggang (Hong Kong), Hong Kong I., 1,250,993
Ethnic groups	Chinese 98%
Languages	Chinese (Cantonese), English, Putonghua
Religions	Buddhist and Taoist 90%, Christian 10%
Life expectancy	80 female, 75 male
Literacy	77%

Politics

Government	Special administrative region of China
Parties	Democratic Foundation, Liberal Democratic Federation, United Democrats, others
Suffrage	Universal, over 21
Memberships	None
Subdivisions	4 areas

Economy

GDP	$119,000,000,000
Per capita	$21,326
Monetary unit	Dollar
Trade partners	Exports: U.S., Germany Imports: Japan, U.S.
Exports	Clothing, textiles, yarn and fabric, footwear, electrical appliances
Imports	Food, transportation equipment, raw materials, manufactures, petroleum

Land

Description	Eastern Asia (islands and mainland area on China's southeastern coast)
Area	414 mi² (1,072 km²)
Highest point	Tai Mo Mtn., 3,140 ft (957 m)
Lowest point	Sea level

Mostly barren hills and islands a century ago, Hong Kong is now covered by scores of residential high-rises, many with spectacular views of the harbor and skyline.

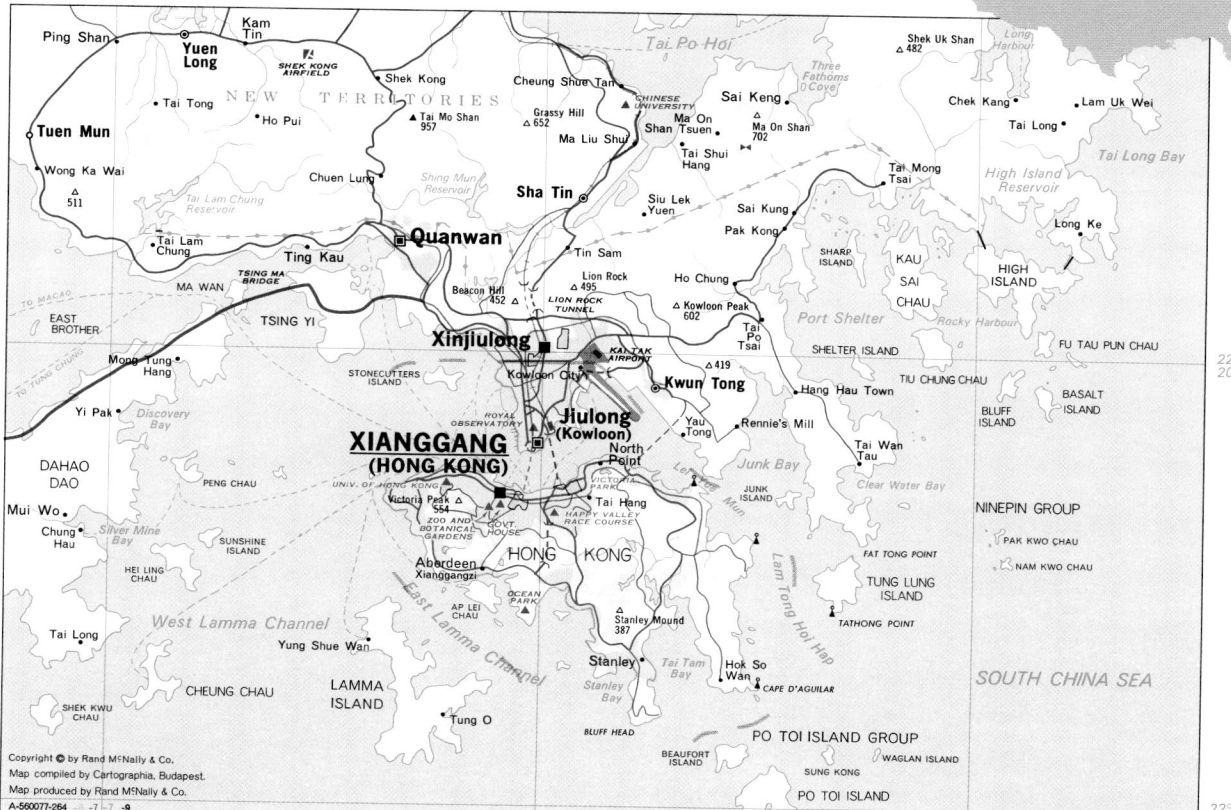

Copyright © by Rand McNally & Co.
Map compiled by Cartographia, Budapest.
Map produced by Rand McNally & Co.
A-560077-264   -7- -7 -9

Scale 1:3,000,000   One inch represents approximately 4.7 miles. One centimeter represents 3 kilometers.

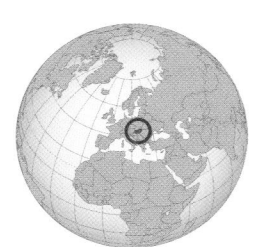

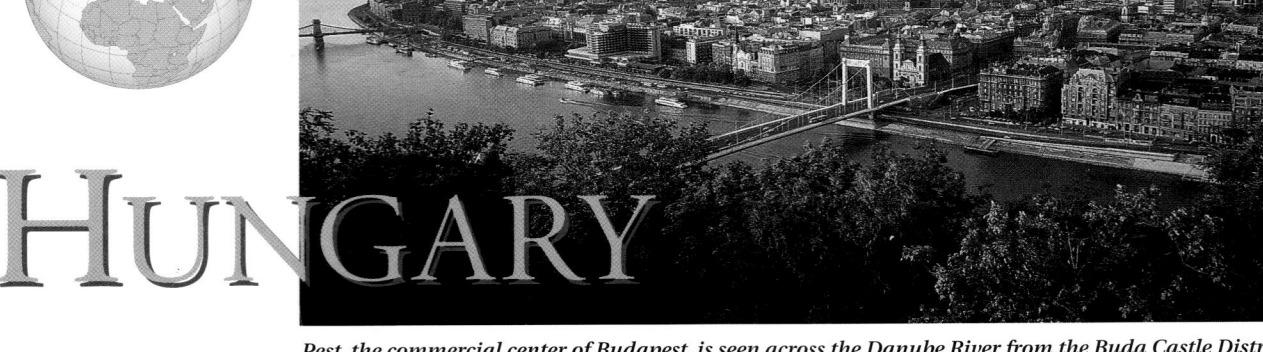

HUNGARY

Pest, the commercial center of Budapest, is seen across the Danube River from the Buda Castle District.

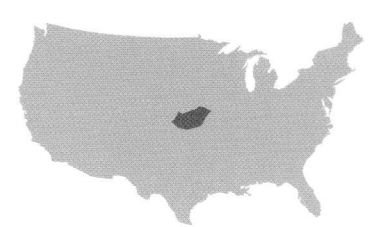

POPULATION COMPARISON
Hungary=4% of U.S.

United States

GDP COMPARISON
Hungary=0.9% of U.S.

United States

ETHNIC GROUPS

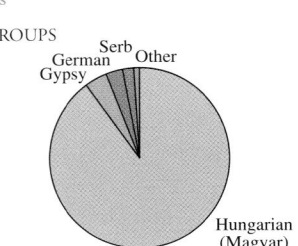

German Serb
Gypsy Other

Hungarian
(Magyar)

POPULATION DISTRIBUTION
Urban   Rural

When Hungary symbolically removed the barbed wire from its border with Austria on a spring morning in 1989, nobody could have known that it would lead to the unraveling of the entire Soviet empire. Like other former communist nations, Hungary's transition to democracy and a market economy has not been easy, although foreign investment is growing.

People
Hungary's major ethnic group and language evolved from Magyar tribes who settled the region in the ninth century. Gypsies, Germans, and other peoples compose minorities. Most people are Roman Catholic and the literacy rate is high. Growth of industry since the 1940s has caused a rural-to-urban population shift.

Economy and the Land
Following World War II, Hungary pursued a program of industrialization, and industries are now being privatized. Agriculture, socialized under Communist rule, will also be returned to private ownership. Farming remains important, with productivity aided by fertile soils and a mild climate. Economic planning was decentralized in 1968, thus Hungary's economy differed from that of other Soviet-bloc nations, permitting some private enterprise. A flat plain dominates the landscape, and the lack of varied terrain results in a temperate climate throughout the country.

History and Politics
In the late 800s Magyar tribes from the east overcame Slavic and Germanic residents and settled the area. Invading Mongols caused much destruction in the thirteenth century. In the early 1500s, after repeated

attacks, the Ottoman Turks dominated central Hungary. By the late seventeenth century, the entire region had come under the rule of Austria's Hapsburgs. Hungary succeeded in obtaining equal status with Austria in 1867, and the dual monarchy of Austria-Hungary emerged. Discontent and nationalistic demands increased until 1914, when a Bosnian Serb killed the heir to the Austro-Hungarian throne. Austria-Hungary declared war on Serbia, and World War I began, resulting in both territory and population losses for Hungary. At the end of the war, in 1918, Hungary became a republic, only to revert to monarchical rule in 1919. Hungary entered World War II on the side of Germany, and Adolf Hitler set up a pro-Nazi government in Hungary in 1944. The Soviet Union invaded that same year, and a Hungarian-Allied peace treaty was signed in 1947. Coalition rule evolved into a Communist government in 1949. In 1956 discontent erupted into rebellion, a new premier declared Hungary neutral, and Soviet forces entered Budapest to quell the uprising. A new constitution, which went into effect in 1990, helped move the nation away from Communist domination. Discontent with the following years of free-market policy resulted in a heavy victory for the Worker's Party, formerly the Socialist Party, in 1994.

Traditional houses, Eger

Hungary at a glance
Official name	Republic of Hungary

People	
Population	10,270,000
Density	286/mi² (110/km²)
Urban	64%
Capital	Budapest, 2,016,774
Ethnic groups	Hungarian (Magyar) 90%, Gypsy 4%, German 3%, Serb 2%
Languages	Hungarian
Religions	Roman Catholic 68%, Calvinist 20%, Lutheran 5%
Life expectancy	74 female, 66 male
Literacy	99%

Politics	
Government	Republic
Parties	Democratic Forum, Free Democrats, Independent Smallholders, Workers', others
Suffrage	Universal, over 18
Memberships	UN
Subdivisions	19 counties, 1 autonomous city

Economy	
GDP	$57,000,000,000
Per capita	$5,531
Monetary unit	Forint
Trade partners	Former Soviet republics, Germany, Austria
Exports	Machinery, food, manufactures, fuel
Imports	Machinery, fuel, manufactures, agricultural products

Land	
Description	Eastern Europe, landlocked
Area	35,919 mi² (93,030 km²)
Highest point	Kékes, 3,327 ft (1,014 m)
Lowest point	Along Tisza River, 256 ft (78 m)

The political changes and improvements to the rail line between Austria and Hungary have sparked greatly increased tourism. Budapest is now three hours by train from Vienna.

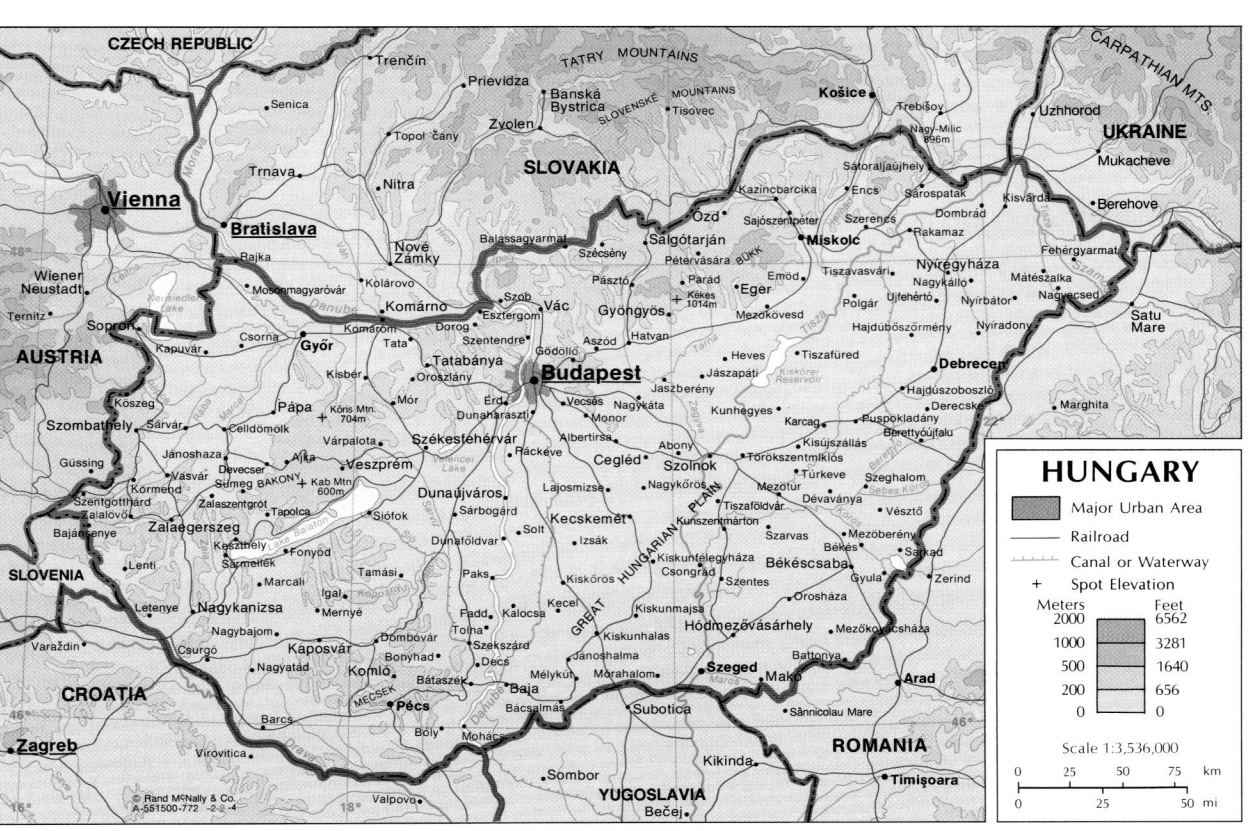

Mountains, fjords, and glaciers dominate much of Iceland's terrain.

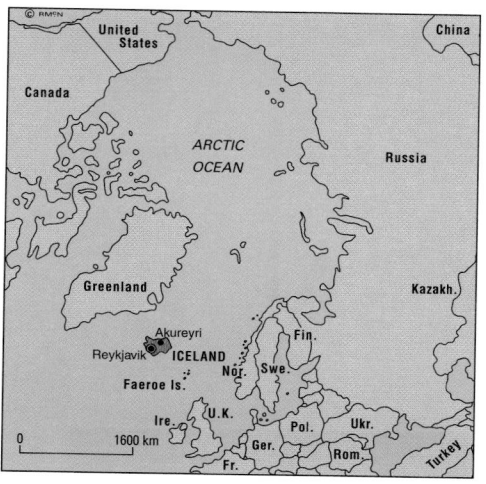

ICELAND

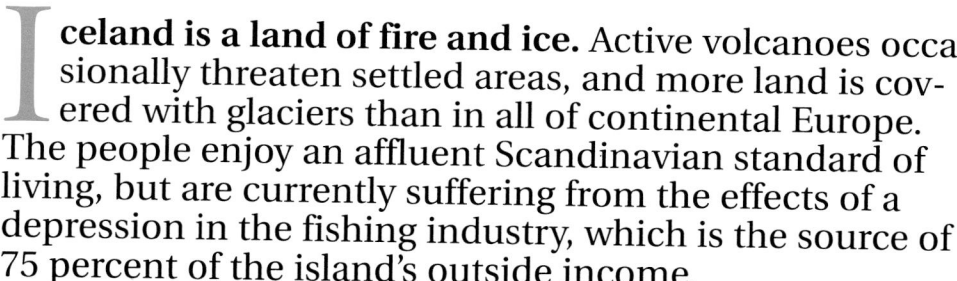

I celand is a land of fire and ice. Active volcanoes occasionally threaten settled areas, and more land is covered with glaciers than in all of continental Europe. The people enjoy an affluent Scandinavian standard of living, but are currently suffering from the effects of a depression in the fishing industry, which is the source of 75 percent of the island's outside income.

Iceland at a glance

Official name	Republic of Iceland

People

Population	265,000
Density	6.7/mi² (2.6/km²)
Urban	91%
Capital	Reykjavík, 100,850
Ethnic groups	Icelander (mixed Norwegian and Celtic)
Languages	Icelandic
Religions	Lutheran 96%, other Christian 3%
Life expectancy	81 female, 76 male
Literacy	100%

Politics

Government	Republic
Parties	Independence, Progressive, Social Democratic, others
Suffrage	Universal, over 18
Memberships	NATO, OECD, UN
Subdivisions	8 regions

Economy

GDP	$4,200,000,000
Per capita	$16,154
Monetary unit	Krona
Trade partners	Exports: U.K., Germany, U.S. Imports: U.S., Germany, Netherlands
Exports	Fish, animal products, aluminum, diatomite
Imports	Machinery and transportation equipment, petroleum, food, textiles

Land

Description	North Atlantic island
Area	39,769 mi² (103,000 km²)
Highest point	Hvannadalshnúkur, 6,952 ft (2,119 m)
Lowest point	Sea level

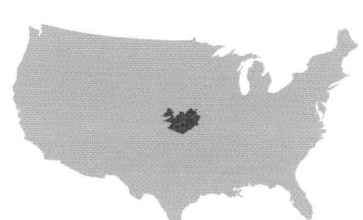

Despite Iceland's northern location, its capital, Reykjavík, has a relatively mild climate, thanks to warm Atlantic currents. Temperatures average between 31 and 53 degrees Fahrenheit year-round. The city's deep harbor never freezes completely.

People

Most Icelanders are of Norwegian or Celtic ancestry, live in coastal cities, and belong to the Lutheran church. Icelandic, the predominant language, has changed little from the Old Norse of the original settlers and still resembles the language of twelfth-century Nordic sagas.

Economy and the Land

Fish, found in the island's rich coastal waters, are the main natural resource and export. Iceland has a long tradition based on fishing, but the industry has recently suffered from decreasing markets and catches. Glaciers, lakes, hot springs, volcanoes, and a lava desert limit agricultural land but provide a scenic terrain. Although the island lies just south of the Arctic Circle, the climate is moderated by the Gulf Stream. Summers are damp and cool, and winters relatively mild but windy. Proximity to the Arctic Circle puts Iceland in the "Land of the Midnight Sun," resulting in periods of twenty-four-hour daylight in June.

POPULATION COMPARISON
Iceland=0.1% of U.S.

United States

GDP COMPARISON
Iceland=0.07% of U.S.

United States

POPULATION DISTRIBUTION
Urban   Rural

History and Politics

Norwegians began settlement of Iceland around the ninth century. The world's oldest parliament, the Althing, was established in Iceland in A.D. 930. Civil wars and instability during the thirteenth century led to the end of independence in 1262, when Iceland came under Norwegian rule. In the fourteenth century Norway was joined to Denmark's realm, and rule of Iceland passed to the Danes. The Althing was abolished in 1800 but re-established in 1843. In the 1918 Act of Union, Iceland became a sovereign state but retained its union with Denmark under a common king. Germany occupied Denmark in 1940 during World War II. British troops, replaced by Americans in 1941, protected Iceland from invasion. Following a 1944 plebiscite, Iceland left its union with Denmark and became an independent republic.

Eruption of Hekla Volcano

Off Iceland's southern coast is Surtsey, a new volcanic island that began forming from eruptions in 1963.

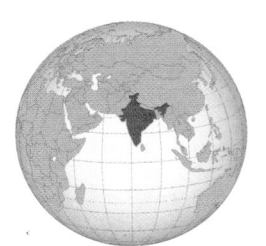

INDIA

Darjeeling, in far northeast India, is a mountain resort famed for its stunning views of the Himalayas. Tea from the plantations lining its hillsides is exported around the world.

(top) Boatload of crops, Dal Lake, Kashmir

(bottom) Camel driver and camel, Thar Desert, Rajasthan

One in six of the world's people lives in India, an ancient land that is home to a myriad of cultures, religions, and peoples. Many of the challenges the country currently faces are related to its enormous population. A growing middle class is offset by the 40 percent of the population still too poor to afford an adequate diet. The cities are overcrowded, and every acre of arable land in the countryside has been planted. But perhaps the most notable aspect of India is that so many people, and so many diverse groups, are generally able to live together in peace.

People

India's population is composed of two main ethnic groups: the Indo-Aryans and the Dravidians. Found mostly in the north are the Indo-Aryans, a central Asian people who arrived in India around 1500 B.C., pushing the Dravidians to the south, where they remain concentrated today. A Mongoloid minority inhabits the mountains of the far north, and aboriginal groups live in the central forests and mountains. There are fifteen official indigenous languages, as well as English, which is spoken by the majority of educated people. India is second only to China in population, and although Hindus are the religious majority, the country also has one of the world's largest Muslim populations. Christians, Sikhs, Jains, and Buddhists comprise additional religious minorities.

Economy and the Land

Economic conditions have improved since India became independent in 1947. Agriculture, upon which most Indians depend, is now more efficient, a result of modernization programs. Industry has expanded as well, and the country ranks high in its number of scientists and skilled laborers. Poverty, unemployment, and underemployment continue to plague the nation, however, partly due to rapid population growth and improved life expectancy. Many natural resources, including coal, iron ore, bauxite, and manganese, remain undeveloped. India comprises three land regions: the Himalayas along the northern border; the Gangetic plain, a fertile northern region; and the peninsula, made up mostly of the Deccan, a plateau region. The climate ranges from temperate to tropical monsoon.

History and Politics

India's civilization dates back to 2500 B.C., when the Dravidians flourished in the region. Aryan tribes invaded about one thousand years later, bringing the indigenous beliefs that evolved into Hinduism, and various empires followed. In the sixth or fifth century B.C., Siddhārtha Gautama, who came to be called Buddha, founded Buddhism, a major influence on Indian life until about A.D. 800. Invasions beginning around A.D. 450 brought the Huns and, during the seventh and eighth centuries, Arab conquerors introduced Islam. The Mogul Empire, under a series of Muslim rulers, began in the 1500s, and the British East India Company established trading posts in the 1600s. By 1757 the East India Company had become India's major power, and by the 1850s the company controlled nearly all present-day India, Pakistan, and Bangladesh. An Indian rebellion in 1857 caused Britain to take over the East India Company's rule. Demands for independence increased after a controversial massacre of Indians by British troops in 1919. By 1920 Mohandas Gandhi had emerged as the leader of an independence campaign based on nonviolent disobedience and noncooperation. The nation gained independence in 1947 and established Pakistan as a separate Muslim state because of Muslim-Hindu hostilities. Ongoing disputes include a border conflict with China that erupted into fighting in 1959 and 1962 and a disagreement with Pakistan over the mainly Muslim region of Kashmir.

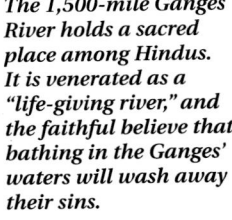

The 1,500-mile Ganges River holds a sacred place among Hindus. It is venerated as a "life-giving river," and the faithful believe that bathing in the Ganges' waters will wash away their sins.

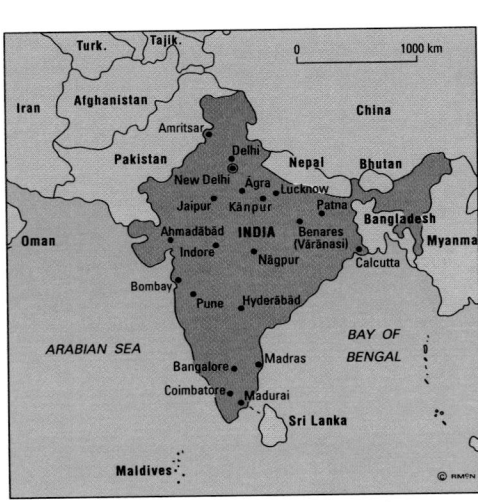

Given its enormous population—more than 12 million—Bombay is surprisingly compact, squeezed into only 239 square miles. The city was an outpost of the British Empire until the 1860s, when the American Civil War disrupted the world supply of cotton. Bombay became a major center of trade in the fiber, which sparked population growth and economic diversification that have continued unabated.

POPULATION COMPARISON
India=346% of U.S.

United States

GDP COMPARISON
India=18% of U.S.

United States

ETHNIC GROUPS

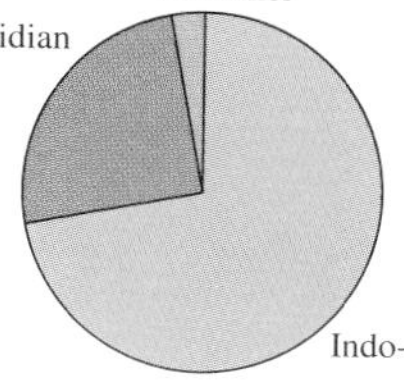

Mongoloid and other
Dravidian
Indo-Aryan

POPULATION DISTRIBUTION

Urban   Rural

(top) Harvesting crops, Himalayan foothills

(bottom) Rooftops of Leh, a town in the Ladākh Range

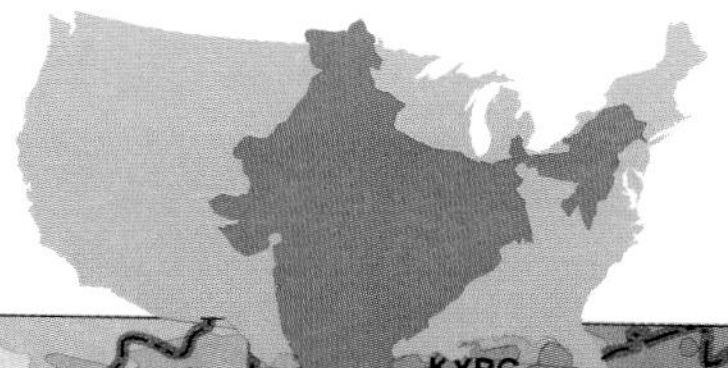

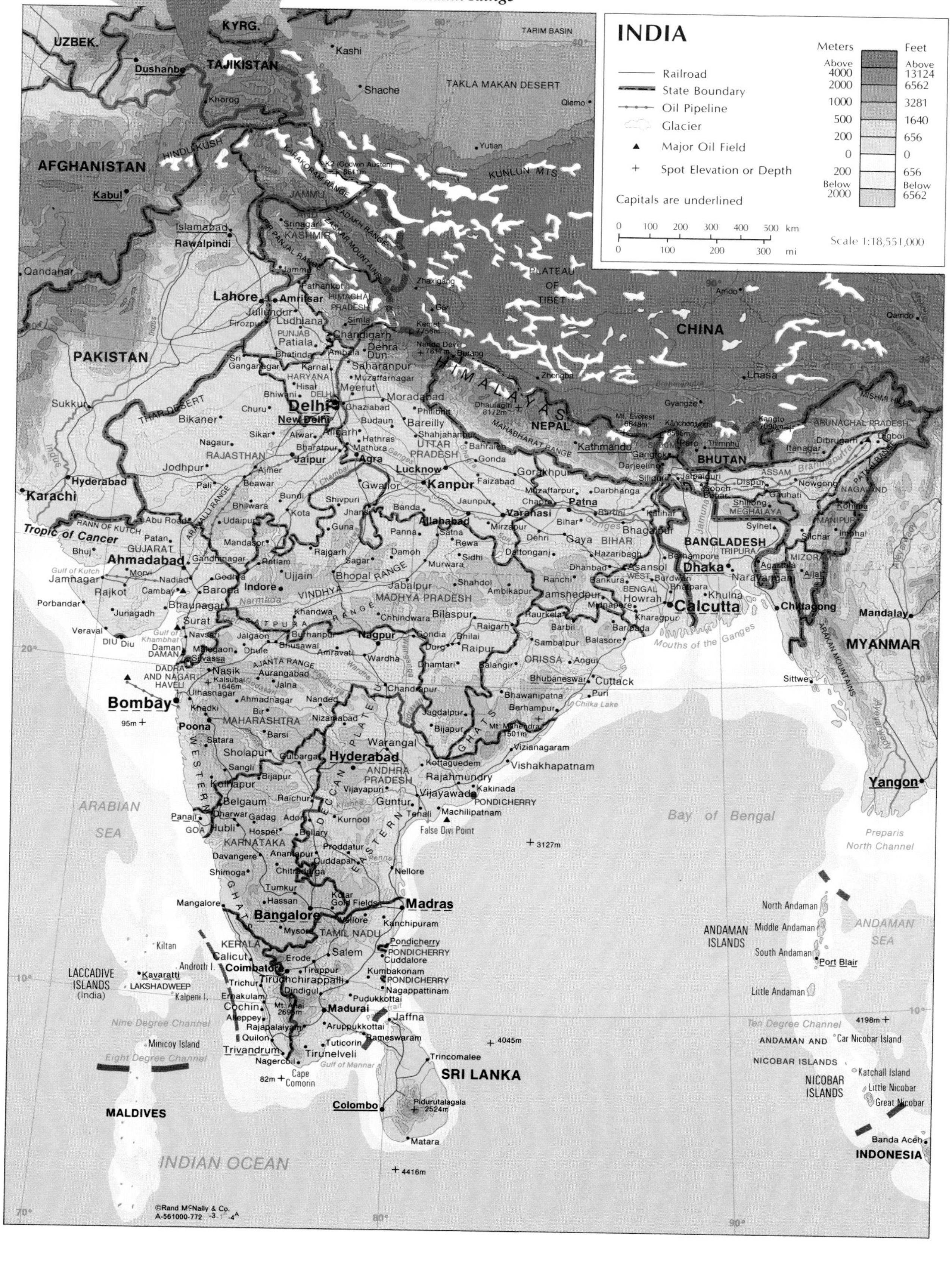

INDIA

Meters		Feet
Above 4000		Above 13124
2000		6562
1000		3281
500		1640
200		656
0		0
200		656
Below 2000		Below 6562

Railroad
State Boundary
Oil Pipeline
Glacier
▲ Major Oil Field
+ Spot Elevation or Depth

Capitals are underlined

0 100 200 300 400 500 km
0 100 200 300 mi
Scale 1:18,551,000

India at a glance

Official name	Republic of India

People

Population	909,150,000
Density	735/mi² (284/km²)
Urban	26%
Capital	New Delhi, 301,297
Ethnic groups	Indo-Aryan 72%, Dravidian 25%, Mongoloid and other 3%
Languages	English, Hindi, Telugu, Bengali, indigenous
Religions	Hindu 80%, Muslim 11%, Christian 2%, Sikh 2%
Life expectancy	61 female, 60 male
Literacy	48%

Politics

Government	Republic
Parties	Congress (I), Communist (Marxist), Janata, Janata Dal, others
Suffrage	Universal, over 18
Memberships	CW, UN
Subdivisions	25 states, 7 union territories

Economy

GDP	$1,170,000,000,000
Per capita	$1,339
Monetary unit	Rupee
Trade partners	Exports: U.S., former Soviet republics, Japan
	Imports: U.S., Japan, Germany
Exports	Gems and jewelry, engineering goods, clothing, textiles, chemicals, tea
Imports	Petroleum, machinery, gems, jewelry, chemicals, iron and steel

Land

Description	Southern Asia
Area	1,237,062 mi² (3,203,975 km²)
Highest point	Kānchenjunga, 28,208 ft (8,598 m)
Lowest point	Sea level

The above information includes part of Jammu and Kashmir.

Bullock cart, Ramnad, Tamil Nadu

©Rand McNally & Co.
A-561000-772

Cut off from the rest of Asia by the snowy peaks of the Himalayas in the north, peninsular India consists of vast plains, plateau regions, and low mountains. This land is hot, humid, and dependent upon seasonal monsoons for rain.

INDONESIA

Indonesia at a glance

Official name	Republic of Indonesia

People	
Population	193,680,000
Density	257/mi² (99/km²)
Urban	29%
Capital	Jakarta, Java I., 8,227,746
Ethnic groups	Javanese 45%, Sundanese 14%, Madurese 8%, coastal Malay 8%
Languages	Bahasa Indonesia (Malay), English, Dutch, indigenous
Religions	Muslim 87%, Protestant 6%, Catholic 3%, Hindu 2%.
Life expectancy	65 female, 61 male
Literacy	77%

Politics	
Government	Republic
Parties	Democracy, Golkar, United Development
Suffrage	Universal, over 17 or married
Memberships	ASEAN, OPEC, UN
Subdivisions	27 provinces

Economy	
GDP	$571,000,000,000
Per capita	$3,067
Monetary unit	Rupiah
Trade partners	Exports: Japan, U.S., Singapore Imports: Japan, U.S., Germany
Exports	Petroleum and natural gas, timber, textiles, rubber, coffee
Imports	Machinery, chemicals, manufactures

Land	
Description	Southeastern Asian islands
Area	752,410 mi² (1,948,732 km²)
Highest point	Jaya Pk., 16,503 ft (5,030 m)
Lowest point	Sea level

The world's fourth most populous country, Indonesia comprises one thousand inhabited islands, and each is a world of its own. Java, the most heavily populated island, is vibrant and overcrowed; Irian Jaya, part of the island of New Guinea, is largely unexplored and home to primitive peoples; and Bali has a lyrical Hindu culture found nowhere else in the world. Extremes of rich and poor coexist in Jakarta: horrific slums surrounding the capital give way to air-conditioned shopping malls filled with the newly affluent.

People

Only three countries—China, India, and the United States—have greater populations than Indonesia. The majority of Indonesians are of Malay stock, which includes several subgroups, such as Javanese, Sundanese, Madurese, and coastal Malay. More than two hundred indigenous languages are spoken, but the official, unifying language is Bahasa Indonesia, a Malay dialect. Most people live in small farm villages and follow ancient customs stressing cooperation. Muslim traders brought Islam to Indonesia, and most of the population is Muslim. Many Indonesians combine spirit worship with Islam or Christianity. Indonesia's rich cultural heritage includes many ancient temples.

Economy and the Land

Indonesia is a leading producer of petroleum in the Far East. The area also has large deposits of minerals and natural gas. Agriculture is still a major economic activity, and rice remains an important crop, though overpopulation threatens the economy and food supply. The nation's more than 13,600 islands form a natural barrier between the Indian and Pacific oceans, making the straits between the islands important for world trade and military strategy. Java, the most industrial and heavily populated island, is characterized by volcanic mountains and narrow fertile plains along the northern coast. Indonesia includes most of Borneo, the third largest island in the world. Other major Indonesian islands are Sulawesi, Sumatra, and Irian Jaya (the western half of New Guinea), which also feature inland mountains and limited coastal plains. The climate is tropical, with seasonal monsoons.

A volcano rises above a farmer plowing his fields on the idyllic island of Bali. Frequent eruptions have damaged the terraced rice paddies which snake around the hillsides.

Mt. Bromo in eastern Java is an active volcano. Indonesia has a total of 60 active volcanoes, which stretch in a line from western Sumatra to the Lesser Sunda Islands.

POPULATION COMPARISON
Indonesia=74% of U.S.

United States

GDP COMPARISON
Indonesia=9% of U.S.

United States

ETHNIC GROUPS

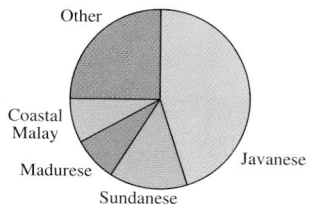

Other

Coastal Malay

Madurese

Sundanese

Javanese

POPULATION DISTRIBUTION

Urban   Rural

Nias Island off the coast of Sumatra is known for its traditional villages and pleasant beaches.

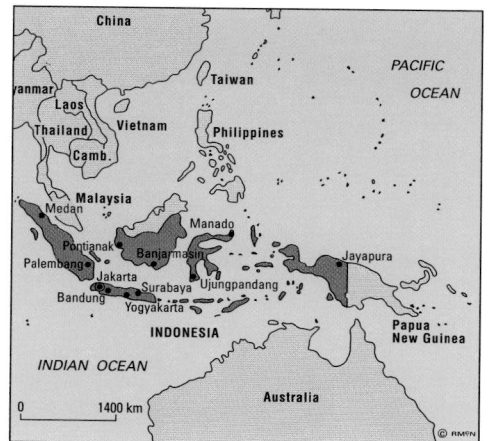

History and Politics

Indonesian civilization is more than 2,500 years old and has produced two major empires with influence throughout Southeast Asia. The Portuguese arrived in the sixteenth century but were outnumbered by the Dutch, who eventually gained control of most of the islands and established a plantation colony. An independence movement began early in the twentieth century and slowly gained momentum. Japan encouraged Indonesian nationalism during World War II. Shortly after the Japanese surrendered in 1945, Indonesia proclaimed itself an independent republic. Economic and political instability led to an attempted Communist coup in 1965. The government has outlawed the Communist party and strengthened relations with the West, at the same time establishing trade talks with China. In annexed East Timor, reports of labor rights violations and human rights abuses continue.

(top) Fishing boats at dawn, Bali

(bottom) Temple at Lake Bratan, Bali

Indonesia is the largest country in Southeast Asia both in number of people and in area. Its 13,677 islands stretch along the equator between the Indian and Pacific oceans.

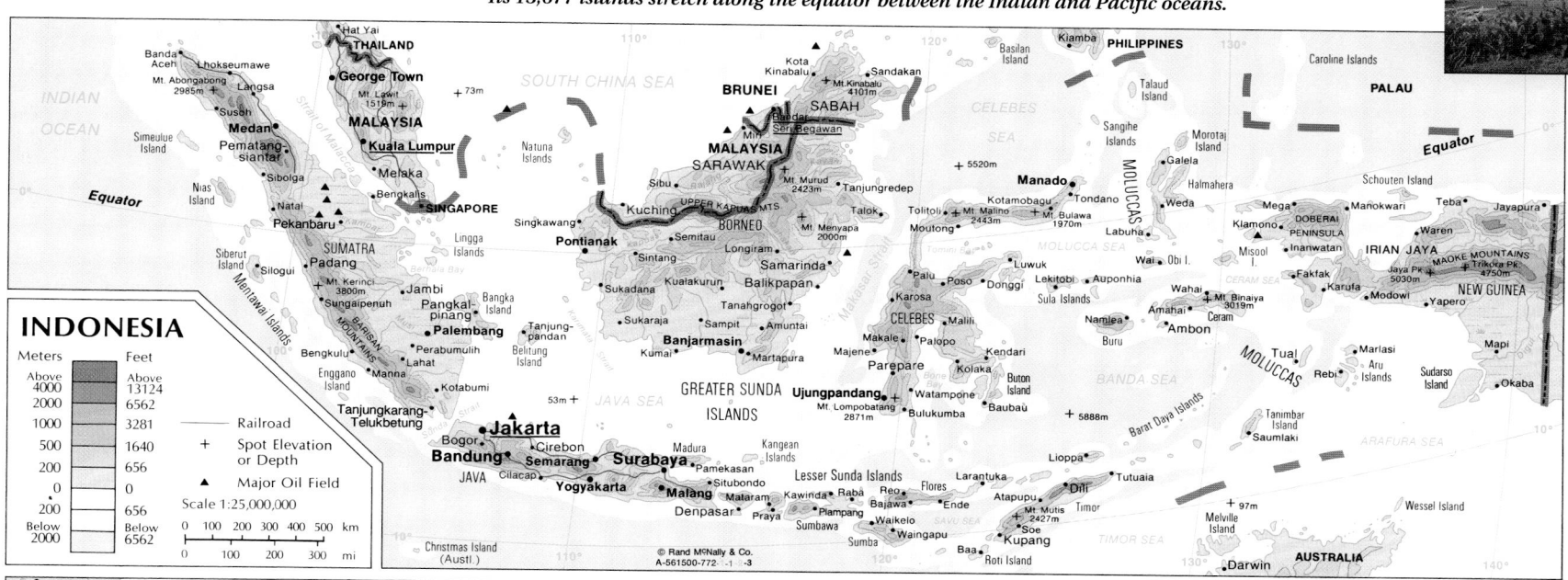

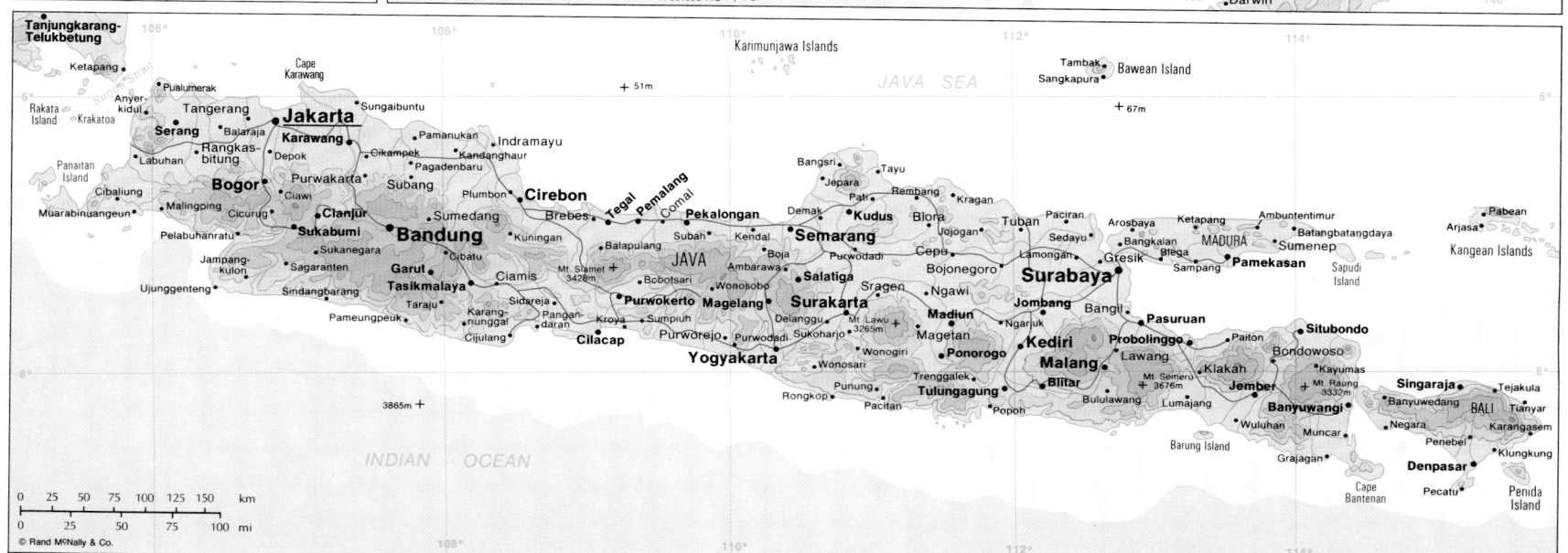

Once the center of the kingdom of Persia, Iran possesses a long history filled with dramatic events. The most recent came in 1979 when Muslim fundamentalists seized power from the Shah, a ruler backed by the United States. The westernized society that had taken root since World War II, thanks to oil revenues, was swept away, and Iran is now governed under strict Islamic law.

IRAN

Iran at a glance

Official name	Islamic Republic of Iran

People

Population	63,810,000
Density	101/mi² (39/km²)
Urban	57%
Capital	Tehrān 6,042,584
Ethnic groups	Persian 51%, Azeri 24%, Kurdish 7%
Languages	Farsi, Turkish dialects, Kurdish
Religions	Shiite Muslim 95%, Sunni Muslim 4%
Life expectancy	68 female, 67 male
Literacy	54%

Politics

Government	Islamic republic
Parties	Militant Clerics Association, Fedaiyin Islam Organization
Suffrage	Universal, over 15
Memberships	OPEC, UN
Subdivisions	24 provinces

Economy

GNP	$303,000,000,000
Per capita	$5,008
Monetary unit	Rial
Trade partners	Exports: Japan, Italy, France Imports: Germany, Japan, Italy
Exports	Petroleum, carpets, fruit, nuts
Imports	Machinery, military supplies, metal works, food, pharmaceuticals

Land

Description	Southwestern Asia
Area	632,457 mi² (1,638,057 km²)
Highest point	Mt. Demavend, 18,386 ft (5,604 m)
Lowest point	Caspian Sea, -92 ft (-28 m)

People

Most Iranians are of Aryan ancestry, descended from an Asiatic people who migrated to the area in ancient times. The Aryan groups include majority Persians and minority Gilani, Mazanderani, Kurds, Lur, Bakhtiari, and Baluchi. Turks and Azeries are the major non-Aryan minorities. Farsi, or Persian, remains the main language. Nearly all Iranians are Muslim, mainly of the Shiite sect, and the country is an Islamic republic, with law based on Islamic teachings. Minority religious groups, especially Baha'is, have been victims of persecution. Due to aridity and a harsh mountain-and-desert terrain, the population is concentrated in the west and north.

Oil production, Ahwaz

Economy and the Land

Iran's previously rapid economic development has slowed as a result of a 1979 revolution and a war with Iraq. Small-scale farming, manufacturing, and trading appear to be current economic trends. Oil remains the most important export, although output has decreased due to changes in economic policy and other factors. Persian carpets also continue as elements of trade. Iran's terrain consists mainly of a central plateau marked by desert and surrounded by mountains; thus agriculture is limited, and the country

remains dependent on imported food. The central region is one of the most arid areas on Earth, and summers throughout most of the country are long, hot, and dry, with higher humidity along the Persian Gulf and Caspian coast. Winters are cold in the mountains of the northwest, but mild on the plain. The Caspian coastal region is generally subtropical.

History and Politics

Iran's history is one of the world's longest, with a civilization dating back several thousand years. Around 1500 B.C., Aryan immigrants began arriving from central Asia, calling the region Iran, or land of the Aryans, and splitting into two groups: the Medes and the Persians. In the sixth century B.C., Cyrus the Great founded the Persian, or Achaemenian, Empire, which came to encompass Babylonia, Palestine, Syria, and Asia Minor. Alexander the Great conquered the region in the fourth century B.C. Various dynasties followed, and Muslim Arabs invaded in the A.D. 600s and established Islam as the major religion. In 1908 oil was discovered in the region, and modernization programs began during the reign of Reza Shah Pahlavi, who came to power in 1925. Despite Iran's declared neutrality in World War II, the Allies invaded, obtaining rights to use the country as a supply route to the Soviet Union. The presence of foreign influences caused nationalism to increase sharply after the war. Mohammad Reza Pahlavi—who succeeded his father, Reza Shah Pahlavi, as shah—instituted social and economic reforms during the sixties,

although many Muslims felt the reforms violated religious law, and resented the increasing Western orientation of the country and the absolute power of the shah. Led by Muslim leader Ayatollah Ruholla Khomeini, revolutionaries seized the government in 1979, declaring Iran an Islamic republic based upon fundamental Islamic principles. Khomeini remained the religious leader of Iran until his death in 1989. In 1988 a long and destructive war with Iraq ended. Hashemi Rafsanjani was elected president two years later. Recent signs of military build-up and the growing strength of the fundamentalist movement throughout the world continue to cause concern in the West.

The Zagros Mountains separate the fertile coastal plains of the Persian Gulf from the rocky highlands and deserts of central Iran.

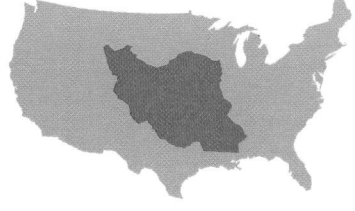

Much of Iran is arid. The Kavir region east of Tehran is uninhabitable, unexplored, and dominated by sharp-edged masses of salt. Numerous faultlines crisscross the west, making the land highly prone to powerful earthquakes.

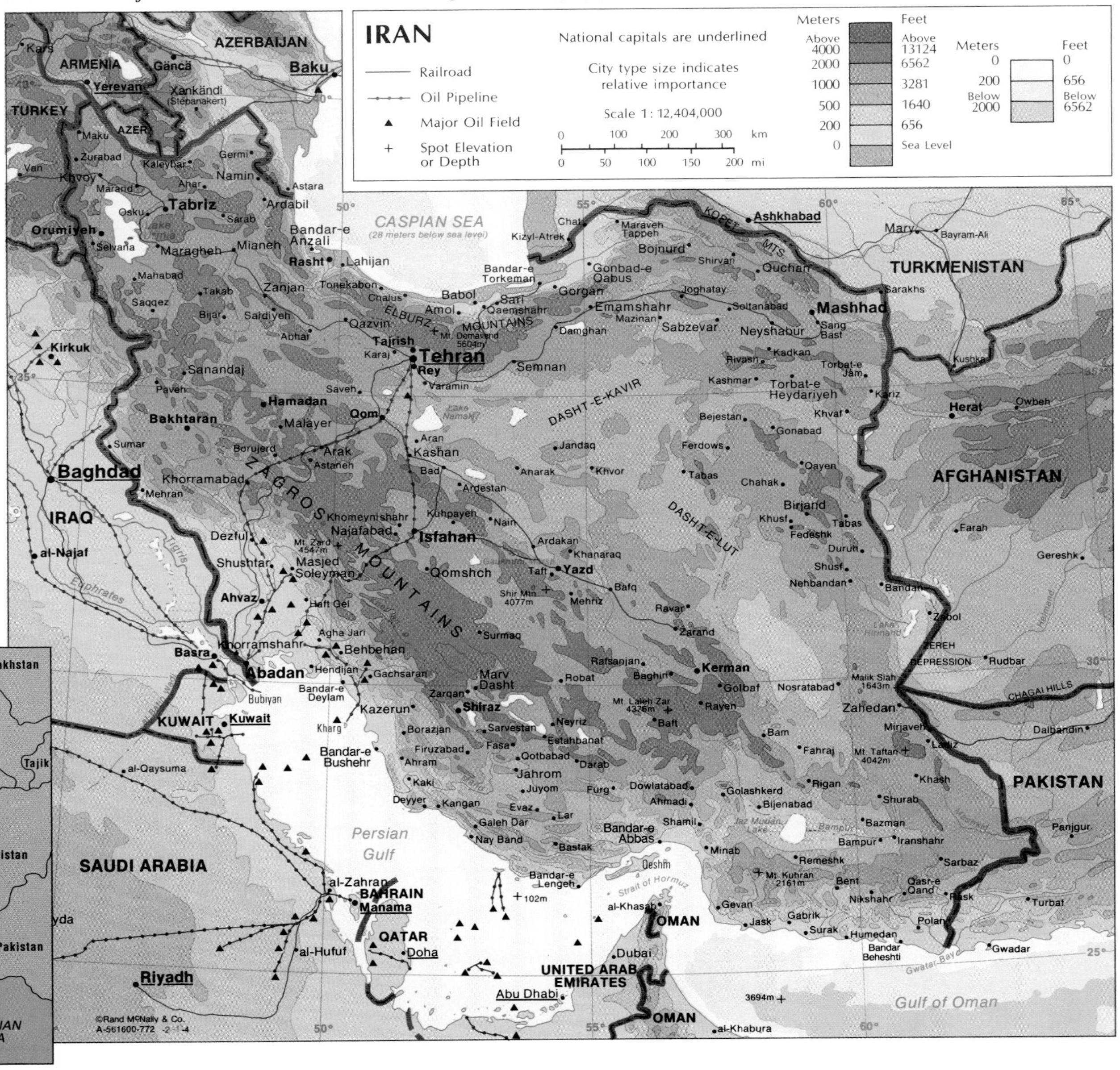

IRAN

National capitals are underlined

——	Railroad
++++	Oil Pipeline
▲	Major Oil Field
+	Spot Elevation or Depth

City type size indicates relative importance

Scale 1: 12,404,000

Meters	Feet
Above 4000	Above 13124
2000	6562
1000	3281
500	1640
200	656
	Sea Level

Meters	Feet
0	0
200	656
Below 2000	Below 6562

©Rand McNally & Co.
A-561600-772 -2-1-4

P**rior to 1979, Iraq was a prosperous country** whose economy was fueled by oil revenues. Then came a decade-long war with Iran that killed thousands of people. This was followed by the invasion of Kuwait in 1990 that sparked an international military response which leveled much of Iraq's industry. At present, the standard of living has plummeted, as United Nations trade sanctions against Iraq and its President Saddam Hussein have taken hold.

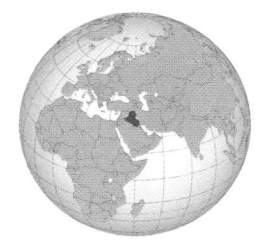

Ruins at Al Hadr in northern Iraq attest to the country's rich historical past. From these highlands, the Sumerians emigrated to Mesopotamia in 3000 B.C. Later civilizations included the Hittites, the Kassites, and the Byzantines.

Iraq at a glance

Official name	Republic of Iraq

People

Population	20,250,000
Density	120/mi² (46/km²)
Urban	72%
Capital	Baghdād, 3,841,268
Ethnic groups	Arab 75%-80%; Kurdish 15-20%; Turkoman, Assyrian, or other 5%
Languages	Arabic, Kurdish, Assyrian, Armenian
Religions	Shiite Muslim 60-65%, Sunni Muslim 32-37%, Christian and others 3%
Life expectancy	68 female, 65 male
Literacy	60%

Politics

Government	Republic
Parties	Ba'th
Suffrage	Universal, over 18
Memberships	AL, OPEC, UN
Subdivisions	15 governorates, 3 autonomous regions

Economy

GNP	$38,000,000,000
Per capita	$2,020
Monetary unit	Dinar
Trade partners	Exports: U.S., Brazil, Turkey, Japan. Imports: Germany, U.S., Turkey, France, U.K.
Exports	Petroleum, fertilizer, sulphur
Imports	Manufactures, food

Land

Description	Southwestern Asia
Area	169,235 mi² (438,317 km²)
Highest point	Unnamed, 11,835 ft (3,607 m)
Lowest point	Sea level

People

Descendants of the founders of one of the world's oldest civilizations inhabit Iraq. Most Iraqis are Muslim Arabs and speak Arabic. The minority Kurds, also mainly Muslim, are concentrated in the northwest; speak their own language, Kurdish; and follow a non-Arab lifestyle. Kurdish demands for self-rule have led to occasional rebellion.

Economy and the Land

Oil is the mainstay of Iraq's economy, and nearly all economic development has focused on the petroleum industry, nationalized in the 1970s. Despite its oil wealth, the Iraqi economy, like the Iranian, was drained by the Iran-Iraq war. Most farmland lies near the Tigris and Euphrates rivers. The terrain is marked by northeastern mountains, southern and western deserts, and the plains of upper and lower Iraq, which lie between the Tigris and Euphrates rivers. The climate is generally hot and dry.

History and Politics

Civilizations such as the Sumerian, Babylonian, and Parthian flourished in the area of the Tigris and Euphrates in ancient times. Once known as Mesopotamia, the region was the setting for many biblical events. After coming under Persian rule in the sixth century B.C., Mesopotamia fell to Alexander the Great in the fourth century B.C. Invading Arabs brought the Muslim religion in the seventh century A.D. and for a time Baghdād was the capital and cultural center of the Arab empire. Thirteenth-century Mongol invaders were followed by Ottoman Turks in the sixteenth century. Ottoman rule continued and, following a British invasion during World War I, Mesopotamia became a British mandate at the end of the war. In 1921 the monarchy of Iraq was established, and independence was gained in 1932. Iraq and other nations formed the Arab League in 1945 and participated in a war against Israel in 1948. Opposition to monarchical rule increased during the 1950s and, after a 1958 military coup, the country was declared a republic. Instability, evidenced by coups, continued into the 1970s. The political climate was further complicated by occasional uprisings by Kurds demanding autonomy. War with Iran, which caused heavy losses on both sides, continued intermittently through the early 1980s, ending in a 1988 cease-fire agreement. In August 1990 Iraq invaded Kuwait and forced the government into exile. A coalition of countries under the military direction of the United States forced Iraq to withdraw in early 1991. After the war the United Nations established "no-fly" zones in northern and southern Iraq to protect Kurdish and Shiite rebels. The UN continues an embargo on trade until Iraq downsizes its military capabilities.

(top) Euphrates River

(bottom) Damascus Street, Baghdad

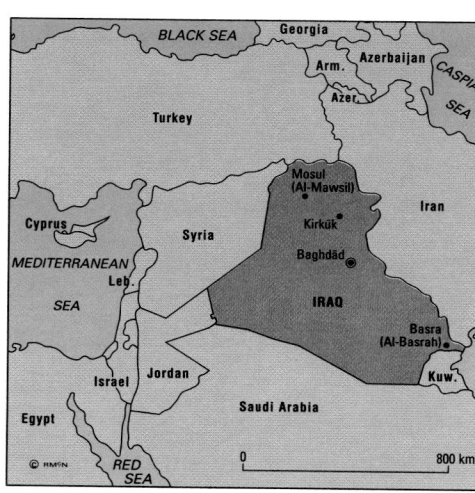

It is generally thought that human civilization began in Mesopotamia, the fertile region cradled by the Tigris and Euphrates Rivers. Archeologists have found evidence of settlements dating back to 10,000 B.C.

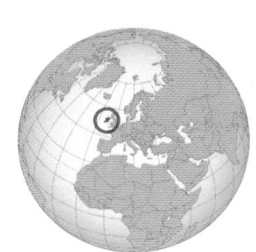

IRELAND

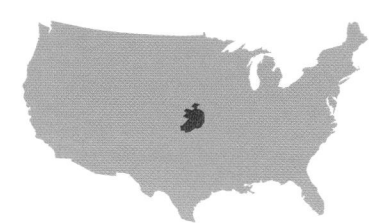

(photo above) Clifden is one of the many quaint towns along Ireland's Atlantic coast.

Ireland is a country of green surrounded by a gray sea. The often cold and brooding weather contrasts with the people, known for their warmth and merriment. A stagnant economy at home compels thousands of Ireland's highly literate citizens to annually seek opportunity elsewhere, primarily in England and the United States.

pastureland, and is surrounded by coastal highlands. The climate is temperate maritime, with mild summers and winters and plentiful rainfall.

History and Politics
Around the fourth century B.C., Ireland's indigenous population was conquered by Gaels, a Celtic tribe, from continental Europe and Great Britain. Christianity was introduced by St. Patrick in A.D. 432, and periodic Viking raids began near the end of the eighth century. In the twelfth century the pope made the Norman king of England, Henry II, overlord of the island; the English intervened in a dispute between Irish kings; and centuries of British influence began. As British control grew, so did Irish Catholic hostility, arising from seizure of land by English settlers, the Protestant Reformation, and the elimination of political and religious freedoms. The Protestant majority of present-day Northern Ireland was established in the 1600s, when land taken from the Irish was distributed to English and Scottish Protestants. In 1801 the British Act of Union established the United Kingdom of Great Britain, and Northern Ireland. Religious freedom was regained in 1829, but the struggle for independence continued. Most of the Irish depended upon potatoes as a staple food, and hundreds of thousands died or emigrated in the 1840s when the crop failed because of a plant disease. Following an armed rebellion, the Irish Free State, a dominion of Great Britain, was created in 1921, with the predominantly Protestant counties in the north remaining under British rule. The nation became a republic in 1949. The explosive issue of reunification with Northern Ireland continues to dominate Irish politics.

The 26 counties of the Republic of Ireland occupy five-sixths of the island. The remaining land consists of the politically troubled six counties of Northern Ireland, a part of the United Kingdom.

People
Most of Ireland's population is descended from the Celts, a people who flourished in Europe and Great Britain in ancient times. Irish Gaelic, a form of ancient Celtic, and English are official languages. Most people are Roman Catholic. Protestants mainly belong to the Church of Ireland, a member of the Anglican Communion. With a long literary tradition, the country has contributed greatly to world literature.

Economy and the Land
Ireland's economy was agricultural until the 1950s, when a program of rapid industrialization began. This expansion resulted in significant foreign investment, especially by the United States. Most of the Irish labor force is unionized. Agriculture continues to play an important role, however, and food is produced for domestic and foreign consumption. The country of Ireland occupies most of the island but excludes Northern Ireland, which is part of the United Kingdom. The fertile central region features green, rolling hills, suitable for farming and

Ireland at a glance
Official name   Ireland

People
Population	3,546,000
Density	131/mi² (50/km²)
Urban	57%
Capital	Dublin, 502,749
Ethnic groups	Irish (Celtic), English
Languages	English, Irish Gaelic
Religions	Roman Catholic 93%, Church of Ireland 3%
Life expectancy	78 female, 73 male
Literacy	98%

Politics
Government	Republic
Parties	Fianna Fail, Fine Gael, Labor, others
Suffrage	Universal, over 18
Memberships	EU, OECD, UN
Subdivisions	26 counties

Economy
GDP	$46,300,000,000
Per capita	$13,135
Monetary unit	Pound (punt)
Trade partners	Exports: U.K., Germany, France Imports: U.K., U.S., Germany
Exports	Chemicals, data processing equipment, machinery, live animals
Imports	Food, animal feed, chemicals, petroleum, machinery, textiles, clothing

Land
Description	Northwestern European island (five-sixths of island of Ireland)
Area	27,137 mi² (70,285 km²)
Highest point	Carrauntoohil, 3,406 ft (1,038 m)
Lowest point	Sea level

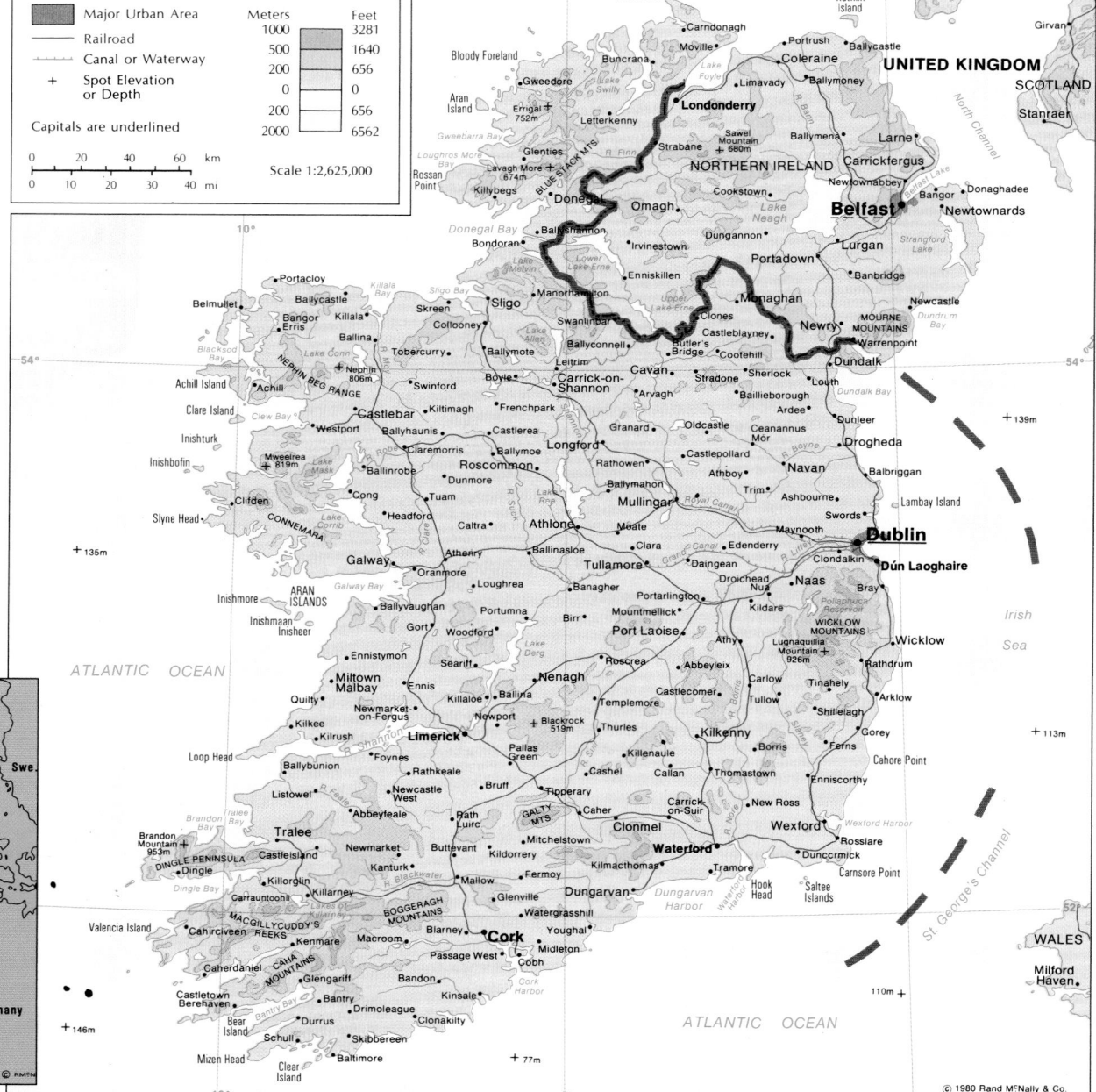

Isle of Man at a glance

Official name   Isle of Man

People

Population	72,000
Density	326/mi² (126/km²)
Urban	74%
Capital	Douglas, 22,214
Ethnic groups	Manx, British
Languages	English, Manx Gaelic
Religions	Anglican, Roman Catholic
Life expectancy	79 female, 73 male

Politics

Government	Crown dependency (U.K. protection)
Parties	None
Suffrage	Universal, over 21
Memberships	None
Subdivisions	None

Economy

GNP	$490,000,000
Per capita	$7,538
Monetary unit	Pound
Trade partners	U.K.
Exports	Textiles, herring, shellfish, meat
Imports	Wood, fertilizer, fish

Land

Description	Northwestern European island
Area	221 mi² (572 km²)
Highest point	Snaefell, 2,036 ft (621 m)
Lowest point	Sea level

Scale 1:1,000,000   One inch represents approximately 16 miles.
One centimeter represents 10 kilometers.

The Isle of Man is linked to England by frequent ferries from Douglas to Heysham and Liverpool. In the summer there are also services to Ireland.

ISLE OF MAN

Located in the Irish Sea between England and Northern Ireland, the Isle of Man was once home to Celtic and Norse peoples. Today, with the decline of fishing, it profits from legions of tourists who come to see the rugged scenery and the island's indigenous tailless Manx cats.

People

Manx, of Celtic descent, compose the majority population on the Isle of Man. Their language, also called Manx, is virtually extinct, having been replaced by English nearly universally on the island. A Crown Dependency of the United Kingdom, the Isle of Man has a minority British population, and the main religion is Anglican.

Economy and the Land

Agricultural activities include livestock raising and dairy farming, and the island's major crops are oats, wheat, barley, and potatoes. Fishing provides for local consumption and export income, and tax incentives have encouraged the development of industry. About 11 percent of the island's income comes from tourism. The Isle of Man is situated midway between Britain and Ireland, and many tourists from the British Isles visit the island annually, attracted by its scenic beauty. In addition, a popular motorcycle race held each year draws international visitors. The rocky coast is marked by cliffs, and moors cover much of the island's interior. Calf of Man, a rocky islet, lies off the southwest shore. The climate is mild.

History and Politics

Irish missionaries came to the Isle of Man early in its history. The Vikings took the island in the ninth century, and it remained under Norwegian control until 1266. Various rulers and owners followed, including the Scots, Welsh, British, and the earls of Salisbury and Derby. In 1765 Britain bought the island from the Duke of Atholl. A self-governing territory of the United Kingdom, the Isle of Man has its own legal system; residents are not subject to British laws and acts, although local laws require British approval. The island also has its own legislature, the one-thousand-year-old Tynwald, which is one of the world's oldest legislative bodies. The Crown is represented in the dependency by a lieutenant governor. The Isle of Man is also famous as the birthplace of the Manx cat.

Two religious shrines dominate the skyline of Jerusalem. The Dome of the Rock, the third-holiest Muslim site, is in the foreground. Behind is the silver domed Church of the Holy Sepulchre, built in the 4th century A.D. The Old City of Jerusalem is covered with holy sites for Jews, Christians, and Muslims.

ISRAEL

Hurrying to worship

An ancient Hebrew kingdom and the birthplace of Christianity, Israel has existed as a country only since 1948. While providing a homeland for Jews, creation of the country has led to decades of conflict with the surrounding Arab nations. Only recently has some accommodation been reached with the Palestinians, the Arab people who were living in Palestine at the time Israel was established. *(continued)*

The desertic Wilderness of Judea, which lies to the west of the Dead Sea, is seen here from Masada, site of the Jewish fortress that fell to the Romans in 73 A.D.

Israel, continued

People

Most Israelis are Jewish immigrants or descendants of Jews who settled in the region in the late 1800s. The two main ethnic groups are the Ashkenazim of central and eastern European origin and the Sephardim of the Mediterranean and Middle East. The non-Jewish population is predominantly Arab and Muslim, and many Palestinians inhabit the Israeli-occupied West Bank, the status of which is still in dispute. Hebrew and Arabic are the official languages, and both are used on documents and currency. Conflict between conservative and liberal Jewish groups has spilled over into the nation's political life.

Economy and the Land

Despite drastic levels of inflation and a constant trade deficit, Israel has experienced continuous economic growth. Skilled labor supports the market economy based on services, manufacturing, and commerce. Taxes are a major source of revenue, as are grants and loans from other countries and income from tourism. The country is poor in natural resources, but through improved irrigation and soil conservation, Israel now produces much of its own food. Because of its limited natural resources, Israel must import most of the raw materials it needs for industry. The region's varied terrain includes coastal plains, central mountains, the Jordan Rift Valley, and the desert region of the Negev. Except in the Negev, the climate is temperate.

History and Politics

Israel comprises much of the historic region of Palestine, known in ancient times as Canaan and the site of most biblical history. Hebrews arrived in this region around 1900 B.C. The area experienced subsequent immigration and invasion by diverse peoples, including Assyrians, Babylonians, and Persians. In 63 B.C. it became part of the Roman Empire, was renamed Judaea and finally, Palestine. In the A.D. 600s, invading Arabs brought Islam to the area and, by the early 1500s when Ottoman Turks conquered the region, Muslims comprised a majority. During the late 1800s, as a result of oppression in eastern Europe, many Jews immigrated to Palestine, hoping to establish a Jewish state. This movement, called Zionism, and the increasing Jewish population led to Arab-Jewish tensions. Turkey sided with Germany in World War I, and after the war the Ottoman Empire collapsed. Palestine became a mandated territory of Britain in 1920. Jewish immigration and Arab-Jewish hostility increased during the years of Nazi Germany. Additional unrest arose from conflicting interpretations of British promises and the terms of the mandate. In 1947 Britain turned to the United Nations for help, and in 1948 the nation of Israel was established. Neighboring Arab countries invaded immediately, and war ensued, during which Israel gained some land. A truce was signed in 1949, but Arab-Israeli wars broke out periodically throughout the fifties, sixties, and seventies. Israel signed a peace treaty with Egypt in 1979, annexed the Golan Heights in 1981, and returned the Sinai to Egypt the following year. The years since have seen continual conflict over the occupation of the Gaza Strip and West Bank. In 1993 an historic accord between Israel and the Palestinians was reached, which gives the Palestinians limited autonomy over the Gaza Strip and the area of Jericho. Continuing peace talks have paved the way for expanded Jewish/Arab relations.

Jerusalem, a city of great religious importance to Jews, Christians and Muslims, has been the cause of religious warfare for thousands of years. With many claims unresolved, an uneasy peace prevails at present.

Israel at a glance

Official name	State of Israel

People

Population	5,059,000
Density	631/mi² (244/km²)
Urban	92%
Capital	Jerusalem, 524,500
Ethnic groups	Jewish 83%, Arab and others 17%
Languages	Hebrew, Arabic
Religions	Jewish 82%, Muslim 14%, Christian 2%, Druze 2%
Life expectancy	78 female, 75 male
Literacy	92%

Politics

Government	Republic
Parties	Labor, Likud, others
Suffrage	Universal, over 18
Memberships	UN
Subdivisions	6 districts

Economy

GDP	$65,700,000,000
Per capita	$14,304
Monetary unit	Shekel
Trade partners	Exports: U.S., Japan, U.K. Imports: U.S., Belgium, Germany
Exports	Diamonds, fruit, textiles and clothing, food, fertilizer
Imports	Military equipment, diamonds, oil, chemicals, machinery, iron and steel

Land

Description	Southwestern Asia
Area	8,019 mi² (20,770 km²)
Highest point	Mt. Meron, 3,963 ft (1,208 m)
Lowest point	Dead Sea, -1,322 ft (-403 m)

The above information excludes Israeli-occupied areas.

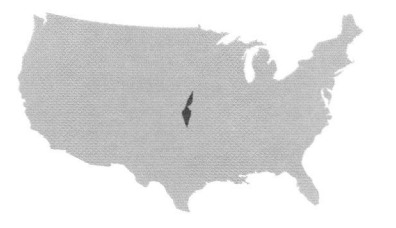

POPULATION COMPARISON
Israel=2% of U.S.

United States

GDP COMPARISON
Israel=1% of U.S.

United States

ETHNIC GROUPS

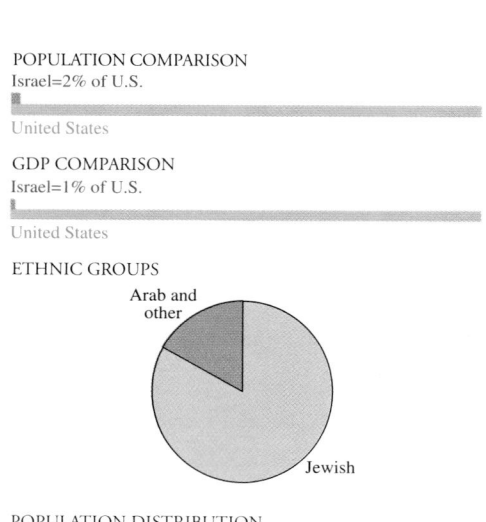

Arab and other

Jewish

POPULATION DISTRIBUTION

Urban   Rural

Boats in the harbor of Acre (Akko), an ancient city located just north of Haifa. Acre has been a trading port since the 9th century B.C, when it was called Ptolemaïs.

Italy is a country of stunning coastlines, and the Amalfi Coast near Salerno is considered to be its finest. Whitewashed villages cling to craggy cliffs that plunge into the crystal-clear waters.

ITALY

Italy has long been a center of Western art and culture. Legacies of the Roman Empire blanket Rome, the brilliance of the Renaissance survives in Florence, and the latest in design and fashion flows out of Milan. The country is notoriously volatile politically—Italian governments change almost annually. Italy's economy is the world's seventh-largest.

People

Italy is populated mainly by Italian Roman Catholics. Most speak Italian, although dialects often differ from region to region. Despite an ethnic homogeneity, the people exhibit diversity in terms of politics and culture. The country has about twelve political parties, and northern inhabitants are relatively prosperous, employed primarily in industry, whereas southerners are generally farmers and often poor. The birthplace of the Renaissance, Italy has made substantial contributions to world culture.

Economy and the Land

The Italian economy is based on private enterprise, although the government is involved in some industrial and commercial activities. Industry and commercial agriculture are centered in the north, which produces steel, textiles, and chemicals. A hilly terrain makes parts of the south unsuited for crop raising, and livestock grazing is a main activity. Tourism is also important; visitors are drawn by the northern Alps, the sunny south, and the Italian cultural tradition. The island of Sicily, lying off the southwest coast, produces fruits, olives, and grapes. Sardinia, a western island, engages in some sheep and wheat raising. Except for the northern Po Valley, narrow areas along the coast, and a small section of the southern peninsula, Italy's terrain is mainly rugged and mountainous. The climate varies from cold in the Alps to mild and Mediterranean in other regions.

History and Politics

Early influences in Italy included Greeks, Etruscans, and Celts. From the fifth century B.C. to the fifth century A.D., the dominant people were Romans descended from Sabines and neighboring Latins, who inhabited the Latium coast. Following the demise of the Roman Empire, rulers and influences included Byzantines; Lombards, an invading Germanic tribe; and the Frankish King Charlemagne, whom the pope crowned emperor of the Romans in 800. During the eleventh century, Italy became a region of city-states, and its cultural life led to the Renaissance, which started in the 1300s. As the city-states weakened, Italy fell victim to invasion and rule by France, Spain, and Austria, with these countries controlling various regions at different times. In 1861 Victor Emmanuel II, the king of Sardinia, proclaimed Italy a kingdom, and by 1871 the nation included the entire peninsula, with Rome as the capital and Victor Emmanuel as king. In 1922 Benito Mussolini, the leader of Italy's Fascist movement, came to power and ruled as dictator until his death at the hands of Italian partisans in 1945. The country allied with Germany in World War II, and a popular resistance movement evolved. Recent politics have been marked by a volatility that has produced frequent changes in government. *(continued)*

(top) Ruins, Roman Forum

(middle) Santa Croce Church, Florence

(bottom) A Lake Como village

Italy at a glance

Official name	Italian Republic

People

Population	57,320,000
Density	493/mi² (190/km²)
Urban	69%
Capital	Rome, 2,693,383
Ethnic groups	Italian (Latin)
Languages	Italian, German, French, Slovene
Religions	Roman Catholic
Life expectancy	80 female, 74 male
Literacy	97%

Politics

Government	Republic
Parties	Democratic Party of the Left, Popular, Socialist, others
Suffrage	Universal, over 18
Memberships	EU, NATO, OECD, UN
Subdivisions	20 regions

Economy

GDP	$967,600,000,000
Per capita	$17,100
Monetary unit	Lira
Trade partners	Exports: Germany, France, U.S. Imports: Germany, France, Netherlands
Exports	Textiles, clothing, metals, transportation equipment, chemicals
Imports	Petroleum, machinery, chemicals, metals, food, agricultural products

Land

Description	Southern Europe
Area	116,324 mi² (301,277 km²)
Highest point	Mont Blanc (Monte Bianco), 15,771 ft (4,807 m)
Lowest point	Sea level

An almost perfectly preserved remnant of ancient Rome, the domed Pantheon is nearly 2,000 years old. The entrance is supported by 16 granite columns. Once a Roman temple, the building is now a church.

POPULATION COMPARISON
Italy=22% of U.S.

United States

GDP COMPARISON
Italy=15% of U.S.

United States

POPULATION DISTRIBUTION
Urban   Rural

An annual boat marathon begins on the San Marco Lagoon in Venice. The city is dominated by the Campanile, or bell tower, on the right. Narrow canals spanned by arched bridges thread among Venice's ancient buildings and squares.

(top) Via del Croce, Rome

(middle) Gondolas and bridges, Venice

(bottom) The Dolomites, northern Italy

ITALY

- Major Urban Area
- Railroad
- Glacier
- + Spot Elevation or Depth

National capitals are underlined

City type size indicates relative importance

Meters	Feet
Above 4000	Above 13124
2000	6562
1000	3281
500	1640
200	656
0	0
200	656
Below 2000	Below 6562

Scale 1:6,145,000

0   50   100   150 km
0   50   100 mi

From Rome north to the Alps, Italy's rolling plains are home to the economic engines of industry that drive Italy. In the south, the pace is slower and the people poorer. Active volcanoes loom over Naples and Sicily.

Port Antonio on Jamaica's north coast is a popular yachting and tourist destination.

JAMAICA

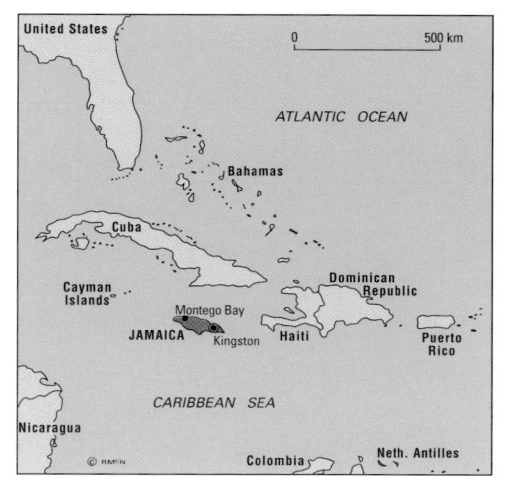

Kingston festival

O nce the chief slave market for the United States, Jamaica is today a highly popular destination for sun-seeking U.S. tourists. Three-quarters of its people are descended from slaves. Many live in abject poverty that contrasts starkly with the luxurious resorts lining the coast.

People

Most Jamaicans are of African or Afro-European descent, and the majority are Christian. English is the official language, but many Jamaicans also speak Creole. Population is concentrated on the coastal plains, where the main commercial crops are also grown.

Economy and the Land

Agriculture is the traditional mainstay, and more than a third of the population is engaged in farming. Sugar cane and bananas are principal crops. Mining is also important, and Jamaica is a leading producer of bauxite. The tropical climate, tempered by ocean breezes, makes the island a popular tourist destination. A mountainous inland region is surrounded by coastal plains and beaches.

History and Politics

Christopher Columbus claimed the island for Spain in 1494. As the enslaved native population died out, blacks were brought from Africa to work plantations. Britain invaded and gained control of Jamaica in the seventeenth century, and for a time the island was one of the most important sugar and slave centers of the New World. In 1838 the British abolished slavery, the plantation economy broke down, and most slaves became independent farmers. Local political control began in the 1930s, and the nation became fully independent in 1962. Since independence the nation has faced problems of unemployment, inflation, and poverty, with periodic social unrest.

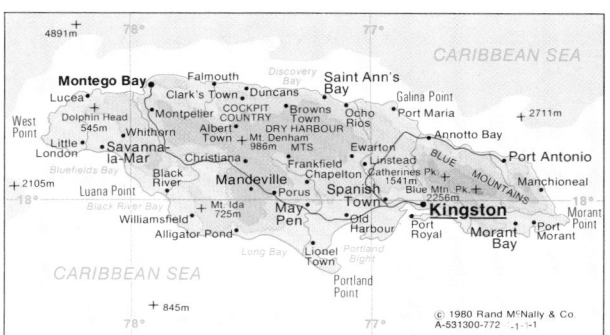

Seaweed-munching manatees can still be found along the southern coast of Jamaica. Inland, the mountains which blanket 80 percent of the island are home to 200 species of birds.

JAMAICA	Meters	Feet		Meters	Feet
	4000	13124		0	0
—— Railroad	2000	6562		200	656
+ Spot Elevation or Depth	1000	3281		Below	Below
	500	1640		2000	6562
Scale 1:3,353,000	200	656			

Jamaica at a glance

Official name	Jamaica

People

Population	2,568,000
Density	605/mi² (234/km²)
Urban	52%
Capital	Kingston, 587,798
Ethnic groups	Black 75%, mixed 13%, East Indian 1%
Languages	English, Creole
Religions	Church of God 18%, Baptist 10%, Anglican 7%, Seventh-Day Adventist 7%
Life expectancy	76 female, 71 male
Literacy	98%

Politics

Government	Parliamentary state
Parties	Labor, People's National
Suffrage	Universal, over 18
Memberships	CW, OAS, UN
Subdivisions	14 parishes

Economy

GDP	$8,000,000,000
Per capita	$3,199
Monetary unit	Dollar
Trade partners	Exports: U.S., U.K., Canada Imports: U.S., U.K., Venezuela
Exports	Bauxite, alumina, sugar, bananas
Imports	Petroleum, machinery, food, manufactures

Land

Description	Caribbean island
Area	4,244 mi² (10,991 km²)
Highest point	Blue Mountain Pk., 7,402 ft (2,256 m)
Lowest point	Sea level

POPULATION COMPARISON
Jamaica=1% of U.S.

United States

GDP COMPARISON
Jamaica=0.1% of U.S.

United States

ETHNIC GROUPS

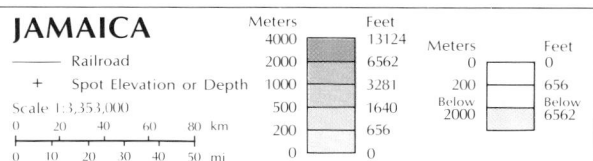

Other
East Indian
Mixed
Black

POPULATION DISTRIBUTION
Urban   Rural

A typical Jamaican house clings to a hillside in the island's interior, where most of the original rain forest has been cut down for timber.

JAPAN

(top) Japan's famed bullet trains

(bottom) Smiling for the camera, Tokyo

(left) The Ginza district is Tokyo's center for shopping. On Sundays, vehicle traffic is banned and shoppers rule the roads.

Mount Fuji, Japan's national symbol

J apan's rise from ashes after World War II has been much heralded. Its powerhouse economy is built on exports—primarily vehicles and electronics—that are in demand worldwide. Although Japan's investments span the globe, the country has been reticent to flex its political muscles abroad. At home, Japanese culture is refined, and the people place great value on politeness, an essential trait when living in so crowded a nation.

Harakura shopping district, Tokyo

People

The Japanese constitute Japan's major ethnic group; there is a small Korean minority. Shintoism and Buddhism are the principal religions. Almost all the population lives on the coastal plains. Japan's culture blends East and West, with karate, tea ceremonies, and kimonos balanced by baseball, fast food, and business suits. Although its arts have been greatly influenced by China, Japan has developed distinctive music, literature, and painting.

Economy and the Land

One of the world's leading industrial powers, Japan is remarkable for its economic growth rate since World War II, considering it has few natural resources. It has also become famous for its innovative technology. Manufacturing is the basis of the economy, and Japan is a leading producer of ships, machinery, cars, and electronic equipment. Its chemical, iron, and steel industries are extremely profitable. Agriculture's part in the economy is small, since little of the rugged island terrain is arable. Fishing still plays a significant role in Japan's economy as Japan maintains one of the world's largest fishing fleets. Overseas trade has expanded rapidly since the 1960s, as Japan requires raw materials for its many industries. Trade barriers and the competitiveness of Japanese products overseas have led to trade deficits among Western nations. Japan's mountainous terrain includes both active and dormant volcanoes; earthquakes occasionally occur. The climate ranges from subtropical to temperate.

History and Politics

Legend states that Japan's first emperor was descended from the sun goddess and came to power around 600 B.C. The arrival of Buddhism, Confucianism, and new technologies from China in the fifth and sixth centuries A.D. revolutionized society. Feuding nobles controlled Japan between 1192 and 1867 and ruled as shoguns, or generals, in the name of the emperor. The warrior class, or samurai, developed early in this period. The arrival of Europeans in the sixteenth century caused fear of an invasion among the shoguns, and in the 1630s they dissolved all foreign contacts. Japan's isolation lasted until 1854, when Commodore Matthew Perry of the United States opened the nation to the West with a show of force. The subsequent Meiji Restoration modernized Japan by adopting Western technologies and legal systems, and by stressing industrialization and education. Japan embarked on military expansion in the late nineteenth century, annexing Korea in 1910 and adding to its holdings after participating in World War I as a British ally. It occupied Manchuria in 1931 and invaded China in 1937. As part of the Axis powers in World War II, Japan attacked United States military bases in Pearl Harbor, Hawaii, in 1941. After the United States dropped atomic bombs on Hiroshima and Nagasaki in 1945, Japan surrendered. Allied forces occupied the nation until 1952, by which time the Japanese had approved a constitution that shifted power from the emperor to the people and abolished the military. With the help of U.S. aid Japan experienced a rapid economic recovery. Foreign trade issues and an economic slump dominated the early 1990s.

(right) Japan has an especially scenic and rocky coastline that is dotted with small islands. This scene is near Nagato at the southwestern tip of Honshu Island.

(bottom) A tram climbs Mt. Usu. Because most live in crowded cities, Japanese place high value on excursions to the countryside. The Showa-Shinzan volcano, seen in the background, appeared during a 1943 eruption and is testament to Japan's unstable geology.

Japan's four main islands—Hokkaido, Honshu, Shikoku and Kyushu—are geologically young and unstable. They are prone to violent earthquakes such as the one that devastated Kobe in 1995.

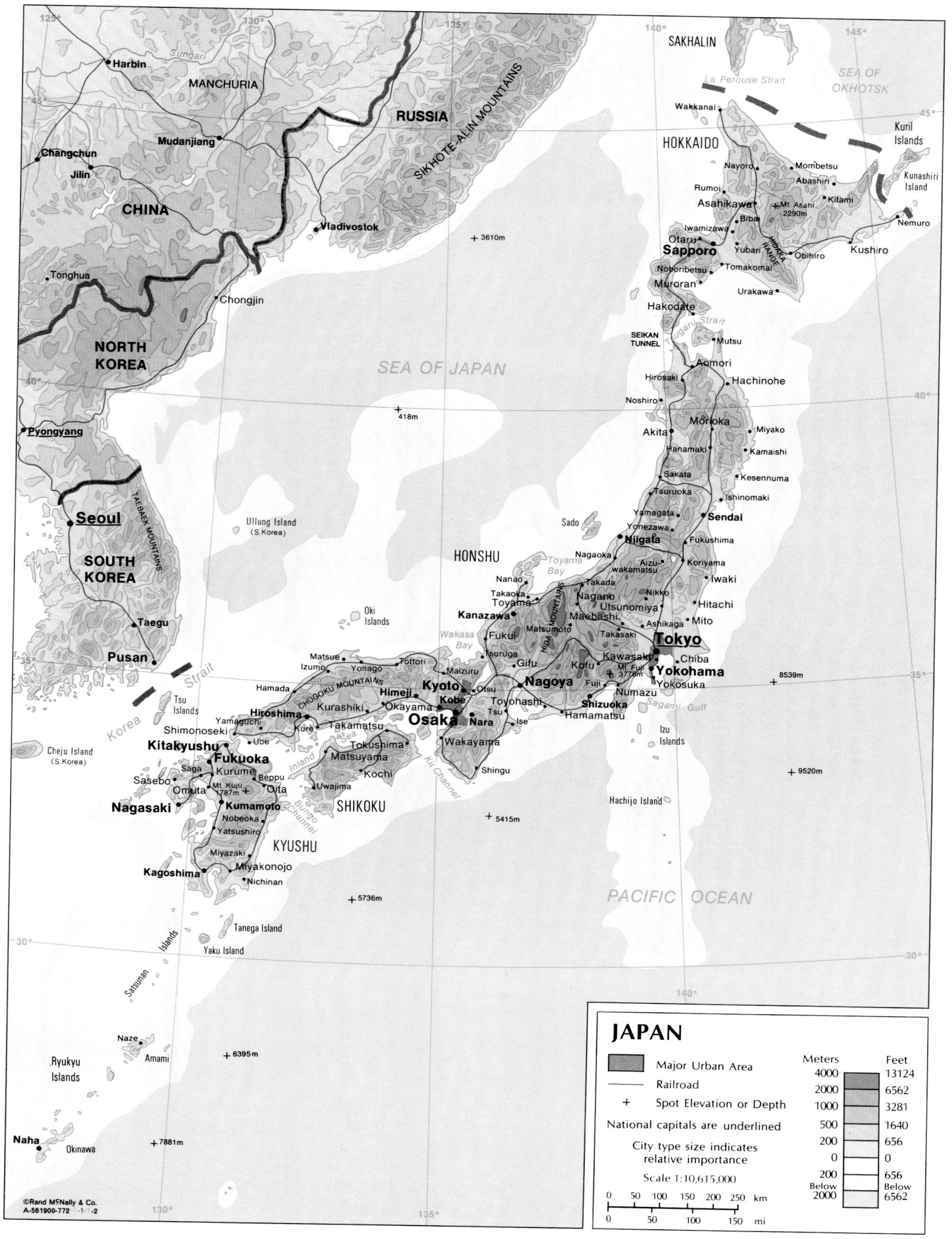

Japan at a glance

Official name   Japan

People

Population	125,360,000
Density	859/mi² (332/km²)
Urban	77%
Capital	Tōkyō, Honshū I., 8,163,573
Ethnic groups	Japanese 99%, Korean
Languages	Japanese
Religions	Buddhist and Shinto
Life expectancy	82 female, 76 male
Literacy	99%

Politics

Government	Constitutional monarchy
Parties	Liberal Democratic, Shinseito, Social Democratic, others
Suffrage	Universal, over 20
Memberships	OECD, UN
Subdivisions	47 prefectures

Economy

GDP	$2,549,000,000,000
Per capita	$20,439
Monetary unit	Yen
Trade partners	Exports: U.S., Germany, Korea Imports: U.S., Indonesia, Korea
Exports	Machinery, motor vehicles, consumer electronics
Imports	Manufactures, fuel, food and raw materials

Land

Description	Eastern Asian islands
Area	145,870 mi² (377,801 km²)
Highest point	Mt. Fuji, 12,388 ft (3,776 m)
Lowest point	Hachiro-gata reclamation area, Honshū I., -13 ft (-4 m)

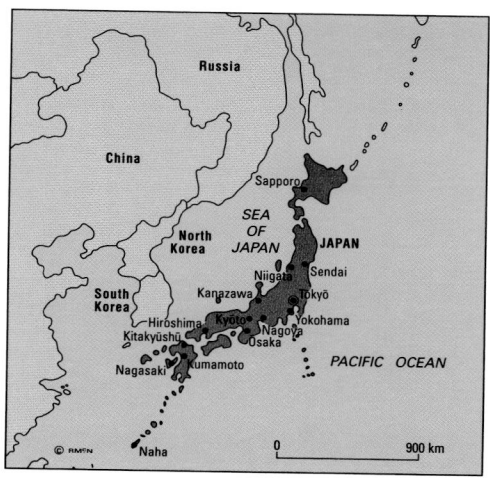

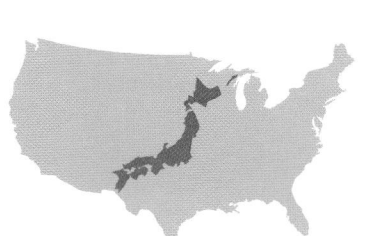

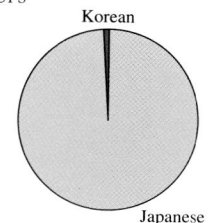

POPULATION COMPARISON
Japan=48% of U.S.

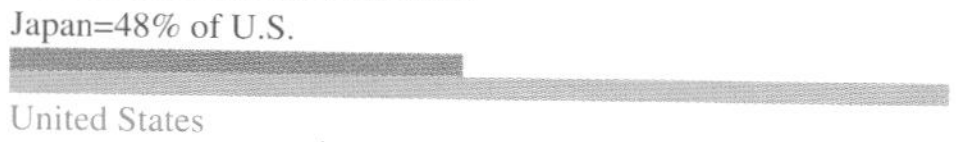

United States

GDP COMPARISON
Japan=40% of U.S.

United States

ETHNIC GROUPS

Korean

Japanese

POPULATION DISTRIBUTION

Urban   Rural

JAPAN

	Meters	Feet
Major Urban Area	4000	13124
Railroad	2000	6562
+ Spot Elevation or Depth	1000	3281
	500	1640
National capitals are underlined	200	656
City type size indicates relative importance	0	0
Scale 1:10,615,000	200	656
	Below 2000	Below 6562

Scale 1:10,615,000

0   50   100   150   200   250 km

0   50   100   150 mi

©Rand McNally & Co.
A-561900-772 -1-1-2

*(top) A beach near Yokohama
(bottom) Rice fields near Kawasaki*

This view of farmland near Kagoshima on southern Kyushu Island attests to the high level of agricultural development in Japan. Although only 15 percent of the country's land is farmed, heavy use of fertilizers and machinery has boosted crop yields in the last 40 years. About half the cropland is used to grow rice, the staple of the Japanese diet.

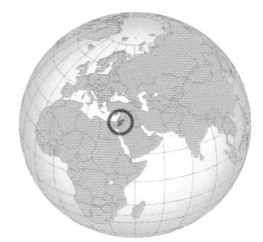

L ying at the crossroads of the Holy Land, Jordan has often been caught up in conflicts between the Jews, Muslims, and Christians. A force of moderation in the region, Jordan has in recent years sought peace with Israel.

JORDAN

The purple peaks of the Jabal Ramm massif in southern Jordan have given the area the name Valley of the Moon.

People

Most Jordanians are Arabs, but there are Circassian, Armenian, and Kurdish minorities, as well as a small nomadic population, the Bedouins, in desert areas. About one-third of all Jordanians are Palestinian refugees, displaced by Arab-Israeli wars. Jordan is the only Arab nation that has granted citizenship to the Palestinians. Arabic is the official language, and most people are Sunni Muslim, legacies of the Muslim conquest in A.D. 600s.

Economy and the Land

A nation with few natural resources, limited rainfall, and little arable land, Jordan has suffered further economic damage from an influx of refugees and the chronic political instability of the Middle East. In a 1967 war with Israel, Jordan lost control of Jerusalem and the West Bank, which made up about half the country's farmland. Agriculture remains the most important activity, and tourism has helped boost a weak economy that relies heavily on foreign aid and investment from the United States and Arab nations. There is some light industry and mining. The Jordan River forms the country's westernmost boundary, and the terrain is marked by deserts, mountains, and rolling plains. The climate ranges from Mediterranean in the West to desert in the East.

History and Politics

Jordan is the site of one of the world's oldest settlements, dating back to about 8000 B.C. The area came under the rule of the Hebrews, Assyrians, Egyptians, Persians, Greeks, and Romans, and around A.D. 636, Arab Muslims. Rule by the Ottoman Turks began in the sixteenth century, and in World War I Arab armies helped the British defeat Turkey. At the end of the war present-day Israel and Jordan became the British mandate of Palestine, which in 1922 was divided into the mandates of Transjordan, lying east of the Jordan River, and Palestine, lying to the West. Transjordan gained full independence in 1946. In 1948 the Palestine mandate created Israel, and Arab-Israeli fighting ensued. After capturing the West Bank, Transjordan was renamed Jordan in 1949. During the Arab-Israeli Six-Day War in 1967, this region and the Jordanian section of Jerusalem fell to Israel. After each war, Jordan's Palestinian-refugee population grew. A 1970 civil war pitted the Jordanian

monarchy against Palestinian guerrillas who sought to overthrow the government. The guerrillas were expelled following the war, but subsequent Arab-Israeli hostilities led to Jordan's recognition of the Palestine Liberation Organization. Although Jordan relinquished all claims to the Israeli-held West Bank area in 1988, the country continues to be involved in discussions on the fate of the Palestinians who live there. Jordan is a constitutional monarchy and has been headed by King Hussein since 1953. In the 1990s, King Hussein's moderate policies were increasingly criticized not only by Palestinian radicals, but also by a growing number of Muslim fundamentalists. However, 1993 parliamentary elections were won by moderates endorsing peace efforts that resulted in a historic peace treaty with Israel in 1994.

Jordan at a glance

Official name	Hashemite Kingdom of Jordan

People

Population	4,028,000
Density	115/mi² (44/km²)
Urban	68%
Capital	'Ammān, 936,300
Ethnic groups	Arab 98%, Circassian 1%, Armenian 1%
Languages	Arabic
Religions	Sunni Muslim 92%, Christian 8%
Life expectancy	70 female, 66 male
Literacy	80%

Politics

Government	Constitutional monarchy
Parties	Muslim Brotherhood
Suffrage	Universal, over 20
Memberships	AL, UN
Subdivisions	8 governorates

Economy

GDP	$11,500,000,000
Per capita	$3,166
Monetary unit	Dinar
Trade partners	Exports: India, Iraq, Saudi Arabia Imports: U.S., Iraq, France
Exports	Phosphates, fertilizer, potash, agricultural products, manufactures
Imports	Petroleum, machinery, transportation equipment, food, live animals

Land

Description	Southwestern Asia
Area	35,135 mi² (91,000 km²)
Highest point	Mt. Ramm, 5,755 ft (1,754 m)
Lowest point	Dead Sea, -1,322 ft (-403 m)

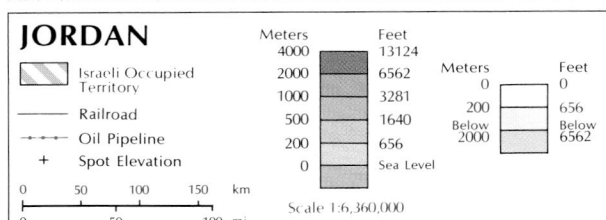

JORDAN

Meters	Feet
4000	13124
2000	6562
1000	3281
500	1640
200	656
0	Sea Level

Israeli Occupied Territory
— Railroad
+ + + Oil Pipeline
+ Spot Elevation

Scale 1:6,360,000

The Jordan River flows into the Dead Sea, a landlocked body of water that is seven times as salty as the ocean. More than 1,300 feet below sea level, it is the lowest body of water in the world.

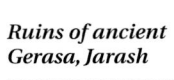

Ruins of ancient Gerasa, Jarash

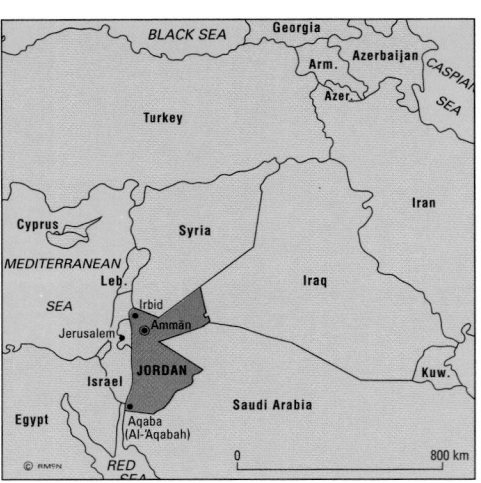

Amman, Jordan's capital, has seen its population mushroom since 1948 due to an influx of Palestinian refugees from the Arab-Israeli wars.

Kazakhs have a long history as nomadic herders. Their traditions are still alive today as the country grapples with its role in the modern world.

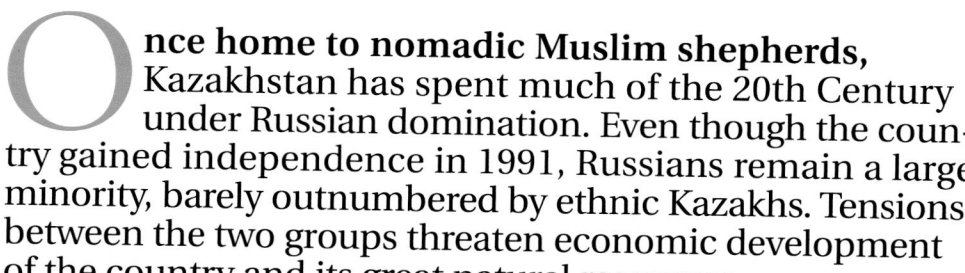

KAZAKHSTAN

Kazakhstan at a glance

Official name	Republic of Kazakhstan

People

Population	17,025,000
Density	16/mi² (6.3/km²)
Urban	57%
Capital	Astana (Akmola), 286,000
Ethnic groups	Kazakh 42%, Russian 37%, Ukrainian 5%, German 5%
Languages	Kazakh, Russian
Religions	Muslim 47%, Russian Orthodox 15%, Lutheran
Life expectancy	73 female, 63 male
Literacy	98%

Politics

Government	Republic
Parties	December Movement, Freedom (Azat), Peoples Congress, Socialist
Suffrage	Universal, over 18
Memberships	CIS, UN
Subdivisions	19 oblasts

Economy

GNP	$60,300,000,000
Per capita	$3,508
Monetary unit	Tenge
Trade partners	Exports: Russia, Ukraine, Uzbekistan Imports: Russia and other former Soviet republics
Exports	Oil, metals, chemicals, grain, wool, meat
Imports	Machinery and parts, industrial materials

Land

Description	Central Asia, landlocked
Area	1,049,156 mi² (2,717,300 km²)
Highest point	Khan Tengri Peak, 22,949 ft (6,995 m)
Lowest point	Karagiye Basin, -433 ft (-132 m)

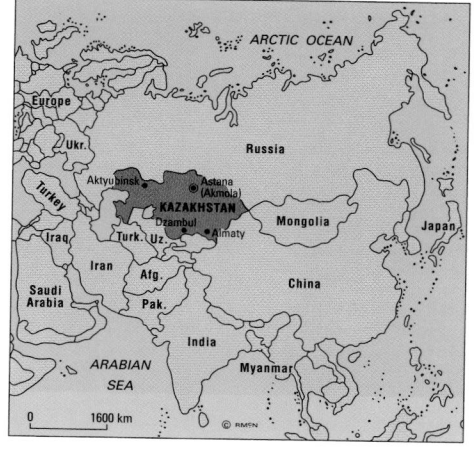

Once home to nomadic Muslim shepherds, Kazakhstan has spent much of the 20th Century under Russian domination. Even though the country gained independence in 1991, Russians remain a large minority, barely outnumbered by ethnic Kazakhs. Tensions between the two groups threaten economic development of the country and its great natural resources.

People

Kazakhstan is the traditional homeland of the Kazakh people, Turkic-speaking descendants of the Mongols. Prior to Soviet control, most Kazakhs were Muslim and nomadic. Immigration into Kazakhstan from other republics has left the Kazakhs with only 42% of the population. Russians are the next largest group, with more than one-third of the population.

Economy and the Land

The world's ninth-largest country in area, Kazakhstan is generally a vast tableland. The climate is harsh and dry, with hot summers and cold winters. Agriculture is concentrated in the north and the irrigated areas of the southeast. Industry, based mainly on the country's vast mineral resources, makes the largest contributions to the economy. Kazakhstan produces large amounts of coal and boasts tremendous undeveloped oil resources.

History and Politics

Two important trade routes brought early travelers through Kazakhstan on their way to China. The people known as the Kazakhs have inhabited the region since the sixteenth century. Russian expansion into the region began in the mid-1700s, and one of the area's most powerful states joined the Russian empire in the mid-1800s. After the Russian revolution, the region was organized into the Kirghiz Autonomous Republic, but then enlarged in 1925 to form the Kazakh Autonomous Republic. Kazakhstan became a Soviet Republic in 1936. As the heartland of the Soviet Union, Kazakhstan was home to the country's space program and hosted much of the nation's nuclear arsenal. Since the breakup of the Soviet Union in late 1991, Kazakhstan has emerged as the leader of the newly independent central Asian states, and has taken a lead in modernizing its economy. In 1993 Kazakhstan voted to dismantle its nuclear weapons. The large Russian minority threatens the stability of the government.

(top) Alakol Lake and Dzungarskij Alatau mountains

(bottom) Wild camel crossing road

Much of Kazakhstan is isolated because the country has few roads and railroads.

KAZAKHSTAN

National capitals are underlined

City type size indicates relative importance

Scale 1:18,500,000

Meters	Feet
Above 4000	Above 13124
2000	6562
1000	3281
500	1640
200	656
0	Sea Level

Meters	Feet
0	0
200	656
Below 2000	Below 6562

— Railroad
•••• Oil Pipeline
▲ Major Oil Field
+ Spot Elevation

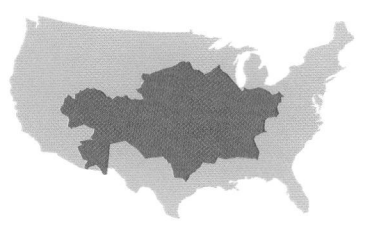

POPULATION COMPARISON
Kazakhstan=6% of U.S.
United States

GDP COMPARISON
Kazakhstan=0.9% of U.S.
United States

ETHNIC GROUPS

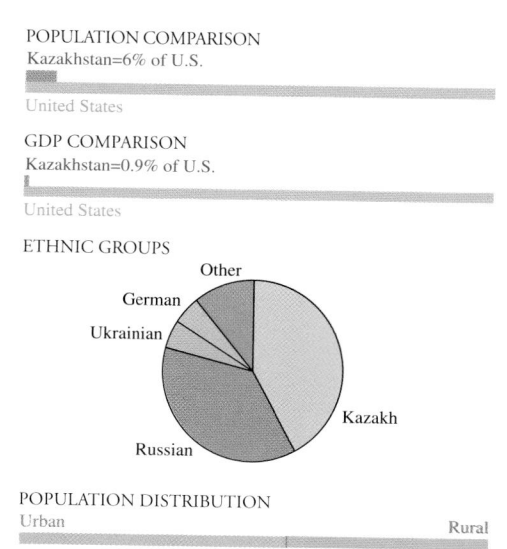

Other
German
Ukrainian
Russian
Kazakh

POPULATION DISTRIBUTION
Urban   Rural

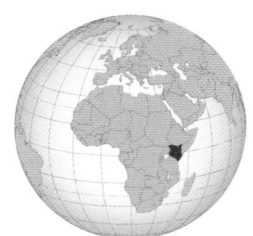

KENYA

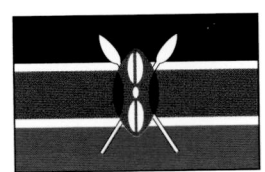

With its numerous national parks sheltering scores of animals, including lions, elephants, and giraffes, Kenya has become the symbol of Africa for many people. After decades of domestic stability and a growing economy, the nation was shocked by tribal and political violence in the early 1990s.

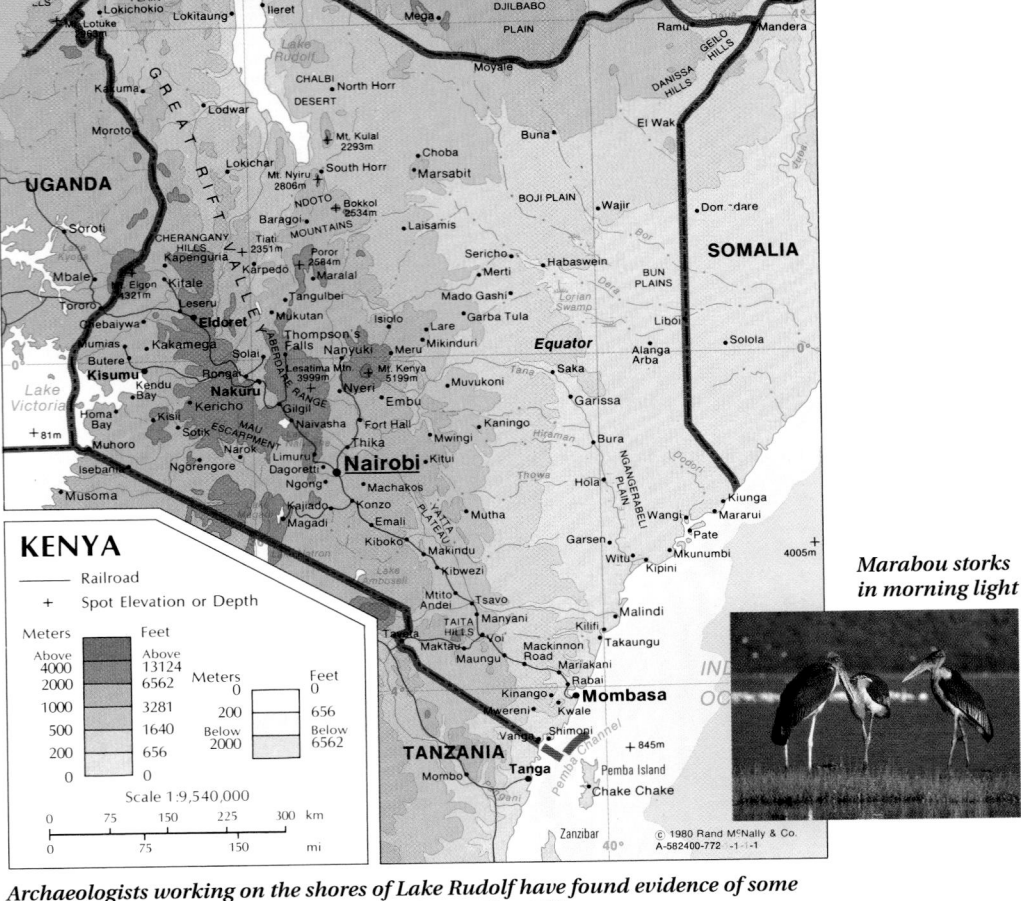

KENYA

— Railroad
+ Spot Elevation or Depth

Meters	Feet
Above 4000	Above 13124
2000	6562
1000	3281
500	1640
200	656
0	0

Meters	Feet
0	0
200	656
Below 2000	Below 6562

Scale 1:9,540,000

0 75 150 225 300 km
0 75 150 mi

© 1980 Rand McNally & Co.
A-582400-772 -1 -1 -1

Marabou storks in morning light

Archaeologists working on the shores of Lake Rudolf have found evidence of some of the earliest humans, dating back some four to five million years.

Kenya at a glance

Official name	Republic of Kenya

People

Population	28,380,000
Density	126/mi² (49/km²)
Urban	24%
Capital	Nairobi, 1,505,000
Ethnic groups	Kikuyu 21%, Luhya 14%, Luo 13%, Kamba 11%, Kalenjin 11%, Kisii 6%, Meru 5%
Languages	English, Swahili, indigenous
Religions	Roman Catholic 28%, Protestant 26%, Animist 18%, Muslim 6%
Life expectancy	61 female, 57 male
Literacy	69%

Politics

Government	Republic
Parties	African National Union, Democratic, Forum for the Restoration of Democracy, others
Suffrage	Universal, over 18
Memberships	CW, OAU, UN
Subdivisions	7 provinces, 1 capital district

Economy

GDP	$33,200,000,000
Per capita	$1,246
Monetary unit	Shilling
Trade partners	Exports: U.K., Germany, Uganda Imports: U.K., Japan, United Arab Emirates
Exports	Tea, coffee, petroleum
Imports	Machinery and transportation equipment, petroleum, iron and steel

Land

Description	Eastern Africa
Area	224,961 mi² (582,646 km²)
Highest point	Kirinyaga (Mt. Kenya), 17,058 ft (5,199 m)
Lowest point	Sea level

Elephants

Tea plantation near Kisumu

People

Nearly all Kenyans are black Africans belonging to one of more than forty different groups, each with its own language and culture. Some groups are nomadic, like the Masai. Arab and European minorities—found mostly along the coast—reflect Kenya's history of foreign rule. Most Kenyans live in the southwestern highlands, raising crops or livestock. Over half of the citizens practice a form of Christianity, while the rest pursue indigenous beliefs or Islam. Swahili, a blend of Bantu and Arabic, is an official language; it serves as a communication link among Kenya's many ethnic groups. English is also an official language. The national slogan of harambee, or "pull together," illustrates the need for cooperation among Kenya's diverse groups. The government promotes such national unity.

Economy and the Land

Scenic terrain, tropical beaches, and abundant wildlife have given Kenya a thriving tourist industry, and land has been set aside for national parks and game preserves. Agriculture is the primary activity, even though the northern three-fifths of the country is semidesert. The most productive soils are found in the southwestern highlands where tea and coffee are the main export crops. Much of the land is also used for raising livestock, another leading economic contributor. Oil from other nations is refined in Kenya, and food processing and cement production are also significant activities. Kenya's climate varies from arid in the north to temperate in the highlands and tropical along the coast.

History and Politics

Remains of early humans dating back more than four million years have been found in Kenya. Settlers from other parts of Africa arrived about 1000 B.C. A thousand years later Arab traders reached the coast, and controlled the area by the eighth century A.D. The Portuguese ruled the coast between 1498 and the late 1600s. Kenya came under British control in 1895 and was known as the East African Protectorate. Opposition to British rule began to mount in the 1940s as Kenyans demanded a voice in government. The Mau Mau rebellion of the fifties, an armed revolt, was an outgrowth of this discontent. Kenya gained independence from Britain in 1963 and became a republic in 1964. Its first president was Jomo Kenyatta, a Kikuyu who had been an active leader in the previous revolt. Recent administrations have pursued a policy of Africanization, under which land and other holdings have been transferred from European to African hands. The first multiparty elections in 26 years were held in December 1992. The incumbent, Daniel arap Moi, won reelection as president despite widespread allegations of voting fraud. Tribal fighting has become a serious problem in the recent years.

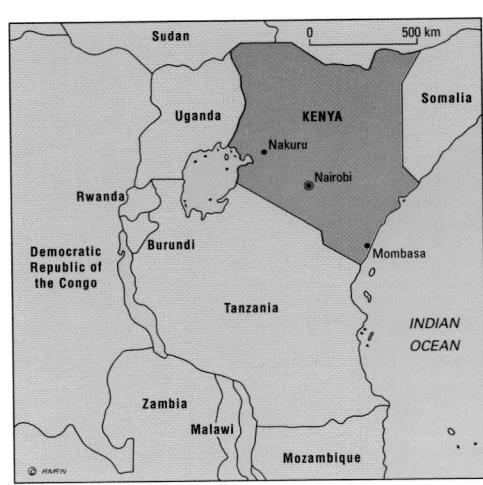

At the base of Mt. Kilimanjaro, Amboseli National Park has one of the world's most striking settings. Lions, cheetahs, and other predators hunt the great herds of wildebeests, zebras, and gazelles.

Scale 1:1,000,000   One inch represents approximately 16 miles.
One centimeter represents 10 kilometers.

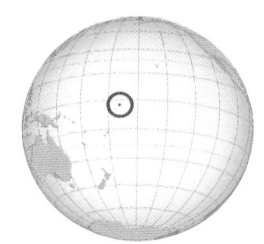

Kiribati at a glance

Official name Republic of Kiribati

People

Population	79,000
Density	252/mi² (97/km²)
Urban	36%
Capital	Bairiki, Tarawa Atoll, 2,226
Ethnic groups	Kiribatian (Micronesian) 98%
Languages	English, Gilbertese
Religions	Roman Catholic 53%, Congregationalist 39%, Bahai 2%
Life expectancy	56 female, 53 male

Politics

Government	Republic
Parties	Christian Democratic, Gilbertese National
Suffrage	Universal, over 18
Memberships	CW
Subdivisions	6 districts

Economy

GDP	$36,800,000
Per capita	$526
Monetary unit	Australian dollar
Trade partners	Exports: Netherlands, Denmark, Fiji
	Imports: Australia, Japan, Fiji
Exports	Fish, copra
Imports	Food, fuel, transportation equipment

Land

Description	Central Pacific islands
Area	313 mi² (811 km²)
Highest point	Unnamed, 246 ft (75 m)
Lowest point	Sea level

KIRIBATI

Coconut-growing and fishing are the main economic activities of Kiribati, a country of 33 islands, 20 of which are inhabited. Isolated in the South Pacific, the islands are home to 79,000 people, most of whom live in traditional thatched huts.

People

The people of Kiribati, a nation of thirty-three islands in the central Pacific, are mostly Micronesian. Almost all the population lives on the Gilbert Islands in small villages and practices Roman Catholicism or Protestantism. English, the official language, and Gilbertese are spoken.

Economy and the Land

A small, unskilled workforce combined with small land area and few natural resources have given Kiribati a subsistence economy. Tourisim is of increasing importance. Copra and fish are the main exports. Kiribati depends on economic aid from Australia, New Zealand, and Great Britain. The islands of Kiribati are almost all coral reefs, composed of hard sand and little soil; many surround a lagoon. The climate is tropical.

History and Politics

Samoa invaded Kiribati in the 1400s. The islands were declared a British protectorate in 1892 and, from 1916 until 1975, the islands were administered as part of the Gilbert and Ellice Islands. Fighting between the United States and Japan took place during World War II on Tarawa Island. The Ellice Islands became independent in 1978 as the nation of Tuvalu, and the Gilbert Islands gained independence as part of the Republic of Kiribati one year later.

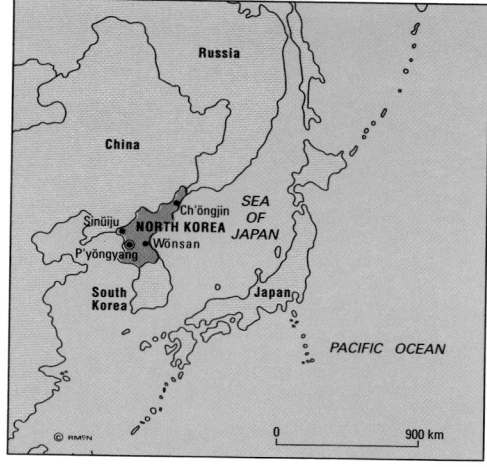

North Korea at a glance

Official name Democratic People's Republic of Korea

People

Population	23,265,000
Density	500/mi² (193/km²)
Urban	60%
Capital	Pyŏngyang, 2,355,000
Ethnic groups	Korean 100%
Languages	Korean
Religions	Buddhist, Chondoist, Confucian
Life expectancy	74 female, 68 male
Literacy	99%

Politics

Government	Socialist republic
Parties	Chondoist Chongu, Social Democratic, Workers'
Suffrage	Universal, over 17
Memberships	UN
Subdivisions	9 provinces, 3 special cities

Economy

GDP	$22,000,000,000
Per capita	$989
Monetary unit	Won
Trade partners	Former Soviet republics, Japan, China
Exports	Minerals, metal products, food, manufactures
Imports	Petroleum, machinery, coal, grain

Land

Description	Eastern Asia
Area	46,540 mi² (120,538 km²)
Highest point	Paektu Mtn., 9,003 ft (2,744 m)
Lowest point	Sea level

KOREA, NORTH

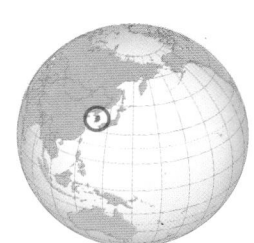

While other Communist countries have liberalized their economies, North Korea has steadfastly refused to change. Closed to outsiders, the country devotes a large part of its limited resources to its massive military forces. North Korea's threat of an invasion of South Korea, and its thinly veiled efforts to develop nuclear weapons, have kept regional tensions high.

People

Despite a history of invasions, North Korea has a homogeneous population with virtually no minorities. Several dialects of Korean are spoken, and North Koreans use the Hankul, or Korean, alphabet exclusively. Korean religions have included Confucianism and Buddhism with Chondoist sects, though the government discourages religious activity. Urban population has grown rapidly since 1953 due to an emphasis on manufacturing. The nation remains more sparsely populated than South Korea.

Economy and the Land

The division of the Korean peninsula after World War II left North Korea with most of the industry and natural resources but little agricultural land and few skilled workers. The country has succeeded in becoming one of the most industrialized nations in Asia and in overcoming its agricultural problems. Most industry is government owned, and mines produce a variety of minerals. Farming is collectivized, and output has been aided by irrigation and other modern practices. The Soviet Union and China aided North Korea's development, but the theory of self-reliance was the government's guiding principle. A central mountainous region is bounded by coastal plains, and the climate is temperate.

History and Politics

History and reference map of North and South Korea follow under KOREA, SOUTH.

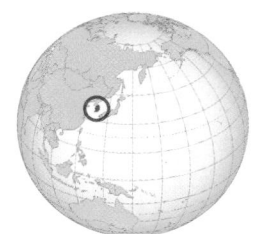

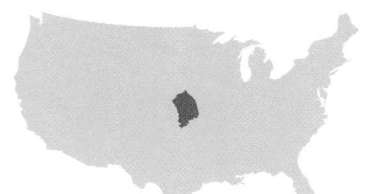

POPULATION COMPARISON
South Korea=17% of U.S.

United States

POPULATION DISTRIBUTION
Urban   Rural

KOREA, SOUTH

In the four decades since the Korean War, South Korea has created from scratch one of the fastest-growing economies in Asia. Its export-driven wealth mirrors that of Japan. Seoul has grown into an affluent city, but with this affluence has come increased worry concerning the intentions of North Korea, only 30 miles away.

Seoul residential neighborhood

Pukhan-san Mountain near Seoul

People

The homogeneous quality of South Korea's population is similar to that of North Korea. Population density, however, is much greater in South Korea, where two million Koreans migrated following World War II. The major language, Korean, is written predominantly in the Hankul, or Korean, alphabet, with some Chinese characters. Christianity is practiced by most South Koreans, although Buddhism and Confucianism have influenced much of life.

Economy and the Land

South Korea was traditionally the peninsula's agricultural zone, and following the 1945 partition of the country, the south was left with little industry and few resources but abundant manpower. The economy has advanced rapidly since 1953, and today agriculture and industry are of almost equal

importance. Rice, barley, and beans are principal crops; electronics and textiles are significant manufactured products. Central mountains give way to plains in the south and west, and the climate is temperate.

History and Politics

Korea's strategic location between Russia, China, and Japan has made it prey to foreign powers. China conquered the northern part of the peninsula in 108 B.C., influencing culture, religion, and government. Mongols controlled Korea for most of the thirteenth and fourteenth centuries. The rule of the Yi dynasty lasted from 1392 to 1910, when Japan annexed Korea. In 1945, following Japan's defeat in World War II, Soviet troops occupied northern Korea while the United States military occupied the south. The Soviet Union, the United States, and Great Britain tried to aid unification of the country but failed. The Soviets opposed a subsequent plan for United Nations-supervised elections. Separate governments were formed in 1948: the northern Democratic People's Republic of Korea and the southern Republic of Korea. Both governments claimed the peninsula, and relations became strained. After several border clashes, North Korea invaded South Korea in 1950. Chinese Communists fought on the side of North Korea, and United States/United Nations forces aided the south. An armistice ended the war in 1953, but a permanent peace treaty has never been signed.

North Korea

The Democratic People's Republic of Korea was established in 1948, several months after the formation of South Korea. The country incurred about three million casualties during the war with South Korea. Following the war, the government moved quickly to modernize industry and the military; North Korea maintains one of the world's largest armies. North Korea's reported development of its nuclear facilities has raised serious concerns worldwide.

South Korea

The Republic of Korea was established on August 15, 1948. The country has since experienced a presidential overthrow, military rule, and a presidential assassination. In 1980 it adopted its fifth constitution since 1948, which initiated the Fifth Republic. The first non-military president in more than thirty years was elected in December 1992.

Korea, South at a glance

Official name	Republic of Korea
People	
Population	44,655,000
Density	1,168/mi² (451/km²)
Urban	72%
Capital	Seoul, 10,627,790
Ethnic groups	Korean
Languages	Korean
Religions	Christian 49%, Buddhist 47%, Confucian 3%.
Life expectancy	74 female, 68 male
Literacy	96%
Politics	
Government	Republic
Parties	Democratic Justice, New Democratic Republican, Peace and Democracy, Reunification Democratic, others.
Suffrage	Universal, over 20
Memberships	UN
Subdivisions	9 provinces, 6 special cities
Economy	
GNP	$424,000,000,000
Per capita	$9,711
Monetary unit	Won
Trade partners	Exports: U.S., Japan, China Imports: Japan, U.S., Germany
Exports	Textiles, clothing, electronic and electrical equipment, footwear.
Imports	Machinery, electronic equipment, oil, steel, transportation equipment
Land	
Description	Eastern Asia
Area	38,230 mi² (99,016 km²)
Highest point	Mt. Halla, 6,398 ft (1,950 m)
Lowest point	Sea level

The fishing town of Sokch'o is 30 miles south of the border with North Korea. Fish is the main source of protein in the diet of South Koreans.

KOREA

	Meters	Feet
	4000	13124
Railroad	2000	6562
Spot Elevation or Depth	1000	3281
	500	1640
Scale 1:7,500,000	200	656
0 50 100 150 km		0
0 50 100 mi		

Meters	Feet
0	0
200	656
Below 2000	Below 6562

© Rand McNally & Co.
A-562100-772 -1-7-2

The Korean Peninsula has long been the bridge from Asia to Japan, 120 miles away across the Korean Strait. The border between the two Koreas is one of the most heavily defended in the world. Thousands of troops from the two sides and from the United States stand in constant readiness.

Fishing was a major part of the Kuwaiti economy before the discovery of oil. While fish are still caught in the Persian Gulf, the great majority of Kuwait's food is imported.

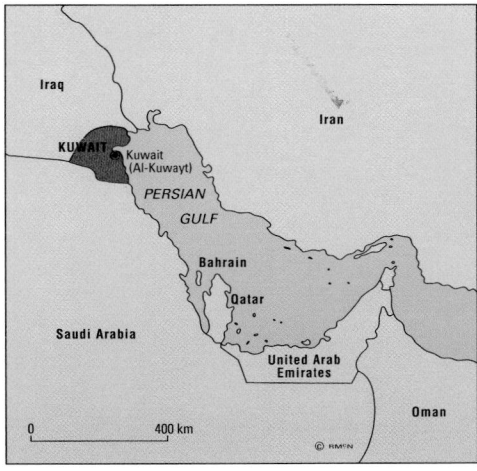

KUWAIT

Kuwait at a glance

Official name	State of Kuwait

People

Population	1,866,000
Density	271/mi² (105/km²)
Urban	96%
Capital	Kuwait, 44,335
Ethnic groups	Kuwaiti 45%, other Arab 35%, South Asian 9%, Iranian 4%
Languages	Arabic, English
Religions	Sunni Muslim 45%, Shiite Muslim 30%, Christian 6%
Life expectancy	78 female, 73 male
Literacy	73%

Politics

Government	Constitutional monarchy
Parties	None
Suffrage	Limited adult male
Memberships	AL, OPEC, UN
Subdivisions	5 governorates

Economy

GDP	$25,700,000,000
Per capita	$10,762
Monetary unit	Dinar
Trade partners	Exports: Iraq, Saudi Arabia, China Imports: U.S., Japan, Germany
Exports	Petroleum
Imports	Food, construction materials, motor vehicles, clothing

Land

Description	Southwestern Asia
Area	6,880 mi² (17,818 km²)
Highest point	Unnamed, 922 ft (281 m)
Lowest point	Sea level

POPULATION COMPARISON
Kuwait=0.7% of U.S.

United States

GDP COMPARISON
Kuwait=0.4% of U.S.

United States

ETHNIC GROUPS

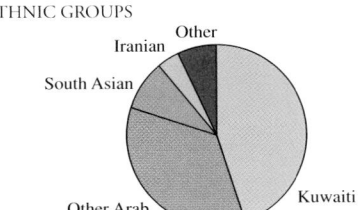

Other
Iranian
South Asian
Other Arab
Kuwaiti

POPULATION DISTRIBUTION
Urban　　　　　　　　　　　　　Rural

Kuwait was the first of the oil-producing Middle Eastern countries to fully share its oil-derived wealth with all of its people. Until it was invaded and annexed by Iraq in 1990, it was a quiet country where the people enjoyed one of the highest standards of living in the world. Since being liberated by a multinational force in 1991, Kuwait has cleaned up and repaired much of the damage, but it now keeps a nervous eye on its neighbor to the north.

People

Kuwait's recent prosperity has drawn emigrants from the Persian Gulf and beyond, giving it a diverse population with Palestinian, Iranian, and Pakistani minorities. The population has risen dramatically since the thirties, when the oil industry began. Arabic is the official language; English is also taught and widely spoken. Almost all residents of Kuwait observe Islam, the state religion. Most belong to the Sunni branch, but there is a sizable Shiite community.

Economy and the Land

The economy centers on the largely government-controlled petroleum industry. Kuwait is one of the world's largest oil producers, and its oil reserves are among the world's most extensive. Iraq's 1990 invasion of Kuwait brought the economy to a standstill when many Kuwaitis and virtually all of the large foreign workforce fled the country. During 1991, burning oil fields, oil slicks, and massive aerial bombardments threatened the environment. Despite the destruction, the Kuwaiti government continues to profit from its many foreign investments as it rebuilds its oil production facilities.

History and Politics

Arab nomads settled Kuwait Bay around A.D. 1700. The Al Sabah dynasty has ruled the nation since the mid-1700s. Alarmed by Turk and Arabic expansion, in 1899 Kuwait signed an agreement with Britain to guarantee Kuwait's defense. Drilling for oil began in 1936, and by 1945 Kuwait had become a major exporter. Independence came in 1961. Iraq immediately made a claim to the state but was discouraged from attacking by the arrival of British troops. Official border agreements have never been made between Kuwait and Iraq. Kuwait briefly cut off oil shipments to Western nations in retaliation for their support of Israel in the 1967 and 1973 Arab-Israeli wars. Kuwait's remarkable oil wealth, which transformed it from a poor nation into an affluent one, has enabled it to offer its citizens a wide range of benefits and to aid other Arab states. Poised at the tip of the Persian Gulf, Kuwait must always be sensitive to the interests of its many neighbors. Kuwait allied itself with Iraq in the 1980–1988 Iran/Iraq war. This did not, however, prevent Iraq from invading Kuwait in August 1990. International outrage resulted in allied military action against Iraq in January 1991. Less than two months later Iraq was forced to withdraw. The constitution, which was suspended in 1976, was revived after the war. In 1992 elections, a number of opposition candidates won seats in the National Assembly, and the process of democratization has begun.

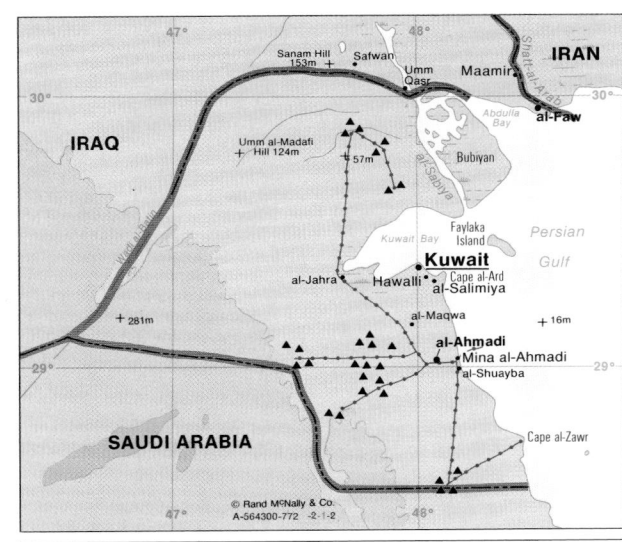

Abandoned Iraqi tanks in the desert following liberation in 1991

KUWAIT

←→←→	Oil Pipeline
▲	Major Oil Field
+	Spot Elevation or Depth

National capitals are underlined

Scale 1:2,969,000

Meters	Feet
1000	3281
500	1640
200	656
0	0
200	656

Until oil wealth began flowing into the country in the 1950s, Kuwait's people were nomadic shepherds and traders. Kuwait City was a small town fortified with a mud wall.

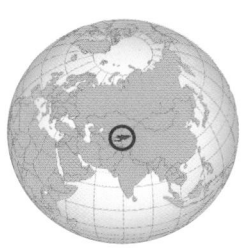

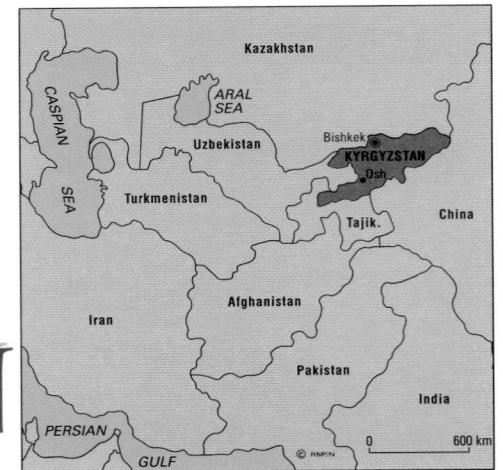

KYRGYZSTAN

O ne of the smallest and poorest of the former Soviet republics, Kyrgyzstan is an isolated, mountainous land with few developed natural resources. However, it stands as a bastion of economic reform and social harmony amidst the turmoil of its neighbors.

Kyrgyzstan at a glance

Official name Kyrgyz Republic

People

Population	4,541,000
Density	59/mi² (23/km²)
Urban	38%
Capital	Bishkek (Frunze), 631,300
Ethnic groups	Kirghiz 52%, Russian 22%, Uzbek 13%
Languages	Kirghiz, Russian
Religions	Muslim 70%, Russian Orthodox
Life expectancy	72 female, 63 male
Literacy	97%

Politics

Government	Republic
Parties	Akayev, Asaba, Democratic Movement
Suffrage	Universal, over 18
Memberships	CIS, UN
Subdivisions	6 oblasts

Economy

GDP	$11,300,000,000
Per capita	$2,450
Monetary unit	Som
Trade partners	Russia, Ukraine, Uzbekistan, Kazakhstan
Exports	Wool, chemicals, cotton, metals, footwear, machinery, tobacco
Imports	Lumber industrial products, ferrous metals, fuel, machinery, textiles, shoes

Land

Description	Central Asia, landlocked
Area	76,641 mi² (198,500 km²)
Highest point	Pobeda Peak, 24,406 ft (7,439 m)
Lowest point	Along Chu River, 1,804 ft (550 m)

The Issyk Kul railway stretches through the desolate reaches of eastern Kyrgyzstan. Mineral resources such as coal, zinc and gold abound in the mountains.

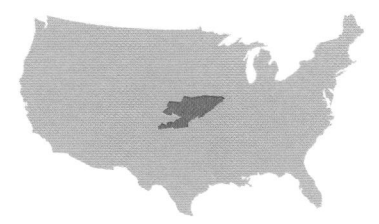

POPULATION COMPARISON
Kyrgyzstan=2% of U.S.

United States

GDP COMPARISON
Kyrgyzstan=0.2% of U.S.

United States

ETHNIC GROUPS

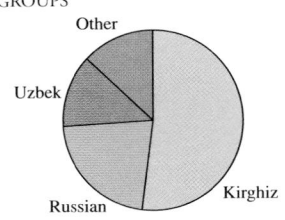

Other
Uzbek
Russian
Kirghiz

POPULATION DISTRIBUTION
Urban   Rural

KYRGYZSTAN

National capitals are underlined

— Railroad
 Glacier
+ Spot Elevation

City type size indicates relative importance

Scale 1:12,500,000

Meters	Feet
Above 4000	Above 13124
2000	6562
1000	3281
500	1640
200	656

Like its neighboring ex-Soviet republics, Kyrgyzstan is isolated and has few roads or railroads.

People

A little more than one-half of the people are Kirghiz, Turkic-speaking descendants of the region's original nomadic herdsmen. The Kirghiz are related to the Mongols. Russians are the next largest ethnic group, followed by the Uzbeks. Ethnic tension exists between the Kirghiz and the Uzbeks, and fighting between the two groups claimed hundreds of lives in 1990. Most people live in the countryside and are engaged in agriculture, although the Russians tend to live in the cities.

Economy and the Land

High, snow-capped mountains dominate the landscape of Kyrgyzstan. Most of the economic activity takes place in the Fergana and Chu Valleys. Temperature and precipitation vary widely with elevation but, in general, the climate is harsh. The land is rich in minerals, including gold, coal, petroleum, natural gas, uranium, lead, zinc, and mercury. Although the Kirghiz were forced to give up their nomadic lifestyle, livestock raising remains important, including goats, sheep, and horses.

History and Politics

The Kirghiz people have lived in the mountains and valleys of Kyrgyzstan since at least the second millennium B.C. Kirghiz warlords controlled the region when it was used as a trade route to China. One of the Kirghiz warlords first turned to Russia for protection in the mid-1800s. By 1870, central Kyrgyzstan had been conquered by Russia, and control was consolidated after the 1917 revolution. It became an autonomous oblast in 1924 and the Kirghiz Soviet Socialist Republic within the Soviet Union in 1936. The Republic of Kyrgyzstan declared itself independent in December 1990 and elected its first President in October 1991. Their independence was internationally recognized in December 1991, after the collapse of the Soviet Union. Kyrgyzstan stands today as an example of a developing democracy.

Shepherd and flock

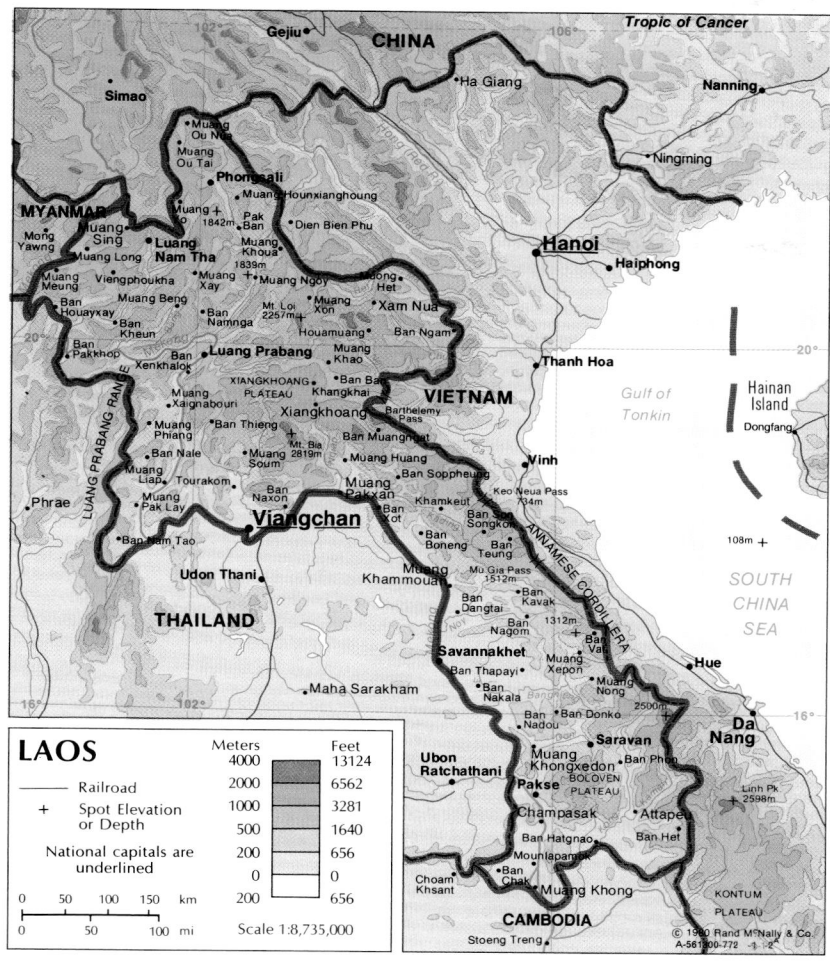

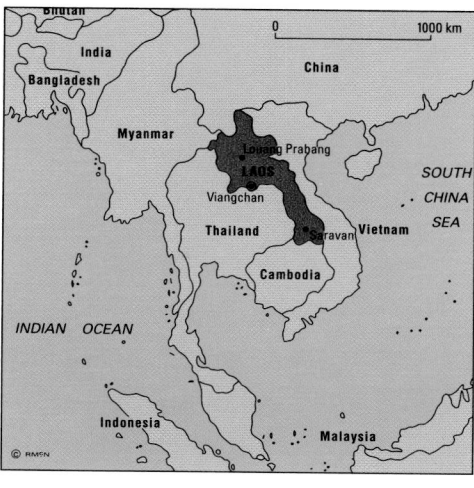

More than half of all Laotians live along the low-lands of the eastern bank of the Mekong River.

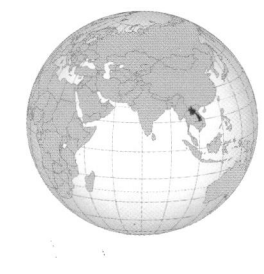

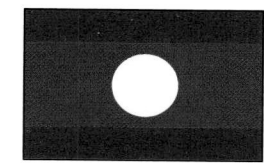

LAOS

Laos is a landlocked and unde-veloped country whose people are predominantly Buddhist. The Communist government has made efforts to loosen the economy, but this has had little effect on the people, most of whom live in villages and devote their energies to subsistence farming of rice and vegetables.

Laos at a glance

Official name	Lao People's Democratic Republic

People

Population	4,768,000
Density	52/mi² (20/km²)
Urban	19%
Capital	Viangchan (Vientiane), 377,409
Ethnic groups	Lao 50%; Thai 20%; Phoutheung 15%; Miao, Hmong, Yao, and others 15%
Languages	Lao, French, English
Religions	Buddhist 85%, Animist and others 15%
Life expectancy	53 female, 50 male
Literacy	84%

Politics

Government	Socialist republic
Parties	People's Revolutionary
Suffrage	Universal, over 18
Memberships	UN
Subdivisions	16 provinces, 1 municipality

Economy

GDP	$4,100,000,000
Per capita	$910
Monetary unit	Kip
Trade partners	Exports: Thailand, Malaysia, Vietnam
	Imports: Thailand, former Soviet republics, Japan, France
Exports	Electricity, wood, coffee, tin
Imports	Food, petroleum, consumer goods, manufactures

Land

Description	Southeastern Asia, landlocked
Area	91,429 mi² (236,800 km²)
Highest point	Mt. Bia, 9,249 ft (2,819 m)
Lowest point	Along Mekong River, 230 ft (70 m)

POPULATION COMPARISON
Laos=2% of U.S.

United States

GDP COMPARISON
Laos=0.06% of U.S.

United States

ETHNIC GROUPS

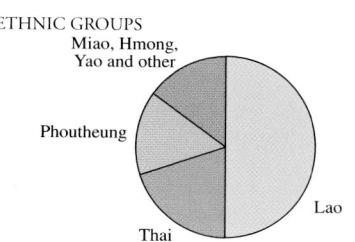

Miao, Hmong, Yao and other

Phoutheung

Lao

Thai

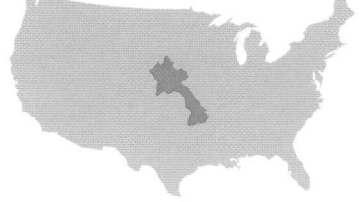

POPULATION DISTRIBUTION
Urban   Rural

People

Laos is populated by many ethnic groups, each with its own customs, religion, and language. Its history of culturally diverse communities is mirrored in the political divisions of recent years. The Lao are numerically and politically dominant, and Lao is the official language. Small Vietnamese and Chinese minorities exist. Most Laotians are rice farmers.

Economy and the Land

Years of warfare, a landlocked position, and a poor transportation system have hindered the development of Laos's economy. Although agriculture is the basis of the economy, very little of the fertile land is cultivated. Substantial mineral deposits and large timber reserves also have not been exploited to their potential. Manufacturing is limited, partly because of an un-skilled workforce. Situated in a mountainous, densely forested region, Laos has a tropical climate and experiences seasonal monsoons.

History and Politics

By A.D. 900 the forerunners of the Lao had arrived from southern China. The first united Lao kingdom was founded in 1353 and included much of modern Thailand. It dissolved into three rival states by the early 1700s, setting the stage for interference by Burma, Vietnam, and Sigam, present-day Thailand. In 1899 France made Laos part of French Indochina. Laos gained some autonomy in 1949, but this period saw the growth of Communist and anti-Communist factions whose rivalry would prevent any unified government until 1975. Although Geneva peace agreements declared Laos neutral in 1954 and 1962, the nation became increasingly embroiled in the Vietnam War as both sides in that conflict entered Laos. A protracted civil war began in 1960 between the Pathet Lao, a Communist faction aided by the North Vietnamese, and government forces backed by the Thai and South Vietnamese. A cease-fire was signed in 1973 and a new coalition government was formed a year later. Following Communist victories in Vietnam and Cambodia, the Pathet Lao gained control in 1975 and established the Lao People's Democratic Republic. Laos began permitting private enterprise in 1986, but has allowed only limited contact with the outside world. Relief agencies were called upon for help after a drought in 1993 decimated the rice harvest.

Laotian children

The first Lao Kingdom was centered around Luang Prabang, in what is now northern Laos, in the 14th century. Today Luang Prabang is a small city boasting historic temples and French colonial mansions.

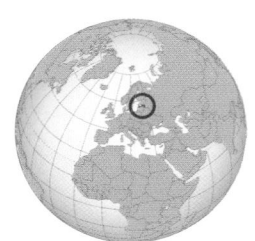

LATVIA

Coastal dunes on the Baltic Sea

LATVIA

		Meters	Feet
— Railroad	National capitals are underlined	200	656
+ Spot Elevation	City type size indicates relative importance	0	0
Scale 1:6,250,000		200	656

Like its neighbor Estonia, Latvia is quickly leaving behind its five decades of Soviet occupation. After some tough economic measures were introduced in the early 1990s, the economy has become market-based, and extensive trade ties are being forged with the European Union. Only 52 percent of the population is ethnic Latvian. The large Russian minority—34 percent of the population—has faced discrimination since independence.

People

The Latvians are closely related to the neighboring Lithuanians, and the Latvian language is one of the oldest in Europe. Many Latvians were killed or deported during World War II and the subsequent Soviet invasion. Today, more than one-third of the people are Russian. Most Latvians are Lutheran or Roman Catholic.

Economy and the Land

Manufacturing is the foundation of the Latvian economy, despite its lack of energy resources. Industrial production is highly diversified. Latvia's farms are efficient, and food is plentiful and varied. Most of the land is low plains, and much is forested. The capital city of Rīga is one of the Baltic region's busiest ports.

History and Politics

Latvian history was profoundly affected by the Teutonic Knights, who ruled the country for more than two hundred years starting in the mid-1300s. They established themselves as landowners and forced the Latvians into serfdom. Latvia was subsequently captured by Poland, Sweden, and Russia. After one hundred years of Russian rule, serfdom in Latvia was eliminated in the early 1700s. An independent Latvian state was established in 1918. Political instability followed and the country descended into fascism. In 1940, the Soviet Union invaded Latvia, ending twenty-two years of Latvian independence. The Latvians resisted Soviet domination and regained their independence in 1991. They have begun a transition to a free market economy.

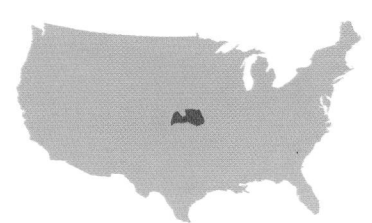

POPULATION COMPARISON
Latvia=1% of U.S.

United States

GDP COMPARISON
Latvia=0.2% of U.S.

United States

ETHNIC GROUPS

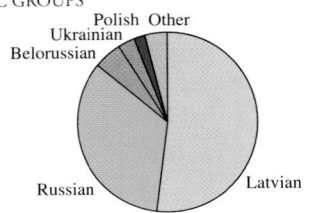

POPULATION DISTRIBUTION
Urban — Rural

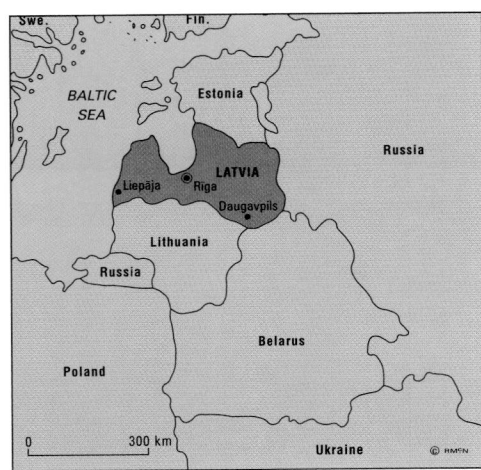

Latvia's capital, Rīga, was one of the great cities of the medieval Hanseatic League. Although heavily influenced by German culture, the city has been dominated by Russia.

Latvia at a glance

Official name	Republic of Latvia

People

Population	2,532,000
Density	103/mi² (40/km²)
Urban	71%
Capital	Rīga, 910,200
Ethnic groups	Latvian 52%, Russian 34%, Belorussian 5%, Ukrainian 3%, Polish 2%
Languages	Lettish, Lithuanian, Russian, other
Religions	Lutheran, Roman Catholic, Russian Orthodox
Life expectancy	76 female, 67 male
Literacy	99%

Politics

Government	Republic
Parties	Harmony and Rebirth for the National Economy, Latvian Way, National Independence Movement, Peasants' Union
Suffrage	Universal, over 18
Memberships	UN
Subdivisions	26 counties, 7 municipalities

Economy

GDP	$13,200,000,000
Per capita	$4,823
Monetary unit	Lat
Trade partners	Russia, Ukraine, other former Soviet republics
Exports	Food, railroad cars, chemicals.
Imports	Machinery, petroleum products, chemicals

Land

Description	Eastern Europe
Area	24,595 mi² (63,700 km²)
Highest point	Gaizina Hill, 1,020 ft (311 m)
Lowest point	Sea level

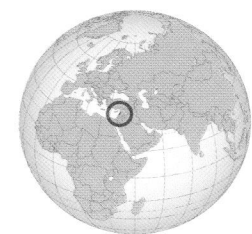

Phoenician ruins guard the entrance to the harbor at Jubayl, the site of ancient Byblos. The forerunners of today's alphabet and syllabic writing were created by the Phoenicians in this ancient town in 1000 B.C.

LEBANON

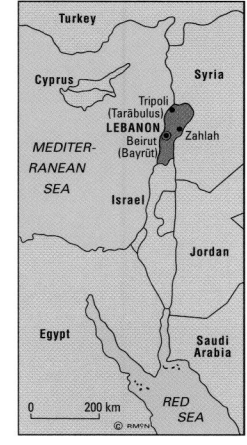

Once known as "the Paris of the Middle East," Beirut suffered massive destruction during years of civil war and religious fighting that began in 1975. A resourceful people, the Lebanese have moved rapidly to rebuild the once-prosperous economy since peace returned to much of the country.

People

Traditionally home to many diverse groups, Lebanon has recently been shaken by the conflicting demands of its population. Almost all Lebanese are of Arab stock, and Arabic and French are the official languages. Palestinian refugees have settled here since the creation of Israel in 1948, many of them living in refugee camps. Lebanon's religious makeup is notable for its variety, encompassing seventeen recognized sects. Islam is now the majority religion, although Christianity continues to be a strong presence. Muslims are divided among the majority Shiite, minority Sunni, and Druze sects, while most Christians are Maronites.

Economy and the Land

Situated strategically between the West and the Middle East, Lebanon has long been a center of commerce. Its economy is fueled by the service sector, particularly banking. Prolonged fighting, beginning with the 1975 civil war, has greatly damaged all economic activity. Much of the workforce is engaged in agriculture, and various crops are grown. The coastal area consists of a plain, behind which lie mountain ranges separated by a fertile valley. The climate is Mediterranean.

History and Politics

The Phoenicians settled parts of Lebanon about 3000 B.C. and were followed by Egyptian, Assyrian, Persian, Greek, and Roman rulers. Christianity came to the area during the Byzantine Empire, around A.D. 325, and Islam followed in the seventh century. In 1516 Lebanon was incorporated into the Ottoman Empire. Between the end of World War I, when the Ottoman Empire collapsed, and 1943, when Lebanon became independent, the nation was a French mandate. After independence, Muslims and Christians shared government power. Opposition to Lebanon's close ties to the West led to a 1958 insurrection, which United States marines put down at the government's request. The Palestine Liberation Organization (PLO), a group working to establish a Palestinian state, began operating from bases in Lebanon. This led to clashes with Israel in the late 1970s and early 1980s. The presence of the PLO divided Muslims, who generally supported it, from Christians, who opposed it. The increasing Muslim population also demanded a greater voice in the government. Civil war between Muslims and Christians broke out in 1975, and fighting slowed the next year with the requested aid of Syrian deterrent forces. Internal instability continued, however, along with Israeli-Palestinian hostilities. In June 1982 Israel invaded Lebanon, driving the PLO from Beirut and the south. Hundreds of Palestinian refugees were killed by the Christian Lebanese forces in September. A multinational peacekeeping force left after falling victim to terrorist attacks. Israel began a gradual withdrawal from Lebanon in 1985, but maintains a buffer zone in southern Lebanon. Syrian troops also occupy parts of the country. Sporadic fighting continues in southern Lebanon. An uneasy peace has returned to Beirut, but sporadic fighting continues in southern Lebanon.

Lebanon at a glance

Official name	Republic of Lebanon

People

Population	3,660,000
Density	912/mi² (352/km²)
Urban	84%
Capital	Beirut, 509,000
Ethnic groups	Arab 95%, Armenian 4%
Languages	Arabic, French, Armenian, English
Religions	Muslim 70%, Christian 30%
Life expectancy	71 female, 67 male
Literacy	80%

Politics

Government	Republic
Parties	Progressive Socialist, Liberal Nationalist, Phalangist, others.
Suffrage	Females, over 21 (with elementary education); males, over 21
Memberships	AL, UN
Subdivisions	6 governorates

Economy

GDP	$6,100,000,000
Per capita	$1,759
Monetary unit	Pound
Trade partners	Exports: Saudi Arabia, Switzerland, Jordan Imports: Italy, France, U.S., Turkey
Exports	Agricultural products, chemicals, textiles, jewelry
Imports	Food, textiles and clothing, machinery and transportation equipment, metals

Land

Description	Southwestern Asia
Area	4,015 mi² (10,400 km²)
Highest point	Mt. Sawda, 10,115 ft (3,083 m)
Lowest point	Sea level

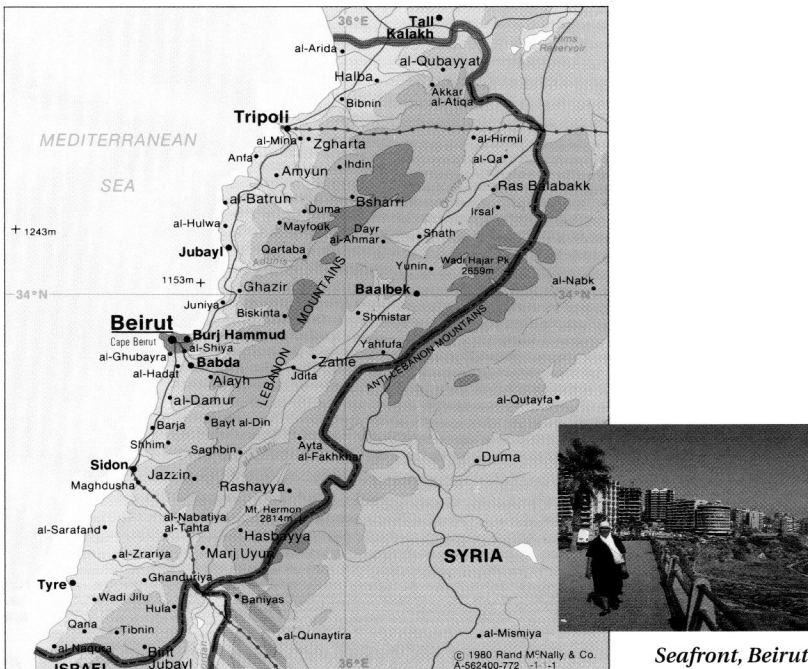

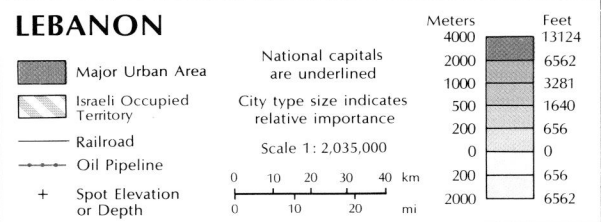

Seafront, Beirut

LEBANON

▨ Major Urban Area	National capitals are underlined
▨ Israeli Occupied Territory	City type size indicates relative importance
── Railroad	Scale 1: 2,035,000
┈┿┈ Oil Pipeline	
+ Spot Elevation or Depth	

Meters	Feet
4000	13124
2000	6562
1000	3281
500	1640
200	656
0	0
200	656
2000	6562

Southern Lebanon is the domain of heavily armed militias backed variously by Israel, Syria, and numerous religious sects and political factions.

POPULATION COMPARISON
Lebanon=1% of U.S.
United States

GDP COMPARISON
Lebanon=0.1% of U.S.
United States

ETHNIC GROUPS

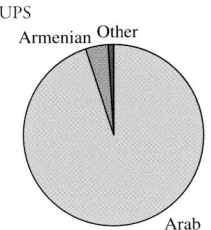

Armenian Other

Arab

POPULATION DISTRIBUTION
Urban   Rural

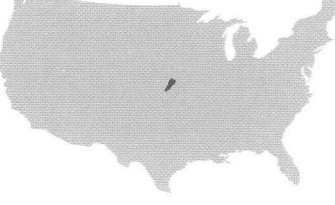

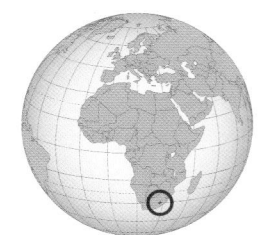

Water projects in Lesotho's mountains will store run-off water and redirect it for sale to South Africa.

LESOTHO

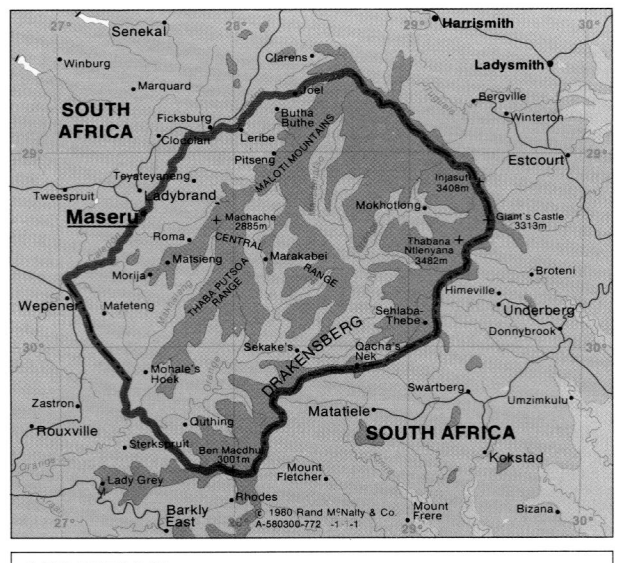

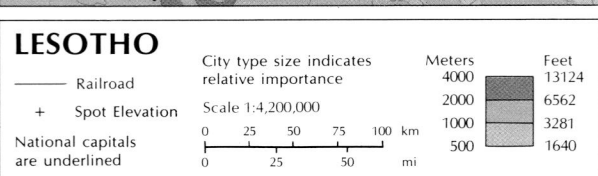

LESOTHO

	City type size indicates relative importance	Meters	Feet
——— Railroad		4000	13124
+ Spot Elevation	Scale 1:4,200,000	2000	6562
	0 25 50 75 100 km	1000	3281
National capitals are underlined	0 25 50 mi	500	1640

People

The Sotho, a black African group, comprise almost all of Lesotho's population. Most Sotho live in the lowlands and raise livestock and crops. The official languages are Sesotho, a Bantu tongue, and English, and the traditional religion is based on ancestor worship, though most Sotho are Roman Catholic. A system of tribal chieftaincy is followed locally.

Economy and the Land

Surrounded by South Africa and having few resources, Lesotho is almost entirely dependent on South Africa for economic survival. Much of the male population must seek employment there, usually spending several months a year in South African mines or industries. Agriculture remains at the subsistence level, and soil erosion threatens production. Livestock raising represents a significant part of Lesotho's economy. Wool and mohair are among the chief exports. Diamond mining, one of the few industries, employs a small portion of the population. Most of the terrain is mountainous; the fairly high elevations give Lesotho a temperate climate.

History and Politics

Refugees from tribal wars in southern Africa arrived in what is now Lesotho between the sixteenth and nineteenth centuries A.D. Chief Moshoeshoe united the Sotho tribes in 1818 and led them in war against the Boers, settlers of Dutch or Huguenot descent. At Moshoeshoe's request, Basutoland came under British protection in 1868. It resisted attempts at absorption by the Union of South Africa and became the independent kingdom of Lesotho in 1966. The military has effectively ruled since 1986, considerably reducing the powers of the hereditary monarchy. Surprise March 1993 election results have given an elected government at least some power. King Moshoeshoe II was restored to the throne in 1995.

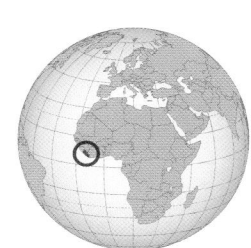

Except for swamps and open land along the coast, Liberia is covered with West Africa's largest rain forest.

LIBERIA

LIBERIA

		Meters	Feet		Meters	Feet
——— Railroad		2000	6562		0	0
+ Spot Elevation		1000	3281		200	656
Scale 1:6,360,000		500	1640		Below 2000	Below 6562
0 50 100 150 km		200	656		0	0
0 50 100 mi		0	0			

People

Most Liberians belong to about twenty indigenous black groups. Few are descended from the freed American slaves who founded modern Liberia, but this group—known as Americo-Liberians—has traditionally been politically dominant. The official language is English, but more than twenty other tongues are also spoken. Most people are farmers and practice traditional religious beliefs, although Islam and Christianity also have adherents. Liberia is the only black African state to escape colonialism.

Economy and the Land

Before the recent war, Liberia owed its healthy economy largely to an open-door policy, which had made its extensive resources attractive to foreign nations. Two of the most important activities, iron-ore mining and rubber production, were developed by western firms. Large timber reserves have not yet been fully exploited. Liberia also profits from the vast merchant fleet registered under its flag. The land is characterized by a coastal plain, plateaus, and low mountains, while the hot, humid climate is marked by distinct wet and dry seasons.

History and Politics

Early settlers are thought to have migrated from the north and east between the twelfth and seventeenth centuries A.D. Trade between Europeans and coastal groups developed after the Portuguese visited the area in the late 1400s. The American Colonization Society, a private United States organization devoted to resettling freed slaves, purchased land in Liberia, and in 1822 the first settlers landed at the site of Monrovia. The settlers declared their independence in 1847, setting up a government based on the United States model and creating Africa's first independent republic. For the next century, the Liberian government endured attempts at colonization by France and Britain, as well as internal tribal opposition. The string of Americo-Liberian rulers was broken in 1980, when a small group of soldiers of African descent toppled the government and imposed martial law. Civilian rule and some degree of harmony were restored in a 1985 election. Dissatisfaction with this government led to civil war in early 1990, resulting in the president's assassination. Peacekeeping forces of West African nations have been attempting to unify the various factions that have since divided the country. There are reports of 100,000 deaths from warfare and widespread starvation.

The Libyan Desert is one of the world's largest. Less than six percent of Libya's land is economically viable. The few people who live away from the fertile coast are clustered around desert oases.

F ew nations bear the imprint of a single personality as profoundly as Libya. Since seizing power in 1969, Colonel Mu'ammar al-Qadhafi has remade Libya into his vision of an Islamic nation. His support of international terrorism has drawn widespread condemnation and severe United Nations sanctions. His efforts to enforce territorial claims in northern Chad have ended disastrously, with the Chad army routing the much better-equipped Libyan army.

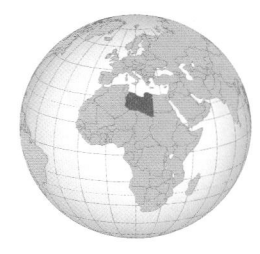

LIBYA

Desert irrigation project

People

Libya, originally settled by Berbers, is largely a mix of Arab and Berber today. Almost all Libyans live along the coast, with some nomadic groups in desert areas. Large migrations from rural areas to the cities have accompanied Libya's oil-based prosperity. Islam is the majority religion, and nearly all Libyans speak Arabic. Traditional social orders still exist, despite centuries of foreign rule.

Economy and the Land

The discovery of oil in 1959 propelled Libya from the ranks of the world's poorest nations to one of its leading oil producers. It has used these revenues to develop industry and agriculture to diversify its economy. Most of Libya is covered by the Sahara Desert, and the limited agriculture has been further hurt by Libyan farmers migrating to the cities. The climate is desert except for the coast, which has moderate temperatures.

History and Politics

For much of its history, Libya was dominated by Mediterranean empires: Phoenician, Carthaginian, Greek, and Roman. In the seventh century A.D. the area was taken by Muslim Arabs, whose language and religion transformed Libyan culture. Although the Ottoman Turks conquered the region in the sixteenth century, local rulers remained virtually autonomous. Italy invaded Libya in 1911, and the country became an Italian colony in 1912. Following World War II, British and French forces occupied the area until a United Nations resolution made Libya an independent nation in 1951. A monarchy ruled until 1969, when a military coup established a republic headed by Colonel Mu'ammar al-Qadhafi. Under his leadership, Libya has backed Arab unity and the Palestinian cause, opposed foreign influences, and created a welfare system. Libya's support of terrorist activities resulted in a controversial United States air strike against the country in 1986. Libya's refusal to turn over accused terrorists has led to United Nations sanctions.

Libya at a glance

Official name	Socialist People's Libyan Arab Jamahiriya

People

Population	5,148,000
Density	7.6/mi² (2.9/km²)
Urban	82%
Capital	Tripoli, 591,062
Ethnic groups	Arab-Berber 97%
Languages	Arabic
Religions	Sunni Muslim 97%
Life expectancy	65 female, 62 male
Literacy	64%

Politics

Government	Socialist republic
Parties	None
Suffrage	Universal, over 18
Memberships	AL, OAU, OPEC, UN
Subdivisions	13 municipalities

Economy

GDP	$32,000,000,000
Per capita	$7,030
Monetary unit	Dinar
Trade partners	Exports: Italy, France, Greece Imports: Italy, Japan, Germany
Exports	Petroleum, peanuts, hides
Imports	Machinery, transportation equipment, food, manufactures

Land

Description	Northern Africa
Area	679,362 mi² (1,759,540 km²)
Highest point	Bikkū Bittī, 7,438 ft (2,267 m)
Lowest point	Sabkhat Ghuzzayil, -154 ft (-47 m)

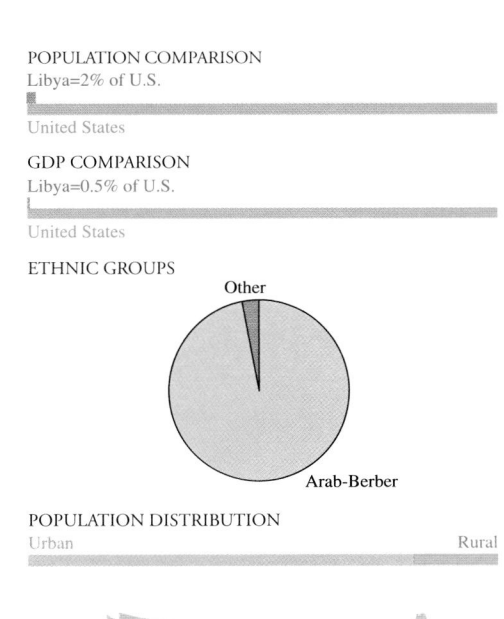

Tripoli means "three cities" in Greek. The Libyan capital gets its name from the trio of towns established by the Phoenicians on the site in the 7th century B.C. Buildings in Tripoli's Old Town date back 1,000 years or more. The modern city, with its geometric street grid, has arisen since World War II.

Work is proceeding on the largest water project in the world, a huge effort to bring water from aquifers under the southern deserts to the coastal cities of the north.

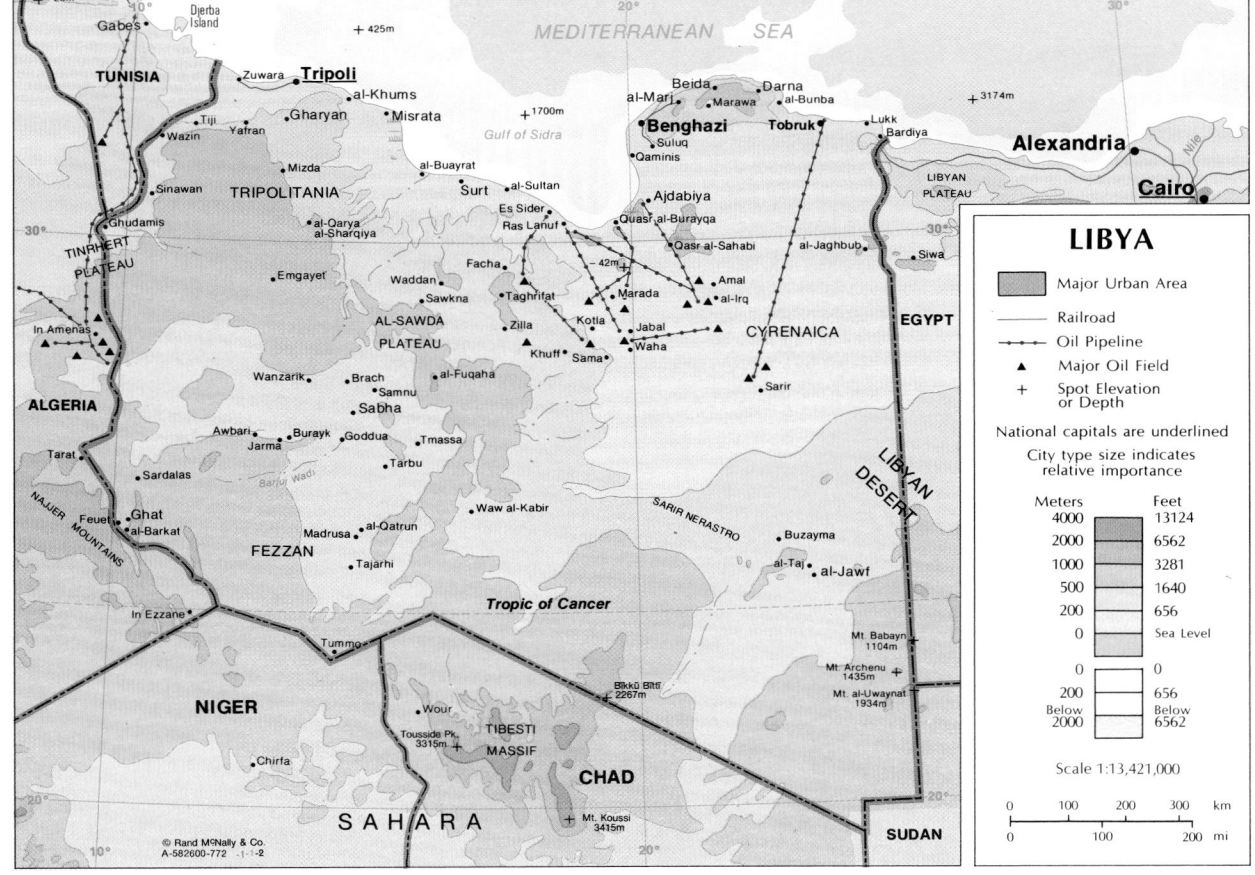

LIBYA

- ▨ Major Urban Area
- Railroad
- Oil Pipeline
- ▲ Major Oil Field
- + Spot Elevation or Depth

National capitals are underlined
City type size indicates relative importance

Meters	Feet
4000	13124
2000	6562
1000	3281
500	1640
200	656
0	Sea Level

0	0
200	656
Below 2000	Below 6562

Scale 1:13,421,000

POPULATION COMPARISON
Libya=2% of U.S.
United States

GDP COMPARISON
Libya=0.5% of U.S.
United States

ETHNIC GROUPS
Other
Arab-Berber

POPULATION DISTRIBUTION
Urban   Rural

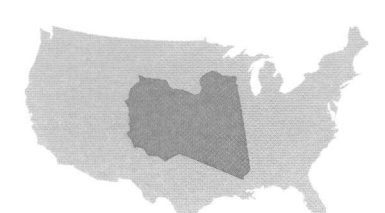

LIECHTENSTEIN

Liechtenstein is indistinguishable, both economically and geographically, from its neighbors Switzerland and Austria. Liberal tax and banking laws have made the tiny country a popular shelter of international fortunes.

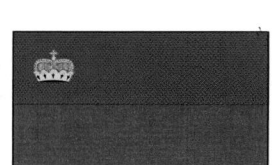

There are no border controls betweeen Liechtenstein and its neighbors, which are home to many of its workers.

Liechtenstein at a glance

Official name	Principality of Liechtenstein

People

Population	30,000
Density	484/mi^2 (188/km^2)
Urban	20%
Capital	Vaduz, 4,887
Ethnic groups	Liechtensteiner (Alemannic) 95%
Languages	German
Religions	Roman Catholic 87%, Protestant 8%
Life expectancy	81 female, 74 male
Literacy	100%

Politics

Government	Constitutional monarchy
Parties	Fatherland Union, Progressive Citizens'
Suffrage	Universal, over 18
Memberships	UN
Subdivisions	11 communes

Economy

GDP	$630,000,000
Per capita	$22,500
Monetary unit	Swiss franc
Trade partners	Switzerland, other Eur. countries
Exports	Machinery, dental products, stamps, hardware, pottery
Imports	Machinery, metal goods, textiles, food, motor vehicles

Land

Description	Central Europe, landlocked
Area	62 mi^2 (160 km^2)
Highest point	Vorder-Grauspitz, 8,527 ft (2,599 m)
Lowest point	Ruggleller Riet, 1,411 ft (430 m)

People

In spite of its location at the crossroads of Europe, Liechtenstein has retained a largely homogeneous ethnicity. Almost all Liechtensteiners are descended from Germanic tribes, and German is the official language. Roman Catholicism is the most widely practiced religion but a Protestant minority also exists. Most of the country is mountainous, and population is concentrated on the fertile plains adjacent to the Rhine River, which forms the country's western boundary. Most Liechtensteiners work in factories or in trades.

Economy and the Land.

The last few decades have seen the economy shift from agricultural to highly industrialized. Despite this growth in industry, Liechtenstein has not experienced a serious pollution problem, and the government continues its work to prevent the problem from occurring. An economic alliance with Switzerland dating from 1923 has been profoundly beneficial to Liechtenstein: the two nations form a customs union and use the same currency. Other important sources of revenue are tourism, the sale of postage stamps, and taxation of foreign businesses

headquartered here. Most of Liechtenstein, one of the world's smallest nations, is covered by the Alps; nonetheless, its climate is mild.

History and Politics

Early inhabitants of what is now Liechtenstein included the Celts, Romans, and Alemanni, who arrived about A.D. 500. The area became part of the empire of the Frankish king Charlemagne in the late 700s, and following Charlemagne's death, it was divided into the lordships of Vaduz and Schellenberg. By 1719, when the state became part of the Holy Roman Empire, the Austrian House of Liechtenstein had purchased both lordships, uniting them as the Imperial Principality of Liechtenstein. The nation's independence dates from the abolition of the empire by France's Napoleon Bonaparte in 1806. Liechtenstein was neutral in both World Wars and has remained unaffected by European conflicts. The government is a hereditary constitutional monarchy; the prince is the head of the House of Liechtenstein, thus chief of state, and the prime minister is the head of government. Women gained the right to vote in 1984.

LITHUANIA

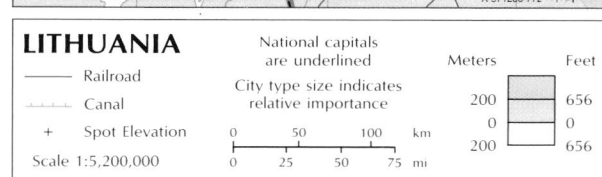

Always ice-free, Klaipèda is a major port. Lithuania's dense network of railways makes it an important transportation center for Eastern Europe.

Lithuania at a glance

Official name	Republic of Lithuania

Politics

Population	3,757,000
Density	149/mi^2 (58/km^2)
Urban	69%
Capital	Vilnius, 596,900
Ethnic groups	Lithuanian 80%, Russian 9%, Polish 8%, Byelorussian 2%
Languages	Lithuanian, Polish, Russian
Religions	Roman Catholic, Lutheran
Life expectancy	77 female, 68 male
Literacy	99%

Economy

Government	Republic
Parties	Christian Democratic, Democratic Labor, Sajudis, Social Democratic
Suffrage	Universal, over 18
Memberships	UN
Subdivisions	44 regions, 11 municipalities

Land

GNP	$12,400,000,000
Per capita	$3,260
Monetary unit	Litas
Trade partners	Russia, Ukraine, other former Soviet republics
Exports	Electronics, petroleum products, food, chemicals
Imports	Petroleum, machinery, chemicals, grain

Land

Description	Eastern Europe
Area	25,212 mi^2 (65,300 km^2)
Highest point	Juozapines Hill, 965 ft (294 m)
Lowest point	Sea level

People

Lithuanians are a Baltic people related to the Latvians. Although about 80 percent of the people are ethnic Lithuanians, Russian immigrants held many key positions in Lithuania under Soviet rule. Lithuanians also chafed under Soviet rules restricting religion because most are devoutly Roman Catholic. Lithuanians are known for their fine singing and splendid choral festivals.

Economy and the Land

Prior to Soviet rule, Lithuania was predominately rural with an agricultural economy based on meat and dairy products. Today the Lithuanian economy is dependent on industrial production, although it lacks significant mineral fuel deposits. The nation

has suffered from a severe oil shortage since independence when the Russians ceased to supply subsidized oil. The land is generally flat. There are fine white-sand beaches along the coastline of the Baltic Sea.

History and Politics

Unlike the neighboring Soviet republics of Latvia and Estonia, Lithuania has had a long tradition of independence. By the mid-1300s, Lithuania extended from the Baltic to the Black seas, and was a major regional power. Close political association with Poland led to a merger in 1569 and eventual annexation by Russia in the late nineteenth century. In 1918, Lithuania again claimed its independence, until it was overtaken by the Soviets in 1940. Stalin killed or

deported about one-third of the Lithuanian population. Friction between Lithuania and the Soviet Union increased after the introduction of glasnost fueled Lithuanian aspirations for independence. A Soviet invasion in early 1991 was followed by international recognition of Lithuania as an independent state later in the year. Disillusionment with their lagging economy led to a surprise victory by the ex-communist Democratic Labor Party in October 1992.

LUXEMBOURG

——	Railroad
+	Spot Elevation

Scale 1:1,087,000

City type size indicates relative importance

National capitals are underlined

Meters	Feet
1000	3281
500	1640
200	656
0	0

0 5 10 15 20 25 km
0 5 10 15 mi.

Most of Luxembourg is rolling hills and valleys. Highly productive family farms occupy half of the land.

Compact Luxembourg has a consistently prosperous economy based on manufacturing, banking, and farming. Because of a chronic labor shortage, the country has negligible unemployment and encourages immigration from other European nations. The quiet capital, also called Luxembourg, is more town than city.

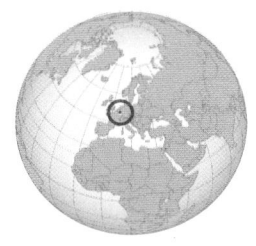

LUXEMBOURG

People
Luxembourg's population bears the imprint of foreign influences, yet retains an individual character. Most Luxembourgers are a blend of Celtic, French, and German stock. French is an official language, as is Luxembourgish, an indigenous German dialect. Roman Catholicism is observed by virtually all the population. There are significant communities of guest workers from several European nations.

Economy and the Land
Luxembourg's steel industry forms the basis of its economy, and the country has compensated for a worldwide drop in the steel market by developing financial services, notably banking. Manufacturing of plastics and chemicals is also important, as is tourism. Luxembourg's trade benefits from the country's membership in the European Community and the Benelux union. Luxembourg has two distinct regions: the mountainous, wooded north and the open, rolling south, known as Bon Pays. The climate is temperate.

History and Politics
The present city of Luxembourg developed from a castle built in A.D. 963 by Count Siegfried of Ardennes. Several heavily fortified towns grew up around the castle, and the area became known as the "Gibraltar of the North" because of those fortifications. The duchy remained semiautonomous until the Burgundians conquered the area in 1443. Various European powers ruled Luxembourg for most of the next four centuries, and in 1815 the duchy was elevated to a grand duchy. It became autonomous in 1839 and was recognized in 1867 as an independent state. Despite Luxembourg's declaration of neutrality, Germany occupied the country in both World Wars.

Luxembourg at a glance
Official name	Grand Duchy of Luxembourg

People
Population	396,000
Density	397/mi² (153/km²)
Urban	84%
Capital	Luxembourg, 75,377
Ethnic groups	Luxembourger (mixed Celtic, French, and German)
Languages	French, Luxembourgish, German
Religions	Roman Catholic 97%, Jewish and Protestant 3%
Life expectancy	79 female, 72 male
Literacy	100%

Politics
Government	Constitutional monarchy
Parties	Christian Socialist, Liberal, Socialist Workers, others
Suffrage	Universal, over 18
Memberships	EU, NATO, OECD, UN
Subdivisions	3 districts

Economy
GDP	$8,700,000,000
Per capita	$22,194
Monetary unit	Franc
Trade partners	Exports: Western European countries, U.S. Imports: Belgium, Germany, France
Exports	Iron and steel products, chemicals, rubber products, glass
Imports	Minerals, metals, food, consumer goods

Land
Description	Western Europe, landlocked
Area	998 mi² (2,586 km²)
Highest point	Buurgplaatz, 1,834 ft (559 m)
Lowest point	Confluence of Moselle and Sûre rivers, 427 ft (130 m)

Macao at a glance
Official name	Macao

People
Population	396,000
Density	57,571/mi² (22,000/km²)
Urban	99%
Capital	Macao, Macao I., 452,300
Ethnic groups	Chinese 95%, Portuguese 3%
Languages	Portuguese, Chinese (Cantonese)
Religions	Buddhist 45%, Roman Catholic 7%
Life expectancy	82 female, 77 male
Literacy	90%

Politics
Government	Chinese territory under Portuguese administration
Parties	Association to Defend the Interests of Macao, Democratic Center, others
Suffrage	Universal, over 18
Memberships	None
Subdivisions	2 districts

Economy
GDP	$3,500,000,000
Per capita	$7,813
Monetary unit	Pataca
Trade partners	Exports: U.S., China, Germany, France Imports: China, Japan
Exports	Textiles, clothing, toys
Imports	Raw materials, food, machinery

Land
Description	Eastern Asia (islands and peninsula on China's southeastern coast)
Area	7.0 mi² (18 km²)
Highest point	Coloane Alto, 571 ft (174 m)
Lowest point	Sea level

People
Situated on the southeastern China coast, 17 miles (27.4 km) west of Hong Kong, Macao is populated almost entirely by Chinese. A former overseas province of Portugal, the island also includes people of Portuguese and mixed Chinese-Portuguese descent. Several Chinese dialects are widely spoken, and Portuguese is the official language. Buddhism is Macao's principal religion; a small percentage of its population are Roman Catholics.

Economy and the Land
Tourism, gambling, and light industry help make up Macao's economy; however, its leading industries are textiles and light manufacturing, which employ the majority of the labor force. Macao has been likened to Hong Kong because of its textile exports, yet it remains a heavy importer, relying on China for drinking water and much of its food supply. The province consists of the city of Macao, located on a peninsula, and the nearby islands of Taipa and Coloane. The climate is maritime tropical, with cool winters and warm summers.

History and Politics
Macao became a Portuguese trading post in 1557. It flourished as the midpoint for trade between China and Japan but declined when Hong Kong became a trading power in the mid-1800s. Macao remained a neutral port during World War II and was economically prosperous. Although the government is nominally directed by Portugal, any policies relating to Macao are subject to China's approval. Macao is the oldest European settlement in the Far East. It will be returned to China in 1999 under a negotiated agreement whereby the present capitalist system will be maintained for fifty years.

Macao's first airport is under construction on the island of Taipa. Frequent, fast hydrofoils and ferries provide shuttle service to Hong Kong, 17 miles east.

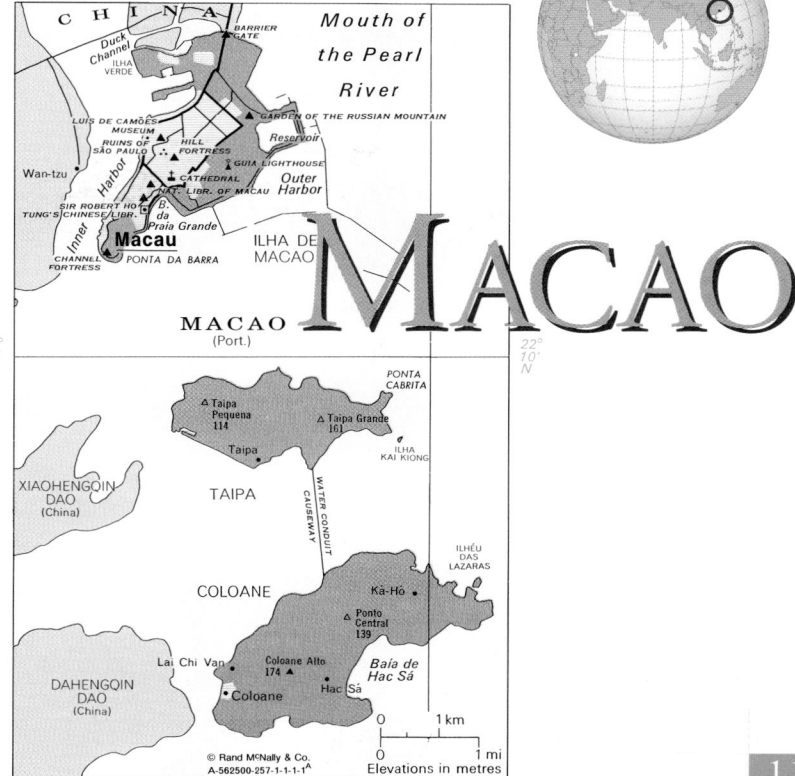

MACAO

People
Most Macedonians are of mixed Serbian and Bulgarian descent, reflected in the country's Slavic dialect. Albanians are the most significant minority. Many Macedonians practice the Orthodox religion, although there is a significant Muslim minority in the western part of the country. Macedonians are proud of their folklore and traditional music.

MACEDONIA

Economy and the Land
Landlocked Macedonia is predominately mountainous, and most of the people are involved in agriculture and herding. Agricultural products include cereal grains, tobacco, and cotton. The country has deposits of iron ore, lead, zinc, nickel, and chromium, but there are no significant mineral fuels.

History and Politics
The country of Macedonia is part of a larger historical region of the same name. Macedonia reached its zenith under the rule of Alexander the Great, who created a vast Macedonian empire in the fourth century B.C. that extended from Egypt to northern India. The empire fell apart after Alexander's death, and Rome then conquered the region. The Slavic people, who were the ancestors of today's Macedonians, migrated to the area in the sixth century A.D. The region suffered numerous invasions over the centuries. After 500 years of Turkish rule, it was finally split between Serbia, Greece, and

Macedonia at a glance

Official name	Republic of Macedonia

People

Population	2,102,000
Density	212/mi² (82/km²)
Urban	54%
Capital	Skopje, 444,900
Ethnic groups	Macedonian 67%, Albanian 21%, Turkish 4%, Serb 2%
Languages	Macedonian, Albanian
Religions	Eastern Orthodox 59%, Muslim 26%, Roman Catholic 4%
Life expectancy	75 female, 71 male
Literacy	89%

Politics

Government	Republic
Parties	Internal Revolutionary Organization-Democratic National Unity, Social Democratic Alliance
Suffrage	Universal, over 18
Memberships	UN
Subdivisions	34 counties

Economy

GDP	$2,200,000,000
Per capita	$1,010
Monetary unit	Denar
Trade partners	Exports: Former Yugoslavian republics, Germany, Greece Imports: Former Yugoslavian republics, Greece, Albania
Exports	Manufactures, machinery and transportation equip., food
Imports	Fuels and lubricants, manufactures, machinery and transport. equip.

Land

Description	Eastern Europe, landlocked
Area	9,928 mi² (25,713 km²)
Highest point	Korab, 9,035 ft (2,754 m)
Lowest point	Along Vardar River, 165 ft (50 m)

Bulgaria in 1913, after serving as a battleground for two Balkan wars. In 1945, the Serbian portion of Macedonia became a full republic of Yugoslavia. It remained part of Yugoslavia until 1991, when it followed the lead of neighboring Yugoslavian republics and declared its independence. International

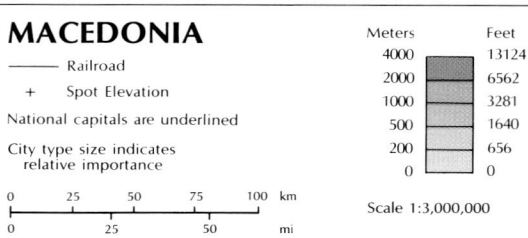

Macedonia is not easily defined geographically. It consists of plains, valleys and mountains. The Greek province of Macedonia is immediately south.

peacekeeping forces in Macedonia are attempting to prevent a spillover of ethnic strife. Greece opposes use of the name "Macedonia." U.S. and European Union recognition of Macedonia in 1994 prompted Greece to cut off Macedonia's main trade route.

People
Most of the population is of mixed African and Indonesian descent. Those who live on the coast, the *cotiers*, are of predominantly African origin, while those on the inland plateau have Asian roots. There is a long-standing rivalry between the cotiers and the inland groups, most of whom belong

MADAGASCAR

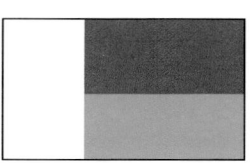

to the Merina people. The official language is Malagasy. Sizable Christian communities exist, but most Malagasy practice indigenous Animist beliefs.

Economy and the Land
Madagascar is chiefly an agricultural nation, with the majority of the workforce engaged in farming or herding. Overpopulation and outmoded cultivation have recently cut into yields of rice, an important crop, and other products. Varied mineral resources, including oil, point to possible expansion. The climate is tropical on the coastal plains and moderate in the inland highlands.

History and Politics
Madagascar's first settlers are thought to be Indonesians, who brought African wives and slaves around two thousand years ago. Arab traders established themselves on the coast in the seventh century. The Portuguese first sighted the island in the 1500s, and other Europeans followed. The Merina kingdom, based in the central plateau, gained control over most of the island in the 1790's. French influence grew throughout the nineteenth century, and in 1896 France made the island a colony after subduing the Merina. Resentment of France rule continued, culminating in an armed revolt in 1947. Full independence came in 1960. After twelve years of

rule by the same president, a coup placed the military in power. A new constitution was adopted in 1975 that established the Democratic Republic of Madagascar. By 1991 there were major protests against the government, and a late 1992 election was won by the opposition.

Madagascar at a glance

Official name	Republic of Madagascar

People

Population	13,645,000
Density	60/mi² (23/km²)
Urban	24%
Capital	Antananarivo, 1,250,000
Ethnic groups	Merina 15%, Betsimisaraka 9%, Betsileo 7%, Tsimihety 4%, Antaisaka 4%, other tribes
Languages	Malagasy, French
Religions	Animist 52%, Christian 41%, Muslim 7%
Life expectancy	57 female, 54 male
Literacy	80%

Politics

Government	Republic
Parties	Advanced Guard of the Revolution, Militants for the Establishment of a Proletarian Regime, others
Suffrage	Universal, over 18
Memberships	OAU, UN
Subdivisions	6 provinces

Economy

GDP	$10,400,000,000
Per capita	$813
Monetary unit	Franc
Trade partners	Exports: France, U.S., Japan Imports: France, U.S., former Soviet republics
Exports	Coffee, vanilla, cloves, petroleum
Imports	Manufactures, machinery, food

Land

Description	Southeastern African island
Area	226,658 mi² (587,041 km²)
Highest point	Maromokotro, 9,436 ft (2,876 m)
Lowest point	Sea Level

The same forces that split Madagascar from Africa are expected eventually to produce another new island, consisting roughly of Ethiopia, Kenya and Tanzania. The process will take several million years.

Malawi at a glance

Official name   Republic of Malawi

People

Population	8,984,000
Density	196/mi² (76/km²)
Urban	12%
Capital	Lilongwe, 233,318
Ethnic groups	Chewa, Nyanja, Tumbuko, Yao, Lomwe, others
Languages	Chichewa, English
Religions	Protestant 55%, Roman Catholic 20%, Muslim 20%
Life expectancy	45 female, 44 male
Literacy	22%

Politics

Government	Republic
Parties	Congress, others
Suffrage	Universal, over 21
Memberships	CW, OAU, UN
Subdivisions	3 regions

Economy

GDP	$6,000,000,000
Per capita	$619
Monetary unit	Kwacha
Trade partners	Exports: U.K., Germany, South Africa Imports: South African countries, U.K., Japan
Exports	Tobacco, tea, sugar, coffee, peanuts
Imports	Food, petroleum, manufactures, transportation equipment

Land

Description	Southern Africa, landlocked
Area	45,747 mi² (118,484 km²)
Highest point	Sapitwa, 9,849 ft (3,002 m)
Lowest point	Along Shire River, 120 ft (37 m)

Beautiful Lake Malawi accounts for 20 percent of the country's total area.

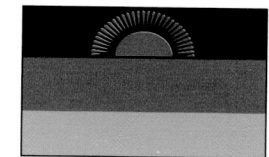

MALAWI

People

Almost all Malawians are black Africans descended from Bantu peoples. The Chewa constitute the majority in the central area, while the Nyanja are dominant in the south and the Tumbuko in the north. Chichewa and English are official languages. The majority of the population is rural, and traditional village customs are prevalent. For the most part, the society is matriarchal. Many Malawians combine Christian or Muslim beliefs with traditional religious practices.

Economy and the Land

A landlocked nation with limited resources and a largely unskilled workforce, Malawi relies almost entirely on agriculture. A recent series of poor harvests, combined with a tripling of the population between 1950 and 1989, has contributed to the decline in agricultural output and consequent food shortages. Among the main exports are tea and tobacco. Many Malawians work part of the year as miners in South Africa, Zambia, and Zimbabwe. Malawi, situated along the Great Rift Valley, has a varied terrain with highlands, plateaus, and lakes. The climate is subtropical, and rainfall varies greatly from north to south.

History and Politics

Archeological findings indicate that Malawi has been inhabited for at least 50,000 years. Bantu-speaking peoples, ancestors of the Malawians, immigrated from the north around A.D. 1400 and soon formed centralized kingdoms. In the 1830s, other Bantu groups, involved in the slave trade, invaded the region. The arrival of Scottish missionary David Livingstone in 1859 began a period of British influence; in 1891 the territory became the British protectorate of Nyasaland. Beginning in 1953, Nyasaland was part of the larger Federation of Rhodesia and Nyasaland. Malawi attained independence in 1964 and became a republic in

With little industry or other development, Malawi has concentrated on agriculture. Tobacco, sugarcane, cotton, and tea have allowed the country to generally post a positive balance of trade—a significant achievement in Africa. Malawi is widely considered one of Africa's most hospitable countries.

1966, with nationalist leader Dr. Hastings Banda as its first president. The Malawi Congress party appointed Banda as president-for-life in 1970, but a 1993 referendum strongly favored the creation of a multiparty system. In May 1994, President Banda, who was the oldest head of state in the world and Africa's longest-ruling dictator, was ousted from office and then charged with the murder of political foes.

Malaysia is one of the fast-developing Asian countries that have come to be known as "the Asian tigers." Kuala Lumpur is a modern city expanding in all directions. Its central district now holds the world's tallest office building, the Petronas Twin Towers. Away from the cities, there are rubber and palm plantations. Many of the surviving rain forests are preserved in national parks.

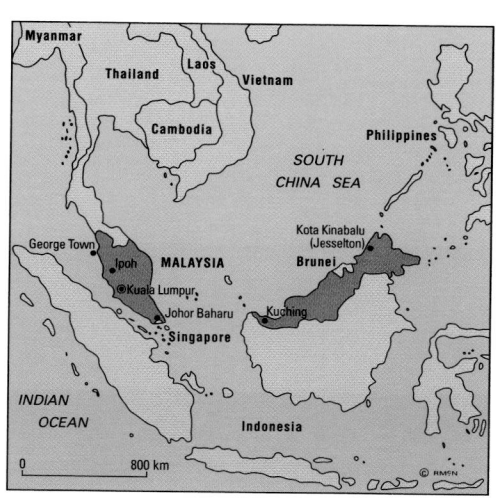

MALAYSIA

Boys play in the waters of Tioman Island, the largest and most beautiful island off Malaysia's east coast in the South China Sea.

People

Malaysia's location at one of Southeast Asia's maritime crossroads has left it with a diverse population, including Malays, Chinese, Indians, and native non-Malay groups. The mostly rural Malays dominate politically, while the predominantly urban Chinese are very active in economic life.

Considerable tension exists between the two groups. Although most Malays speak Malay and practice Islam, Malaysia's ethnic groups have resisted assimilation; Chinese, Indian, and Western languages and beliefs are also part of the culture. Most Malaysians live in Peninsular Malaysia. *(continued)*

Malaysia at a glance

Official name   Malaysia

People

Population	19,505,000
Density	153/mi² (59/km²)
Urban	43%
Capital	Kuala Lumpur, 919,610
Ethnic groups	Malay and other indigenous 59%, Chinese 32%, Indian 9%.
Languages	Malay, Chinese dialects, English, Tamil
Religions	Muslim 53%, Buddhist 17%, Chinese religions 12%, Hindu 7%
Life expectancy	73 female, 69 male
Literacy	78%

Politics

Government	Constitutional monarchy
Parties	Democratic Action, Islamic, National Front
Suffrage	Universal, over 21
Memberships	ASEAN, CW, UN
Subdivisions	13 states, 2 federal territories

Economy

GDP	$141,000,000,000
Per capita	$7,568
Monetary unit	Ringgit
Trade partners	Exports: Singapore, U.S., Japan Imports: Japan, U.S., Singapore
Exports	Manufactures, petroleum, timber, rubber, palm oil, textiles
Imports	Food, petroleum, manufactures, machinery, chemicals

Land

Description	Southeastern Asia (includes part of the island of Borneo)
Area	127,320 mi² (329,758 km²)
Highest point	Mt. Kinabalu, 13,455 ft (4,101 m)
Lowest point	Sea level

Kuala Lumpur, Malaysia's capital

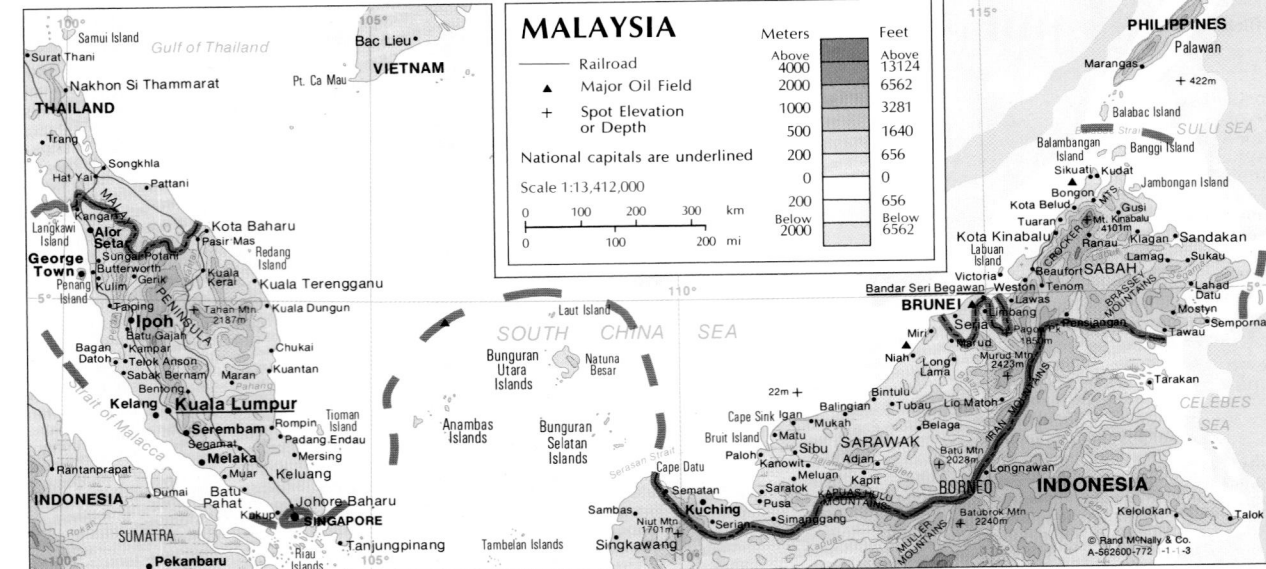

Economy and the Land

The economy is one of the healthiest in the region, supported by multiple strengths in agriculture, mining, forestry, and fishing. The nation is one of the world's leading producers of rubber, palm oil, and tin, and one of the Far East's largest petroleum exporters. Manufacturing is also being developed. Malaysia consists of the southern portion of the Malay Peninsula and the states of Sarawak and Sabah on northern Borneo. The land features swampy areas, mountains, and rain forests. The climate is tropical and very humid.

History and Politics

The Malay Peninsula has been inhabited since the late Stone Age. Hindu and Buddhist influences were widespread from the ninth through the fourteenth centuries A.D., after which Islam was introduced. In 1511 the Portuguese seized Melaka, a trading center, but were soon replaced, first by the Dutch in 1641 and then by the British in 1795. By the early 1900s, Britain was in control of present-day Malaysia and Singapore, the areas which were occupied by Japan during World War II. Following the war, the Federation of Malaya was created, a semiautonomous state under British authority. A guerrilla war ensued, waged by Chinese Communists and others who opposed the British. The country gained full independence in 1963 with the unification of Malaysia. Singapore seceded in 1965. Government attempts in 1993 to curb the powers of hereditary rulers threatens peace in the country.

Malaysia's economic life is centered on the mainland. The states of Sabah and Sarawak on the island of Borneo comprise 60 percent of Malaysia's area and are more rural and agricultural.

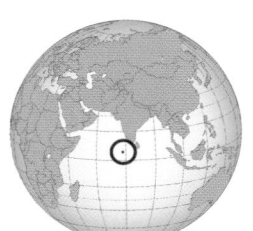

MALDIVES

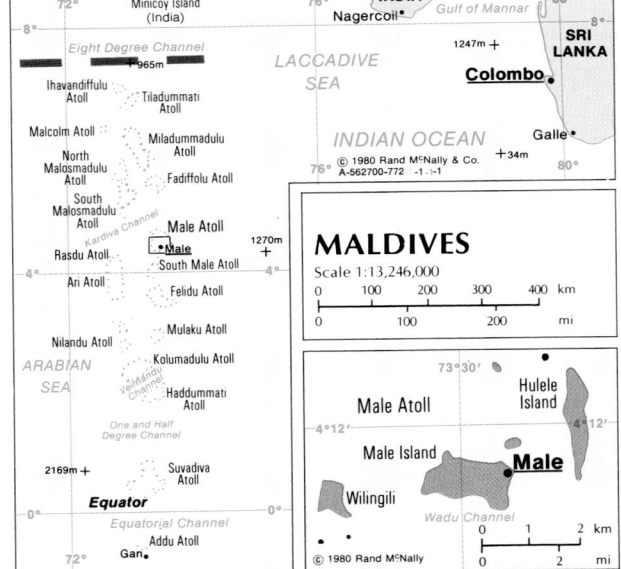

None of the Maldives islands rises more than ten feet above the Indian Ocean. The islands are protected from storms by barrier reefs.

A chain of some 1,100 islands—220 of which are inhabited—the Maldives together total only 115 square miles of land. With little room for agriculture, the islands depend upon fishing and a rapidly growing tourism industry.

People

Most Maldivians are descended from Sinhalese peoples from Sri Lanka; southern Indians, or Dravidians; and Arabs. Nearly all Maldivians are Sunni Muslims and speak Divehi. The population is concentrated on Male, the capital island.

Economy and the Land

The nation draws on its advantages as a union of eleven hundred islands to fuel its economy: tourism, shipping, and fishing are the mainstays. With limited arable land and infertile soil, agriculture is marginal. The Maldives, flat coral islands, form a chain of nineteen atolls. Seasonal monsoons mark the tropical climate.

History and Politics

The Maldives are believed to have been originally settled by southern Indian peoples. Arab sailors brought Islam to the islands in the twelfth century A.D. Although a Muslim sultanate remained in power with only two interruptions from 1153 until 1968, the Portuguese and Dutch controlled the islands intermittently between the 1500s and the 1700s. The Maldives were a British protectorate from 1887 to 1965, when they achieved independence. They declared the country a republic three years later.

Maldives at a glance

Official name   Republic of Maldives

People

Population	251,000
Density	2,183/mi² (842/km²)
Urban	29%
Capital	Male', Male I., 55,130
Ethnic groups	Maldivian (mixed Sinhalese, Dravidian, Arab, and black)
Languages	Divehi
Religions	Sunni Muslim
Life expectancy	62 female, 65 male
Literacy	92%

Politics

Government	Republic
Parties	None
Suffrage	Universal, over 21
Memberships	CW, UN
Subdivisions	19 districts, 1 capital city

Economy

GDP	$140,000,000
Per capita	$651
Monetary unit	Rufiyaa
Trade partners	Exports: U.S., U.K., Sri Lanka Imports: Singapore, Germany, Sri Lanka
Exports	Fish, clothing
Imports	Consumer goods, manufactures, petroleum products

Land

Description	Indian Ocean islands
Area	115 mi² (298 km²)
Highest point	Unnamed, 10 ft (3 m)
Lowest point	Sea level

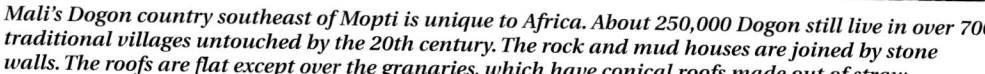

Mali at a glance

Official name   Republic of Mali

People

Population	9,585,000
Density	20/mi² (7.7/km²)
Urban	24%
Capital	Bamako, 658,275
Ethnic groups	Mande 50%, Fulani 17%, Voltaic 12%, Songhai 6%
Languages	French, Bambara, indigenous
Religions	Sunni Muslim 90%, Animist 9%, Christian 1%
Life expectancy	48 female, 44 male
Literacy	32%

Politics

Government	Republic
Parties	Alliance for Democracy, National Committee for Democratic Initiative, Sudanese Union-African Democratic Rally
Suffrage	Universal, over 21
Memberships	OAU, UN
Subdivisions	8 regions, 1 capital district

Economy

GDP	$5,800,000,000
Per capita	$663
Monetary unit	CFA franc
Trade partners	Exports: Cote d'Ivoire, Senegal, former Soviet Union Imports: France, Cote d'Ivoire, Senegal
Exports	Livestock, peanuts, fish, cotton, animal hides
Imports	Textiles, vehicles, petroleum, machinery, sugar, grain

Land

Description	Western Africa, landlocked
Area	482,077 mi² (1,248,574 km²)
Highest point	Hombori Mtn., 3,789 ft (1,155 m)
Lowest point	Along Senegal River, 72 ft (22 m)

POPULATION COMPARISON
Mali=4% of U.S.

United States

GDP COMPARISON
Mali=0.09% of U.S.

United States

ETHNIC GROUPS

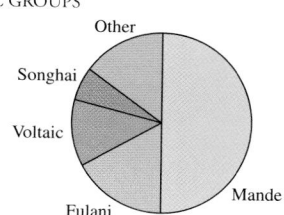

Other
Songhai
Voltaic
Fulani
Mande

POPULATION DISTRIBUTION

Urban   Rural

Mali's Dogon country southeast of Mopti is unique to Africa. About 250,000 Dogon still live in over 700 traditional villages untouched by the 20th century. The rock and mud houses are joined by stone walls. The roofs are flat except over the granaries, which have conical roofs made out of straw.

MALI

L ittle remains of Mali's legacy as a medieval Islamic center of trading and art. The country struggles to feed its people amidst political turmoil and drought. Wide areas of land once suitable for grazing have turned to desert.

People
The majority of Malians belong to one of several black groups, although there is a small non-black nomadic population. Most Malians are farmers who live in small villages. The official language is French, but most people communicate in Bambara, a market language. The population is concentrated in the basins of the Niger and Senegal rivers in the south. Heirs of three ancient empires, Malians have produced a distinct culture.

Economy and the Land
One of the world's poorest nations, Mali depends primarily on agriculture but is limited by a climate that produces drought and a terrain that is almost half desert. Mineral reserves have not been exploited because of poor transportation and power facilities. Food processing and textiles account for most industry. A landlocked country, Mali faces a growing national debt due to its dependence on foreign goods. The climate is hot and dry, with alternating dry and wet seasons.

History and Politics
Parts of present-day Mali once belonged to the Ghana, Mali, and Songhai empires. These wealthy empires, which ruled from about A.D. 300 to 1600, traded with the Mediterranean world and were centers of Islamic learning. Fierce native resistance delayed colonization by the French until 1904, when French Sudan, as the area was called, was made part of French West Africa. In 1959 it joined Senegal to form the Federation of Mali. Senegal soon withdrew from the union, and French Sudan declared itself the Republic of Mali in 1960. A military coup overthrew the republic, a socialist state, in 1968. This government, in turn, was overthrown, and the country has since moved haltingly toward democracy. Nomadic Tuareg rebels have negotiated a peace agreement.

Bani Lake, Mopti

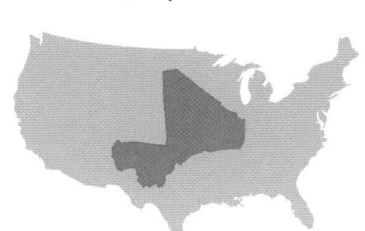

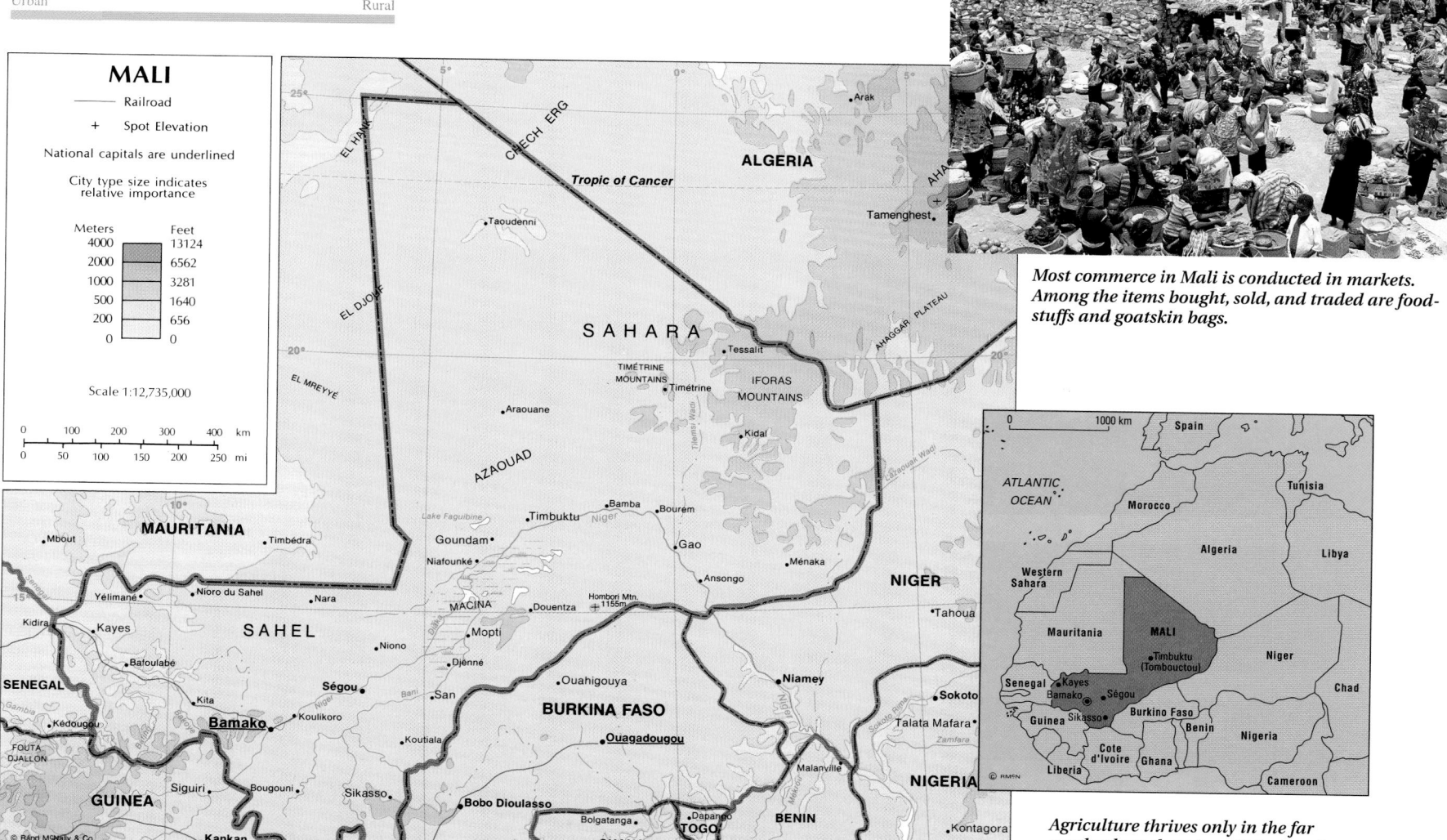

MALI

— Railroad

+ Spot Elevation

National capitals are underlined

City type size indicates relative importance

Meters	Feet
4000	13124
2000	6562
1000	3281
500	1640
200	656
0	0

Scale 1:12,735,000

0 100 200 300 400 km
0 50 100 150 200 250 mi

Most commerce in Mali is conducted in markets. Among the items bought, sold, and traded are foodstuffs and goatskin bags.

Agriculture thrives only in the far south where there is sufficient and reliable rainfall to permit planting.

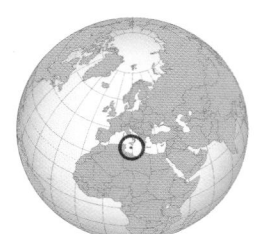

Rather than coming to conquer Malta, as was the case for centuries, visitors today come to enjoy its warm, dry climate and to study its many ancient sites.

MALTA

People
Malta's diverse population reflects centuries of rule by Arabs, Normans, and British. The official languages are English and Maltese, the latter a blend of Arabic and a Sicilian dialect of Italian. Roman Catholicism is practiced by the majority of residents. Malta is one of the world's most densely populated nations.

Economy and the Land
Situated strategically between Europe and Africa, Malta became an important military site for foreign powers with the opening of the Suez Canal in 1869. Its economy, shaped by the patterns of war and peace in the Mediterranean, has recently turned toward commercial shipbuilding, construction, manufacturing, and tourism. Its soil is poor, and most food is imported. Although there are many natural harbors and hundreds of

miles of coastline, fishing is not a major source of income. Malta, with its hilly terrain, is subtropical in summer and temperate the rest of the year.

History and Politics
The Phoenicians and Carthaginians first colonized the island of Malta between 1000 and 600 B.C. After becoming part of the Roman and Byzantine empires, Malta was ruled successively by Arabs, Normans, and various feudal lords. In the 1500s the Holy Roman Emperor Charles V ceded Malta to the Knights of St. John of Jerusalem, an order of the Roman Catholic church. The Knights' reign, marked by cultural and architectural achievements, ended with surrender to France's Napoleon Bonaparte in 1798. The Maltese resisted French rule, however, and offered control to Britain, becoming part of the United Kingdom in 1814. Throughout

both World Wars, Malta was a vital naval base for the Allied forces. It achieved independence from Britain in 1964 and became a republic ten years later. In 1979 the last British and North Atlantic Treaty Organization (NATO) military forces departed, and Malta declared its neutrality.

Malta at a glance

Official name	Republic of Malta

People
Population	368,000
Density	3,016/mi² (1,165/km²)
Urban	87%
Capital	Valletta, 9,199
Ethnic groups	Maltese (mixed Arab, Sicilian, Norman, Spanish, Italian, and English)
Languages	English, Maltese
Religions	Roman Catholic 98%
Life expectancy	78 female, 74 male
Literacy	84%

Politics
Government	Republic
Parties	Labor, Nationalist
Suffrage	Universal, over 18
Memberships	CW, UN
Subdivisions	6 regions

Economy
GDP	$2,400,000,000
Per capita	$6,723
Monetary unit	Lira
Trade partners	Exports: Italy, Germany, U.K. Imports: Italy, U.K., Germany
Exports	Clothing, textiles, footwear, ships
Imports	Food, petroleum, machinery, manufactures

Land
Description	Mediterranean island
Area	122 mi² (316 km²)
Highest point	Unnamed, 829 ft (253 m)
Lowest point	Sea level

The Marshall Islands are coral atolls growing atop ancient volcanoes which rise from the sea floor.

With few natural resources other than simple agriculture and fishing, the Marshall Islands are heavily dependent upon the United States for assistance. After World War II, the U.S. exploited the islands' isolated location, using Bikini and Enewetak for testing nuclear weapons.

MARSHALL ISLANDS

Marshall Islands at a glance

Official name	Republic of the Marshall Islands

People
Population	55,000
Density	786/mi² (304/km²)
Urban	48%
Capital	Majuro (island)
Ethnic groups	Micronesian
Languages	English, indigenous, Japanese
Religions	Protestant, Roman Catholic
Life expectancy	64 female, 61 male
Literacy	93%

Politics
Government	Republic (U.S. protection)
Parties	None
Suffrage	Universal, over 18
Memberships	UN
Subdivisions	None

Economy
GDP	$63,000,000
Per capita	$1,575
Monetary unit	U.S. dollar
Trade partners	U.S., Japan
Exports	Copra, agricultural products, handicrafts
Imports	Food, beverages, building materials

Land
Description	North Pacific islands
Area	70 mi² (181 km²)
Highest point	Unnamed, 80 ft (24 m)
Lowest point	Sea level

People
Most Marshall Islanders are Micronesian, although there is a Polynesian minority. Both English and Malay-Polynesian languages are spoken on the islands.

Economy and the Land
The main industry of the Marshall Islands is coconuts, and many islanders continue to practice subsistence farming and fishing. The islands remain dependent on economic aid from the United States. Part of the area of the Pacific Ocean known as Micronesia, the two major island groups are the eastern Ratak Chain and the western Ralik Chain. The coral islands are mostly flat and low-lying, and the climate is hot and rainy.

History and Politics
The history of the Marshall Islands prior to the arrival of Europeans is largely unknown, but it is likely that the earliest settlers came from Southeast Asia. The islands received their name from Captain John Marshall, a Briton who reached the Marshalls in 1788. In the 1880s, the Marshall Islands became a German protectorate, and in 1914, during World War I, Japan seized the islands. During World War II, the United States captured the islands from Japan, and in 1947,

the Marshall Islands were incorporated into the Trust Territory of the Pacific Islands established by the United Nations, and placed under the protection of the United States. In the late 1940s and early 1950s, the United States conducted dozens of nuclear test explosions throughout the Marshall Islands. The United States continues to provide compensation to those victimized by radiation-related illnesses and destruction of property, but the displaced inhabitants of Bikini Atoll insist that the United States should restore their island's environment. In 1986, the Marshall Islands became self-governing, when a compact of free association with the United States was finalized. Official recognition of the new republic did not come until 1991, when the United Nations removed the Marshall Islands from the trusteeship.

Martinique at a glance

Official name   Department of Martinique

People

Population	384,000
Density	904/mi² (349/km²)
Urban	75%
Capital	Fort-de-France, 99,844
Ethnic groups	Black or mulatto 90%, white 5%
Languages	French, Creole
Religions	Roman Catholic 95%
Life expectancy	79 female, 73 male
Literacy	93%

Politics

Government	Overseas department (France)
Parties	Rally for the Republic, Union for French Democracy, Union of the Left, others
Suffrage	Universal, over 18
Memberships	None
Subdivisions	3 arrondissements

Economy

GDP	$2,000,000,000
Per capita	$6,061
Monetary unit	French franc
Trade partners	Exports: France, Guadeloupe, French Guiana Imports: France, United Arab Emirates, U.K.
Exports	Petroleum products, bananas, rum, pineapples
Imports	Petroleum products, food, construction materials, vehicles, clothing

Land

Description	Caribbean island
Area	425 mi² (1,100 km²)
Highest point	Montagne Pelée, 4,583 ft (1,397 m)
Lowest point	Sea level

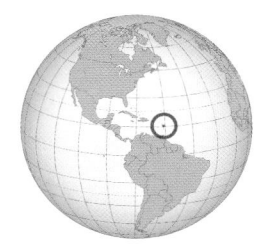

The French impressionist painter Gauguin celebrated Martinique in a series of paintings recording its idyllic beauty. The population is highly literate and mostly employed serving the growing tourist industry.

MARTINIQUE

People

Blacks and people of mixed black-and-French ancestry compose the majority group on Martinique. The culture is a unique blend of French and West Indian life-styles.

Economy and the Land

Martinique's tropical climate and beautiful scenery attract many visitors each year. Agriculture provides additional income, and major products include bananas, sugar, and rum. Forested mountains cover much of the island.

History and Politics

Carib Indians inhabited the island when Christopher Columbus first sighted it in 1493. Columbus didn't come ashore until his 1502 voyage, and Indian hostility discouraged colonization. French settlement began in 1635, and except for short periods of British rule, the island has remained in French hands. In 1946 Martinique became an overseas department of France.

Scale 1:1,000,000   One inch represents approximately 16 miles.
One centimeter represents 10 kilometers.

Prior to 1902, St-Pierre was Martinique's primary city. Then Mt. Pelée erupted, destroying the city and killing 30,000 people. The volcano has been dormant since.

For most of this century Mauritania's economy was centered around iron ore exports, but a worldwide glut of the commodity has depressed prices and wiped out demand. With little arable land, Mauritania will have increasing problems feeding its population.

People

Most Mauritanians are Moors, descendants of Arabs and Berbers, or of mixed Arab, Berber, and black descent. The Moors, who speak Arabic, are mostly nomadic herdsmen. The remainder of the population is composed of black Africans, who speak several languages and farm in the Senegal River valley. Virtually all Mauritanians are Muslim. Proportionally, the nomadic population has declined recently because of long periods of drought, although overall population is increasing.

Economy and the Land

Mauritania's economy is based on agriculture, with many farmers producing only subsistence-level outputs. Crop production, confined chiefly to the Senegal River valley, has recently fallen because of drought and outmoded cultivation methods. Mining of high-grade iron-ore deposits is the main industrial activity, although fishing and fish processing are also important. Inadequate transportation and communication systems have crippled the economy. In addition to the river valley, land regions include a northern desert and southeastern grasslands. Mauritania has a hot, dry climate.

History and Politics

Berbers began settling in parts of the area around A.D. 300 and established a network of caravan trading routes. From this time until the late 1500s, sections of the south were dominated by the Ghana, the Mali, and finally the Songhai empires. Contact with Europeans grew between the 1600s and 1800s, and in 1920 France made Mauritania a colony. Mauritania attained independence in 1960, although Morocco claimed the area and did not recognize the state until 1970. During the late 1970s, Mauritania became embroiled in a war with Morocco and the

Mauritania at a glance

Official name   Islamic Republic of Mauritania

People

Population	2,228,000
Density	5.6/mi² (2.2/km²)
Urban	47%
Capital	Nouakchott, 285,000
Ethnic groups	Mixed Moor and black 40%, Moor 30%, black 30%
Languages	Arabic, Pular, Soninke, Wolof
Religions	Sunni Muslim 100%
Life expectancy	50 female, 46 male
Literacy	34%

Politics

Government	Republic
Parties	Assembly for Democratic Unity, Democratic and Social Republican, Union of Democratic Forces-New Era
Suffrage	Universal, over 18
Memberships	AL, OAU, UN
Subdivisions	12 regions, 1 capital district

Economy

GDP	$2,200,000,000
Per capita	$1,085
Monetary unit	Ouguiya
Trade partners	Exports: Japan, France, Spain Imports: France, Spain, Senegal
Exports	Iron ore, fish
Imports	Food, manufactures, petroleum, machinery

Land

Description	Western Africa
Area	395,956 mi² (1,025,520 km²)
Highest point	Mt. Ijill, 3,002 ft (915 m)
Lowest point	Sebkha de Ndrhamcha, -10 ft (-3 m)

Polisario Front, a Western Saharan nationalist group, for control of Western Sahara. Mauritania withdrew its claim to the area in 1979. A new constitution providing for universal suffrage was approved in 1991, and multiparty elections have been held. There are repeated reports of discrimination against the black population.

MAURITANIA

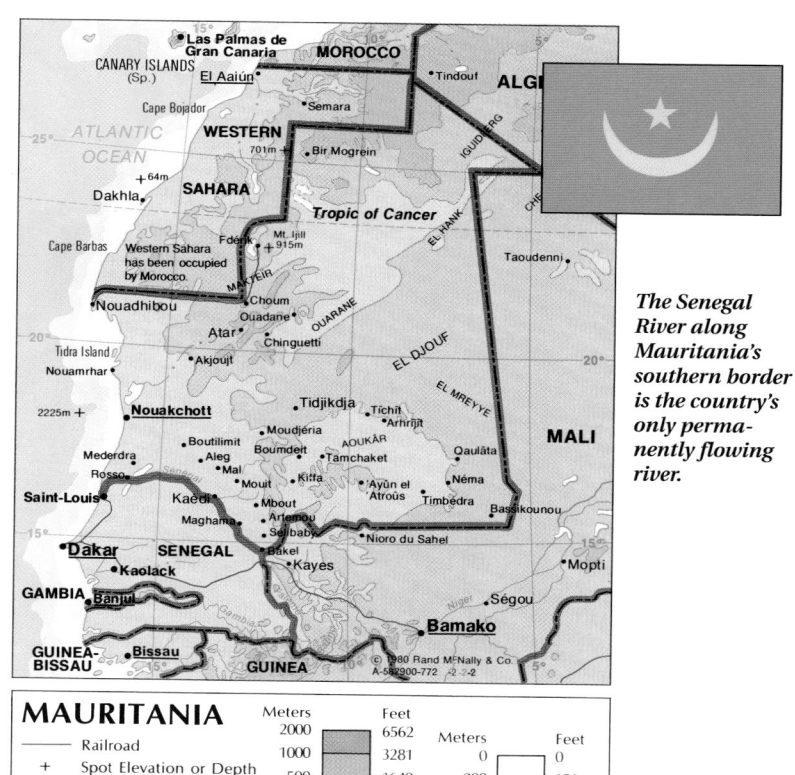

The Senegal River along Mauritania's southern border is the country's only permanently flowing river.

MAURITANIA	Meters	Feet		Meters	Feet
—— Railroad	2000	6562			
+ Spot Elevation or Depth	1000	3281		0	0
Scale 1:21,455,000	500	1640		200	656
0 100 200 300 400 500 km	200	656		Below 2000	Below 6562
0 100 200 300 mi	0	Sea level			

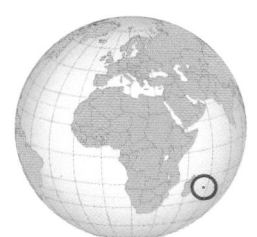

Despite its large population, Mauritius has preserved many of its picturesque villages as well as its crystal-clear coastal waters.

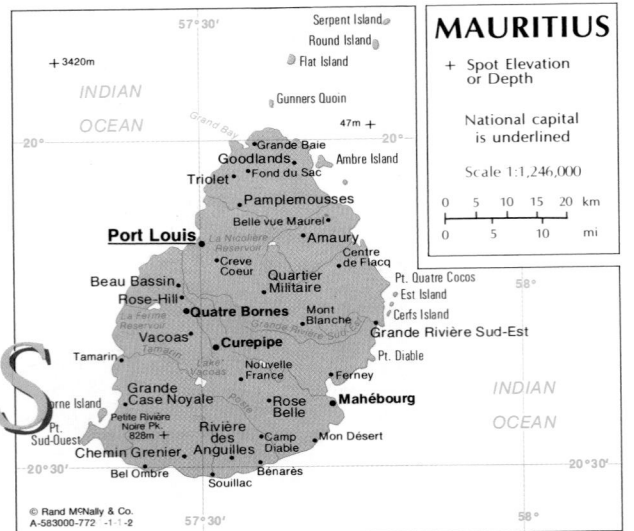

MAURITIUS

+ Spot Elevation or Depth

National capital is underlined

Scale 1:1,246,000

0 5 10 15 20 km
0 5 10 mi

© Rand McNally & Co.
A-583000-772 -1-1-2

MAURITIUS

Mauritius at a glance

Official name	Republic of Mauritius

People

Population	1,120,000
Density	1,423/mi² (550/km²)
Urban	41%
Capital	Port Louis, Mauritius I., 141,870
Ethnic groups	Indo-Mauritian 68%, Creole 27%, Sino-Mauritian 3%, Franco-Mauritian 2%
Languages	English, Creole, Bhojpuri, French, Hindi, Tamil, others
Religions	Hindu 52%, Roman Catholic 28%, Muslim 17%
Life expectancy	74 female, 67 male
Literacy	83%

Politics

Government	Republic
Parties	Labor, Militant Socialist Movement, Militant Movement, Social Democratic, others
Suffrage	Universal, over 18
Memberships	CW, OAU, UN
Subdivisions	9 districts

Economy

GDP	$8,600,000,000
Per capita	$7,847
Monetary unit	Rupee
Trade partners	Exports: U.K., France, U.S. Imports: France, China, U.S., South Africa
Exports	Textiles, sugar, manufactures
Imports	Manufactures, machinery, food, petroleum, chemicals

Land

Description	Indian Ocean island
Area	788 mi² (2,040 km²)
Highest point	Piton de la Petite Rivière Noire, Piton, 2,717 ft (828 m)
Lowest point	Sea level

The above information includes dependencies.

The small, densely populated islands of **Mauritius** are among the most ethnically diverse lands in the world. Sizable populations of Indians, Malays, Chinese, black Africans, British, and French all coexist. Mauritius has avoided the woes of many small island nations with a diversified and growing economy based on exports and tourism.

People

Mauritius's diverse ethnicity is largely the product of its past as a sugar-producing colony. Creoles are descendants of African slaves and European plantation owners, while the Indian community traces its roots to laborers who replaced the Africans after slavery was abolished. There are also people of Chinese and French descent. Franco-Mauritians now compose most of the nation's elite. English is the official tongue, although a French creole and many other languages are also spoken. Religious activity is similarly varied and includes Hinduism, Christianity and Islam.

Economy and the Land

Once heavily dependent on the production of sugar, Mauritius was wise enough to diversify its economy as the price of sugar fell. Tourism has become important, as well as international finance and light industry, earning Mauritius a reputation as Africa's Hong Kong. The nation includes the island of Mauritius, Rodrigues Island, Agalega Islands, and Cargados Carajos Shoals. The climate is tropical.

History and Politics

Although visited by Arab, Malay, and Portuguese sailors between the tenth and sixteenth centuries A.D., Mauritius was uninhabited until 1598, when the Dutch claimed it. They abandoned the island in 1710, and five years later the French made it their colony. During the 1700s, the French used Mauritius, which they called île de France, as a naval base and established plantations worked by imported slaves. The British ousted the French in 1810 and outlawed slavery soon afterward. In the nineteenth century indentured workers from India replaced the slaves. Mauritius began its history as an independent state in 1968 with a system of parliamentary democracy, and became a republic in 1992.

Comoros has claimed Mayotte, but has not pressed the issue. The island has the only deep-water port in the Comoros archipelago.

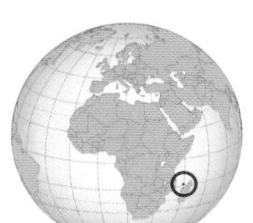

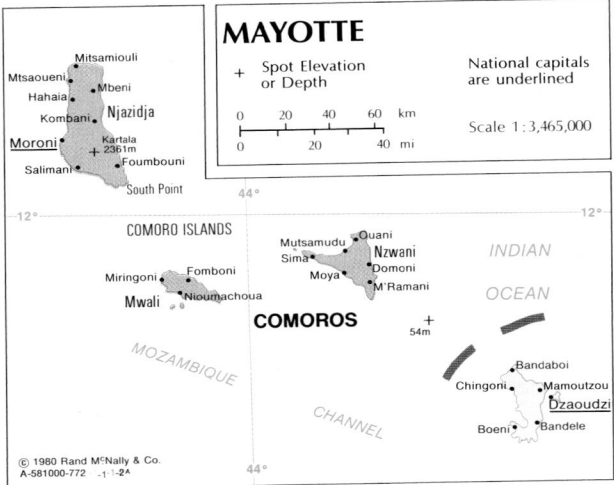

MAYOTTE

+ Spot Elevation or Depth

National capitals are underlined

0 20 40 60 km
0 20 40 mi

Scale 1:3,465,000

© 1980 Rand McNally & Co.
A-581000-772 -1-1-2A

MAYOTTE

Mayotte at a glance

Official name	Territorial Collectivity of Mayotte

People

Population	95,000
Density	660/mi² (254/km²)
Capital	Dzaoudzi (de facto), Dzaoudzi Island, 5,865; Mamoutzou (future), Mayotte Island
Ethnic groups	Mahorais
Languages	French, Swahili (Mahorian)
Religions	Sunni Muslim 99%
Life expectancy	60 female, 55 male

Politics

Government	Territorial collectivity (France)
Parties	Democratic Rally, Popular Movement, Rally for the Republic
Suffrage	Universal, over 18
Memberships	None
Subdivisions	17 communes

Economy

Monetary unit	French franc
Trade partners	Exports: France, Comoros, Reunion. Imports: France, Kenya, S. Africa
Exports	Perfume oils, vanilla
Imports	Building materials, transportation equipment, rice, clothing, flour

Land

Description	Southeastern African islands
Area	144 mi² (374 km²)
Highest point	Bénara, 2,165 ft (660 m)
Lowest point	Sea level

Alone among the Comoros islands, Mayotte twice voted to remain a French territory. This was in many ways necessitated by the island's poverty: Mayotte relies heavily on France for financial assistance and food.

People

Of Malagasy descent, Mahorais are the main ethnic group on French-ruled Mayotte, and most of the population is Sunni Muslim. French, the official language, is used for commercial affairs, but most Mahorais speak Mahorian, an Arab dialect of Swahili. Both the French and Malagasy cultures have influenced the people of Mayotte.

Economy and the Land

Mayotte's cash crops include ylang-ylang, vanilla, coffee, copra, cinnamon, and cloves. The economy and future development of Mayotte are heavily dependent upon French aid. The territorial collectivity comprises the volcanic island of Mayotte; the small island of Pamanzi; and several other islands. The climate is tropical.

History and Politics

Part of the Comoro archipelago, Mayotte shares much of its early history with the nation of Comoros. The islands served as a link between Madagascar and the African mainland, and Mayotte became a crossroads for invading Africans, Arabs, Indonesians, and Malagasy. In 1843 France took the island of Mayotte, then eventually expanded its control to the other Comoro islands. When Comoros became independent in 1975, Mayotte remained under French rule. In 1976 Mayotte's people again voted to retain their ties with France and not join the independent country of Comoros.

Cardon cactus grow on Baja California. Much of the peninsula is arid, the ideal condition for Mexico's many hundreds of species of cactus.

MEXICO

Mexico has a history far richer than that of any other nation in North America. The Mayan civilization lasted for 2,000 years and erected pyramids which rival those of Egypt. Later, the Aztecs built a complex society centered on what is now Mexico City. Today, most Mexicans are descended from these empires as well as from the Spaniards, who conquered Mexico in the 1500s. As the government strives for closer ties to its neighbors, Mexico's economy and politics remain volatile and cause for popular dissent. *(continued)*

(top) Playa Cerritos, Baja California

(bottom) Pyramid of the Sun, near Mexico City

MEXICO

— Railroad
State Boundary
Oil Pipeline
▲ Major Oil Field
+ Spot Elevation or Depth

Capitals are underlined

City type size indicates relative importance

Scale 1:13,469,000

Meters	Feet
Above 4000	Above 13124
2000	6562
1000	3281
500	1640
200	656
0	Sea Level
0	0
200	656
Below 2000	Below 6562

0 100 200 300 400 km
0 100 200 mi

From the arid plains of the north to the tropical jungles of the south, Mexico is a widely varied land. The center of the country is dominated by high mountains which surround Mexico City and trap the pollution generated by its 14 million inhabitants.

People

Most Mexicans are mestizos, descended from Indians and the Spaniards who conquered Mexico in the 1500s. Spanish is spoken by most inhabitants, and Roman Catholicism is the most popular religion. Another major ethnic group is comprised of indigenous Indians, or Amerindians, some of whom speak only Indian languages and hold traditional religious beliefs. Mexico's rapid population growth has contributed to poverty among rural dwellers, spurring a migration to the cities. Due to its mild climate and fertile soils, Mexico's central plateau is home to most of the population.

Economy and the Land

Mexico is a leading producer of petroleum and silver, a growing manufacturer of iron, steel, and chemicals, and an exporter of coffee and cotton. Foreign visitors—drawn by archeological sites and warm, sunny weather—make tourism an important activity. Despite economic gains made since the mid-1900s in agriculture and industry, Mexico recently has been troubled by inflation, declining oil prices, rising unemployment, and a trade deficit that has grown with the need for imported materials. In recent years the peso has been significantly devalued, and banks have been nationalized to help reduce a massive international debt. Austerity plans and foreign aid are expected to help revitalize the economy. Terrain and climate are greatly varied, ranging from tropical jungles along the coast to desert plains in the north. A temperate central plateau is bounded by rugged mountains in the south, east, and west.

History and Politics

Farm settlements grew in the Valley of Mexico between 6500 and 1500 B.C., and during the subsequent 3,000 years Mexico gave birth to the great civilizations of the Olmec, Maya, Toltec, and Aztec Indians. The Aztec Empire was overthrown by the Spanish in 1521, and Mexico became the viceroyalty of New Spain. Although there was much dissatisfaction with Spanish rule, rebellion did not begin until 1810. Formal independence came in 1821. Mexico lost considerable territory, including Texas, to the United States during the Mexican War, from 1846 to 1848. During subsequent years, power changed hands frequently as liberals demanding social and economic reforms battled conservatives. A brief span of French imperial rule, from 1864 to 1867, interrupted the struggle. Following a revolution that started in 1910, a new socialist constitution was adopted in 1917, and progress toward reform began, culminating in the separation of church and state and the redistribution of land. Mexico joined the U.S. and Canada in approving the North American Free Trade Agreement in 1992. Momentum for political change developed after the January 1994 peasant rebellion in the state of Chiapas.

Mexico at a glance

Official name	United Mexican States

People

Population	93,860,000
Density	124/mi² (48/km²)
Urban	73%
Capital	Mexico City, 8,235,744
Ethnic groups	Mestizo 60%, Amerindian 30%, white 9%
Languages	Spanish, indigenous.
Religions	Roman Catholic 89%, Protestant 6%
Life expectancy	74 female, 67 male
Literacy	87%

Politics

Government	Republic
Parties	Cardenist Front of the Nationalist Reconstruction, Institutional Revolutionary, National Action, others
Suffrage	Universal, over 18
Memberships	OAS, UN
Subdivisions	31 states, 1 federal district

Economy

GDP	$740,000,000,000
Per capita	$8,588
Monetary unit	Peso
Trade partners	Exports: U.S., Japan, Spain Imports: U.S., Germany, Japan
Exports	Petroleum, petroleum products, coffee, shrimp, engines, motor vehicles
Imports	Grain, manufactures, agricultural machinery, electrical equipment

Land

Description	Southern North America
Area	759,534 mi² (1,967,183 km²)
Highest point	Pico de Orizaba, 18,406 ft (5,610 m)
Lowest point	Laguna Salada, -26 ft (-8 m)

The Basilica de Nuestra Senora de Guanajuato and the Templo de la Compania dominate the center of Guanajuato. The scenic city is built on a ravine in central Mexico.

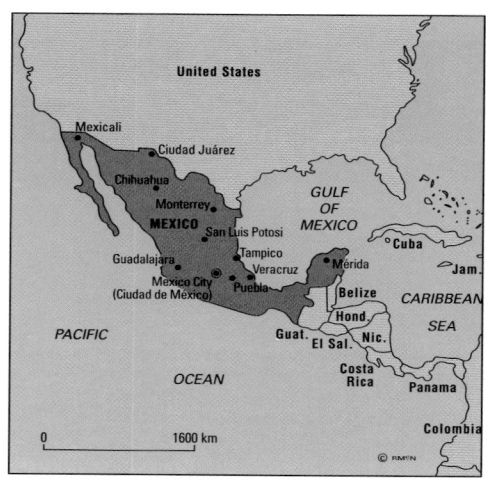

POPULATION COMPARISON
Mexico=36% of U.S.

United States

GDP COMPARISON
Mexico=6% of U.S.

United States

ETHNIC GROUPS

White Other

Amerindian

Mestizo

POPULATION DISTRIBUTION

Urban   Rural

Tabuca Street, Mexico City

Women bargain for pots at the central market of Puebla, the capital of the state of Puebla, in central Mexico.

(left)
Horse-drawn cart, near Mazatlán

(right)
Sailboat, Cancun

The Avenue San Juan de Letran is one of Mexico City's many bustling thoroughfares. The mountains in the distance ring the city.

People

Most inhabitants of Chuuk, Yap, Kosrae, and Pohnpei—the four states of the Federated States of Micronesia—are Micronesian, a group of mixed Melanesian, Polynesian, and Malaysian origin. Eight native languages are spoken, and English is the unifying language.

Economy and the Land

Subsistence farming and fishing are the primary activities for most islanders. Coconuts are the main cash crop. The states are heavily dependent on economic assistance from the United States, which will continue until 2001. Each of the four states comprises a number of islands and, together with the territory of Palau, form the Caroline Islands, made up of volcanic and coral islands. The climate is tropical.

Micronesia at a glance

Official name	Federated States of Micronesia

People

Population	122,000
Density	450/mi² (174/km²)
Urban	19%
Capital	Kolonia, 6,169 (de facto); Paliker (future)
Ethnic groups	Micronesian, Polynesian
Languages	English, indigenous
Religions	Protestant, Roman Catholic
Life expectancy	69 female, 65 male
Literacy	90%

Politics

Government	Republic (U.S. protection)
Parties	None
Suffrage	Universal, over 18
Memberships	UN
Subdivisions	4 states

Economy

GNP	$150,000,000
Per capita	$1,389
Monetary unit	U.S. dollar
Trade partners	U.S., Japan
Exports	Copra, pepper, fish, handicrafts, coconut oil

Land

Description	North Pacific islands
Area	271 mi² (702 km²)
Highest point	Ngihneni, 2,566 ft (782 m)
Lowest point	Sea level

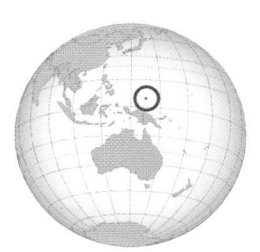

MICRONESIA, FEDERATED STATES OF

History and Politics

The ancestors of today's population probably arrived in the region more than twenty-five hundred years ago. Spanish and German competition for the islands came to an end in 1899, when Germany purchased the Caroline Islands and most of the Mariana Islands from Spain. Japan controlled the islands from World War I until 1947, when the islands became part of the Trust Territory of the Pacific Islands. The trust territory was established by the United Nations and placed under United States administration. In 1978, Chuuk, Yap, Kosrae, and Pohnpei, along with the Marshall Islands and Palau, voted on a constitution that would have united all of Micronesia into a single entity. The Marshall Islands and Palau rejected the proposal, but Chuuk, Yap, Kosrae, and Pohnpei elected to become the Federated States of Micronesia. The United States recognized the Micronesian constitution in 1979, and in 1982 a compact of free association was signed. The compact received final approval in 1986 and the country became self-governing. However, full independence was not achieved until 1991, when the United Nations officially removed the Federated States of Micronesia from trusteeship status. A new capital is planned at Palikir on the island of Pohnpei.

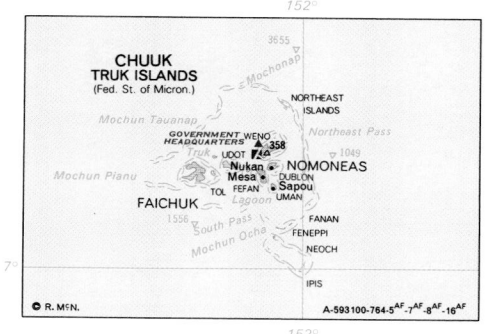

Scale 1:1,000,000 One inch represents approximately 16 miles. One centimeter represents 10 kilometers.

Scale 1:3,000,000 One inch represents approximately 47 miles. One centimeter represents 30 kilometers.

The Federated States of Micronesia consist of two types of islands. Yap and its neighbors were formed by folds in the Earth's crust. The other islands were formed from coral growing atop old ocean-floor volcanoes. This second type of island is common throughout the Pacific.

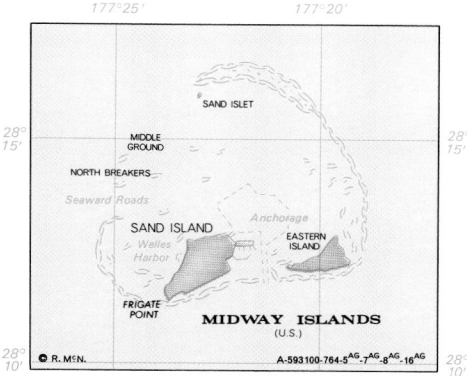

Scale 1:300,000 One inch represents approximately 4.7 miles. One centimeter represents 3 kilometers.

The Midway Islands are home to many large seafaring birds, including the Gooneys, a type of albatross noted for its crash landings.

MIDWAY ISLANDS

People

Midway has no native peoples. In the past United States military personnel and government employees constituted the territory's population. Military facilities were closed in 1993.

Economy and the Land

Since 1993 the military has been engaged in an environmental clean-up in order to turn the islands over to the United States Department of Interior, which will maintain the islands as a wildlife refuge. The bird life protected here includes albatross, frigate birds, and terns. The islands of Midway are situated approximately 1,200 miles (1,931 kilometers) northwest of the U.S. state of Hawaii. The unincorporated territory is made up of a coral atoll that encircles two islands, Sand and Eastern. The climate is tropical.

History and Politics

In 1859 Captain N.C. Brooks of the Hawaiian ship *Gambia* discovered the uninhabited islands, and for a time Midway was known as Brooks Island. Captain William Reynolds was the next American to arrive, and in 1867, sailing on the U.S.S. Lackawana, he claimed Midway as a United States possession. United States president Theodore Roosevelt declared Midway a naval reservation in 1903, and a cable relay station was erected that same year. Development of the islands by the United States continued, and in the 1930s a commercial airport and facilities for housing airplane travelers overnight were built. In 1939 construction workers from the United States began turning Eastern Island into a submarine and air base. By August 1941 their work had been completed; in December of that year the Japanese attacked Midway on their return flight from the bombing of Pearl Harbor. Throughout World War II, the Japanese were unable to capture the islands. From June 4 to June 6, 1942, United States warplanes attacked a Japanese fleet off the shores of Midway. Four of Japan's aircraft carriers and one cruiser were destroyed in the battle, virtually crippling the Japanese navy. Losses on the United States side included an aircraft carrier and a destroyer. This sea-and-air battle became known as the Battle of Midway, and many believe the United States victory at Midway was the turning point of the war in the Pacific. The Midway Islands' political status is that of unincorporated territory of the United States.

Midway Islands at a glance

Official name	Midway Islands

People

Population	500
Density	250/mi² (96/km²)
Capital	None
Ethnic groups	American
Languages	English
Religions	Protestant, Roman Catholic

Politics

Government	Unincorporated territory (U.S.)
Parties	None
Memberships	None

Land

Description	North Pacific islands
Area	2.0 mi² (5.2 km²)
Highest point	12 ft (4 m)
Lowest point	Sea level

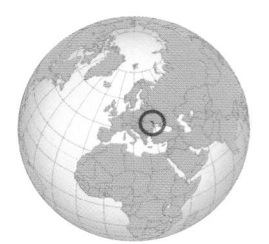

Since independence, Moldova has adopted economic reforms with a fervor unmatched by other former Soviet republics. Its fertile land is the breadbasket of Eastern Europe and ensures the Moldovans a healthy economy based on food exports. Major cash crops include wine grapes, fruits, and vegetables.

MOLDOVA

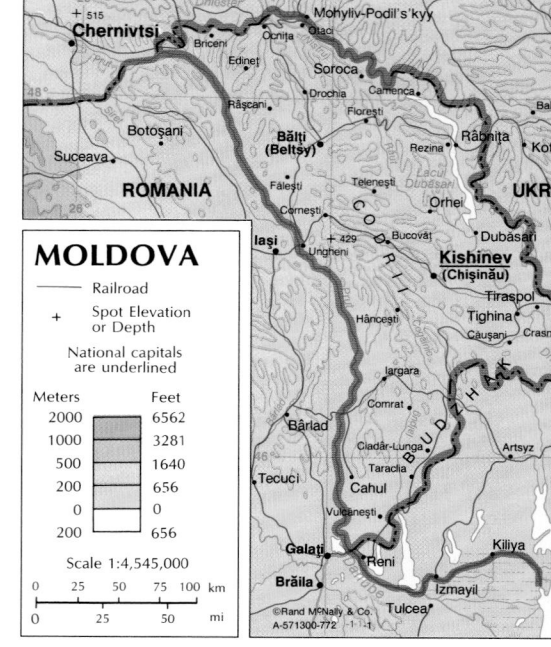

The southern 40 percent of Moldova is highly fertile and is almost entirely farmland. Some 3,000 rivers drain into the Black Sea.

Moldova at a glance

Official name	Republic of Moldova

People

Population	4,377,000
Density	336/mi² (130/km²)
Urban	47%
Capital	Kishinev, 676,700
Ethnic groups	Moldovan 65%, Ukrainian 14%, Russian 13%, Gagauz 4%, Jews 2%
Languages	Romanian (Moldovan), Russian
Religions	Eastern Orthodox 99%
Life expectancy	72 female, 64 male
Literacy	99%

Politics

Government	Republic
Parties	Agrarian Democratic, Christian Democratic Popular Front, Democratic, Democratic Labor, Social Democratic
Suffrage	Universal, over 18
Memberships	UN
Subdivisions	None

Economy

GNP	$16,300,000,000
Per capita	$3,643
Monetary unit	Leu
Trade partners	Former Soviet republics
Exports	Food, wine, tobacco, textiles and footwear, machinery, chemicals
Imports	Oil, gas, coal, machinery, food, automobiles, consumer durables

Land

Description	Eastern Europe, landlocked
Area	13,012 mi² (33,700 km²)
Highest point	Unnamed, 1,407 ft (429 m)
Lowest point	Along Dniester River, 3 ft (1 m)

People

After the Soviet Union wrested Moldova from Romanian control, it claimed that the Moldovans were a distinct ethnic group with their own language. In fact, Moldovans claim Romanian ancestry, and their language is virtually the same as Romanian. Most people also speak Russian, and there are substantial Russian and Ukrainian minorities.

Economy and the Land

Most of Moldova is gently rolling plains, rising to wooded hills in the central part of the country. Much of the land is suitable for agriculture, and wheat, grapes, and other fruits are important crops. Although agriculture and food processing dominate the economy, Moldova also has some light manufacturing. The country has no significant energy resources.

History and Politics.

Formerly known as Bessarabia, this region was ruled by Romanian-speaking Moldovan princes since the 1300s. Bessarabia fell under the control of the Ottoman Turks from the 1600s until 1812, when the Turks were defeated by Russia. In 1918 control went to Romania and the territory was subsequently shifted back and forth between the two countries. In 1944 the Soviet Union defeated Romania and the Moldavian Soviet Socialist Republic was established. Moldovans began agitating for greater autonomy within the Soviet Union as early as 1989. It gained its independence in December 1991, after the demise of the Soviet Union. A new 1994 constitution established Moldova as a neutral republic. A referendum provided for the withdrawal of foreign troops and special status for the Dniester region, occupied by ethnic Russians.

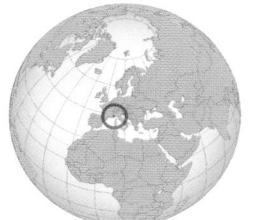

MONACO

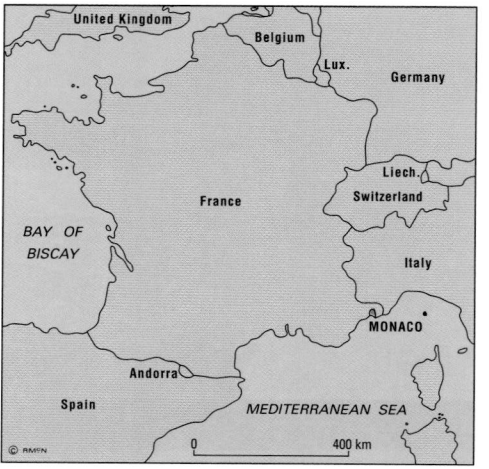

Less than one square mile in size, Monaco is entirely built-up. Luxurious highrises surround the harbor.

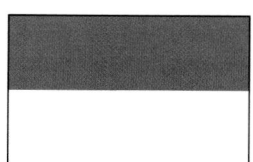

People

Monaco is inhabited mostly by French citizens, while Monegasques—citizens of indigenous descent—and various Europeans form the rest of the population. Many foreigners have taken up residence, drawn by the country's tax benefits. French is the official language. Monegasque, a blend of French and Italian, is also spoken, as are French, Italian, and English. Most residents are Roman Catholic.

Economy and the Land

Monaco's scenic seaside location, mild Mediterranean climate, and renowned gambling casino in Monte Carlo make it a popular tourist haven. Consequently, tourism forms the backbone of the economy. Production of chemicals, food products, and perfumes, among other light industries, are additional sources of income. Monaco also profits from many foreign businesses, which are attracted by the favorable tax climate and headquartered in the principality. France and Monaco form a customs union

for a mutually beneficial trade system; the French franc is Monaco's official currency. The world's second smallest independent state in area—after Vatican City—Monaco has four regions: the old city of Monaco-Ville, site of the royal palace; Monte Carlo, the resort and major tourist center; La Condamine, the port area; and Fontvieille, the rapidly growing industrial section.

History and Politics

Known to the Phoenicians, Greeks, and Romans, the region became a Genoese colony in the twelfth century A.D. Around the turn of the fourteenth century, the area was granted to the Grimaldi family of Genoa. France, Spain, and Sardinia had intermittent control of Monaco from 1400 until 1861, when its autonomy was recognized by the Franco-Monegasque Treaty. Another treaty, providing for French protection of Monaco, was signed in 1918. The absolute rule of Monaco's princes ended with the 1911 constitution. Monaco joined the United Nations in 1993.

Monaco at a glance

Official name	Principality of Monaco

People

Population	31,000
Density	44,286/mi² (16,316/km²)
Urban	100%
Capital	Monaco, 31,000
Ethnic groups	French 47%, Monegasque 16%, Italian 16%, English 4%, Belgian 2%, Swiss 1%
Languages	French, English, Italian, Monegasque
Religions	Roman Catholic 95%
Life expectancy	81 female, 74 male

Politics

Government	Constitutional monarchy
Parties	Action, Democractic Union Movement, National and Democratic Union, Socialist
Suffrage	Universal, over 25
Memberships	UN
Subdivisions	3 communes

Economy

GDP	$475,000,000
Per capita	$16,379
Monetary unit	French franc

Land

Description	Southern Europe (on the southeastern coast of France)
Area	0.7 mi² (1.9 km²)
Highest point	Unnamed, 459 ft (140 m)
Lowest point	Sea level

MONGOLIA

Mongolia is one of the world's oldest countries. Life for its people has changed little since the country was at the zenith of its political power in the 13th century. Most Mongolians survive the harsh climate by raising livestock in widely scattered settlements. Mongolia has the world's highest ratio of livestock to people—animals outnumber humans fifteen to one.

An encampment of nomads on the windswept plain near the Mongolian capital of Ulan Bator. The nomads take shelter in yurts, the traditional tents of Central Asia. Made of leather skins stretched over a collapsible wood frame, yurts are easily moved, but are very strong in the face of the region's harsh weather.

Schoolchildren, Ulan Bator

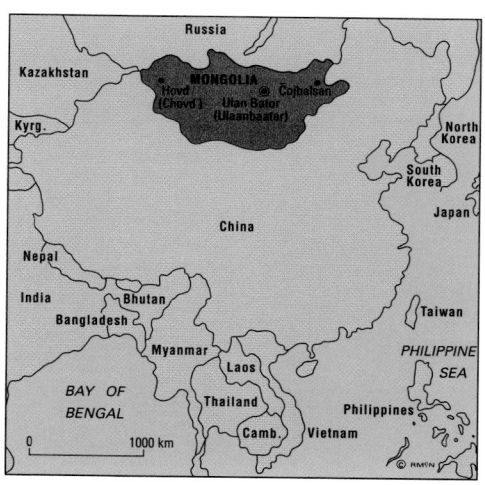

Mongolia at a glance

Official name Mongolia

People

Population	2,462,000
Density	4.1/mi² (1.6/km²)
Urban	58%
Capital	Ulan Bator, 575,000
Ethnic groups	Mongol 90%, Kazakh 4%, Chinese 2%, Russian 2%
Languages	Khalkha Mongol, Turkish dialects, Russian, Chinese
Religions	Shamanic, Tibetan Buddhist, Muslim
Life expectancy	65 female, 62 male
Literacy	90%

Politics

Government	Republic
Parties	Democratic, National Progress, National Renaissance, People's Revolutionary, Social Democratic
Suffrage	Universal, over 18
Memberships	UN
Subdivisions	18 provinces, 3 municipalities

Economy

GDP	$2,800,000,000
Per capita	$1,199
Monetary unit	Tughrik
Trade partners	Exports: Former Soviet republics, China, Japan
	Imports: Former Soviet republics, Austria, China
Exports	Copper, livestock, animal products, cashmere, wool, hides
Imports	Machinery, fuel, food, consumer goods, chemicals, building materials

Land

Description	Central Asia, landlocked
Area	604,829 mi² (1,566,500 km²)
Highest point	Kuyten-Uul, 14,350 ft (4,374 m)
Lowest point	Höh Lake, 1,814 ft (553 m)

People

Mongols, a central Asian people, make up the vast majority of Mongolia's population. Khalkha Mongol is the predominant language. Turkic-speaking Kazakhs, as well as Russians and Chinese, comprise minorities. Tibetan Buddhism was once the most common religion; however, during the years of communist rule the government discouraged religious practice. The traditional nomadic way of life is becoming less common, as recent government policies have led to urbanization and settled agriculture.

Economy and the Land

Mongolia's economy, long based on the raising of livestock, has been shaped by the ideal grazing land found in most of the country. Livestock outnumber people in Mongolia by a ratio of fifteen to one. Significant economic changes have taken place since the collapse of the Soviet economy, because 90% of Mongolia's trade was with Russia and Eastern Europe. Market reform during the current transition period has produced great economic hardship. Mongolia's terrain varies from mountains in the north and west to steppe in the east and desert in the south. Located in the heart of Asia, remote from any moderating body of water, Mongolia has a rigorous continental climate with little precipitation.

History and Politics

Mongolian tribes were united under the warlord Genghis Khan around A.D. 1200, and he and his successors built one of history's largest land empires. In 1691 the Manchu dynasty of China subdued Outer Mongolia, as the area was then known, but allowed the Mongol rulers autonomy. Until the Mongols ousted the Chinese in 1911, Outer Mongolia remained a Chinese province. In 1912 the state accepted Russian protection but was unable to prevent a subsequent Chinese advance, and in 1919 Outer Mongolia again became a Chinese province. In 1921 a combined Soviet and Mongolian force defeated Chinese and Belorussian, or White Russian, troops, and the Mongolian People's Republic was declared in 1924. A mutual-assistance pact was signed by Mongolia and Russia in 1966. In 1989 the Soviets agreed to withdraw most of their troops from Mongolia. Increasing pressure for democratization led to the country's first free, multiparty elections in August 1990. A new constitution, describing Mongolia as a republic with parliamentary government, was adopted in 1992.

POPULATION COMPARISON
Mongolia=0.9% of U.S.

United States

GDP COMPARISON
Mongolia=0.04% of U.S.

United States

ETHNIC GROUPS
Russian
Chinese   Other
Kazakh

Mongol

POPULATION DISTRIBUTION
Urban   Rural

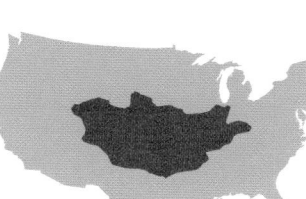

Mongolia's arid land swallows its few rivers and streams. Most disappear into salt lakes, marshes, or desert sand.

Once a pleasant Caribbean island with a budding tourism industry, Montserrat has been devastated since 1995 by eruptions of the Soufriere Hills volcano. The island's remaining residents now live in crowded conditions on the northern part of the island.

MONTSERRAT

Stone tower on historic Galway's Plantation

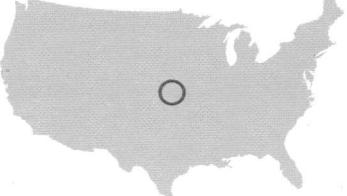

Smoke and ash billow from the Soufriere Hills volcano. A short distance away lies Plymouth, Montserrat's capital.

This photo shows one of Montserrat's few beaches prior to the 1995 volcanic eruption. Tourism, as well as light industry, had begun to replace traditional economic pursuits such as fishing. Today, with much of the island covered in ash and mud, the economy is in shambles.

People

Most of Montserrat's people are black descendants of African slaves, nearly all are English speaking, and the majority belong to the Anglican church. A number of the island's early settlers were Irish, and traces of an Irish brogue can still be heard in the speech of some residents. The culture, however, is distinctly West Indian.

Economy and the Land

The late 1970s and early 1980s saw an influx of light industry to Montserrat, with companies taking advantage of the island's tax benefits. Until recently, agriculture had been on the decline, but emphasis on the production of Sea Island cotton and vegetable crops helped to revive that sector somewhat. Tourism is an important economic contributor, yet the island remains unspoiled by commercialism. The volcanic island of Montserrat is rugged and mountainous, and climate is tropical.

History and Politics

Christopher Columbus reached the island in 1493, naming it after the Spanish monastery of Santa Maria de Montserrat. In 1632 British and Irish settlers arrived from St. Christopher, and later in the seventeenth century many more Irish immigrants came to Montserrat via Virginia. Sugar cultivation began in 1650, and Africans were bought as slaves to work on the plantations. In 1664 the French took the island, and the British were not able to regain control until four years later. In 1782 France again overpowered the British for possession of Montserrat, but it returned to British rule the next year. Slavery was ended in 1834, and the island's sugar, lime, and cotton industries declined soon after. In 1966 Montserrat residents chose to remain a colony rather than become an associate state of the United Kingdom. Although some islanders desire independence, most seem to prefer colonial status. In 1995 the Soufriere Hills volcano began to erupt, forcing the evacuation of Plymouth, the capital city. Since then, about 9,000 Montserratians have fled the island. The remaining residents have criticized the British government's relief effort as inadequate.

POPULATION COMPARISON
Montserrat=0.005% of U.S.

United States

GDP COMPARISON
Montserrat=0.001% of U.S.

United States

ETHNIC GROUPS

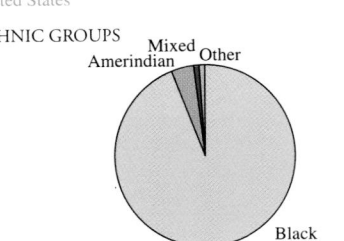

Mixed Other
Amerindian

Black

POPULATION DISTRIBUTION

Urban   Rural

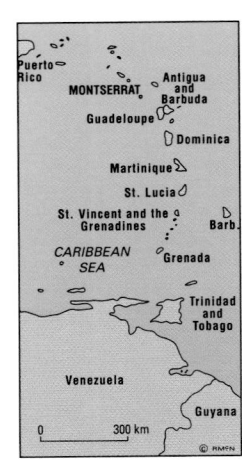

Montserrat's central location in the Leeward Islands puts it squarely on the seasonal hurricane path. It regularly suffers severe storm damage.

Tinerhir is a typical village of mud-brick buildings in the Todra Valley in Morocco's interior. The river banks are lined with palm and date plantations.

MOROCCO

Moroccan cities team with life and energy. The medinas—old Arabic trading quarters—are vast labyrinths that have been centers of trading and commerce for centuries. In Marrakech, tourists mingle with Berber tribesmen bringing their camels to market after long desert journeys. Morocco's countryside is a mix of rugged mountains, shifting sands, and fertile regions of citrus orchards.

People

Moroccans, virtually homogeneous in race and culture, are mostly a mix of Arab and Berber stocks and speak Arabic. A few Berber dialects are spoken in rural mountain areas, and French and Spanish, the colonial tongues, are common in business and government. The majority of people are Sunni Muslim. The population is concentrated west of the Atlas Mountains, which border the Sahara Desert. Rural people are migrating to cities, where the standard of living is higher.

Economy and the Land

Although agriculture employs much of the workforce and is an important activity, the nation depends on mining for most of its income. Morocco is a leading exporter of phosphates, but has other mineral reserves

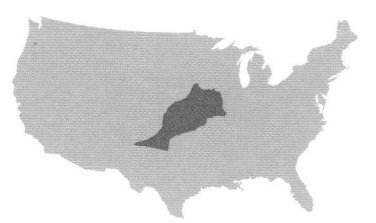

as well. Fishing and tourism are growing sources of revenue. Recently, severe drought, rising dependency on imported oil, and a costly war in Western Sahara have slowed productivity, while investments by Arab countries have bolstered the economy. Morocco, with its varied terrain of desert, forests, and mountains, has an equally varied climate that is semitropical along the coast, and desert beyond the Atlas Mountains.

History and Politics

In ancient times, Morocco was a province of Carthage and Rome. Vandals and Byzantine Greeks, the subsequent rulers, were followed in the A.D. 700s by Arabs, who brought Islam. Morocco's strategic position awakened the interest of colonial powers in the 1800s, and by 1912 the area was divided into French and Spanish protectorates. A nationalist movement began in the 1920s, occasionally bringing violence, but not until 1956 did Morocco become independent from France. The last of Spain's holdings in Morocco were returned in 1969. War broke out in

1976, when Morocco claimed the northern part of Western Sahara and was challenged by the Saharan nationalist Polisario Front. Mauritania surrendered its claim in 1979 and Morocco quickly established claim to the entire territory. Negotiations over the final disposition of Western Sahara have been sporadic. King Hassan shares power with directly elected groups under a complex formula.

Sand dunes, Sahara Desert

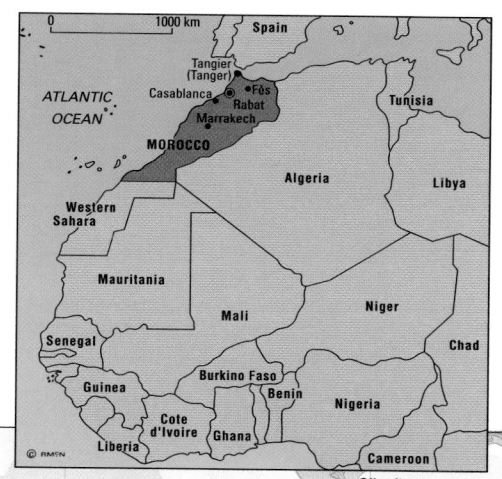

Morocco at a glance

Official name Kingdom of Morocco

People

Population	26,890,000
Density	156/mi² (60/km²)
Urban	46%
Capital	Rabat, 518,616
Ethnic groups	Arab-Berber 99%
Languages	Arabic, Berber dialects, French
Religions	Muslim 99%
Life expectancy	65 female, 62 male
Literacy	50%

Politics

Government	Constitutional monarchy
Parties	Constitutional Union, Istiqlal, Popular Movement, Socialist Union of Popular Forces, others
Suffrage	Universal, over 21
Memberships	AL, UN
Subdivisions	36 provinces, 2 prefectures

Economy

GDP	$70,300,000,000
Per capita	$2,603
Monetary unit	Dirham
Trade partners	Exports: France, Spain, Italy Imports: France, Spain, Iraq
Exports	Food, manufactures, phosphates
Imports	Machinery, manufactures, raw materials, fuel, food

Land

Description	Northwestern Africa
Area	172,414 mi² (446,550 km²)
Highest point	Mt. Toubkal, 13,665 ft (4,165 m)
Lowest point	Sebkha Tah, -180 ft (-55 m)

The above information excludes Western Sahara.

Until the middle part of this century, much of Morocco's northern coast belonged to Spain. Today only two Spanish enclaves remain: Ceuta and Melilla.

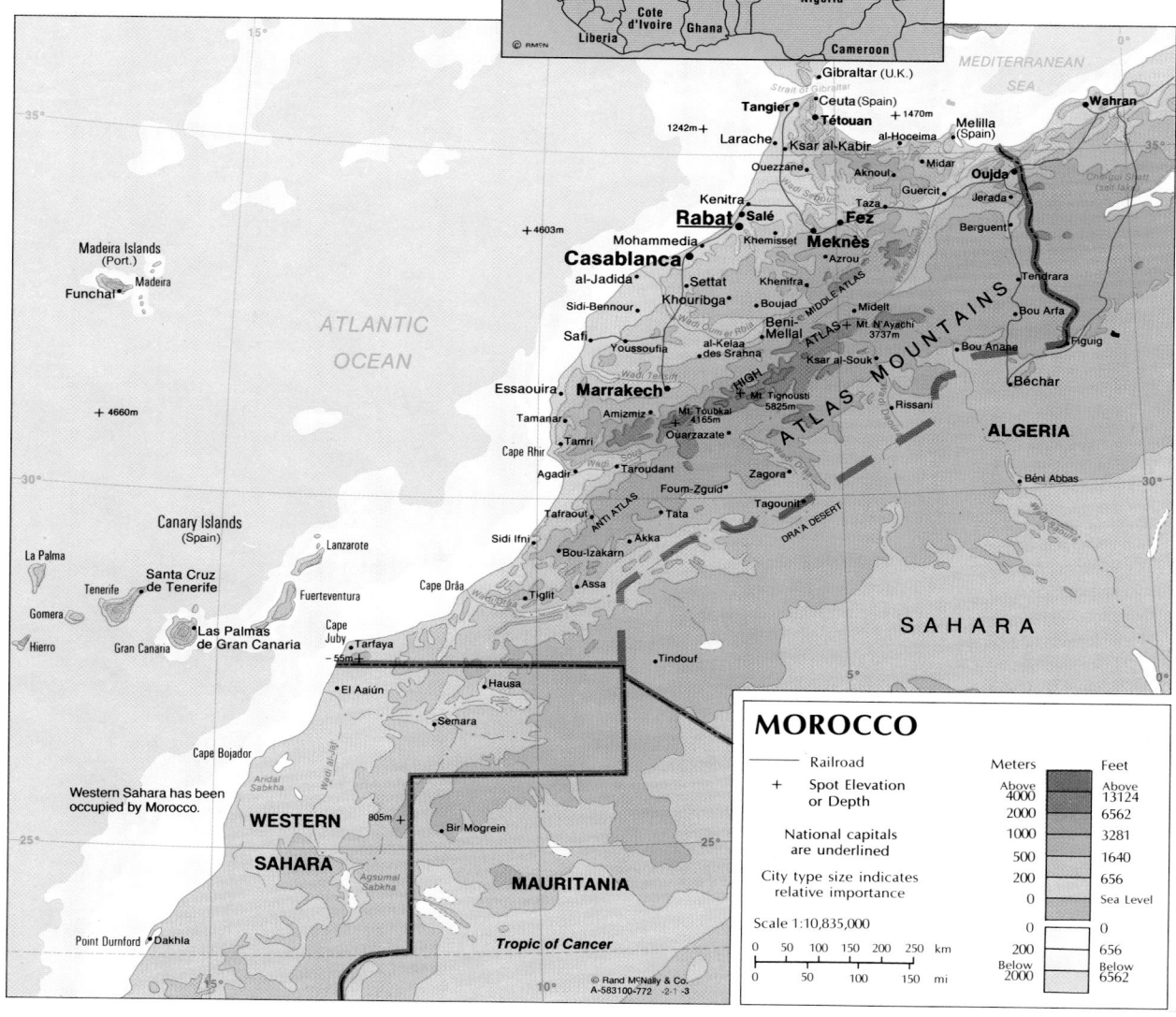

MOROCCO

		Meters	Feet
Railroad		Above 4000	Above 13124
+ Spot Elevation or Depth		2000	6562
		1000	3281
National capitals are underlined		500	1640
		200	656
City type size indicates relative importance		0	Sea Level
Scale 1:10,835,000		0	0
0 50 100 150 200 250 km		200	656
0 50 100 150 mi		Below 2000	Below 6562

Western Sahara has been occupied by Morocco.

© Rand McNally & Co.
A-563100-772 3-1-3

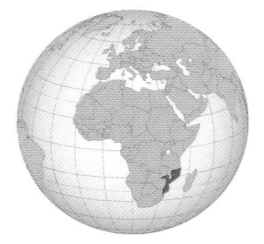

(left) Mozambican boy

(right) Children play in marshes near the coastal town of Quelimane. Much of Mozambique's coast is marshy; the weather is generally hot and humid.

MOZAMBIQUE

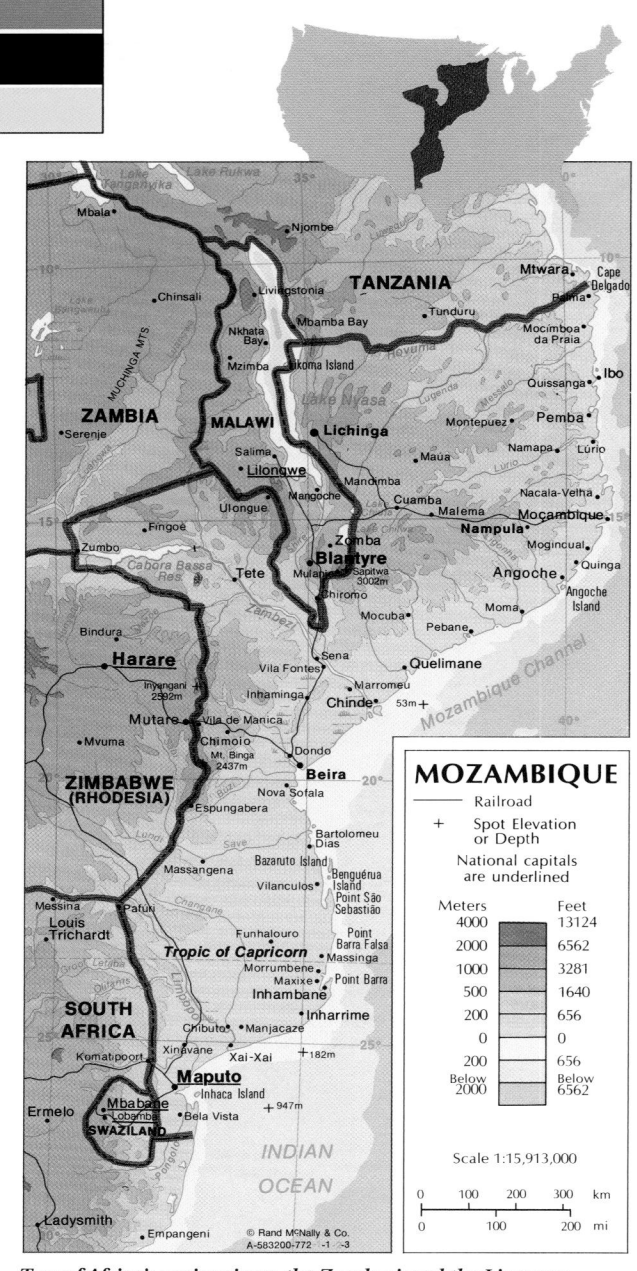

MOZAMBIQUE

— Railroad
+ Spot Elevation or Depth

National capitals are underlined

Meters		Feet
4000		13124
2000		6562
1000		3281
500		1640
200		656
0		0
200		656
Below 2000		Below 6562

Scale 1:15,913,000

0 100 200 300 km
0 100 200 mi

© Rand McNally & Co.
A-583200-772 -1 -3

Two of Africa's major rivers, the Zambezi and the Limpopo, flow through Mozambique.

Refugees from Mozambique's civil war struggle with their day-to-day existence in a camp along the border with Zimbabwe. Over two million people fled the fighting which tore through the country in the early 1990s.

Mozambique's many economic resources, including agriculture, hydropower, and transportation, were squandered during a horrific civil war in the 1980s. A drought made life even worse for most Mozambicans. Any government elected after the recent tentative steps to democracy faces enormous difficulties restoring Mozambique's health.

People

Black Africans belonging to about ten groups compose the vast majority of the population. Most black Mozambicans live in rural areas, while small European and Asian minorities live primarily in urban centers. Traditional African religions are followed by a majority, while others practice Islam and Christianity. Although Portuguese is the official language, most blacks speak Bantu tongues.

Economy and the Land

Mozambique's underdeveloped economy is largely the product of its colonial past, during which its human and natural resources were neglected. Recent political developments in southern Africa have created more economic woes, as lucrative trade agreements with racially divided neighbors have ceased. While the mainstays of the economy are agriculture and transport services, fishing and mining are also being developed. The Marxist government allowed some private enterprise, and foreign aid is important. The climate is tropical or subtropical along the coastal plain that covers nearly half of the country, with cooler conditions in the western high plateaus and mountains.

History and Politics

Bantu-speaking peoples settled in present-day Mozambique around the first century A.D. Subsequent immigrants included Arab traders in the 800s and the Portuguese in the late 1400s. European economic interest in the area was hindered by lucrative trading with other colonies, and Mozambique wasn't recognized as a Portuguese colony until 1885. Policies instituted by the Portuguese benefited European settlers and Portugal, but overlooked the welfare of Mozambique and its native inhabitants. In the early 1960s the country made clear its opposition to foreign rule, with the formation of the Front for the Liberation of Mozambique, a Marxist nationalist group that initiated an armed campaign against the Portuguese. In 1975 Mozambique became an independent state, but fighting between the socialist government and opposition forces continued. A new constitution passed in 1990 marked the end of single-party rule in Mozambique. The civil war, resulting in a million casualties and nearly two million refugees, finally ended in October 1992. A fragile peace and the return of over one million refugees was complicated by the worst drought of the century. The country's first multiparty elections were held in October 1994.

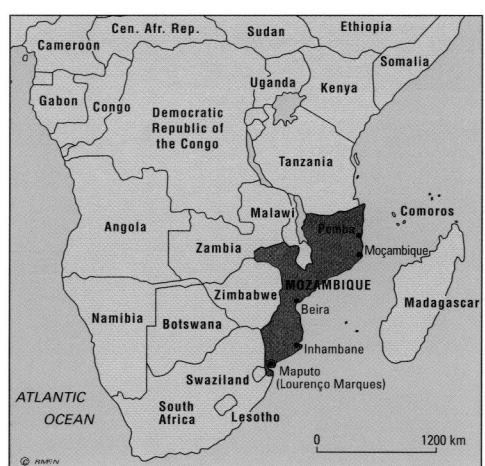

POPULATION COMPARISON
Mozambique=7% of U.S.

United States

GDP COMPARISON
Mozambique=0.2% of U.S.

United States

POPULATION DISTRIBUTION
Urban   Rural

Mozambique at a glance

Official name	Republic of Mozambique

People

Population	17,860,000
Density	58/mi² (22/km²)
Urban	27%
Capital	Maputo, 1,069,727
Ethnic groups	Makua, Lomwe, Thonga, others
Languages	Portuguese, indigenous.
Religions	Tribal religionist 60%, Roman Catholic and other Christian 30%, Muslim
Life expectancy	48 female, 45 male
Literacy	33%

Politics

Government	Republic
Parties	Front for the Liberation of Mozambique, others
Suffrage	Universal, over 18
Memberships	OAU, UN
Subdivisions	10 provinces, 1 independent city

Economy

GDP	$9,800,000,000
Per capita	$620
Monetary unit	Metical
Trade partners	Exports: U.S., Germany, Japan Imports: Former Soviet republics, South African countries, Portugal
Exports	Cashews, sugar, copra, fruit
Imports	Food, clothing, farm equipment, petroleum

Land

Description	Southern Africa
Area	308,642 mi² (799,380 km²)
Highest point	Mt. Binga, 7,995 ft (2,437 m)
Lowest point	Sea level

Myanmar at a glance

Official name   Union of Myanmar

People

Population	44,675,000
Density	171/mi² (66/km²)
Urban	25%
Capital	Yangon (Rangoon), 2,513,023
Ethnic groups	Bamar (Burmese) 69%, Shan 9%, Kayin 6%, Rakhine 5%
Languages	Burmese, indigenous
Religions	Buddhist 89%, Muslim 4%, Christian 4%
Life expectancy	59 female, 56 male
Literacy	81%

Politics

Governement	Provisional military government
Parties	National League for Democracy, National Unity Party, others
Suffrage	Universal, over 18
Memberships	UN
Subdivisions	7 divisions, 7 states

Economy

GDP	$41,000,000,000
Per capita	$952
Monetary unit	Kyat
Trade partners	Exports: Southeast Asian countries, India, Japan Imports: Japan, Western European countries, China
Exports	Teak, rice, oilseed, metals, rubber, gems
Imports	Machinery and transportation equipment, chemicals, food

Land

Description	Southeastern Asia
Area	261,228 mi² (676,577 km²)
Highest point	Mt. Hkakabo, 19,296 ft (5,881 m)
Lowest point	Sea level

People

The population of Myanmar is highly diverse, with many ethnic groups including Tibetan-related Bamar, who compose the majority; Kayin, who inhabit mainly the south and east; and Thai-related Shan, found on the eastern plateaus. Diversity results in many languages, although Burmese predominates. Buddhist monasteries and pagodas dot the landscape, and minority religions include Christianity, indigenous beliefs, and Islam. The primarily rural population is concentrated in the fertile valleys and on the delta of the Irrawaddy River.

Economy and the Land

Fertile soils, dense woodlands, and mineral deposits provide a resource base for agriculture, forestry, and mining. Myanmar has been beset with economic problems, however, caused mainly by the destruction of World War II, as well as post-independence instability. Today agriculture continues as the economic mainstay. The hot, wet climate is ideal for rice production. In addition, dense forests provide for a timber industry, and resource deposits include petroleum and various minerals. Myanmar's economic future most likely depends on exploitation of natural resources and political stability. The terrain is marked by mountains, rivers, and forests, and the climate is tropical.

History and Politics

Myanmar's Chinese and Tibetan settlers were first united in the eleventh century. Independence ended with the invasion of Mongols led by Kublai Khan, followed by national unification in the fifteenth and eighteenth centuries. Annexation to British

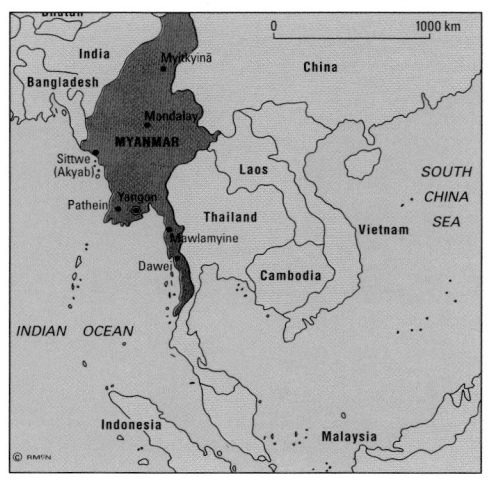

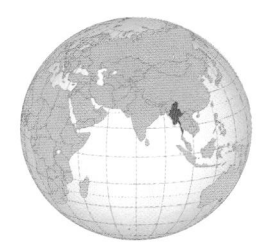

Houses are built above marshes in Shwenyaung, a water-rich town near scenic Inle Lake in central Myanmar. Some nearby villages are built on pontoons and are entirely afloat.

MYANMAR

Long known to English speakers as Burma, Myanmar was until recently one of the world's most politically isolated countries. The few visitors allowed in found an undeveloped country that seemed to be living in the past. The government is somewhat more liberal now. Like many Third World countries that are rich in cultural heritage and natural beauty, Myanmar is pinning much of its future economic hope on developing tourism.

India in the nineteenth century ended Myanmar's monarchy. During World War II, Japanese occupation and subsequent Allied-Japanese conflicts caused much economic and physical damage. Myanmar officially became independent in 1948. After initial stability, the government was unable to withstand separatist and political revolts, and military rule has alternated with civilian governments. The latest attempts to reestablish democracy were thwarted when the results of elections in 1990 were contested by ninety-three opposition parties. The military government refused to relinquish control or hold new elections. The 1991 Nobel Peace Prize award to the country's main opposition leader, Aung San Suu Kyi, focused world attention on continued human rights abuses. Reforms were enacted in 1992 to appease public opinion, but reports of abuses continue.

POPULATION COMPARISON
Myanmar=17% of U.S.

United States

GDP COMPARISON
Myanmar=0.6% of U.S.

United States

ETHNIC GROUPS

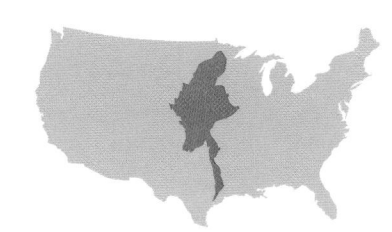

Other, Rakhine, Kayin, Shan, Bamar (Burmese)

POPULATION DISTRIBUTION
Urban   Rural

Away from the capital of Yangon, large portions of Myanmar are under the control of rebel forces who are illegally clear-cutting the once-vast hardwood forests. The timber is smuggled to buyers in Thailand.

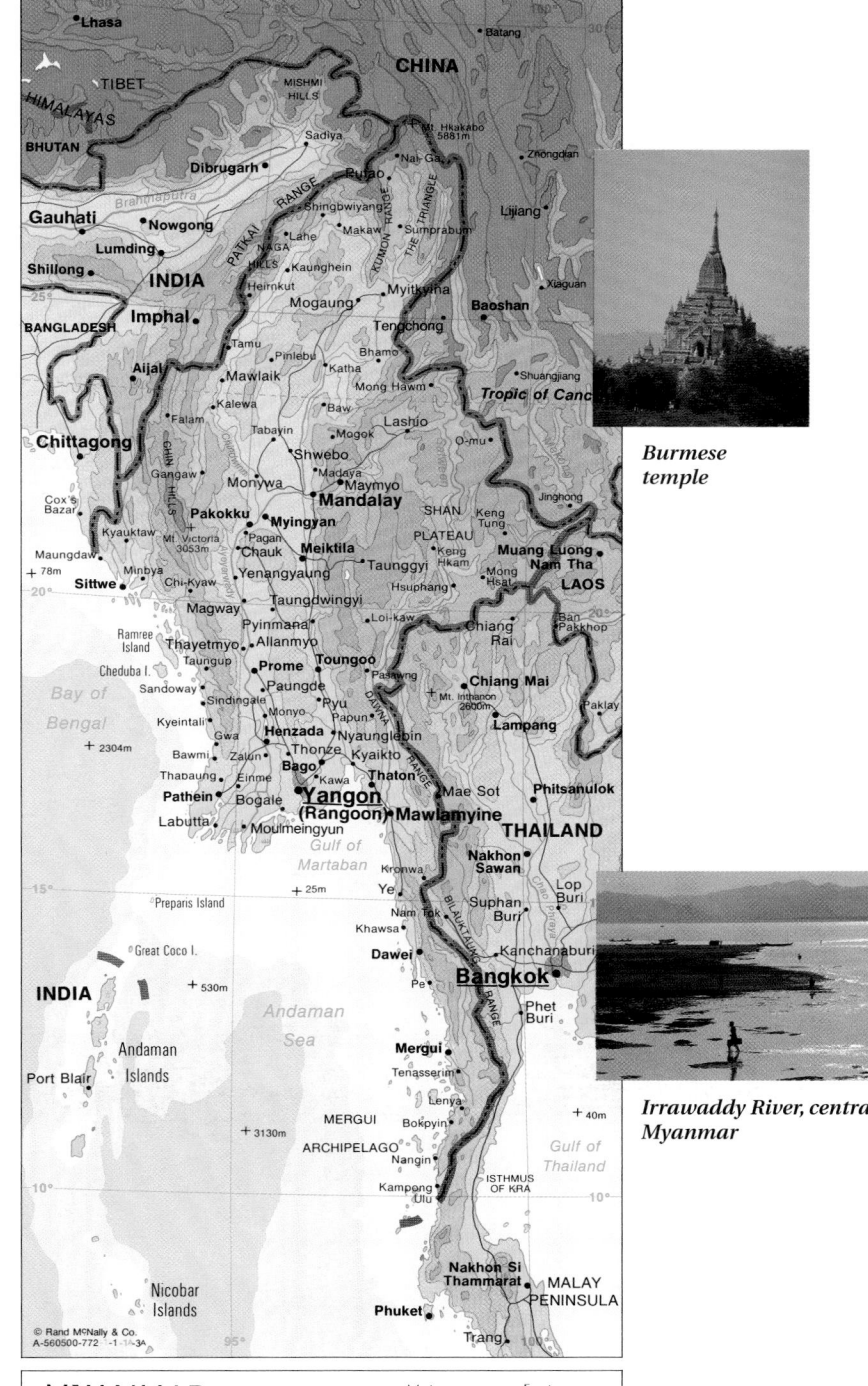

Burmese temple

Irrawaddy River, central Myanmar

MYANMAR

	Meters	Feet
Major Urban Area	Above 4000	Above 13124
Railroad	2000	6562
	1000	3281
Spot Elevation or Depth	500	1640
	200	656
National capitals are underlined	0	0
	200	656
Scale 1:13,888,000	Below 2000	Below 6562

0 100 200 300 400 km
0 100 200 mi

NAMIBIA

Himba tribespeople, Kaukauveld

Namibia at a glance

Official name Republic of Namibia

People

Population	1,623,000
Density	5.1/mi² (2.0/km²)
Urban	28%
Capital	Windhoek, 114,500.
Ethnic groups	Ovambo 49%, Kavango 9%, Damara 8%, Herero 7%, white 7%, mixed 7%
Languages	English, Afrikaans, German, indigenous
Religions	Lutheran and other Protestant, Roman Catholic, Animist
Life expectancy	60 female, 58 male
Literacy	38%

Politics

Government	Republic
Parties	Democratic Turnhalle Alliance, South West Africa People's Organization, United Democratic Front, others
Suffrage	Universal, over 18
Memberships	CW, OAU, UN
Subdivisions	13 regions

Economy

GDP	$3,850,000,000
Per capita	$2,402
Monetary unit	South African rand
Trade partners	Exports: Switzerland, South Africa, Germany Imports: South Africa, Germany, U.S.
Exports	Uranium, diamonds, zinc, copper, meat, fish
Imports	Food, petroleum and fuel, machinery and equipment

Land

Description	Southern Africa
Area	318,253 mi² (824,272 km²)
Highest point	Brandberg, 8,461 ft (2,579 m)
Lowest point	Sea level

Namibia is emerging as an independent nation after years of interference in its internal affairs by Angola and South Africa. It has some of the richest diamond mines in the world, but the wealth they produce has not found its way to Namibia's impoverished people.

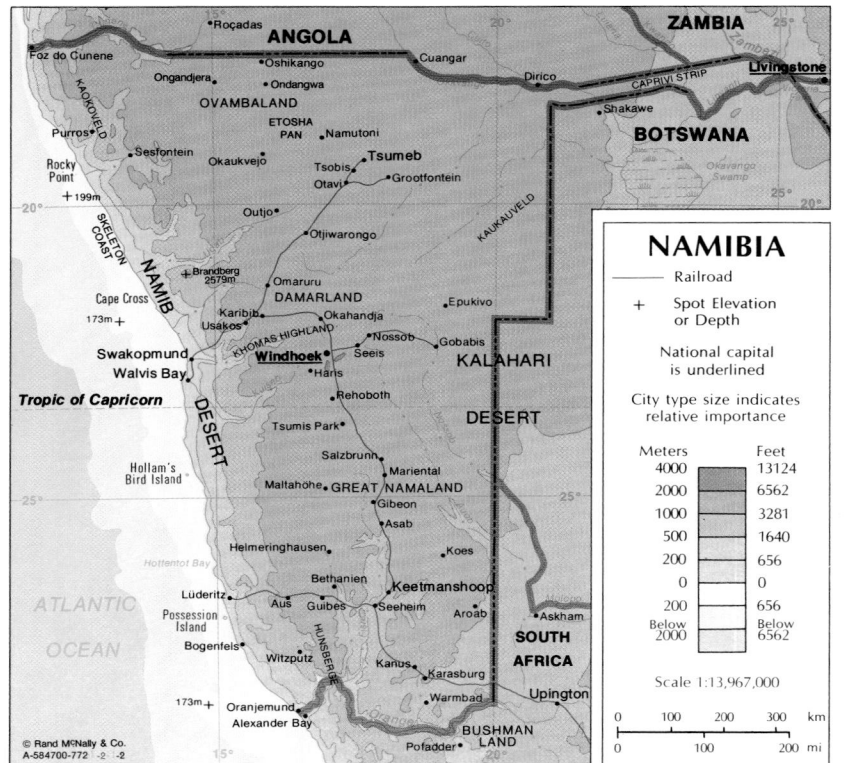

The forbidding Namib Desert along Namibia's coast kept the European colonial powers at bay until the late 19th century.

People
The largest ethnic group is black African, composed of many indigenous peoples. South Africans, Britons, and Germans constitute the white minority. Black Namibians speak various native dialects, while the majority of whites speak Afrikaans. Blacks still follow traditional customs and religions, but a considerable number have converted to Christianity.

Economy and the Land
Namibia's economy is based on the mining of diamonds, copper, lead, and other minerals. Agriculture makes a marginal contribution, but livestock raising is important. Manufacturing remains undeveloped because of an unskilled work force, and Namibia imports most of its finished goods from South Africa, its partner in a customs union. A variety of factors, including continuing drought and political instability, have held back economic growth. Namibia consists of a high plateau that encompasses the Namib Desert and part of the Kalahari Desert. The climate is subtropical.

History and Politics
Bushmen were probably the area's first inhabitants, followed by other African peoples. European exploration of the coast began in the A.D. 1500s, but the coastal desert prevented foreign penetration. In 1884 Germany annexed all of the territory except for the coastal enclave of Walvis Bay, which had been claimed by Britain in 1878. After South African troops ousted the Germans from the area during World War I, the League of Nations mandated Namibia, then known as South West Africa, to South Africa. Following World War II, the United Nations requested that the territory become a trusteeship. South Africa refused

to cooperate. In 1966 the United Nations revoked South Africa's mandate, yet South Africa kept control of Namibia. Beginning in the 1960s, the South West Africa People's Organization (SWAPO), a Namibian nationalist group with Communist support, made guerrilla raids on South African forces from bases in Zambia and later from Angola. In 1989, after years of continued pressure, an assembly was elected to draft a constitution. Independence was achieved in 1990. In 1994, Namibia's first post-independence election resulted in a major victory for SWAPO.

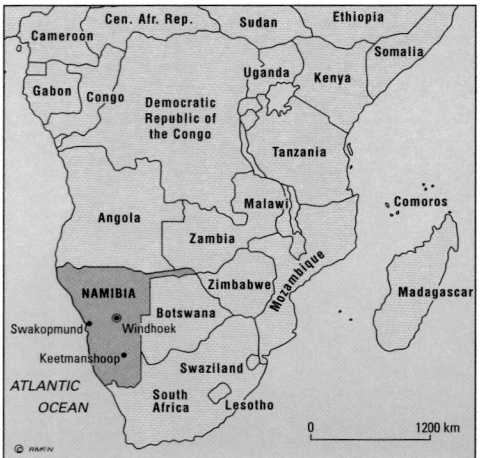

POPULATION COMPARISON
Namibia=0.6% of U.S.

United States

GDP COMPARISON
Namibia=0.06% of U.S.

United States

ETHNIC GROUPS

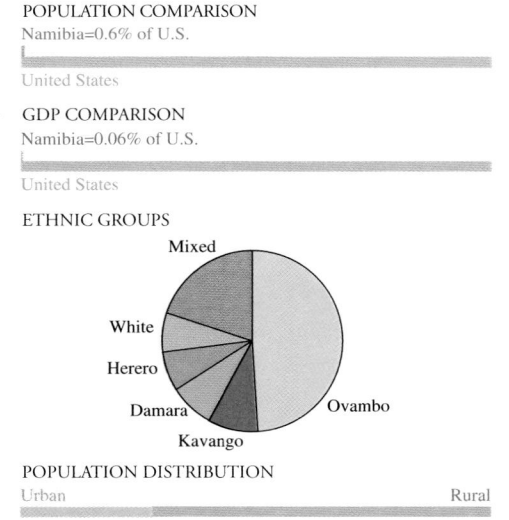

Mixed

White

Herero

Damara

Kavango

Ovambo

POPULATION DISTRIBUTION
Urban   Rural

Sand dunes dominate the land at Sossusvlei in Namibia's Namib-Naukluft Park. At 1,000 feet, the dunes are thought to be the world's tallest. During the rainy season, the plain surrounded by the dunes becomes a fresh-water lake.

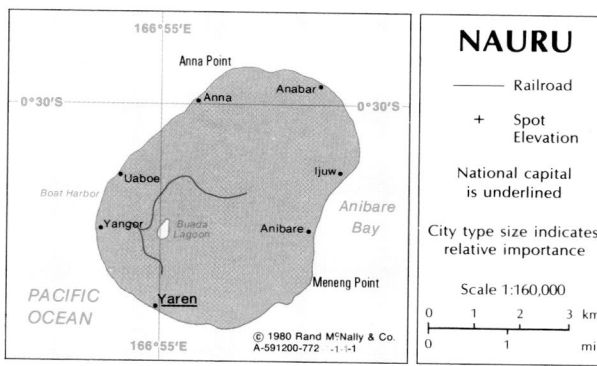

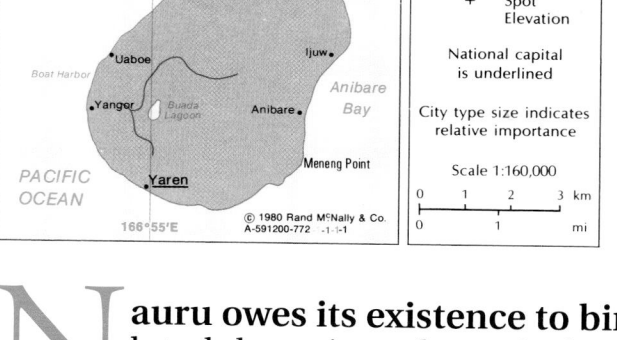

The smallest republic in the world, Nauru imports virtually everything its people need, including drinking water.

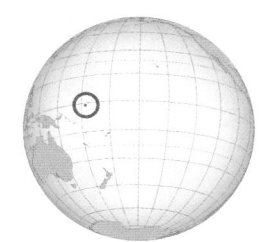

NAURU

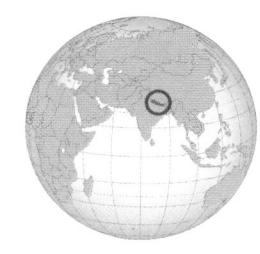

Nauru owes its existence to birds, whose accumulated droppings through the millennia formed the island. Mining the resulting rich phosphate deposits has given Nauruans one of the highest per capita incomes of any country in the world. It is thought that mining will cease to be economically viable by the year 2000, and Nauru faces many questions about its future.

People
Indigenous Nauruans are a mix of Polynesian, Micronesian, and Melanesian stock, and many residents are from other Pacific islands. Nauruan is the language of most inhabitants, but English is widely spoken. Nearly all Nauruans are Christian.

Economy and the Land
The economy depends primarily on its sole resource, phosphates; the government is establishing trust funds to support islanders when the resource is depleted. Mining has destroyed 80 percent of the island; with agriculture limited, the country must import nearly all of its food. Nauru is one of the smallest countries in the world. Most of the coral island is a plateau, and the climate is tropical.

History and Politics
Nauru was most likely settled by castaways from nearby islands. Noted by a British explorer in 1798, Nauru remained autonomous until it came under German control in 1881. In 1914 Germany surrendered the island, and it was subsequently mandated to Australia, Britain, and New Zealand. World War II brought occupation by Japan. Nauru reverted to Australian rule in 1947 as a trusteeship. It became independent in 1968 and gained control of European interests in the phosphate industry in 1970. The country is preparing for the near future when phosphate is gone and the people must develop a new economy and restore the land.

NEPAL

Annapurna, a 26,504-foot Himalayan peak that is the world's 11th highest, looms above a traditional thatched-roof Nepalese house.

Nepal is a mysterious land, and the people living among its peaks generally shun foreign contact. The capital, Kathmandu, is exotic and medieval, dominated by a Hindu monastery high on a hillside. Forty percent of the people are undernourished, and literacy and life expectancy are both low. Tourism plays an increasing role as the government seeks to boost the economy. Visitors are drawn by the many isolated and exotic cultures scattered throughout the Himalayas.

People
Nepal's mixed population results from migrations over the centuries from India, Tibet, and central Asia. Most of Nepal's ruling families have been of Indian descent, and Nepali, the official language, is derived from Sanskrit, an ancient Indian language. Although the majority of the population practices Hinduism, Nepal is the birthplace of Buddha and has been greatly influenced by Buddhism as well. The importance of both religions is reflected in the more than twenty-seven hundred shrines in the Kathmandu Valley. Most Nepalese are rural farmers.

Economy and the Land
Because of geographic remoteness and a political policy of isolation lasting until the 1950s, Nepal's economy is one of the least developed in the world. Agriculture, concentrated chiefly in the south, is the most significant activity, even though most of Nepal is covered by the Himalayas, the world's highest mountains. This range—which includes Mount Everest, the world's highest peak—has made tourism increasingly lucrative. Nepal has potential in hydroelectricity and forestry, but inadequate transportation routes, overpopulation, and deforestation present obstacles to development. Nepal has received financial aid from many nations, partly because of its strategic location between India and China. The climate varies from subtropical in the flat, fertile south to temperate in the central hill country. Himalayan summers are cool and winters severe.

continued

Nepal boasts eight of the world's ten highest peaks, including Mount Everest, the world's highest, which straddles the border with China. The government sharply limits the number of mountain-climbing permits issued each year.

History and Politics

Several small Hindu-Buddhist kingdoms had emerged in the Kathmandu Valley by about A.D. 300. These states were unified in the late 1700s by the founder of the Shah dynasty. The Rana family wrested control from the Shahs in 1846 and pursued an isolationist course, which thwarted foreign influence but stunted economic growth. Opposition to the Ranas mounted during the 1930s and 1940s, and in 1951 the Shah monarchy was restored by a revolution. In 1962 the king established a government that gave the crown dominance and abolished political parties. A 1980 referendum narrowly upheld this system. In November 1990 a pro-democracy movement forced the king to approve a new constitution providing for a multiparty structure and the country's new status as a constitutional monarchy. In 1991, the Nepali Congress Party became the first democratically elected administration in Nepal, followed in 1994 by a reformist Communist Party which became the first democratically elected Communist government in Asia.

Nepal at a glance

Official name Kingdom of Nepal

People

Population	21,295,000
Density	375/mi² (145/km²)
Urban	11%
Capital	Kathmandu, 421,258
Ethnic groups	Newar, Indian, Tibetan, Gurung, Magar, Tamang, Bhotia, Sherpa, others
Languages	Nepali, Maithali, Bhojpuri, other indigenous
Religions	Hindu 90%, Buddhist 5%, Muslim 3%
Life expectancy	53 female, 54 male
Literacy	26%

Politics

Government	Constitutional monarchy
Parties	Communist/United Marxist and Leninist, Congress, United People's Front, others
Suffrage	Universal, over 18
Memberships	UN
Subdivisions	14 zones

Economy

GDP	$20,500,000,000
Per capita	$1,009
Monetary unit	Rupee
Trade partners	Exports: U.S., Germany, India Imports: India, Singapore, Japan
Exports	Clothing, carpets, leather goods, grain
Imports	Petroleum, fertilizer, machinery

Land

Description	Southern Asia, landlocked
Area	56,827 mi² (147,181 km²)
Highest point	Mt. Everest, 29,028 ft (8,848 m)
Lowest point	Unnamed, 197 ft (60 m)

NETHERLANDS

Maastricht, which is set on the Meuse (Maas) River near the Belgian and German borders, is surrounded by hills which belie the Netherlands' image as a flat country. The Maastricht Treaty, which paved the way for closer economic and political ties among the countries of the European Union, was signed in Maastricht in 1992.

The Netherlands is home to an industrious and affluent people who have reclaimed much of their flat country from the sea. Although generally conservative, the Dutch place great value on tolerance of others. This is most evident in freewheeling Amsterdam. Rotterdam is the world's busiest port and handles goods both from the country's many industries and from the rest of Europe. Much of the land in the Netherlands is devoted to agriculture, including dairy farms and fields of the famous tulips.

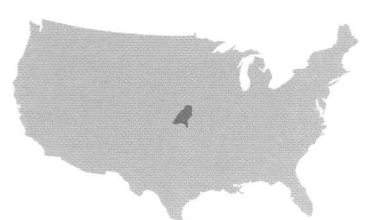

People

The major ethnic group is the Dutch, for the most part a mixture of French, Scandinavian, and Celtic peoples. There are small minorities from the former Dutch possessions of Indonesia and Suriname. Dutch is the official language, but many Netherlanders also speak English or German. Although most Dutch are Christian, the nation has a history of religious tolerance that has drawn countless refugees of other faiths.

Economy and the Land

A variety of manufacturing strengths—notably the metal, chemical, and food-processing industries—fuels the prosperous economy. Tourism and the production of natural gas are also important. Due to a lack of natural resources, the Netherlands must import many goods. The country benefits from its strategic position and has enjoyed success in shipping and trade. Much of the Netherlands, including most farmland, has been reclaimed from the sea through artificial drainage. The land is almost uniformly flat, and proximity to the sea produces a mild, damp climate. The Kingdom of the Netherlands includes the Netherlands Antilles, two groups of Caribbean islands, and Aruba.

History and Politics

The Germanic tribes of the area were conquered in 58 B.C. by the Romans, who were driven out in the A.D. 400s by the Franks. As part of the Low Countries with Belgium and Luxembourg, the Netherlands was dominated successively by Charlemagne, the dukes of Burgundy, the Hapsburgs, and rulers of Spain. Spanish persecution of

Dutch Protestants led to a revolt that in 1581 created the Republic of the United Netherlands. In the 1600s the Netherlands became a maritime as well as a colonial power, and produced many masterpieces in painting. But a series of wars with England and France ending in 1714 spelled the end of Dutch influence, and the nation fell to France in 1795. With the defeat of Napoleon Bonaparte of France in 1815, the Netherlands was united with Belgium and became an independent kingdom. Belgium seceded in 1830. The Netherlands declared its neutrality in both World Wars but was occupied by Germany from 1940 to 1945. World War II cost the country many lives and much of its economic strength. Membership in several international economic unions aided recovery. In recent years the Netherlands has been actively involved in the European Union.

Amsterdam's concentric canals such as the Herengracht, shown here, were avenues of commerce during the 17th and 18th centuries. Merchants vied for space along their banks with tall buildings built of brick and stone. Today the canals offer a quiet respite in the busy city. The buildings now house apartments, hotels, and shops.

The Netherlands is justifiably famous for its tulips, which are exported to all parts of the world. Their colors span the spectrum. Actually a native of Turkey, the tulip was a major part of the Dutch economy by 1600.

Netherlands at a glance

Official name Kingdom of the Netherlands

People

Population	15,425,000
Density	954/mi² (368/km²)
Urban	89%
Capital	Amsterdam (designated), 713,407; The Hague (seat of government), 445,287
Ethnic groups	Dutch (mixed Scandinavian, French, and Celtic) 96%
Languages	Dutch
Religions	Roman Catholic 36%, Dutch Reformed 19%, Calvinist 8%
Life expectancy	81 female, 74 male
Literacy	99%

Politics

Government	Constitutional monarchy
Parties	Christian Democratic Appeal, Labor, Liberal, others
Suffrage	Universal, over 18
Memberships	EU, NATO, OECD, UN
Subdivisions	12 provinces

Economy

GDP	$262,800,000,000
Per capita	$17,301
Monetary unit	Guilder
Trade partners	Exports: Germany, Belgium, France Imports: Germany, Belgium, U.K.
Exports	Agricultural products, food and tobacco, natural gas, chemicals
Imports	Raw materials, consumer goods, transportation equipment, petroleum, food

Land

Description	Western Europe
Area	16,164 mi² (41,864 km²)
Highest point	Vaalserberg, 1,053 ft (321 m)
Lowest point	Prins Alexander polder, -23 ft (-7 m)

NETHERLANDS

Major Urban Area
Railroad
Canal or Waterway
▲ Major Oil Field
+ Spot Elevation or Depth
Dike

National capitals are underlined
City type size indicates relative importance

Scale 1:1,950,000

(top) Windmill at sunset

(bottom) Dairy cows

The Netherlands has invested enormous sums building vast tidal barriers along its southern coast. They are designed to protect the country from floods, such as the one in 1953 which destroyed hundreds of towns and killed thousands of people.

A n affluent tourist trade and liberal banking laws have given the Netherlands Antilles a much higher standard of living than most Caribbean islands. In the south, on Curaçao, Willemstad is a thriving city known for its Dutch colonial architecture. In the north, sparsely populated Saba and St. Eustatius are popular with those who want to get away from it all.

NETHERLANDS ANTILLES

The Netherlands Antilles include the southern part of St. Maarten (not shown on map), which is Dutch. The northern two-thirds is called St. Martin and is part of French Guadeloupe.

People
The people of the Netherlands Antilles are of mixed African, Carib Indian, and European descent. Most people are multi-lingual, and languages include Dutch, English, and Papiamento, which combines Spanish, Dutch, Portuguese, English, and Indian elements.

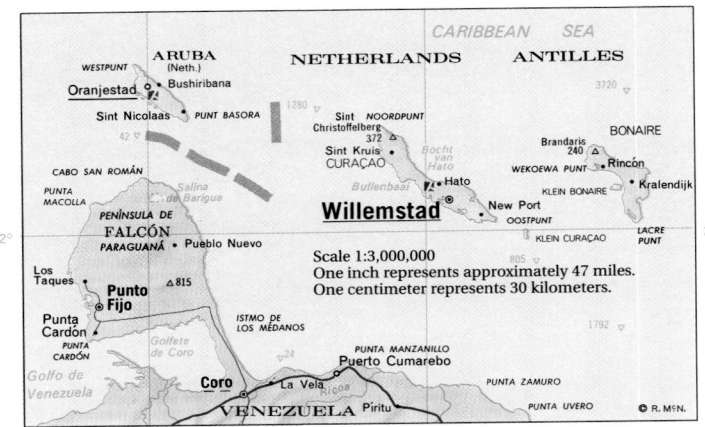

Economy and the Land
The bases of the islands' economy are financial services, petroleum refining, and tourism. Tax incentives have drawn some industry. Poor soils and aridity limit agriculture. The mainly volcanic St. Maarten, St. Eustatius, and Saba make up the northern island group; the coral islands of Curaçao and Bonaire constitute the southern islands. The climate is tropical.

History and Politics
Carib Indians were the original inhabitants of the northern islands, and Caiquetio Indians resided on the islands to the south. Christopher Columbus reached the northern islands in 1493, and the Spanish arrived at the southern islands in 1499. In the 1630s both groups came under Dutch rule. Some of the islands saw brief periods of French and British rule, but since 1816 all the islands have been under Dutch control. The Netherlands Antilles are a self-governing territory of the Netherlands. Aruba was part of the territory until 1986.

The main island of New Caledonia is believed to have once been part of the Australian continent.

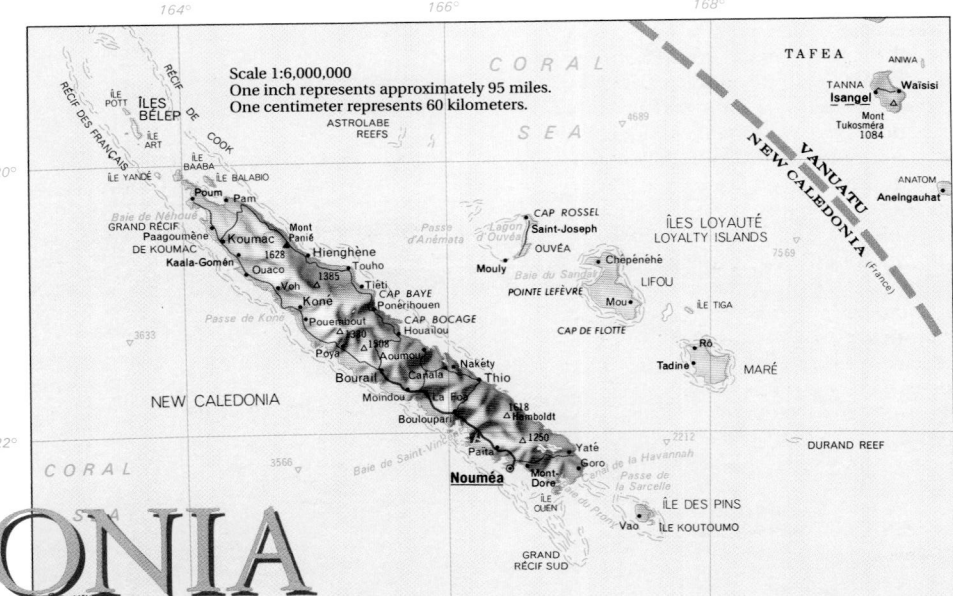

NEW CALEDONIA

N ew Caledonia's relaxed pace was interrupted in 1988 after voters decided to remain part of France. Violent clashes erupted, sparked by those people in favor of independence. Peace has now returned to the islands.

People
The Melanesian, or Kanak, comprise the largest ethnic group in New Caledonia, a group of Pacific islands northeast of Australia. People of French descent make up the second largest group, with Asians and Polynesians composing significant minorities. New Caledonia's status as an overseas French territory is reflected in its languages, which include French as well as regional dialects, and in a population that is largely Christian.

Economy and the Land
The principal economic activity, the mining and smelting of nickel, has fallen off in recent years. Small amounts of coffee and copra are exported, and tourism is important in the capital. Possessing few resources, New Caledonia imports almost all finished products from France. The main island, also called New Caledonia, is mountainous and accounts for almost 90 percent of the territory's land area. Smaller islands include the Isle of Pines, Loyalty and Bélep islands. The climate is tropical.

History and Politics
New Caledonia was settled by Melanesians about 2000 B.C. Europeans first reached the main island in 1774, when Captain James Cook of Britain gave it its present name. In 1853 France annexed New Caledonia and used the main island as a penal colony until the turn of the century. During World War II the islands served as a base for the United States military. Officially a French overseas territory since 1946, New Caledonia experienced violence in the 1980s, stemming from the desire of the Kanak population for independence. An independence referendum is planned for 1998, although the Kanaks may gain some form of autonomy earlier.

Queenstown is a year-round mountain resort on Lake Wakatipu in the southern part of South Island. First settled by gold miners in the mid-1800s, the region is largely untouched by development.

NEW ZEALAND

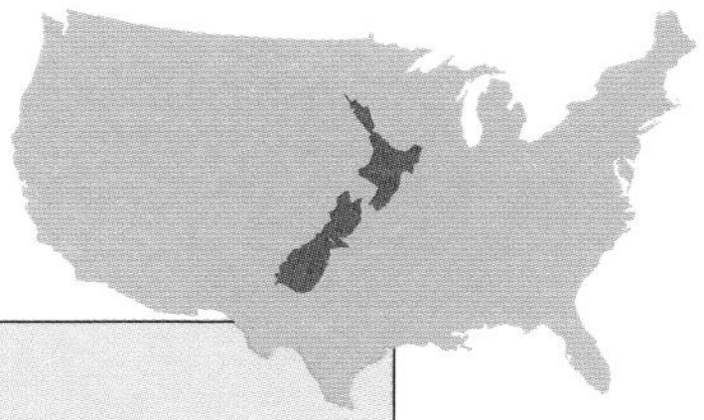

People

The majority of New Zealanders are descended from Europeans, mostly Britons, who arrived in the 1800s. The indigenous Maoris, of Polynesian descent, form the largest minority. After a period of decline following the arrival of the Europeans, the Maori population has been increasing. The major languages are English, the official tongue, and Maori. Most New Zealanders live on North Island. Christian religions are observed by many residents, and the Maoris have incorporated some Christian elements into their beliefs.

Economy and the Land

Success in agriculture and trade has allowed New Zealand to overcome its small work force, remoteness from major markets, and a relative lack of natural resources. A terrain with much ideal grazing land and a climate that is temperate year-round have encouraged cattle and sheep farming. Manufacturing, including the food-processing and paper industries, is an expanding sector, as is tourism. New Zealand consists of two large islands—North Island and South Island—and many smaller islands scattered throughout the South Pacific. The nation administers several island territories. The scenic terrain is greatly varied, ranging from fjords and mountains to a volcanic plateau.

History and Politics

The Maori, the original settlers, are thought to have arrived around A.D. 1000. In 1642 they fought off the Dutch, the first Europeans to reach the area. Captain James Cook of Britain charted the islands in the late 1700s. Soon after, European hunters and traders, drawn by the area's whales, seals, and forests, began to arrive. Maori chiefs signed the 1840 Treaty of Waitangi, establishing British sovereignty, and British companies began to send settlers to New Zealand. Subsequent battles between settlers and Maoris ended with the Maoris' defeat in 1872, but European diseases and weapons continued to reduce the Maori population. In 1907 New Zealand became a self-governing dominion of Britain; formal independence came forty years later. New Zealand supported Britain in both World Wars, but foreign policy has recently focused on Southeast Asia and the South Pacific. The country has banned vessels carrying nuclear weapons through its waters. Compensation has begun to Maori groups for land claims going back to 1840.

New Zealand was one of the last places on Earth to be settled by humans. The Polynesians arrived about 1,000 years before the Dutch, who came in 1642. Two centuries of British settlers built a prosperous country based on raising sheep. Government efforts to diversify the economy have been only moderately successful; much of the land remains a mix of grazing sheep and dramatic beauty.

New Zealand at a glance

Official name	New Zealand

People

Population	3,558,000
Density	34/mi² (13/km²)
Urban	84%
Capital	Wellington, North I., 150,301
Ethnic groups	European origin 86%, Maori 10%, Samoan and other Pacific islander 4%
Languages	English, Maori
Religions	Anglican 24%, Presbyterian 18%, Roman Catholic 15%, Methodist 5%
Life expectancy	79 female, 73 male
Literacy	99%

Politics

Government	Parliamentary state
Parties	Alliance, Labor, National, others
Suffrage	Universal, over 18
Memberships	CW, OECD, UN
Subdivisions	14 regions

Economy

GDP	$53,000,000,000
Per capita	$15,241
Monetary unit	Dollar
Trade partners	Exports: Australia, Japan, U.S. Imports: Australia, U.S., Japan
Exports	Wool, lamb, mutton, beef, fruit, fish, cheese, manufactures, chemicals
Imports	Petroleum, manufactures, motor vehicles, machinery

Land

Description	South Pacific islands
Area	104,454 mi² (270,534 km²)
Highest point	Mt. Cook, 12,316 ft (3,754 m)
Lowest point	Sea level

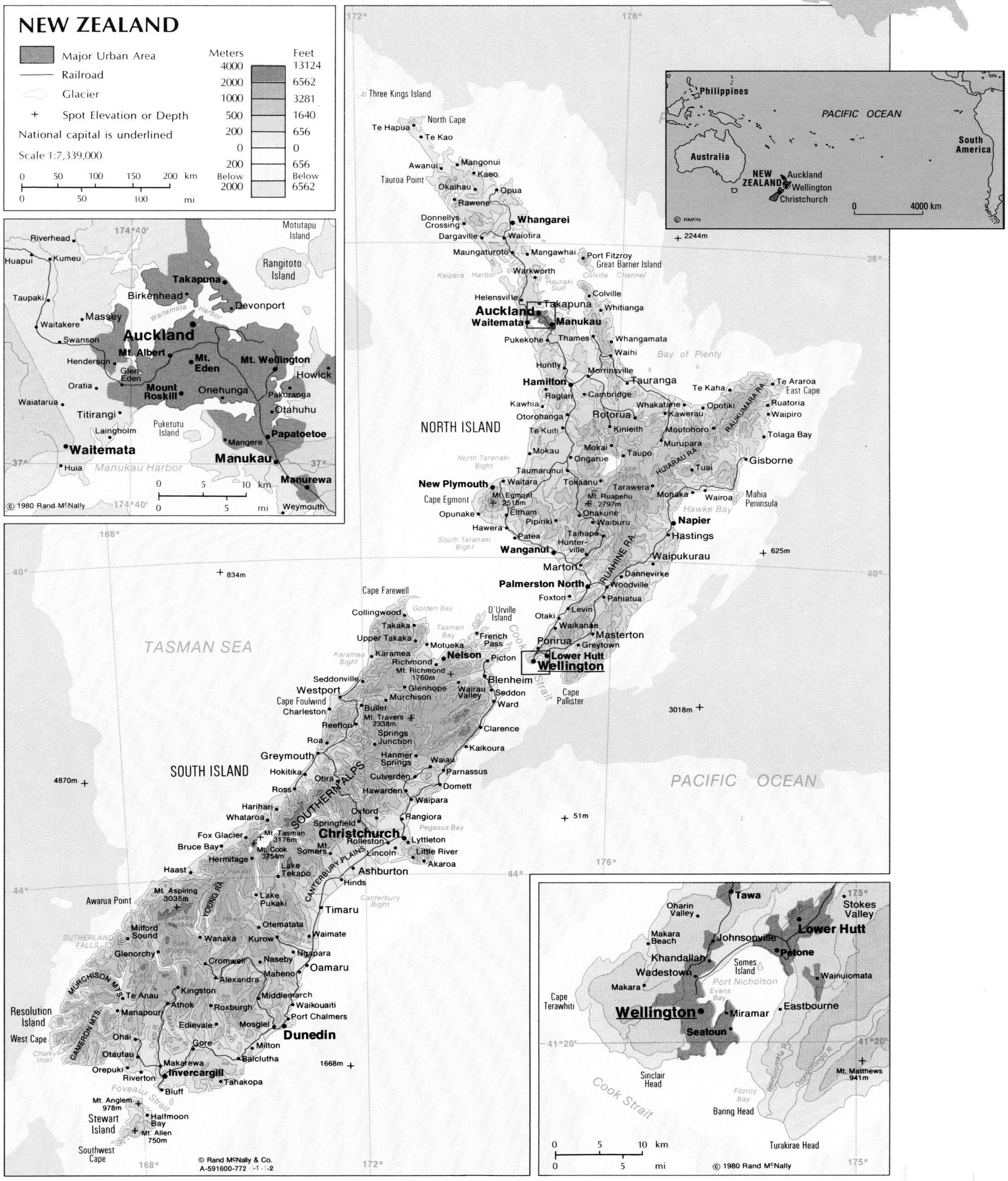

NEW ZEALAND

- Major Urban Area
- Railroad
- Glacier
- \+ Spot Elevation or Depth
- National capital is underlined

Scale 1:7,339,000

Meters	Feet
4000	13124
2000	6562
1000	3281
500	1640
200	656
0	0
200 Below 2000	656 Below 6562

New Zealand's climate is moderated by Pacific currents and trade winds. The northern reaches of North Island are sub-tropical. South Island is more temperate; its southern reaches are at times chilled by winds from the Antarctic.

A terrible earthquake in 1972 marked the start of almost two decades of bitter political fighting that tore at the heart of Nicaragua. The country is now struggling to become a stable democracy. It has many natural resources and the lowest population density in Central America.

Melons at market

NICARAGUA

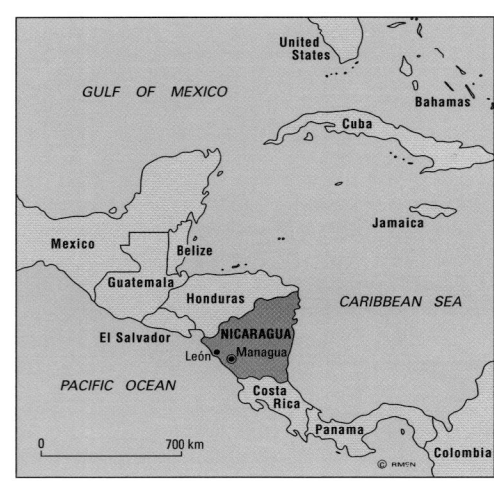

Managua, Nicaragua's capital, is prone to devastating earthquakes. A severe temblor in 1972 leveled much of the city and killed thousands of people, a disaster from which the city has yet to completely recover. Masaya, an active volcano, looms just to the southeast.

People
Nicaraguan society closely reflects the nation's history as a Spanish colony: most of its inhabitants are Spanish-speaking, Roman Catholic, and mestizo, a mix of Indian and European stocks. Indian and black communities are found mostly in the Caribbean region. The educational level has improved in the past decade.

Nicaraguan children

Economy and the Land
Nicaragua is chiefly an agricultural nation, relying on the production of textiles, coffee, and sugar. A large foreign debt inherited from the previous regime, and continuing political instability, have severely hindered economic prosperity. The nation also suffers from a reliance on imported goods. In 1985 the currency was sharply devalued, and the United States, formerly a chief trading partner, announced a trade embargo. The terrain includes a low-lying Pacific region, central highlands, and a flat Caribbean area. The climate is tropical.

History and Politics
Spanish conquistadores, who came via Panama in 1522 to what is now Nicaragua, found a number of independent Indian states. Nicaragua was ruled by Spain as part of Guatemala until it became independent in 1821. In 1823 the former Spanish colonies of the region formed the Federation of Central America, a union which collapsed in 1838, resulting in the independent Republic of Nicaragua. For the next century, Nicaragua was the stage both for conflict between the Liberal and Conservative parties and for United States military and economic involvement.

Members of the Somoza family, who had close ties to America, directed a repressive regime from 1936 to 1979, when the widely-supported Sandinistas overthrew the government. The Sandinistas, led by Daniel Ortega, were opposed by rival political parties and the Contras, rebels linked to the former Somoza administration and backed by the United States. Five Central American countries reached an agreement in 1987 on a plan to dismantle Contra forces. In 1990 elections, Ortega was defeated by Violeta Chamorro of the National Opposition Union. Despite the disbanding of the Contras in 1990, the situation remains unstable as Chamorro tries to placate the still powerful Sandinistas and revise the moribund economy.

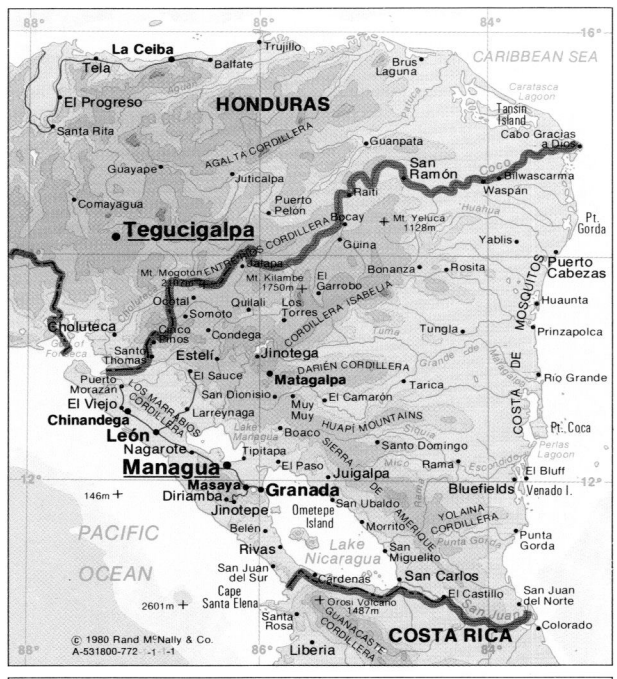

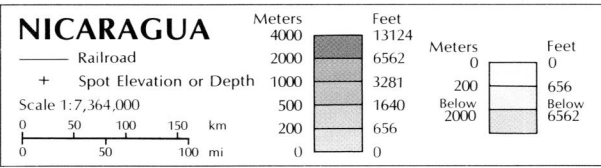

NICARAGUA

	Meters	Feet
	4000	13124
—— Railroad	2000	6562
+ Spot Elevation or Depth	1000	3281

	Meters	Feet
	0	0
	200	656
	Below 2000	Below 6562

Scale 1:7,364,000

	500	1640
	200	656
	0	0

0 50 100 150 km
0   50   100 mi

© 1980 Rand McNally & Co.
A-531800-772 -1 -1

Lake Nicaragua features several picturesque islands formed by volcanoes. The United States once planned a trans-ocean canal across Nicaragua that would have passed through the lake and the surrounding lowlands.

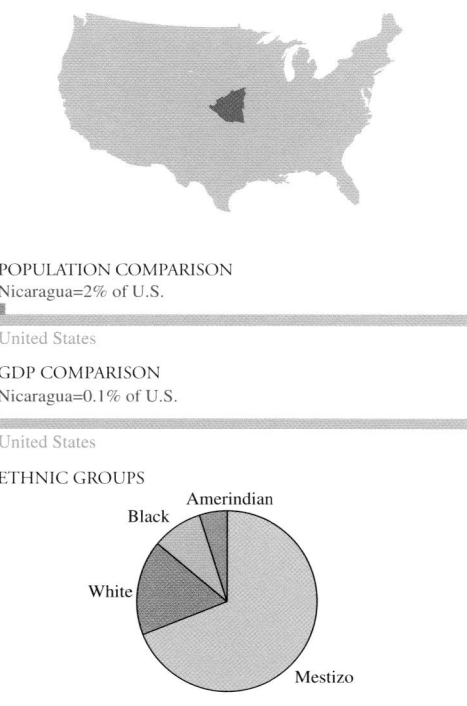

POPULATION COMPARISON
Nicaragua=2% of U.S.

United States

GDP COMPARISON
Nicaragua=0.1% of U.S.

United States

ETHNIC GROUPS

- Amerindian
- Black
- White
- Mestizo

POPULATION DISTRIBUTION
Urban   Rural

Nicaragua at a glance

Official name	Republic of Nicaragua

People

Population	4,438,000
Density	89/mi² (34/km²)
Urban	60%
Capital	Managua, 682,000
Ethnic groups	Mestizo 69%, white 17%, black 9%, Amerindian 5%
Languages	Spanish, English, indigenous
Religions	Roman Catholic 95%
Life expectancy	69 female, 65 male
Literacy	57%

Politics

Government	Republic
Parties	National Opposition Union, Sandinista National Liberation Front
Suffrage	Universal, over 16
Memberships	OAS, UN
Subdivisions	16 departments

Economy

GDP	$6,400,000,000
Per capita	$1,628
Monetary unit	Cordoba
Trade partners	Exports: Belgium, Cuba, Germany Imports: Former Soviet republics, Mexico
Exports	Coffee, cotton, sugar, bananas, seafood, meat, chemicals
Imports	Petroleum, food, chemicals, machinery, clothing

Land

Description	Central America
Area	50,054 mi² (129,640 km²)
Highest point	Mt. Mogotón, 6,913 ft (2,107 m)
Lowest point	Sea level

NIGER

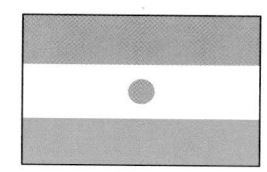

Camels are the traditional mounts of Tuareg tribesmen. Ranging across the Sahel, the Tuareg were once fierce fighters who raided villages and passing caravans. More peaceful today, they are one of the five principal ethnic groups in Niger.

D welling in a land of desert and frequent drought, Niger's people have always led difficult lives. With a lack of natural resources, and a government reliant on foreign—mostly French—aid for its operating expenses, it is likely that Niger will continue to be a land of hardship.

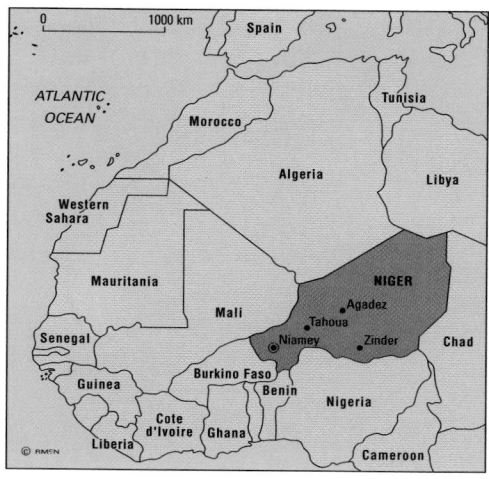

Niger at a glance

Official name   Republic of Niger

People

Population	9,125,000
Density	19/mi² (7.2/km²)
Urban	20%
Capital	Niamey, 392,165
Ethnic groups	Hausa 56%, Djerma 22%, Fulani 9%, Tuareg 8%, Beriberi 4%
Languages	French, Hausa, Djerma, indigenous
Religions	Muslim 80%, Animist and Christian 20%
Life expectancy	48 female, 45 male
Literacy	28%

Politics

Government	Provisional military government
Parties	National Movement for the Development of Society, Social Democratic Convention, Unity and Democracy
Suffrage	Universal, over 18
Memberships	OAU, UN
Subdivisions	7 departments

Economy

GDP	$5,400,000,000
Per capita	$659
Monetary unit	CFA franc
Trade partners	Exports: France, Nigeria Imports: France, U.S., Cote d'Ivoire, Nigeria
Exports	Uranium, livestock products, cowpeas, onions
Imports	Petroleum, raw materials, machinery, transportation equipment, electronics

Land

Description	Western Africa, landlocked
Area	489,191 mi² (1,267,000 km²)
Highest point	Idoûkâl-en-Taghès, 6,634 ft (2,022 m)
Lowest point	Along Niger River, 650 ft (198 m)

People

Nearly all Nigeriens are black Africans belonging to culturally diverse groups. The Hausa and the Djerma, farmers who live mostly in the south, constitute the two largest groups. The remaining Nigeriens are nomadic herders who inhabit the northern desert regions. Although the official language is French, most inhabitants speak indigenous tongues. Islam is the most commonly observed religion, but some Nigeriens follow indigenous and Christian beliefs.

Economy and the Land

Niger's economy is chiefly agricultural, although arable land is scarce and drought common. The raising of livestock, grain, beans, and peanuts accounts for most farming activity. Uranium mining, a growing industry, has become less productive recently due to a slump in the world uranium market. Mountains and the Sahara Desert cover most of northern Niger, while the south is savanna. The climate is hot and dry.

History and Politics

Because of its central location in northern Africa, Niger was a crossroads for many peoples during its early history and was dominated by several African empires before European explorers arrived in the 1800s. The area was placed within the French sphere of influence in 1885, but not until 1922 did France make Niger a colony of French West Africa. Gradual moves toward autonomy were made during the forties and fifties, and Niger became fully independent in 1960. Unrest caused in part by a prolonged drought led to a coup in 1974 and the establishment of a military government. A December 1992 referendum gave overwhelming approval to a new multiparty constitution. Frequent clashes with the Tuareg ethnic groups in the north have abated since a truce was signed in 1994.

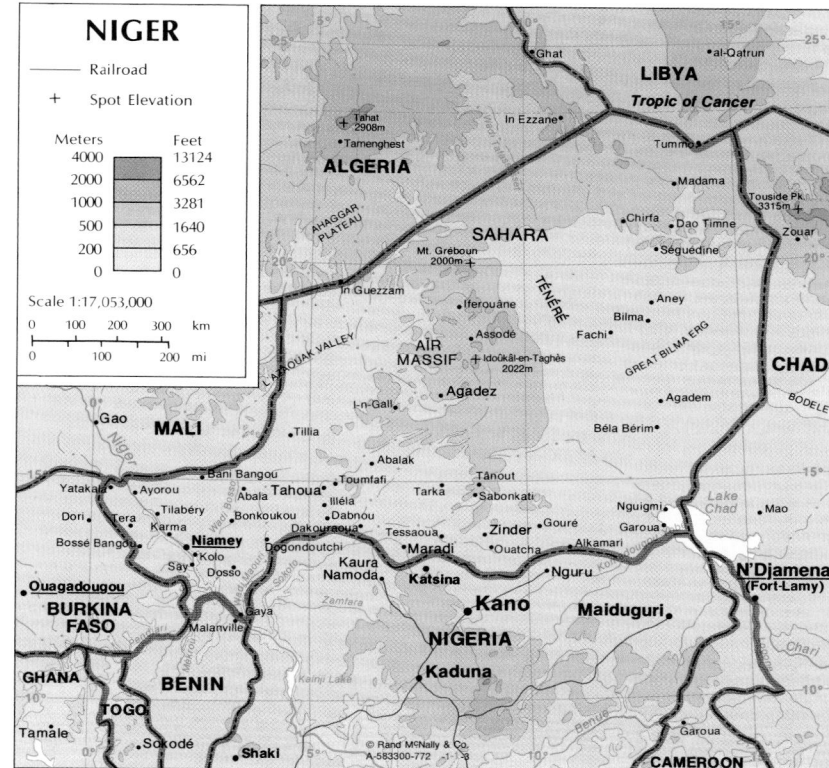

Niger's only permanent river is the Niger; its only lake is a portion of Lake Chad in its southeast corner. Rainfall is less than 20 inches annually in the south. Some parts of the north never receive rain.

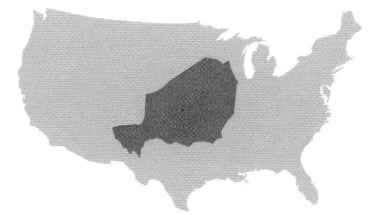

POPULATION COMPARISON
Niger=4% of U.S.

United States

GDP COMPARISON
Niger=0.08% of U.S.

United States

ETHNIC GROUPS

POPULATION DISTRIBUTION
Urban   Rural

*(top) Nigerien girls
(bottom) Merchant*

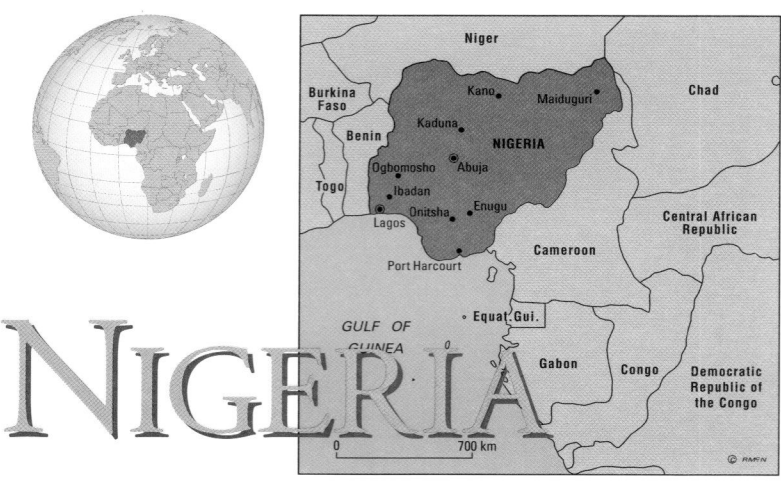

NIGERIA

The Fulani of northern Nigeria are renowned cattle-herders. They regularly cross the Niger border with their animals, and Fulani villages can be found in both countries. Nigerian Fulani are centered around Kano, a thousand-year-old trading center whose Old City consists of hundreds of narrow, winding streets.

Nigeria is Africa's most populous country. Never united before its independence from Great Britain in 1960, it is a mix of many different peoples, cultures, and religions. This diversity has led to many violent clashes. Rural dwellers, drawn to the cities and their oil wealth, live in slums as grim as any in the world.

(top) Leki Lagoon, near Lagos
(bottom) Unusual rock formation near Wase, central Nigeria

People

Nigeria, Africa's most populous nation, contains more than 200 distinct black African groups. The largest groups are the Hausa and the Fulani, who dominate the north; the Yoruba, found primarily in the southwest; and the Ibo, who live in the southeast and have historically been active in government and trade. Most Hausa and Fulani are Muslim, and a sizable Christian community is found mainly in the south. Religious violence between Christians and Muslims erupts periodically, as in 1982 when hundreds were killed. Nigerians commonly combine traditional beliefs with Islam or Christianity. Indigenous tongues are more widely spoken than English, the official language. Competition among Nigeria's many ethnic groups has threatened national unity.

Economy and the Land

Nigeria's economy is based on mining and agriculture. Petroleum is very important to the Nigerian economy, but a number of factors—including unskilled labor, poor power facilities, and the worldwide dip in oil prices—have silenced the oil boom of the 1970s and slowed development in other areas. In 1983 and 1985 the government expelled millions of illegal aliens in an effort to revive the economy. The terrain is diverse, encompassing tropical forest, savanna, and semidesert. The climate is predominantly tropical.

History and Politics

From around 500 B.C. to about A.D. 200 the region was home to the sophisticated Nok civilization. Later cultures that dominated parts of the area included the Hausa, Fulani, and Yoruba. The Portuguese arrived in the 1400s, but the British gained control over the following centuries, uniting the region in 1914 as the Colony and Protectorate of Nigeria. Nigerian calls for self-rule culminated in independence in 1960. Internal tensions began to wrack the new nation, and in 1966 two military coups took place. After subsequent massacres of Ibo, that group declared eastern Nigeria the autonomous state of Biafra. A three-year civil war followed, ending in 1970 with Biafra's surrender. Government development and the oil boom speeded economic recovery. Subsequent years have seen coups and elections which install short-lived regimes, while political instability continues. In a transparent attempt to retain control, June 1993 elections were annulled by the military, and democracy has been put on hold.

POPULATION COMPARISON
Nigeria=37% of U.S.

United States

GDP COMPARISON
Nigeria=2% of U.S.

United States

POPULATION DISTRIBUTION
Urban   Rural

Nigeria at a glance

Official name	Federal Republic of Nigeria

People

Population	97,300,000
Density	273/mi² (105/km²)
Urban	35%
Capital	Lagos (de facto), 1,213,000; Abuja (designated), 250,000
Ethnic groups	Hausa, Fulani, Yoruba, Ibo, others
Languages	English, Hausa, Fulani, Yorbua, Ibo, indigenous
Religions	Muslim 50%, Christian 40%, Animist 10%
Life expectancy	54 female, 51 male
Literacy	51%

Politics

Government	Provisional military government
Parties	National Republican Convention, Social Democratic
Suffrage	Universal, over 21
Memberships	CW, OAU, OPEC, UN
Subdivisions	30 states, 1 capital territory

Economy

GDP	$95,100,000,000
Per capita	$1,037
Monetary unit	Naira
Trade partners	Exports: U.S., France, Netherlands Imports: U.K., Germany, U.S., France
Exports	Petroleum, cocoa, rubber
Imports	Manufactures, machinery, chemicals, raw materials

Land

Description	Western Africa
Area	356,669 mi² (923,768 km²)
Highest point	Mt. Waddi, 7,936 ft (2,419 m)
Lowest point	Sea level

NIGERIA
— Railroad
—•— Oil Pipeline
▲ Major Oil Field
+ Spot Elevation or Depth
National capitals are underlined
Scale 1:8,500,000

Meters	Feet
4000	13124
2000	6562
1000	3281
500	1640
200	656
0	0
Below 2000	Below 6562

© 1980 Rand McNally & Co.
A-583400-772 -1 -2

Before the boundaries of Lake Chad were settled, Nigeria, Chad, Cameroon, and Niger frequently fought over the lake. The situation was complicated by the lake's great fluctuations in size, caused by seasonal monsoon rains.

Niue at a glance

Official name	Niue

People

Population	1,900
Density	19/mi² (7.3/km²)
Urban	23%
Capital	Alofi, 706
Ethnic groups	Polynesian
Languages	English, indigenous
Religions	Church of Niue 76%, Mormon 12%, Roman Catholic 5%

Politics

Government	Self-governing territory (New Zealand protection)
Parties	Niue Island Party
Suffrage	Universal, over 18
Memberships	None
Subdivisions	14 village councils

Economy

GDP	$2,000,000
Per capita	$833
Monetary unit	New Zealand dollar
Trade partners	Exports: New Zealand Imports: New Zealand, Fiji
Exports	Coconut cream, lime products, honey, footballs, taro, yams
Imports	Food, live animals, manufactures, machinery, fuel, chemicals

Land

Description	South Pacific island
Area	100 mi² (259 km²)
Highest point	220 ft (67 m)
Lowest point	Sea level

Scale 1:1,000,000
One inch represents approximately 16 miles.
One centimeter represents 10 kilometers.

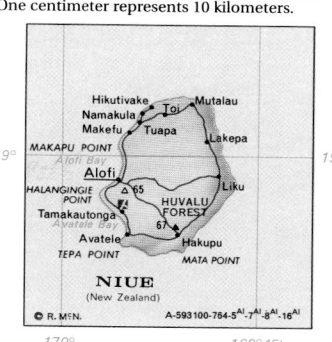

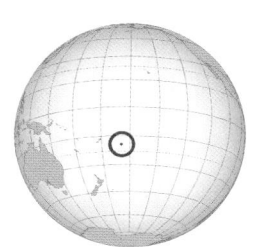

Niue is one of the world's largest coral islands. Two-thirds of the land is farmed.

People
Niue has a mainly Polynesian population that speaks indigenous tongues. Because of Niue's association with New Zealand, English is widely spoken.

Economy and the Land
The economy is heavily dependent upon foreign aid, mostly from New Zealand. Poor soil and an erratic climate produce mostly subsistence farming. Although most residents have emigrated to New Zealand, the current government is offering incentives to entice people to return. The coral island's climate is tropical.

History and politics
More than one thousand years ago Niue's first inhabitants arrived either from Samoa or another eastern Pacific island. In 1774 Captain James Cook of Britain came to Niue, calling it Savage Island because of the hostility of the inhabitants. The island did not come under British rule until 1900. In 1901 Niue was annexed to New Zealand, and the island became a self-governing territory of New Zealand in 1974.

NIUE

Norfolk Island at a glance

Official name	Territory of Norfolk Island

People

Population	2,700
Density	193/mi² (75/km²)
Capital	Kingston
Ethnic groups	Norfolk Islander (mixed European and Tahitian), Australian, New Zealander
Languages	English, Norfolk
Religions	Anglican 39%, Uniting Church 16%, Roman Catholic 12%

Politics

Government	External territory (Australia)
Suffrage	Universal, over 18
Memberships	None
Subdivisions	None

Economy

Monetary unit	Australian dollar
Trade partners	Australia, Pacific island countries, New Zealand
Exports	Postage stamps, Norfolk Island pine seeds, palm seeds, avocados
Imports	Food, manufactures

Land

Description	South Pacific island
Area	14 mi² (36 km²)
Highest point	Mt. Bates, 1,047 ft (319 m)
Lowest point	Sea level

NORFOLK ISLAND

Norfolk Island's population comprises descendants of *Bounty* mutineers, called "islanders," and immigrants from Australia and New Zealand, or "mainlanders." Tourism is the main economic contributor. Of volcanic origin, Norfolk Island has a subtropical climate. Captain James Cook arrived at the uninhabited island in 1774, and for a time Norfolk served as a penal colony. In 1914 the island became an external territory of Australia.

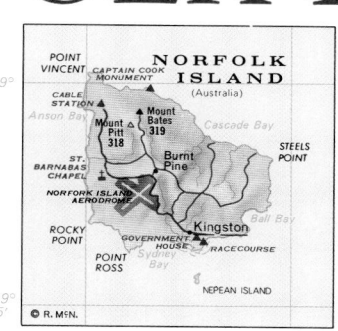

Scale 1:300,000   One inch represents approximately 4.7 miles.
One centimeter represents 3 kilometers.

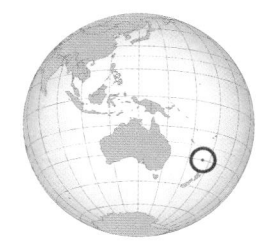

Norfolk Island's gentle, rolling green hills are surrounded by rugged cliffs. The peaks are covered with pine trees first planted by convicts.

Northern Mariana Islands

Official name	Commonwealth of the Northern Mariana Islands

People

Population	51,000
Density	277/mi² (107/km²)
Urban	16%
Capital	Saipan Island
Ethnic groups	Chamorro, Carolinian and other Micronesian, Caucasian, Japanese, Chinese, Korean
Languages	English, Chamorro, Carolinian
Religions	Roman Catholic and other Christian, tribal religionist
Life expectancy	69 female, 66 male
Literacy	97%

Politics

Government	Commonwealth (U.S. protection)
Parties	Democratic, Republican
Suffrage	Universal, over 18
Memberships	None
Subdivisions	4 municipalities

Economy

GDP	$541,000,000
Per capita	$11,761
Monetary unit	U.S. dollar
Exports	Manufactures, clothing, vegetables, beef, pork
Imports	Food, construction equipment, raw materials

Land

Description	North Pacific islands
Area	184 mi² (477 km²)
Highest point	3,166 ft (965 m)
Lowest point	Sea level

NORTHERN MARIANA ISLANDS

The Chamorros, of mixed descent, are a majority on the Northern Mariana Islands. Most income derives from tourism. The islands' climate is tropical. Inhabited for more than three thousand years, the Northern Marianas were ruled by Spain, Germany, and Japan. In 1947 the United Nations declared the Northern Marianas part of the Trust Territory of the Pacific Islands, under United States administration. In 1990, the Northern Marianas became a U.S. commonwealth territory.

Scale 1:1,000,000   One inch represents approximately 16 miles.
One centimeter represents 10 kilometers.

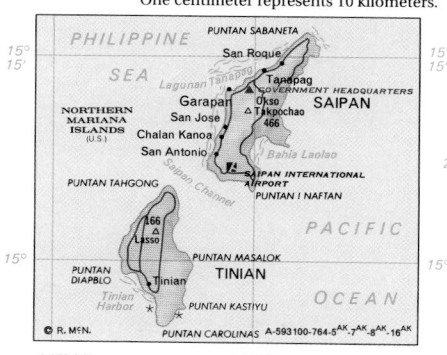

Warm Pacific waters fill the lagoons of the Northern Mariana Islands. Each of the islands is lined with beaches.

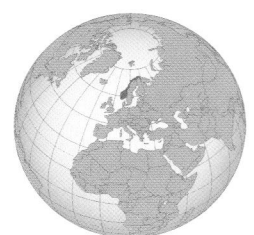

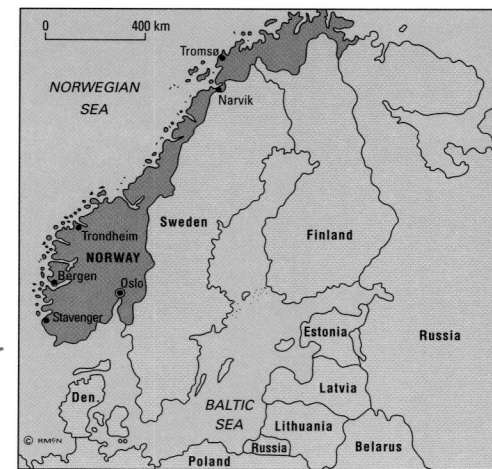

NORWAY

Stretched across the top of Europe, Norway has a jagged, 2,100-mile-long coast with countless fjords which have been carved out by glaciers over the eons. The country's hardy people have built a nation where high government taxes are used to insure a comfortable life for everyone. Fishing, trade, and oil production are the economic mainstays.

Norway at a glance

Official name	Kingdom of Norway

People

Population	4,339,000
Density	29/mi² (11/km²)
Urban	75%
Capital	Oslo, 470,204
Ethnic groups	Norwegian (Scandinavian), Lapp
Languages	Norwegian, Lapp, Finnish
Religions	Lutheran 89%, other Protestant and Roman Catholic 4%
Life expectancy	81 female, 74 male
Literacy	99%

Politics

Government	Constitutional monarchy
Parties	Center, Conservative, Labor, Progress, others
Suffrage	Universal, over 18
Memberships	NATO, OECD, UN
Subdivisions	19 counties

Economy

GDP	$89,500,000,000
Per capita	$20,775
Monetary unit	Krone
Trade partners	Exports: U.K., Sweden, Germany Imports: Sweden, Germany, U.K., U.S.
Exports	Petroleum, natural gas, fish, ships and boats, aluminum, pulp and paper
Imports	Machinery, fuels and lubricants, transportation equipment, chemicals

Land

Description	Northern Europe
Area	149,412 mi² (386,975 km²)
Highest point	Galdhøpiggen, 8,100 ft (2,469 m)
Lowest point	Sea level

The above information includes Svalbard and Jan Mayen.

Hjelmland, east of Stavanger

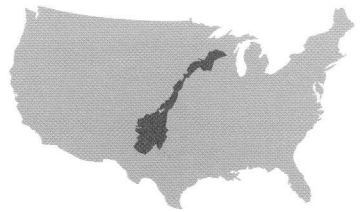

POPULATION COMPARISON
Norway=2% of U.S.

United States

GDP COMPARISON
Norway=1% of U.S.

United States

POPULATION DISTRIBUTION
Urban   Rural

People

Because of its relatively remote location in far northern Europe, Norway has seen few population migrations and possesses a virtually homogeneous population, which is predominantly Germanic, Norwegian-speaking, and Lutheran. Small communities of Lapps and Finns live in the far north, while most Norwegians live in the south and along the coast. The people enjoy many government-provided social services and programs.

Economy and the Land

Norway's economy, based on shipping, trade, and the mining of offshore oil and natural gas, takes its shape from the nation's proximity to several seas. Shipbuilding, fishing, and forestry are also important activities. Norway is a leading producer of hydroelectricity. Combined with some government control of the economy, these lucrative activities have given the nation a high standard of living and fairly low unemployment. Most of Norway is a high plateau covered with mountains. The Gulf Stream gives the nation a much milder climate than other places at the same latitude.

History and Politics

Parts of present-day Norway were inhabited by about 9000 B.C. Germanic tribes began immigrating to the area about 2000 B.C. Between A.D. 800 and 1100, Viking ships from Norway raided coastal towns throughout Western Europe and also colonized Greenland and Iceland. Unified around 900, Norway was subsequently shaken by civil war, plague, and the end of its royal line. It entered a union with Denmark in 1380, becoming a Danish province in 1536. Around the end of the Napoleonic Wars, in 1814, Norway became part of Sweden. A long struggle against Swedish rule ended in 1905 as Sweden recognized Norwegian independence, and a Danish prince was made king. Norway was neutral in World War I but endured German occupation during World War II. In 1967 the government initiated a wide-ranging social-welfare system.

During the Cold War, Norway was the only member of NATO to share a border with the Soviet Union. Nearly one-third of Norway lies within the Arctic Circle; the frozen north is home to many more reindeer than people.

Seaside villages like Alesund have found their traditional reliance on fishing supplanted by industry. However, modern trawlers continue to supply the great amounts of frozen cod, canned sardines, and canned herring that are exported each year.

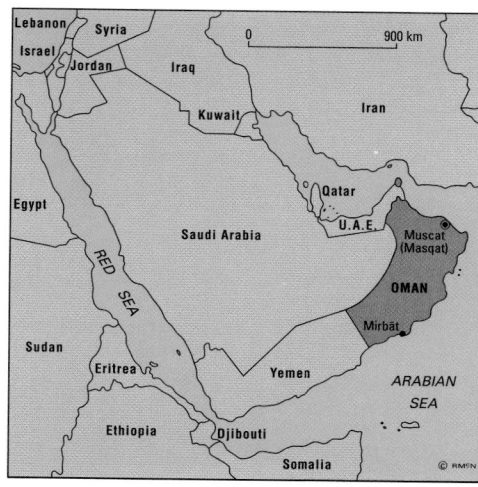

O man was known as Muscat and Oman until 1970. In that year the ruling sultan was deposed by his son, who consolidated political power to the diminutive state of Oman in the north, renaming the country in the process. With an average summer temperature in some places of 120 degrees, Oman is one of the hottest places on Earth.

OMAN

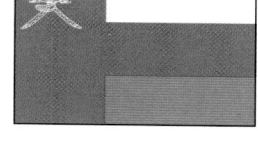

People

Most of Oman's population is Arab, Arabic-speaking, and belongs to the Ibadite sect of Islam. Other forms of Islam are also practiced. There is a significant foreign community that includes Indians, Baluchis from Pakistan, and East African blacks. Many of them are guest workers in the oil industry.

Economy and the Land

Once a mainstay of Oman's economy, oil revenues declined as prices fell throughout the 1980s. The mining of natural gas and copper is being developed, as are agriculture and fishing. A central position in the politically volatile Persian Gulf and revolutionary internal strife have led Oman to devote a considerable portion of its budget to defense. Land regions include a coastal plain and interior mountains and desert. Oman's land borders are undefined and in dispute. A desert climate prevails over most areas except the coast, which has humid conditions.

History and Politics

Islam came to Muscat and Oman, as the nation was known before 1970, in the seventh century A.D. The Portuguese gained control of parts of the coast in 1508 but were driven out in 1650 by the Arabs. At about this time the hereditary sultanate—which absorbed the political power formerly held by the Ibadite religious leaders, or imams—was founded. Close relations with Britain, cemented in a 1798 agreement and subsequent treaties, have continued to the present. Conflicts between the sultan and Omanis, who wanted to be ruled exclusively by their imam, erupted intermittently after 1900, and in 1959 the sultan defeated the rebels with British help and outlawed the office of imam. Marxist insurgency was put down in 1975. Sultan Qaboos bin Said, who overthrew his father's regime in 1970, has liberalized some policies and worked to modernize the nation. Oman is still somewhat isolated and discourages foreign contacts.

Oman at a glance

Official name Sultanate of Oman

People

Population	2,089,000
Density	25/mi² (9.8/km²)
Urban	11%
Capital	Muscat, 30,000
Ethnic groups	Arab, Baluchi, Zanzibari, Indian
Languages	Arabic, English, Baluchi, Urdu, Indian dialects
Religions	Ibadite Muslim 75%, Sunni Muslim, Shiite Muslim, Hindu
Life expectancy	72 female, 68 male

Politics

Government	Monarchy
Parties	None
Suffrage	None
Memberships	AL, UN
Subdivisions	7 regions

Economy

GDP	$6,400,000,000
Per capita	$10,142
Monetary unit	Rial
Trade partners	Exports: United Arab Emirates, Saudi Arabia, U.K. Imports: United Arab Emirates, Japan, U.K.
Exports	Petroleum, fish, copper metal, fruits and vegetables
Imports	Machinery, transportation equipment, manufactures, food, livestock

Land

Description	Southwestern Asia
Area	82,030 mi² (212,457 km²)
Highest point	Mt. Sham, 9,957 ft (3,035 m)
Lowest point	Sea level

POPULATION COMPARISON
Oman=0.8% of U.S.

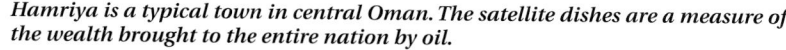

United States

GDP COMPARISON
Oman=0.3% of U.S.

United States

POPULATION DISTRIBUTION
Urban   Rural

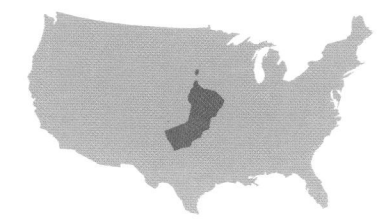

Hamriya is a typical town in central Oman. The satellite dishes are a measure of the wealth brought to the entire nation by oil.

Boys and young camel, near the Yemeni border

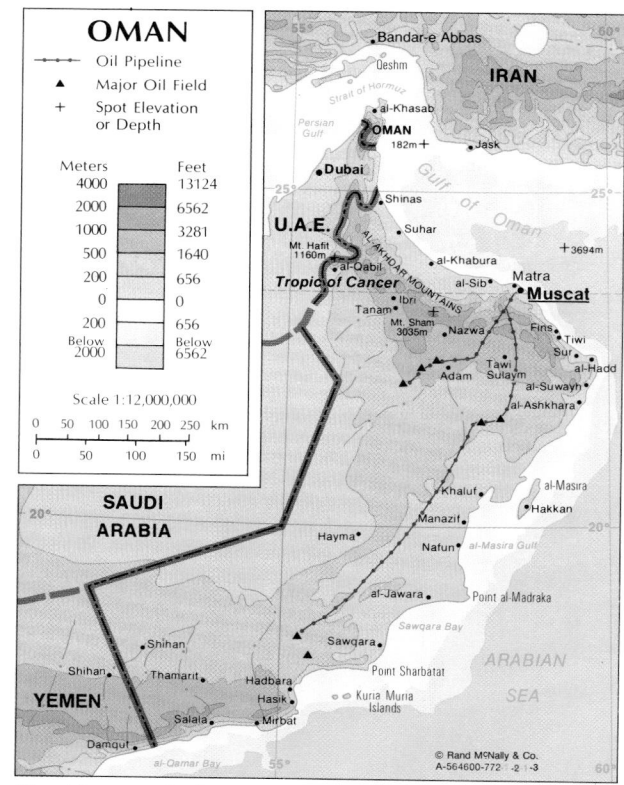

Frankincense, the fragrant treasure of biblical lore, is extracted from trees growing in the Dhofar region in the southwest, one of the very few parts of Oman that isn't desert.

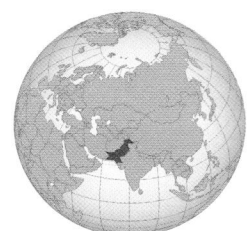

PAKISTAN

The Karakoram Range sweeps across Kashmir in the north of Pakistan. India has claimed the same territory, and there have been occasional border clashes. The Hunza District shown here is shaped by glaciers which have formed deep gorges.

Badshahi Mosque, Lahore

People

Pakistan's varied ethnicity is the product of centuries of incursions by different races. Today each people is concentrated in a different region and speaks its own language; English and Urdu, official languages, are not widely spoken. The Punjabis compose the largest ethnic group and traditionally have been influential in government and commerce. Virtually all of Pakistan, which was created as a Muslim homeland, follows Islam. Spurred by poor living conditions and a lack of jobs, many Pakistanis work abroad.

Economy and the Land

Despite recent progress in manufacturing, agriculture remains the economic mainstay. Improvement in farming techniques has increased productivity. Government planning and foreign assistance have aided all sectors, but Pakistan remains troubled by population growth, unskilled labor, a trade deficit, and an influx of refugees fleeing the war in Afghanistan. Pakistan's terrain includes mountains, fertile plains, and desert. The climate is continental, with extremes in temperature.

History and Politics

Around 2500 B.C., the Indus Valley civilization flourished in the area of modern Pakistan. Various empires and immigrants

followed, including Aryans, Persians, and Greeks. Invading Arabs introduced Islam to the region in the A.D. 700s. In the 1500s the Mogul Empire of Afghanistan came to include nearly all of present-day Pakistan, India, and Bangladesh, and as that empire declined, various peoples ruled the area. Through wars and treaties, the British presence in Asia expanded, and by the early twentieth century British India included all of modern Pakistan. Because of hostilities between British India's Muslims and Hindus, the separate Muslim nation of Pakistan was created when British India gained independence in 1947. With its boundaries drawn around the Muslim population centers, Pakistan was formed from the northeastern and northwestern parts of India, and its eastern region was separated from the west by more than 1,000 miles (1,600 km). East Pakistanis felt that power was unfairly concentrated in the west, and in 1971 a civil war erupted. Aided by India, East Pakistan won the war and became the independent nation of Bangladesh. After the death of President Mohammed Zia in 1988, the people elected Benazir Bhutto, who revived the People's party of her father, a previous president. She was ousted in 1990 but reinstated as Prime Minister in 1993. Political violence has escalated as ethnic groups and Islamic fundamentalists struggle for power.

Historic tensions with India have caused the Pakistani government to devote large sums to the military, despite a fast-growing population and massive infrastructure needs. The country has benefited from foreign aid from the United States, owing to its strategic location amidst Russia, China, India and Iran. Pakistan was a major source of support for Afghan rebels during the years of Soviet occupation of Afghanistan.

POPULATION COMPARISON
Pakistan=48% of U.S.

United States

POPULATION DISTRIBUTION
Urban   Rural

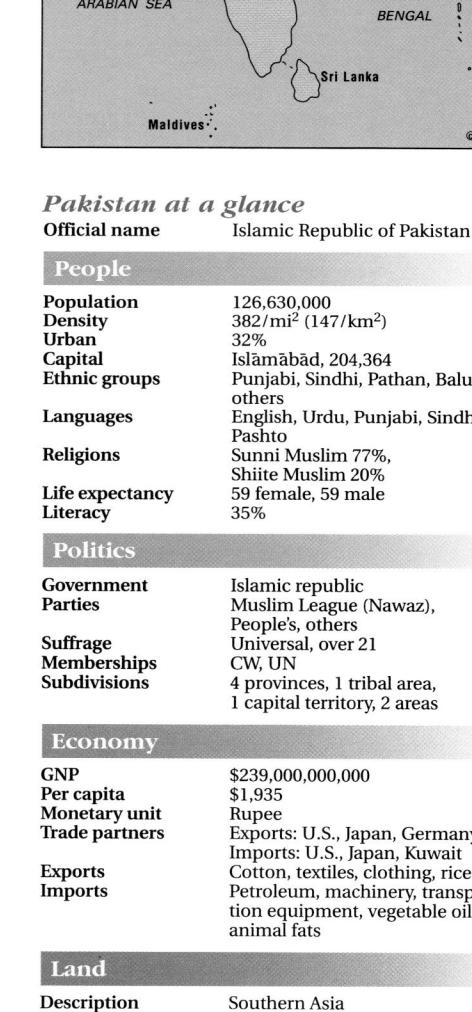

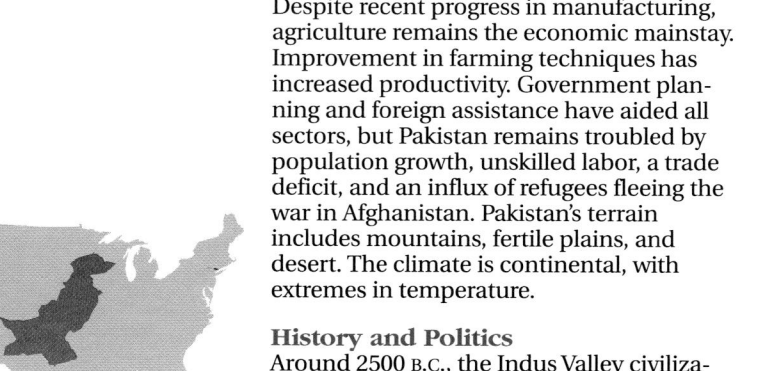

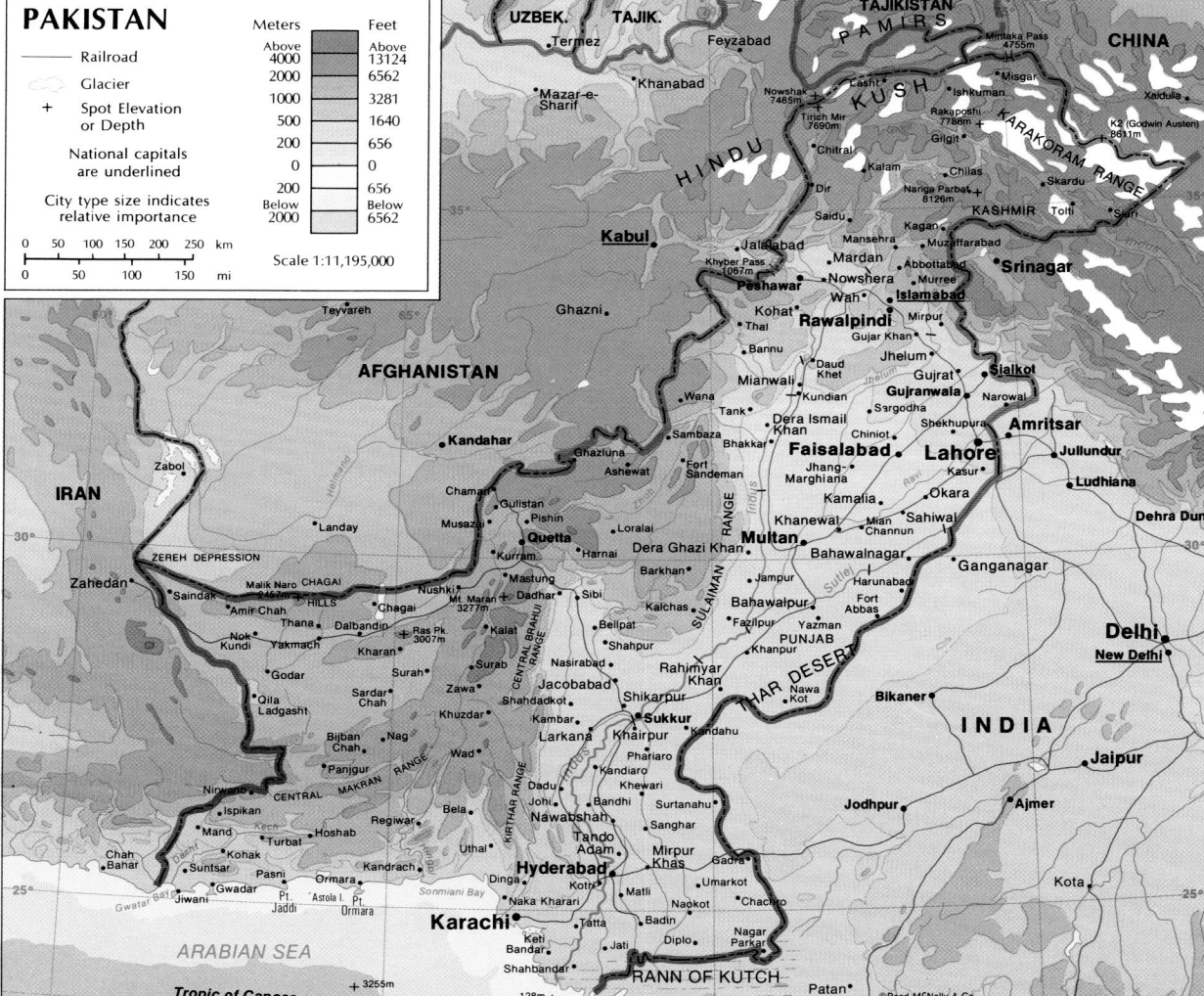

Pakistan has three distinct geographic regions. The northern highlands are a region of formidable mountains. The west is a varied, arid landscape of mountains, plateaus, and basins. The south is a fertile plain of rivers.

Pakistan at a glance

Official name	Islamic Republic of Pakistan

People

Population	126,630,000
Density	382/mi² (147/km²)
Urban	32%
Capital	Islāmābād, 204,364
Ethnic groups	Punjabi, Sindhi, Pathan, Baluchi, others
Languages	English, Urdu, Punjabi, Sindhi, Pashto
Religions	Sunni Muslim 77%, Shiite Muslim 20%
Life expectancy	59 female, 59 male
Literacy	35%

Politics

Government	Islamic republic
Parties	Muslim League (Nawaz), People's, others
Suffrage	Universal, over 21
Memberships	CW, UN
Subdivisions	4 provinces, 1 tribal area, 1 capital territory, 2 areas

Economy

GNP	$239,000,000,000
Per capita	$1,935
Monetary unit	Rupee
Trade partners	Exports: U.S., Japan, Germany Imports: U.S., Japan, Kuwait
Exports	Cotton, textiles, clothing, rice
Imports	Petroleum, machinery, transportation equipment, vegetable oils, animal fats

Land

Description	Southern Asia
Area	339,732 mi² (879,902 km²)
Highest point	K2, 28,250 ft (8,611 m)
Lowest point	Sea level

The above information includes part of Jammu and Kashmir.

Scale 1:3,000,000   One inch represents approximately 47 miles.
One centimeter represents 30 kilometers.

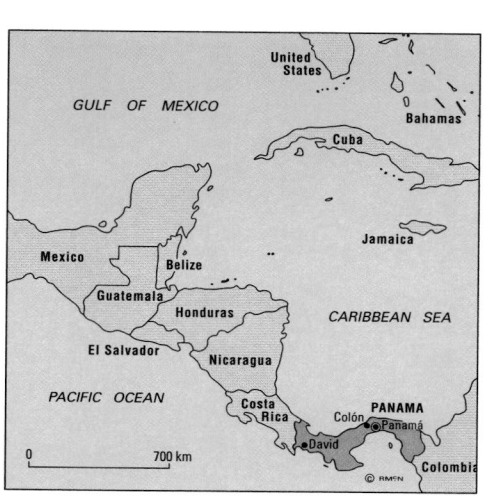

Palau at a glance

People	
Population	17,000
Density	87/mi² (33/km²)
Urban	51%
Capital	Koror, Babelthuap Island, 9,018
Ethnic groups	Palauan (Mixed Polynesian, Malayan, and Melanesian)
Languages	Angaur, English, Japanese, Palauan, Sonsorolese, Tobi
Religions	Roman Catholic, Protestant, tribal religionist
Life expectancy	73 female, 69 male
Literacy	92%

Politics	
Government	Republic
Parties	None
Suffrage	Universal, over 18
Memberships	UN
Subdivisions	16 states

Economy	
GDP	$32,000,000
Per capita	$2,286
Monetary unit	U.S. dollar
Trade partners	U.S., Japan
Exports	Fish, copra, handicrafts
Imports	Food, consumer goods

Land	
Description	North Pacific islands
Area	196 mi2 (508 km²)
Highest point	804 ft (245 m)
Lowest point	Sea level

Official name — Republic of Palau

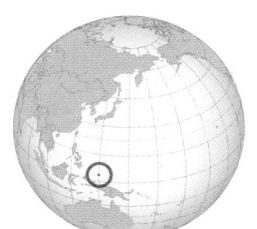

PALAU

The eight inhabited islands of the Republic of Palau, the last trust territory of the United Nations administered by the United States, became independent in 1994. Although the islands offer stunning scenery and a tropical climate, they have had difficulty developing a significant tourism industry because of their remote location.

People

Palau's majority group is Micronesian, and languages include English as well as Malay-Polynesian tongues. The islands are divided into six states, each with its own governor, but the village chiefs continue to wield power as well

Economy and the Land

Government jobs provide for much employment, but the service sector is on the rise as tourism expands. Foreign investment has increased as well. Phosphate deposits on the island of Angaur once fueled a prosperous export industry, but reserves were depleted in 1955, and economic plans include further exploration and exploitation of natural resources. The United States continues to supply economic assistance. Palau is made up of a group of islands in the Caroline Islands. The northern islands in the group are volcanic, and the southern islands are coral. The climate is tropical.

History and Politics

The Spanish seafarer Ruy Lopez de Villalobos was the first to sight the Palau Islands, in 1543. Spaniards controlled the islands until 1899, when Spain sold Palau to Germany. Following World War I, Palau came under Japan's jurisdiction as a League of Nations mandate. Japan invested in improvements for certain islands, constructing a naval base on Beliliou, and soon an influx of Japanese settlers boosted the islands' population. Some of World War II's bloodiest battles between the United States and Japan took place at Beliliou in 1944. War memorials for both Japanese and American soldiers stand on the island today, and the remains of warships and planes are found in the offshore waters. After the war, in 1947, Palau along with the Northern Marianas, the islands of the Federated States of Micronesia, and the Marshall Islands were declared a United Nations trust territory under United States administration. Palau adopted a constitution in 1980, declaring itself the Republic of Palau, and a constitutional government was installed in 1981. Palau became independent in 1994, thus ending the U.N. Trusteeship. Palau has voted for a compact of free association with the U.S. which provides the islands with financial assistance and the U.S. with a strategic military foothold in the South Pacific.

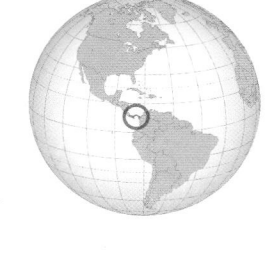

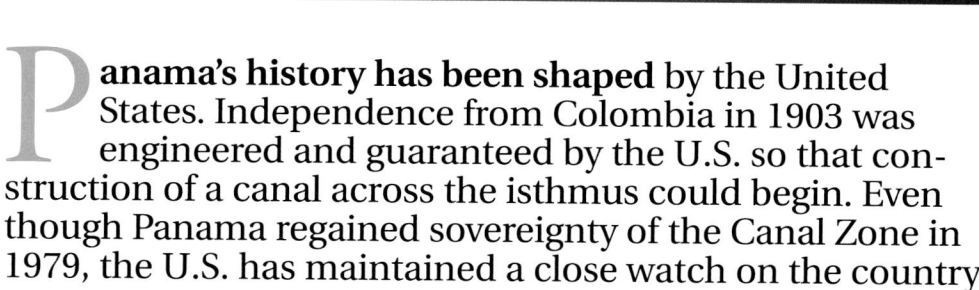

PANAMA

Gatun Lake is the large artificial body of water that was formed when the locks and dams of the Panama Canal were constructed early in the century. The many islands were once the tops of hills. One, Barro Colorado, is home to hundreds of species of animals and is a nature preserve administered by the Smithsonian Institution of the United States.

Panama's history has been shaped by the United States. Independence from Colombia in 1903 was engineered and guaranteed by the U.S. so that construction of a canal across the isthmus could begin. Even though Panama regained sovereignty of the Canal Zone in 1979, the U.S. has maintained a close watch on the country.

POPULATION COMPARISON
Panama=1% of U.S.

United States

GDP COMPARISON
Panama=0.2% of U.S.

United States

ETHNIC GROUPS

POPULATION DISTRIBUTION
Urban   Rural

People

Most Panamanians are mestizos, a mixture of Spanish and Indian stocks. Indigenous Indians, blacks from the West Indies, and whites form the remaining population. A Spanish legacy is reflected by the official language, Spanish, and the predominance of Roman Catholicism. Most people live near the Panama Canal. A wealthy elite has traditionally directed the government and economy.

Economy and the Land

Because of its location, Panama has been a strategic center for trade and transportation. The 1914 opening of the Panama Canal, connecting the Atlantic and Pacific oceans, accentuated these strengths and has provided additional revenue and jobs; the canal area is now Panama's most economically developed region. Agriculture is an important activity; and oil refining, food processing, fishing, and financial services all contribute to the economy as well. *(continued)*

The Panama Canal cannot accommodate many modern ships, such as super tankers, because they are too wide for its now comparatively narrow locks. Such vessels must sail around Cape Horn, just as clipper ships did in the 1800s.

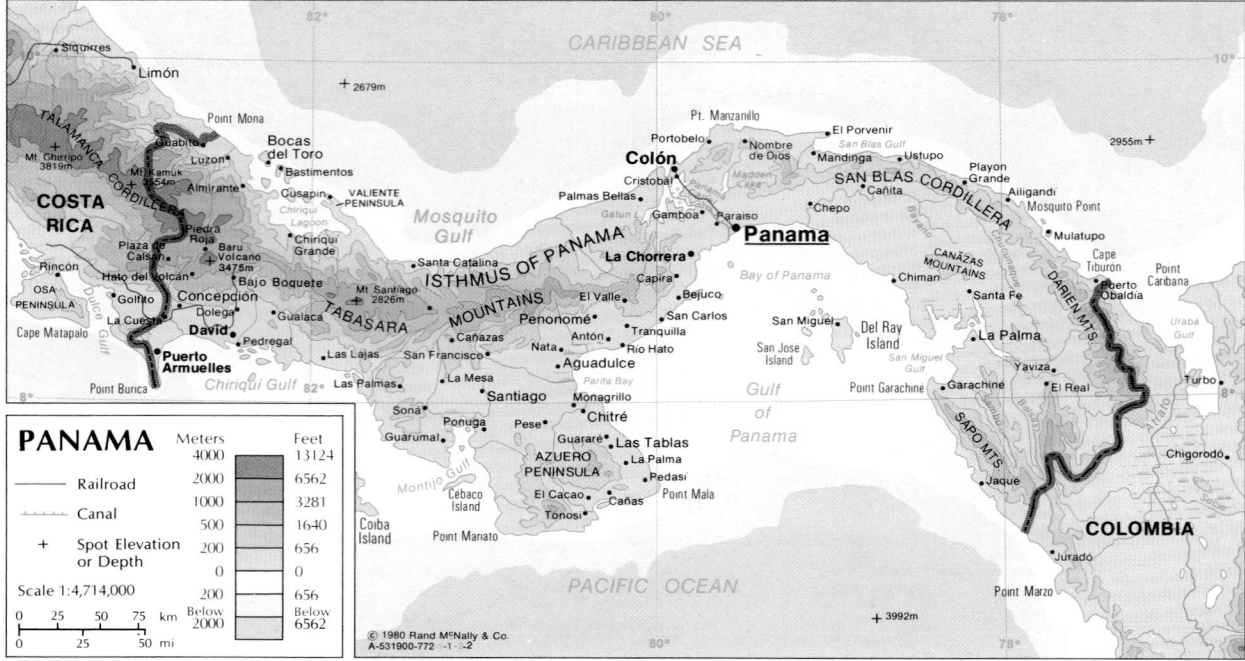

People

Population	2,654,000
Density	91/mi² (35/km²)
Urban	53%
Capital	Panamá, 411,549
Ethnic groups	Mestizo 70%, West Indian 14%, white 10%, Amerindian 6%
Languages	Spanish, English
Religions	Roman Catholic 85%, Protestant 15%
Life expectancy	75 female, 71 male
Literacy	88%

Politics

Government	Republic
Parties	Christian Democrat, Nationalist Republican Liberal Movement, Authentic Liberal, others
Suffrage	Universal, over 18
Memberships	OAS, UN
Subdivisions	9 provinces, 1 intendency

Economy

GDP	$11,600,000,000
Per capita	$4,540
Monetary unit	Balboa
Trade partners	Exports: U.S., Germany, Costa Rica. Imports: U.S., Ecuador, Japan
Exports	Bananas, shrimp, sugar, clothing, coffee
Imports	Machinery, petroleum, food, manufactures, chemicals

Land

Description	Central America
Area	29,157 mi² (75,517 km²)
Highest point	Baru Volcano, 11,401 ft (3,475 m)
Lowest point	Sea level

Cuna Indian girl, San Blas Islands, off Panama's northern coast

Panama will have to adjust to the economic and technical losses that will accompany the end of United States operation of the canal in 1999. The country has a mountainous interior and a tropical climate.

History and Politics

Originally inhabited by Indians, Panama became a Spanish colony in the early 1500s and served as a vital transportation center. In 1821 it overcame Spanish rule and entered the Republic of Greater Colombia. After Colombia vetoed a United States plan to build a canal across the narrow isthmus, Panama, encouraged by the United States, seceded from the republic and became independent in 1903. Eleven years later, America completed the canal and established control over it and the Panama Canal Zone. Dissatisfaction with this arrangement resulted in several anti-American riots in the fifties and sixties. A 1968 coup placed the Panamanian National Guard in power, and the movement to end American control of the Canal Zone gained momentum. In 1979 the sovereignty of the Canal Zone was transferred to Panama; it will gain control of the canal in 1999. Beginning in 1994 military bases began reverting to Panamanian control. General Manuel Noriega maintained a repressive and corrupt control of the government until U.S. military forces invaded and overthrew him in 1989. Elections in May 1994 returned the reformed party of Noriega to power.

New Guinea and the other islands around the Bismarck Sea represent one of the world's last great frontiers. Each year explorers and scientists make new discoveries.

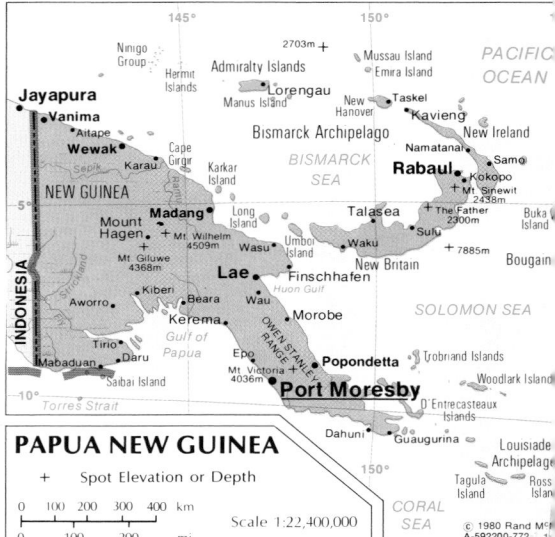

PAPUA NEW GUINEA

People

Population	3,989,000
Density	22/mi² (8.6/km²)
Urban	16%
Capital	Port Moresby, New Guinea I., 193,242
Ethnic groups	Melanesian, Papuan, Negrito, Micronesian, Polynesian
Languages	English, Motu, Pidgin, indigenous
Religions	Roman Catholic 22%, Lutheran 16%, United Church 8%, Anglican 5%
Life expectancy	57 female, 55 male
Literacy	52%

Politics

Government	Parliamentary state
Parties	Pangu (United), People's Action, People's Democratic Movement, People's Progress, others
Suffrage	Universal, over 18
Memberships	CW, UN
Subdivisions	19 provinces, 1 capital district

Economy

GDP	$3,400,000,000
Per capita	$859
Monetary unit	Kina
Trade partners	Exports: Japan, Germany, Korea. Imports: Australia, Japan, U.S.
Exports	Copper, gold, coffee, lumber, palm oil, cocoa, lobster
Imports	Machinery and transportation equipment, food, fuel, chemicals

Land

Description	South Pacific islands
Area	178,704 mi² (462,840 km²)
Highest point	Mt. Wilhelm, 14,793 ft (4,509 m)
Lowest point	Sea level

People

Almost all inhabitants are Melanesians belonging to several thousand culturally diverse and geographically isolated communities. More than seven hundred languages are spoken, but most people also speak Motu or a dialect of English. European missionaries brought Christianity, but faiths based on spirit and ancestor worship predominate. The traditions of village life remain strong.

Economy and the Land

The economic supports are agriculture, which employs most of the workforce, and copper and gold mining. Papua New Guinea has other mineral resources, as well as potential for forestry. The nation consists of the eastern half of New Guinea Island, plus New Britain, New Ireland, Bougainville, and six hundred smaller islands. Terrain includes mountains, volcanoes, broad valleys, and swamps; the climate is tropical.

History and Politics

Settlers from Southeast Asia are thought to have arrived as long as fifty thousand years ago. Isolated native villages were found by the Spanish and Portuguese in the early 1500s. In 1884 Germany annexed the northeastern part of the island of New Guinea and its offshore islands, and Britain took control of the southeastern section and its islands. Australia assumed administration of the British territory, known as Papua, in 1906 and seized the German regions, or German New Guinea, during World War I. The League of Nations granted Australia a mandate to New Guinea in 1920. After being occupied by Japan in World War II, Papua and New Guinea were united as an Australian territory from 1945 to 1946. Papua New Guinea gained independence in 1975. A separatist movement in Bougainville continues to plague the central government.

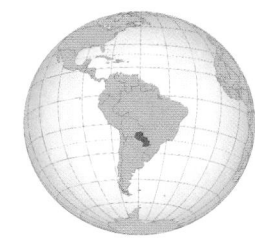

Asunción, capital of Paraguay, is the only sizable city in the country. The quiet center still features traditional low-rise Spanish buildings such as these shown here around the Plaza de los Heroes. The city lies at the juncture of the Pilcomayo and Paraguay Rivers.

PARAGUAY

Over ninety percent of Paraguayans live in the fertile region east of the Paraguay River. The vast, arid Chaco region in the west is home to only two percent of the population.

People

Paraguay's population displays a homogeneity unusual in South America; most people are a mix of Spanish and Guarani Indian ancestry, are Roman Catholic, and speak both Spanish and Guarani. The small number of unassimilated Guarani live mostly in western Paraguay, known as the Gran Chaco. There are some foreign communities, mostly German, Japanese, and Brazilian. Culture combines Spanish and Indian traditions.

Economy and the Land

Agriculture—based on cotton, soybeans, and cattle—forms the keystone of the economy. Forestry also contributes significantly to Paraguay's exports. the lack of direct access to the sea, unskilled labor, and a history of war and instability have resulted in an underdeveloped economy; manufacturing in particular has suffered. The world's largest hydroelectric project, the Itaipu Dam, was completed in 1988. Paraguay has two distinct regions, divided by the Paraguay River: the semiarid Gran Chaco plains in the west, and the temperate, fertile east, where most farming takes place.

History and Politics

The indigenous Guarani formed an agricultural society centered around what is now Asunción. Portuguese and Spanish explorers arrived in the early 1500s, and the region subsequently gained importance as the center of Spanish holdings in southern South America. During the 1700s, Jesuit missionaries worked to convert thousands of Indians to Roman Catholicism. After gaining independence in 1811, Paraguay was ruled by a succession of dictators. A disastrous war against Argentina, Brazil, and Uruguay from 1865 to 1870 cost the nation half its population. Another war against Bolivia from 1932 to 1935 increased Paraguay's territory but further weakened its stability. A military coup in 1989 ended the 35-year regime of General Stroessner, but the 1993 election of a civilian leader brought little change. The country is still controlled by the military.

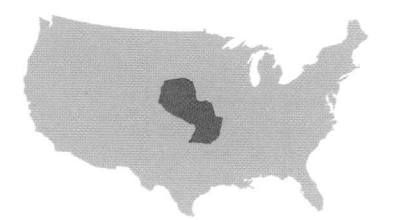

Paraguay and its neighbor Bolivia are the only landlocked countries in South America.

Paraguay at a glance

Official name	Republic of Paraguay

People

Population	4,400,000
Density	28/mi² (11/km²)
Urban	48%
Capital	Asunción, 502,426
Ethnic groups	Mestizo 95%, white and Amerindian 5%
Languages	Spanish, Guarani
Religions	Roman Catholic 90%, Mennonite and other Protestant
Life expectancy	70 female, 65 male
Literacy	90%

Politics

Government	Republic
Parties	Authentic Radical Liberal, Colorado, others
Suffrage	Universal, over 18
Memberships	OAS, UN
Subdivisions	19 departments, 1 city

Economy

GDP	$15,200,000,000
Per capita	$3,038
Monetary unit	Guarani
Trade partners	Exports: Brazil, Netherlands Imports: Brazil, Argentina, Algeria, U.S.
Exports	Cotton, soybeans, wood, vegetable oil, coffee, tung oil, meat
Imports	Machinery, manufactures, petroleum, fuel, raw materials, food

Land

Description	Central South America, landlocked
Area	157,048 mi² (406,752 km²)
Highest point	Unnamed, 2,625 ft (800 m)
Lowest point	Confluence of Paraná and Paraguay rivers, 151 ft (46 m)

POPULATION COMPARISON
Paraguay=2% of U.S.

United States

GDP COMPARISON
Paraguay=0.2% of U.S.

United States

ETHNIC GROUPS

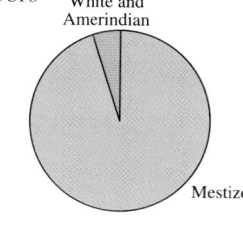
White and Amerindian

Mestizo

POPULATION DISTRIBUTION
Urban   Rural

Cattle, southern Paraguay

Boys on horseback survey a ranch near San Ignacío, 50 miles north of the Argentinean border. Cattle are Paraguay's greatest agricultural resource, although the country's isolated location restricts exports.

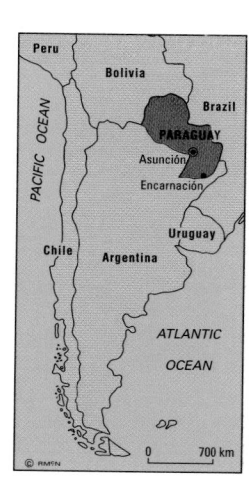

PERU

The Urubamba Valley in the Peruvian highlands is the center of Inca ruins. Stones in some of the long abandoned cities weigh more than 300 tons. Archeologists can only speculate about how they were moved.

Peru at a glance

Official name   Republic of Peru

People

Population	23,095,000
Density	47/mi² (18/km²)
Urban	70%
Capital	Lima, 371,122
Ethnic groups	Amerindian 45%, mestizo 37%, white 15%
Languages	Quechua, Spanish, Aymara
Religions	Roman Catholic
Life expectancy	67 female, 63 male
Literacy	85%

Politics

Government	Republic
Parties	American Popular Revolutionary Alliance, New Majority-Change 90, Popular Action, United Left
Suffrage	Universal, over 18
Memberships	OAS, UN
Subdivisions	24 departments, 1 constitutional province

Economy

GDP	$70,000,000,000
Per capita	$3,044
Monetary unit	Sol
Trade partners	Exports: U.S., Japan, U.K. Imports: U.S., Panama, Germany, Argentina
Exports	Copper, fishmeal, zinc, petroleum, lead, silver, coffee, cotton
Imports	Food, machinery, transportation equipment, iron and steel, chemicals

Land

Description	Western South America
Area	496,225 mi² (1,285,216 km²)
Highest point	Huascarán, 22,133 ft (6,746 m)
Lowest point	Sea level

Ancient cities of the Incas, colonial opulence of the Spaniards, and stunning scenery make Peru a cultural and visual standout. Sadly, political insurrection and terrorism brought bloodshed to the land during much of the 1980s. The economy and tourism are slowly recovering.

Ruins of Machu Picchu, north of Cusco

People

Peru's Indian population constitutes the nation's largest ethnic group and the largest Indian concentration in North or South America. Although whites make up the third-largest group after Indians and mestizos, they have historically controlled much of the wealth. The Indians are often geographically and culturally remote from the ruling classes and generally live in poverty. Most Peruvians practice Roman Catholicism.

Economy and the Land

Considerable natural resources have made Peru a leader in the production of minerals—notably copper, lead, and silver—and in fishing. The food-processing, textile, and oil-refining industries also contribute. Productivity has been slowed by a mountainous terrain that impedes transport and communication, earthquakes and other natural disasters, a largely unskilled workforce, and years of stringent military rule. Climate varies from arid to mild in the coastal desert to temperate but cool in the Andean highlands, and hot and humid in the eastern jungles and plains.

History and Politics

Several Native American cultures arose in the region between 900 B.C. and A.D. 1200, the last of which was the Incan. Excavation began in 1987 of the richest pre-Hispanic ruler ever discovered, further documenting the sophistication of these cultures. Builders of an empire stretching from Colombia to Chile, the Inca were conquered by the Spanish in 1533. For almost the next three hundred years, Peru was a harshly ruled Spanish colony and center for colonial administration. Peru achieved independence from Spain in 1821, largely through the efforts of José de San Martín of Argentina and Simón Bolívar of Venezuela, although Spain did not formally recognize Peruvian independence until 1879. Military officers ruled the country through the rest of the century. In 1883, Chile and Bolivia defeated Peru in the War of the Pacific, and the country lost its valuable southern nitrite region. Fernando Belaúnde Terry, a moderate reformer, was elected in 1963. A military junta ousted him in 1968, nationalizing some industries and instituting land reform. Inflation and unemployment caused dissatisfaction and a 1975 coup. Elections in 1980 and 1985 restored democratic leadership. However, economic chaos has since destabilized the government and allowed the growth of the Shining Path, a terrorist guerrilla movement. Alberto Fujimori, elected in 1990, has controlled the Shining Path and improved the economy, although the distribution of wealth remains uneven.

Cusco, a city of 200,000, is the present regional capital of the department which encompasses the Urubamba Valley. The city was the capital of the Inca empire, and many of its buildings are constructed on foundations of stone first cut by the Incas.

PERU

Legend	
——	Railroad
+++	Oil Pipeline
▲	Major Oil Field
+	Spot Elevation or Depth

Meters	Feet
Above 4000	Above 13124
2000	6562
1000	3281
500	1640
200	656
0	0
200	656
Below 2000	Below 6562

Scale 1:14,667,000

0 50 100 150 200 km
0 50 100 150 mi

© Rand McNally & Co.
A-541100-772 -1-1-2

The Andes form Peru's spine. Melting snow from their peaks combines with other run-offs and tributaries to form the Amazon River.

POPULATION COMPARISON
Peru=9% of U.S.

United States

GDP COMPARISON
Peru=1% of U.S.

United States

ETHNIC GROUPS

White — Other
Mestizo — Amerindian

POPULATION DISTRIBUTION
Urban   Rural

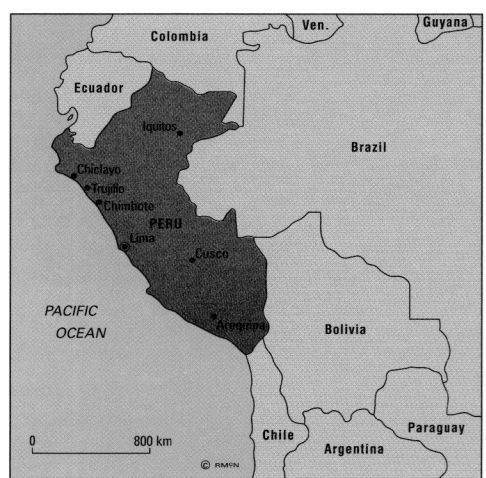

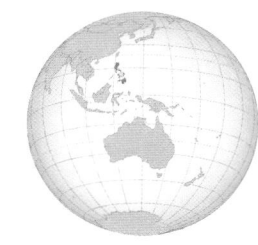

Cattle descend a hilly path on a ranch on Luzon, the largest and most important island of the Philippines. The lowlands have fertile soil that is excellent for farming. At higher elevations, the soil is poor and rocky and is best suited for cattle grazing.

PHILIPPINES

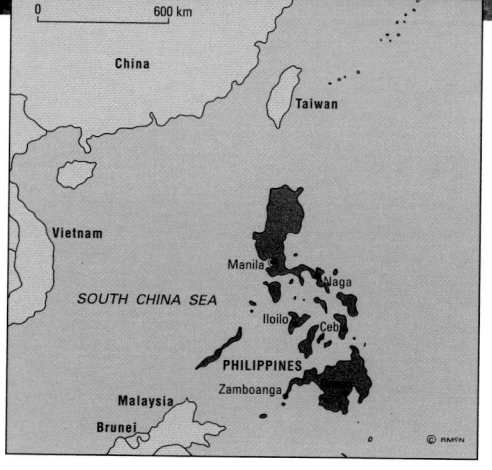

The Philippines are an almost ungraspable collection of over 7,000 tropical islands. The culture derives from Malayan, American and Spanish influences, and exists in myriad permutations throughout the islands. Politics and religions span the spectrum and have been the frequent cause of violent upheaval. The government has all but ceded some islands to communist rebels. Administering the Philippines has proven a nearly impossible task, and many officials have shown a greater penchant for scandal than leadership.

People
Nearly all Filipinos are descended from Malay peoples. The majority are Roman Catholic, a reflection of centuries of Spanish rule. A Muslim minority has begun agitating for autonomy. Although nearly ninety native languages and dialects are spoken, Pilipino and English are the official languages. The wide gap between rich and poor, inherited from a plantation economy, has concentrated wealth in the hands of the landowners.

Economy and the Land
Philippines is a primarily agricultural nation, relying on rice, sugar, coconuts, and wood. Fishing is an important activity. Considerable reserves of copper, nickel, and chromite make mining important. Manufacturing is developing through government incentives. A dependence on imported goods, along with inadequate but growing power and transport systems, has hampered growth. The archipelago of more than seven thousand islands is marked by mountains, volcanoes, forests, and inland plains. The climate is tropical and includes a typhoon season.

History and Politics
The islands are thought to have been settled by Negritos about thirty thousand years ago. Beginning about 3000 B.C., Malay immigrants arrived. By A.D. 1565 the area was under Spanish control, and the Roman

Catholic church had considerable influence throughout the Spanish period. In the late 1800s a movement for independence developed but was put down first by the Spanish and then by the United States, which gained the islands in 1898 after defeating Spain in the Spanish-American War. Japan occupied the Philippines during World War II. Independence came in 1946 and was followed by a rebellion by Communists demanding land reform; the rebels were defeated in 1954. Ferdinand Marcos was elected president in 1965 and, in the face of opposition from many quarters, declared martial law in 1972. Marcos lifted martial law in 1981 but was defeated in a 1986 presidential election by

Corazon Aquino, wife of assassinated opposition leader Benigno Aquino. Marcos eventually fled the island, and Aquino assumed power until 1992. The closing of Clark Air Base and Subic Bay Naval Base in 1992 ended an era of United States military presence in the Philippines. There is increasing conflict between Muslim and Christian factions, particularly in the Muslim-majority southern islands.

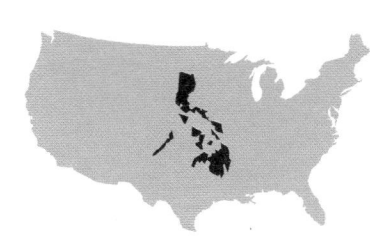

POPULATION COMPARISON
Philippines=26% of U.S.

United States

GDP COMPARISON
Philippines=3% of U.S.

United States

ETHNIC GROUPS

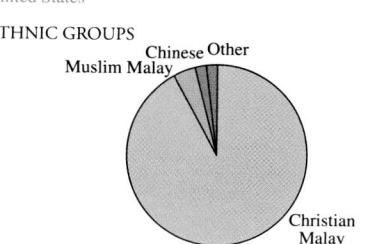
Chinese Other
Muslim Malay
Christian Malay

POPULATION DISTRIBUTION
Urban   Rural

Philippines at a glance
Official name Republic of the Philippines

People

Population	67,910,000
Density	586/mi² (226/km²)
Urban	43%
Capital	Manila, Luzon I., 1,598,918
Ethnic groups	Christian Malay 92%, Muslim Malay 4%, Chinese 2%
Languages	English, Pilipino, Tagalog
Religions	Roman Catholic 83%, Protestant 9%, Muslim 5%, Buddhist and others 3%
Life expectancy	67 female, 63 male
Literacy	90%

Politics

Government	Republic
Parties	Democratic Filipino Struggle, Nationalist People's Coalition, People Power-National Union of Christian Democrats
Suffrage	Universal, over 15
Memberships	ASEAN, UN
Subdivisions	73 provinces

Economy

GDP	$171,000,000,000
Per capita	$2,611
Monetary unit	Peso
Trade partners	Exports: U.S., Japan Imports: U.S., Japan, China
Exports	Electrical equipment, textiles, minerals, agricultural products, coconut
Imports	Raw materials, machinery, petroleum.

Land

Description	Southeastern Asian islands
Area	115,831 mi² (300,000 km²)
Highest point	Mt. Apo, 9,692 ft (2,954 m)
Lowest point	Sea level

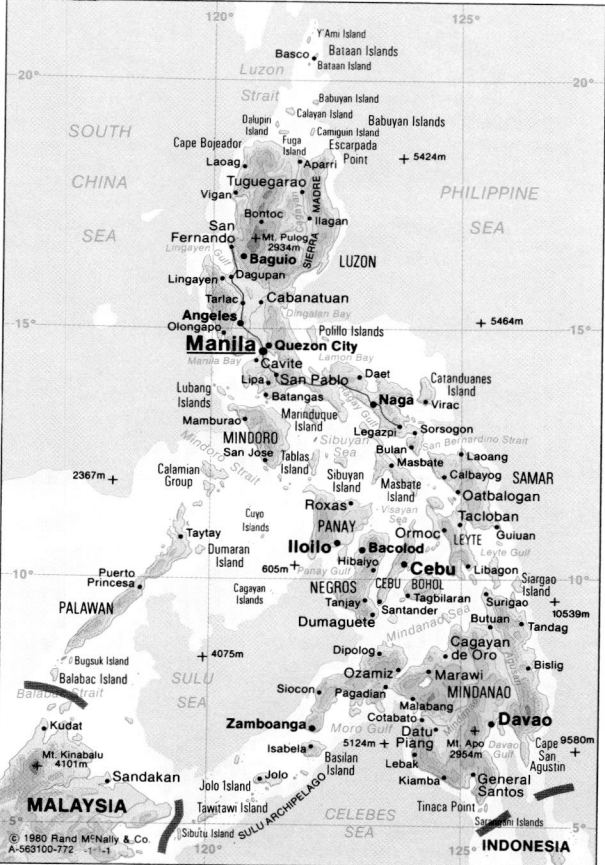

PHILIPPINES

	Meters	Feet
Railroad	Above 4000	Above 13124
Spot Elevation or Depth	2000	6562
	1000	3281
	500	1640
	200	656
	0	0

Meters	Feet
0	0
200	656
Below 2000	Below 6562

Scale 1:16,000,000

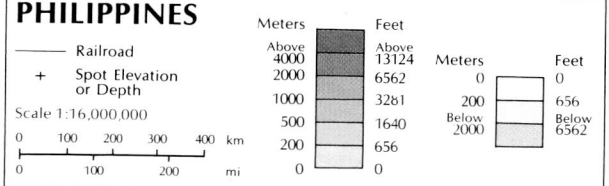

The 11 largest Philippine islands account for 94 percent of the land.

Pitcairn Island is the isolated home to fewer than 100 people, most of whom are descendants of mutineers from the H.M.S. *Bounty* and their Polynesian cohorts. The island is very fertile, and the islanders have no trouble growing all they need. Goods are bartered between them and no money is used.

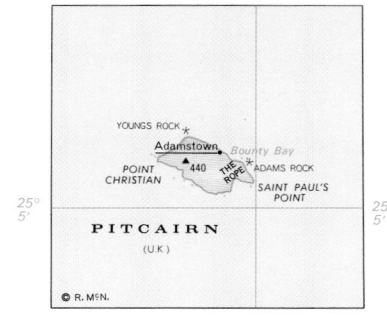

PITCAIRN

People
The population of Pitcairn is of mixed European and Tahitian ancestry, most descendants of British sailor Fletcher Christian and his fellow mutineers from H.M.S. *Bounty*. Uninhabited for about three years in the late 1850s, Pitcairn has been permanently occupied since 1859. In the past decades emigration to New Zealand has been an ongoing trend.

Economy and the Land
Fertile soil provide for subsistence farming and some export crops as well. Many islanders also engage in fishing and sell handicrafts to the passengers of the ships that dock here. Pitcairn is a rugged, volcanic island, and its shores are nearly inaccessible. The colony includes the uninhabited islands of Henderson, Dulcie, and Oeno. The climate is mild.

History and Politics
More than six hundred years ago, Polynesians likely lived on Pitcairn off and on, but it was uninhabited when the

British admiral Philip Carteret arrived in 1767, naming the island after the midshipman who first sighted it. In 1789 crew members of H.M.S. *Bounty*, led by Fletcher Christian, carried out a mutiny in the South Pacific, and the following year Christian, eight other mutineers, six Tahitian women, and twelve Tahitian men left Tahiti and sailed to Pitcairn. Violence marked the community's early days; by 1800 John Adams was the only surviving adult male. In 1808 a United States ship inadvertently arrived at the island, yet Pitcairn remained largely unheard of until 1814 when the British ships *Briton* and *Tagus* reached its shores. Between 1814 and 1831 the population grew from forty to eighty-six, and concern about drought and dwindling resources caused the Pitcairners to leave for Tahiti. Unable to adjust to the lifestyle of the island, they returned to Pitcairn six months later. In 1838 the islanders obtained a constitution and universal adult suffrage, and most Pitcairners trace the island's colonial status back to this time. Pitcairn was again evacuated when the United Kingdom arranged for resettlement on Norfolk Island in 1856, but forty-three Pitcairners returned to the island between 1859 and 1864. Pitcairn was officially made a British colony under the Settlements Act of 1887, and the island continues as a colony of the United Kingdom.

Pitcairn Island is connected to the outside world by very infrequent calls by ships. Its major source of outside revenue is postage stamp sales to collectors.

Pitcairn at a glance

Official name	Pitcairn, Henderson, Ducie and Oeno Islands

People

Population	100
Density	5.3/mi² (2.0/km²)
Capital	Adamstown, Pitcairn Island, 59
Ethnic groups	Mixed European and Tahitian
Languages	English, Tahitian
Religions	Seventh Day Adventist 100%

Politics

Government	Dependent territory (U.K.)
Suffrage	Universal, over 18
Memberships	None
Subdivisions	None

Economy

Monetary unit	New Zealand dollar
Exports	Fruits, vegetables, curios
Imports	Fuel, machinery, building materials, flour, sugar

Land

Description	South Pacific islands
Area	19 mi² (49 km²)
Highest point	1,445 ft (440 m)
Lowest point	Sea level

POLAND

Vendors and cafés enliven the Old Market Place in Warsaw. Few historic buildings survived World War II unscathed; much of the city was reconstructed after the war. Unlike this square, most of Warsaw's buildings are charmless structures built during the Communist era.

Historically, Poland has been on the major invasion route between eastern and western Europe. Successive armies of French, Germans, Russians, and others have laid waste to the gently rolling countryside and its peasant farmers. In the 1980s, it was the Poles' turn to fight, as they spent the decade protesting Communist domination. Since shaking off Soviet control, the hardworking country has struggled to build both a democracy and a free-market economy.

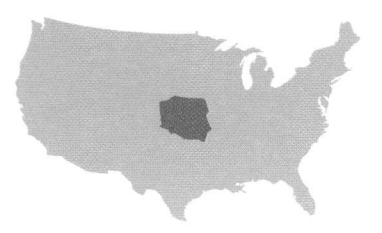

Torun, central Poland

POPULATION COMPARISON
Poland=15% of U.S.

United States

GDP COMPARISON
Poland=3% of U.S.

United States

ETHNIC GROUPS

Other

Polish

POPULATION DISTRIBUTION
Urban   Rural

The village of Zakopane is set high in the Tatra Mountains, just across the border from Slovakia. The region is characterized by jagged peaks and placid meadows. Vacationing Poles flock here for the hiking and skiing.

People
Poland's homogeneous population is partially a result of Nazi persecution during World War II, which virtually obliterated the Jewish community and led to the emigration of most minorities. Roman Catholicism, practiced by almost all Poles, remains a unifying force. The urban population has risen in the postwar period because of government emphasis on industrialization.

Economy and the Land
Government policies since the war transformed Poland from an agricultural nation into an industrial one. Machinery and textiles are important products. Since the collapse of communism in eastern Europe, an entrepreneurial spirit has taken hold. Privatization is proceeding, but slowly, in

order to keep inflation and unemployment under control. Poland has a mostly flat terrain—except for mountains in the south—and a temperate climate.

History and Politics
Slavic tribes inhabited the region of modern Poland several thousand years ago. The Piast dynasty began in the A.D. 900s and established Roman Catholicism as the official religion. In the sixteenth century, the Jagiellonian dynasty guided the empire to its height of expansion. A subsequent series of upheavals and wars weakened Poland, and from the 1770s to the 1790s it was partitioned three times, finally disappearing as an independent state. In 1918, following the Allies' World War I victory, Poland regained its independence and, through the 1919 Treaty of Versailles, much

of its former territory. World War II began with Germany's invasion of Poland in 1939. With the end of the war, Poland came under Communist control and Soviet domination. Antigovernment strikes and riots, some spurred by rising food prices, erupted periodically. In the first free election since Communist control, the trade union Solidarity, led by Lech Walesa. won an overwhelming victory in 1989. The nation is still struggling with the transition from a communist to a capitalist economy, and communism remains a strong influence.

Poland at a glance
Official name	Republic of Poland

People
Population	38,730,000
Density	320/mi² (123/km²)
Urban	62%
Capital	Warsaw, 1,644,500
Ethnic groups	Polish (mixed Slavic and Teutonic) 98%
Languages	Polish
Religions	Roman Catholic 95%
Life expectancy	76 female, 67 male
Literacy	99%

Politics
Government	Republic
Parties	Democratic Left Alliance, Democratic Union, Labor, Peasant, others
Suffrage	Universal, over 18
Memberships	UN
Subdivisions	49 provinces

Economy
GDP	$180,400,000,000
Per capita	$4,706
Monetary unit	Zloty
Trade partners	Exports: Former Soviet republics, Germany, U.K. Imports: Former Soviet republics, Germany, Austria
Exports	Machinery, metals, chemicals, fuel, food
Imports	Machinery, fuel, chemicals, food, manufactures

Land
Description	Eastern Europe
Area	121,196 mi² (313,895 km²)
Highest point	Rysy, 8,199 ft (2,499 m)
Lowest point	Raczki Elbląskie, -7 ft (-2 m)

POLAND
- Major Urban Area
- Railroad
- Canal or Waterway
- + Spot Elevation

National capitals are underlined

Scale 1:4,800,000

Meters	Feet
4000	13124
2000	6562
1000	3281
500	1640
200	656
0	Sea Level

0 25 50 75 100 km
0 25 50 75 mi

© Rand McNally & Co.
A-552500-772

Poland's borders have shifted often, owing to wars and a lack of strong natural features at the eastern and western extremes.

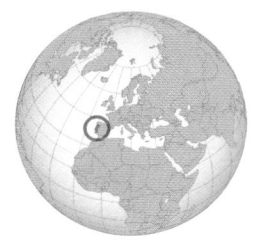

Portugal's maritime location has been one of the main factors in its history. Explorers sailed forth from Lisbon in the 15th and 16th centuries: Vasco da Gama was the first to sail around the Cape of Good Hope, and Ferdinand Magellan led a voyage that was the first to circumnavigate the world. Portugal's rich past has faded, and today the country is one of Europe's smallest and poorest. Per capita income is only 55 percent of the European Union's average.

PORTUGAL

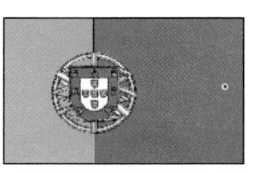

Albufeira is the largest resort on Portugal's Algarve Coast. Its street signs are in English out of deference to the hordes of tourists who visit each year. Away from the glitter, the Old Quarter is a showcase of Moorish architecture.

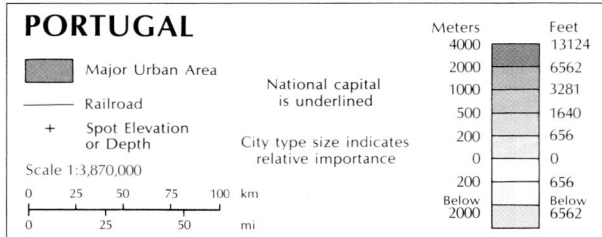

People

Although many foreign invaders have been drawn by Portugal's long coastline, today the population is relatively homogeneous. One group of invaders, the Romans, laid the basis for the chief language, Portuguese, which developed from Latin. The only significant minority is composed of black Africans from former colonies. Most Portuguese are rural and belong to the Roman Catholic church, which has had a strong influence on society.

Economy and the Land

The mainstays of agriculture and fishing were joined in the mid-1900s by manufacturing, chiefly of textiles, clothing, cork products, metals, and machinery. A variety of social and political ills contributing to Portugal's status as one of Europe's poorest nations include: past wars with African colonies, an influx of colonial refugees, and intraparty violence. Tourism is increasingly important, but agriculture has suffered from outdated techniques and a rural-to-urban population shift. The terrain is mostly plains and lowlands, with some mountains; the climate is mild and sunny.

History and Politics

Inhabited by an Iberian people about five thousand years ago, the area was later visited by Phoenicians, Celts, and Greeks before falling to the Romans around the first century B.C. The Romans were followed by Germanic Visigoths and in A.D. 711 by North African Muslims, who greatly influenced Portuguese art and architecture. Spain absorbed Portugal in 1094, and Portugal declared its independence in 1143. About one hundred years later, the last of the Muslims was expelled. Portugal's golden age—during which its navigators

explored the globe and founded colonies in South America, Africa, and the Far East—lasted from 1385 to the late 1500s. Rival European powers soon began to seize Portuguese holdings. In 1580 Spain invaded Portugal, ruling until 1640, when the Spanish were driven out and independence reestablished. After the 1822 loss of Brazil, Portugal's most valuable colony, and decades of opposition, a weakened monarchy was overthrown in 1910. The hardships of World War I battered the newly established republic, and in 1926 its parliamentary democracy fell to a military coup. Antonio Salazar became prime minister in 1932, ruling as a virtual dictator until 1968. Salazar's favored treatment of the rich and his refusal to relinquish Portugal's colonies aggravated the economic situation. A 1974 coup toppled Salazar's successor and set up a military government, events that sparked violence among political parties. Almost all Portuguese colonies gained independence during the next two years, A democratic government was adopted in 1976; varying coalitions have since ruled the nation.

Portugal at a glance

Official name	Portuguese Republic

People

Population	9,907,000
Density	279/mi² (108/km²)
Urban	34%
Capital	Lisbon, 807,167
Ethnic groups	Portuguese (Mediterranean), black
Languages	Portuguese
Religions	Roman Catholic 97%, Protestant 1%
Life expectancy	78 female, 71 male
Literacy	85%

Politics

Government	Republic
Parties	Communist, Social Democratic, Socialist, others.
Suffrage	Universal, over 18
Memberships	EU, NATO, OECD, UN
Subdivisions	18 districts, 2 autonomous regions

Economy

GDP	$91,500,000,000
Per capita	$8,583
Monetary unit	Escudo
Trade partners	Exports: Germany, France, Spain Imports: Spain, Germany, France
Exports	Textiles, cork and paper products, canned fish, wine, timber resin, machinery
Imports	Machinery and transportation equipment, agricultural products, chemicals

Land

Description	Southwestern Europe
Area	35,516 mi² (91,985 km²)
Highest point	Pico Point, 7,713 ft (2.351 m)
Lowest point	Sea level

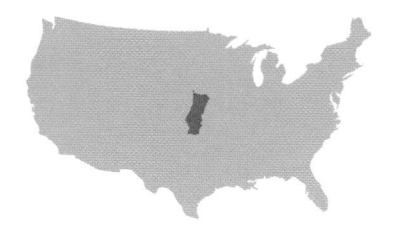

POPULATION COMPARISON
Portugal=4% of U.S.

United States

GDP COMPARISON
Portugal=1% of U.S.

United States

POPULATION DISTRIBUTION
Urban   Rural

The booming Algarve coast in southern Portugal is one of Europe's most popular beachside resort areas.

PUERTO RICO

San Juan, Puerto Rico's capital, was founded by the Spanish in 1508. Massive fortifications were begun in 1533 to protect the settlement's strategic location. El Morro fortress, now a national park, is a major tourist attraction.

Puerto Rico is the first Caribbean island where industrial output has surpassed agriculture. Trade policies put in place by the United States have encouraged enormous investment by U.S. companies. While most Puerto Ricans support continued ties with the U.S., groups in favor of full independence have often protested violently.

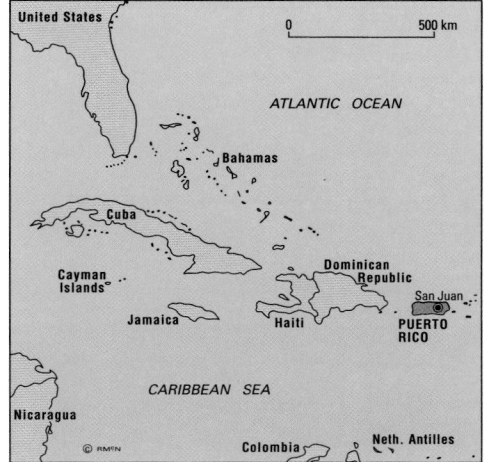

Beach and palm trees

Puerto Rico at a glance

Official name	Commonwealth of Puerto Rico

Politics

Population	3,625,000
Density	1,031/mi² (418/km²)
Urban	74%
Capital	San Juan, 426,832
Ethnic groups	Puerto Rican (mixed Spanish and black)
Languages	Spanish, English
Religions	Roman Catholic 85%, Protestant and other 15%
Life expectancy	78 female, 72 male
Literacy	89%

Politics

Government	Commonwealth (U.S. protection)
Parties	New Progressive, Popular Democratic, others
Suffrage	Universal, over 18
Memberships	None
Subdivisions	78 municipalities

Economy

GNP	$26,800,000,000
Per capita	$7,596
Monetary unit	U.S. dollar
Trade partners	U.S.
Exports	Pharmaceuticals, electronics, clothing, canned tuna, rum
Imports	Chemicals, clothing, food, fish, petroleum

Land

Description	Caribbean island
Area	3,515 mi² (9,104 km²)
Highest point	Punta Mtn., 4,389 ft (1,338 m)
Lowest point	Sea level

People

Puerto Rico's chief language, Spanish, and religion, Roman Catholicism, reflect this American commonwealth's past under Spanish rule. Most of the population is descended from Spaniards and black African slaves. A rising population has caused housing shortages and unemployment. Many Puerto Ricans live in the United States, mostly in New York City.

Economy and the Land

Once dependent on such plantation crops as sugar and coffee, Puerto Rico is now a manufacturing nation, specializing in food processing and electrical equipment. Commonwealth incentives for foreign investors aided this transformation, also known as Operation Bootstrap, after World War II. Foreign visitors, attracted by the tropical climate, make tourism another important activity. A lack of natural resources and fluctuations in the United States economy have hurt economic development. The island's terrain is marked by mountains, lowlands, and valleys.

History and Politics

The original inhabitants, the Arawak Indians, were wiped out by Spanish colonists, who first settled the island in 1508. Despite successive attacks by the French, English, and Dutch, Puerto Rico remained under Spanish control until 1898, when the United States took possession after the Spanish-American War. A civil government under a United States governor was set up in 1900; seventeen years later Puerto Ricans were made United States citizens. In 1952 the island became a self-governing commonwealth. This status was upheld in a referendum in 1967, and again in 1993 after fierce internal debate.

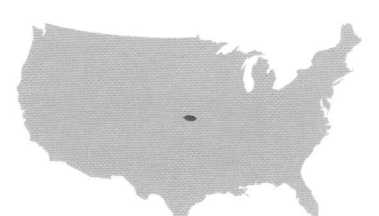

POPULATION COMPARISON
Puerto Rico=1% of U.S.

United States

POPULATION DISTRIBUTION

Urban   Rural

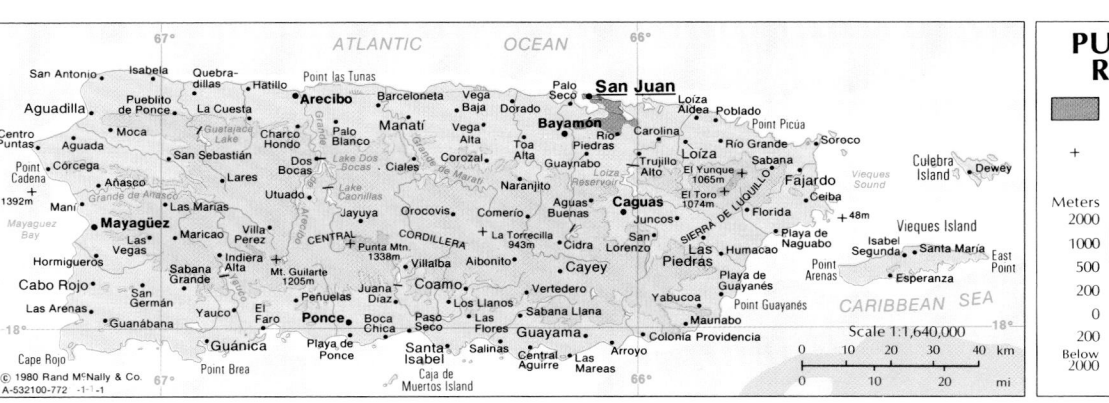

Puerto Rico is the smallest of the four large islands that make up the Greater Antilles. The others are, in increasing order of size: Jamaica, Hispaniola and Cuba.

Qatar occupies a strategic position in the central Persian Gulf. Past its shores sail supertankers with oil destined for much of the world.

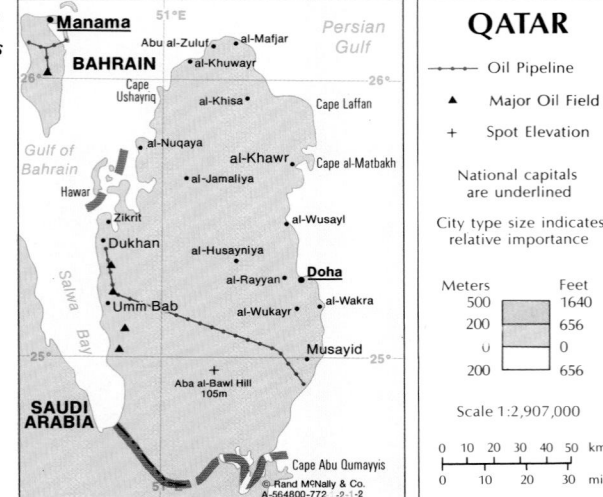

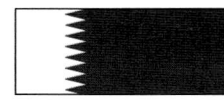

QATAR

Qatar at a glance

Official name	State of Qatar

Politics

Population	519,000
Density	118/mi² (45/km²)
Urban	90%
Capital	Doha, 217,294
Ethnic groups	Arab 40%, Pakistani 18%, Indian 18%, Iranian 10%
Languages	Arabic, English
Religions	Muslim 95%
Life expectancy	73 female, 68 male
Literacy	76%

Politics

Government	Monarchy
Parties	None
Suffrage	None
Memberships	AL, OPEC, UN
Subdivisions	9 municipalities

Economy

GDP	$8,800,000,000
Per capita	$17,886
Monetary unit	Riyal
Trade partners	Exports: Japan, Brazil, United Arab Emirates Imports: U.K., Japan, U.S., Italy
Exports	Petroleum, steel, fertilizer
Imports	Food, beverages, animal and vegetable oils, chemicals, machinery

Land

Description	Southwestern Asia
Area	4,412 mi² (11,427 km²)
Highest point	Aba al Bawl Hill, 344 ft (105 m)
Lowest point	Sea level

Qatar exemplifies the remarkable changes oil has brought to the petroleum-producing Middle East countries. Its capital, Doha, was once a tiny fishing village. Today, it is home to glistening hotels and office buildings. Qatar's people, whose ancestors scratched out an existence in the desert, are now among the world's most affluent, thanks to free-flowing oil revenues.

People

Qatar's population is distinguished by a relatively high proportion of Iranians, Pakistanis, and Indians, who began arriving during the oil boom of the 1950s. Most Qataris are Sunni Muslims and live in or near Doha, the capital. In recent years the government has encouraged the nomadic Bedouins to take up settled lifestyles. Despite a political trend toward a modern welfare state, Qatar retains many elements of a traditional Islamic society.

Economy and the Land

Oil provides the great majority of Qatar's income, while extensive reserves of natural gas await exploitation. The government has made moves toward economic diversification, investing in agriculture and industry; fertilizer and cement are important new products. Most of Qatar is stony desert, and the climate is hot and arid.

History and Politics

No strong central government existed in Qatar before Saudi Muslims gained control in the late eighteenth century. Ottoman Turks occupied the region from 1872 to 1916, when Qatar became a British protectorate. Although oil was discovered in 1940 on the western side of Qatar's peninsula, the outbreak of World War II postponed exploitation for another nine years. Qatar became independent in 1971 after failing to agree on the terms of a union with eight Persian Gulf sheikdoms—today the United Arab Emirates and Bahrain. Oil revenues have been used to improve housing, transportation, and public health.

Reunion is dominated by sugarcane plantations. While many Western Europeans and Indians live in affluent enclaves, the indigenous people often live in squalor. This economic disparity has led to tensions and riots. France is trying to alleviate Reunion's chronic unemployment.

Reunion at a glance

Official name	Department of Reunion

People

Population	660,000
Density	681/mi² (263/km²)
Urban	64%
Capital	Saint-Denis, 84,400
Ethnic groups	Reunionese (mixed French, African, Malagasy, Chinese, Pakistani, and Indian)
Languages	French, Creole
Religions	Roman Catholic 94%
Life expectancy	80 female, 69 male
Literacy	79%

Politics

Government	Overseas department (France)
Parties	Communist, Rally for the Republic, Union for Democracy
Suffrage	Universal, over 18
Memberships	None
Subdivisions	4 arrondissements

Economy

GDP	$3,370,000,000
Per capita	$6,241
Monetary unit	French franc
Trade partners	Exports: France, Comoros, Madagascar, Japan Imports: France, Bahrain, Germany, Italy
Exports	Sugar, rum and molasses, perfume oils, lobster, vanilla, tea
Imports	Manufactures, food, beverages, tobacco, machinery and transportation equipment

Land

Description	Indian Ocean island
Area	969 mi² (2,510 km²)
Highest	Piton des Neiges, 10,072 ft (3,070 m)
Lowest	Sea level

REUNION

People

Reunion has a racially mixed population, mainly descended from French settlers, African slaves, and Asian laborers. French is the official language, but most inhabitants speak a creole dialect. The mainly Roman Catholic population is densely concentrated in the lowland areas along the coast. Social stratification is rigid.

Economy and the Land

Reunion's traditional coffee crop was replaced by sugar early on, and sugar continues as an economic mainstay today. Industry is based on the production of sugar by-products, such as rum and molasses. Unemployment is a problem, and the island remains dependent upon French aid. The mountainous terrain is marked by one active and several extinct volcanoes. The tropical climate is subject to occasional cyclones and trade winds, which bring high rainfall to the south and southeast.

History and Politics

Although known to the Arabs and the Portuguese, Reunion was uninhabited when French settlement began in the 1660s. First called Bourbon, the island originally served as a stopover on the French shipping route to India. The French soon developed coffee and sugar plantations, bringing slaves from Africa to work them. British-French rivalry for control of the area led to brief British rule during the early 1800s. After several name changes, from Bourbon to Reunion to Bonaparte and back to Bourbon again, in 1848 the French settled on the name Reunion. After the abolition of slavery, indentured laborers were brought form Indochina, India, and eastern Africa. Reunion was a French colony until 1946, when it became an overseas department.

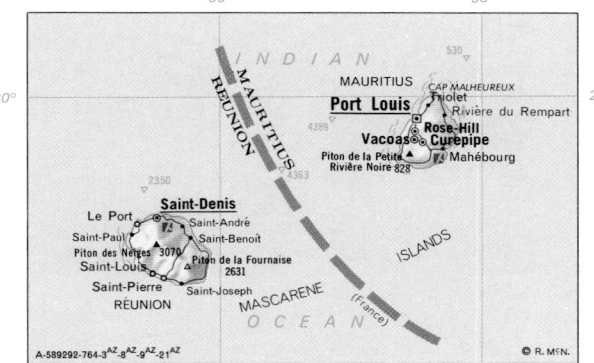

Scale 1:6,000,000 One inch represents approximately 95 miles.
One centimeter represents 60 kilometers.

Reunion's interior features volcanic cones and craters. At least one cone is still geologically active.

ROMANIA

Romania owes its name and language to its time as part of the Roman Empire. Successive waves of invaders have made it a part of their empires, most recently the Soviets after World War II. Since the revolution in 1989, Romania has tried to breathe life into its stagnant economy.

(photo at left) The Evangelical Cathedral dominates the center of Sibiu, an industrial city northwest of Bucharest. It was founded by Saxons in the 12th century.

People

The majority population of Romania belongs to the Romanian Orthodox church and traces its roots to Latin-speaking Romans, Thracians, Slavs, and Celts. Minorities, concentrated in Transylvania and areas north and west of Bucharest, are mainly Roman Catholic Hungarians and Germans. Other minorities include Gypsies, Serbs, Croats, Ukrainians, Greeks, Turks, and Armenians. Almost all inhabitants speak Romanian, although minority groups often speak other languages.

Economy and the Land

When Romania became a Communist country in the 1940s, the government began to turn the country from agriculture to industry. The economy is now based on such major products as iron and steel. Although Romania remains less developed than many other European countries, it has experienced postwar growth in its gross national product. Most agriculture is collectivized, and corn and wheat are major crops. The transition to a market economy has been slow and troubled. Romania's terrain is

marked by a south-to-northeast plateau that curves around several mountain ranges, including the Carpathians, found in the northern and central regions. The climate is continental, with cold, snowy winters and warm summers.

History and Politics

First colonized by the Dacians, a Thracian tribe, around the fourth century B.C., the area became the Roman province of Romania in the second century A.D. Invading Bulgars, Goths, Huns, Magyars, Slavs, and Tartars followed the Romans. Between 1250 and 1350, the independent Romanian principalities of Walachia and Moldavia emerged. In the fifteenth and sixteenth centuries, Ottoman Turks conquered the principalities and, following a Russian-Turkish war, Russians occupied the states. In 1861 Walachia and Moldavia were united as Romania, in 1878 they gained independence, and in 1881 Romania was proclaimed a kingdom. Oppression and a concentration of land and wealth among the aristocracy marked the nation's government, and in 1907 its army quelled a rebellion. In 1919, after a World

War I alliance with the Allies, Romania gained Transylvania and other territories. Instability and dissatisfaction, spurred by worldwide economic depression, continued through the 1930s. With the cooperation of Romanian leadership, Germany occupied the country in World War II. In 1944 Soviet troops entered Romania, and the nation subsequently joined the Allies. A Communist government was established in 1945, and in 1947 the king was forced to abdicate, and Romania officially became a Communist country. Initially Romania's policies were closely tied to those of the Soviet Union; but renewed nationalism in the sixties led to several independent policy decisions. Nicolae Ceausescu's twenty-four years of harsh, repressive leadership led to a popular revolt and his execution in 1989. Elections held by an interim government in 1990 were won by the National Salvation Front (former Communists). The country approved a new constitution in December 1991 that allowed multiparty representation. There have been periodic riots over continued government failure to improve economic conditions.

Gathering hay, Transylvania

Romania at a glance

Official name	Romania

Politics

Population	22,745,000
Density	248/mi² (96/km²)
Urban	54%
Capital	Bucharest, 2,064,474
Ethnic groups	Romanian (mixed Latin, Thracian, Slavic, and Celtic) 89%, Hungarian 9%
Languages	Romanian, Hungarian, German
Religions	Romanian Orthodox 70%, Roman Catholic 6%, Protestant 6%
Life expectancy	73 female, 67 male
Literacy	96%

Politics

Government	Republic
Parties	Democratic Convention, National Salvation Front, National Unity, Social Democracy
Suffrage	Universal, over 18
Memberships	UN
Subdivisions	40 counties, 1 municipality

Economy

GDP	$63,700,000,000
Per capita	$2,746
Monetary unit	Leu
Trade partners	Exports: Former Soviet republics, Italy, Germany Imports: Former Soviet republics, Iran, Egypt
Exports	Machinery and transportation equipment; fuel, minerals, and metals
Imports	Fuel, minerals, and metals; machinery and transportation equipment; chemicals

Land

Description	Eastern Europe
Area	91,699 mi² (237,500 km²)
Highest point	Moldoveanu, 8,346 ft (2,544 m)
Lowest point	Sea level

ROMANIA

Meters	Feet
4000	13124
2000	6562
1000	3281
500	1640
200	656
0	0
200	656
2000	6562

—— Canal
—— Railroad
—•—•— Oil Pipeline
▲ Major Oil Field
+ Spot Elevation

Scale 1:5,000,000

© Rand McNally & Co.
A-552700-772 -2 -4

The dark forests and misty valleys of the Transylvanian Alps have given rise to many tales and much folklore.

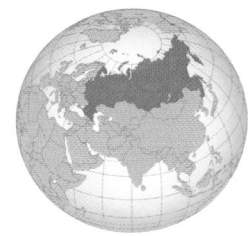

RUSSIA

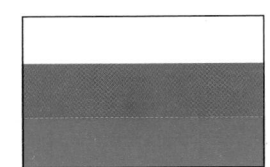

Russia is every bit as diverse as [...] uld indicate. St. Petersburg in the w[...]rk of European art and architectu[...]ria is home to Asiatic Eskimos whose live[...] little in centuries. In between live 75 dist[...]s with their attending languages and cultu[...]s predominate throughout the land, [...]y decades when they held the reins o[...] Communist Party. With no democra[...] grappling with a myriad of changes [...] collapse of the Soviet Union.

People

The Russians are a Slavic people who have occupied the land between the Baltic and Black seas for at least fifteen hundred years. Russia is also home to many other ethnic groups, including the Tatars, Yakuts, Ossetians, and Buryats. Many of the minority ethnic groups reside in their own autonomous regions. The Russian church is the largest of the Eastern Orthodox churches, and dates back to A.D. 988. Once discouraged under Communist rule, religion is now experiencing a revival. Russians are known for their many great contributions to the arts and sciences.

Econ[...]

Before [...] quent [...] nation [...] my. De[...] indust[...] plague[...] shorta[...] The So[...] other C[...] 1980s, [...] trade v[...] is the l[...] is wide[...] minera[...]

Arkhangelsk is a port on the White Sea in western Russia. Icebound for half the year, it is busy during the other half with ships exporting Siberian goods such as lumber and grain.

Russia stretches almost halfway around the world. The legendary Trans-Siberian Express takes eight days to cover the 5,500 miles from Moscow to Vladivostok.

(top) The Kremlin and St. Basil's Cathedral, Moscow

(middle) Hermitage Museum and Admiralty Tower, St. Petersburg

(bottom) Commuters at bus stop, morning rush hour, Moscow

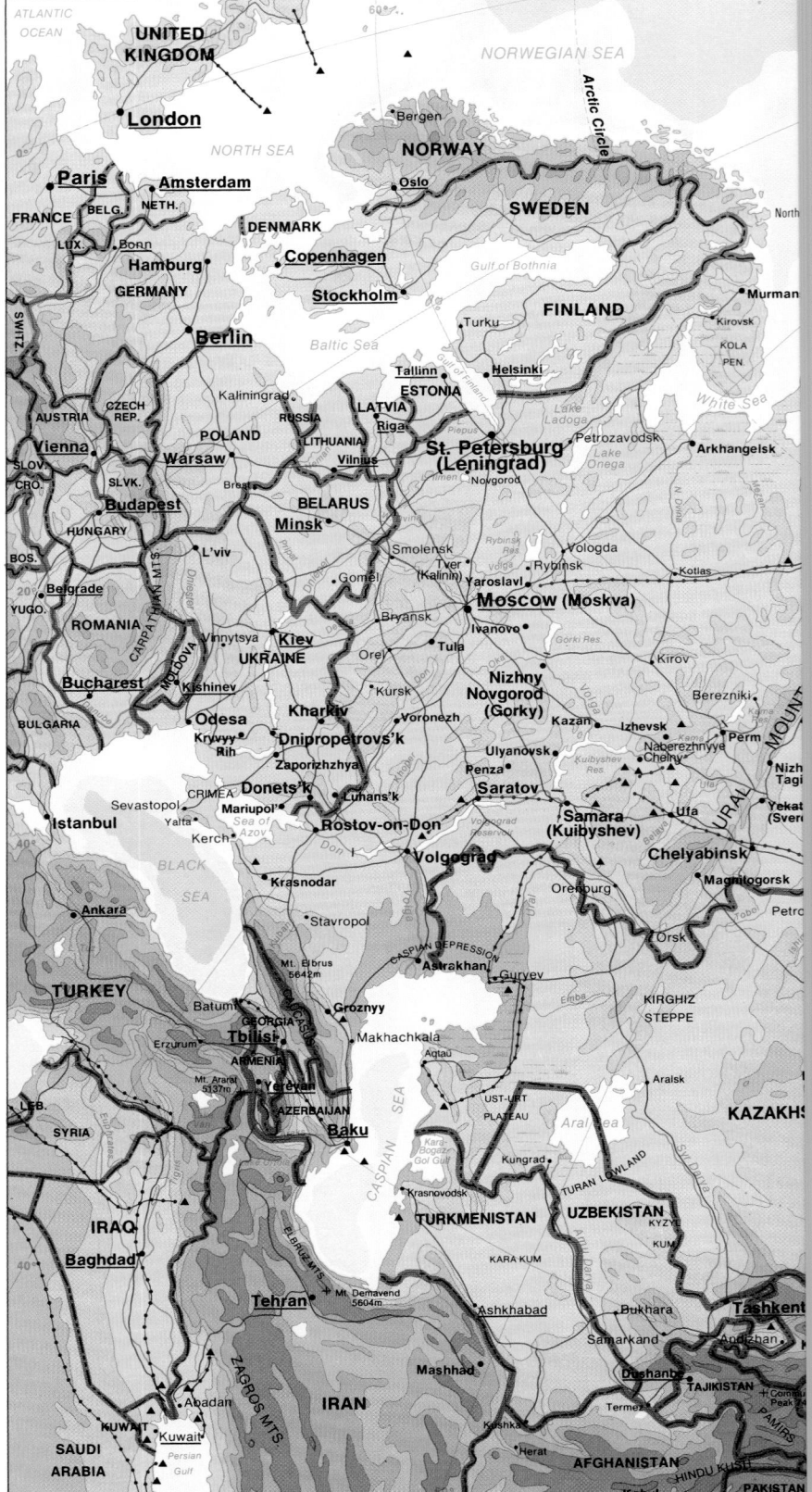

Tankers at anchor, Black Sea

The snow belies the fact that it is spring in frigid Siberia as a woman leads her herd of reindeer on their annual migration. Few roads reach into the isolated Yamal Peninsula in far northern Siberia.

Parts of Moscow's Kremlin date from the 12th century, when a fortress was built on the site. Today the sprawling complex contains structures from every century since then. Home of the Russian President, the Kremlin's east side faces Red Square.

some of the world's most fertile land, long winters and hot, dry summers make agriculture difficult and risky.

History and Politics

Inhabited as early as the Stone Age, what is now Russia was much later invaded by the Scythians, Sarmatians, Goths, Huns, Bulgars, Slavs, and others. By A.D. 989, Byzantine cultural influence had become predominant. Various groups and regions were slowly incorporated into a single state. In 1547, Ivan the Terrible was crowned czar of all Russia, beginning a tradition of czarist rule and expansionism. The borders of all the Russian empire in the mid-1800s roughly approximated those of the former Soviet Union. Czarist rule continued until the 1917 Russian Revolution, when the Bolsheviks came to power and named Vladimir Lenin as head of the first Soviet government. The Bolsheviks established a new, experimental Communist state based on the works of economist Karl Marx. A bitter civil war ensued as all private property was seized by the government. Many areas that had been under the control of czarist Russia enjoyed a brief period of independence before Joseph Stalin succeeded Lenin as head of state, reclaimed the lost territories, and initiated a series of political purges that lasted through the 1930s. The Soviet Union became embroiled in World War II, siding with the Allies, losing over twenty million people, and suffering widespread destruction of its cities and countryside. It emerged from the war with extended influence, however, having annexed part of Finland and occupying many Eastern European nations. In the years following World War II, the Soviet Union and the United States and their allies were engaged in a "cold war," which was characterized by escalating production of nuclear weapons and severe restrictions on travel and communications between the two sides. Mikhail Gorbachev took office in 1985 and introduced a new era of reform and government restructuring. The new political climate resulted in the end of the cold war and the ultimate breakup of the Soviet Union. Russia emerged as an independent state in late 1991. Russian president Boris Yeltsin rose to prominence as the leader of Russia and emphasized economic reform and closer ties with all Western nations. Political and economic instability continue to plague the new Russian state. *(continued)*

RUSSIA

Legend	
——	Railroad
⋯⋯	Canal or Waterway
——	Oil Pipeline
▲	Major Oil Field
+	Spot Elevation or Depth

Capitals are underlined
City type size indicates relative importance

Scale 1:25,929,000

Meters Above	Feet Above
4000	13124
2000	6562
1000	3281
500	1640
200	656
0	Sea Level

Meters	Feet
0	656
200	
Below 2000	Below 6562

0 200 400 600 km.
0 200 400 mi

© Rand McNally & Co.
A-570000-772

Russia, continued

Combines harvest wheat on the farms around Krasnodar near the Black Sea. Despite fertile soil, Russian agriculture has been hampered by years of misman-agement and central planning during the Communist era.

A metallurgical plant belches smo[...] mountains. Russia is the most poll[...] of Soviet economic policies that str[...] the environment.

Siberian woman

Russia at a glance

Official name	Russian Federation

People

Population	150,500,000
Density	23/mi^2 (8.8/km^2)
Urban	74%
Capital	Moscow, 8,801,500
Ethnic groups	Russian 82%, Tatar 4%, Ukrainian 3%, Chuvash 1%
Languages	Russian, Tatar, Ukrainian
Religions	Russian Orthodox, Muslim
Life expectancy	74 female, 64 male
Literacy	99%

Politics

Government	Republic
Parties	Democratic, Democratic Russia, Movement for Democratic Reforms, People's
Suffrage	Universal, over 18
Memberships	CIS, UN
Subdivisions	21 republics, 1 autonomous oblast, 49 oblasts, 6 krays, 10 autonomous okrugs, 2 cities

Economy

GDP	$775,400,000,000
Per capita	$5,152
Monetary unit	Ruble
Trade partners	Western and eastern European countries, Japan
Exports	Petroleum and natural gas, lumber, coal, nonferrous metals, chemicals
Imports	Machinery and equipment, chemi-cals, consumer goods, grain, meat

Land

Description	Eastern Europe and Northern Asia
Area	6,592,849 mi^2 (17,075,400 km^2)
Highest point	Mt. Elbrus, 18,510 ft (5,642 m)
Lowest point	Caspian Sea, -92 ft (-28 m)

POPULATION COMPARISON
Russia=57% of U.S.

United States

GDP COMPARISON
Russia=12% of U.S.

United States

ETHNIC GROUPS

Other
Chuvash
Ukrainian
Tatar
Russian

POPULATION DISTRIBUTION
Urban   Rural

Green islets contrast with the [...] in eastern Russia. At over 2,7[...] the 12th-longest river in the [...] for much of the Lena's water.

(left) Sunset on the Neva River, St. Petersburg
(right) Siberian town, Lake Baikal

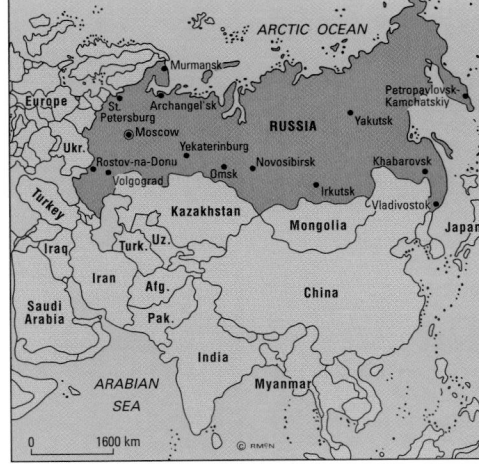

A shepherd watches over his flock from horseback in the Altai Mountains in Siberia. Despite development schemes to exploit the region's tremendous resources, most of Siberia's people lead lives little changed by modernity.

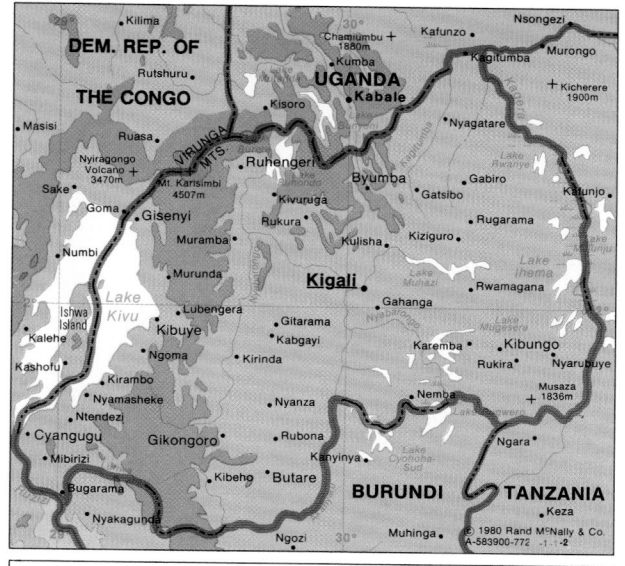

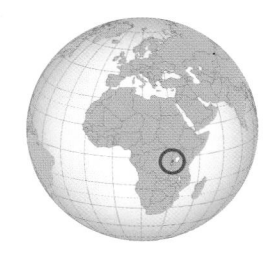

Rwanda's tragic history mirrors that of its equally tragic neighbor, Burundi. The usually amicable relations between the Hutu and Tutsi tribes periodically explode into orgies of killing and retribution. Those who survive often endure severe hardship as refugees in neighboring countries.

RWANDA

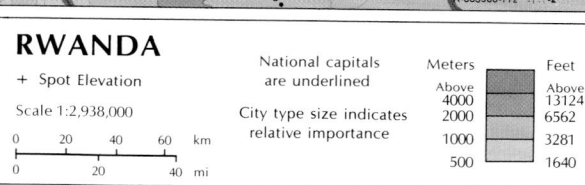

Rwanda's rich and varied wildlife includes rare mountain gorillas which are marginally protected in national parks and in other reserves.

People

Most Rwandans are Hutus, mainly farmers of Bantu stock. Minorities include the Tutsis, a pastoral people that dominated politically until a Hutu rebellion in 1959, and the Twa, Pygmies descended from the original population. Both French and Kinyarwanda are official languages, but most speak Kinyarwanda, a Bantu tongue. Roman Catholicism is the major religion, and minority groups practice indigenous beliefs as well as Protestantism and Islam. A high population density and a high birthrate characterize Rwanda.

Economy and the Land

Agriculture is Rwanda's major activity, although the country is plagued by the erosion and overpopulation of arable land. Many Rwandans practice subsistence farming, while coffee and tea are major export crops. The production and export of minerals, partly fueled by foreign investment, is also important. The country's landlocked position and underdeveloped transportation system hinder economic growth. The terrain consists mainly of grassy uplands and hills,

with volcanic mountains in the west and northwest. The climate is mild.

History and Politics

The Twa, the region's original inhabitants, were followed by the Hutus. The Tutsis most likely arrived about the fourteenth century, subjugating the weaker Hutus and becoming the region's dominant force. The areas of present-day Rwanda and Burundi became part of German East Africa in the 1890s. In 1919, following World War I, the region was mandated to Belgium as Ruanda-Urundi, and following World War II, Ruanda-Urundi was made a United Nations trust territory under Belgian administration. In 1959 a Hutu revolt against Tutsi domination resulted in the death of many Tutsis and the flight of many more. After gaining independence in 1962, the former territory split into the countries of Rwanda and Burundi. The military overthrew the nation's first president in 1973. Ethnic violence erupted after the death in April 1994 of President Habyarimana in a plane crash. The ruling Hutu tribe and the minority Tutsis engaged in bloody reprisals resulting in perhaps the greatest flood of refugees in Africa's history.

Rwanda at a glance

Official name	Republic of Rwanda

Politics

Population	7,343,000
Density	722/mi² (279/km²)
Urban	6%
Capital	Kigali, 232,733
Ethnic groups	Hutu 90%, Tutsi 9%, Twa (Pygmy) 1%
Languages	French, Kinyarwanda, Kiswahili
Religions	Roman Catholic 65%, Animist 25%, Protestant 9%
Life expectancy	48 female, 45 male
Literacy	50%

Politics

Government	Republic
Parties	Democratic Republican, Liberal, Republican National Movement for Democracy and Development
Suffrage	Universal adult
Memberships	OAU, UN
Subdivisions	10 prefectures

Economy

GDP	$6,800,000,000
Per capita	$898
Monetary unit	Franc
Trade partners	Exports: Italy, Belgium, France Imports: Belgium, Japan, Kenya
Exports	Coffee, tea, tin, cassiterite, wolframite, pyrethrum
Imports	Textiles, food, machinery, steel, petroleum, cement

Land

Description	Eastern Africa, landlocked
Area	10,169 mi² (26,338 km²)
Highest point	Mt. Karisimbi, 14,787 ft (4,507 m)
Lowest point	Along Ruzizi River, 3,117 ft (950 m)

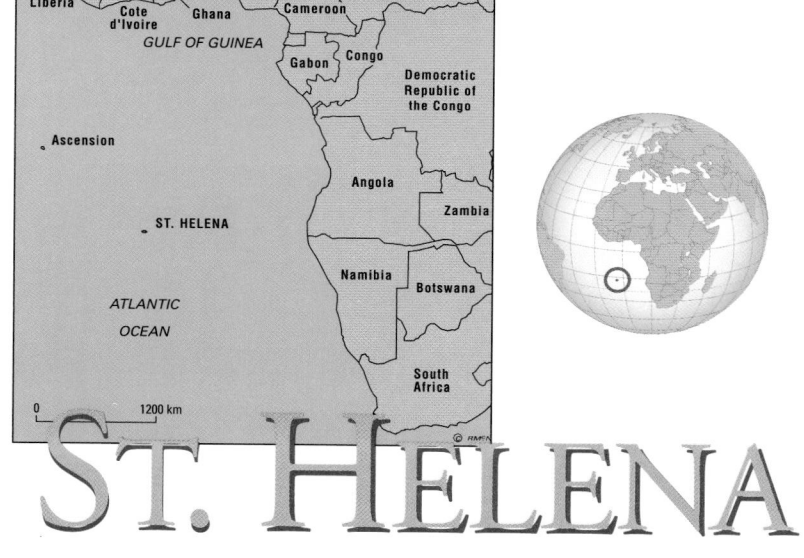

St. Helena at a glance

Official name	St. Helena

People

Population	7,000
Density	58/mi² (22/km²)
Urban	17%
Capital	Jamestown, St. Helena I., 1,413
Ethnic groups	Mixed European, Asian, African
Languages	English
Religions	Anglican 86%, Jehovah's Witness 5%, Baptist 3%
Life expectancy	76 female, 72 male
Literacy	98%

Politics

Government	Dependent territory (U.K.)
Parties	Labor, Progressive
Subdivisions	2 dependencies, 1 admin. area

Economy

Monetary unit	Pound
Trade partners	Exports: South Africa, U.K. Imports: U.K., South Africa
Exports	Fish, handicrafts
Imports	Food, beverages, tobacco, fuel oil, animal feed, building materials

Land

Description	South Atlantic islands
Area	121 mi² (314 km²)
Highest point	Queen Mary's Pk., 6,760 ft (2,060 m)
Lowest point	Sea level

People

Most of the inhabitants of the island of St. Helena are of mixed European, Asian, and African heritage. St. Helena is a British colony with a distinctly British culture; English is the language spoken on the island, and the major religion is Anglican. Most people work as laborers or farmers, but many islanders have emigrated to Ascension Island, a dependency of St. Helena, in order to find employment.

Economy and the Land

Subsistence farmers grow crops for local consumption, producing mainly corn, potatoes, and vegetables. Other agricultural activity includes the raising of sheep, cattle, and goats. A plentiful supply of fish is found in the offshore waters. In the 1970s a crafts industry was established on the island, and handicrafts, together with fish, constitute the island's principal exports. However, the colony remains dependent upon economic aid from the United Kingdom. The terrain of this volcanic island is rugged and mountainous. The climate is mild, cooled by South Atlantic trade winds. In addition to the main island of St. Helena, the colony includes the dependencies of Ascension Island and the Tristan da Cunha archipelago, made up of the islands of Tristan da Cunha, Gough, Inaccessible, and Nightingale. These islands are also of volcanic origin.

History and Politics

The Portuguese navigator João de Nova reached the uninhabited island in 1502, naming it St. Helena after the mother of the Emperor Constantine the Great. It was not until the late 1500s, however, that St. Helena became widely known, and, in time, it evolved into a stopover for ships traveling the trade routes from Europe to the East Indies. The Dutch were first to officially claim the island, annexing St. Helena to the Netherlands in 1633. They did not, however, attempt settlement. Administration by the British East India Company began in 1659, and the company's administration and British annexation became offi-

ST. HELENA

cial in 1661. The British were able to withstand a Dutch attempt to take the island in 1673. From 1815 until his death in 1821 Napoleon Bonaparte was exiled on St. Helena, and it is mainly for this that the island is known today. In 1834 St. Helena became a colony, with administration of the island shifting from the East India Company to the British Crown. In 1922 the British government made Ascension Island a dependency of St. Helena, and in 1938 administration of the Tristan da Cunha island group passed to the St. Helena colony as well. In 1942, during World War II, a weather and radio station was built on the island of Tristan da Cunha by a South African defense unit. The British navy used the station for the rest of the war.

Tourism has come only recently to this small island nation in the Caribbean. Previously, sugar was the major industry. Free education has given the people a high literacy rate. Although the islands became fully independent in 1983, they remain part of the Commonwealth, with the British monarch as head of state.

ST. KITTS AND NEVIS

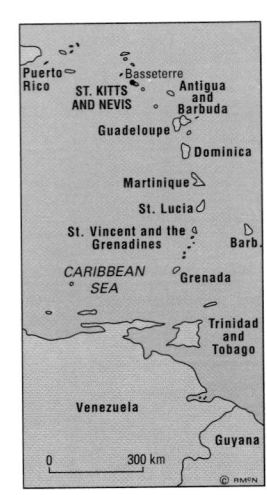

Alexander Hamilton, a major figure in the birth of the United States, was born at Fort Charles on Nevis.

People
Most of the inhabitants of the islands of St. Kitts, often called St. Christopher, and Nevis are of black African descent. The primarily rural population is concentrated along the coast. English is spoken throughout the islands, and most people are Protestant, especially Anglican, evidence of former British rule.

Economy and the Land
Agriculture and tourism are the economic mainstays of St. Kitts and Nevis. Sugarcane is a major crop, cultivated mainly on St. Kitts Island, while Nevis Island produces cotton, fruits, and vegetables. Agriculture also provides for sugar processing, the major industrial activity. A tropical climate, beaches, and a scenic mountainous terrain provide an ideal setting for tourism.

History and Politics
The islands were first inhabited by Arawak Indians, who were displaced by the warlike Caribs. In 1493 Christopher Columbus sighted the islands, and in the 1600s British settlement of both islands began, along with

---

St. Lucia is known for its breathtaking mountain scenery that includes an active volcano and Gros Piton, 2,500-foot-high seaside peak.

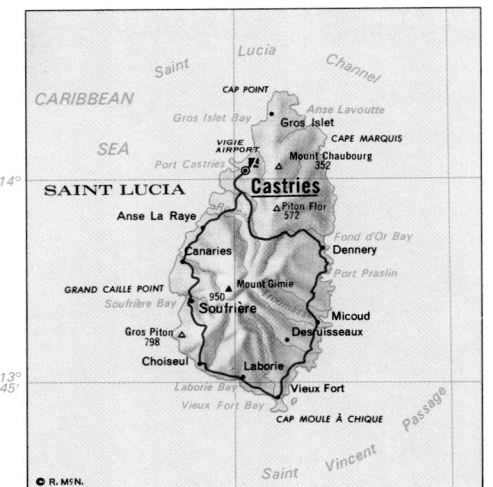

Scale 1:1,000,000   One inch represents approximately 16 miles.
One centimeter represents 10 kilometers.

ST. LUCIA

Despite its small size, St. Lucia has a fast-growing economy based on tourism and bananas. Modern communications and a well-educated workforce have made it a data processing center. The people are mostly descendants of African slaves brought to work the sugar plantations that existed throughout the Caribbean during colonial times.

People
St. Lucia's population is composed mainly of descendants of black African slaves, and minority groups include people of African-European descent, whites, and East Indians. During the colonial period, the island frequently shifted from British to French control, and its culture reflects both British and French elements. Although English is widely spoken, many St. Lucians speak a French dialect. Roman Catholicism is the main religion, and the Protestant minority includes Anglicans.

Economy and the Land
Agriculture remains important, and principal crops include bananas and cocoa. Tax incentives and relative political stability have caused an increase in industrial development and foreign investment, mainly from the United States. Tourism is becoming increasingly important, with visitors drawn by the tropical climate, mountain scenery, and excellent beaches.

History and Politics
Arawak Indians arrived between the A.D. 200s and 400s and were conquered by the Caribs

St. Pierre and Miquelon

Official name   Territorial Collectivity of St. Pierre and Miquelon

People

Population	7,000
Density	72/mi² (28/km²)
Urban	91%
Capital	St. Pierre, St. Pierre Island, 5,371
Ethnic groups	French descent
Languages	French
Religions	Roman Catholic 98%
Life expectancy	77 female, 74 male
Literacy	99%

Politics

Government	Territorial collectivity (France)
Parties	Socialist, Union for French Democracy
Suffrage	Universal, over 18

Economy

GDP	$60,000,000
Per capita	$8,824
Monetary unit	French franc
Trade partners	Exports: U.S., France, Canada Imports: Canada, France
Exports	Fish, fox and mink pelts
Imports	Meat, clothing, fuel, electrical equipment, machinery, building materials

Land

Description	North Atlantic islands (south of Newfoundland)
Area	93 mi² (242 km²)
Highest point	Morne de la Grande Montagne, (784 ft (239 m)
Lowest point	Sea level

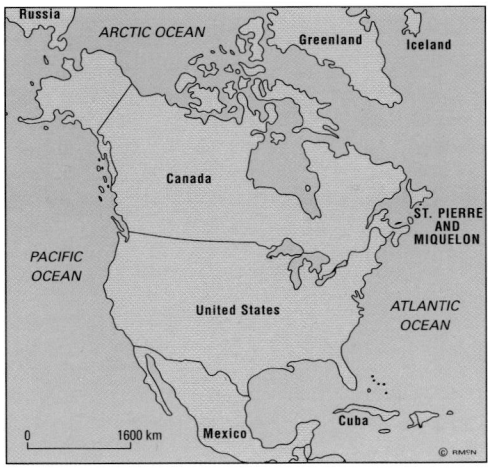

St. Pierre and Miquelon are only for the hardy. They are cold, wet, and windy, with long periods of mist and fog.

People

Lying off the coast of Newfoundland in Canada, the territorial collectivity of St. Pierre and Miquelon is the last vestige of France's former North American empire. Most of the colony's inhabitants are Roman Catholic descendants of Norman stock. French is spoken throughout the islands, and the literacy rate of 99% is among the highest in the world.

Economy and the Land

The islands of St. Pierre and Miquelon are barren, rocky, and frequently covered in fog. Agricultural activity is minimal; thin soil and little vegetation cover the islands' granite masses. St. Pierre and Miquelon lie near the fish-rich waters of the Grand Banks. Fishing is the main economic activity and major employer. The primary export is fish, which makes up 88 percent of the total export trade. After fish, shellfish provide for six percent and fishmeal five percent of exported goods. During the annual fishing season, European as well as local vessels are found in the waters surrounding the islands. Because of the Gulf Stream, St. Pierre's harbor remains ice-free throughout the winter, and the island is on a shipping route that connects with Sydney, Australia. The territorial collectivity of St. Pierre and Miquelon is made up of a number of small islands in addition to the two main islands of St. Pierre and Miquelon. The climate is mild and humid, moderated by the Gulf Stream.

History and Politics

Basque fishermen found their way to the islands in the sixteenth century, and French settlement began in the seventeenth century. In 1713 the British captured the islands, but the 1763 Treaty of Paris returned the islands to French hands. The same treaty ceded the French colony of Acadia to Britain, and when many French inhabitants of Acadia were forced to relocate, some of these established permanent settlements on St. Pierre and Miquelon. British-French rivalry for possession continued, and the British were able to regain control of the islands two more times in the next decades. In 1814 French rule was finally established, with the stipulation that France could not fortify the islands. From 1816 to 1976 the islands were a French overseas territory, and they became self-governing in 1956. A French territorial collectivity, the islands are governed by a privy council and a nineteen-member general council, which the voters of St. Pierre and Miquelon elect by direct vote. The term of each representative is six years. The islands are represented in France by one senator and one councilor, while an appointed commissioner represents France's interests on the islands.

ST. PIERRE AND MIQUELON

St. Vincent and the Grenadines at a glance

Official name   St. Vincent and the Grenadines

Politics

Population	110,000
Density	733/mi² (284/km²)
Urban	20%
Capital	Kingstown, St. Vincent I., 15,466
Ethnic groups	Black 82%, mixed 14%, East Indian 2%, white 1%
Languages	English, French
Religions	Anglican 42%, Methodist 21%, Roman Catholic 21%, Baptist 6%
Life expectancy	73 female, 70 male
Literacy	96%

Politics

Government	Parliamentary state
Parties	Labor, New Democratic
Suffrage	Universal, over 18
Memberships	CW, OAS, UN
Subdivisions	5 parishes

Economy

GDP	$215,000,000
Per capita	$1,870
Monetary unit	East Caribbean dollar
Trade partners	Exports: U.K., Trinidad and Tobago, U.S. Imports: U.S., U.K.
Exports	Bananas, eddoes and taro, arrowroot starch, tennis racquets, flour
Imports	Food, machinery, chemicals, fuel

Land

Description	Caribbean islands
Area	150 mi² (388 km²)
Highest point	Soufrière, 4,048 ft (1,234 m)
Lowest point	Sea level

People

The people of St. Vincent are mainly descended from black African slaves. The colonial influences of Britain and France are evident in the languages and religions. English is the official language, though a French patois is also spoken. Most people are Anglican, Methodist, or Roman Catholic.

Economy and the Land

St. Vincent's economy is based on agriculture, especially banana production. tourism also plays a role, both on the main island of St. Vincent and in the Grenadines. St. Vincent is the largest island, and about one hundred smaller islands make up the Grenadines. The terrain is mountainous, with coastlines marked by sandy beaches, and the climate is tropical.

History and Politics

The indigenous Arawak Indians were conquered by the Caribs about 1300. Christopher Columbus probably reached the area in 1498. Although the Caribs fought the Europeans, the British began settling St. Vincent in the 1760s. A period of French control began in 1779, and the islands were returned to the British in 1783. St. Vincent and the Grenadines remained under British rule until they gained independence in 1979.

ST. VINCENT AND THE GRENADINES

Scale 1:1,000,000   One inch represents approximately 16 miles.
One centimeter represents 10 kilometers.

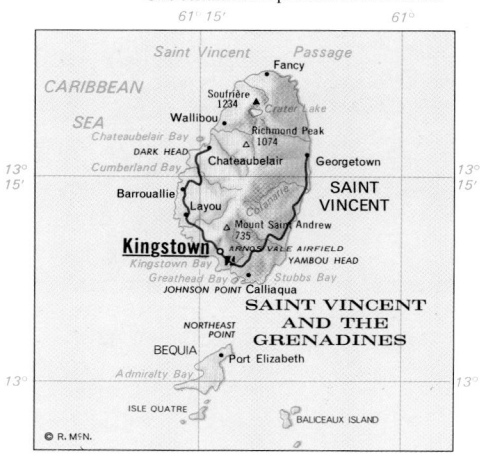

The Grenadines, a string of tiny islands south of St. Vincent, are popular with sailors, who anchor their yachts and explore the deserted beaches.

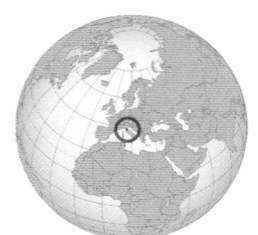

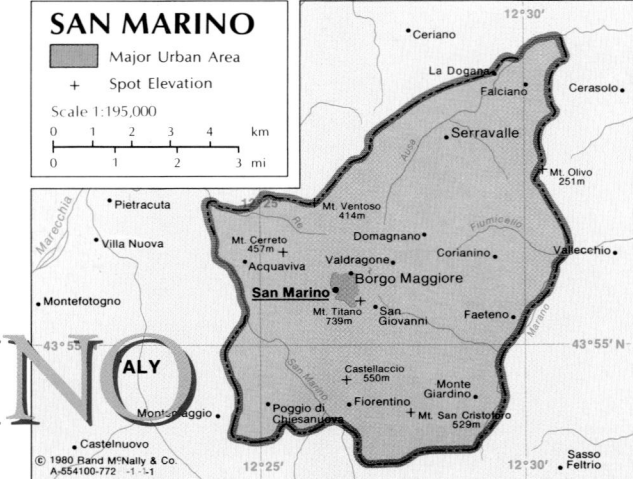

SAN MARINO
Major Urban Area
+ Spot Elevation
Scale 1:195,000

San Marino at a glance

Official name	Republic of San Marino

Politics

Population	24,000
Density	1,000/mi² (393/km²)
Urban	92%
Capital	Marino, 2,794
Ethnic groups	Sanmarinese (mixed Latin, Adriatic, and Teutonic), Italian
Languages	Italian
Religions	Roman Catholic
Life expectancy	85 female, 77 male
Literacy	96%

Politics

Government	Republic
Parties	Christian Democratic, Progressive Democratic, Socialist, others
Suffrage	Universal, over 18
Memberships	UN
Subdivisions	9 municipalities

Economy

GDP	$370,000,000
Per capita	$16,087
Monetary unit	Italian lira
Trade partners	Italy
Exports	Building materials, lime, wood, chestnuts, wheat, wine
Imports	Consumer goods

Land

Description	Southern Europe, landlocked
Area	24 mi² (61 km²)
Highest point	Monte Titano, 2,425 ft (739 m)
Lowest point	Unnamed, 164 ft (50 m)

SAN MARINO

T he third-smallest independent state in Europe, San Marino claims to be the oldest, with a history dating back to the 4th century. Each year millions of tourists visit its old town. Many buy collectable stamps, a major source of revenue.

People
San Marino, completely surrounded by Italy, has strong ethnic ties to the Italians, combining Latin, Adriatic, and Teutonic roots. Italian is the main language, and Roman Catholicism the major religion. Despite San Marino's similarities to Italy, its tradition of independence has given its citizens a strong national identity.

Economy and the Land
Close economic ties between San Marino and Italy have produced a mutually beneficial customs union: Italians have no customs restrictions at San Marino's borders, and San Marino receives annual budget subsidiary payments from Italy. Most San Marinese are employed in agriculture; livestock raising is a main activity, and crops include wheat and grapes. Tourism and the sale of postage stamps are major economic contributors, as is industry, which produces construction materials for export. Located in the Apennine Mountains, San Marino has a rugged terrain and a generally moderate climate.

History and Politics
San Marino is considered the world's oldest republic. Tradition has it that Marinus, a Christian stonecutter seeking religious freedom in a time of repressive Roman rule, founded the state in the fourth century A.D. Partly because of the protection afforded by its mountainous terrain, San Marino has been able to maintain continuous independence despite attempted invasions. In the 1300s the country became a republic, and the pope recognized its independent status in 1631. San Marino signed its first treaty of friendship with Italy in 1862. In its foreign relations, the country maintains a distinct identity and status.

SAO TOME AND PRINCIPE
+ Spot Elevation or Depth
National capital is underlined
Scale 1:3,454,000

Gulf of Guinea

Sao Tome and Principe at a glance

Official name	Democratic Republic of Sao Tome and Principe

Politics

Population	127,000
Density	341/mi² (132/km²)
Urban	42%
Capital	São Tomé, São Tomé I., 5,245
Ethnic groups	Black, mixed black and Portuguese, Portuguese
Languages	Portuguese, Fang
Religions	Roman Catholic, Evangelical Protestant, Seventh Day Adventist
Life expectancy	65 female, 61 male
Literacy	57%

Politics

Government	Republic
Parties	Democratic Convergence-Reflection Group, Movement for the Liberation
Suffrage	Universal, over 18
Memberships	OAU, UN
Subdivisions	7 districts

Economy

GDP	$50,000,000
Per capita	$407
Monetary unit	Dobra
Trade partners	Exports: Germany, Netherlands, China; Imports: Portugal, Germany, Angola, China
Exports	Cocoa, copra, coffee, palm oil
Imports	Machinery and electrical equipment

Land

Description	Western African islands
Area	372 mi² (964 km²)
Highest point	São Tomé Peak, 6,640 ft (2,024 m)
Lowest point	Sea level

SAO TOME AND PRINCIPE

M uch of Sao Tome's and Principe's land is devoted to cocoa production, the main component of the economy. However, government mismanagement has cut yields by 50 percent since independence in 1975.

People
Descendants of African slaves and people of Portuguese-African heritage compose most of Sao Tome and Principe's population. Colonial rule by Portugal is evidenced by the predominance of the Portuguese language and Roman Catholicism. The majority of the population lives on São Tomé.

Economy and the Land
Cocoa dominates Sao Tome and Principe's economy. Copra and palm-oil production are also important, and fishing plays an economic role as well. Through the development of vegetable crops, the government hopes to diversify agricultural output, as much food must now be imported. Part of an extinct volcanic mountain range, Sao Tome and Principe have a mostly mountainous terrain. The climate is tropical.

History and Politics
When Portuguese explorers arrived in the 1400s, Sao Tome and Principe were uninhabited. Early settlers included Portuguese convicts and exiles. Cultivation of the land and importation of slaves led to a thriving sugar economy by the mid-1500s. In the 1800s, following slave revolts and the decline of sugar production, coffee and cocoa became the islands' mainstays, and soon large Portuguese plantations, called *rocas*, were established. Slavery was abolished by Portugal in 1876, but an international controversy arose in the early 1900s when it was found that Angolan contract workers were being treated as virtual slaves. Decades of unrest led to the 1953 Batepa Massacre, in which Portuguese rulers killed several hundred rioting African workers. A movement for independence began in the late 1950s, and following a 1974 change of government in Portugal, Sao Tome and Principe became independent in 1975. The country has established ties with other former Portuguese colonies in northern Africa since gaining independence. The first presidential elections were held in March 1990.

Most of Saudi Arabia has a desert climate, characterized by exceptionally high daytime temperatures for much of the year. The north receives less than one inch of rain annually; the south even less.

SAUDI ARABIA

S audi Arabia reigns as the world's largest exporter of oil. A fact of greater importance to many people is that the desert kingdom is the location of Mecca, the holiest city in Islam and the birthplace of the prophet Muhammad. Every Muslim hopes to make a *hajj*, or pilgrimage, to Mecca's shrine at least once.

People

Saudi Arabia is inhabited primarily by Arab Muslims descended from Semitic peoples who settled in the region several thousand years ago. The petroleum industry has attracted a sizable minority of Arabs from other nations, Europeans, and non-Arab Muslims from Africa and Asia. The country's official language is Arabic, although English is used among educated Saudis in business and international affairs. Islam dominates Saudi life, and nearly all the people belong to the religion's Sunni branch. Various forms of Christianity and traditional religions are practiced among foreign workers and indigenous minority groups. Most live in urban areas, but some Bedouin tribes preserve their nomadic way of life.

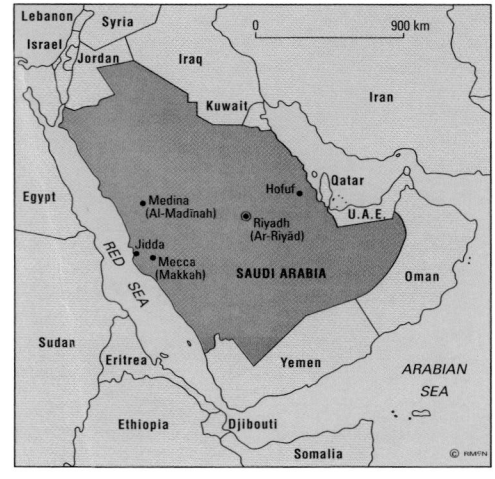

Economy and the Land

The economy of Saudi Arabia has been shaped by its vast deserts and huge petroleum and natural gas reserves. The hot, mostly arid climate has prevented agricultural abundance and stability: the country must import nearly all its food. Oil was discovered in the 1930s, but the country did not begin rapid economic development until the reserves were aggressively exploited following World War II. Saudi Arabia is one of the world's leading exporters of petroleum, possessing the largest concentration of known oil reserves in the world. The government is seeking to diversify the economy, improve transportation and communication lines, and build agricultural output. Private enterprise and foreign investment are encouraged. Saudi Arabia is divided into the western highlands bordering the Red Sea, a central plateau, northern deserts, the huge Rub al Khali desert in the south, and the eastern lowlands. Only the coastal regions receive appreciable rainfall, and some inland desert areas may go without rain for several years.

History and Politics

Even though Saudi Arabia established prosperous trade routes thousands of years ago, its history begins with the founding of Islam by Muhammad in the early A.D 600s. By the end of that century, Mecca and Medina were established as political and

religious centers of Islam and remain so today. The territory split into numerous states that warred among themselves for over a thousand years. The Ottoman Turks gained control over the coastal region of Hejaz in the early 1500s, while Britain set up protectorates along the southern and eastern coasts of Arabia during the 1800s. The Saud family dynasty, founded in the 1400s, managed to remain a dominant religious and political force. Members of the dynasty fought to establish the supremacy of Islamic law and unite the various clans into one nation. In 1932 Ibn Saud proclaimed the Kingdom of Saudi Arabia and established a Saud monarchy that has continued despite dissension within the royal family. Since the 1960s Saudi Arabia has aggressively sought to upgrade local governments, industry, education, the status of women, and the standard of living, while maintaining Islamic values and traditions. Saudi Arabia is a dominant member of the Organization of Petroleum Exporting Countries (OPEC). Despite disagreements with the West and continuing conflicts with Israel, the country maintains strong diplomatic and economic ties with Western nations. During the Gulf War, Saudi Arabia received help from a coalition of nations to protect its borders from Iraqi invasion. The ruling family continues to resist both democratic and extreme fundamentalist influences.

Super tankers loading oil

Saudi Arabia at a glance

Official name	Kingdom of Saudi Arabia

People

Population	18,190,000
Density	22/mi² (8.5/km²)
Urban	77%
Capital	Riyadh, 1,250,000
Ethnic groups	Arab 90%, Afro-Asian 10%
Languages	Arabic
Religions	Muslim 100%
Life expectancy	71 female, 68 male
Literacy	62%

Politics

Government	Monarchy
Parties	None
Suffrage	None
Memberships	AL, OPEC, UN
Subdivisions	14 emirates

Economy

GDP	$194,000,000,000
Per capita	$12,136
Monetary unit	Riyal
Trade partners	Exports: Japan, U.S., Singapore Imports: U.S., Japan, U.K.
Exports	Petroleum
Imports	Manufactures, transportation equipment, construction materials, food

Land

Description	Southwestern Asia
Area	830,000 mi² (2,149,690 km²)
Highest point	Mt. Sawda, 10,522 ft (3,207 m)
Lowest point	Sea level

Saudi Arabia's southern and eastern borders are undefined. This unpopulated and desolate area is called Rub Al-Khali—the Empty Quarter.

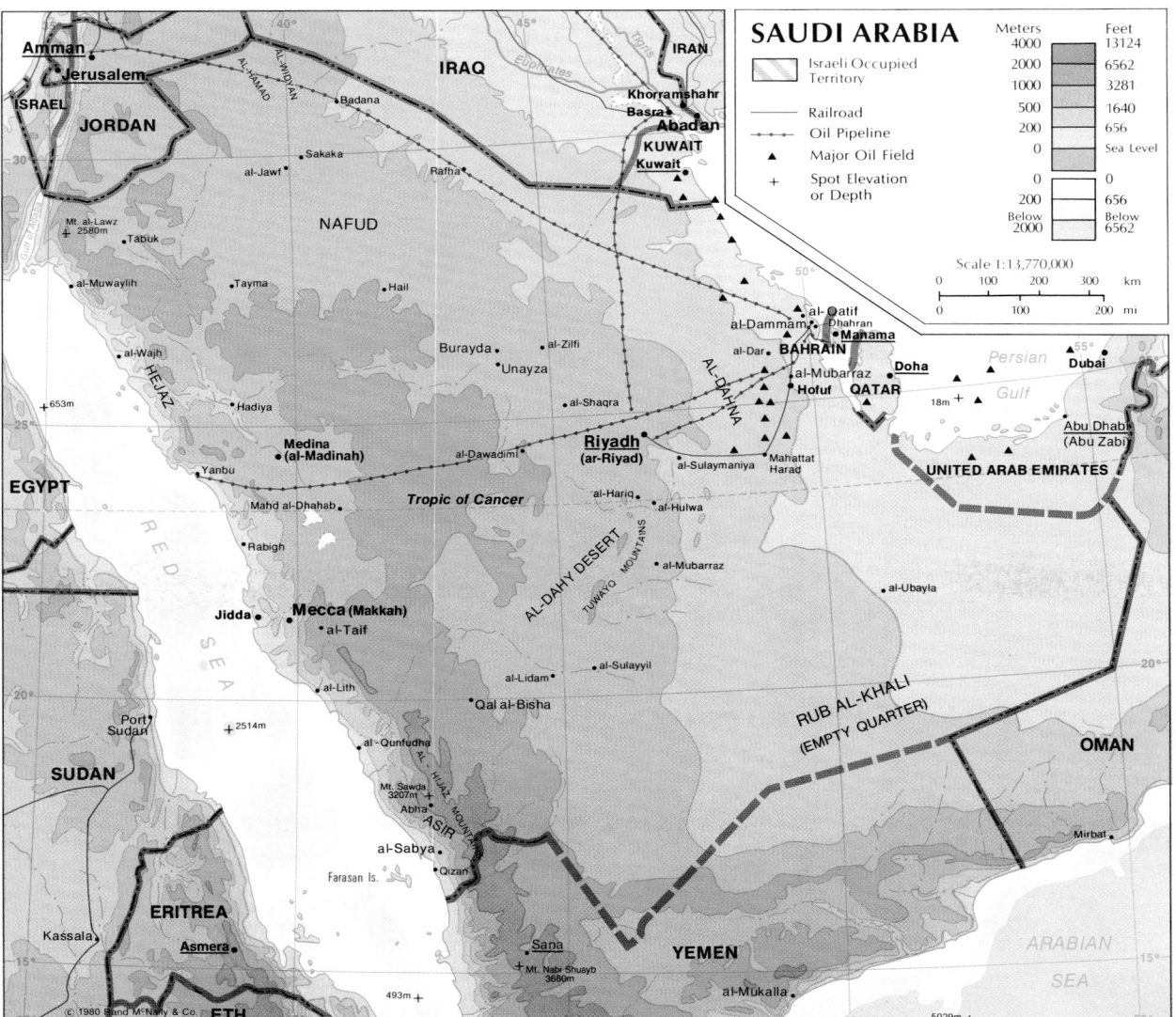

The Senegal River forms the northern border that divides Senegal from Mauritania. Besides serving as a vital transportation route, the river is home to hippopotamuses, turtles, crocodiles, and many species of fish.

SENEGAL

Malinké girls

Although Senegal possesses French Africa's strongest economy, the country's future is threatened by the falling price of peanuts, its principal export, and by several years of bad weather. The fast-growing population also threatens to outstrip the country's resources.

People
Most Senegalese are black Africans from many ethnic groups, each with its own customs and language. The country has many immigrants from other African nations. While French is the official language, Wolof is widely spoken. Islam is the religion of the vast majority. Senegal is mainly a rural nation of subsistence farmers.

Economy and the Land
The mainstays of the economy are petroleum, agriculture, fishing, and mining. Tourism is a rapidly growing new industry. Manufactured goods, fish, peanuts, and petroleum products rank as Senegal's primary exports. Agricultural output is often hurt by irregular weather patterns, and the country must import nearly all its energy. Senegal has one of the finest transportation systems in Africa. Small plateaus, low massifs, marshy swamps, and a sandy coast highlight the terrain, which is mainly flat. The climate is marked by dry and rainy seasons, with differing precipitation patterns in the south and the more arid north.

History and Politics
The area that is now Senegal has been inhabited by black Africans since prehistoric times. When Europeans first established trade ties with the Senegalese in the mid-1400s, the country had been divided into several independent kingdoms. By the early 1800s France had gained control of the region and in 1895 made Senegal part of French West Africa. In 1959 Senegal joined with French Sudan, or present-day Mali, to form the Federation of Mali, which became independent in 1960. However, Senegal withdrew from the federation later in the year to found the independent Republic of Senegal. The new government was plagued by coup attempts and an economy crippled by the severe droughts of the late 1960s and early 1970s. A socialist government has ruled the country since 1960.

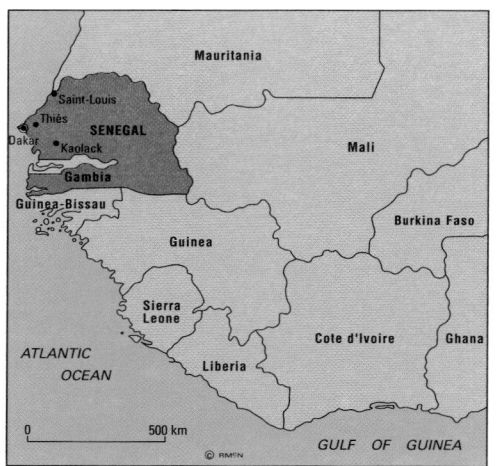

Senegal at a glance

Official name	Republic of Senegal

People

Population	8,862,000
Density	117/mi² (45/km²)
Urban	40%
Capital	Dakar, 1,490,450
Ethnic groups	Wolof 44%, Fulani 23%, Serer 15%, Diola 6%, Malinke 5%
Languages	French, Wolof, Fulani, Serer, indigenous
Religions	Muslim 94%, Christian 5%
Life expectancy	50 female, 48 male
Literacy	38%

Politics

Government	Republic
Parties	Democratic, Socialist, others
Suffrage	Universal, over 18
Memberships	OAU, UN
Subdivisions	10 regions

Economy

GDP	$11,800,000,000
Per capita	$1,503
Monetary unit	CFA franc
Trade partners	Exports: France, India, Mali, Italy. Imports: France, Nigeria, Italy
Exports	Manufactures, fish, peanuts, petroleum products, phosphates
Imports	Manufactures, food, petroleum, machinery

Land

Description	Western Africa
Area	75,951 mi² (196,712 km²)
Highest point	Unnamed, 1,906 ft (581 m)
Lowest point	Sea level

POPULATION COMPARISON
Senegal=3% of U.S.

United States

GDP COMPARISON
Senegal=0.2% of U.S.

United States

ETHNIC GROUPS

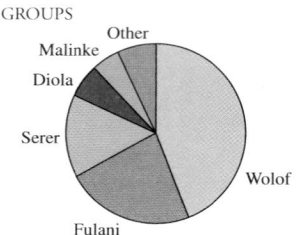

Other
Malinke
Diola
Serer
Wolof
Fulani

POPULATION DISTRIBUTION
Urban   Rural

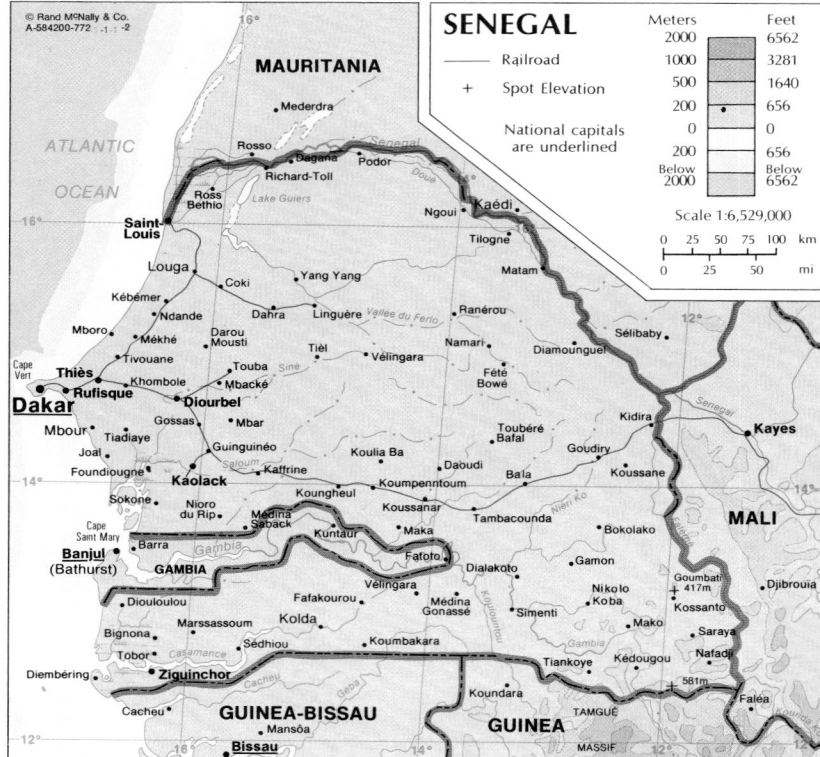

SENEGAL

	Meters	Feet
Railroad	2000	6562
Spot Elevation	1000	3281
	500	1640
	200	656
National capitals are underlined	0	0
	200	656
	Below 2000	Below 6562

Scale 1:6,529,000

0 25 50 75 100 km
0 25 50 mi

Efforts to form a closer bond between Senegal and Gambia have not reached fruition, although the two countries enjoy friendly relations.

The Old Town on Goree Island is overlooked by Dakar, Senegal's capital, in the distance. Dakar is a major center of business and banking in west Africa. Its port is one of the continent's busiest.

Seychelles at a glance

Official name   Republic of Seychelles

People

Population	75,000
Density	429/mi² (166/km²)
Urban	59%
Capital	Victoria, Mahé I., 23,000
Ethnic groups	Seychellois (mixed Asian, African, and European)
Languages	English, French, Creole
Religions	Roman Catholic 90%, Anglican 8%
Life expectancy	73 female, 66 male
Literacy	85%

Politics

Government	Republic
Parties	People's Progressive Front, Democratic
Suffrage	Universal, over 17
Memberships	CW, OAU, UN
Subdivisions	23 districts

Economy

GDP	$407,000,000
Per capita	$5,899
Monetary unit	Rupee
Trade partners	Exports: France, Kuwait, Reunion. Imports: S. Africa, U.K., Kuwait
Exports	Fish, copra, cinnamon bark
Imports	Manufactures, food, tobacco, beverages, machinery and transportation equipment

Land

Description	Indian Ocean islands
Area	175 mi² (453 km²)
Highest point	Mt. Seychelles, 2,969 ft (905 m)
Lowest point	Sea level

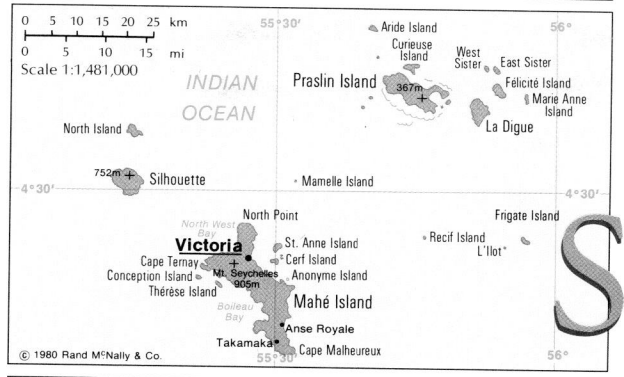

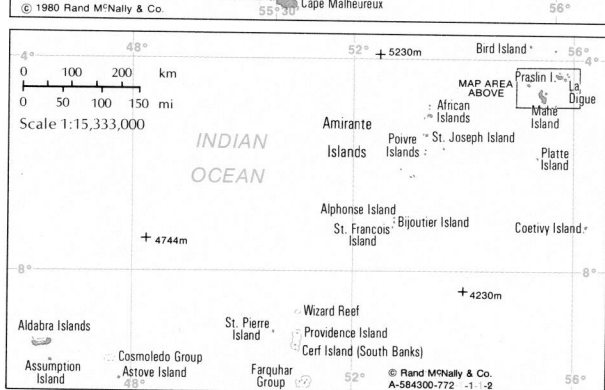

SEYCHELLES

The granite island of Mahé is home to 90 percent of the islands' population and has peaks reaching almost 3,000 feet. The 70-some islands formed from coral are all uninhabited.

People
The majority of Seychellois are of mixed African, European, and Asian ancestry. The islands' culture combines French and African elements, and although the official languages of French and English are widely spoken, most also speak a creole dialect of French. Many of the more than one hundred islands are coral atolls, unable to support human life. The population is concentrated on Mahé, the largest island; the remaining part lives mainly on Praslin and La Digue islands.

Economy and the Land
The basis of the economy is tourism, with foreign visitors attracted by the tropical climate, white-sand beaches, and exotic flora and wildlife found on the granite islands. Mountainous granite islands, which contain fertile soils for growing cinnamon and coconuts, and flat coral islands comprise the Seychelles.

History and Politics
The Portuguese reached the uninhabited islands in the early 1500s. For more than two hundred years, the islands served as little more than pirates' havens. France claimed them in 1756. By the 1770s white planters and African slaves had begun to settle Mahé. After a French-English war, France ceded the islands to Britain in 1814. Seychelles achieved independence in 1976.

Sierra Leone at a glance

Official name   Republic of Sierra Leone

People

Population	4,690,000
Density	168/mi² (65/km²)
Urban	32%
Capital	Freetown, 469,776
Ethnic groups	Temne 30%, Mende 30%, other African
Languages	English, Krio, Mende, Temne, indigenous
Religions	Muslim 30%, Animist 30%, Christian 10%
Life expectancy	45 female, 41 male
Literacy	21%

Politics

Government	Transitional military government
Suffrage	Universal, over 18
Memberships	CW, OAU, UN
Subdivisions	3 provinces, 1 area

Economy

GDP	$4,500,000,000
Per capita	$1,017
Monetary unit	Leone
Trade partners	Exports: U.S., U.K., Netherlands. Imports: U.K., U.S., Germany
Exports	Rutile, bauxite, cocoa, diamonds, coffee
Imports	Machinery, food, petroleum, manufactures

Land

Description	Western Africa
Area	27,925 mi² (72,325 km²)
Highest point	Bintimani, 6,381 ft (1,945 m)
Lowest point	Sea level

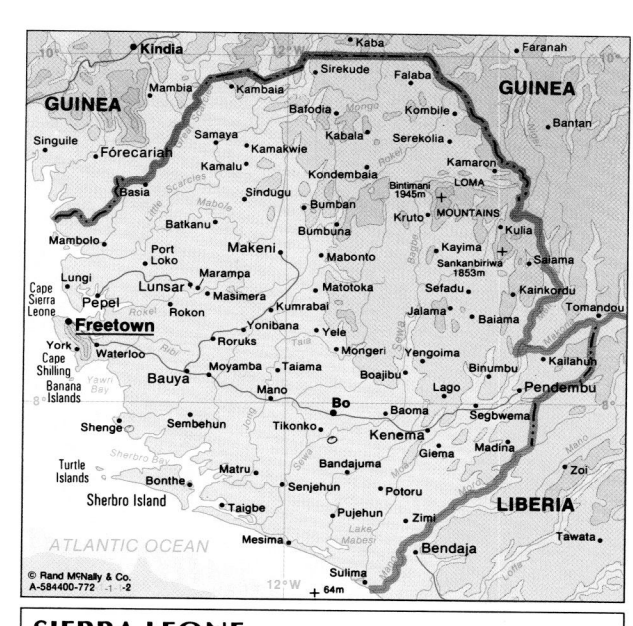

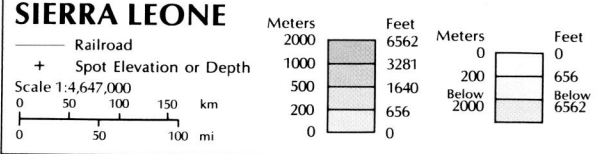

SIERRA LEONE

A great variety of wildlife resides in Sierra Leone's two national parks, north of the village of Kamakwie, but a lack of roads discourages visitors.

People
The population of Sierra Leone is divided into nearly twenty main ethnic groups. The two major groups are the Temne in the north and west and the Mende in the south. Descendants of freed American slaves, who settled in Freetown on the coast, make up a sizable Creole minority. English is the official language, but most of the people speak local African tongues. The Creoles speak Krio, a dialect of English. Most people practice Islam or various local religions, and a small number are Christian.

Economy and the Land
Sierra Leone is one of the world's largest producers of industrial and commercial diamonds. The nation also mines bauxite and rutile. Poor soil, a fluctuating tropical climate, and traditional farming methods keep crop yields low. Sierra Leone is one of Africa's poorest countries. Rice, coffee, and cocoa are important crops. To improve agricultural production, the government is clearing some of the coastal mangrove swamplands. The interior of Sierra Leone is marked by a broad coastal plain in the north and by mountains and plateaus that rise along the country's northern and eastern borders. During the wet season Sierra Leone receives heavy rainfall in the Freetown area and significantly less in the north.

History and Politics
When the Portuguese reached the region in 1460, they found the area inhabited by the Temne. The British followed the Portuguese in the 1500s. Europeans took slaves from the area for the New World until Britain abolished the slave trade. In 1787 Englishman Granville Sharp settled nearly four hundred freed black American slaves in what is now Freetown. Britain declared the peninsula a colony in 1808 and a protectorate in 1896. In 1961 Sierra Leone became an independent nation with a constitution and parliamentary form of government. A military takeover in 1967 was short-lived, and the constitution was rewritten in 1971 to make the country a republic. After years of corrupt one-party rule, the leaders of a military coup in 1992 promised to end corruption and organize democratic elections. Fighting against a strong rebel movement has killed 50,000 people since 1991 and has been very destructive to the economy.

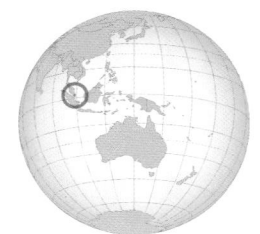

Singapore's relentless pursuit of wealth and order has made it the richest country in Asia, after Japan. The central district's skyline dramatically attests to the country's economic achievements. But adherence to the government's strict rules regulating nearly every aspect of life has dulled Singapore's once-vibrant tapestry of cultures.

SINGAPORE

Just 30 years ago, Singapore's skyline was no more than a jumble of low-rise buildings dating from the pre-war British colonial era. The greatest growth came in the 1980s, when mega-structures such as the 63-story Overseas Union Bank building were erected.

People
Singapore is one of the most densely populated nations in the world. Most of the population is Chinese. A significant minority is Malay, and the remainder is European or Indian. Singapore's languages include Chinese, English, Malay, and Tamil. The main religions—Taoism, Buddhism, Islam, Christianity, and Hinduism—reflect the cultural diversity of the nation. A mixture of Western and traditional customs and dress characterize Singapore's society. Nearly all of the population lives in the city of Singapore, on Singapore Island.

Economy and the Land
Singapore is a leading Asian economic power. The city of Singapore is well known as a financial center and major harbor for trade. The nation's factories produce a variety of goods, such as chemicals, electronic equipment, and machinery, and are among the world leaders in petroleum refining. Singapore has few natural resources, however, and little arable land. Most agricultural output is consumed domestically; the country must import much of its raw mate-

Beach on Sentosa Island

rials and food. The nation consists of one main island, which is characterized by wet lowlands, and many small offshore islets. Cool sea breezes and a tropical climate make Singapore an attractive spot for tourists.

History and Politics
Present-day Singapore has been inhabited since prehistoric times. From the 1100s to the 1800s, Singapore served mainly as a trading center and refuge for pirates. The British East India Company, the major colonial force in India, realized Singapore's strategic importance to British trade and gained possession of the harbor in 1819. Singapore became a crown colony in 1826. As the port prospered, the island's population grew rapidly. Following World War II, the people of Singapore moved from internal self-government to independence in 1965. The government continues to work in partnership with the business community to further Singapore's growth. Singapore's standard of living is one of the highest in eastern Asia. The country's first presidential elections were held in August 1993.

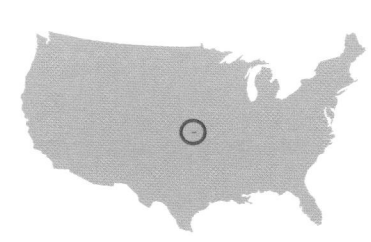

Singapore at a glance

Official name	Republic of Singapore

People

Population	2,921,000
Density	11,894/mi² (4,593/km²)
Urban	100%
Capital	Singapore, 2,921,000
Ethnic groups	Chinese 76%, Malay 15%, Indian 6%
Languages	Chinese (Mandarin), English, Malay, Tamil
Religions	Taoist 29%, Buddhist 27%, Muslim 16%, Christian 10%, Hindu 4%
Life expectancy	77 female, 72 male
Literacy	88%

Politics

Government	Republic
Parties	Democratic, People's Action, Workers', others
Suffrage	Universal, over 20
Memberships	ASEAN, CW, UN
Subdivisions	None

Economy

GDP	$42,400,000,000
Per capita	$15,078
Monetary unit	Dollar
Trade partners	Exports: U.S., Malaysia, Japan Imports: Japan, U.S., Malaysia
Exports	Petroleum, rubber, electronics, manufactures
Imports	Machinery, petroleum, chemicals, manufactures, food

Land

Description	Southeastern Asian island
Area	246 mi² (636 km²)
Highest point	Timah Hill, 545 ft (166 m)
Lowest point	Sea level

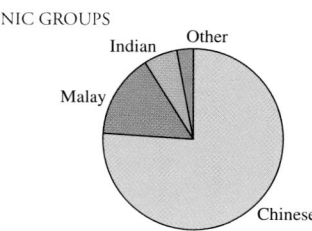

POPULATION COMPARISON
Singapore=1% of U.S.

United States

GDP COMPARISON
Singapore=0.7% of U.S.

United States

ETHNIC GROUPS

POPULATION DISTRIBUTION
Urban   Rural

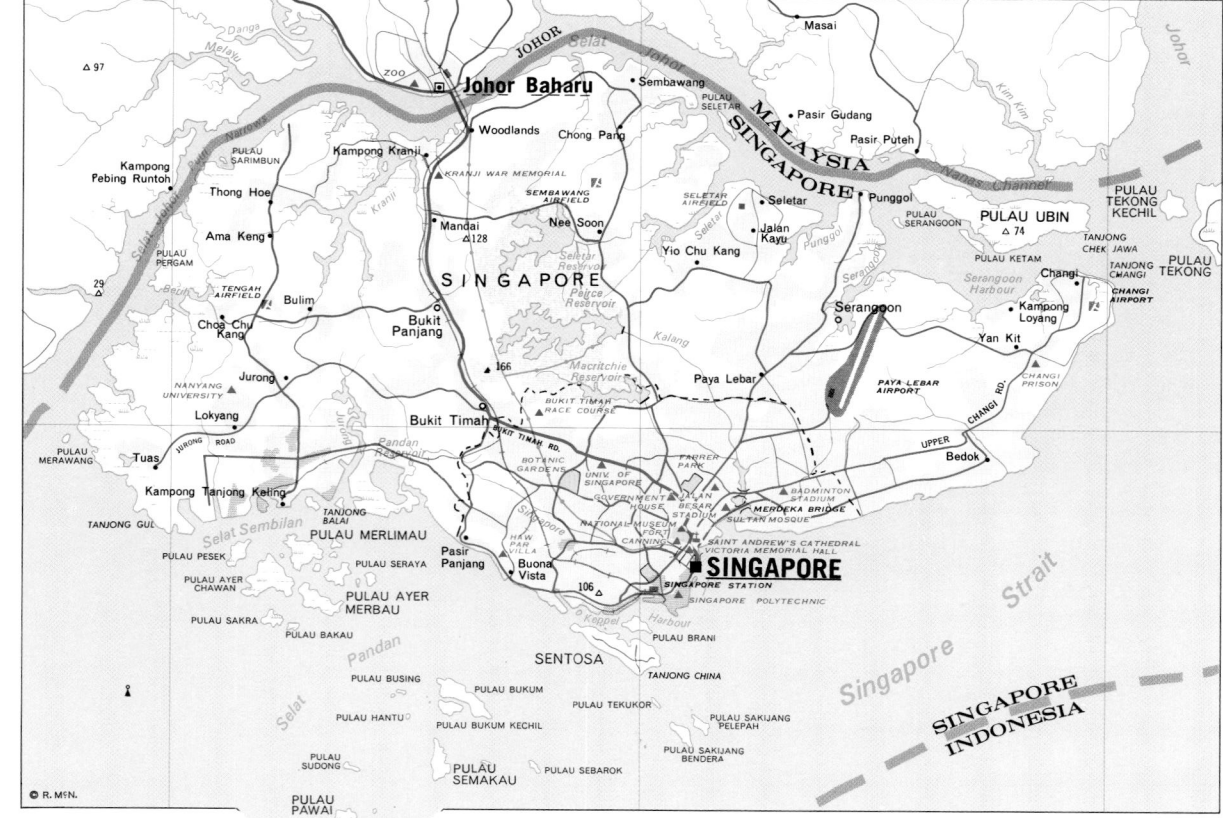

Singapore is the transportation crossroads of Asia. Its airport receives flights from around the region and around the world. Its harbor hosts freighters carrying goods to every continent. From Singapore it is even possible to travel by train all the way north to Bangkok, and beyond.

SLOVAKIA

The Tatra Mountains line Slovakia's border with Poland. Part of the Carpathian Range, their highest point is Gerlach Peak, which rises to 8,711 feet.

Slovakia at a glance
Official name Slovak Republic

People

Population	5,353,000
Density	283/mi² (109/km²)
Capital	Bratislava, 441,453
Ethnic groups	Slovak 86%, Hungarian 11%, Gypsy 2%
Languages	Slovak, Hungarian
Religions	Roman Catholic 60%, Protestant 8%, Orthodox 4%
Life expectancy	77 female, 68 male

Politics

Government	Republic
Parties	Christian Democratic Movement, Democratic Left, Movement for Democracy, Nationalist
Suffrage	Universal, over 18
Memberships	UN
Subdivisions	4 regions

Economy

GDP	$31,000,000,000
Per capita	$5,863
Monetary unit	Koruna
Trade partners	Czech Republic, former Soviet republics, Germany, Poland
Exports	Machinery and transportation equipment; chemicals; fuels, minerals, and metals
Imports	Machinery and transportation equipment, fuels and lubricants, manufactures

People

Description	Eastern Europe, landlocked
Area	18,933 mi² (49,035 km²)
Highest point	Gerlach Peak, 8,711 ft (2,655 m)
Lowest point	Along Bodrog River, 308 ft (94 m)

POPULATION COMPARISON
Slovakia=2% of U.S.

United States

GDP COMPARISON
Slovakia=0.5% of U.S.

United States

ETHNIC GROUPS

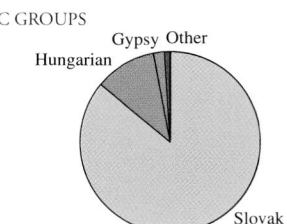

Czechoslovakia's emergence from the Eastern Bloc in 1989 was but the first step towards independence for the Slovak people. They were the driving force which split off Slovakia from the Czech Republic in 1993. Ironically, separation will be much harder for Slovakia, with its obsolete industries and weak economy.

People
The people of Slovakia are related to the Czechs, but they are culturally linked to the Hungarians rather than the Germans. The Slovak language is similar to Czech and has the same roots. Slovakia has a large Hungarian minority, and Hungarians complain that the Slovaks are trying to eliminate their language and culture. Roman Catholicism is the main religion. The Slovaks are proud of their literary heritage and their artistic achievements.

Economy and the Land
Slovakia suffers from both high inflation and unemployment as it struggles to create a new economy in the aftermath of eastern European communism. Although some industrialization took place under communist rule, agriculture remains an important economic activity. Most agriculture takes place in the fertile Hungarian Plain in the south. The nation has important mineral deposits, but lacks any significant energy resources. Slovakia is bounded on the north and east by the Carpathian Mountains.

History and Politics
Slavic people settled Slovakia in the fifth century, and were incorporated into the Moravian state that was established in the ninth century. Slovakia fell under Hungarian rule in the early tenth century, and little economic or social development took place for three hundred years, until Hungary's grasp on the region began to weaken and the Slovaks began to make contact with the outside world. Slovakia remained under Hungarian rule despite a growing nationalist movement that gained momentum throughout the nineteenth century. After Austria-Hungary was defeated in World War I, the Slovaks and the Czechs were united to form the independent nation of Czechoslovakia in 1918. The Slovaks, who had envisioned a federal state, were angered by the centrist government that was established and extremists began demanding separation less than ten years after the nation was formed. The Slovak separatist movement remained active until it was obliterated by the communists who took over Czechoslovakia after World War II. In 1968 Czechoslovakia adopted a liberal reform plan that called for greater autonomy for Slovakia, but the invasion of the Warsaw Pact countries prevented the plan from being implemented. Communist rule ended in 1989, and Slovakia gained full independence in 1993. Slovakia is moving very slowly towards democracy, although the present government has privatized as little as politically possible.

Electric tram, Bratislava

Slovakia has large deposits of iron ore under its forest-covered hills.

SLOVAKIA

Major Urban Area	
Railroad	
Canal	

Capitals are underlined

Meters	Feet
4000	13124
2000	6562
1000	3281
500	1640
200	656
0	0

0 20 40 60 80 100 km
0 20 40 60 mi

Scale 1:4,938,000

©Rand McNally & Co
A-550500-772

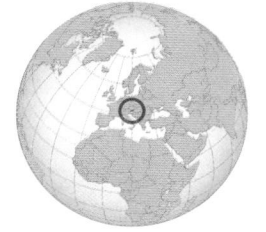

SLOVENIA

Slovenia's standard of living has approached that of neighboring Austria and Hungary. But the violence tearing the other former Yugoslavian republics has torn Slovenia as well. While not subject to the same destruction, Slovenia has faced economic hardship as its former trade routes have been disrupted.

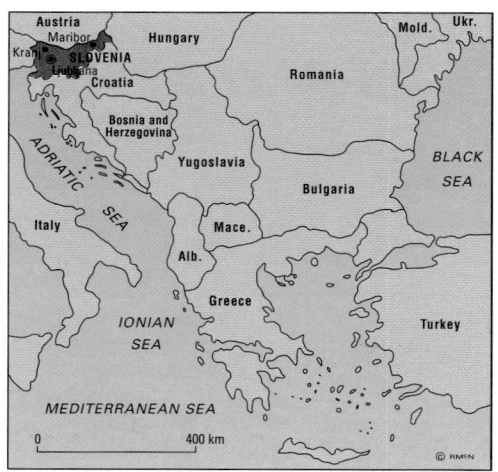

People
The Slovenes managed to keep their own language and traditions only by resisting centuries of unrelenting pressure to adopt German culture. Most people are Roman Catholic, and their religion is an important part of their national identity. Slovenia is also home to small Croatian and Serbian minorities.

Economy and the Land
Slovenia has had a well-developed industrial sector since the mid-1800s. Most people are engaged in industry. Before it achieved independence in 1991, prosperity in Slovenia was greater than in the other Yugoslavian republics. Slovenia's economy is very well-rounded, and despite the mountainous terrain, agriculture is also an important activity. Major crops are potatoes, hops, hemp, and flax. Dairy farming is also an important agricultural activity. Coal and timber are produced in abundance.

History and Politics
Until the 1990s, Slovenia had never been an independent nation in modern times. Ancestors of the modern Slovenes are believed to have arrived in the region around A.D. 600. By the eighth century, they had been conquered by the Franks and were converted to Roman Catholicism by the emperor Charlemagne. The Slovenes were serfs under German feudal lords until the region came under the control of the Austro-Hungarian Hapsburg empire in the late 1200s. The Hapsburgs maintained control for seven hundred years, although the

area was subjected to occasional Turkish raids. The German-speaking Hapsburg empire attempted to impose its language on the Slovenian people, who resisted and continued to speak their own Slavic language. Slovenia became part of Yugoslavia in 1918. During World War II, Slovenia was divided among Germany, Italy, and Hungary. Once again, the Germans attempted to eliminate Slovenian culture by killing the Slovenes in concentration camps or forcing them to migrate to other parts of Yugoslavia. Slovenia gained considerable autonomy after Yugoslavia was reconstituted as a federal Communist republic following the war. Under Communist rule, many Slovenians resented their obligation to support Serbia and the other poorer Yugoslavian republics. Without massive demonstrations or public unrest, the nation slowly moved towards a more peaceful separation from the rest of Yugoslavia. In June 1991, Slovenia, along with neighboring Croatia, declared its independence from Yugoslavia. Shortly after the announcement, the Yugoslavian army made a brief attempt to thwart the will of the people before ordering its troops out of Slovenia. Slovenia received international recognition in January 1992. A lack of public-sector reform has slowed economic development.

SLOVENIA

		Meters	Feet
		4000	13124
— Railroad	City type size indicates relative importance	2000	6562
		1000	3281
+ Spot Elevation	Scale 1:3,371,000	500	1640
		200	656
National capitals are underlined		0	0
		200	656

Scale: 0 25 50 75 km / 0 25 50 mi

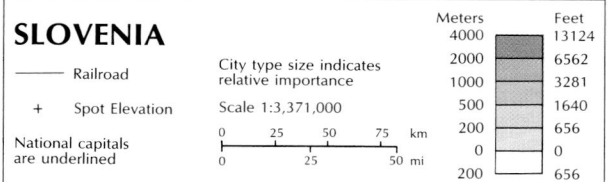

Slovenia's short Adriatic coast is heavily polluted from the years of unbridled industrial development during the Communist era.

Old Town and castle, Ljubljana

POPULATION COMPARISON
Slovenia=0.8% of U.S.

United States

GDP COMPARISON
Slovenia=0.2% of U.S.

United States

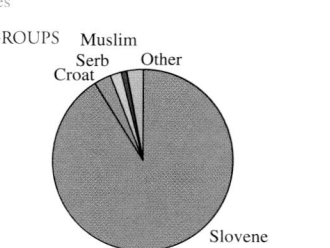

ETHNIC GROUPS — Muslim, Serb, Croat, Other, Slovene

POPULATION DISTRIBUTION
Urban — Rural

Slovenia at a glance

Official name	Republic of Slovenia

People

Population	1,930,000
Density	255/mi² (98/km²)
Urban	49%
Capital	Ljubljana, 233,200
Ethnic groups	Slovene 91%, Croat 3%, Serb 2%, Muslim 1%
Languages	Slovenian, Serbo-Croatian
Religions	Roman Catholic 96%, Muslim 1%
Life expectancy	78 female, 70 male
Literacy	99%

Politics

Government	Republic
Parties	Christian Democratic, Greens, Liberal Democratic, National Democratic, Social Democratic, Socialist
Suffrage	Universal, over 18; over 16, if employed
Memberships	UN
Subdivisions	None

Economy

GDP	$15,000,000,000
Per capita	$7,634
Monetary unit	Tolar
Trade partners	Exports: former Yugoslavian republics, Austria, Italy Imports: former Yugoslavian republics, Germany
Exports	Machinery and transportation equipment, manufactures, chemicals, food
Imports	Machinery and transportation equipment, manufactures, chemicals

Land

Description	Eastern Europe
Area	7,820 mi² (20,253 km²)
Highest point	Triglav, 9,396 ft (2,864 m)
Lowest point	Sea level

Solomon Islands at a glance

Official name Solomon Islands

People

Population	393,000
Density	36/mi² (14/km²)
Urban	15%
Capital	Honiara, Guadalcanal I., 30,413
Ethnic groups	Melanesian 93%, Polynesian 4%, Micronesian 2%
Languages	English, indigenous
Religions	Anglican 34%, Roman Catholic 19%, Baptist 17%, United Church 11%
Life expectancy	73 female, 68 male

Politics

Government	Parliamentary state
Parties	National Action, National Unity and Reconciliation, People's Alliance
Suffrage	Universal, over 21
Memberships	CW, UN
Subdivisions	7 provinces, 1 town

Economy

GDP	$900,000,000
Per capita	$2,795
Monetary unit	Dollar
Trade partners	Exports: Japan, U.K., Thailand Imports: Australia, Japan
Exports	Fish, wood, copra, palm oil
Imports	Machinery, fuel, food

Land

Description	South Pacific islands
Area	10,954 mi² (28,370 km²)
Highest point	Mt. Makarakomburu, 8,028 ft (2,447 m)
Lowest point	Sea level

The body of water at the center of the Solomon Islands known as "The Slot" was the scene of fierce naval warfare during World War II. Scores of Japanese and American ships litter its bottom.

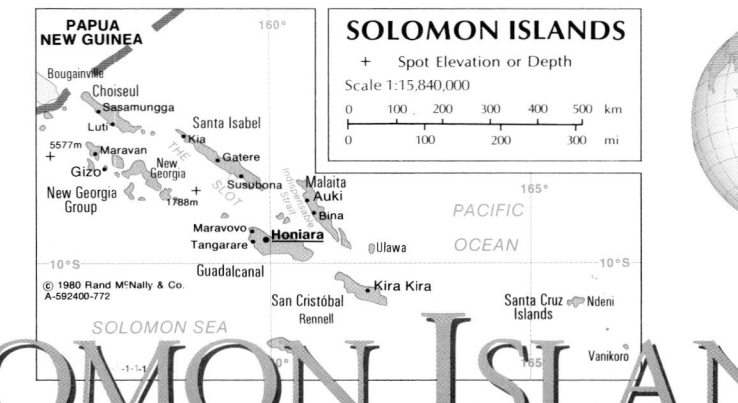

SOLOMON ISLANDS

People
Over 90 percent of the people are Melanesian, and the remainder are Polynesian, European, Chinese, and Micronesian. English is the official language, but some ninety local languages are also spoken. Most people are Anglican, Roman Catholic, Baptist, or other Protestants. The population is primarily rural, and much of its social structure is patterned on traditional village life.

Economy and the Land
The economy is based on subsistence farming and exports of fish, wood, copra, and some spices and palm oil. Tourism is of growing importance. Food, machinery, gasoline, and manufactured goods must be imported. Terrain ranges from forested mountains to low-lying coral atolls. The climate is warm and moist, with heavy annual rainfall.

History and Politics
Hunter-gatherers lived on the islands as early as 1000 B.C. Because of disease and native resistance, early attempts at colonization failed, and Europeans did not firmly establish themselves until the mid-1800s. Britain declared the islands a protectorate in 1893. The area was the site of fierce battles between the Japanese and Allied forces during World War II, and following the war, moves were made toward independence. In 1978 the Solomon Islands adopted a constitution and became a sovereign nation.

Somalia at a glance

Official name Somalia

People

Population	7,187,000
Density	29/mi² (11/km²)
Urban	24%
Capital	Mogadishu, 600,000
Ethnic groups	Somali 85%, Bantu
Languages	Arabic, Somali, English, Italian
Religions	Sunni Muslim
Life expectancy	49 female, 45 male
Literacy	24%

Politics

Government	None
Parties	United Somali Congress
Suffrage	Universal, over 18
Memberships	AL, OAU, UN
Subdivisions	18 regions

Economy

GDP	$3,400,000,000
Per capita	$567
Monetary unit	Shilling
Trade partners	Exports: Saudi Arabia, United Arab Emirates Imports: Italy, Bahrain, U.K.
Exports	Bananas, livestock, fish, hides and skins
Imports	Petroleum, food, construction materials

Land

Description	Eastern Africa
Area	246,201 mi² (637,657 km²)
Highest point	Shimbiris, 7,897 ft (2,407 m)
Lowest point	Sea level

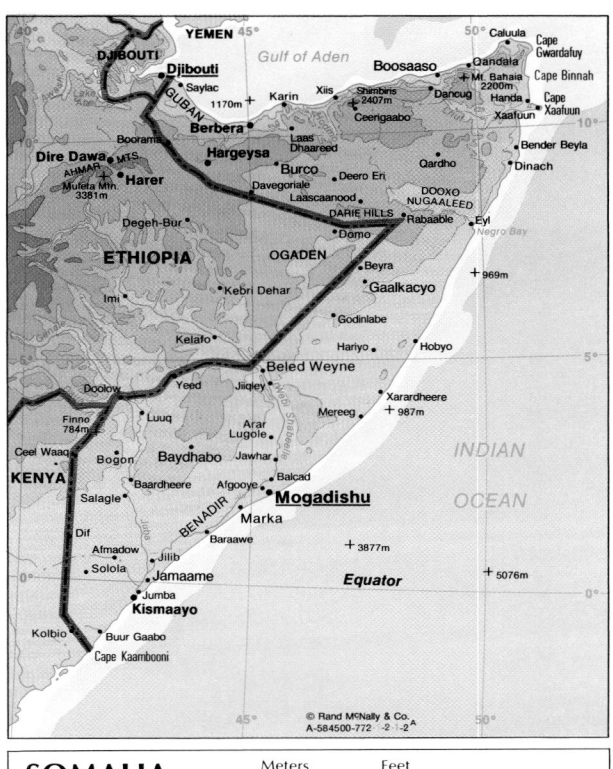

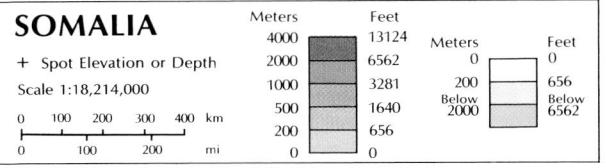

SOMALIA

Relations between Somalia and Ethiopia have been strained over the issue of the Ogaden Desert. Although the desert is surrounded on two sides by Somalia and peopled mostly with Somalis, Ethiopia has held on to it stubbornly.

People
Unlike the population in many African nations, the people of Somalia are remarkably homogeneous in their language, culture, and identity. Most are nomadic or seminomadic herders; only a quarter of the people have settled in permanent communities in southern Somalia. While Arabic and Somali are official languages, English and Italian are also spoken. Nearly all the Somali people are Sunni Muslims.

Economy and the Land
Somalia is a developing country that has not exploited its rich deposits of iron ore and gypsum. There is little manufacturing. The economy is agricultural, though activity is restricted to the vicinity of the rivers and certain coastal districts. A hot climate with recurring droughts, as well as a lack of railroads and paved highways, hamper economic development. The terrain ranges from central and southern flatlands to northern hills.

History and Politics
In the A.D. 800s or 900s, Arabs converted the ancestors of the Somalis who settled the region to Islam. They fought many religious wars with the Christian kingdom of Ethiopia between the 1300s and 1500s. The British, Italians, and French arrived in the region in the latter half of the 1800s and divided the Somali territory among themselves, with Ethiopia seizing Ogaden in the west. After World War II, Italy was made administrator of its former colony to prepare it for independence. In 1960 British Somaliland and Italian Somalia joined to form an independent republic. Since that time, Somalia has had many border clashes with Kenya and Ethiopia over the rights of Somalis living in these countries to determine their own destiny. Military leaders staged a successful coup in 1969, and subsequently changed the nation's name to Somali Democratic Republic and abolished all political parties. Military activity has since resulted in a civil war, famine, and the killing of thousands of civilians. Rebel forces overcame the government in January 1991, and Northern Somalia seceded in May 1991. Clan-based fighting led to mass starvation and the deaths of hundreds of thousands of people. In late 1992 the U.S. military intervened in an attempt to reduce chaos and enable world-wide relief efforts to proceed safely. The United Nations took over the operation in 1993, withdrawing in 1995.

SOUTH AFRICA

During the 1970s and 1980s, South Africa was treated as a pariah around the world for its racist policies of apartheid. The first free elections open to all South Africans were held in 1994 and were won easily by candidates of the African National Party, which had led the struggle against apartheid. A sprawling land rich in ethnic diversity, natural resources, and wildlife, South Africa faces innumerable challenges in the years ahead as it strives to bring economic justice to all its people, while preserving an economy that is far and away the most developed on the continent.

People
South Africa's population consists of four groups: black, white, colored, and Asian. Black African groups make up the majority population. The minority whites are either Afrikaners—of Dutch, German, and French descent—or British. Coloreds, people of mixed white, black, and Asian heritage, and Asians, primarily from India, make up the remaining population. Afrikaans and English are the official languages, although the blacks, coloreds, and Asians speak their own languages as well. The dominant religions are Christian; however, many groups follow traditional practices. For decades the South African government enforced apartheid, a policy of racial segregation widely criticized for violating the rights of blacks, coloreds, and Asians.

Economy and the Land
The discovery of gold and diamonds in South Africa in the late 1800s shaped the nation's prosperous economy. Revenues from mining promoted industry, and today South Africa is one of the richest and most highly developed countries in Africa. Mining remains a mainstay, as does agriculture; the nation is almost self-sufficient in food production. Many effects of apartheid, including discriminatory systems of education and job reservation, kept the majority population from the benefits of national prosperity. The varied landscape features coastal beaches, plateaus, mountains, and deep valleys. The climate is temperate.

History and Politics
Southern Africa has been inhabited for many thousands of years. Ancestors of the area's present African population had settled there by the time Portuguese explorers reached the Cape of Good Hope in the late 1400s. The first white settlers, ancestors of today's Afrikaners, established colonies in the seventeenth century. Britain gained control of the area in the late eighteenth century, and relations between Afrikaners and the British soon became strained. To escape British rule, many Afrikaners

Most of South Africa is a plate-shaped plateau at an elevation of 3,000 to 6,500 feet. Deforestation for lumber and to allow grazing has left few of South Africa's many original forests intact. The only surviving rain forest is at the southern tip.

SOUTH AFRICA

Meters	Feet
4000	13124
2000	6562
1000	3281
500	1640
200	656
0	0
200	656
Below 2000	Below 6562

Major Urban Area
Railroad
Province Boundary
+ Spot Elevation or Depth

Scale 1:15,147,000

©Rand McNally & Co.
A-584600-772 -3 -3

Rural family

Pretoria

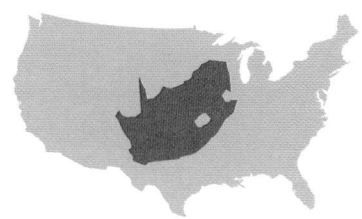

POPULATION COMPARISON
South Africa=17% of U.S.

United States

GDP COMPARISON
South Africa=3% of U.S.

United States

ETHNIC GROUPS

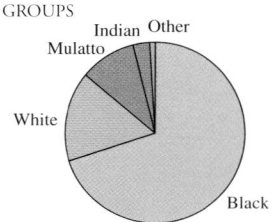

Indian Other
Mulatto
White
Black

POPULATION DISTRIBUTION
Urban   Rural

168

Along with Rio de Janeiro and San Francisco, Cape Town has one of the world's most beautiful settings. The city stretches from the shores of the Atlantic Ocean on the Cape of Good Hope peninsula up the slopes of 3,500-foot Table Mountain. The old part of the city is rich with Dutch, French and British influences. Each of those European colonial powers played a role in Cape Town's history.

migrated northward to lands occupied by black Africans. The discovery of gold and diamonds in the late 1800s brought an influx of Europeans and further strained relations between Afrikaners and the British, with both groups striving for control of valuable mineral deposits. Two wars broke out, and in 1902 the British defeated the Afrikaners, or Boers, and incorporated the Boer territories into the British Empire. The British also subdued black Africans, and in 1910 they formed the white-controlled Union of South Africa. Afrikaner nationalism grew in the early twentieth century and led to the formation of the National party, which gained control in 1924 and again in 1948. The party began the apartheid system of separation of the races in the late 1940s, and subsequent decades saw increasing apartheid legislation and racial tension. In 1951 South Africa embarked on a program to create a white majority by setting up "independent" black republics, or homelands, within its borders. During the 1980s, the government began to force blacks to move into the homelands and to renounce their citizenship, thereby sparking international outcry. Foreign and internal pressure forced the government to respond with reforms and to dismantle apartheid. The 1990 release of Nelson Mandela, leader of the African National Congress (ANC), after 27 years in prison, paved the way for a new South Africa. Under the leadership of Mandela and President de Klerk, the country was led to relatively peaceful elections in April 1994. Mandela was elected president and an interim constitution abolishing the homelands was established.

South Africa at a glance

Official name	Republic of South Africa

People

Population	44,500,000
Density	94/mi² (36/km²)
Urban	49%
Capital	Pretoria (administrative), 525,583; Cape Town (legislative), 854,616; Bloemfontein (judicial), 126,867
Ethnic groups	Black 70%, white 14%, mulatto (coloured) 9%, Indian 3%
Languages	Afrikaans, English, Xhosa, Sotho, Tswana, Zulu, others
Religions	Black Independent 19%, Dutch Reformed 14%, Roman Catholic 10%
Life expectancy	66 female, 60 male
Literacy	76%

Politics

Government	Republic
Parties	African National Congress, Conservative, Democratic, National, others
Suffrage	Universal, over 18
Memberships	CW, OAU, UN
Subdivisions	9 provinces

Economy

GDP	$171,000,000,000
Per capita	$5,176
Monetary unit	Rand
Trade partners	Exports: Italy, Japan, U.S. Imports: Germany, Japan, U.K.
Exports	Gold, minerals and metals, food, chemicals
Imports	Machinery, transportation equipment, chemicals, oil, textiles

Land

Description	Southern Africa
Area	471,010 mi² (1,219,909 km²)
Highest point	eNjesuthi, 11,306 ft (3,446 m)
Lowest point	Sea level

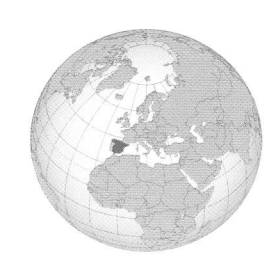

SPAIN

The white-washed village of Casares spills down a hillside in southern Spain near Gibraltar. A United Nations World Heritage Site, it is a splendid example of the villages known as "pueblos blancos" that dot the rolling hills between Seville and Grenada.

The legacy of Spanish influence around the world rivals that of other great powers of history. At home, Spanish culture is spiced by the many lands Spain explored and colonized. This exuberant blend has its own interpretation in each of the country's distinct regions. Recent Spanish history has been as varied and dramatic as the culture. After many years of civil war and dictatorship, Spain's democracy is firmly established. Today Spain plays an increasingly important role in European affairs. (continued)

Spain at a glance

Official name	Kingdom of Spain

People

Population	39,260,000
Density	201/mi² (78/km²)
Urban	78%
Capital	Madrid, 3,102,846
Ethnic groups	Spanish (mixed Mediterranean and Teutonic)
Languages	Spanish (Castilian), Catalan, Galician, Basque
Religions	Roman Catholic 99%
Life expectancy	80 female, 75 male
Literacy	95%

Politics

Government	Constitutional monarchy
Parties	Convergence and Unity, Popular, Social Democratic Center, Socialist Workers, United Left, others
Suffrage	Universal, over 18
Memberships	EU, NATO, OECD, UN
Subdivisions	17 autonomous communities

Economy

GDP	$498,000,000,000
Per capita	$12,719
Monetary unit	Peseta
Trade partners	Exports: U.S., Japan, U.K. Imports: Germany, U.S., U.K.
Exports	Transportation equipment, manufactures, food, machinery
Imports	Machinery, transportation equipment, fuel, manufactures, food

Land

Description	Southwestern Europe
Area	194,885 mi² (504,750 km²)
Highest point	Pico de Teide, 12,188 ft (3,715 m)
Lowest point	Sea level

Alcala Street and the Metropolis Building, Madrid

The 15th-century Cathedral is located at the heart of Barcelona's Gothic Quarter.

POPULATION COMPARISON
Spain=15% of U.S.

United States

GDP COMPARISON
Spain=8% of U.S.

United States

POPULATION DISTRIBUTION
Urban — Rural

Ibiza is one of Spain's Balearic Islands in the Mediterranean. With its white-washed houses and twisting alleys, it resembles one of the Greek Islands far to the east. A one-time trading port for the Phoenicians in the 10th century B.C., the 221-square-mile island is now popular with tourists year-round.

People

The population of Spain is a mixture of ethnic groups from northern Europe and the area surrounding the Mediterranean Sea. Spanish is the official language; however, several regional dialects of Spanish are commonly spoken. The Basque minority, one of the oldest surviving ethnic groups in Europe, lives mainly in the Pyrenees in northern Spain, preserving its own language and traditions. Since the 1978 constitution, Spain has not had an official religion, yet nearly all its people are Roman Catholic. Spain has a rich artistic tradition, blending Moorish and Western cultures.

Economy and the Land

Spain has benefited greatly from an economic-restructuring program that began in the 1950s. The nation has concentrated on developing industry, which now employs over 30 percent of the population. The chemical industry, high technology, electronics, and tourism are important sources of revenue. The agricultural contribution to the economy has declined to about half of peak production. Spain's terrain is mainly composed of a dry plateau area; mountains cover the northern section, and plains extend down the country's eastern coast. The climate in the eastern and southern regions is Mediterranean, while the northwest has more rainfall and less sunshine throughout the year.

History and Politics

Spain is among the oldest inhabited regions in Europe. A Roman province for centuries, Spain was conquered by the Visigoths in the A.D. 500s, only to change hands again in the 700s when the Arab-Berbers, or Moors, seized control of all but a narrow strip of northern Spain. Christian kings reclaimed the country from the eleventh to the fourteenth centuries. Controlled by the three kingdoms of Navarre, Aragon, and Castile, Spain was united in the late 1400s under King Ferdinand and Queen Isabella. At the height of its empire, Spain claimed territory in North and South America, northern Africa, Italy, and the Canary Islands. However, a series of wars burdened Spain financially, and in the 1500s, under King Philip II, the country entered a period of decline. Throughout the 1700s and 1800s, the nation lost most of its colonial possessions through treaty or revolution. In 1936 a bitter civil war erupted between an insurgent fascist group and supporters of the republic. General Francisco Franco, leader of the successful insurgent army, ruled as dictator of Spain from the end of the war until his death in 1975. Since Franco's death, King Juan Carlos has led the country toward a more democratic form of government. Spain has prospered but has had to grapple with separatist movements in Catalonia and the Basque region.

With an average elevation of greater than 2,100 feet, Spain ranks as the second-highest country in Europe, after Switzerland. Spain's numerous mountain systems include the Pyrenees, the Cantabrian Mountains, the Iberian Mountains, the Sierra Morena, and the Sierra Nevada.

Tea is the principal export of Sri Lanka. Here, workers pick the flavorful leaves on a plantation near the southern town of Nuwara Eliya.

SRI LANKA

Washing an elephant

The island country of Sri Lanka is a beautiful land of rain forests and fertile plains. It is also a land of intractable violence, brought on by decades of strife between the majority Sinhalese and the minority Tamils, who live in the north.

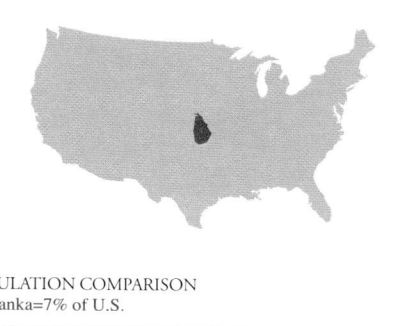

POPULATION COMPARISON
Sri Lanka=7% of U.S.

United States

GDP COMPARISON
Sri Lanka=8% of U.S.

United States

ETHNIC GROUPS

Indian Tamil / Other / Moor / Ceylon Tamil / Sinhalese

POPULATION DISTRIBUTION
Urban / Rural

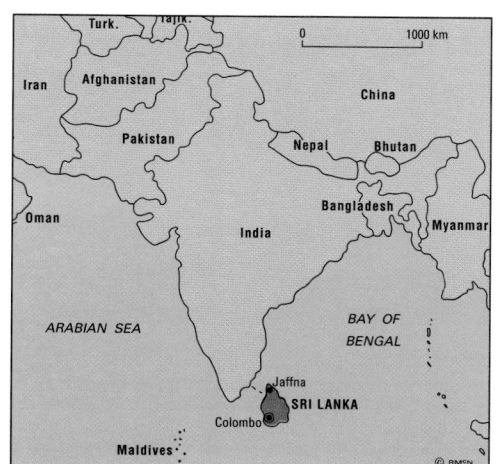

People
The two principal groups in Sri Lanka are the majority Sinhalese and the minority Tamils. Other minorities include the Moors; Burghers, who are descendants of Dutch, Portuguese, and British colonists; Malays; and Veddah aborigines. Sinhala, Tamil, and English are official languages. Most Sinhalese are Buddhist, most Tamils are Hindu, and the majority of the Moors and Malays are Muslims.

Economy and the Land
Sri Lanka's economy is based on agriculture, which employs nearly half the people in producing tea, rubber, and coconuts. Sri Lanka also hopes to become self-sufficient in rice, thus reducing imports of this staple. Industrial production has increased, and major exports include rubber and textile products. The country also sponsors several internal-development programs. However, continuing high government subsidy and welfare policies threaten economic growth. A low coastal plain, mountainous and forested southern interior, and tropical climate characterize Sri Lanka.

History and Politics
The Sinhalese dynasty was founded by a northern Indian prince in about 500 B.C. Later, the Tamils from southern India settled in the north of Sri Lanka. European control began in the 1500s, when the Portuguese and Dutch ruled the island. It became a British possession in 1796 and the independent nation of Ceylon in 1948. In 1972 it changed its name to Sri Lanka. Tensions between the ruling Sinhalese and the minority Tamils have resulted in violence. A cease-fire was signed in 1995.

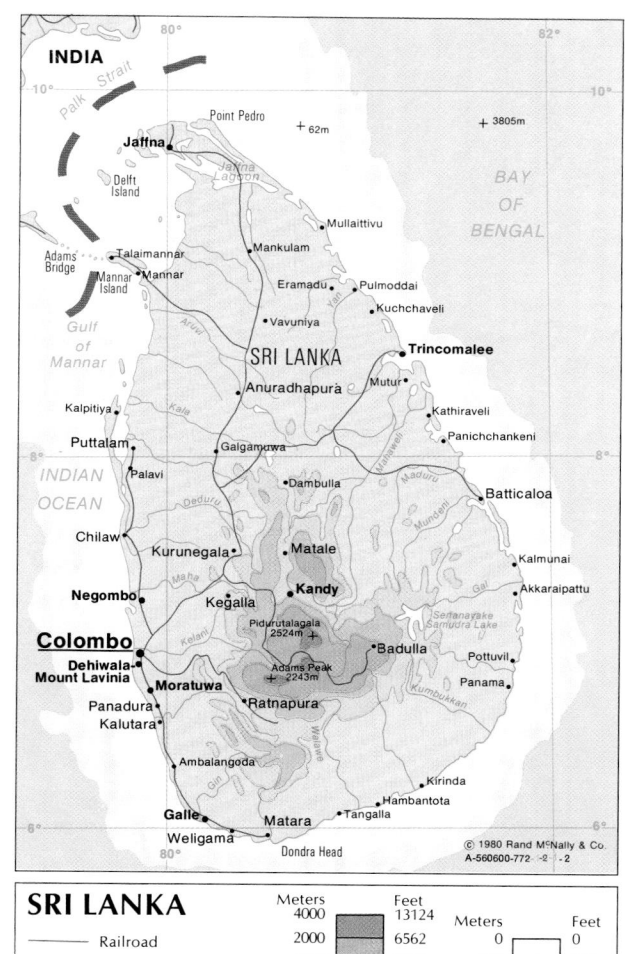

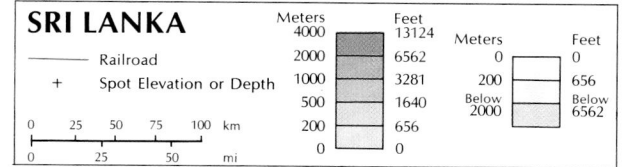

SRI LANKA

— Railroad
+ Spot Elevation or Depth

Meters	Feet
4000	13124
2000	6562
1000	3281
500	1640
200	656
0	0

Meters	Feet
0	0
200	656
Below 2000	Below 6562

0 25 50 75 100 km
0 25 50 mi

More than 2,000 years ago, early inhabitants of Sri Lanka built a system of reservoirs and canals to harness the island's many rivers and abundant rainfall for agriculture. Some of the system is still used today.

Sri Lanka at a glance

Official name	Democratic Socialist Republic of Sri Lanka

People

Population	18,240,000
Density	731/mi² (282/km²)
Urban	21%
Capital	Colombo (designated), 612,000; Sri Jayawardenapura (seat of government), 108,000
Ethnic groups	Sinhalese 74%, Ceylon Tamil 10%, Moor 7%, Indian Tamil 6%
Languages	English, Sinhala, Tamil
Religions	Buddhist 69%, Hindu 15%, Muslim 8%, Christian 8%
Life expectancy	74 female, 70 male
Literacy	88%

Politics

Government	Socialist republic
Parties	Freedom, Tamil Independents, United National, others
Suffrage	Universal, over 18
Memberships	CW, UN
Subdivisions	8 provinces

Economy

GDP	$53,500,000,000
Per capita	$3,016
Monetary unit	Rupee
Trade partners	Exports: U.S., Germany, U.K. Imports: Japan, Iran, U.S.
Exports	Textiles and clothing, teas, petroleum, coconut, rubber
Imports	Food, textiles, petroleum, machinery

Land

Description	Southern Asian island
Area	24,962 mi² (64,652 km²)
Highest point	Pidurutalagala, 8,281 ft (2,524 m)
Lowest point	Sea level

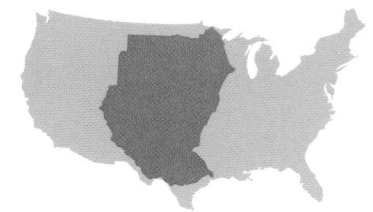

Until it was abandoned by the British in the 1930s, Port Sawakin (Suakin) was Sudan's only port. Today, Port Sudan to the north handles maritime traffic, and this colonial relic is a fascinating warren of crumbling buildings.

SUDAN

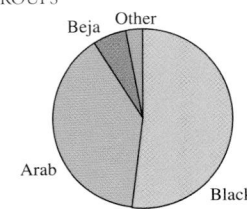

POPULATION COMPARISON
Sudan=10% of U.S.

United States

GDP COMPARISON
Sudan=0.3% of U.S.

United States

ETHNIC GROUPS

Beja Other

Arab

Black

POPULATION DISTRIBUTION
Urban   Rural

Africa's largest country, Sudan straddles the border between the Arab north and the Black south. These two divergent peoples have clashed frequently during Sudan's history, which dates back to the ancient Egyptian dynasties. In recent years, combatants have used food as a weapon, obstructing United Nations famine relief efforts in areas controlled by their opponents.

Men and camels at watering hole

People
Sudan's population is composed of two distinct cultures—black African and Arab. African blacks of diverse ethnicity are a majority and are concentrated in the south, where they practice traditional lifestyles and beliefs and speak indigenous languages. Arabic-speaking Muslims, belonging to several ethnic groups, live mainly in northern and central regions.

Economy and the Land
The economy is based on agriculture; and irrigation has made arid Sudan a leading producer of cotton, although the land is vulnerable to drought. Forests provide for production of gum Arabic, used in making candy and perfumes, while other crops include peanuts and sesame seeds. Economic activity is concentrated near the Nile River and its branches, as well as near water holes and wells. The mostly flat terrain is marked by eastern and western mountains; southern forests and savanna give way to swampland, scrubland, and northern desert. The climate varies from desert in the north to tropical in the south.

History and Politics
Egypt mounted repeated invasions of what is now northern Sudan beginning about 300 B.C. Sudan remained a collection of small independent states until 1821, when Egypt conquered and unified the northern portion. Egypt was unable to establish control over the south, which was often raided by slavers. In 1881 a Muslim leader began uniting various groups in a revolt against Egyptian rule, and success came four years later. His successor ruled until 1898, when British and Egyptian forces reconquered the land. Renamed the Anglo-Egyptian Sudan, the region was ruled jointly by Egypt and Britain, with British administration dominating. Since gaining independence in 1956, a series of military coups, a continuing civil war, and severe famine have burdened Sudan with political and economic instability.

Sudan at a glance

Official name	Republic of the Sudan

People

Population	25,840,000
Density	27/mi² (10/km²)
Urban	23%
Capital	Khartoum, 473,597
Ethnic groups	Black 52%, Arab 39%, Beja 6%
Languages	Arabic, Nubian and other indigenous, English
Religions	Sunni Muslim 70%, indigenous 25%, Christian 5%
Life expectancy	53 female, 51 male
Literacy	27%

Politics

Government	Provisional military government
Parties	None
Suffrage	None
Memberships	AL, OAU, UN
Subdivisions	9 states

Economy

GDP	$21,500,000,000
Per capita	$748
Monetary unit	Dinar
Trade partners	Exports: Saudi Arabia, Thailand, Egypt Imports: Saudi Arabia, U.K., Germany
Exports	Cotton, sesame, gum arabic, peanuts
Imports	Food, petroleum, manufactures, machinery, medicine and chemicals, textiles

Land

Description	Eastern Africa
Area	967,500 mi² (2,505,813 km²)
Highest point	Kinyeti, 10,456 ft (3,187 m)
Lowest point	Sea level

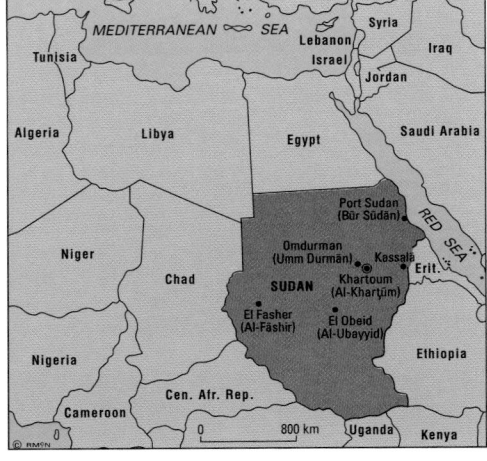

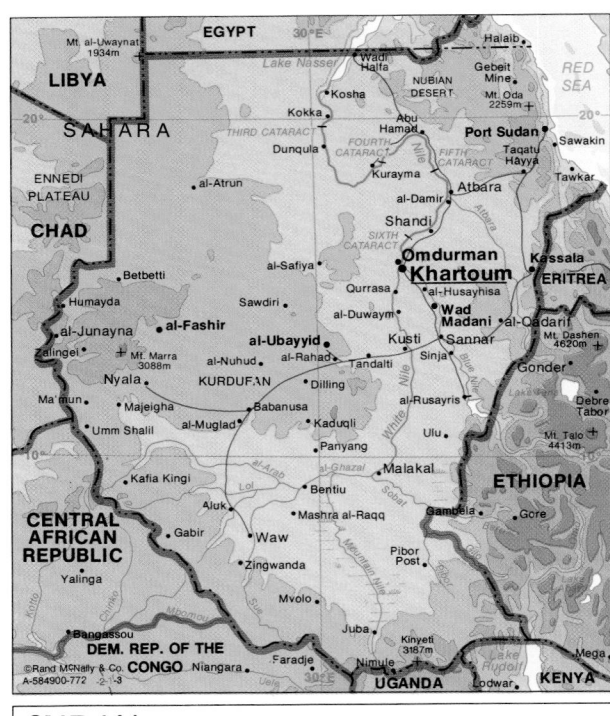

Although Sudan is traversed by the Nile and a number of its tributaries, most of the country is an infertile desert. Where crops are grown—in areas south of Khartoum—droughts occur frequently.

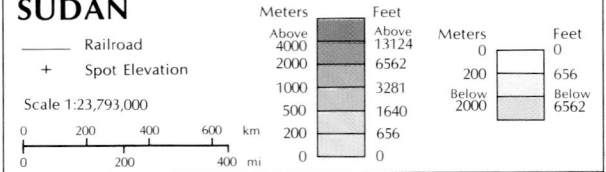

Most Sudanese, such as this woman in front of her thatched hut, are dependent upon the land. Much of the country is prone to drought which disrupts farming and can quickly plunge the nation into famine.

Possessing a myriad of flora and fauna, Suriname is a land of tropical rain forests. A small population and minimal development ensure that it will stay this way for years to come.

People
Descendants of East Indians and Creoles—of mixed European-black African heritage—compose Suriname's two major groups. Black African slaves and contract laborers, imported from the east, resulted in various ethnic populations. Minority groups include the Javanese; Bush Negroes, a black group; Amerindians, descendants of Arawak and Caribs; Chinese; and Europeans. Dutch is the official language, but most groups have preserved their distinct language, culture, and religion.

Economy and the Land
The economy is based on mining and metal processing, and bauxite and alumina are the major exports. Agriculture plays an economic role as well and, together with fishing and forestry, offers potential for expansion. A narrow coastal swamp, central forests and savanna, and southern jungle-covered hills mark the country's terrain. The climate is tropical.

Suriname at a glance

Official name	Republic of Suriname
People	
Population	426,000
Density	6.7/mi² (2.6/km²)
Urban	48%
Capital	Paramaribo, 241,000
Ethnic groups	East Indian 37%, Creole 31%, Javanese 15%, black 10%, Amerindian 3%, Chinese 2%.
Languages	Dutch, Sranan Tongo, English, Hindustani, Javanese
Religions	Hindu 27%, Protestant 25%, Roman Catholic 23%, Muslim 20%
Life expectancy	73 female, 68 male
Literacy	95%
Politics	
Government	Republic
Parties	Democratic Alternative '91, New Democratic, New Front
Suffrage	Universal, over 18
Memberships	OAS, UN
Subdivisions	10 districts
Economy	
GDP	$1,170,000,000
Per capita	$2,833
Monetary unit	Guilder
Trade partners	Exports: Norway, Netherlands, U.S. Imports: U.S., Netherlands Antilles, Trinidad and Tobago
Exports	Alumina, bauxite, aluminum, rice, wood
Imports	Machinery, petroleum, food, cotton, manufactures
Land	
Description	Northeastern South America
Area	63,251 mi² (163,820 km²)
Highest point	Juliana Mtn., 4,035 ft (1,230 m)
Lowest point	Sea level

A Surinamese boy climbs a bamboo pole to cut down nuts from the crests of palm trees.

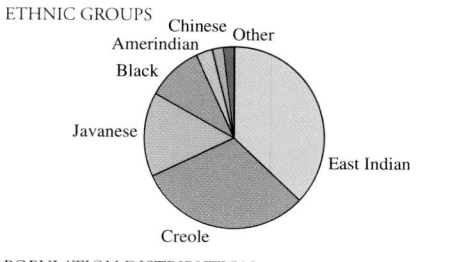

Girls fishing

History and Politics
Prior to the arrival of Europeans, present-day Suriname was inhabited by indigenous Indians. Christopher Columbus sighted the coast in 1498, but the area's lack of gold slowed Spanish and Portuguese exploration. The British established the first settlement in 1651, and in 1665 Jews from Brazil erected the first synagogue in the Western Hemisphere. In 1667 the British traded the area to the Netherlands for the Dutch colony of New Amsterdam—present-day Manhattan, New York. Subsequent wars and treaties shifted ownership of Suriname among the British, French, and Dutch until 1815, when the Netherlands regained control. In 1954 Suriname became an autonomous part of the Netherlands, with status equal to that of the Netherlands Antilles. Suriname gained independence in 1975. In 1980 the military seized power and established a military-civilian government soon after. However, the military has retained considerable control. A general election in May 1991 resulted in a degree of democratic representation.

POPULATION COMPARISON
Suriname=0.2% of U.S.

United States

GDP COMPARISON
Suriname=0.02% of U.S.

United States

ETHNIC GROUPS

Chinese Other
Amerindian
Black
Javanese
East Indian
Creole

POPULATION DISTRIBUTION
Urban   Rural

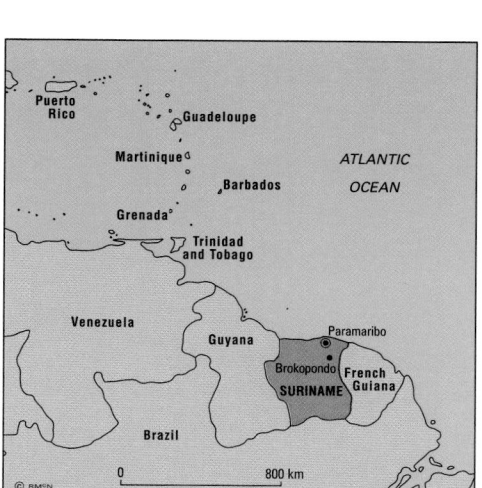

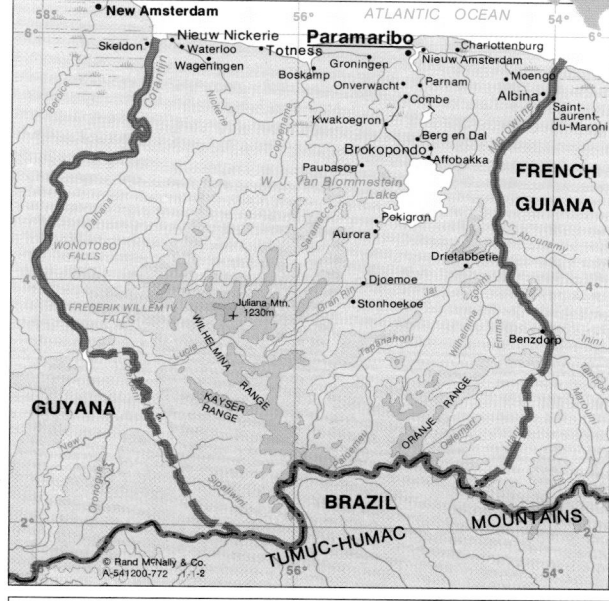

SURINAME

		Meters	Feet
Railroad	National capitals are underlined	2000	6562
+ Spot Elevation	City type size indicates relative importance	1000	3281
		500	1640
0 25 50 75 100 125 km	Scale 1:6,360,000	200	656
0 25 50 75 mi		0	0
		200	656

Most of Suriname's people live along the coast. The remote and unpopulated borders with Guyana and French Guiana are in dispute.

Suriname is a land of water. Numerous rivers drain the rain forest's precipitation into the Atlantic Ocean. The climate is humid and tropical, with an average rainfall of about 86 inches and an average annual temperature of 81 degrees Fahrenheit.

173

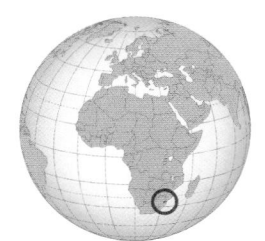

Swaziland

The royal house of Swaziland dates back 400 years; it is one of Africa's last ruling dynasties. Arguments for democracy are countered by royalists who note the country's long and stable history. Swaziland has a close and dependent economic relationship with South Africa.

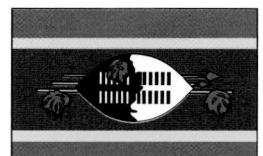

Large areas of the Highveld in the west of Swaziland have been planted with pine and eucalyptus trees; these are the largest planted forests in Africa.

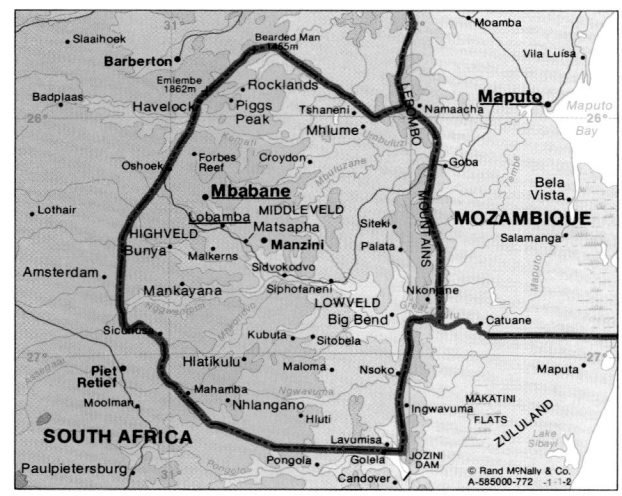

SWAZILAND
— Railroad
+ Spot Elevation
National capitals are underlined
City type size indicates relative importance
Scale 1:3,214,000
0 25 50 75 km
0 25 50 mi

Meters	Feet
4000	13124
2000	6562
1000	3281
500	1640
200	656
0	0
200	656

© Rand McNally & Co.
A-585000-772 -1-1-2'

People
About 95 percent of the people of Swaziland are black Africans called Swazi, though small minorities of white Europeans and Zulus also live in the country. The two official languages are English and siSwati. Government and official business is conducted primarily in English. More than half the Swazi belong to Christian churches, while others practice traditional African religions.

Economy and the Land
Most Swazi are subsistence farmers. Cattle are highly prized for their own sake but are being used increasingly for milk, meat, and profit. Europeans own nearly half the land in Swaziland and raise most of the cash crops, including fruits, sugar, tobacco, cotton, and wood. Although mining has declined in recent years, Swaziland has deposits of coal, pottery clay, gold, and tin. The country's mountains and forests have brought a growing tourist industry. The climate is temperate.

History and Politics
According to legend, the Swazi originally came from the area near Maputo. British traders and Dutch farmers from South Africa first reached Swaziland in the 1830s; more whites arrived in the 1880s when gold was discovered. Swazi leaders unknowingly granted many concessions to the whites at this time. After the Boer War, Britain assumed administration of Swaziland and ruled until 1967. Swaziland became independent in 1968. The British designed a constitution, but many Swazi thought it disregarded their traditions and interests. In 1973 King Sobhuza abolished this constitution, suspended the legislature, and appointed a commission to produce a new constitution. Sobhuza ruled until his death in 1982, and King Mswati III was installed in

1986. The king has committed to a greater degree of democracy, but no political parties are allowed and 1993 elections were not considered open.

Swaziland at a glance
Official name	Kingdom of Swaziland

People
Population	889,000
Density	133/mi² (51/km²)
Urban	26%
Capital	Mbabane (administrative), 38,290; Lobamba (legislative)
Ethnic groups	Swazi 97%, European 3%
Languages	English, siSwati
Religions	African Protestant and other Christian 60%, tribal religionist 40%
Life expectancy	60 female, 56 male
Literacy	64%

Politics
Government	Monarchy
Parties	None
Suffrage	None
Memberships	CW, OAU, UN
Subdivisions	4 districts

Economy
GDP	$2,300,000,000
Per capita	$2,486
Monetary unit	Lilangeni
Trade partners	Exports: South Africa, Western European countries, Canada Imports: South Africa, Japan, Belgium
Exports	Soft drink concentrates, sugar, wood, fruit
Imports	Transportation equipment, machinery, petroleum, food, chemicals

Land
Description	Southern Africa, landlocked
Area	6,704 mi² (17,364 km²)
Highest point	Emlembe, 6,109 ft (1,862 m)
Lowest point	Along Usutu River, 70 ft (21 m)

SWEDEN

Sweden avoided the destruction of World War II by observing a strict neutrality: it sold goods to both the Nazis and the Allies. The Swedish government guarantees the welfare of the people to a degree unmatched elsewhere in the world. Health care, education, and many other services are free. In recent years, competition from less-heavily-taxed countries has hurt Swedish firms in world markets.

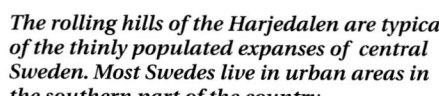

The rolling hills of the Harjedalen are typical of the thinly populated expanses of central Sweden. Most Swedes live in urban areas in the southern part of the country.

Sweden at a glance

Official name	Kingdom of Sweden

People

Population	8,981,000
Density	52/mi² (20/km²)
Urban	84%
Capital	Stockholm, 674,452
Ethnic groups	Swedish (Scandinavian) 92%, Finnish, Lapp
Languages	Swedish, Lapp, Finnish
Religions	Lutheran (Church of Sweden) 94%, Roman Catholic 2%
Life expectancy	81 female, 75 male
Literacy	99%

Politics

Government	Constitutional monarchy
Parties	Center, Moderate, Liberal, Social Democratic, others
Suffrage	Universal, over 18
Memberships	EU, NATO, OECD, UN
Subdivisions	24 counties

Economy

GDP	$153,700,000,000
Per capita	$17,833
Monetary unit	Krona
Trade partners	Exports: Germany, U.K., U.S. Imports: Germany, U.S., U.K.
Exports	Machinery, transportation equipment, paper, pulp and wood, iron and steel
Imports	Manufactures, petroleum, chemicals, transportation equipment, food

Land

Description	Northern Europe
Area	173,732 mi² (449,964 km²)
Highest point	Mt. Kebne, 6,926 ft (2,111 m)
Lowest point	Sea level

POPULATION COMPARISON
Sweden=3% of U.S.

United States

GDP COMPARISON
Sweden=2% of U.S.

United States

ETHNIC GROUPS

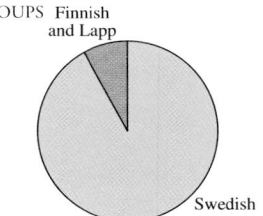

Finnish and Lapp

Swedish

POPULATION DISTRIBUTION

Urban   Rural

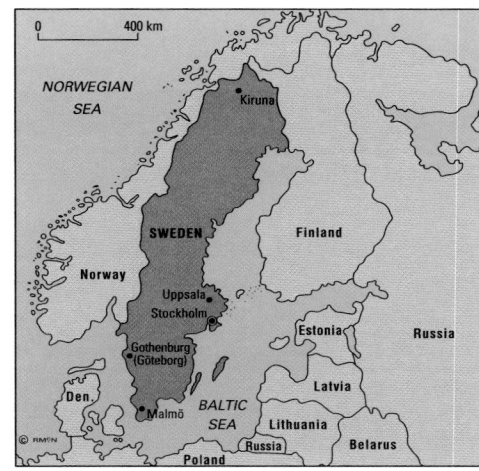

Built on 13 islands at the confluence of Lake Mälaren and the Baltic Sea, Stockholm has close links to water, and it is sometimes referred to as "the Venice of the North." Canals and channels wending through the landscape are used by boats transporting people, goods and mail.

While native Lapps living north of the Arctic Circle have suffered discrimination at the hands of the majority, Sweden is known for its tolerance and is often first to offer asylum to refugees fleeing totalitarianism.

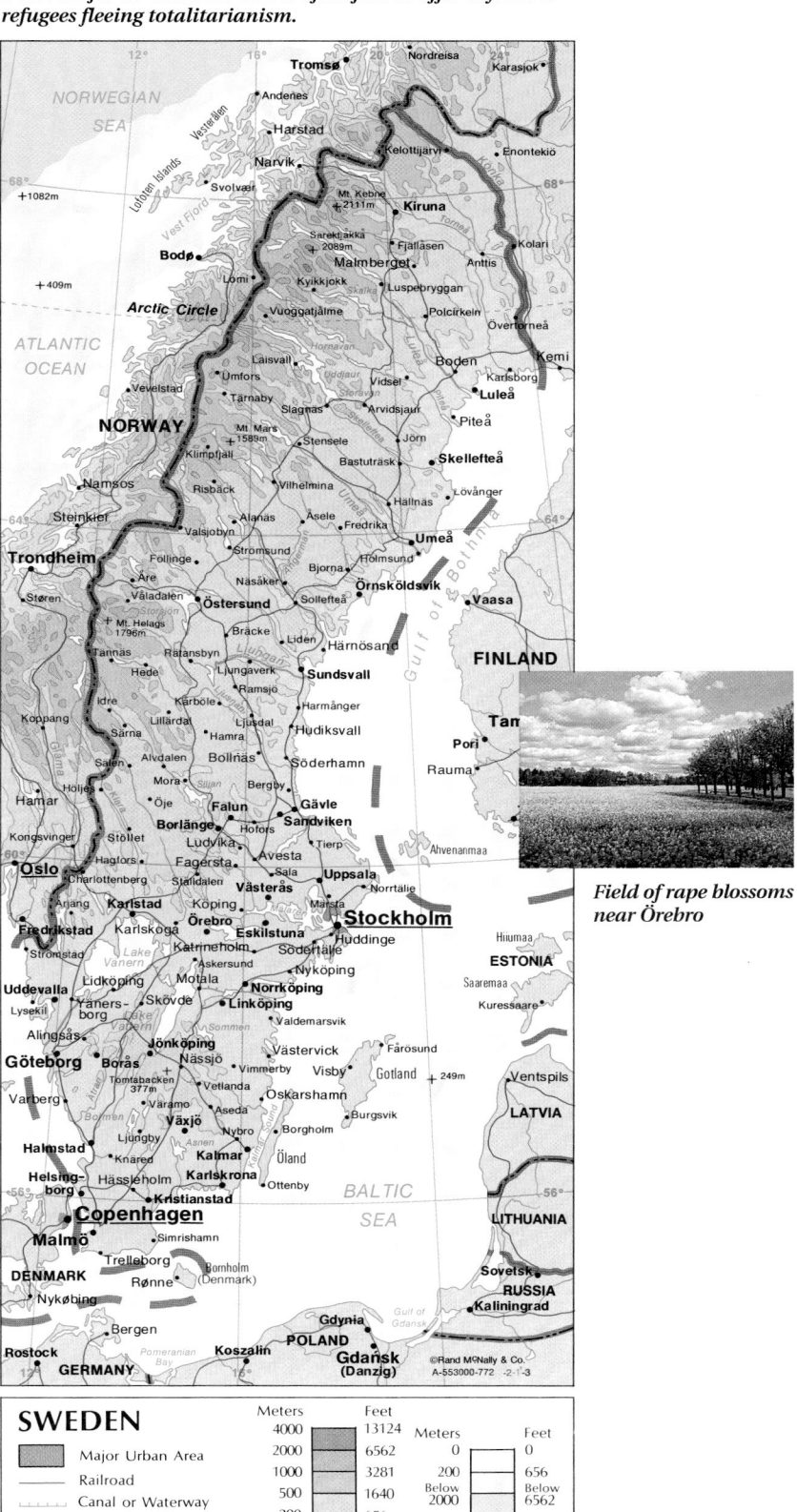

Field of rape blossoms near Örebro

People

The most significant minorities in the largely urban Swedish population are Swedes of Finnish origin and a small number of Lapps. Sweden is also the home of immigrants from other Nordic countries, Yugoslavia, Greece, and Turkey. Swedish is the main language, although Finns and Lapps often speak their own tongues. English is the leading foreign language, especially among students and younger people.

Economy and the Land

Sweden has one of the highest standards of living in the world. Taxes are also high, but the government provides exceptional benefits for most citizens, including free education and medical care, pension payments, four-week vacations, and payments for child care. The nation is industrial and bases its economy on its three most important natural resources—timber, iron ore, and water power. The iron and steel industry produces high-quality steel used in ball bearings, precision tools, agricultural machinery, aircraft, automobiles, and ships. Swedish farmers rely heavily on dairy products and livestock, and most farms are part of Sweden's agricultural-cooperative movement. Sweden's varied terrain includes mountains, forests, plains, and sandy beaches. The climate is temperate, with cold winters in the north. Northern Sweden lies in the "Land of the Midnight Sun" and experiences periods of twenty-four hours of daylight in summer and darkness in winter.

History and Politics

Inhabitants of what is now Sweden began to trade with the Roman Empire about 50 B.C. Sailing expeditions by Swedish Vikings began about A.D. 800. In the fourteenth century the kingdom came under Danish rule, but declared its independence in 1523. The Swedish king offered protection to the followers of Martin Luther, and Lutheranism was soon declared the state religion. By the late 1660s, Sweden had become one of the great powers of Europe; it suffered a military defeat by Russia in 1709, however, and gradually lost most of its European possessions. An 1809 constitution gave most of the executive power of the government to the king. Despite this, the power of the Parliament gradually increased, and parliamentary rule was adopted in 1917. A 1975 constitution reduced the king's role to a ceremonial one. Sweden remained neutral during both world wars. Except for 1976-82, when Sweden was run by a conservative coalition, the country had a Socialist government until February 1990, when it failed to carry Parliament in an economic reform bill. By 1994 the Socialist party was back in power.

SWEDEN

▨	Major Urban Area
—	Railroad
—	Canal or Waterway
+	Spot Elevation or Depth

Meters	Feet
4000	13124
2000	6562
1000	3281
500	1640
200	656
0	0

Meters	Feet
0	0
200	656
Below 2000	Below 6562

Scale 1:9,257,000

Skarhamn is a seaside town near the industrial city of Göteborg.

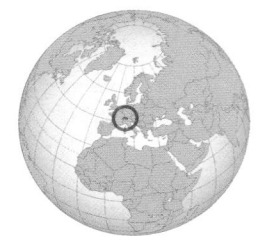

In Graubünden, Switzerland's biggest and least populated canton, small villages nestle in the shadows of the Alps. The spoken language changes from one valley to the next: German to Italian to Romansch, each in a variety of dialects.

SWITZERLAND

Bern, the capital of Switzerland, has a series of high promenades overlooking the Aare River which cleaves the city.

Conservative and reticent, Switzerland is the world's oldest stable democracy. Living in villages nestled in rugged terrain, the Swiss enjoy an affluence matched by few countries. Neutrality is so ingrained in the Swiss soul that the nation has refused to join the United Nations or any other international political group.

People

About seven hundred years ago, the Swiss began joining together for mutual defense, but preserved their regional differences in language and customs. The country has four official languages: German, French, Italian, and Romansch, which is spoken by a minority. Dialects often differ from community to community. The population is concentrated on a central plain located between mountain ranges.

Economy and the Land

The Alps and Jura Mountains cover nearly 70 percent of Switzerland, making much of the land unsuited for agriculture but a good basis for a thriving tourist industry. The central plain contains rich cropland and holds Switzerland's major cities and manufacturing facilities, many specializing in high-quality, precision products. Switzerland is also an international banking and finance center. Straddling the ranges of the central Alps, Switzerland features

mountains, hills, and plateaus. The temperate climate varies with altitude.

History and Politics

Helvetic Celts inhabited the area of present-day Switzerland when Julius Caesar conquered the region, annexing it to the Roman Empire. As the Roman Empire declined, northern and western Germanic tribes began a series of invasions, and in the 800s the region became part of the empire of the Frankish king Charlemagne. In 1291 leaders of the three Swiss cantons, or regions, signed an agreement declaring their freedom and promising mutual aid against any foreign ruler. The confederation was the beginning of modern Switzerland. Over the next few centuries Switzerland became a military power, expanding its territories until 1515, when it was defeated by France. Soon after, Switzerland adopted a policy of permanent neutrality. The country was again conquered by France during the French Revolution; however, after Napoleon's final defeat in 1815, the Congress of Vienna guaranteed Switzerland's neutrality, a guarantee that has never been broken.

Switzerland at a glance

Official name Swiss Confederation

People

Population	7,244,000
Density	454/mi² (170/km²)
Urban	62%
Capital	Bern, 136,338
Ethnic groups	German 65%, French 18%, Italian 10%, Romansch 1%
Languages	German, French, Italian, Romansch
Religions	Roman Catholic 48%, Protestant 44%
Life expectancy	81 female, 75 male
Literacy	99%

Politics

Government	Republic
Parties	Christian Democratic People's, People's, Radical Democratic, Social Democratic, others
Suffrage	Universal, over 18
Memberships	OECD
Subdivisions	26 cantons

Economy

GDP	$149,100,000,000
Per capita	$21,773
Monetary unit	Franc
Trade partners	Exports: Germany, France, Italy Imports: Germany, France, Italy
Exports	Machinery, precision instruments, metals, food, clothing and textiles
Imports	Agricultural products, machinery and transportation equipment, chemicals

Land

Description	Central Europe, landlocked
Area	15,943 mi² (41,293 km²)
Highest point	Dufourspitze, 15,203 ft (4,634 m)
Lowest point	Lago Maggiore, 633 ft (193 m)

POPULATION COMPARISON
Switzerland=3% of U.S.

United States

GDP COMPARISON
Switzerland=2% of U.S.

United States

ETHNIC GROUPS

Romansch
Other
Italian
French
German

POPULATION DISTRIBUTION
Urban   Rural

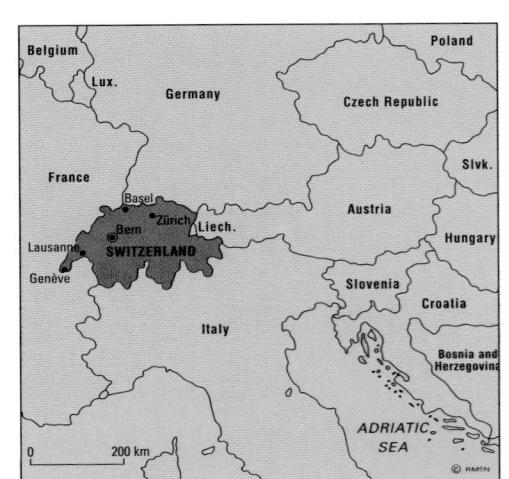

SWITZERLAND

Major Urban Area
National capitals are underlined
Railroad
Canal
Glacier
Spot Elevation

Scale 1:2,174,000

Meters	Feet
Above 4000	Above 13124
2000	6562
1000	3281
500	1640
200	656
0	0

The monumental Swiss Alps, with peaks like Matterhorn and Jungfrau, are Switzerland's great natural resource, drawing hundreds of thousands of free-spending tourists to their spectacular vistas each year.

The hill town of Al Housn overlooks farmland below. Because so much of the country is desert, less than one-third of Syria's land can be cultivated. The most common crops are wheat, barley, and cotton.

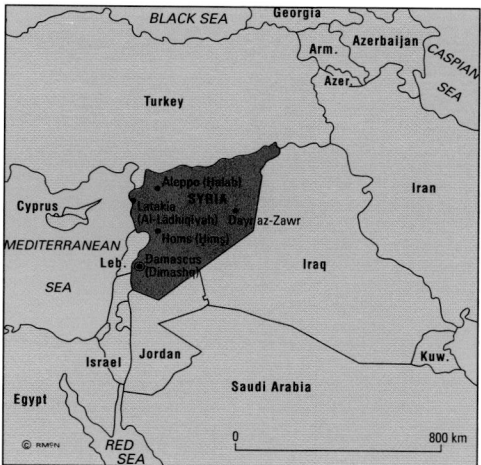

SYRIA

Syria at a glance

Official name	Syrian Arab Republic

People

Population	14,100,000
Density	197/mi² (76/km²)
Urban	50%
Capital	Damascus, 1,549,932
Ethnic groups	Arab 90%, Kurdish, Armenian, and other 10%
Languages	Arabic, Kurdish, Armenian, Aramaic, Circassian
Religions	Sunni Muslim 74%, other Muslim 16%, Christian 10%
Life expectancy	69 female, 65 male
Literacy	64%

Politics

Government	Socialist republic
Parties	Arab Socialist, Arab Socialist Resurrectionist (Baath), Communist
Suffrage	Universal, over 18
Memberships	AL, UN
Subdivisions	14 districts

Economy

GDP	$81,700,000,000
Per capita	$5,807
Monetary unit	Pound
Trade partners	Exports: Former Soviet republics, Italy, France
	Imports: France, Germany, U.S.
Exports	Petroleum, agricultural products, textiles, phosphates
Imports	Food, metals, machinery, textiles, petroleum

Land

Description	Southwestern Asia
Area	71,498 mi² (185,180 km²)
Highest point	Mt. Hermon, 9,232 ft (2,814 m)
Lowest point	Near Sea of Galilee, -656 ft (-200 m)

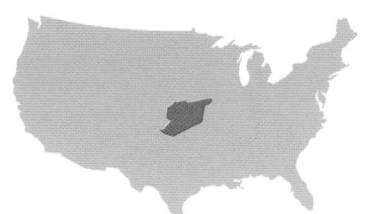

POPULATION COMPARISON
Syria=5% of U.S.

United States

GDP COMPARISON
Syria=0.5% of U.S.

United States

ETHNIC GROUPS
Kurdish, Armenian and other

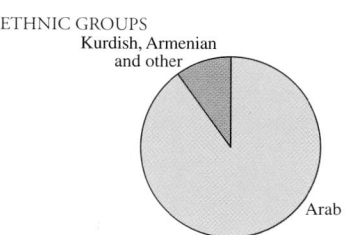

Arab

POPULATION DISTRIBUTION
Urban ——— Rural

The end of World War II meant peace for much of the world. For the Middle East it marked the beginning of five violent decades that have seen Arabs fighting both Israel and other Arabs. Syria has been at the center of much of this conflict. Its troops remain in Lebanon and it continues to press Israel for a return of the Golan Heights.

People

Most Syrians are Arabic-speaking descendants of Semites, a people who settled the region in ancient times. The majority are Sunni Muslim, and Islam is a powerful cultural force. Only a small percentage are Christian. Non-Arab Syrians include Kurds and Armenians, who speak their own languages and maintain their own customs. French is widely understood, and English is spoken in larger cities. The population is evenly divided between urban and rural settlements.

Economy and the Land

Syria is a developing country with great potential for economic growth. Textile manufacturing is a major industry, and oil, the main natural resource, provides for expanding activity in oil refining. The plains and river valleys are fertile, but rainfall is irregular and irrigation is necessary to sustain agriculture. Most farms are small; cotton and wheat are their major products. The terrain is marked by mountains, the Euphrates River valley, and a semiarid plateau. The climate is hot and dry, with relatively cold winters.

History and Politics

Syria was the site of one of the world's most ancient civilizations, and Damascus and other Syrian cities were centers of world trade as early as 2500 B.C. Greater Syria, as the area was called until the end of World War I, originally included much of modern Israel, Jordan, Lebanon, and parts of Turkey. The region was occupied and ruled by several empires, including the Phoenician, Assyrian, Babylonian, Persian, and Greek, before coming under Roman rule in 64 B.C. During subsequent years, Christianity arose in the part of Greater Syria called Palestine. In 636 the region fell to Arab Muslims, who governed until 1260, when Egypt gained control. Syria became part of the Turkish Ottoman Empire in 1516. During World War I, Syria aided Britain in defeating the Turks and Germans in return for independence. After the war, however, the League of Nations divided Greater Syria into four mandates—Syria, Lebanon, Palestine, and Transjordan—and placed Syria under French control. When Syria gained independence in 1946, many nationals wanted to reunite Greater Syria, but the United Nations made part of Palestine into the Jewish state of Israel. Tensions between Israel and Syria erupted in war in 1967 and 1973 and remain unresolved. In the 1980s Syria assumed a role in Lebanon's affairs and maintains a military presence there.

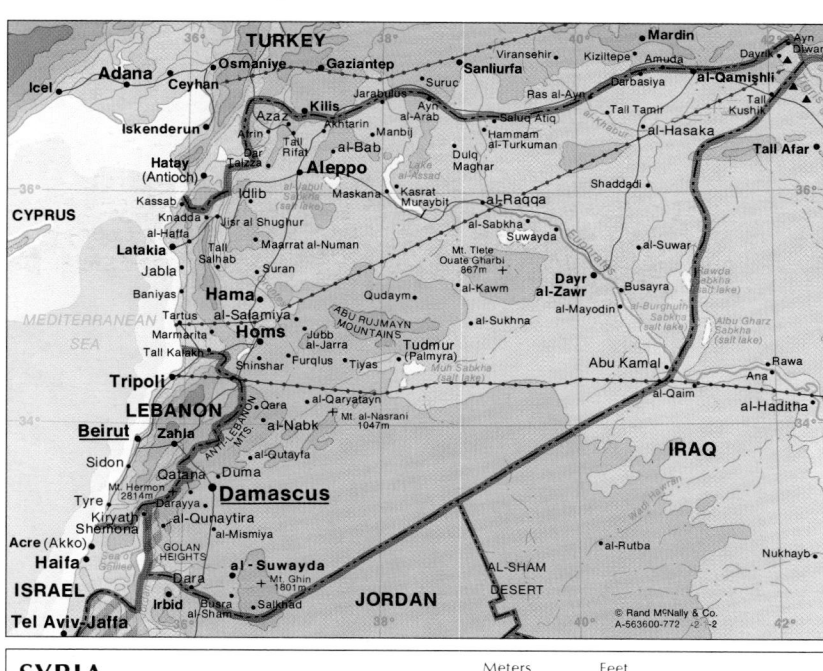

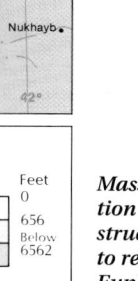

Third-century ruins, Palmyra

SYRIA

		Meters	Feet		
▨ Israeli Occupied Territory	+ Spot Elevation or Depth	4000	13124		
—— Railroad	National capitals are underlined	2000	6562	Meters	Feet
⊶⊶ Oil Pipeline	Scale 1:6,971,000	1000	3281	0	0
▲ Major Oil Field		500	1640	200	656
	0 50 100 150 km	200	656	Below 2000	Below 6562
	0 50 100 mi	0	Sea Level		

© Rand McNally & Co.
A-563600-772 -1 -2

Massive dams and irrigation projects under construction in Turkey threaten to reduce the flow of the Euphrates River, one of Syria's few sources of water.

177

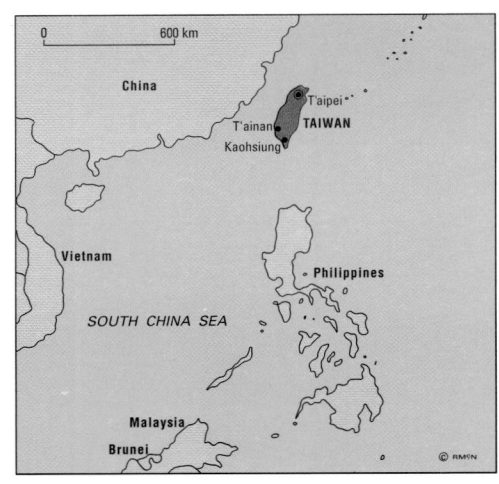

A lone boat crosses Sun Moon Lake at dawn. The lake provides a rare refuge for Taiwanese seeking to escape the bustle and chaos of their overcrowded island.

TAIWAN

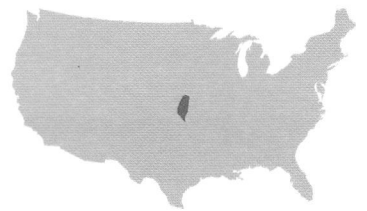

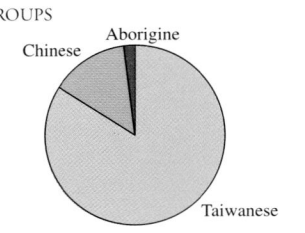

Once merely a refuge for the exiled Nationalist government of China, Taiwan's swift economic growth has allowed it to emerge from the shadow of the mainland as it concentrates on its new role of importance in Asia. Although each government is officially hostile to the other, the Chinese talent for commerce has resulted in many unofficial economic ties between Taiwan and the mainland.

Street in T'aipei

People

The majority of Taiwan's inhabitants are descendants of Chinese who migrated from the coast of China in the eighteenth and nineteenth centuries. In 1949, when the Communists came to power in mainland China, many educated Chinese fled to Taiwan. A small group of aborigines, which lives in the mountains in central Taiwan, is most likely of Malay-Polynesian origin. Taiwan's languages are mainly various dialects of Chinese, a Fujian dialect, and a dialect known as "Hakka." Most religious practices combine Buddhist and Taoist beliefs with the Confucian ethical code.

Economy and the Land

Since World War II, Taiwan's economy has changed from agriculture to industry. A past emphasis on light industry, producing mainly consumer goods, has shifted to technology and heavy industry. Although only one-quarter of the island is arable, farmland is intensely cultivated, with some areas producing two and three crops a year. Though rice, sugarcane, fruits, tea, and fishing are important, much food must be imported. The island's terrain is marked by steep eastern mountains sloping to a fertile western region. The capital of T'aipei administers the Penghu Islands and about twenty off-shore islands as well as the island of Taiwan. The climate is maritime subtropical.

History and Politics

Chinese migration to Taiwan began as early as A.D. 500. Dutch traders claimed the island in 1624 as a base for trade with China and Japan. It was ruled by China's Manchu dynasty from 1683 until 1895, when China ceded Taiwan to Japan after the first Sino-Japanese war. Following World War II, China regained possession of Taiwan. A civil war in mainland China between Nationalist and Communist forces ended with the victory of the Communists in 1949. Nationalist leader Chiang Kai-shek fled to Taiwan, proclaiming T'aipei the provisional capital of Nationalist China. In 1971 the People's Republic of China replaced Taiwan in the United Nations. While the Republic of China still maintains it is the legitimate ruler of all China, nearly all nations now recognize the mainland's People's Republic of China. While reunification talks between the two governments have taken place since 1993, there is also a significant movement supporting independence from mainland China.

Taiwan at a glance

Official name	Republic of China

People

Population	21,150,000
Density	1,522/mi² (587/km²)
Urban	71%
Capital	T'aipei, 2,706,453
Ethnic groups	Taiwanese 84%, Chinese 14%, aborigine 2%
Languages	Chinese (Mandarin), Taiwanese (Min), Hakka
Religions	Buddhist, Confucian, and Taoist 93%, Christian 5%
Life expectancy	78 female, 72 male
Literacy	91%

Politics

Government	Republic
Parties	Democratic Progressive, Kuomintang (Nationalist), others
Suffrage	Universal, over 20
Memberships	None
Subdivisions	16 counties, 7 municipalities

Economy

GDP	$224,000,000,000
Per capita	$10,674
Monetary unit	Dollar
Trade partners	Exports: U.S., Japan Imports: Japan, U.S., Germany
Exports	Machinery, textiles, metals, food, wood
Imports	Machinery, metals, chemicals, petroleum, food

Land

Description	Eastern Asian island
Area	13,900 mi² (36,002 km²)
Highest point	Yu Mtn., 13,114 ft (3,997 m)
Lowest point	Sea level

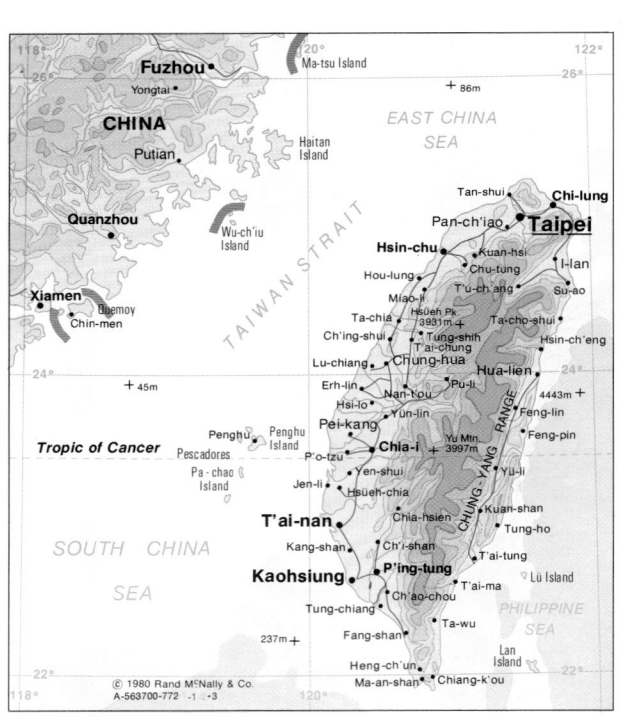

TAIWAN

	Meters	Feet			
— Railroad	4000	13124		Meters	Feet
+ Spot Elevation	2000	6562		0	0
	1000	3281		200	656
Scale 1:5,400,000	500	1640		Below 2000	Below 6562
0 25 50 75 100 125 km	200	656			
0 25 50 75 mi	0	0			

© 1980 Rand McNally & Co.
A-563700-772 -1 -3

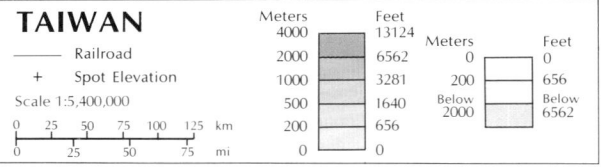

Little of Taiwan is untouched by development. T'aipei's wealth is offset by severe air and water pollution.

With an excellent natural harbor, Kaohsiung is the fastest growing city in Taiwan. Much of the nation's huge volume of exports passes through its ports.

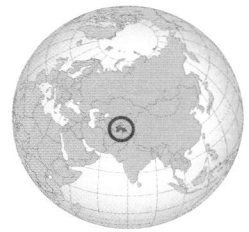

TAJIKISTAN

Tajikistan has the lowest standard of living of any former Soviet republic. A costly civil war in 1992 has been followed by ongoing government turmoil. Hidden from the world amongst its many mountains and glaciers, Tajikistan is almost forgotten.

People

The Tajik people are indistinguishable from the neighboring Uzbeks, although the country also includes many minority groups indigenous to the Pamir Mountains in the west. The Tajik language is closely related to Farsi, the principal language of Iran. The country is home to many people who were born in Uzbekistan, as well as many Russians. Islam has always been widely practiced in Tajikistan, even when the country was under Soviet rule. Most people live in small towns throughout the mountains. Folklore is important to the Tajiks, who are known for their colorful legends and poetry.

Economy and the Land

Cotton is among the country's principal crops, and irrigation allows production of fruits and grains. Cattle breeding is also an important agricultural activity. Tajikistan has many minerals, including coal, petroleum, uranium, lead, zinc, and others. Despite these significant resources, Tajikistan has the lowest standard of living of all of the former Soviet republics. The elevation of more than one-half of the country lies above ten thousand feet. The climate is harsh and precipitation is low. Earthquakes are common.

History and Politics

Iranian people are known to have lived in the region of Tajikistan since the first century B.C. Arabs brought Islam to the region between the seventh and eighth centuries A.D. Tajikistan came under Russian control in 1895 as part of a region known as Turkestan. There was substantial local resistance to the implementation of communism following the Russian Revolution, and several years of armed struggle ensued. The country became an Autonomous Republic within the Soviet Union in 1924 and a Soviet Socialist Republic in 1929. It declared its sovereignty in September 1991 and achieved full independence after the breakup of the Soviet Union the following December. Communists and Islamic fundamentalists have been fighting for control of the country since 1992.

With the support of forces in neighboring Afghanistan, Muslim rebels refuse to agree to peace with the government of Tajikistan.

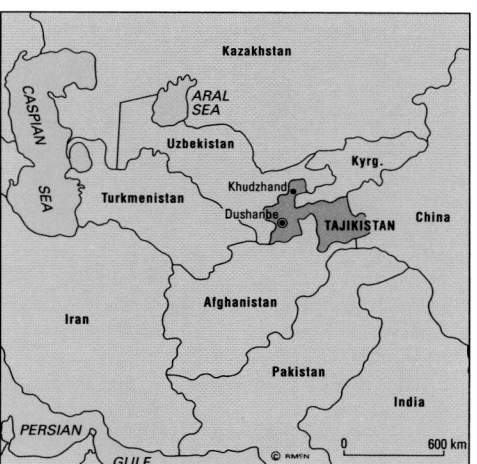

Tajikistan at a glance

Official name	Republic of Tajikistan

People

Population	6,073,000
Density	110/mi^2 (42/km^2)
Urban	33%
Capital	Dushanbe, 582,400
Ethnic groups	Tajik 62%, Uzbek 24%, Russian 8%
Languages	Tajik, Uzbek, Russian
Religions	Sunni Muslim 80%, Shiite Musilm 5%
Life expectancy	71 female, 66 male
Literacy	96%

Politics

Government	Republic
Parties	Democratic, Islamic Renaissance, Rostakhez (Rebirth)
Suffrage	Universal, over 18
Memberships	CIS, UN
Subdivisions	1 autonomous region, 3 regions

Economy

GDP	$23,940,000,000
Per capita	$4,654
Monetary unit	Russian ruble
Trade partners	Russia, Kazakhstan, Ukraine, Uzbekistan
Exports	Aluminum, cotton, fruit, vegetable oil, textiles
Imports	Chemicals, machinery and transportation equipment, textiles, food

Land

Description	Central Asia, landlocked
Area	55,251 mi^2 (143,100 km^2)
Highest point	Communism Peak, 24,590 ft (7,495 m)
Lowest point	Along Syr Darya River, 984 ft (300 m)

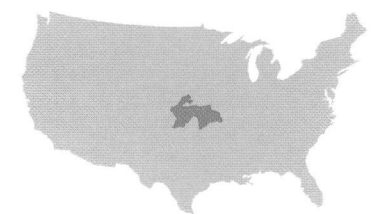

POPULATION COMPARISON
Tajikistan=2% of U.S.

United States

GDP COMPARISON
Tajikistan=0.1% of U.S.

United States

ETHNIC GROUPS

Other
Russian
Uzbek
Tajik

POPULATION DISTRIBUTION
Urban   Rural

Most of Tajikistan is rugged mountains. The Pamir range, shown here, has several peaks over 20,000 feet. Many valleys contain massive glaciers; one glacier is 44 miles long.

TANZANIA

Tanzania at a glance

Official name	United Republic of Tanzania

People

Population	28,350,000
Density	83/mi² (32/km²)
Urban	21%
Capital	Dar es Salaam (de facto), 1,096,000; Dodoma (legislative), 85,000
Ethnic groups	African 99%
Languages	English, Swahili, indigenous
Religions	Animist 33%, Muslim 33%, Christian 33%
Life expectancy	52 female, 49 male
Literacy	46%

Politics

Government	Republic
Parties	Revolutionary
Suffrage	Universal, over 18
Memberships	CW, OAU, UN
Subdivisions	25 regions

Economy

GDP	$16,700,000,000
Per capita	$591
Monetary unit	Shilling
Trade partners	Exports: Germany, U.K Imports: U.K., Japan, Germany
Exports	Coffee, cotton, sisal, tea, cashews, meat, tobacco, diamonds, gold
Imports	Manufactures, machinery and transportation equipment, cotton, petroleum, food

Land

Description	Eastern Africa
Area	341,217 mi² (883,749 km²)
Highest point	Kilimanjaro, 19,340 ft (5,895 m)
Lowest point	Sea level

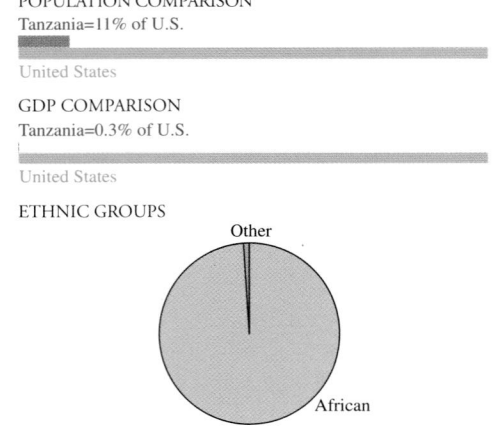

Mt. Kilimanjaro at dusk

Tanzania features some of Africa's most stunning scenery, including Mount Kilimanjaro, the highest peak on the continent. The nearby Serengeti Plain is home to a vast amount of wildlife. As the country has developed its tourism facilities, it has also turned to western nations for development aid.

People
The largely rural African population of Tanzania consists of more than 130 ethnic groups; most speak a distinct language. Religious beliefs are nearly evenly divided among Christian, Muslim, and traditional religions.

Economy and the Land
Agriculture accounts for the most export earnings and employs 80 percent of the workforce. Yet two-thirds of the land cannot be cultivated because of lack of water and tsetse-fly infestation. Mainland farmers grow cassava, corn, and beans, while other cash crops include coffee and cashews. Zanzibar and Pemba islands are famous sources of cloves. Diamonds, salt, and iron are important mineral resources. Hot, humid coastal plains; an arid central plateau; and temperate lake and highland areas characterize mainland Tanzania. The climate is equatorial and includes monsoons.

History and Politics
The northern mainland has fossil remains of some of humanity's earliest ancestors. Subsequent early inhabitants were gradually displaced by Bantu farmers and Nilotes. Arabs were trading with coastal groups as early as the eighth century, and by the early 1500s the Portuguese had claimed the coastal region. They were displaced in the 1700s by Arabs, who subsequently established a lucrative slave trade.

Germans began colonizing the coast in 1884 and six years later signed an agreement with Great Britain, which secured German dominance along the coast and made Zanzibar a British protectorate. After World War I, Britain received part of German East Africa from the League of Nations as a mandate and renamed it Tanganyika. The area became a trust territory under the United Nations following World War II. The country achieved independence in 1961, and two years later Zanzibar received its independence as a constitutional monarchy under the sultan. A 1964 revolt by the African majority overthrew the sultan, and Zanzibar and Tanganyika subsequently united and became known as Tanzania. Tanzania developed a special African brand of Socialism in the 1960s, which served as a model throughout the continent. In 1992 it moved from single to multiparty politics.

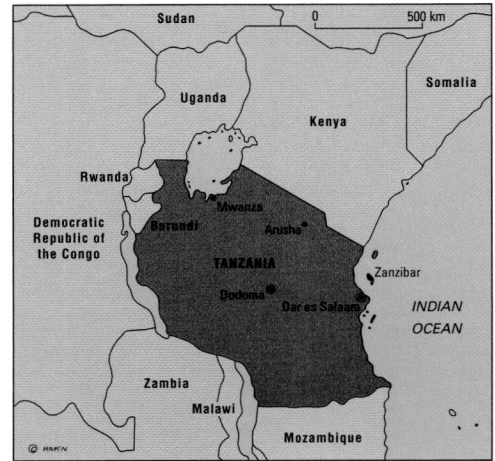

POPULATION COMPARISON
Tanzania=11% of U.S.

United States

GDP COMPARISON
Tanzania=0.3% of U.S.

United States

ETHNIC GROUPS

Other

African

POPULATION DISTRIBUTION

Urban   Rural

Zanzibar and Pemba are ancient Arab trading centers. Mainland Tanzania combines the cultures of more than 100 tribal groups.

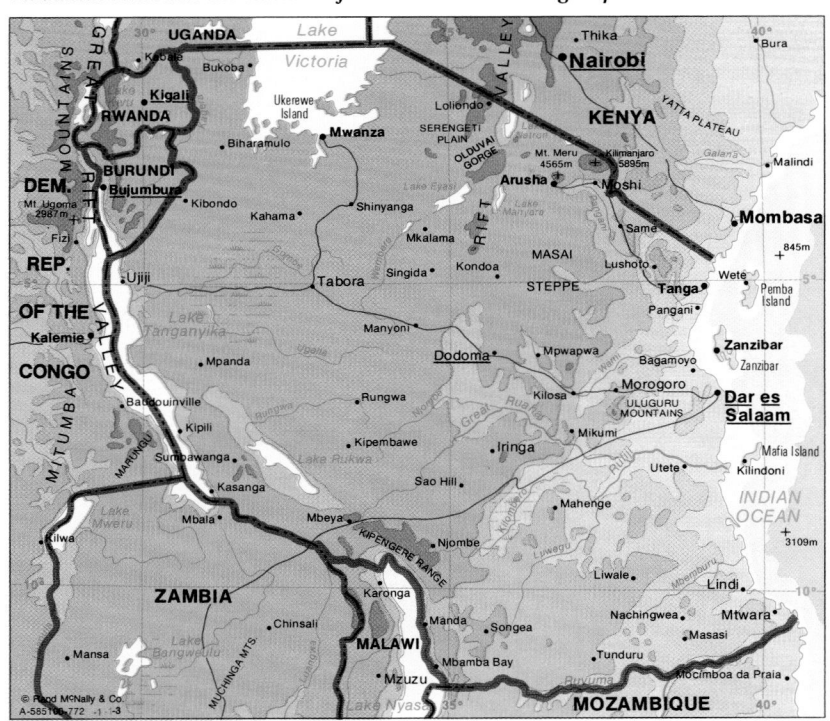

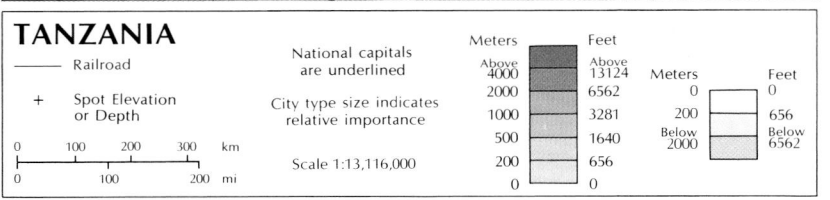

TANZANIA

— Railroad

National capitals are underlined

+ Spot Elevation or Depth

City type size indicates relative importance

Scale 1:13,116,000

Meters	Feet
Above 4000	Above 13124
2000	6562
1000	3281
500	1640
200	656
0	0

Meters	Feet
0	0
200	656
Below 2000	Below 6562

A woman walks amidst rice paddies at sunset at Kalasin in eastern Thailand. Although rice has historically been Thailand's leading export, it is rapidly being overtaken by industrial goods and electronics. However, rice continues to be a vital part of most Thai meals.

POPULATION COMPARISON
Thailand=22% of U.S.

United States

GDP COMPARISON
Thailand=5% of U.S.

United States

ETHNIC GROUPS

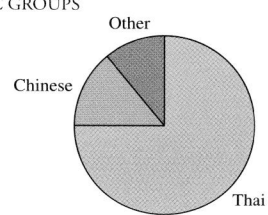

Other
Chinese
Thai

POPULATION DISTRIBUTION

Urban   Rural

Thailand at a glance

Official name   Kingdom of Thailand

People

Population	58,870,000
Density	302/mi² (117/km²)
Urban	22%
Capital	Bangkok, 5,620,591
Ethnic groups	Thai 75%, Chinese 14%
Languages	Thai, indigenous
Religions	Buddhist 95%, Muslim 4%
Life expectancy	72 female, 67 male
Literacy	93%

Politics

Government	Constitutional monarchy
Parties	Chart Thai, Democratic, Force of Truth (Palang Dharma), Justice Unity (Samakki Tham), New Aspiration
Suffrage	Universal, over 21
Memberships	ASEAN, UN
Subdivisions	73 provinces

Economy

GDP	$323,000,000,000
Per capita	$5,566
Monetary unit	Baht
Trade partners	Exports: U.S., Japan, Singapore Imports: Japan, U.S., Singapore
Exports	Machinery and manufactures, food, crude materials
Imports	Machinery and manufactures, chemicals, fuel, crude materials

Land

Description	Southeastern Asia
Area	198,115 mi² (513,115 km²)
Highest point	Mt. Inthanon, 8,530 ft (2,600 m)
Lowest point	Sea level

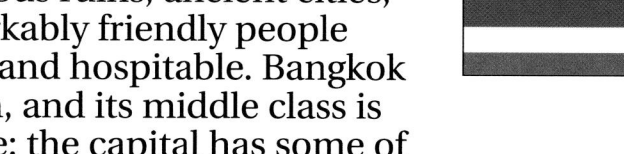

Lanta Island is one of dozens of islands along Thailand's Andaman Sea coast.

THAILAND

A s legions of visitors each year can attest, Thailand is a land of great allure. Religious ruins, ancient cities, huge Buddhas, and a remarkably friendly people make the country both fascinating and hospitable. Bangkok is experiencing tremendous growth, and its middle class is burgeoning. But success has a price: the capital has some of the worst congestion found anywhere in the world.

People
Thailand's society is relatively homogeneous. More than 80 percent of its people speak varying dialects of Thai and share a common culture and common religion, Buddhism. Chinese immigrants are a substantial minority. Thai society is rural, with most people living in the rice-growing regions. The government has sponsored a successful family-planning program, which has greatly reduced the annual birth rate.

Economy and the Land
With an economy based on agriculture, Thailand exports large quantities of rice each year. Forests produce teak and rattan, and tin is another valuable natural resource. Tourism is the largest source of foreign income. Future industrialization may hinge on deposits of coal and natural gas. Thailand is experiencing a period of prosperity and economic growth which provides an ideal climate for foreign investment. A mountainous and heavily forested nation, Thailand has a tropical climate, dominated by monsoons, high temperatures, and humidity.

History and Politics
Thai communities were established as early as 4000 B.C., although a Thai kingdom founded in the thirteenth century A.D. began the history of modern Thailand. In the late 1700s Burmese armies overwhelmed the kingdom. Rama I, founder of the present dynasty, helped to drive the invaders from the country in 1782. He subsequently renamed the nation Siam and established a capital at Bangkok. Siam allowed Europeans to live within its borders during the period of colonial expansion, but the nation never succumbed to foreign rule. As a result, Siam was the only South and Southeast Asian country never colonized by a European power. In 1932 a revolt changed the government from an absolute monarchy to a constitutional monarchy. Military officers assumed control in 1938, and the nation reverted to its former name, Thailand, in 1939. The country was invaded by Japan in World War II. Following the war, Thailand was ruled by military officers until 1973, when civilians seized control and instigated a period of democracy that ended in 1976, when the military again took control. In May 1992, soldiers opened fire on anti-government demonstrators, killing at least 50 people. Ensuing outrage led to the formation of a new, more democratic government.

Washing clothes, Bangkok

Thailand's Andaman Sea coast is lined with hundreds of unusual islands formed from ancient rocks. Their stark formations rise hundreds of feet from the sea. Palms cling to gaps in the sheer faces.

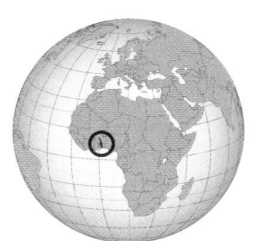

Togo

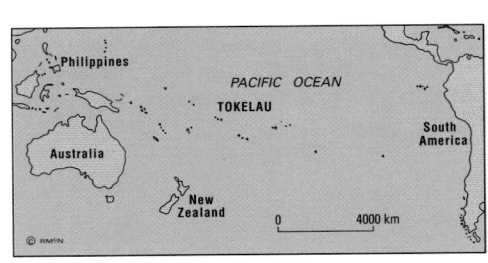

TOGO

- —— Railroad
- + Spot Elevation

National capitals
are underlined

City type size indicates
relative importance

Meters	Feet
1000	3281
500	1640
200	656
0	0
200	656
Below 2000	Below 6562

Scale 1:5,228,000

0 25 50 75 km
0   25   50 mi

Borders determined by colonial powers rather than natural features means that Togo has no unifying element, such as a mountain range or river.

Togo at a glance
Official name   Republic of Togo

People
Population	4,332,000
Density	198/mi² (76/km²)
Urban	29%
Capital	Lomé, 500,000
Ethnic groups	Ewe, Mina, Kabye, others
Languages	French, Ewe, Mina, Kabye, Dagomba
Religions	Animist 70%, Christian 20%, Muslim 10%
Life expectancy	57 female, 53 male
Literacy	43%

Politics
Government	Provisional military government
Parties	Rally of the People
Suffrage	Universal adult
Memberships	OAU, UN
Subdivisions	21 prefectures

Economy
GDP	$3,300,000,000
Per capita	$819
Monetary unit	CFA franc
Trade partners	Exports: Canada, France, Spain, Italy
	Imports: France, Netherlands, Germany
Exports	Phosphates, cocoa, coffee, cotton, manufactures, palm kernels
Imports	Food, fuel, manufactures, machinery

Land
Description	Western Africa
Area	21,925 mi² (56,785 km²)
Highest point	Mont Agou, 3,235 ft (986 m)
Lowest point	Sea level

People
Almost all the people of Togo are black Africans, coming primarily from the Ewe, Kabye, and Mina ethnic groups. Most of the population lives in the south and practices traditional religions. Significant Christian and Muslim minorities exist.

Economy and the Land
Togo is an agricultural country, but productive land is scarce. Fishing is a major industry in the coastal areas. Togo has one of the world's largest phosphate reserves. Much of Togo is mountainous, with a sandy coastal plain. The climate is hot and humid.

History and Politics
Togo's original inhabitants were probably the ancestors of the present-day central mountain people. Ewes entered the south in the 1300s, and refugees from war-torn northern countries settled in the north between the 1500s and 1800s. For two hundred years, European ships raided the coastal region in search of slaves. In 1884 Germany claimed the territory. After World War I Togoland became a League of Nations mandate governed by Britain and France. The mandate was made a United Nations trust territory following World War II and remained under British and French administration. British

Togoland voted to join the Gold Coast and nearby British-administered territories in 1957 and became the independent nation of Ghana. French Togoland voted to become a republic in 1956 with internal self-government within the French Union, although the United Nations did not accept this method of ending the trusteeship. Togo peacefully severed its ties with France in 1960 and gained independence the same year. Internal political strife and military dominance of the government have characterized Togo's years of independence.

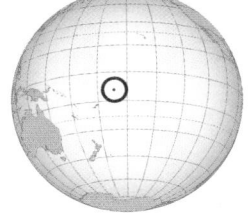

Tokelau

People
Most of Tokelau's people are Polynesian, but widespread intermarriage in the nineteenth century between Polynesians and beachcombers of American, Portuguese, Scottish, French, and German stock gave many a mixed ancestry. Tokelauan, a language with similarities to Samoan and Tuvaluan, is spoken throughout the islands. The Tokelauans share some cultural characteristics with Samoans, but the lifestyle of the atolls is more closely related to that of Tuvalu. All Tokelauans are Christian, either Congregational or Roman Catholic. A resettlement program beginning in the 1960s and lasting until the mid-1970s resulted in the emigration of many Tokelauans to New Zealand.

Economy and the Land
Tokelau has few natural resources, and inhabitants are dependent upon money sent from relatives who have emigrated to New Zealand. Agriculture provides for the production of copra, but all other farming is done at the subsistence level. Coconuts, breadfruit, papaw, and other fruits are grown for food. In an attempt to diversify crop production, the government has tested various types of seeds, but poor-quality soil continues to limit the potential of agriculture. Fish and shellfish are found throughout the waters around the islands, and the islanders hope to improve the size of the catch through the use of various mechanical aids. Industrial activities include the production of copra, woodwork, and woven craft items, such as mats and bags. Tokelau consists of three coral atolls: Atafu, Nukunonu, and Fakaofo. The climate is tropical.

History and Politics
According to tradition, the ancestors of today's population came from Samoa, Rarotonga, and Nanumanga. In 1765 a British commodore sighted the uninhabited island of Atafu, and another Briton came upon Atafu and Nukunonu in 1791. The Europeans did not know of the island of Fakaofo until 1835, when an American whaling ship sailed past. Following nearly twenty years under unofficial British administration, the islands of Tokelau formally became a British protectorate in 1889. Britain placed the islands with Western Samoa, then Tonga, and then Gilbert and Ellice Islands Colony. Administrative problems arose, however, because of distance, and New Zealand began administering the islands from Western Samoa in 1925. In 1948 the Tokelau Islands Act placed the islands within the international boundaries of New Zealand. The islands continue as a territory of New Zealand.

Tokelau at a glance
Official name   Tokelau

People
Population	1,500
Density	326/mi² (125/km²)
Capital	None
Ethnic groups	Tokelauan and other Polynesian 100%
Languages	English, Tokelauan
Religions	Congregationalist 67%, Roman Catholic 30%

Politics
Government	Island territory (New Zealand)
Suffrage	Universal adult
Subdivisions	None

Economy
GDP	$1,000,000
Per capita	$556
Monetary unit	New Zealand dollar
Trade partners	New Zealand
Exports	Stamps, copra, handicrafts
Imports	Food, building materials, fuel

Land
Description	South Pacific Islands
Area	4.6 mi² (12 km²)
Highest point	16 ft (5 m)
Lowest point	Sea level

Tonga at a glance

Official name: Kingdom of Tonga

People

Population	110,000
Density	382/mi² (147/km²)
Urban	35%
Capital	Nuku'alofa, Tongatapu I., 21,265
Ethnic groups	Tongan (Polynesian)
Languages	Tongan, English
Religions	Methodist 47%, Roman Catholic 16%, Free Church 14%, Church of Tonga 9%
Life expectancy	70 female, 66 male
Literacy	100%

Politics

Government	Constitutional monarchy
Parties	None
Suffrage	Literate adults, over 21 (males must be taxpayers)
Memberships	CW
Subdivisions	3 island groups

Economy

GDP	$200,000,000
Per capita	$1,942
Monetary unit	Pa'anga
Trade partners	Exports: New Zealand, U.S., Australia Imports: New Zealand, Australia, Fiji
Exports	Coconut oil, copra, bananas, taro, vanilla beans, fruits and vegetables
Imports	Food, machinery and transportation equip., manufactures, fuel

Land

Description	South Pacific islands
Area	288 mi² (747 km²)
Highest point	Unnamed, 3,432 ft (1,046 m)
Lowest point	Sea level

People

Almost all Tongans are Polynesian and follow Methodist and other Christian religions. About two-thirds of the population lives on the main island of Tongatapu.

Economy and the Land

Tonga's economy is dominated by both subsistence and plantation agriculture,

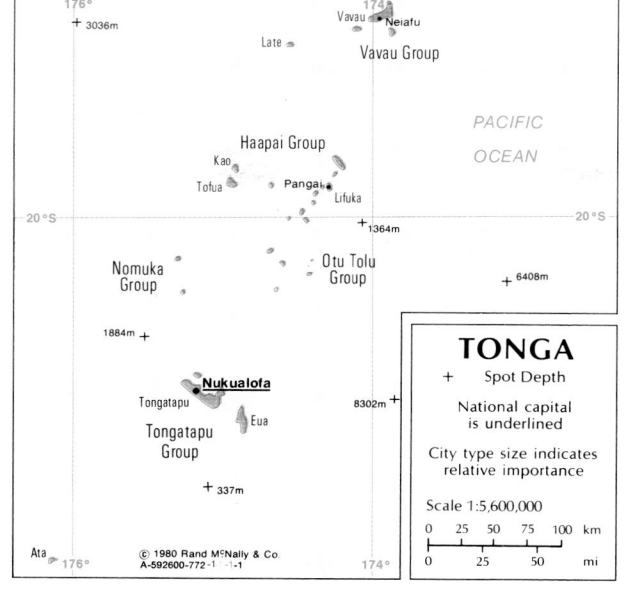

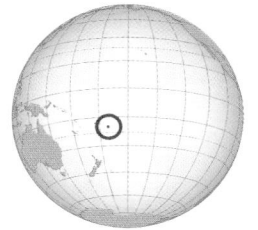

Located just west of the International Date Line, Tonga is the first country in the world to greet each new day.

TONGA

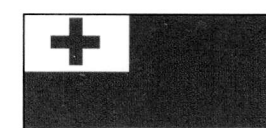

Comprising 170 volcanic islands and coral atolls, Tonga is one of the last surviving Polynesian kingdoms. The monarchy has existed since the 10th century; its influence once extended as far as Hawaii.

while manufacturing is almost nonexistent. Most o the islands are coral reefs, and many have fertile soil. The climate is subtropical.

History and Politics

Tonga has been settled since at least 500 B.C. In the late 1700s, a civil war broke out among three lines of kings who sought to establish rulership. In 1822 Wesleyan Methodist missionaries converted one of the warring kings to Christianity. His faction prevailed, and he ruled as George Tupou I, founder of the present dynasty. Tonga came under British protection in 1900 but retained its autonomy in internal matters. The nation became fully independent in 1970. Elections in 1993 highlighted the growth of two movements: the status quo as a constitutional monarchy, versus a pro-democracy faction.

Trinidad and Tobago at a glance

Official name: Republic of Trinidad and Tobago

People

Population	1,281,000
Density	647/mi² (250/km²)
Urban	65%
Capital	Port of Spain, Trinidad I., 50,878
Ethnic groups	Black 41%, East Indian 41%, mixed 16%, white 1%
Languages	English, Hindi, French, Spanish
Religions	Baptist 40%, Anglican 19%, Methodist 16%, Church of God 11%
Life expectancy	74 female, 69 male
Literacy	95%

Politics

Government	Republic
Parties	National Alliance for Reconstruction, People's National Movement
Suffrage	Universal, over 18
Memberships	CW, OAS, UN
Subdivisions	10 administrative areas

Economy

GDP	$10,400,000,000
Per capita	$7,957
Monetary unit	Dollar
Trade partners	Exports: U.S., Barbados, Netherlands Antilles Imports: U.S., Venezuela, U.K.
Exports	Petroleum, steel, fertilizer, sugar, cocoa, coffee, fruit
Imports	Raw materials, machinery, manufactures

Land

Description	Caribbean islands
Area	1,980 mi² (5,128 km²)
Highest point	El Cerro del Aripo, 3,085 ft (940 m)
Lowest point	Sea level

People

The two islands of Trinidad and Tobago form a single country, but Trinidad has nearly all the land mass and population. About 80 percent of all Trinidadians are either black African or East Indian, and about 20 percent are European, Chinese, and of mixed descent. Most Tobagonians are black African. The official language is English, and most people are Protestant.

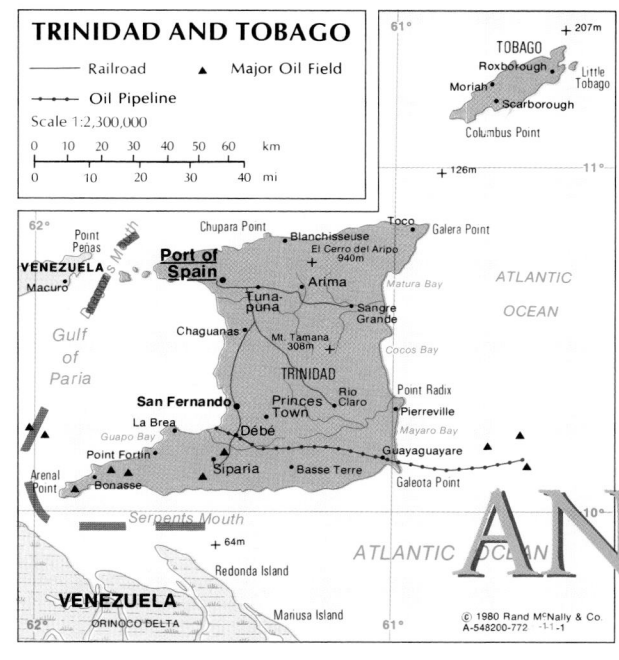

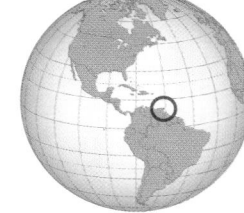

Separated by a narrow channel from the mainland, Trinidad is much like Venezuela in appearance. Tobago, twenty miles to the north, is mountainous and uncrowded.

TRINIDAD AND TOBAGO

Oil wealth has given Trinidad and Tobago a higher standard of living than many other Latin American countries. But declining production has hurt the economy, and the islands must find new forms of income.

Economy and the Land

Agriculture and tourism are important, but the economy is based on oil, which accounts for about 80 percent of the nation's exports. Trinidad is also one of the world's chief sources of natural asphalt and possesses supplies of natural gas. Tropical rain forests, scenic beaches, and fertile farmland characterize the islands.

History and Politics

Trinidad was occupied by Arawak Indians when Christopher Columbus arrived and claimed the island for Spain in 1498. The island remained under Spanish rule until 1797, when the British captured it and ruled for more than 150 years. Tobago changed hands among the Dutch, French, and British until 1814, when Britain took control. In 1888 Trinidad and Tobago became a single British colony, and achieved independence in 1962. The racially diverse society is beginning to agitate for a more balanced representation in the government. In August 1990 Muslim militants kidnapped a large number of government officials in an unfocused and failed attempt to force the Prime Minister to resign. However, the militants retain a hold on the country's politics.

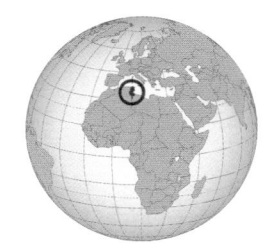

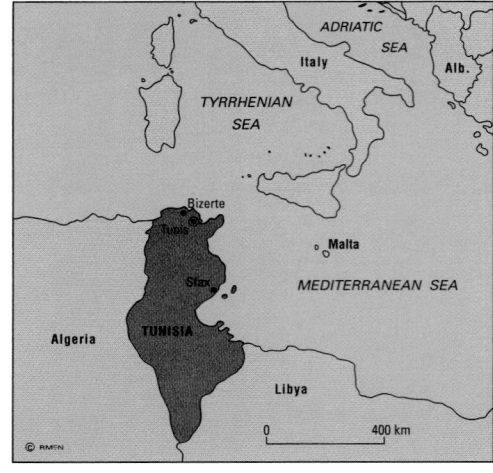

TUNISIA

A **succession of empires** have left their cultural and social marks on Tunisia. The Phoenicians were first, followed by the Romans, Byzantines, Arabs, Ottomans, and the French. Away from the coast, the nomadic Berber culture adds its own unique influence. Modern Tunisia is prosperous and stable and is visited by scores of European tourists annually.

Merchant and his wares, Djerba Island

People
Tunisians are descended from a mix of Berber and Arab ethnic groups. Nearly all Tunisians are Muslim. Arabic is the official language, but French is widely spoken. Tunisia is a leader in the Arab world in promoting rights for women. A large middle class and equitable land distribution characterize its society.

Economy and the Land
Tunisia is an agricultural country; wheat, barley, citrus fruits, and olives are important crops. Oil from deposits discovered in the 1960s supplies domestic needs and serves as a major export, along with phosphates and other chemicals. Tourism is a growing industry, and despite an unemployment problem, Tunisia has a more balanced economy than many of its neighbors. Tunisia's terrain ranges from a well-watered and fertile northern area to more arid central and southern regions.

History and Politics
Phoenicians began the Carthaginian Empire in Tunisia about 1100 B.C. In 146 B.C. Romans conquered Carthage and ruled Tunisia for six hundred years. Arab Muslims from the Middle East gained control of most of North Africa in the seventh century, influencing the religion and overall culture of the region. Tunisia became part of the Turkish Ottoman Empire in the late 1500s, and in 1881 France succeeded in establishing a protectorate in the area. Nationalistic calls for Tunisian independence began before World War I and gained momentum by the 1930s. When Tunisia gained independence in 1956, more than half of the European population emigrated, severely damaging the economy. A year later Tunisia abolished its monarchy and became a republic. The first multiparty parliament was elected in March 1994. Muslim fundamentalist parties are banned.

Tunisia at a glance
Official name	Republic of Tunisia

People

Population	8,606,000
Density	139/mi² (54/km²)
Urban	56%
Capital	Tunis, 596,654
Ethnic groups	Arab 98%, European 1%
Languages	Arabic, French
Religions	Muslim 98%, Christian 1%
Life expectancy	69 female, 67 male
Literacy	65%

Politics

Government	Republic
Parties	Constitutional Democratic Rally, Movement of Democratic Socialists
Suffrage	Universal, over 20
Memberships	AL, OAU, UN
Subdivisions	23 governorates

Economy

GDP	$34,300,000,000
Per capita	$4,038
Monetary unit	Dinar
Trade partners	Exports: France, Italy, Germany Imports: France, Italy, Germany
Exports	Hydrocarbons, agricultural products, phosphates and chemicals
Imports	Manufactures, petroleum, food

Land

Description	Northern Africa
Area	63,170 mi² (163,610 km²)
Highest point	Mt. Chambi, 5,066 ft (1,544 m)
Lowest point	Chott el Gharsa, -56 ft (-17 m)

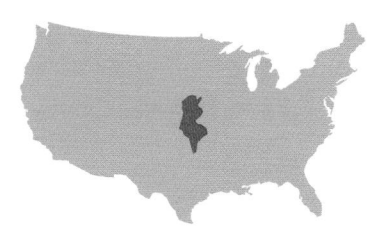

POPULATION COMPARISON
Tunisia=3% of U.S.

United States

GDP COMPARISON
Tunisia=0.5% of U.S.

United States

ETHNIC GROUPS

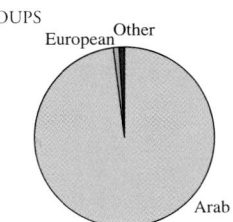

European   Other
Arab

POPULATION DISTRIBUTION
Urban   Rural

The fishing village of Ghar el Melh (Porto Farina) has a Mediterranean climate owing to its location on the Gulf of Tunis. Rain falls during the warm winter months. The summers are hot and dry, conditions which draw ever-growing numbers of European vacationers to northern Tunisia's beaches.

Tunisia's climate ranges from dry near the coast to very dry inland. There is very little annual rainfall near Libya and the northern edge of the Sahara Desert.

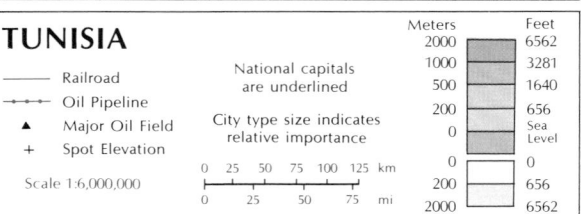

TUNISIA

——	Railroad
+++++	Oil Pipeline
▲	Major Oil Field
+	Spot Elevation

National capitals are underlined

City type size indicates relative importance

Scale 1:6,000,000

Meters	Feet
2000	6562
1000	3281
500	1640
200	656
0	Sea Level
0	0
200	656
2000	6562

0 25 50 75 100 125 km
0 25 50 75 mi

© Rand McNally & Co.
A-585300-772

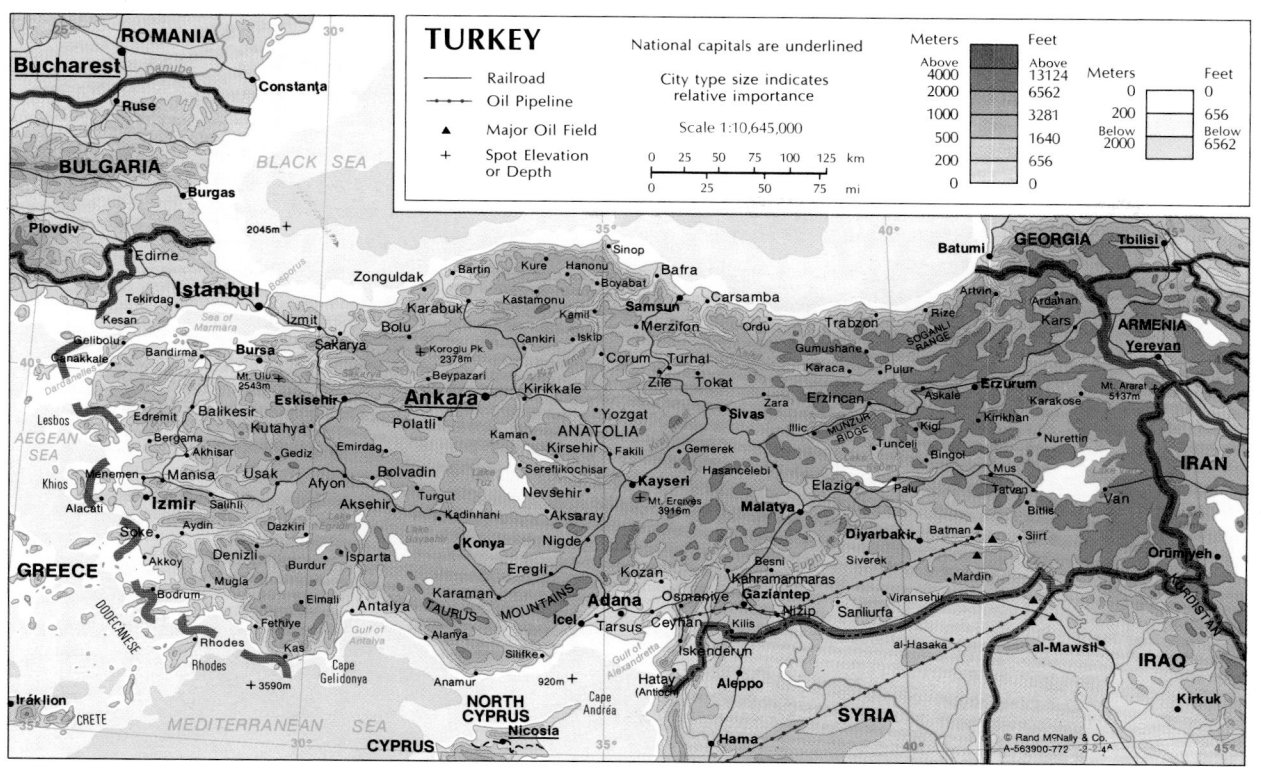

TURKEY

National capitals are underlined

—— Railroad
+-+-+ Oil Pipeline
▲ Major Oil Field
+ Spot Elevation
or Depth

City type size indicates
relative importance

Scale 1:10,645,000

Meters	Feet
Above 4000	Above 13124
2000	6562
1000	3281
500	1640
200	656
0	0

Meters	Feet
0	0
200	656
Below 2000	Below 6562

TURKEY

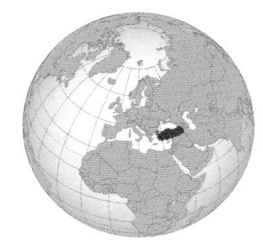

The narrow waterways linking the Black Sea with the Mediterranean are of great strategic importance. During the Cold War, they were major shipping lanes for the Soviet Union.

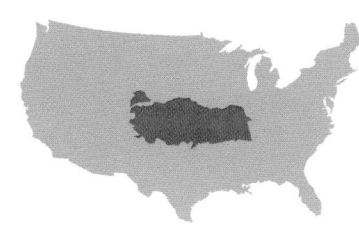

S**traddling the border between Europe and Asia,** Turkey is influenced by both. Its government looks west for trade wealth and political stability. The people look east for the roots of their Muslim rites and rituals. Invaders from both directions, including Hittites, Greeks, and Romans, have left their imprint on Turkey. The country's archeological sites are without compare.

People

Most Turks are descended from an Asian people who migrated from Russia and Mongolia around A.D. 900. About half the Turkish population lives in cities and half in rural areas. Kurds, the largest minority, live in the country's mountainous regions. Arabs and whites compose smaller minorities. The population is mainly Sunni Muslim. The changing status of women and the influence of Islam on daily life are key issues in Turkish society.

Economy and the Land

More than half the workers in this developing country are farmers, but industrialization has increased greatly since 1950. The most productive lands are in the mild coastal regions, although wheat and barley are grown in the desert-like plateau area. The government owns or controls many important industries, transportation services, and utilities, while most small farms and manufacturing companies are privately owned. The climate is Mediterranean along the coast, but temperature extremes are typical in the inland plateau.

History and Politics

Hittites began to migrate to the area from Europe or central Asia around 2000 B.C. Successive dominant groups included Phrygians, Greeks, Persians, and Romans. Muslims and Christians battled in the area during the Crusades of the eleventh and twelfth centuries. In the 1300s Ottoman

Turks began to build what would become a vast empire for six hundred years. Mustafa Kemal founded the Republic of Turkey in 1923, after the collapse of the Ottoman Empire. In 1960 the Turkish government was overthrown by Turkish military forces, who subsequently set up a provisional government, adopted a new constitution, and held free elections. In the 1960s and 1970s, disputes with Greece over Cyprus, populated by majority Greeks and minority Turks, flared into violence, and radical groups committed terrorist acts against the government. Turkey's generals assumed power in 1980 and restored order to the country. The government returned to civilian rule in 1984 and in 1993 elected its first woman prime minister. The militant Kurdish minority insurrection continues to defy military and political resolution. Also, militant fundamentalist Muslims are a growing problem.

Plowing by horsepower, central Turkey

The resort town of Alanya lies at the base of a large promontory dominated by the 13th-century Alâeddin Castle. The surrounding coastline is lined with beaches and caves.

POPULATION COMPARISON
Turkey=24% of U.S.

United States

GDP COMPARISON
Turkey=5% of U.S.

United States

ETHNIC GROUPS

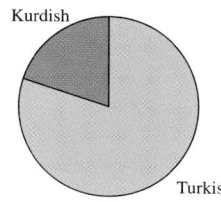

Kurdish

Turkish

POPULATION DISTRIBUTION

Urban   Rural

Turkey at a glance

Official name	Republic of Turkey

People

Population	62,030,000
Density	206/mi² (80/km²)
Urban	61%
Capital	Ankara, 2,559,471
Ethnic groups	Turkish 80%, Kurdish 20%
Languages	Turkish, Kurdish, Arabic
Religions	Muslim
Life expectancy	70 female, 65 male
Literacy	81%

Politics

Government	Republic
Parties	Correct Way, Motherland, Social Democratic Populist
Suffrage	Universal, over 21
Memberships	NATO, OECD, UN
Subdivisions	74 provinces

Economy

GDP	$312,400,000,000
Per capita	$5,329
Monetary unit	Lira
Trade partners	Exports: Germany, Italy, U.S. Imports: Germany, U.S., Italy
Exports	Steel, chemicals, fruits, vegetables, tobacco, meat products
Imports	Petroleum, machinery, transportation equipment, metals, chemicals

Land

Description	Southeastern Europe and southwestern Asia
Area	300,948 mi² (779,452 km²)
Highest point	Mt. Ararat, 16,804 ft (5,122 m)
Lowest point	Sea level

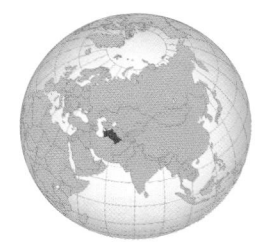

Once dependent upon cattle and cotton, Turkmenistan has begun to reap the benefits of its large oil reserves. Petroleum has insulated the country from the economic shocks that other countries in the region have suffered.

TURKMENISTAN

Wild camels roam the long sand ridges of the Kara Kum, a desert which accounts for more than 70 percent of Turkmenistan's land area. Some Turkmen continue their nomadic lives, but most are now farmers in the irrigated eastern region.

People

Almost three-quarters of the people are Turkmen, although there are Russian and Uzbek minorities. Before the Russian Revolution, the Turkmen were nomads who were organized into tribes and clans. Under Communist rule, many people turned to agriculture. The Turkmen speak a Turkish dialect of the same name.

Economy and the Land

Most of Turkmenistan is a vast desert. Like most deserts, the climate is characterized by extreme variations in temperature. Agriculture takes place in the country's river valleys and oases, and cotton is the most significant crop. Grapes, melons, and vegetables are also grown. Animal husbandry is a traditional activity, and sheep, horses, and camels are raised. The sheep provide wool for the country's famous handmade Oriental carpets. Petroleum and natural gas are among Turkmenistan's most impor-tant mineral resources. Only 10 percent of the people of Turkmenistan are engaged in industry.

History and Politics

In ancient times, Turkmenistan was part of the Persian Empire. Arabs invaded the region in the eighth century, bringing Islam. Turkic tribes conquered Turkmenistan in the tenth century, followed by the Mongols and the Uzbeks. The area was incorporated into Russian Turkestan in 1881. In 1925, Turkestan became a Soviet Socialist Republic within the Soviet Union. Turkmenistan was slow to make its claim to independence from the Soviet Union following the abortive coup against President Mikhail Gorbachev and the subsequent disbanding of the Soviet Communist party. The country gained full independence with the rest of the former Soviet republics in December 1991. Communists continue to dominate Turkmenistan's politics, and democratic institutions have not been established. With no opposition, the incumbent Turkmen Democratic Party was returned to power in 1994, and President Niazov's term was extended to 2002. Unlike many of its neighbors, Turkmenistan has not experienced ethnic strife, but there are signs of dissent over the autocratic rule and the austere economic circumstances that most people endure.

Turkmenistan at a glance

Official name	Turkmenistan

People

Population	4,000,000
Density	21/mi² (8.3/km²)
Urban	45%
Capital	Ashkhabad, 412,200
Ethnic groups	Turkmen 73%, Russian 10%, Uzbek 9%, Kazakh 2%
Languages	Turkmen, Russian, Uzbek
Religions	Muslim 87%, Eastern Orthodox 11%
Life expectancy	69 female, 61 male
Literacy	97%

Politics

Government	Republic
Parties	Democratic
Suffrage	Universal, over 18
Memberships	CIS, UN
Subdivisions	4 oblasts

Economy

GDP	$13,000,000,000
Per capita	$3,347
Monetary unit	Manat
Trade partners	Russia, Ukraine, Uzbekistan
Exports	Natural gas, oil, chemicals, cotton, textiles, carpets
Imports	Machinery and parts, plastics and rubber, consumer durables, textiles

Land

Description	Central Asia, landlocked
Area	188,456 mi² (488,100 km²)
Highest point	Unnamed, 10,299 ft (3,139 m)
Lowest point	Akdzhakaya Basin, -266 ft (-81 m)

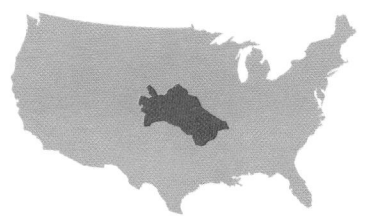

POPULATION COMPARISON
Turkmenistan=2% of U.S.

United States

GDP COMPARISON
Turkmenistan=0.2% of U.S.

United States

ETHNIC GROUPS

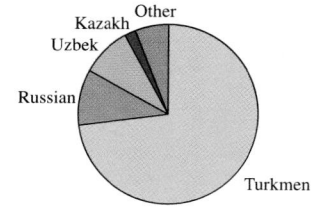

Other
Kazakh
Uzbek
Russian
Turkmen

POPULATION DISTRIBUTION
Urban   Rural

Oil rigs, Cheleken

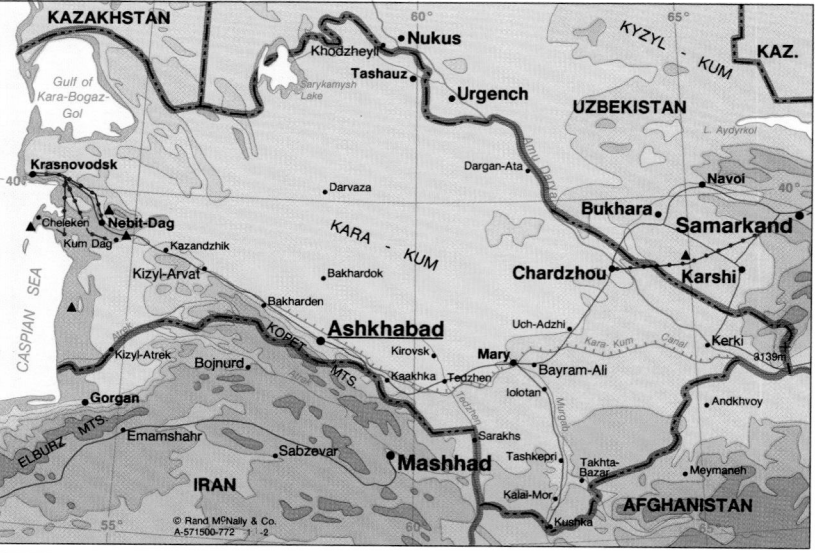

TURKMENISTAN

——	Railroad
········	Canal
+—+—+	Oil Pipeline
▲	Major Oil Field
+	Spot Elevation

National capitals are underlined

Scale 1:12,000,000

Meters	Feet
4000	13124
2000	6562
1000	3281
500	1640
200	656
0	Sea Level

Meters	Feet
0	0
200	656
2000	6562

Except for the Kopet Mountains in the south, Turkmenistan is essentially flat.

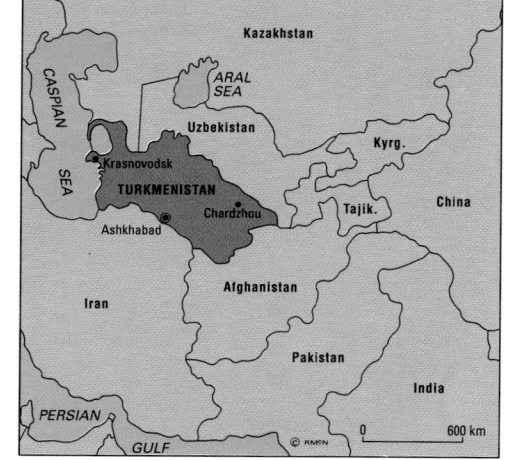

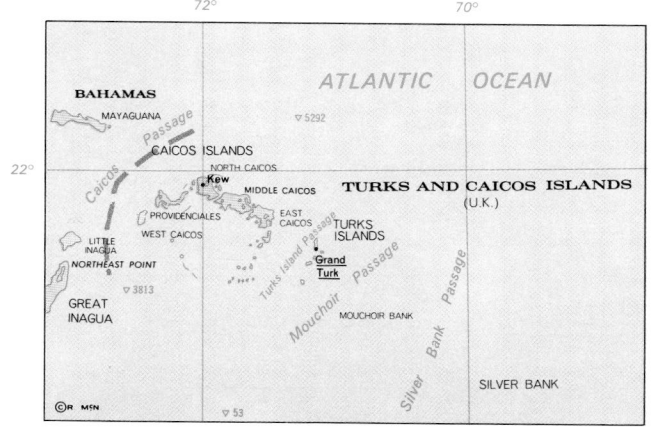

Of the 30 islands and cays that comprise the Turks and Caicos, only eight are inhabited. All are low-lying, with limestone flats and mangrove swamps.

TURKS AND CAICOS ISLANDS

Turks and Caicos at a glance

Official name	Turks and Caicos Islands

People

Population	14,000
Density	73/mi² (28/km²)
Urban	51%
Capital	Grand Turk, Grand Turk Island, 3,691
Ethnic groups	Mixed 63%, black 33%, white 3%
Languages	English
Religions	Baptist 40%, Anglican 20%, Methodist 19%, Church of God 8%
Life expectancy	77 female, 73 male
Literacy	98%

Politics

Government	Dependent territory (U.K.)
Parties	People's Democratic Movement, Progressive National
Suffrage	Universal, over 18
Memberships	None
Subdivisions	3 districts

Economy

GDP	$69,000,000
Per capita	$6,900
Monetary unit	U.S. dollar
Trade partners	U.S., U.K.
Exports	Lobster, conch
Imports	Food, beverages, tobacco, clothing

Land

Description	Caribbean islands
Area	193 mi² (500 km²)
Highest point	157 ft (48 m)
Lowest point	Sea level

The Turks and Caicos Islands have followed the familiar path of other Caribbean islands. Tourism and off-shore banking and insurance are the bases for the economy, due to the lack of other resources.

People
The population of Turks and Caicos is mostly black. English is the main language, although Haitian Creole is spoken by a group of immigrants. A trend of emigration is reversing as the islands' economy develops and employment opportunities expand.

Economy and the Land
Since the completion of a major resort in 1984, Turks and Caicos's tourism industry has expanded, with visitors drawn by the beautiful beaches and offshore coral reefs. Financial services are on the rise as well; tax benefits, coupled with minimal government control, continue to attract foreign investors. More than thirty islands and cays compose Turks and Caicos. Six of the main islands are inhabited, along with several of the cays. The terrain is flat with some low hills. The climate is tropical, tempered by trade winds.

History and Politics
The islands' first inhabitants were the Lucayan Indians. It is likely that present-day Turks and Caicos, rather than San Salvador in the Bahamas, was Christopher Columbus's first New World landfall in 1492. The Spaniard Ponce de Léon arrived in 1515, and soon the islands became a center for pirate activity. In 1678 settlers from Bermuda made their way to the islands, establishing a sea salt operation that endured as a successful enterprise until 1964. Until the 1760s, when the British secured the islands, Turks and Caicos saw invasions by both the Spanish and French. Following the American Revolution, British Loyalists fled the United States for Turks and Caicos, establishing a plantation economy fueled by slaves. At various times the islands were joined with the Bahamas and Jamaica, and when Jamaica gained independence in 1962, Turks and Caicos became a separate colony.

Tuvalu is a small island group of unspoiled beauty but limited natural resources. With only one small hotel and a few cafés, it has few visitors. Most of Tuvalu's annual budget comes from a trust fund established by Australia, New Zealand, and the United Kingdom.

TUVALU

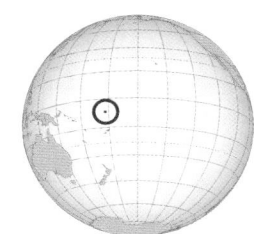

Tuvalu at a glance

Official name	Tuvalu

People

Population	10,000
Density	1,000/mi² (385/km²)
Capital	Funafuti, Funafuti I., 2,191
Ethnic groups	Tuvaluan (Polynesian)
Languages	Tuvaluan, English
Religions	Congregationalist (Church of Tuvalu) 97%
Life expectancy	64 female, 61 male

Politics

Government	Parliamentary state
Parties	None
Suffrage	Universal, over 18
Memberships	CW
Subdivisions	1 town council, 7 island councils

Economy

GNP	$6,400,000
Per capita	$727
Monetary unit	Dollar, Australian dollar
Trade partners	Exports: Fiji, Australia, New Zealand Imports: Australia, New Zealand, U.K.
Exports	Copra
Imports	Food, animals, fuel, machinery, manufactures

Land

Description	South Pacific islands
Area	10 mi² (26 km²)
Highest point	Unnamed, 16 ft (5 m)
Lowest point	Sea level

People
The small island nation of Tuvalu has a largely Polynesian population centered in rural villages. Tuvaluans speak the Tuvaluan language, derived from Polynesian, and many also speak English, reflecting ties with England.

Economy and the Land
The soil of the Tuvaluan coral-reef islands is poor, and there are few natural resources other than coconut palms. Copra and developed film are the primary exports, and many Tuvaluans weave mats and baskets for export. Tuvalu has minimal manufacturing and no mining. The nation consists of nine islands, most of them atolls surrounding lagoons. The climate is tropical.

History and Politics
Tuvalu's first inhabitants were probably Samoan immigrants. The islands were not seen by Europeans until 1568 and came under British control in the 1890s. Then called the Ellice Islands by Europeans, they were combined with the nearby Gilbert Islands in 1916 to form the Gilbert and Ellice Islands Colony. The island groups were separated in 1975. The Ellice Islands were renamed Tuvalu and gained independence in 1978. One year later, the Gilbert Islands became part of independent Kiribati.

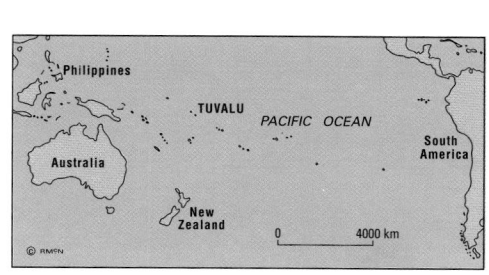

None of Tuvalu's islands have any natural sources of fresh water. All needs are met by rainwater catchment basins.

187

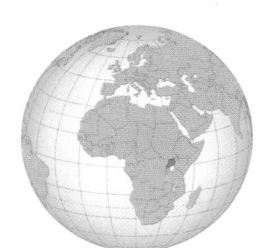

UGANDA

Sudanese refugees carry grass for huts, near Adjumani. Sudan's ongoing civil war has caused thousands of people to flee into southern Uganda.

Winston Churchill called Uganda "the Pearl of Africa" before its independence in 1962. But years of dictatorship, civil war, and an unbridled military have taken their toll. Now Uganda is engaged in a painful recovery, and perhaps the pearl will regain its luster.

People

Primarily a rural nation, Uganda has a largely African population, which is composed of various ethnic groups. Numerous differences divide Uganda's peoples and have traditionally inspired conflict. Though English is the official language, Luganda and Swahili are widely used, along with indigenous Bantu and Nilotic languages. Most Ugandans are Christian, but Muslims and followers of traditional beliefs compose significant minorities.

Economy and the Land

Despite attempts to diversify the economy, the country remains largely agricultural. Uganda meets most of its own food needs and grows coffee, cotton, and tea commercially. Copper deposits account for most mining activity. Though Uganda straddles the equator, temperatures are modified by altitude. Most of the country is plateau, and Uganda benefits from its proximity to several major lakes.

History and Politics

Arab traders who traveled to the interior of Uganda in the 1830s found sophisticated kingdoms that had developed over several centuries. Trying to track the source of the Nile River, British explorers arrived in the 1860s and were followed by European missionaries. Britain quickly became a dominant force in eastern Africa, and part of modern Uganda became a British protectorate in 1894. Subsequent border adjustments brought Uganda to its present boundaries in 1926. After increasing demands for independence, moves toward autonomy began in the mid-1950s. Independence came in 1962, followed by internal conflicts and power struggles. In 1971 Major General Idi Amin Dada led a successful coup against President Obote and declared himself president. His dictatorship was rife with corruption, economic decline, and disregard for human rights, and he was driven into exile in 1979. In July 1993 the ancient kingdom of Buganda was symbolically restored and Ronald Mutebi crowned as king. A Constituent Assembly was elected in 1994 to draft a constitution.

Uganda at a glance

Official name	Republic of Uganda

People

Population	18,270,000
Density	196/mi^2 (76/km^2)
Urban	11%
Capital	Kampala, 773,463
Ethnic groups	Ganda, Nkole, Gisu, Soga, Turkana, Chiga, Lango, Acholi
Languages	English, Luganda, Swahili, indigenous
Religions	Roman Catholic 33%, Protestant 33%, Muslim 16%, Animist
Life expectancy	43 female, 41 male
Literacy	48%

Politics

Government	Republic
Parties	National Resistance Movement
Suffrage	Universal, over 18
Memberships	CW, OAU, UN
Subdivisions	33 districts

Economy

GDP	$24,100,000,000
Per capita	$1,384
Monetary unit	Shilling
Trade partners	Exports: U.S., U.K., France Imports: Kenya, U.K., Italy
Exports	Coffee, cotton, tea
Imports	Petroleum products, machinery, textiles, metals, transportation equipment

Land

Description	Eastern Africa, landlocked
Area	93,104 mi^2 (241,139 km^2)
Highest point	Margherita Pk., 16,763 ft (5,109 m)
Lowest point	Along Albert Nile River, 2,000 ft (610 m)

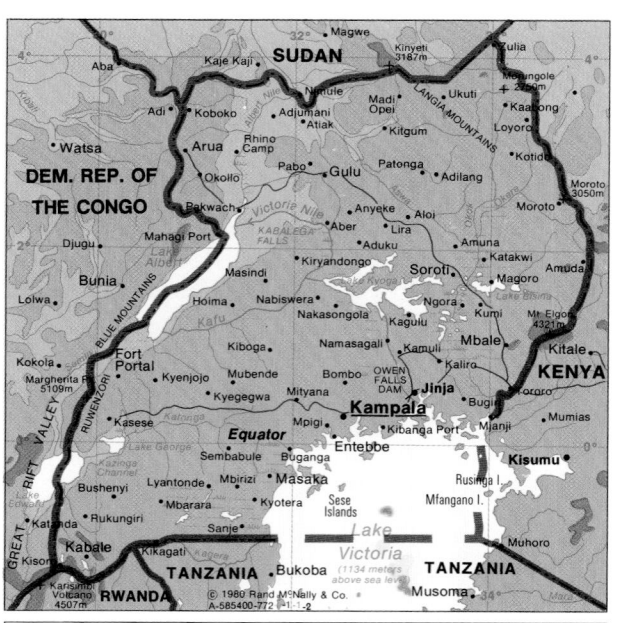

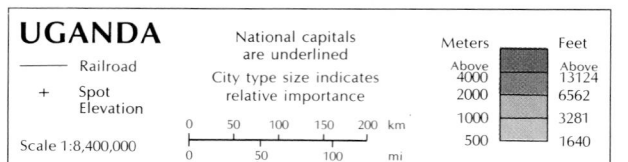

UGANDA

		Meters	Feet
National capitals are underlined		Above 4000	Above 13124
City type size indicates relative importance		2000	6562
		1000	3281
		500	1640

Railroad
+ Spot Elevation

Scale 1:8,400,000

0 50 100 150 200 km
0 50 100 mi

POPULATION COMPARISON
Uganda=7% of U.S.

United States

GDP COMPARISON
Uganda=0.4% of U.S.

United States

POPULATION DISTRIBUTION
Urban _____ Rural

Unlike many African countries to the north and west, Uganda receives abundant rainfall and has fertile soil.

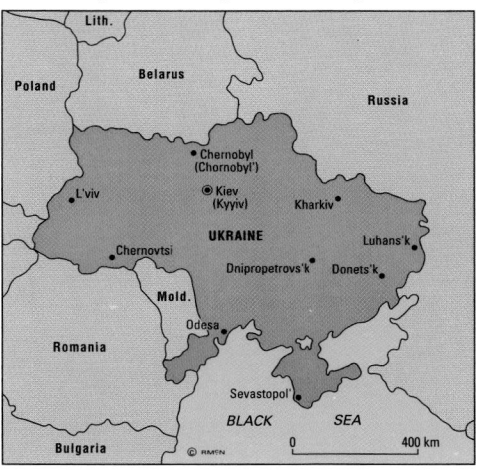

Ukraine was the agricultural heart of the Soviet Union. Today, crops grown on the rolling steppes, such as the corn shown here, provide valuble export income for the country.

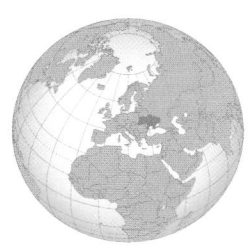

UKRAINE

The richest former Soviet republic after Russia, Ukraine has suffered from internal dissent and lack of direction since independence. Its once great industrial and agricultural output has fallen sharply. However, increasing numbers of Ukrainians are turning to the rich black soil and developing their own small farms.

People

The size of the population of newly independent Ukraine is second only to Russia among the former Soviet republics. Although there are more than one hundred minority groups, ethnic Ukrainians account for almost three-quarters of the population. Ukrainians are Slavic people, and their language is closely related to Russian and Belorussian. The Ukrainians are proud of their traditional stories, music, and art.

Economy and the Land

The land is almost entirely flat plains. The topography and the extremely fertile soils combine to make Ukraine one of the world's most outstanding agricultural areas. Major crops include grain, potatoes, meat, and milk. The country is also rich in mineral resources, including petroleum, coal, iron ore, and manganese. Industry is well developed in the eastern part of the country, and Ukraine boasts powerful steel and chemical industries. The coast of the Crimean Peninsula on the Black Sea is a famous resort area owing to its warm Mediterranean climate. Unlike many former Soviet republics, Ukraine has a very well developed transportation system.

History and Politics

Ukraine's first inhabitants were agricultural tribesmen who made their homes in the fertile river valleys. Slavic people found their way to the area around the fourth century A.D. In the ninth century, a dynasty centered at Kiev, called the Kievan Rus, was founded by the Scandinavian Varangians. This kingdom is considered the foundation of both the modern Ukrainian and Russian states. Kiev was destroyed during the Tatar-Mongol invasion in 1237. In the late 1300s Ukraine was part of the Lithuanian empire, and was later governed by Poland. The Ukrainians were made serfs under Polish rule, and religious rivalry between the Orthodox Ukrainians and the Roman Catholic Poles exacerbated the situation. Ukrainians who rebelled and fled from serfdom came to be known as Cossacks. The Cossacks established their own colonies and led several revolts against Polish rule and also against the Tatars. Eventually, the Cossacks turned to the Russians for protection and the first treaty was signed in 1654. By the late 1700s the Cossacks began to chafe under czarist rule, but the Russians managed to keep the territory under its control despite numerous revolts. Ukraine declared its independence after the Russian Revolution in 1917, but the new nation was soon invaded by Germany. Bolshevik troops drove the Germans out and the country became a Soviet Socialist Republic in 1922. In the 1930s agricultural land was seized by the government and devastating political purges followed. Most of the farmers were killed, and millions of people died in the ensuing famine. Ukraine was again ravaged during the German invasion of the Soviet Union during World War II. The country prospered in the years after the war, but nationalist sentiments were revived during the upheaval accompanying Gorbachev's rule. The nuclear accident at the Chernobyl nuclear power plant in 1986 contributed to the people's growing desire for greater control over their own territory. A referendum in Ukraine in early December 1991 called for complete independence from the Soviet Union and ultimately prompted the final collapse of the USSR in late 1991. Anger over rampant inflation and general economic chaos resulted in a 1994 presidential election promising reform. Crimea continues to press for independent status.

Soviet-era tractor on soybean farm near Donetsk

Ukraine at a glance

Official name	Ukraine

People

Population	52,140,000
Density	224/mi^2 (86/km^2)
Urban	67%
Capital	Kiev (Kyyiv), 2,635,000
Ethnic groups	Ukrainian 73%, Russian 22%
Languages	Ukrainian, Russian, Romanian, Polish
Religions	Ukrainian Orthodox, Ukrainian Catholic
Life expectancy	75 female, 75 male
Literacy	97%

Politics

Government	Republic
Parties	Democratic Rebirth, Green, Peasant Democratic, People's, Republican, Social Democratic, Ukrainian Socialist
Suffrage	Universal, over 18
Memberships	CIS, UN
Subdivisions	1 republic, 24 oblasts

Economy

GDP	$205,400,000,000
Per capita	$3,951
Monetary unit	Karbovanets
Trade partners	Russia, Belarus, Kazakhstan
Exports	Coal, electricity, metals, chemicals, machinery, transportation equipment
Imports	Machinery, transportation equipment, chemicals, textiles

Land

Description	Eastern Europe
Area	233,090 mi^2 (603,700 km^2)
Highest point	Mt. Hoverla, 6,762 ft (2,061 m)
Lowest point	Sea level

Only five percent of Ukraine is mountainous. The rest of the country is home to the fertile plains that were the breadbasket of the Soviet Union.

UKRAINE

Meters	Feet
4000	13124
2000	6562
1000	3281
500	1640
200	656
0	0
200	656
Below 2000	Below 6562

Railroad
Spot Elevation

Scale 1:9,000,000

0 50 100 150 200 km
0 50 100 mi

© Rand McNally & Co.
A-571600-772 -1- -1

I n the early 1970s, seven undeveloped Arab sheikdoms merged to become the United Arab Emirates. In the following decades, oil wealth transformed the country into a modern and affluent state.

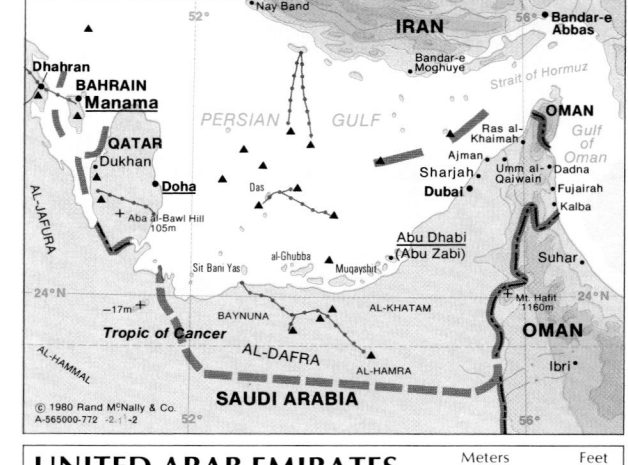

UNITED ARAB EMIRATES

United Arab Emirates at a glance

Official name	United Arab Emirates

People

Population	2,855,000
Density	88/mi^2 (34/km^2)
Urban	81%
Capital	Abu Dhabi, 242,975
Ethnic groups	South Asian 50%, native Emirian 19%, other Arab 23%
Languages	Arabic, Farsi, English, Hindi, Urdu
Religions	Sunni Muslim 80%, Shiite Muslim 16%
Life expectancy	74 female, 70 male
Literacy	68%

Politics

Government	Federation of monarchs
Parties	None
Suffrage	None
Memberships	AL, OPEC, UN
Subdivisions	7 emirates

Economy

GDP	$63,800,000,000
Per capita	$24,633
Monetary unit	Dirham
Trade partners	Exports: Japan, France, U.S. Imports: Japan, U.K., U.S.
Exports	Petroleum, natural gas, dried fish, dates
Imports	Food, manufactures, machinery

Land

Description	Southwestern Asia
Area	32,278 mi^2 (83,600 km^2)
Highest point	Mt. Yibir, 6,346 ft (1,934 m)
Lowest point	Sea level

People

The United Arab Emirates is a predominantly urban federation of seven independent states, each with its own ruling emir. The indigenous population is mostly Arab and Muslim, but only a small percentage of residents are United Arab Emirates citizens. Other groups include foreigners attracted by jobs in industry, especially Asians and Western Europeans. Arabic is the official language, but Farsi and English are widely spoken. The nation's population enjoys one of the highest per capita incomes in the world, as well as free medical and educational facilities.

Economy and the Land

Most of the United Arab Emirates is desert, which explains agriculture's small economic role. However, the federation is rich in oil, and major deposits—primarily in Abu Dhabi—account for nearly all of the Emirian national budget. The United Arab Emirates has tried to diversify its economy through production of natural gas, ammonia, and building materials. To attract tourists, airport expansion and hotel development are also on the rise.

The United Arab Emirates was originally to include Qatar as its eighth sheikdom, but negotiations failed and Qatar chose an independent course.

History and Politics

Centuries ago, Arab rulers gained control of the region, formerly called the Trucial Coast, and Islam spread to the area in the A.D. 600s. In 1820 Arabian emirs signed the first of a number of treaties with the United Kingdom. Mutual self-interest led to an 1892 treaty that granted Britain exclusive rights to Trucial territory and government activity in return for military protection. Britain formally withdrew from Trucial affairs in 1971, and six of the Trucial emirates entered into a loose federation called the United Arab Emirates, which included Abu Dhabi, Dubai, Ash Shāriqah, 'Ajmān, Umm al Qaywayn, and Al Fujayrah. The seventh, Ra's al Khaymah, joined in early 1972. Because each emirate has a great deal of control over its internal affairs and economic development, the growth of federal powers has been slow. Defense spending is on the increase, however, and growing Arab nationalism may lead to a more centralized government.

UNITED KINGDOM

London is one of the world's great cities. The Thames River passes some of its most famous monuments, such as the Parliament Building and the Tower of London. Efforts in recent years to clean up the river have been highly successful. It was once so polluted that Londoners often hung perfumed sheets in their Thames-facing windows to counter its foul odor.

C omprising England, Scotland, Wales, Northern Ireland, and a host of tiny dependent territories scattered around the globe, the United Kingdom is a shadow of its former self. A century ago, the sun never set on the British Empire, which included Australia, Canada, India, and much of Africa. While its influence has waned, the U.K.'s great historical legacy will endure for centuries.

St. Paul's Cathedral, London

Tunnbridge Wells, Kent

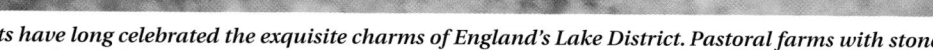

Poets have long celebrated the exquisite charms of England's Lake District. Pastoral farms with stone cottages dot the landscape, and misty lakes abound.

People

The ancestry of modern Britons reflects many centuries of invasions and migrations from Scandinavia and the European continent. Today Britons are a mixture of Celtic, Roman, Anglo-Saxon, Norse, and Norman influences. English is the predominant language, although Celtic languages such as Welsh and Scottish Gaelic are also spoken. Anglican is the dominant religion in England, while many Scots practice Presbyterianism. A sizable minority is Roman Catholic. The population is primarily urban and suburban, with a significant percentage living in the southeastern corner of England.

Economy and the Land

A land of limited natural resources, the United Kingdom has relied on trading and, more recently, manufacturing to achieve economic strength. Access to the sea is a traditional economic and political asset. The country maintains a large merchant fleet, which at one time dominated world trade. The industrial revolution developed quickly in Great Britain, and the country continues to be a leading producer of transportation equipment, metal products, and other manufactured goods. Although climate and limited acreage have hindered agricultural development, intensive, mechanized farming methods have allowed the nation to produce half of its food supply. Livestock raising is especially important. Additional contributors to the country's industry are extensive deposits of coal and iron, which make mining important. London is well known as an international financial center. The United Kingdom includes Scotland, England, Wales, Northern Ireland, and several offshore islands. The varied terrain is marked by several mountain ranges, moors, rolling hills, and plains. The climate is tempered by the sea and is subject to frequent changes. Great Britain administers many overseas possessions.

History and Politics

Little is known of the earliest inhabitants of Britain, but evidence such as Stonehenge indicates the existence of a developed culture before the Roman invasion in the 50s B.C. Britain began to trade with the rest of Europe while under Roman rule. The Norman period after A.D. 1066 fostered the establishment of many cultural and political traditions that continue to be reflected in British life. Scotland came under the British Crown in 1603, and in 1707 England and Scotland agreed to unite as Great Britain. Ireland had been conquered by the early seventeenth century, and the 1801 British Act of Union established the United Kingdom of Great Britain and Ireland. Although colonial and economic expansion had taken Great Britain to the Far East, America, Africa, and India, the nation's influence began to diminish at the end of the nineteenth century as the industrial revolution strengthened other nations. World War I significantly weakened the United Kingdom and during the period following World War II, which saw the demise of an empire, many colonies gained independence. The Conservative party has governed the country since 1979. The issue of peace for Northern Ireland continues to dominate the country's political scene. *(continued)*

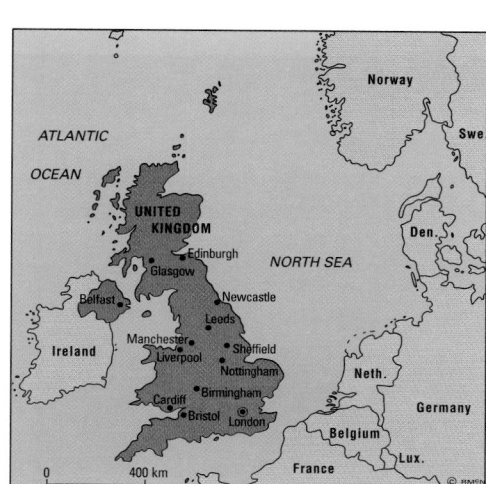

Tucked into the west side of England, Wales has its own distinct Celtic culture and language. Many of its cities and towns boast massive stone castles that once guarded the kingdom. Hikers prize the network of trails in the rolling hills.

Cottage, Devonshire

Edinburgh, Scotland

United Kingdom, continued

When people think of the United Kingdom, they often think of England in particular. London and its surroundings have been the heart of Britain for over 1,000 years.

United Kingdom at a glance

Official name   United Kingdom of Great Britain and Northern Ireland

People

Population	58,430,000
Density	620/mi² (239/km²)
Urban	89%
Capital	London, England, 6,574,009
Ethnic groups	English 82%, Scottish 10%, Irish 2%, Welsh 2%
Languages	English, Welsh, Scots Gaelic
Religions	Anglican 47%, Roman Catholic 9%, Presbyterian 3%, Methodist 1%
Life expectancy	79 female, 74 male
Literacy	99%

Politics

Government	Parliamentary monarchy
Parties	Conservative, Labor, Liberal Democratic, others
Suffrage	Universal, over 18
Memberships	CW, EU, NATO, OECD, UN
Subdivisions	2 countries, 1 principality, 1 province

Economy

GDP	$980,200,000,000
Per capita	$16,932
Monetary unit	Pound sterling
Trade partners	Exports: U.S., Germany, France. Imports: Germany, U.S., France
Exports	Manufactures, machinery, fuel, chemicals, transportation equipment
Imports	Manufactures, machinery, food

Land

Description	Northwestern European islands
Area	94,249 mi² (244,101 km²)
Highest point	Ben Nevis, 4,406 ft (1,343 m)
Lowest point	Holme Fen, England, -9 ft (-3 m)

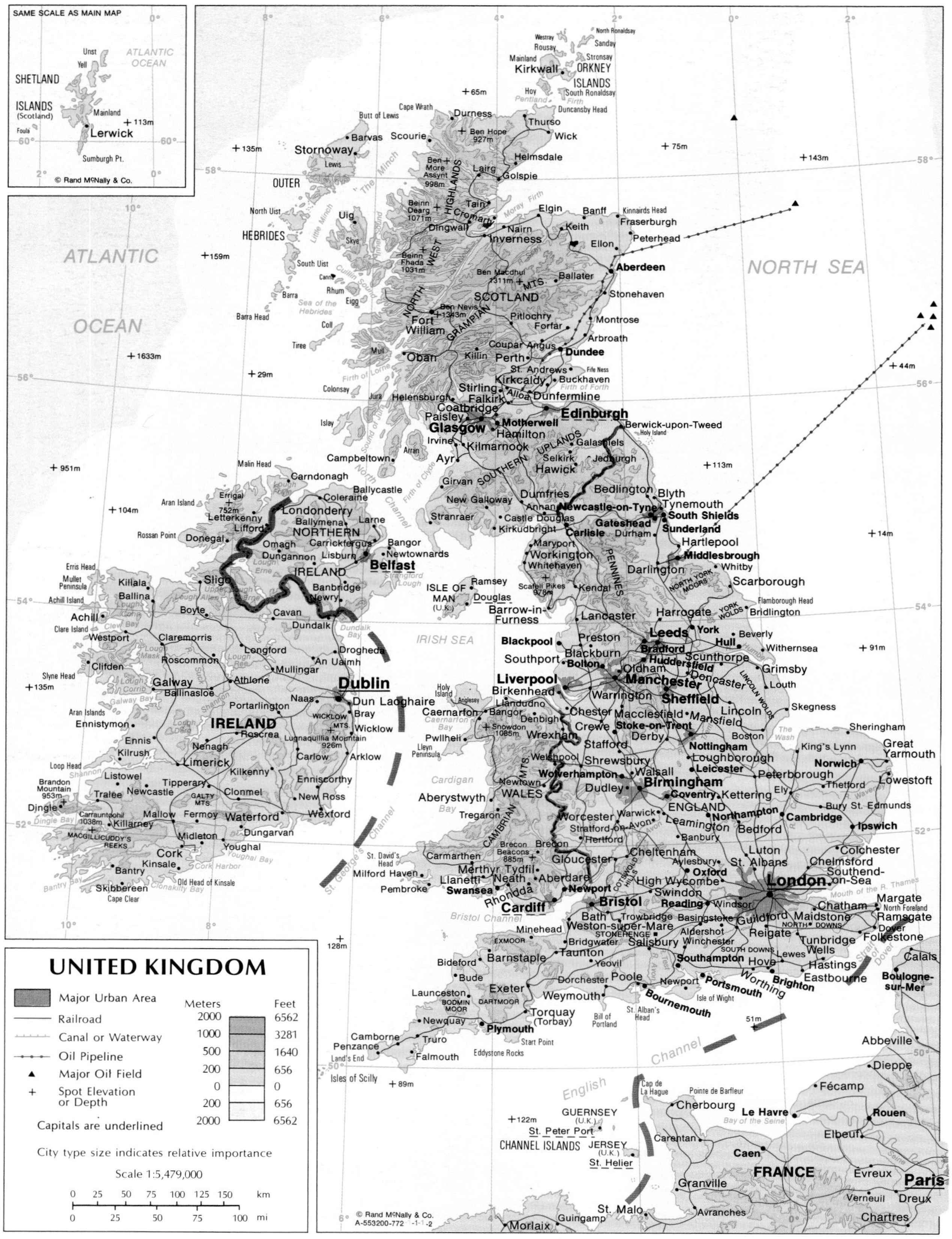

Kyle, Scotland

Swansea, Wales

UNITED KINGDOM

- Major Urban Area
- Railroad
- Canal or Waterway
- Oil Pipeline
- ▲ Major Oil Field
- + Spot Elevation or Depth

Meters	Feet
2000	6562
1000	3281
500	1640
200	656
0	0
200	656
2000	6562

Capitals are underlined

City type size indicates relative importance

Scale 1:5,479,000

© Rand McNally & Co.
A-553200-772 -1'-2

The Scottish Highlands are a remote region of the United Kingdom revered for their breathtaking scenery. Chiseled granite mountains overlook the icy pure waters of lakes, or "lochs" as the Scottish call them.

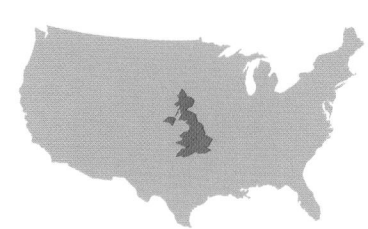

POPULATION COMPARISON
United Kingdom=22% of U.S.
United States

GDP COMPARISON
United Kingdom=15% of U.S.
United States

ETHNIC GROUPS

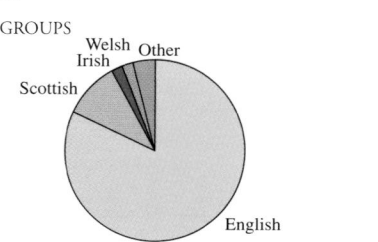

Welsh Other
Irish
Scottish
English

POPULATION DISTRIBUTION
Urban   Rural

UNITED STATES

As settlers spread west from the original East Coast colonies, the concept of the "frontier" has played an integral role in American life and lore. Today, Alaska, with its vast open spaces such as the Tatana River shown here, is America's last frontier.

The Lincoln and Washington Monuments and the Capitol, Washington, D.C.

Admired, reviled, emulated and debated, the United States inspires strong feelings around the globe. As the sole remaining world superpower, the country wields influence unmatched by any other. Its vast landscape, diverse people, and tradition of personal freedom are unequaled. For many of the world's people, going to the U.S. is the trip of a lifetime; for others—as it has been for generations—it is a journey to a new life. Even those who never set foot in North America cannot escape the United States' pervasive cultural influences, which have spread to every corner of the world.

People

The diverse population of the United States is mostly composed of whites, many descended from eighteenth-and nineteenth-century immigrants; blacks, mainly descended from African slaves; peoples of Spanish and Asian origin; and indigenous Indians, Inuit, and Hawaiians. Religions encompass the world's major faiths, but Christianity predominates. English is the predominant language, though Spanish is spoken by many, and other languages are often found in ethnic enclaves.

Economy and the Land

The United States is an international economic power, and all sectors of the economy are highly developed. Fertile soils produce high crop yields, with considerable land under cultivation. Mineral output includes petroleum and natural gas, coal, copper, lead, and zinc; but high consumption makes the United States dependent on foreign oil. The country is a leading manufacturer, with a well-developed service sector. Mountains, prairies, woodlands, and deserts mark its vast terrain. The climate varies regionally, from mild year-round along the Pacific coast and in the South to temperate in the Northeast and Midwest. In addition to forty-eight contiguous states, the country includes the subarctic state of Alaska and the tropical state of Hawaii, an island group in the Pacific. *(continued)*

A field of barley in the state of Washington calls to mind the "amber waves of grain" mentioned in the song "America the Beautiful." Family farms once formed the foundation of American society. Now supplanted by much larger corporate-owned operations, the family farm is fading as an American way of life.

United States, continued

History and Politics

Thousands of years ago, Asiatic peoples, ancestors of American Indians, crossed the Bering Strait land bridge and spread across North and South America. Vikings reached North America around A.D. 1000, and Christopher Columbus arrived in 1492. Following early explorations by Portugal and Spain, England established a colony at Jamestown, Virginia, in 1607. Thirteen British colonies waged a successful war of independence against England from 1775 to 1783. United States expansion continued westward throughout the nineteenth century. The issues of black slavery and states' rights led to the American Civil War from 1861 to 1865, a struggle that pitted the North against the South and resulted in the end of slavery. Opportunities for prosperity accompanied the industrial revolution in the late nineteenth century and led to a large influx of immigrants. From 1917 to 1918 the country joined with the Allies in World War I. A severe economic depression began in 1929, and the United States did not really recover until World War II stimulated industry and the economy in general. In 1945 the use of the atomic bomb on Japan ended the war and changed the course of history. The Civil Rights Act of 1964 and the Vietnam War, 1961–75, ushered in an era of great social progress and turmoil in the United States. Technological advances were unparalleled with man's entry into space and the first landing on the moon in 1969. The 1980s saw increasing concern with a deteriorating environment and the nuclear arms race. Unemployment, a sluggish economy, a trade deficit, crime, and health care reform were the greatest concerns of Americans in the early 1990s.

ETHNIC GROUPS

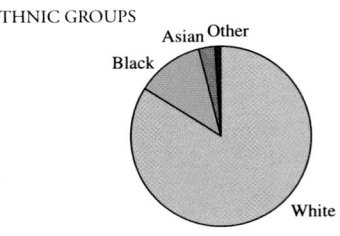

POPULATION DISTRIBUTION

Urban   Rural

(below) Wyoming's Grand Tetons are reflected in the Snake River. Grand Teton National Park and the adjoining Yellowstone National Park together contain some of the United States' most spectacular scenery.

(below right) The Carp River flows through an autumnal scene in Michigan's Upper Peninsula. Despite massive development around cities, the United States still contains much wilderness.

194

Na Pali coast, Kauai, Hawaii

Miami Beach, Florida

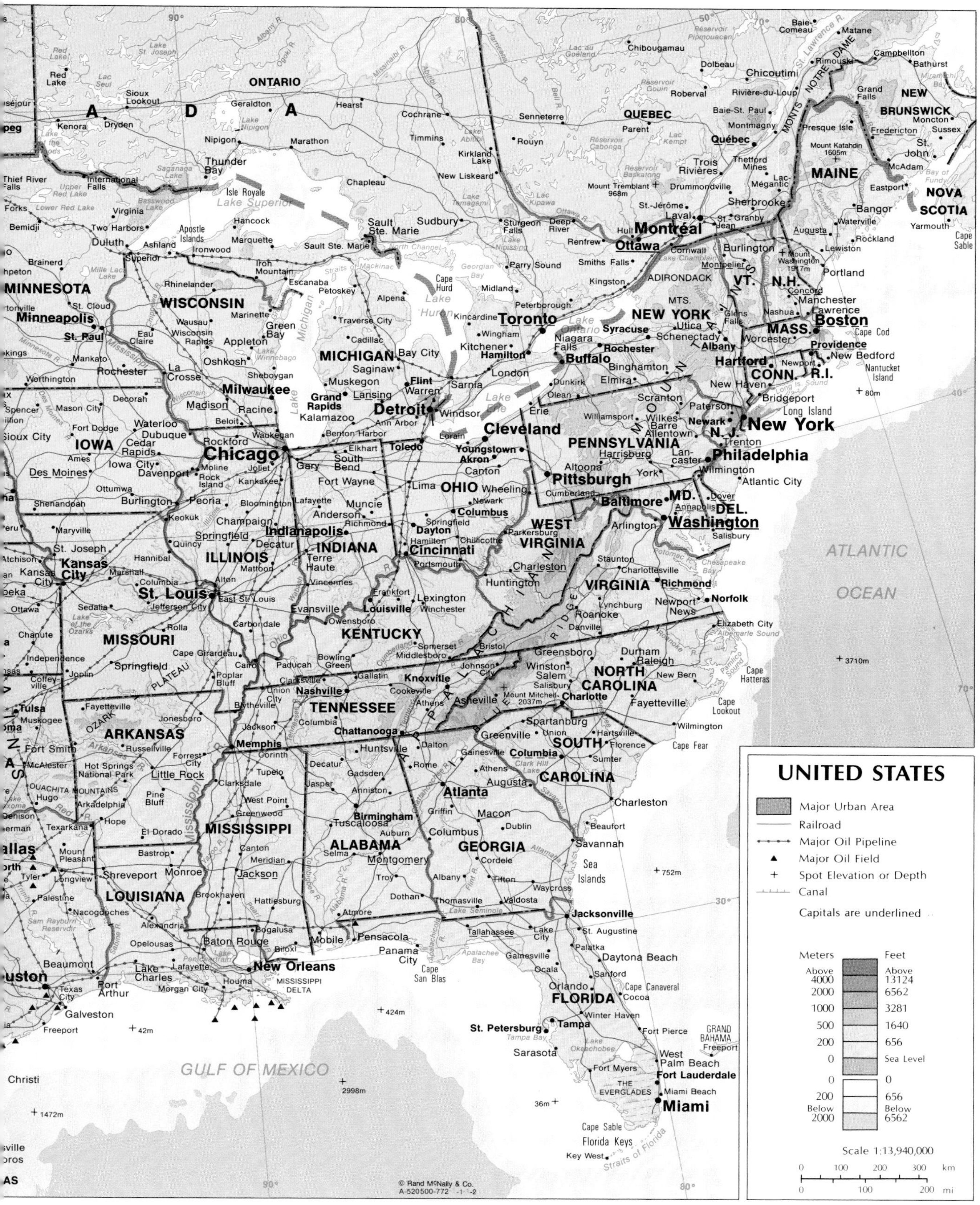

Maine is renowned for its rugged, rocky coast-line. The coast is only 228 miles long by air, but if all of its inlets and crags are measured, it is over 3,400 miles long.

Chicago, Illinois and Lake Michigan

Horse farm near Lexington, Kentucky

Americans have a long tradition of mobility. The centers of population continue to shift as people move in search of better lives. The second-largest city in the United States, Los Angeles, was a small town before World War II.

UNITED STATES

▨	Major Urban Area
	Railroad
•┼•┼•	Major Oil Pipeline
▲	Major Oil Field
+	Spot Elevation or Depth
	Canal
	Capitals are underlined

Meters		Feet
Above 4000		Above 13124
2000		6562
1000		3281
500		1640
200		656
0		Sea Level
0		0
200		656
Below 2000		Below 6562

Scale 1:13,940,000

0   100   200   300 km
0   100   200 mi

© Rand McNally & Co.
A-520500-772 -1- -2

A school bus transports its charges through the archetypal western landscape of Arizona's Monument Valley. Long a favorite with movie-makers, the valley is home to a Navajo Indian reservation.

Los Angeles, California was America's boom-town for much of the 20th century. Its aerospace and entertainment industries led a diverse economy that seemed to know no bounds. In recent years, however, the city has had to grapple with a myriad of challenges, many of which are linked to its still-growing population fueled by immigrants drawn from around the world. The city's renowned freeways, such as the Harbor freeway shown here passing downtown Los Angeles, are crowded around the clock.

(continued)

*Cypress Swamp,
South Carolina*

*Cattle graze on a farm near Iowa City, Iowa. With slightly over 100,000 farms, Iowa is a leading agricultural state that produces
a wide variety of crops and livestock. Much of the one billion bushels of corn Iowa produces annually is used as cattle feed.*

United States, continued

United States at a glance

Official name	United States of America

People

Population	262,530,000
Density	69/mi^2 (27/km^2)
Urban	75%
Capital	Washington, D.C., 606,900
Ethnic groups	White 84%, black 12%, Asian 3%
Languages	English, Spanish
Religions	Baptist and other Protestant 56%, Roman Catholic 28%, Jewish 2%
Life expectancy	79 female, 73 male
Literacy	98%

People

Government	Republic
Parties	Democratic, Republican
Suffrage	Universal, over 18
Memberships	NATO, OECD, OAS, UN
Subdivisions	50 states, 1 district

Economy

GDP	$6,379,000,000,000
Per capita	$24,877
Monetary unit	Dollar
Trade partners	Exports: Canada, Japan, Mexico Imports: Canada, Japan, Mexico
Exports	Machinery, automobiles, raw materials, manufactures, agricultural products
Imports	Petroleum, machinery, automobiles, manufactures, raw materials, food

Land

Description	Central North America
Area	3,787,425 mi^2 (9,809,431 km^2)
Highest point	Mt. McKinley, 20,320 ft (6,194 m)
Lowest point	Death Valley, California, -282 ft (-86 m)

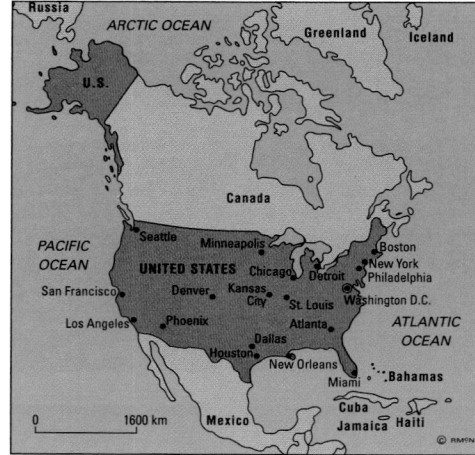

*Prickly Pear Cactus
in flower, Chisos
Mountains, Texas*

*The great Mississippi River drains America's
heartland, from western Pennsylvania to Idaho.
Shown here near New Orleans, it has played a
central role in the country's history. In the 19th
century, steamboats like this replica were active
throughout most of the river's length, from
Minnesota to Louisiana.*

*New York City is
America's first city.
The Statue of Liberty,
shown here against
the World Trade
Center and other
skyscrapers of lower
Manhattan, has
welcomed millions
of immigrants from
around the world to
the United States.*

About 68,000 square miles in size, Uruguay is dwarfed by its neighbors Brazil and Argentina. Those countries are respectively about 3,200,000 and 1,000,000 square miles in size.

Gauchos driving cattle, south of Aiguá

URUGUAY

Uruguay at a glance

Official name	Oriental Republic of Uruguay

People

Population	3,317,000
Density	48/mi² (19/km²)
Urban	89%
Capital	Montevideo, 1,251,647
Ethnic groups	White 88%, mestizo 8%, black 4%
Languages	Spanish
Religions	Roman Catholic 66%, Protestant 2%, Jewish 2%
Life expectancy	76 female, 69 male
Literacy	96%

Politics

Government	Republic
Parties	Broad Front, Colorado, National (Blanco)
Suffrage	Universal, over 18
Memberships	OAS, UN
Subdivisions	19 departments

Economy

GDP	$19,000,000,000
Per capita	$6,030
Monetary unit	Peso
Trade partners	Exports: Brazil, U.S., Germany Imports: Brazil, Argentina, U.S.
Exports	Hides and leather goods, beef, wool, fish, rice
Imports	Fuel, metals, machinery, transportation equipment, chemicals

Land

Description	Eastern South America
Area	68,500 mi² (177,414 km²)
Highest point	Cerro Catedral, 1,686 ft (514 m)
Lowest point	Sea level

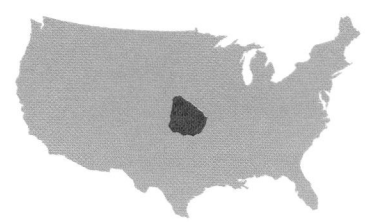

POPULATION COMPARISON
Uruguay=1% of U.S.

United States

GDP COMPARISON
Uruguay=0.3% of U.S.

United States

ETHNIC GROUPS

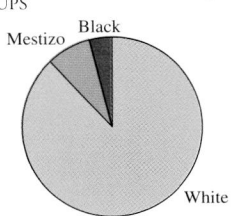

Black
Mestizo
White

POPULATION DISTRIBUTION
Urban   Rural

Uruguay's main feature, a long, rolling plain, is the heart of the country's economy. The plain supports large ranches devoted to raising livestock, especially cattle, sheep, and goats. This scene shows the countryside near Dolores.

U ruguay, the second-smallest country in South America, is sandwiched between the two largest, Argentina and Brazil. Uruguay's culture is overshadowed by the cultures of these two giant neighbors, and blends traits of both.

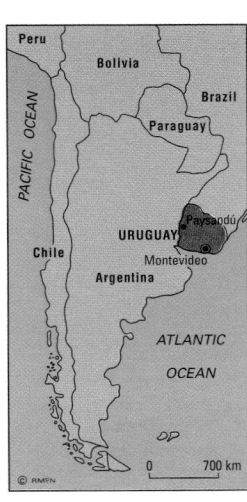

People

Most Uruguayans are white descendants of nineteenth- and twentieth-century immigrants from Spain, Italy, and other European countries. Mestizos, of Spanish-Indian ancestry, and blacks round out the population. Spanish is the dominant language, and Roman Catholicism is the major religion, with small Protestant and Jewish minorities. About one-third of all Uruguayans claim to follow no religion.

Economy and the Land

Uruguay's fertile soil, grassy plains, and temperate climate provide the basis for agriculture and are especially conducive to livestock raising. The country has virtually no mineral resources, and petroleum exploration has been unrewarding. However, refinement of imported fuel is a major industry, and Uruguay has significant hydroelectric potential.

History and Politics

Uruguay's original inhabitants were Indians. In the 1680s the Portuguese established the first European settlement, followed by a Spanish settlement in the 1720s. By the 1770s Spain had gained control of the area, but in the 1820s Portugal once again came to power, annexing present-day Uruguay to Brazil. When nationalistic feelings in the early nineteenth century led to an 1828 war by Uruguayan patriots and Argentina against Brazil, the country achieved independence. Political unrest, caused in part by economic depression, resurfaced in the 1970s, leading to military intervention in the government and the jailing of thousands of political prisoners. The country restored its civilian government in 1985. The first democratic elections in twenty years were won by the Centrist Colorado party, which is expected to introduce economic reforms.

197

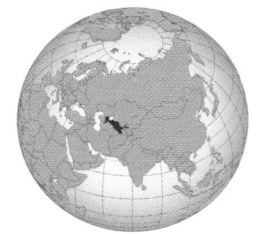

The world's third-largest exporter of cotton, Uzbekistan grows its crops on only 20 percent of its land, the fertile river valleys.

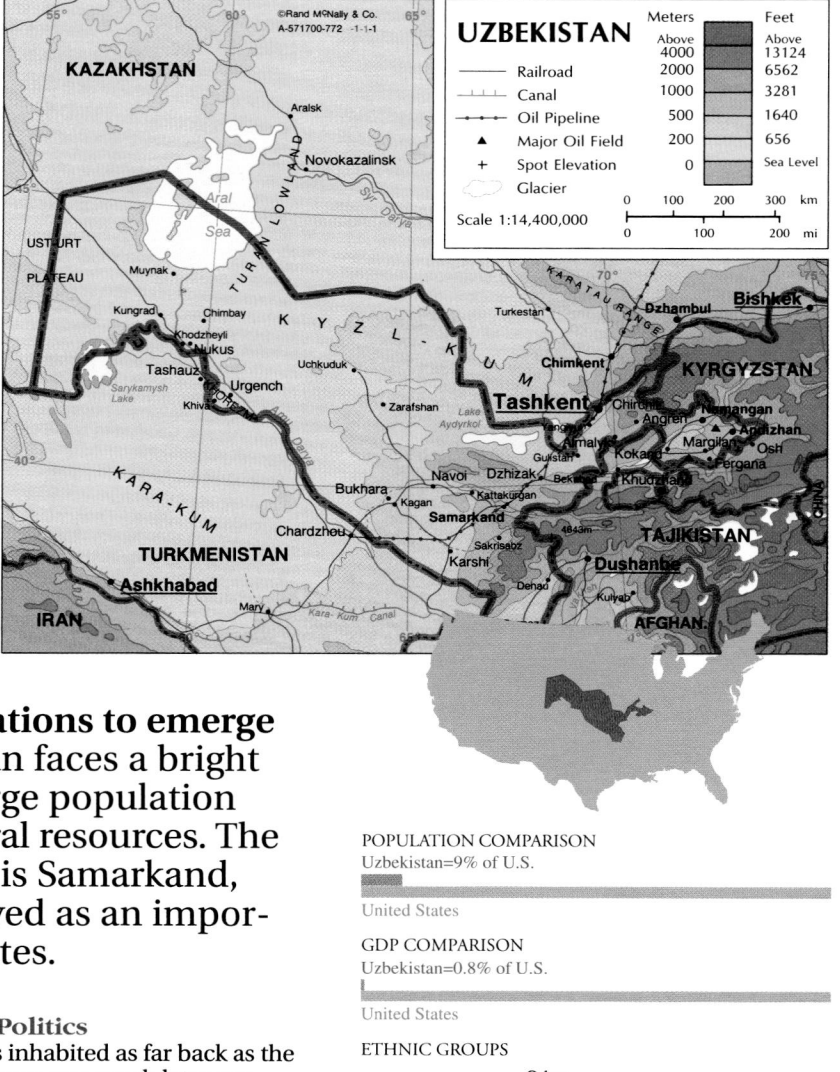

UZBEKISTAN

Picking cotton, Samarkand

Although it is one of the poorer nations to emerge from the Soviet Union, Uzbekistan faces a bright economic future, thanks to its large population and tremendous untapped oil and mineral resources. The republic's oldest and second-largest city is Samarkand, which for more than 2,500 years has served as an important stopping point on Asian trading routes.

People

The third most populous of the former Soviet republics, Uzbekistan is a land of many ethnic groups. Ethnic Uzbeks account for more than 70 percent of the population. Other ethnic groups include Russians, Tajiks, Kazakhs, and Tatars. The Uzbeks speak a Turkish dialect and adhere to Islam.

Economy and the Land

Irrigation allows for the production of cotton, and Uzbekistan is one of the world's largest producers, although it hopes to diversify its economy and end its dependence on cotton. Fruit and silk are produced in the mountain valleys. Gold, uranium, natural gas, and other minerals are mined in abundance. Western Uzbekistan is a flat desert that rises to mountains in the eastern part of the country. Most of the population and economic activity is based in valleys that cross eastern Uzbekistan. Uzbekistan exports electricity to other former Soviet central Asian republics, and it is the region's largest machinery producer.

History and Politics

Uzbekistan was inhabited as far back as the Stone Age. The area was much later conquered by the Turks, the armies of Alexander the Great, the Arabs, and the Mongols. Uzbekistan was under the rule of the Mongol-Turk Tamerlane dynasty from the thirteenth to the sixteenth centuries. Various sovereign khanates ruled the land until Russia annexed Uzbekistan in 1885 as part of the region then known as Turkestan. After the Russian revolution, Uzbekistan attempted to establish a western-style democracy, but the Soviets took over in 1924, and it was admitted to the Soviet Union the following year. Uzbekistan gained independence in 1991, following the dissolution of the Soviet Union. At first Uzbeks struggled to establish a new economy and form of government, but rising Islamic fundamentalism in neighboring Tajikistan has prompted a return to conservative government policies and a moratorium on reform. A new constitution, adopted December 1992, promised freedom and multiparty democracy. However, on the same day several opposition politicians were arrested. Elections in 1994 proved that power is still firmly in the hands of ex-communists and a centralized economic system. Economic reform has been moderately effective.

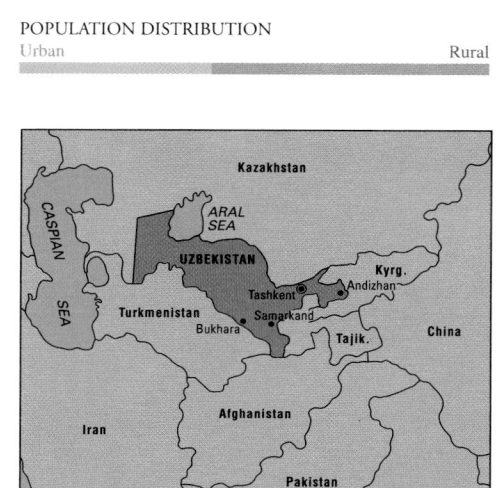

A young shepherd tends to his cattle and sheep in the Zeravshan Mountains. Two-thirds of Uzbekistan's people live in rural areas.

Uzbekistan at a glance

Official name Republic of Uzbekistan

People

Population	22,860,000
Density	132/mi^2 (51/km^2)
Urban	41%
Capital	Tashkent, 2,113,300
Ethnic groups	Uzbek 71%, Russian 8%, Tajik 5%, Kazakh 4%
Languages	Uzbek, Russian
Religions	Muslim 88%, Eastern Orthodox 9%
Life expectancy	72 female, 65 male
Literacy	97%

Politics

Government	Republic
Parties	ERK, People's Democratic
Suffrage	Universal, over 18
Memberships	CIS, UN
Subdivisions	1 republic, 11 oblasts

Economy

GDP	$53,700,000,000
Per capita	$2,454
Monetary unit	Som
Trade partners	Russia, Ukraine, eastern European countries
Exports	Cotton, gold, textiles, fertilizers, vegetable oil
Imports	Machinery, manufactures, grain and other food

Land

Description	Central Asia, landlocked
Area	172,742 mi^2 (447,400 km^2)
Highest point	Unnamed, 15,233 ft (4,643 m)
Lowest point	Mynbulak Basin, -39 ft (-12 m)

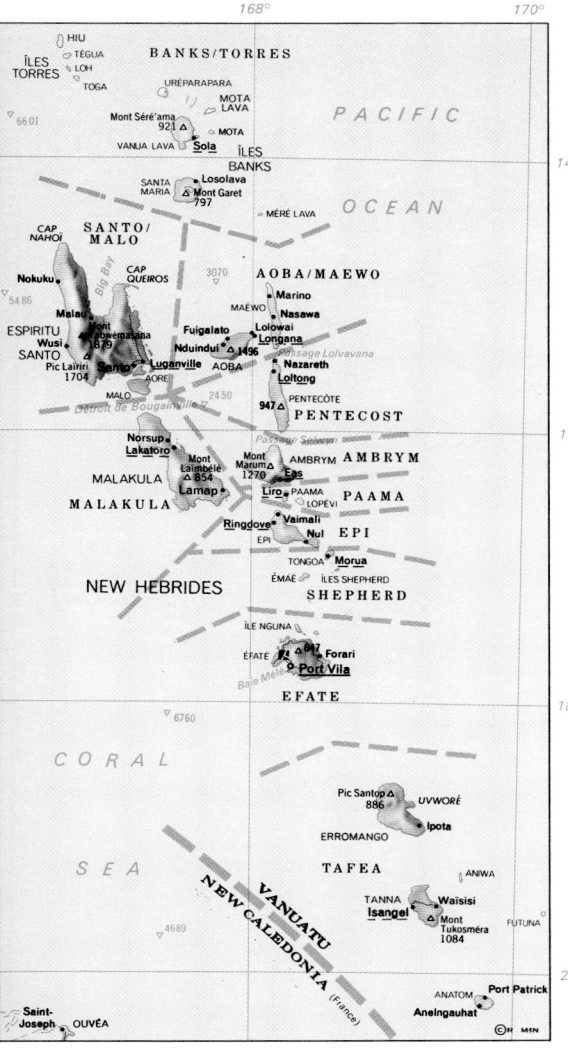

Scale 1:6,000,000 One inch represents approximately 95 miles.
One centimeter represents 60 kilometers.

One of the world's most unusual rituals occurs each May on Pentecost Island. Men and boys build 70-foot towers and then dive headfirst to the ground. Vines tied to their ankles stop them inches before they hit the ground.

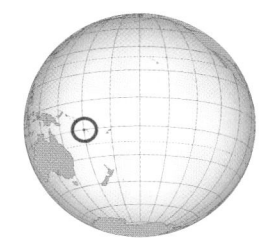

Formerly known as the New Hebrides islands, Vanuatu is a remote South Pacific mixture of primitive Melanesian peoples, decaying colonial plantations, and relics from World War II. Active volcanoes dot the twelve major islands, and there are frequent earthquakes.

VANUATU

People
The majority of Vanuatuans are Melanesian. Europeans and Polynesians compose minorities. Languages include English and French, the languages of former rulers; and Bislama, a mixture of English and Melanesian. Most Vanuatuans are Christian, although indigenous religions are also practiced.

Economy and the Land
The economy is based on agriculture, and copra is the primary export crop. Fishing is also important, as is the growing tourist business. Narrow coastal plains, mountainous interiors, and a mostly hot, rainy climate characterize the more than eighty islands of Vanuatu.

History and Politics
In 1606 Portuguese explorers encountered indigenous Melanesian inhabitants on islands that now compose Vanuatu. Captain James Cook of Britain charted the islands in 1774 and named them the New Hebrides after the Hebrides islands of Scotland. British and French merchants and missionaries began to settle the islands in the early 1800s. To resolve conflicting interests, Great Britain and France formed a joint naval commission to oversee the area in 1887 and a condominium government in 1906. Demands for autonomy began in the 1960s, and the New Hebrides became the independent Republic of Vanuatu in 1980. The first national election since independence was held in 1991.

Vanuatu at a glance

Official name	Republic of Vanuatu
People	
Population	161,000
Density	34/mi² (13/km²)
Urban	19%
Capital	Port-Vila, Efate I., 18,905
Ethnic groups	Ni-Vanuatu (Melanesian) 92%, European 2%, other Pacific Islander 2%
Languages	Bislama, English, French
Religions	Presbyterian 37%, Anglican 15%, Roman Catholic 15%, other Protestant
Life expectancy	61 female, 57 male
Literacy	53%
Politics	
Government	Republic
Parties	National (Vanua'aku Pati), Union of Moderate Parties, others
Suffrage	Universal, over 18
Memberships	CW, UN
Subdivisions	11 island councils
Economy	
GDP	$142,000,000
Per capita	$979
Monetary unit	Vatu
Trade partners	Exports: Netherlands, Japan, France Imports: Australia, New Zealand, Japan
Exports	Copra, cocoa, meat, fish, timber
Imports	Transportation equipment, food, manufactures, raw materials, chemicals
Land	
Description	South Pacific islands
Area	4,707 mi² (12,190 km²)
Highest point	Mont Tabwémasana, 6,165 ft (1,879 m)
Lowest point	Sea level

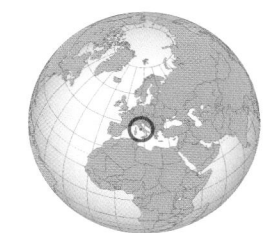

VATICAN CITY

Vatican City has its own train station on a rarely used spur off the Italian railways.

People
The Vatican City, the smallest independent state in the world, is the administrative and spiritual center of the Roman Catholic church and home to the pope, the church's head. The population is composed of administrative and diplomatic workers of more than a dozen nationalities; Italians and Swiss predominate. A military corps known as the Swiss Guard also resides here. Roman Catholicism is the only religion. The official language is Italian, although acts of the Holy See are drawn up in Latin.

Economy and the Land
The Vatican City does not engage in commerce per se; however, it does issue its own coins and postage stamps. In addition, it is the destination of thousands of tourists and pilgrims each year. Lying on a hill west of the Tiber River, the Vatican City is an urban enclave in northwestern Rome, Italy. The Vatican City enjoys a mild climate moderated by the Mediterranean Sea.

History and Politics
For centuries the popes of the Roman Catholic church ruled the Papal States, an area across central Italy which included Rome. The popes' temporal authority gradually was reduced to the city of Rome, which itself was eventually annexed by the Kingdom of Italy in 1870. Denying these rulings, the pope declared himself a prisoner in the Vatican, a status that lasted fifty-nine years. The Vatican City has been an independent sovereign state since 1929, when Italy signed the Treaty of the Lateran in return for papal dissolution of the Papal States. The pope heads all branches of government, though day-to-day responsibilities are delegated to staff members.

Vatican City at a glance

Official name	State of the Vatican City
People	
Population	1,000
Density	5,000/mi² (2,500/km²)
Urban	100%
Capital	Vatican City, 1,000
Ethnic groups	Italian, Swiss, other
Languages	Italian, Latin, other
Religions	Roman Catholic
Literacy	100%
Politics	
Government	Monarchical-sacerdotal state
Parties	None
Suffrage	Roman Catholic cardinals less than 80 years old
Memberships	None
Subdivisions	None
Economy	
Monetary unit	Lira
Land	
Description	Southern Europe, landlocked (within the city of Rome, Italy)
Area	0.2 mi² (0.4 km²)
Highest point	Unnamed, 249 ft (76 m)
Lowest point	Unnamed, 62 ft (19 m)

199

VENEZUELA

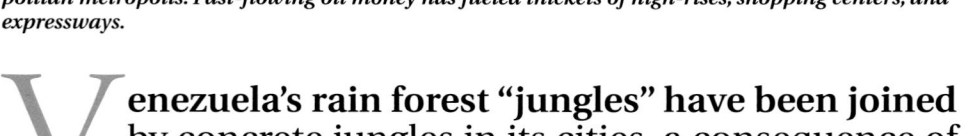

Set in a once-lush valley surrounded by densely forested mountains, Caracas is a vibrant and cosmopolitan metropolis. Fast-flowing oil money has fueled thickets of high-rises, shopping centers, and expressways.

Fishing boats at Sunset, Margarita Island

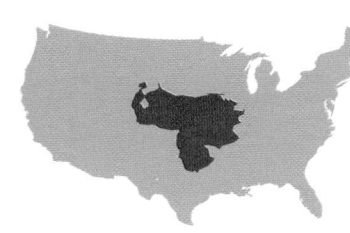

Venezuela's rain forest "jungles" have been joined by concrete jungles in its cities, a consequence of its great oil wealth. Oil production is greater than in any other country outside of the Middle East. Venezuela's cities are among the world's most modern, but in the rain forests which occupy more than half the land, there are few people and much has yet to be explored.

POPULATION COMPARISON
Venezuela=8% of U.S.

United States

GDP COMPARISON
Venezuela=3% of U.S.

United States

ETHNIC GROUPS
Black, Indian, White, Mestizo

POPULATION DISTRIBUTION
Urban   Rural

People
Spanish colonial rule of Venezuela is reflected in its predominantly mestizo population, people of Spanish-Indian blood, and its official language of Spanish. Minorities include Europeans, blacks, and Indians, who generally speak local languages. Nearly all Venezuelans are Roman Catholic, further evidence of former Spanish domination. Protestants and lesser numbers of Jews and Muslims compose small minorities, and traditional religious practices continue among some Indians.

Economy and the Land
Since the expansion of the petroleum industry in the 1920s, Venezuela has experienced rapid economic growth, but unevenly distributed wealth, a high birthrate, and fluctu-ations in the price of oil have hampered the economy. Partly because of the emphasis on oil production, agriculture has declined; its contribution to the gross national product is minimal, and Venezuela must import much of its food. Manufacturing and hydroelectric power are being developed. The varied Venezuelan landscape is dominated by the Andes Mountains, a coastal zone, high plateaus, and plains, or llanos. The climate is tropical, but temperatures vary with altitude. Most of the country experiences rainy and dry seasons.

History and Politics
The original inhabitants of modern Venezuela included Arawak and Carib Indians. In 1498 Christopher Columbus was the first European to visit Venezuela. The area became a colony of Spain and was briefly under German rule. Independence was achieved in 1821 under the guidance of Simón Bolívar, Venezuela's national hero. Venezuela became a sovereign state in 1830. The nineteenth century saw political instability and revolutionary fervor, followed by a succession of dictators in the twentieth century. Since 1958, Venezuela has tried to achieve a representational form of government and has held a number of democratic elections. The fall in oil prices, for a country heavily dependent upon oil export, has been an economic hardship in recent years. Abortive coups and presidential corruption have underscored Venezuela's continuing political instability.

Venezuela at a glance
Official name   Republic of Venezuela

People
Population	21,395,000
Density	61/mi² (23/km²)
Urban	91%
Capital	Caracas, 1,822,465
Ethnic groups	Mestizo 67%, white 21%, black 10%, Indian 2%
Languages	Spanish, Amerindian
Religions	Roman Catholic 96%, Protestant 2%
Life expectancy	74 female, 67 male
Literacy	88%

Politics
Government	Republic
Parties	Democratic Action, Movement Toward Socialism, Social Christian, others
Suffrage	Universal, over 18
Memberships	OAS, OPEC, UN
Subdivisions	20 states, 2 territories, 1 dependency, 1 district

Economy
GDP	$161,000,000,000
Per capita	$8,436
Monetary unit	Bolivar
Trade partners	Exports: U.S., Japan, Colombia, Netherlands Imports: U.S., Germany, Italy
Exports	Petroleum, bauxite and aluminum, iron ore, agricultural products
Imports	Food, chemicals, manufactures, machinery and transportation equipment

Land
Description	Northern South America
Area	352,145 mi² (912,050 km²)
Highest point	Bolívar Peak, 16,427 ft (5,007 m)
Lowest point	Sea level

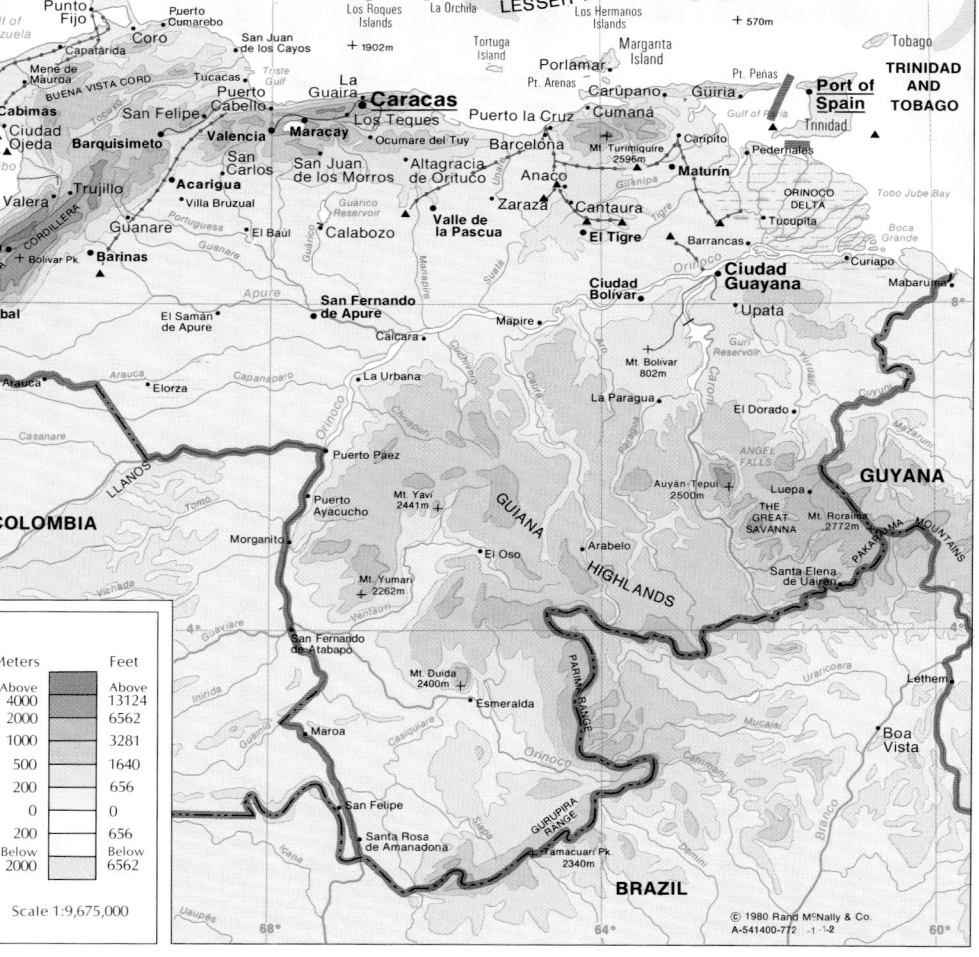

VENEZUELA
— Railroad
···· Oil Pipeline
▲ Major Oil Field
+ Spot Elevation or Depth

National capitals are underlined

City type size indicates relative importance

Meters	Feet
Above 4000	Above 13124
2000	6562
1000	3281
500	1640
200	656
0	0
200	656
Below 2000	Below 6562

0 50 100 150 200 250 km
0 50 100 150 mi
Scale 1:9,675,000

© 1980 Rand McNally & Co.
A-541400-772 -1 '-2

Explorer Amerigo Vespucci named Venezuela for Venice, Italy, after he encountered Indians living in houses perched on stilts above water.

Vietnam is a fertile land populated with rice farmers. After World War II its name became synonymous with tragedy, first for France and then for the United States. Communist forces eventually took control of the entire country, and much of the 1980s was spent rebuilding from the decades of turmoil. Recently, Vietnam has rejoined the world stage and has sought friendship with the same Americans it once so bitterly fought.

Street in Ho Chi Minh City

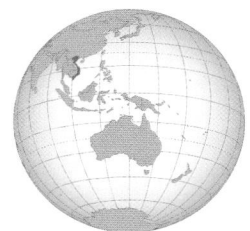

VIETNAM

With its narrow middle and plump extremes, Vietnam is often described by natives as a bamboo pole supporting two bowls of rice.

People

Despite centuries of foreign invasion and domination, the people of Vietnam remain remarkably homogeneous; ethnic Vietnamese compose the majority of the population. Chinese influence is seen in the major religions of Buddhism and Taoism. Most people live along two rivers, the Red in the north and the Mekong in the south, separated by mountains. The official language is Vietnamese, but a history of foreign intervention is reflected in wide use of French, English, Chinese, and Russian.

Vietman at a glance

Official name	Socialist Republic of Vietnam
People	
Population	73,760,000
Density	579/mi² (223/km²)
Urban	20%
Capital	Hanoi, 905,939
Ethnic groups	Kinh 87%, Hoa 2%, Tay 2%
Languages	Vietnamese, French, Chinese, English, Khmer, indigenous
Religions	Buddhist, Taoist, Roman Catholic, indigenous, Islamic
Life expectancy	66 female, 62 male
Literacy	88%
Politics	
Government	Socialist republic
Parties	Communist
Suffrage	Universal, over 18
Memberships	UN
Subdivisions	50 provinces, 3 municipalities
Economy	
GNP	$72,000,000,000
Per capita	$1,034
Monetary unit	Dong
Trade partners	Japan, Singapore, Thailand, eastern European countries
Exports	Agricultural products, handicrafts, coal, minerals
Imports	Petroleum, steel, railroad equipment, chemicals, pharmaceuticals, cotton
Land	
Description	Southeastern Asia
Area	127,428 mi² (330,036 km²)
Highest point	Phan Si Pang, 10,312 ft (3,143 m)
Lowest point	Sea level

Economy and the Land

The Vietnamese economy has struggled to overcome the effects of war and the difficulties inherent in unifying the once-divided country. Agriculture, centered in the fertile southern plains, continues to employ nearly 70 percent of the people. Vietnam intends to expand its war-damaged mining industry, which has been slowed by lack of skilled personnel and a poor transportation network. Vietnam's economic picture is not likely to improve until the country can resolve its political and social problems. The landscape of Vietnam ranges from mountains to plains, and the climate is tropical.

History and Politics

The first Vietnamese lived in what is now northern Vietnam. After centuries of Chinese rule, Vietnam finally became independent in the 1400s, but civil strife continued for nearly two centuries. French missionary activity began in the early seventeenth century, and by 1883 all of present-day Vietnam, Cambodia, and Laos were under French rule. When Germany occupied France during World War II, control of French Indochina passed to the Japanese until their defeat in 1945. The French presence continued until 1954, when Vietnamese Communists led by Ho Chi Minh gained control of North Vietnam. United States aid to South Vietnam began in 1961 and ended, after years of conflict, with a cease-fire in 1973. Communist victory and unification of the country as the Socialist Republic of Vietnam was achieved in 1975. Vietnamese military policy resulted in fighting with China and the occupation of Cambodia until 1989. A U.S. economic embargo was lifted in 1994, and the economic picture is likely to improve as the country attracts foreign investors.

POPULATION COMPARISON
Vietnam=28% of U.S.

United States

ETHNIC GROUPS

Other
Tay
Hao

Kinh

POPULATION DISTRIBUTION
Urban   Rural

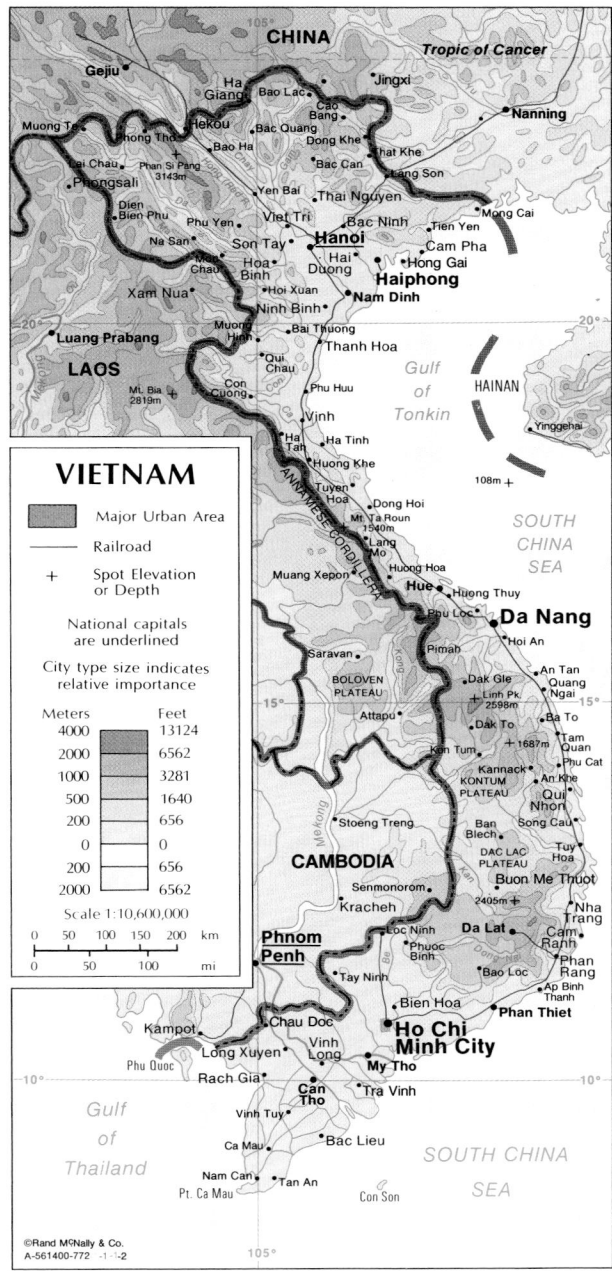

VIETNAM

Major Urban Area
— Railroad
+ Spot Elevation or Depth

National capitals are underlined

City type size indicates relative importance

Meters	Feet
4000	13124
2000	6562
1000	3281
500	1640
200	656
0	0
200	656
2000	6562

Scale 1:10,600,000
0 50 100 150 200 km
0 50 100 mi

©Rand McNally & Co.
A-561400-772 -1 -2

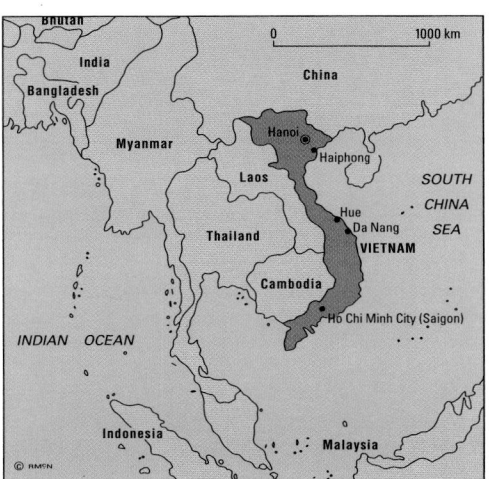

Steps serve as streets in Sa Pa, a village less than 25 miles from the border with China. Numerous hill tribes live in the remote mountains of northern Vietnam, largely untouched by the influences of modern life.

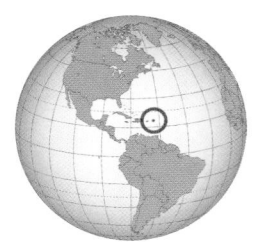

The Virgin Islands are a single chain of islands divided between the United States and the United Kingdom. The U.S. gained possession of its three main islands in 1917 when it bought them as part of a deal that saw Greenland go to Denmark. The British islands were the haunt of Dutch pirates until the British gained control in the 17th century.

VIRGIN ISLANDS

Virgin Islands (U.S.) at a glance

Official name	Virgin Islands of the United States

People

Population	97,000
Density	729/mi² (282/km²)
Urban	47%
Capital	Charlotte Amalie, St. Thomas Island, 12,331
Ethnic groups	Black 80%, white 15%
Languages	English, Spanish, Creole
Religions	Baptist 42%, Roman Catholic 34%, Episcopalian 17%
Life expectancy	77 female, 74 male

Politics

Government	Unincorporated territory (U.S.)
Parties	Democratic, Independent Citizens' Movement, Republican
Suffrage	Universal, over 18
Memberships	None
Subdivisions	3 islands

Economy

GDP	$1,200,000,000
Per capita	$10,526
Monetary unit	U.S. dollar
Trade partners	U.S., Puerto Rico
Exports	Refined petroleum products
Imports	Crude petroleum, food, consumer goods, building materials

Land

Description	Caribbean islands
Area	133 mi² (344 km²)
Highest point	Crown Mountain, 1556 ft (474 m)
Lowest point	Sea level

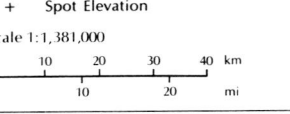
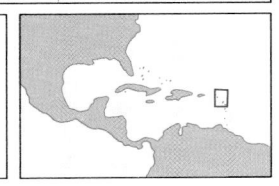

Many of the Virgin Islands' original rain forests have been destroyed, but the islands are popular with tourists for their other natural features, including beaches and reefs.

VIRGIN ISLANDS

+ Spot Elevation

Scale 1:1,381,000

© 1980 Rand McNally & Co. A-532300-772 -1-1-1

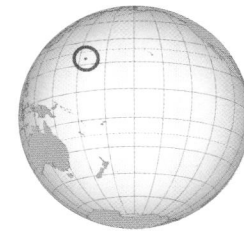

WAKE ISLAND

Wake Lagoon is enclosed by the V-shaped islands and an encircling coral reef.

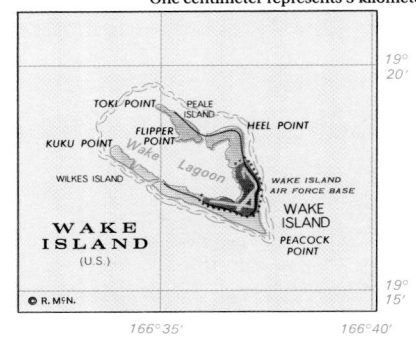

Scale 1:300,000 One inch represents approximately 4.7 miles. One centimeter represents 3 kilometers.

WAKE ISLAND (U.S.)

© R. MSN.

People

A possession of the United States, Wake Island has a population of about three hundred employees of the United States government and military. The three islets have no indigenous population, and there are no ethnic groups other than the Americans. For a period of several months during 1975, however, a large group of Vietnamese refugees en route to the United States was held here until transportation could be arranged. The United States government has considered using Wake Island as the relocation site for former inhabitants of the Bikini Atoll, which will remain uninhabitable well into the twenty-first century because of radiation resulting from United States nuclear weapon tests.

Economy and the Land

Wake Island is a United States military base and the site of an American weather station. The workforce consists of Air Force personnel, civilians employed by the Air Force, and employees of the National Oceanographic and Atmospheric Administration. Commercial as well as military flights use Wake Island as a stopover, generally only in emergency situations during flights from Honolulu to Tokyo or Guam. The atoll, situated midway between Hawaii and Guam, is made up of three

islets: Wake, Peale, and Wilkes. The climate is tropical, with occasional typhoons.

History and Politics

Pacific tradition holds that early Marshall Islanders used the three islets as a collection ground for birds and turtles. The first European to arrive was the Spanish explorer Mendana, who came in 1568 and found the atoll uninhabited. More than two centuries later, in 1796, the British sea captain William Wake reached the island and gave it his name. During the eighteenth century, seafarers knew the atoll as Halcyon and Helsion as well as Wake Island, and a United States expedition led by Commodore Wilkes officially charted Wake Island in 1840. The Americans built a cable relay station on Wake Island in 1899, annexing the island to the United States. The island's significance was its location; a commercial air station, constructed in 1935, provided a stopover point for flights to the East, and in 1939 the United States military established a naval and air base. Following the bombing of Pearl Harbor and the capture of Guam in 1941, the Japanese seized Wake Island. American bombing raids continued from 1942 until 1945, but the Japanese were able to hold the island, and United States personnel did not return until after the Japanese surren-

dered to Allies in 1945. After a period of administration by the United States Federal Aviation Administration, jurisdiction of the island passed to the United States Air Force. Wake Island is currently administered by the Air Force in conjunction with the United States Department of the Interior.

Wake Island at a glance

Official name	Wake Island

People

Population	300
Density	100/mi2 (38/km2)
Capital	None
Ethnic groups	American
Languages	English
Religions	Protestant, Roman Catholic

Politics

Government	Unincorporated territory (U.S.)
Memberships	None

Economy

Imports	Food, manufactures

Land

Description	North Pacific island
Area	3.0 mi² (7.8 km²)
Highest point	21 ft (6 m)
Lowest point	Sea level

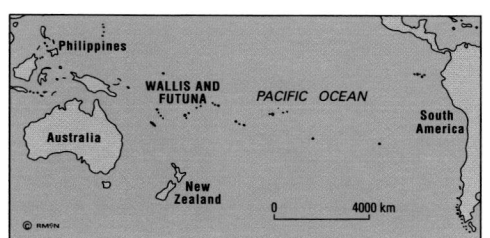

The island of Alofi off Futuna is uninhabited.

People

The French overseas territory of Wallis and Futuna consists of two main island groups, and the population is made up of Roman Catholic Polynesians. Despite this seeming homogeneity, each island has its own language. Inhabitants of Wallis Island, known locally as Uvea, speak Wallisian, or East Uvean, a tongue related to Tongan. Futunan, often called East Futunan, is spoken on Futuna Island, and this language is related to Samoan. Although the majority of the people over age forty-five cannot speak French, it remains the official language. The current birthrate in the islands is high, and more than half the population is under twenty years old.

Economy and the Land

Most islanders engage in subsistence activities, and family income comes mainly from government employment or money sent home by emigrants working in New Caledonia. Small-scale crop production can, for the most part, meet the needs of the islanders, but a lack of fertile land, inefficient farming methods, soil depletion, and traditional division of the land into tiny plots leave little hope for the development of a successful farm industry. One-time coconut plantations on Wallis ceased operation following a beetle infestation, and production of copra on Futuna is minimal. Fishing remains important throughout the islands and fish are the staple of the islanders' diet. There is potential for a tourism industry; however, local chiefs generally oppose development of the islands for tourism, and hotel facilities and restaurants remain minimal. Two island groups make up Wallis and Futuna. Wallis consists of a main volcanic island and about nineteen uninhabited islets. Futuna and nearby Alofi were formerly known as the Hoorn Islands. Futuna, not to be confused with the island of Futuna in Vanuatu, is mountainous, and because Alofi has no fresh-water supply, the small island remains without a permanent population. The climate is tropical, with a cyclone season between October and March.

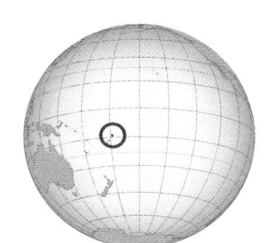

WALLIS AND FUTUNA

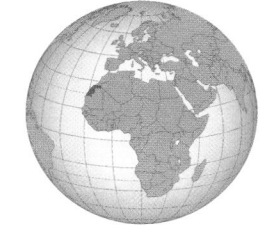

History and Politics

Wallis was probably settled in the mid-1400s or 1500s by immigrants from Tonga, and rivalry between chiefs marked its early years. The first settlers on Futuna likely came from Samoa, and tradition holds that some inhabitants are descendants of crew members of a Marshall Islands ship that docked on Futuna early in the island's history. In 1616 Dutch mariners reached Futuna and Alofi, naming them the Hoorn Islands for a town in the Netherlands. Captain Samuel Wallis of Britain came to Wallis in 1767, and he was followed by other Europeans in 1781 and 1791. French missionaries began their work in 1830s, and after initial hostilities and the murder of a priest on Futuna, Roman Catholicism was universally accepted on the islands. In 1842 local chiefs requested protection from the French government, and Wallis and Futuna became a French protectorate in 1887. Following a 1959 referendum to change the islands' status, Wallis and Futuna became an overseas territory of France in 1961.

Wallis and Futuna at a glance

Official name	Territory of the Wallis and Futuna Islands

People

Population	14,000
Density	143/mi2 (55/km2)
Capital	Matu-Utu, Uvea Island, 815
Ethnic groups	Polynesian
Languages	French, Wallisian
Religions	Roman Catholic
Life expectancy	72 female, 71 male
Literacy	50%

Politics

Government	Overseas territory (France)
Parties	People's Local Union, Rally for the Republic, Union for French Democracy
Suffrage	Universal, over 18
Memberships	None
Subdivisions	3 districts

Economy

GDP	$25,000,000
Per capita	$1,563
Monetary unit	CFP franc
Trade partners	France, Australia, New Zealand
Exports	Copra, handicrafts
Imports	Food, manufactures, transportation equipment, fuel

Land

Description	South Pacific islands
Area	98 mi² (255 km²)
Highest point	Mont Puke, 1,719 ft (524 m)
Lowest point	Sea level

People

Most Western Saharans are nomadic Arabs or Berbers. Because these nomads often cross national borders in their wanderings, the population of Western Sahara is in a constant state of flux. Islam is the principal religion, and Arabic is the dominant language.

Economy and the Land

Most of Western Sahara is desert, with a rocky, barren soil that severely limits agriculture. Mining of phosphate deposits began in 1972, and phosphates are now the primary export. Western Sahara is almost completely arid; rainfall is negligible, except along the coast.

History and Politics

By the fourth century B.C. Phoenicians and Romans had visited the area. Spain explored the region in the sixteenth century and gained control of the region in 1860, but Spanish Sahara was not designated a province of Spain until 1958. When Spanish control ceased in 1976, the area became known as Western Sahara. Mauritania and Morocco subsequently divided the territory, and Morocco gained control of valuable phosphate deposits. Fighting soon broke out between an independence movement, the Polisario Front, and troops from Morocco and Mauritania. In 1979 Mauritania gave up its claim to the area and withdrew. After years of conflict, Morocco and the Polisario Front agreed in 1988 to a cease-fire and a referendum to offer Western Saharans a choice between independence and integration with Morocco. The UN's attempts to organize the referendum have consistently been thwarted.

WESTERN SAHARA

Western Sahara at a Glance

Official name	Western Sahara

People

Population	215,000
Density	2.1/mi² (0.8/km²)
Urban	57%
Capital	El Aaiún, 93,875
Ethnic groups	Arab, Berber
Languages	Arabic
Religions	Muslim
Life expectancy	46 female, 44 male

Politics

Government	Occupied by Morocco
Memberships	None
Subdivisions	None

Economy

GNP	$60,000,000
Per capita	$300
Monetary unit	Moroccan dirham
Trade partners	Morocco
Exports	Phosphates
Imports	Fuel, food

Land

Description	Northwestern Africa
Area	102,703 mi² (266,000 km²)
Highest point	Unnamed, 2,640 ft (805 m)
Lowest point	Sea level

There are few cities in the Western Sahara, and none of the few roads linking the villages are paved.

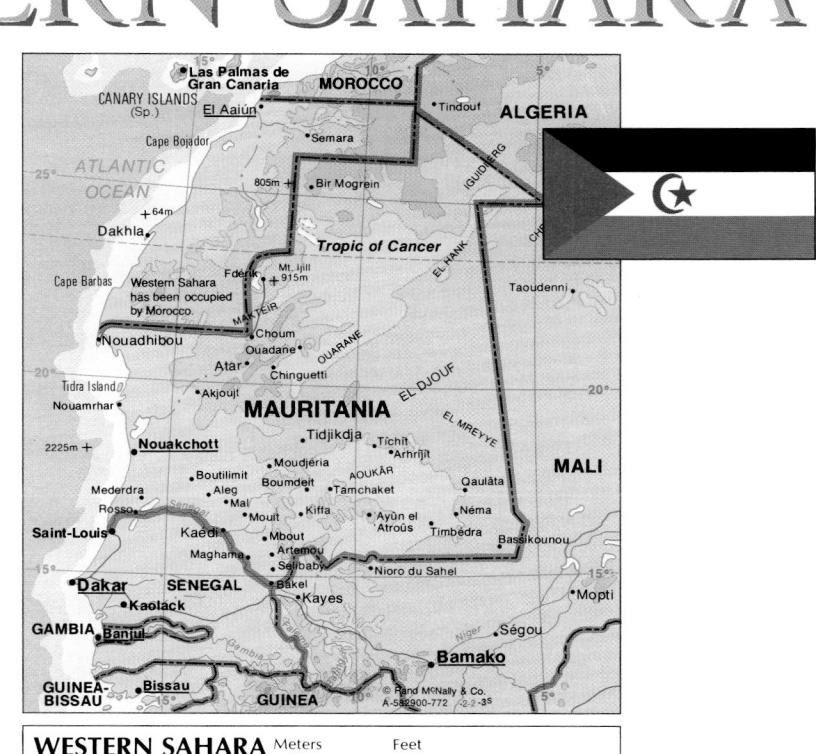

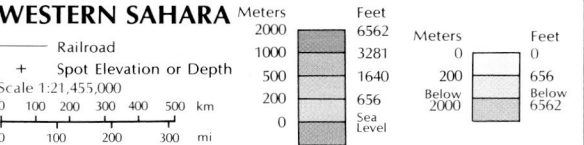

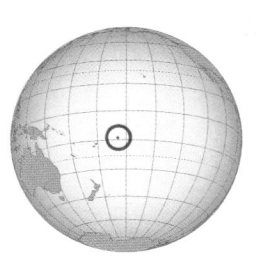

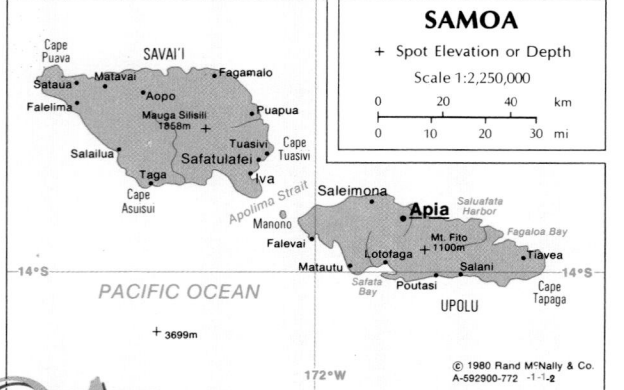

Samoa's annual rainfall of 275 inches is more than sufficient to support the dense green jungles covering the center of the islands.

SAMOA (FORMERLY WESTERN SAMOA)

People

Most Samoans are of Polynesian descent, and a significant minority are of mixed Samoan and European heritage. Most of the population is Christian and practices a variety of faiths introduced by European missionaries and traders. Samoan and English are the principal languages.

Economy and the Land

The tropical climate of Samoa, which is composed of volcanic islands, is suited for agriculture—the country's chief economic support. Bananas, coconuts, and tropical fruits are the most important crops.

History and Politics

Polynesians settled the Samoan islands more than two thousand years ago. Dutch explorers visited the islands in the early 1700s, and English missionaries arrived in 1830. Rivalry between the islands' royal families increased, along with competition among the United Kingdom, the United States, and Germany. In 1900 the islands were divided between the U.S., which called its portion Eastern Samoa, and Germany, which called its portion Western Samoa. By the end of World War I, New Zealand had gained control of Western Samoa. Growing demand for independence led to United Nations intervention and gradual steps toward self-government. The islands became fully independent in 1962. The nation maintains friendly relations with New Zealand and neighboring Pacific islands. In June 1997 the government officially changed the country's name from Western Samoa to Samoa.

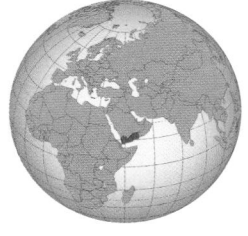

Because it is crossed by a historic trading route between Africa and Asia, Yemen has a rich and still largely undiscovered archeological heritage under its desert sands. For much of this century, Yemen has been divided into north and south entities. The two Yemens have been unified, although not always peacefully, since 1990.

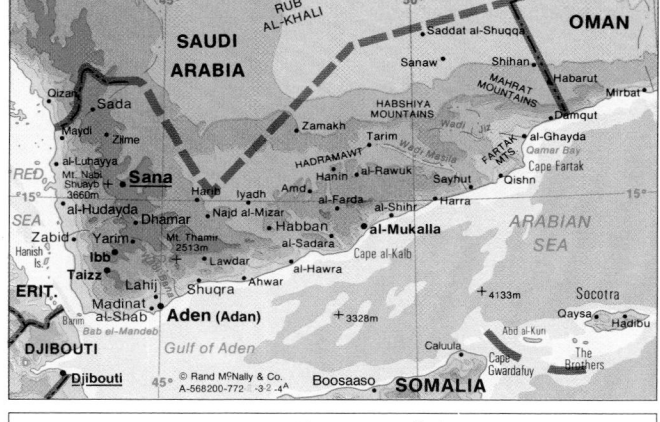

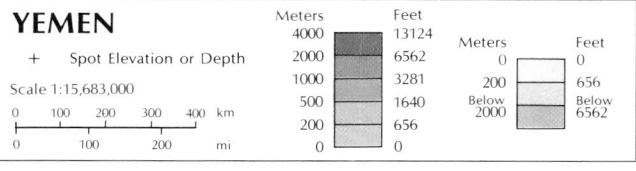

Under unification, the northern city of Sana is Yemen's capital. The port city of Aden is the center of commerce.

YEMEN

People

Most inhabitants of Yemen are Arab, with small minorities of Indians, Pakistanis, and East Africans. Islam is the predominant religion, while Arabic is the language of Yemen. The population includes both Sunni and Shiite Muslims. Small numbers of Christians, Hindus, and Jews also exist. Most of the population lives in the western part of the country.

Economy and the Land

Much of northwestern Yemen has a terrain suited for agriculture, the backbone of the nation's economy. However, ineffective agricultural techniques combined with regional instability often hinder production. Industrial activity is growing slowly, with production based on domestic resources, but exploitation of oil, iron ore, and salt deposits is financially prohibitive at this time. Subsistence farming and nomadic herding characterize the drier, eastern part of the country. Yemen varies from arid lowlands to fertile, well-cultivated highlands. The climate is temperate in the highlands and hot and dry in the lowlands.

History and Politics

Between 1200 B.C. and 525 A.D., trade empires occupied the area of present-day Yemen, and it was part of the Kingdom of Sheba in the 900s B.C. Christian and Jewish societies thrived before the seventh century, when Islam was introduced. The region's flourishing economy made it a focal point in the development of Islam. The country was divided since the early sixteenth century, when the Ottoman Empire conquered northwestern Yemen. The Turks stayed in power until 1918, when the Turkish military withdrew and gave control to the Zaidis, who established a monarchy. The Imam Badr was overthrown in 1962, when the Yemeni army proclaimed creation of the Yemen Arab Republic. Meanwhile, Aden and the southeastern part of the country were under British domination since 1839, and became a protectorate in the 1930s. By the mid-1960s, Aden had become the focus of Arab nationalists, and in 1967 Britain granted independence to the People's Republic of South Yemen. After a coup by a Marxist faction in 1970, the country's name changed to the People's Democratic Republic of Yemen. Border clashes between the two Yemens were frequent during the 1970s but relations improved throughout the 1980s, and the two countries merged to form the Republic of Yemen in 1990. Four years later civil war broke out, fueled by dual military forces. The war was won by the North, and unity was restored.

Montenegro and **Serbia** are the only two remaining Yugoslavian republics. Prior to the breakup which began in 1991, the country also included Bosnia and Herzegovina, Croatia, Macedonia, and Slovenia.

YUGOSLAVIA

Much of Yugoslavia's coast is undeveloped, like this stretch near Petrovac.

People

The population of Yugoslavia is mainly Serbs, although there are important Montenegrin, Albanian, and Hungarian minorities. Relations between the Orthodox Serbs and the Muslim Albanians are particularly tense in Kosovo province, where the Albanians form the majority.

Economy and the Land

Before the breakup of Yugoslavia in 1991, most industry was located in the republics of Croatia and Slovenia. As a result, the new Yugoslavia is struggling to improve its industrial base and move away from an agricultural economy. Economic conditions, which improved rapidly after World War II, are now poor as a result of political instability and failed economic restructuring. The nation has many mineral resources, including coal. Much of the land is hilly or mountainous, although there are broad, fertile river valleys.

History and Politics

The area now known as Yugoslavia was originally inhabited by the Thracians and the Illyrians, who were eventually con-

quered by the Roman Empire. These people were in turn overtaken by Slavs who migrated to the area from Poland and Russia in the seventh century. Orthodox Christianity came to the area in the tenth century. In the thirteenth century, Serbia was established as an independent kingdom, and it was then that it gained control over Montenegro. The Ottoman Turks conquered the region in the mid-1300s, and Turkey held the area for almost five hundred years. The nation gained its independence in 1878, but was politically and economically dominated by Austria. Calls for Slavic unity began in the early 1800s. In 1914, a Slavic patriot assassinated Archduke Ferdinand of Austria-Hungary and triggered World War I. The Kingdom of Serbs, Croats, and Slovenes was formed in 1918. Fighting among the various groups encouraged King Alexander I to declare himself dictator in 1929 and change the country's name to Yugoslavia, which was retained

after Alexander's assassination in 1934. Germany and the other Axis powers invaded Yugoslavia during World War II. After the war, Josip Broz Tito assumed leadership, and Yugoslavia became a Communist republic. Tito's policy of nonalignment caused the Soviet Union to break off diplomatic relations from 1948 to 1955. After Tito's death in 1980, the country was governed by a presidency rotating amongst the republics. In June 1991, the federation began to break apart as Croatia and Slovenia declared their independence, followed by Macedonia and then Bosnia and Herzegovina, leaving Serbia and Montenegro as the remaining Yugoslav republics. Continuing aggression against its neighboring former republics has led to international economic sanctions and an economy in shambles. By 1994 sanctions were eased as Yugoslavia vowed to end support to Bosnian Serbs.

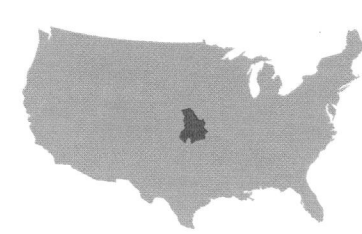

Sheep and shepherd

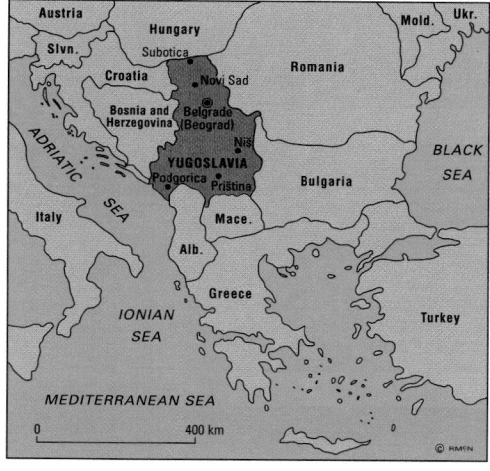

Yugoslavia at a glance

Official name	Socialist Federal Republic of Yugoslavia

People

Population	10,765,000
Density	273/mi² (105/km²)
Capital	Belgrade, 1,136,786
Ethnic groups	Serb 63%, Albanian 14%, Montenegrin 6%, Hungarian 4%
Languages	Serbo-Croatian 95%, Albanian 5%
Religions	Orthodox 65%, Muslim 19%, Roman Catholic 4%
Life expectancy	75 female, 69 male
Literacy	89%

Politics

Government	Republic
Parties	Former Communist, Serbian Radical, Serbian Renewal
Suffrage	Universal, over 18; over 16 if employed
Memberships	None
Subdivisions	2 republics (2 autonomous provinces)

Economy

GDP	$10,000,000,000
Per capita	$937
Monetary unit	Dinar
Trade partners	Exports: Former Yugoslav republics, former Soviet republics
Exports	Machinery and transportation equipment, manufactures, chemicals, food
Imports	Machinery, fuels and lubricants, manufactures, chemicals, food

Land

Description	Eastern Europe
Area	39,449 mi² (102,173 km²)
Highest point	Đaravica, 8,714 ft (2,656 m)
Lowest point	Sea level

YUGOSLAVIA

Major Urban Area
— Railroad
— Canal or Waterway
···· Republic Boundary
--- Autonomous Region Boundary
+ Spot Elevation or Depth

Scale 1:4,752,000

Meters	Feet
4000	13124
2000	6562
1000	3281
500	1640
200	656
0	0
200	656
2000	6562

0 25 50 75 100 125 km
0 25 50 75 mi

City type size indicates relative importance

©Rand McNally & Co.
A-553400-772 -3-/-3A

Yugoslavia has thus far escaped the destruction brought about by ethnic warfare in neighboring Bosnia and Herzegovina.

Lake Kariba

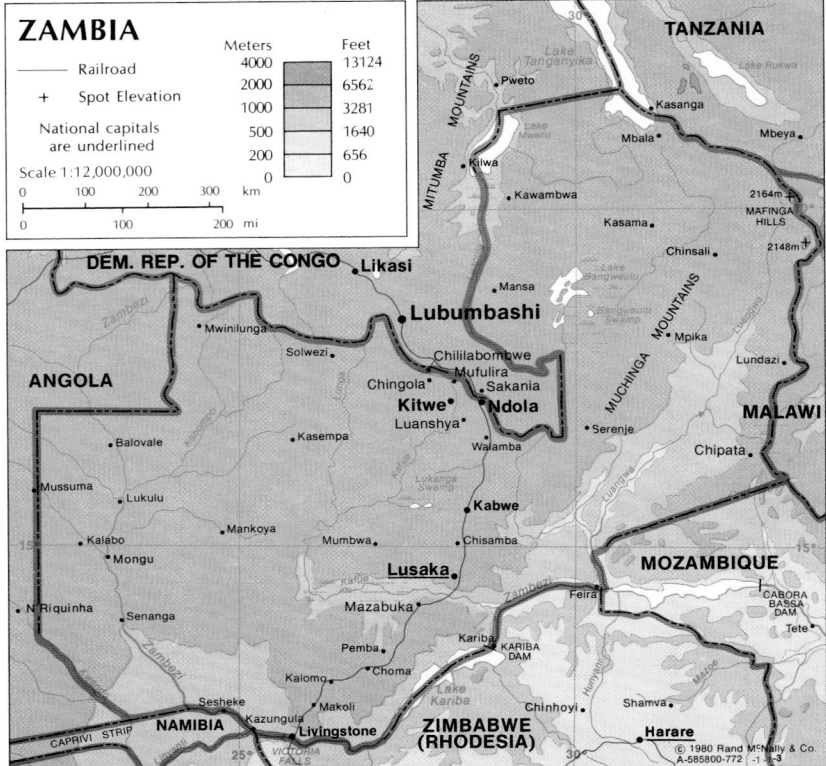

ZAMBIA

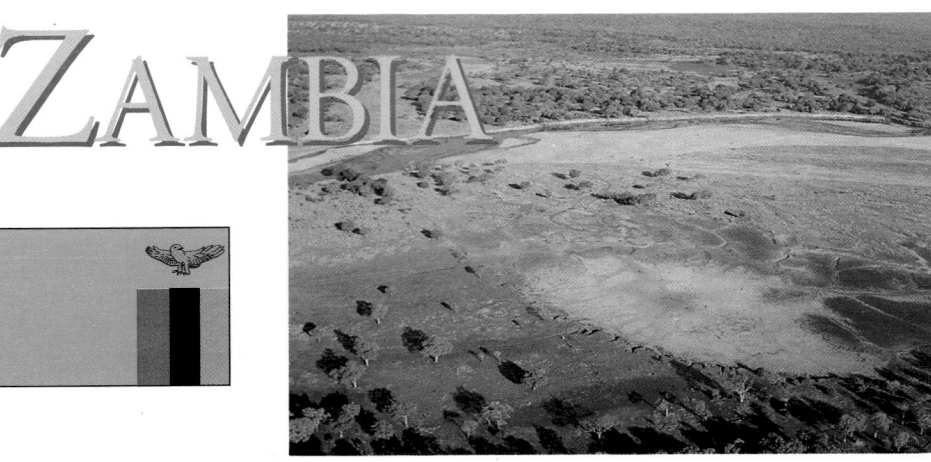

Most of Zambia is arid savanna, and thus poorly suited to agriculture. Frequent droughts and infestation by the disease-carrying tsetse fly further limit economic activity.

Zambia is an example of colonialism at its worst.

It was formed from the remnants of other lands, and its boundaries were drawn with no regard for tribal demarcations or natural features. This lack of cohesiveness has led to near-permanent political turmoil.

People

Virtually all Zambians are black Africans belonging to one of more than seventy Bantu-speaking ethnic groups. Besides the indigenous Bantu languages, many speak English, a reflection of decades of British influence. Although most Zambians are Christian, small minorities are Hindu, Muslim, or hold indigenous beliefs. Many Zambians are subsistence farmers in small villages; however, the mining industry has caused many people to move to urban areas, where wages are rising.

Economy and the Land

The economy is based on copper, Zambia's major export. In an attempt to diversify the economy, the government has emphasized the development of agriculture to help achieve an acceptable balance of trade. Zambia is a subtropical nation marked by high plateaus and great rivers.

History and Politics

European explorers in the nineteenth century discovered an established society of Bantu-speaking inhabitants. In 1888 Cecil Rhodes and the British South Africa Company obtained a mineral-rights concession from local chiefs; and Northern and Southern Rhodesia, now Zambia and Zimbabwe, came under British influence. Northern Rhodesia became a British protectorate in 1924. In 1953 Northern Rhodesia was combined with Southern Rhodesia and Nyasaland, now Malawi, to form a federation, despite African-nationalist opposition to the white-controlled minority government in Southern Rhodesia. The federation was dissolved in 1963, and Northern Rhodesia became the independent Republic of Zambia in 1964. In late 1991 the first multiparty election in decades brought a landslide victory for democratic forces, as well as a sound rejection of socialism. Zambia is now undergoing a painful conversion to capitalism.

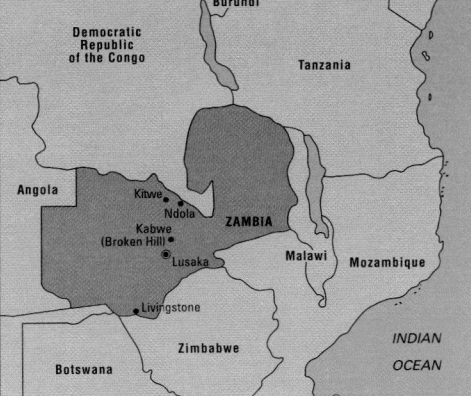

Zambia at a glance

Official name	Republic of the Zambia

People

Population	8,809,000
Density	30/mi² (12/km²)
Urban	42%
Capital	Lusaka, 982,362
Ethnic groups	African 99%, European 1%
Languages	English, Tonga, Lozi, other indigenous
Religions	Christian 50-75%, Muslim and Hindu 24-49%
Life expectancy	45 female, 44 male
Literacy	73%

Politics

Government	Republic
Parties	Movement for Multiparty Democracy, United National Independence
Suffrage	Universal, over 18
Memberships	CW, OAU, UN
Subdivisions	9 provinces

Economy

GDP	$7,300,000,000
Per capita	$861
Monetary unit	Kwacha
Trade partners	Exports: Japan, Germany, U.K. Imports: South African countries, U.K., U.S.
Exports	Copper, zinc, cobalt, lead, tobacco
Imports	Machinery, transportation equipment, food, fuel, manufactures

Land

Description	Southern Africa, landlocked
Area	290,586 mi² (752,614 km²)
Highest point	Unnamed, 7,100 ft (2,164 m)
Lowest point	Along Zambezi River, 1,081 ft (329 m)

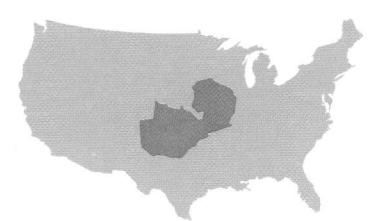

POPULATION COMPARISON
Zambia=3% of U.S.

United States

GDP COMPARISON
Zambia=0.1% of U.S.

United States

ETHNIC GROUPS

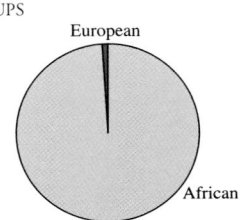

European

African

POPULATION DISTRIBUTION
Urban   Rural

Zambia's Bemba people survive by growing millet, a grain eaten much like rice. Here, a group of women use sticks to grind millet into a flour which is used to make unleavened bread.

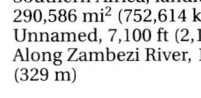

A solitary elephant ambles across the plains of Hwange National Park, the largest game preserve in Zimbabwe. Established in 1927, the 8,700-square-mile park is also home to giraffes, lions, jackals and many other species.

Women's farming co-op near Masvingo

POPULATION COMPARISON
Zimbabwe=4% of U.S.

United States

GDP COMPARISON
Zimbabwe=0.3% of U.S.

United States

ETHNIC GROUPS

Other
White
Ndebele
Shona

POPULATION DISTRIBUTION
Urban   Rural

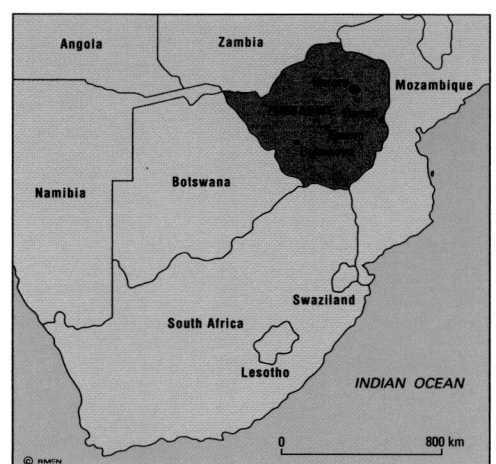

ZIMBABWE

Sunset over Victoria Falls

Sorghum growing near Masvingo

A s Rhodesia, Zimbabwe tried to preserve a white-dominated government similar to that of neighboring South Africa. Years of struggle resulted in free elections in 1979. A major focus of the new government was encouraging people to continue farming as opposed to moving to the cities in search of work. Economic management has been mostly effective and growth has kept pace with the population.

People

The great majority of Zimbabweans are black Africans of Bantu descent, with a small but economically significant minority of white Europeans. Most Zimbabweans are subsistence farmers who live in small villages. The influence of British colonization is seen in the official language, English, and in the influence of Christianity.

Economy and the Land

Zimbabwe's natural mineral resources have played a key role in the country's sustained economic growth. The subtropical climate supports the exportation of many agricultural products and makes large-scale cattle ranching feasible. Though primarily a landlocked country of high plateaus, transportation of goods is facilitated by an excellent system of paved roads and railways.

History and Politics

Zimbabwe was populated by Bantu groups until European exploration in the nineteenth century. British influence began in 1888, when Cecil Rhodes and the British South Africa Company obtained mineral rights to the area from local chiefs. Eventually, the region was divided under British rule as Southern Rhodesia, or present-day Zimbabwe, and Northern Rhodesia, or modern Zambia. In 1953, Southern Rhodesia, Northern Rhodesia, and Nyasaland, now Malawi, formed a federation that ended in discord after ten years; Zambia and Malawi gained their independence, and Southern Rhodesia, which remained under British control, became Rhodesia. In response to British pressure to accept black-majority rule, Rhodesian whites declared independence from the United Kingdom in 1965, which led to economic sanctions imposed by the United Nations. These sanctions and years

of antigovernment violence finally forced agreement to the principle of black-majority rule. In 1980 the Zimbabwe African National Union-Patriotic Front won a majority of seats in the House of Representatives, and Rhodesia became independent Zimbabwe. A depressed economy in recent years has increased racial tensions.

Zimbabwe at a glance

Official name	Republic of Zimbabwe

People

Population	11,075,000
Density	73/mi² (28/km²)
Urban	29%
Capital	Harare, 681,000
Ethnic groups	Shona 71%, Ndebele 16%, white 1%
Languages	English, Shona, Sindebele
Religions	Mixed Christian and Animist 50%, Christian 25%, Animist 24%
Life expectancy	57 female, 54 male
Literacy	67%

Politics

Government	Republic
Parties	African National Union, Unity Movement
Suffrage	Universal, over 18
Memberships	CW, OAU, UN
Subdivisions	8 provinces

Economy

GDP	$15,900,000,000
Per capita	$1,590
Monetary unit	Dollar
Trade partners	Exports: South Africa, U.K., Germany Imports: South Africa, U.K., U.S
Exports	Tobacco, gold, ferrochrome, cotton
Imports	Machinery and transportation equipment, manufactures, chemicals, fuel

Land

Description	Southern Africa, landlocked
Area	150,873 mi² (390,759 km²)
Highest point	Inyangani, 8,504 ft (2,592 m)
Lowest point	Confluence of Sabi and Lundi rivers, 530 ft (162 m)

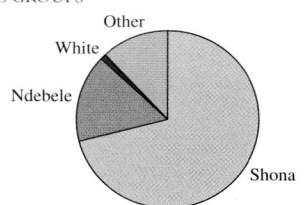

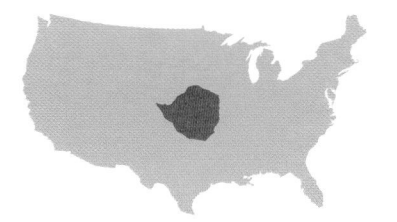

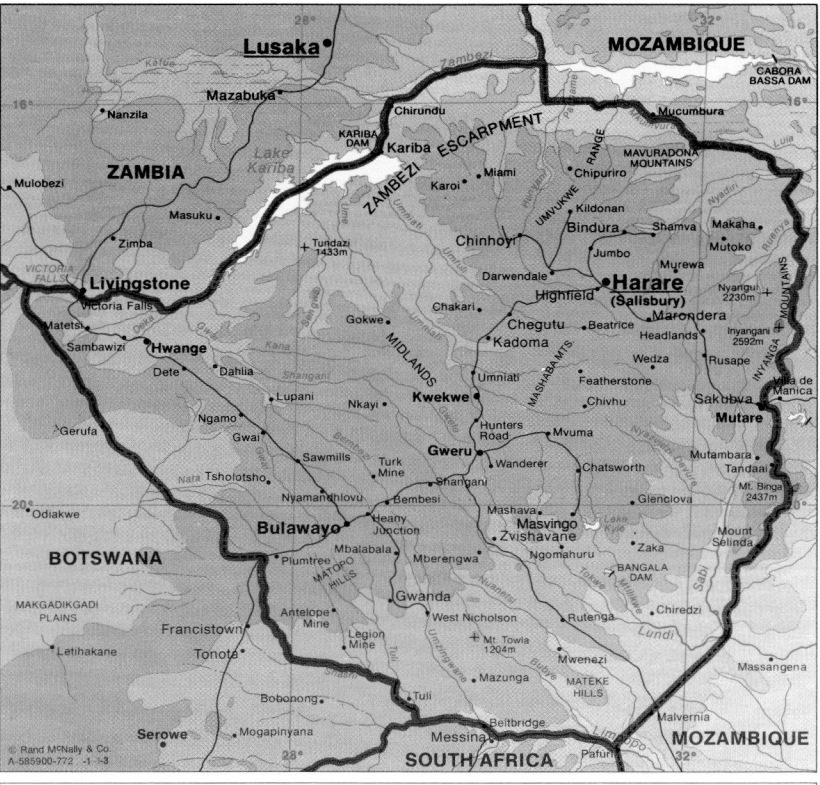

ZIMBABWE

— Railroad
+ Spot Elevation

National capitals are underlined
City type size indicates relative importance

0   50   100   150   200 km
0   50   100   150   mi

Scale 1:7,512,000

Meters	Feet
4000	13124
2000	6562
1000	3281
500	1640
200	656
0	0

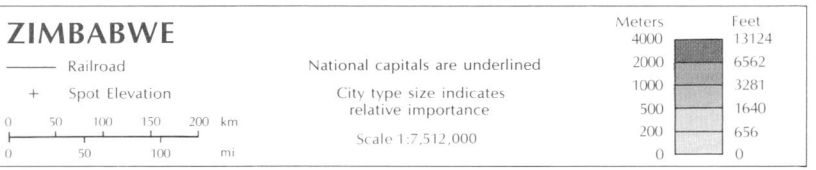

Natural beauty and expansive game parks are major tourist draws for Zimbabwe. Victoria Falls, where the Zambezi River plunges into a deep chasm, is one of the greatest sights in Africa.

INDEX

Introduction to the Index

This universal index includes in a single alphabetical list approximately 8,700 names of features that appear on the reference maps. Each name is followed by the name of the country or continent in which it is located, a map-reference key and a page reference.

Names
The names of cities appear in the index in regular type. The names of all other features appear in *italics*, followed by descriptive terms (hill, mtn., state) to indicate their nature.

Names that appear in shortened versions on the maps are spelled out in full in the index. The portions of these names omitted from the maps are enclosed in brackets — for example, Acapulco [de Juárez].

Abbreviations of names on the maps have been standardized as much as possible. Names that are abbreviated on the maps are generally spelled out in full in the index.

Country designations follow the names of all places in the index. The locations of places in the United States, Canada, and the United Kingdom are further defined by abbreviations that indicate the state, province, or political division in which each is located.

All abbreviations used in the index are defined in the List of Abbreviations below.

Alphabetization
Names are alphabetized in the order of the letters of the English alphabet. Spanish *ll* and *ch*, for example, are not treated as distinct letters. Furthermore, diacritical marks are disregarded in alphabetization — German or Scandinavian *å* or *ö* are treated as *a* or *o*.

The names of physical features may appear inverted, since they are always alphabetized under the proper, not the generic, part of the name, thus: 'Gibraltar, Strait of'. Otherwise every entry, whether consisting of one word or more, is alphabetized as a single continuous entity. 'Lakeland', for example, appears after 'La Crosse' and before 'La Salle'. Names beginning with articles (Le Havre, Den Helder, Al Manşūrah) are not inverted. Names beginning 'St.', 'Ste.' and 'Sainte' are alphabetized as though spelled 'Saint'.

In the case of identical names, towns are listed first, then political divisions, then physical features. Entries that are completely identical are listed alphabetically by country name.

Geographic Coordinates and Page References
The geographic coordinates and page references are found in the last two columns of each entry.

Geographic coordinates for point features, such as cities and mountain peaks, indicate the locations of the symbols. For extensive areal features, such as countries or mountain ranges, locations are given for the approximate centers of the features. Those for linear features, such as canals and rivers, are given for the locations of the terminating points or mouths.

The page number generally refers to the main map for the country in which the feature is located. Page references to two-page maps always refer to the left-hand page.

List of Abbreviations

Afg.	Afghanistan	Ct., U.S.	Connecticut, U.S.	*is.*	islands	N.H., U.S.	New Hampshire, U.S.	Sol. Is.	Solomon Islands
Afr.	Africa	*ctry.*	country	Isr.	Israel	Nic.	Nicaragua	Som.	Somalia
Ak., U.S.	Alaska, U.S.	C.V.	Cape Verde	Jam.	Jamaica	Nig.	Nigeria	Sp. N. Afr.	Spanish North Africa
Al., U.S.	Alabama, U.S.	Cyp.	Cyprus	Jer.	Jericho Area	N. Ire., U.K.	Northern Ireland, U.K.	Sri L.	Sri Lanka
Alb.	Albania	Czech Rep.	Czech Republic	Jord.	Jordan	N.J., U.S.	New Jersey, U.S.	*state*	state, republic, canton
Alg.	Algeria	D.C., U.S.	District of Columbia,	Kaz.	Kazakhstan	N. Kor.	North Korea	St. Hel.	St. Helena
Alta., Can.	Alberta, Can.		U.S.	Kir.	Kiribati	N.M., U.S.	New Mexico, U.S.	St. K./N	St. Kitts and Nevis
Am. Sam.	American Samoa	De., U.S.	Delaware, U.S.	Ks., U.S.	Kansas, U.S.	N. Mar. Is.	Northern Mariana	St. Luc.	St. Lucia
anch.	anchorage	Den.	Denmark	Kuw.	Kuwait		Islands	*stm.*	stream (river, creek)
And.	Andorra	*dep.*	dependency, colony	Ky., U.S.	Kentucky, U.S.	Nmb.	Namibia	S. Tom./P.	Sao Tome and
Ang.	Angola	*depr.*	depression	Kyrg.	Kyrgyzstan	Nor.	Norway		Principe
Ant.	Antarctica	*dept.*	department, district	*l.*	lake, pond	Norf. I.	Norfolk Island	St. P./M.	St. Pierre and
Antig.	Antigua and Barbuda	*des.*	desert	La., U.S.	Louisiana, U.S.	N.S., Can.	Nova Scotia, Can.		Miquelon
Ar., U.S.	Arkansas, U.S.	Dji.	Djibouti	Lat.	Latvia	Nv., U.S.	Nevada, U.S.	*strt.*	strait, channel, sound
Arg.	Argentina	Dom.	Dominica	Leb.	Lebanon	N.W. Ter.,	Northwest Territories,	St. Vin.	St. Vincent and the
Arm.	Armenia	Dom. Rep.	Dominican Republic	Leso.	Lesotho	Can.	Can.		Grenadines
Aus.	Austria	D.R.C.	Democratic Republic	Lib.	Liberia	N.Y., U.S.	New York, U.S.	Sur.	Suriname
Austl.	Australia		of the Congo	Liech.	Liechtenstein	N.Z.	New Zealand	*sw.*	swamp, marsh
Az., U.S.	Arizona, U.S.	Ec.	Ecuador	Lith.	Lithuania	Oc.	Oceania	Swaz.	Swaziland
Azer.	Azerbaijan	El Sal.	El Salvador	Lux.	Luxembourg	Oh., U.S.	Ohio, U.S.	Swe.	Sweden
b.	bay, gulf, inlet,	Eng., U.K.	England, U.K.	Ma., U.S.	Massachusetts, U.S.	Ok., U.S.	Oklahoma, U.S.	Switz.	Switzerland
	lagoon	Eq. Gui.	Equatorial Guinea	Mac.	Macedonia	Ont., Can.	Ontario, Can.	Tai.	Taiwan
Bah.	Bahamas	Erit.	Eritrea	Madag.	Madagascar	Or., U.S.	Oregon, U.S.	Taj.	Tajikistan
Bahr.	Bahrain	*est.*	estuary	Malay.	Malaysia	Pa., U.S.	Pennsylvania, U.S.	Tan.	Tanzania
Barb.	Barbados	Est.	Estonia	Mald.	Maldives	Pak.	Pakistan	T./C. Is.	Turks and Caicos
B.C., Can.	British Columbia,	Eth.	Ethiopia	Man., Can.	Manitoba, Can.	Pan.	Panama		Islands
	Can.	Eur.	Europe	Marsh. Is.	Marshall Islands	Pap. N. Gui.	Papua New Guinea	*ter.*	territory
Bdi.	Burundi	Faer. Is.	Faeroe Islands	Mart.	Martinique	Para.	Paraguay	Thai.	Thailand
Bel.	Belgium	Falk. Is.	Falkland Islands	Maur.	Mauritania	P.E.I., Can.	Prince Edward Island,	Tn., U.S.	Tennessee, U.S.
Bela.	Belarus	Fin.	Finland	May.	Mayotte		Can.	Tok.	Tokelau
Ber.	Bermuda	Fl., U.S.	Florida, U.S.	Md., U.S.	Maryland, U.S.	*pen.*	peninsula	Trin.	Trinidad and Tobago
Bhu.	Bhutan	*for.*	forest, moor	Me., U.S.	Maine, U.S.	Phil.	Philippines	Tun.	Tunisia
B.I.O.T.	British Indian Ocean	Fr.	France	Mex.	Mexico	Pit.	Pitcairn	Tur.	Turkey
	Territory	Fr. Gu.	French Guiana	Mi., U.S.	Michigan, U.S.	*pl.*	plain, flat	Turk.	Turkmenistan
Bngl.	Bangladesh	Fr. Poly.	French Polynesia	Micron.	Federated States of	*plat.*	plateau, highland	Tx., U.S.	Texas, U.S.
Bol.	Bolivia	Ga., U.S.	Georgia, U.S.		Micronesia	Pol.	Poland	U.A.E.	United Arab Emirates
Bos.	Bosnia and	Gam.	Gambia	Mid. Is.	Midway Islands	Port.	Portugal	Ug.	Uganda
	Herzegovina	Gaza	Gaza Strip	*mil.*	military installation	P.R.	Puerto Rico	U.K.	United Kingdom
Bots.	Botswana	Geor.	Georgia	Mn., U.S.	Minnesota, U.S.	*prov.*	province, region	Ukr.	Ukraine
Braz.	Brazil	Ger.	Germany	Mo., U.S.	Missouri, U.S.	Que., Can.	Quebec, Can.	Ur.	Uruguay
Bru.	Brunei	Gib.	Gibraltar	Mol.	Moldova	*reg.*	physical region	U.S.	United States
Br. Vir. Is.	British Virgin Islands	Golan	Golan Heights	Mon.	Monaco	*res.*	reservoir	Ut., U.S.	Utah, U.S.
Bul.	Bulgaria	Grc.	Greece	Mong.	Mongolia	Reu.	Reunion	Uzb.	Uzbekistan
Burkina	Burkina Faso	Gren.	Grenada	Monts.	Montserrat	*rf.*	reef, shoal	Va., U.S.	Virginia, U.S.
c.	cape, point	Grnld.	Greenland	Mor.	Morocco	R.I., U.S.	Rhode Island, U.S.	*val.*	valley, watercourse
Ca., U.S.	California, U.S.	Guad.	Guadeloupe	Moz.	Mozambique	Rom.	Romania	Vat.	Vatican City
Cam.	Cameroon	Guat.	Guatemala	Mrts.	Mauritius	Rw.	Rwanda	Ven.	Venezuela
Camb.	Cambodia	Gui.	Guinea	Ms., U.S.	Mississippi, U.S.	S.A.	South America	Viet.	Vietnam
Can.	Canada	Gui.-B.	Guinea-Bissau	Mt., U.S.	Montana, U.S.	S. Afr.	South Africa	V.I.U.S.	Virgin Islands (U.S.)
Cay. Is.	Cayman Islands	Guy.	Guyana	*mth.*	river mouth or	Sask., Can.	Saskatchewan, Can.	*vol.*	volcano
Cen. Afr.	Central African	Hi., U.S.	Hawaii, U.S.		channel	Sau. Ar.	Saudi Arabia	Vt., U.S.	Vermont, U.S.
Rep.	Republic	*hist.*	historic site, ruins	*mtn.*	mountain	S.C., U.S.	South Carolina, U.S.	Wa., U.S.	Washington, U.S.
Christ. I.	Christmas Island	*hist. reg.*	historic region	*mts.*	mountains	*sci.*	scientific station	Wake I.	Wake Island
C. Iv.	Cote d'Ivoire	Hond.	Honduras	Mwi.	Malawi	Scot., U.K.	Scotland, U.K.	Wal./F.	Wallis and Futuna
clf.	cliff, escarpment	Hung.	Hungary	Mya.	Myanmar	S.D., U.S.	South Dakota, U.S.	W.B.	West Bank
co.	county, parish	*i.*	island	N.A.	North America	Sen.	Senegal	Wi., U.S.	Wisconsin, U.S.
Co., U.S.	Colorado, U.S.	Ia., U.S.	Iowa, U.S.	N.B., Can.	New Brunswick, Can.	Sey.	Seychelles	W. Sah.	Western Sahara
Cocos Is.	Cocos Islands	Ice.	Iceland	N.C., U.S.	North Carolina, U.S.	Sing.	Singapore	*wtfl.*	waterfall
Col.	Colombia	*ice*	ice feature, glacier	N. Cal.	New Caledonia	S. Geor.	South Georgia	W.V., U.S.	West Virginia, U.S.
Com.	Comoros	Id., U.S.	Idaho, U.S.	N. Cyp.	North Cyprus	S. Kor.	South Korea	Wy., U.S.	Wyoming, U.S.
cont.	continent	Il., U.S.	Illinois, U.S.	N.D., U.S.	North Dakota, U.S.	S.L.	Sierra Leone	Yugo.	Yugoslavia
Cook Is.	Cook Islands	In., U.S.	Indiana, U.S.	Ne., U.S.	Nebraska, U.S.	Slvk.	Slovakia	Yukon, Can.	Yukon Territory, Can.
C.R.	Costa Rica	Indon.	Indonesia	Neth.	Netherlands	Slvn.	Slovenia	Zam.	Zambia
crat.	crater	I. of Man	Isle of Man	Neth. Ant.	Netherlands Antilles	S. Mar.	San Marino	Zimb.	Zimbabwe
Cro.	Croatia	Ire.	Ireland	Newf., Can.	Newfoundland, Can.				

A

B

T